The Diplomacy of Involvement

The Diplomacy *of* Involvement

American Economic Expansion across the Pacific, 1784–1900

DAVID M. PLETCHER

University of Missouri Press
Columbia and London

Copyright © 2001 by
The Curators of the University of Missouri
University of Missouri Press, Columbia, Missouri 65201
Printed and bound in the United States of America
All rights reserved
5   4   3   2   1   05   04   03   02   01

Library of Congress Cataloging-in-Publication Data

Pletcher, David M.
    The diplomacy of involvement : American economic expansion
across the Pacific, 1784–1900 / David M. Pletcher.
        p.   cm.
    Includes bibliographical references and index.
    ISBN 0-8262-1315-4 (alk. paper)
    1. United States—Foreign economic relations—Pacific Area.   2. Pacific
Area—economic relations—United States.   3. United States—Foreign
relations—Pacific Area.   4. Pacific Area—Foreign relations—United States.
    5. United States—Commerical policy—History.   I. Title.
HF1456.5.P3 P56   2001
337.7309—dc21   2001018917

♾ This paper meets the requirements of the
American National Standard for Permanence of Paper
for Printed Library Materials, Z39.48, 1984.

Designer: Stephanie Foley
Typesetter: Bookcomp, Inc.
Printer and binder: Thomson-Shore, Inc.
Typeface: Minion

To Nuba M. Pletcher and Jean Hutchinson Pletcher

The Diplomacy of American Expansionism—Nineteenth Century

The Diplomacy of Annexation: Texas, Oregon, and the Mexican War

The Diplomacy of Trade and Investment: American Economic Expansion in the Hemisphere, 1865–1900

The Diplomacy of Involvement: American Economic Expansion across the Pacific, 1784–1900

Contents

Acknowledgments

MANY PERSONS AND INSTITUTIONS have helped me in the research and writing of this book. Indiana University generously granted me regular sabbatical leaves while I was an active member of its faculty and since my retirement has extended the use of its considerable research resources. Near the beginning of this project I held a National Archives Fellowship, which enabled me to spend a semester in Washington using the documentary resources available in the Archives stacks. There I also had the advice and help of the late Albert Leisinger.

My home library throughout my research has been that of Indiana University, whose staff has given unfailing and skilled help, especially in the divisions of government documents, microfilms, and interlibrary loans. Many other libraries have also made materials available, especially the following: the Library of Congress, the New York Public Library, the Indiana Historical Library, Indianapolis; the Rutherford B. Hayes Memorial Library, Fremont, Ohio; the Rhees Library, University of Rochester, Rochester, New York; and the Library of the University of Chicago. Other libraries have let me use their materials on interlibrary loan.

Many persons have read portions of this manuscript or related writings of mine, offered suggestions and given encouragement where needed, in particular the following: David L. Anderson, William H. Becker, Robert H. Ferrell, James F. Goode, Donald J. Lisio, Irene D. Neu, Robert E. Quirk, Martin Ridge, Walter V. and Marie V. Scholes, Lynn Struve, Paul A. Varg, Jeff Wasserstrom, and George M. Wilson. The maps were prepared by John M. Hollingsworth.

The Diplomacy of Involvement

Introduction

EWS OF THE FIRST AMERICAN commercial treaty with China (1844) caused a flurry of excitement in business circles. The leading trade journal of the day, *Merchants' Magazine*, likened the event to "the discovery of a new continent ready peopled with a rich, industrious people, numbering 200,000,000 with wants in unison with the customs of the nations of Europe."[1] This sort of wide-eyed enthusiasm persisted for the rest of the century. Nearly forty years later, for example, the *American Exporter* detailed the profitable opportunities China presented to American merchants and investors:

> No greater field for commercial enterprise can be found than that offered in the vast and undeveloped markets of China for our manufacturers and farmers. . . . Its vast rivers and canals present unrivaled scope for steam navigation, and its wide plains and valleys offer matchless facilities for railways. . . .
> China is open to almost all our manufactures. . . . The spirit of the age has entered this vast empire, and it stands upon the threshold of the New World and offers to America the greater share of a trade which has enriched every community which has been able to command it.[2]

A kind of economic Manifest Destiny embraced the whole Pacific basin. During the heady years after the Mexican War the *Alta California* (San Francisco) predicted: "We shall become the factors for the entire Pacific coast. . . . The whole Pacific seas are before us and invite us to occupy them with our trade. We cannot escape our destiny if we would. . . . The Yankee, with his clipper ships—with his steamers—with his enterprise, his skill, his unceasing activity, will defeat his great rival [England]." William H. Seward told a Pacific railroad convention that a transcontinental line would even threaten British supremacy in the Indian trade. Throughout Asia and Australasia, he said, connecting steamers would bring drugs, spices, teas, and silks to American shores in exchange for surplus American meats, cereals, and cotton goods, accompanied by "the Bible, the Printing Press, the Ballot Box, and the Steam Engine." In 1868 the *New York Herald* declared: "The whole Pacific world is thus bound up with the growing prosperity of the United States. . . . Ours is the favored position. We

---

1. *Merchants' Magazine* 12 (January 1845): 79–80. After some uncertainty about Chinese population, later writers usually fixed on estimates of three or four hundred million. But a few made a strong case for a much lower figure. William Barclay Parsons, *An American Engineer in China*, 291–303.
2. *American Exporter* 7 (May 1881): 37.

stand between two worlds. We must benefit by—perhaps at last absorb—the wealth of both."[3]

Outside China, two Pacific areas in particular attracted mid–nineteenth century commercial expansionists: Japan and Hawaii. In 1845 a congressman asked, "Where can we now find a better field of enterprise than . . . the empire of Japan and the kingdom of Corea, with their aggregate population of sixty or seventy millions?" A few years later the *Democratic Review* declared that "the opening of commerce with Japan is demanded by reason, civilization, progress, and religion." After trade with Japan had begun, the *New York Herald* added: "Destiny has marked out the North Pacific as our own. . . . We do not want Japanese territory, but we do wish to benefit by Japanese trade. The European Powers must not be allowed to take an undue advantage, and it is our duty and our interest to see that they do not."[4] Hawaii seemed to the *Oregon Statesman* "the West Indies of the Pacific Coast," and in the 1860s a few believed that "it is considered only a question of time when the Eagle will gather these little islands under his wing. The 'pear may be hardly ripe!' but I think it will fall into the right basket when it does fall."[5]

Other influences reinforced the attraction of markets, such as exotic cultures and ancient civilizations. In China the most important noneconomic factor— more significant to many Americans than mere trade—was the opening of a new missionary field to save the souls and heal the bodies of the "benighted heathen." In 1875 there were more than two hundred American missionaries in China, about half of the total American population there. By 1900 both figures had been multiplied by five.[6] A final expansionist factor was geopolitics, the influence of economic and social geography on the national power of the United States. As early as 1852, while a senator, Seward called for the annexation of Hawaii, predicting in an often-quoted phrase that the Pacific would become "the chief theatre of events in the world's great hereafter." By the 1890s a vocal minority of publicists and politicians had created a network of expansionist measures, including an isthmian canal, island bases, subsidized shipping, and lower tariffs, all justified in part by increased trade in the Pacific and the Far East.[7]

3. *San Francisco Daily Alta California*, n.d., reprinted in *Merchants' Magazine* 24 (June 1851): 780. Seward is quoted in Walter G. Sharrow, "William Henry Seward and the Basis for the American Empire," 339. *New York Herald*, May 16, 1868.

4. United States, 28th Cong., 2d sess., *House Document 138*, 2. *United States Magazine and Democratic Review* 30 (April 1852): 332. *New York Herald*, May 1, 1868.

5. *Oregon Statesman*, November 3, 1859, quoted in Sylvester K. Stevens, *American Expansion in Hawaii, 1842–1898*, 45. Zephaniah Spalding, quoted in Merze Tate, *Hawaii: Reciprocity or Annexation?* 57.

6. Theodore Christlieb, *Protestant Foreign Missions, Their Present State: A Universal Survey*, 192–94. Charles F. Remer, *Foreign Investments in China*, 250.

7. William H. Seward, *The Works of William H. Seward*. Seward also wrote of San Francisco as "the Suez of the continent" and "the Constantinople of American empire." For samples of later rhetoric see H. C. Taylor, "The Control of the Pacific," 407–16; George W. Melville, "Our Future in the Pacific—What We Have There to Hold and Win," 281–96.

From the beginning the two principal goals of this trade, the China coast and the Pacific islands, were linked together. During its early years American ships sought out the islands for commodities such as sandalwood, *bêche-de-mer* (dried sea slugs), and birds' nests, which they might sell to the Chinese in return for tea and silk. Eventually the whaling industry and direct trade between the islands and the United States grew up, but American expansionists usually viewed the islands as stepping stones to the Golden East and established steamship lines to reach both goals. The Alaska coast passed through the same evolution, furnishing sea otter and seal furs for the China trade and later fish and more furs for the United States. In the case of Japan, navigation as well as trade drew the Americans, for ships approaching Canton and Shanghai could hardly avoid the offshore archipelago. A few expansionists, such as Matthew Fontaine Maury, advocated the "great circle" route from Central America to Shanghai via California, Alaska, and the Aleutian Islands as the shortest way to the Far East, but bad weather and the lack of northern markets kept most Yankee ships in the central Pacific.

Although the attraction of the China market and to a lesser extent the tropical products of the Pacific islands constituted a powerful pull factor, American foreign commerce was also pushed outward by forces operating within the United States. For nearly a century after independence the domestic market seemed more than adequate for American farmers and manufacturers. However, growth and maladjustments during the 1840s and 1850s raised occasional questions, and an article advocating the opening of Japan concluded: "The policy, then, of our republic is to . . . multiply our markets and increase our factors, both at home and abroad. . . . Every consumer of our necessaries, made such by supplying us with luxuries, is a new source of wealth to our country."[8]

During the five-year depression after 1873 complaints arose against a system of protective tariffs, fostered by the Civil War, that seemed to block access to foreign markets for American surplus wheat, textiles, and ironware. According to a "glut thesis" put forward by tariff reformers, the country must have either a general lowering of tariffs or, if that were too much for conservatives, a series of reciprocity treaties with likely trade partners whereby each country would lower a few schedules of duties to facilitate trade with the other. This pressure for tariff reform affected American relations with Europe and the Western Hemisphere more than those with the Far East and the Pacific, but beginning in the 1850s it became a determining factor in U.S. policy toward Hawaii.

Not long after Americans established trade with China, they made their first foreign investments in the Far East as they built warehouses and wharves at Canton, the center of that trade. Similar installations appeared a few years later in Hawaii and a few other Pacific islands as well as trading posts and small forts on the northwest coast. The first large-scale systematic investment in the Pacific was probably the holdings of Claus Spreckels, the sugar baron of Hawaii, who created plantations, irrigation systems, and a steamship line to San Francisco after

---

8. "Japan," *United States Magazine and Democratic Review* 30 (October 1852).

the reciprocity treaty of 1875. The first American investment in China outside of direct trade facilities was a steamship line on the Yangtze River that operated profitably from 1862 to 1876. During the 1880s and early 1890s the success of two long railroad systems in Mexico (the Mexican Central and the Mexican National, both financed largely with American capital) proved that railroad investments abroad were feasible, and promoters appeared in China with grandiose plans.[9] These proved premature, for American capitalists could not provide the requisite funds, and the Chinese government was unwilling to grant sufficiently attractive concessions. In most cases the Japanese government would not even negotiate with American promoters, preferring to reserve its railroads and steamship lines for budding Japanese capital.

In 1881 the *American Protectionist* warned the United States government to "keep a watchful eye on European intrigues in the Far East in order to retain the customers for American industry."[10] Through the last half of the nineteenth century the combination of American interests and foreign rivalries increasingly involved the United States in the international politics of the whole Pacific area. From the beginning, American merchants and sea captains had to deal with the competition of the British, fortified by their head start, their naval power, and their monopolistic East India Company. Sometimes it was useful to cooperate with them or profit from their aggressiveness toward the Chinese, as in the case of the First Anglo-Chinese War (the "Opium War," 1839–1841), which led to the first American treaty with China. The Anglo-American rivalry extended to the Pacific islands and Japan, and at times France joined the competition for trade and influence. After midcentury Russia became a competitor for influence in China, and later Germany as well. During the 1860s and 1870s the Japanese hurriedly adapted western economic and social methods and goals to their needs, and they proved able imitators in power politics too.

To combat this rivalry in and around the Pacific, the U.S. government followed an intermittent expansionist policy during the last half of the nineteenth century that gradually involved it in commitments ever farther from home. In 1867 it annexed Alaska, and seven years later it backed up its growing Hawaiian trade with a reciprocity treaty—but only after hesitation and two false starts. During the 1880s Washington committed itself to a dangerously aggressive policy in the remote South Pacific Samoan island group, where Americans had almost no economic stake.

In East Asia involvement also developed at about the same time. During the early 1860s an enterprising minister to China, Anson Burlingame, experimented with a policy of Anglo-American cooperation, but it did not satisfy either party and was soon abandoned. American diplomats gave moderate support to American citizens whom the Japanese hired to advise in or direct the modernization

9. Thomas Kevin O'Horo, "American Foreign Investments and Foreign Policy: The Railroad Experience, 1865–1898." David M. Pletcher, *The Diplomacy of Trade and Investment: American Economic Expansion in the Hemisphere, 1865–1900,* chap. 3.

10. *American Protectionist* 1 (February 5, 1881): 37.

projects. During the 1880s the United States "opened" the onetime "hermit na-tion" of Korea to foreign trade, just as it was becoming the arena of a Sino-Japanese power struggle. In 1894–1895 Japan invaded Korea and northern China with its new, crack army and navy and humiliated the colossus. Through these complica-tions the United States maintained its neutrality with considerable difficulty.

By the 1890s the American government had become more closely involved in Pacific and Far Eastern affairs than either its leaders or the American public realized. American residents of Hawaii fomented a revolution against the native government, but when they petitioned for annexation to the United States, the Cleveland administration, shocked at the sudden proposal, put them off. Several years earlier an alarming naval crisis with Britain and Germany over Samoa was resolved with some difficulty and an awkward joint administration improvised. Even more serious, the European powers, aroused by the Chinese weakness in the war with Japan, prepared in 1897 to divide up China into "spheres of influence." American expansionists feared for their trade and investment interests in northern China, but could not take an overt stand because of their country's developing diplomatic crisis with Spain over Cuba.

The brief Spanish-American War, which followed immediately, solved the problem in an unexpected way. The war was fought mainly in the Caribbean, but the American occupation of Spain's Philippine Islands, undertaken for reasons of naval and political strategy, redirected the United States' Far Eastern policies. The annexation of the islands gave the nation a military base off the Chinese coast and greatly strengthened America's concern for its economic interests. The first sign of this new concern was the Open Door notes (1899), in which Secretary of State John Hay proposed a policy of equal access to Chinese trade, long an informal American policy. In the following year the United States became involved in helping the European powers and Japan put down a rebellion in China, and soon the Americans were playing a full-scale role in Far Eastern affairs, lending money to China, actively supporting American merchants and promoters, and keeping warships and marines close at hand for emergencies. In the Pacific meanwhile the United States annexed Hawaii, as it had long considered doing, but arranged to divide the Samoan Islands with Britain and Germany.

Nineteenth-century economic realities fell far short of American hopes. By 1900, more than a century of American trade with China had developed only a small market, greatly inferior to those in Europe, Canada, and Latin America. According to available statistics, the American annual trade with China amounted to about $8 million in 1865 and increased to about $52 million by 1900. This represented only about 2 percent of America's total foreign trade for that year. Im-ports consistently outran exports; in two years during that period the unfavorable trade ratio was more than twenty to one. Although few in the Civil War period would have expected it, American annual trade with Japan rose somewhat faster— from about $3 million in 1870 to about $62 million in 1900 (about 2.3 percent of total foreign trade). American nonmissionary (i.e., business) investments in China have been estimated at about $3 million in 1830, about $7 million in 1875, and just under $20 million in 1900. (The last-named figure represented only about 2.5 percent of all foreign investments in China.) American trade with the Pacific in 1900 (defined as Australasia and Oceania) stood at about $70 million, of which about two-fifths went to Hawaii.[11]

The often frustrating experiences of nineteenth-century American merchants and promoters in the Pacific and the Far East and the involvement of the American government need to be understood as background to the larger-scale political and economic operations of the United States during the eventful twentieth century. This book is intended to show how experimental, often improvised, policies developed in the Pacific and the Far East. There are many questions to be answered. Why did American trade figures disappoint the confident expectations of economic expansionists? How much and what sort of support did merchants and promoters receive from their government? How did businessmen, expansionist publicists, and government react to foreign rivals? How well did the Pacific involvement serve the best interests of the American people? More detailed questions will also contribute to our understanding. How did Americans view the spectacular development of Japan? Why were they so successful in developing influence in Hawaii? Why did they err so badly in trying to apply similar procedures in Samoa?

Since the area to be covered is vast, it is impossible to follow one grand chronology. I shall begin with a general chapter outlining developments during the first sixty years of American activity, 1784–1844. Then three chapters will follow, reviewing American economic expansion, 1845–1895, in the areas of the Pacific where Americans were most active—Alaska, Hawaii, and Samoa. The next four chapters will deal with American trade, investments, and economic policy in China, Japan, and finally Korea. Two chapters will deal with events during the culminating years of international wars affecting the Pacific and especially the Far East, 1895–1900. The book will conclude with a brief view of changed conditions after 1900 and general conclusions.

When the nineteenth century ended, the United States was only half prepared to play a major role in the Pacific basin and East Asia, as its improvisations and errors of subsequent years demonstrated. This account will help to explain the economic aspects of this incomplete preparation.

11. U.S., Department of Commerce, Bureau of the Census, *Historical Statistics of the United States, Colonial Times to 1970,* 2, 903–7. Percentages computed by author.

I

The
Pacific *and the*
Far East *as* **Fields**
for **Expansion,**
1784-1890

1

The Chinese Magnet and
the Pacific Distances, 1784–1844

O N THE MORNING of February 22, 1784, a 360-ton square-sterned ship flying the new flag of the United States left New York Harbor after exchanging salutes with the harbor forts. This was the *Empress of China,* bound for the Cape of Good Hope and the Far East, to open American trade with China. She carried 30 tons of ginseng, a medicinal root regarded by the Chinese as a miraculous cure-all, 2,600 fur skins, smaller amounts of lead and cotton, and $20,000 in silver coin. Her wealthy owners, who could afford such a speculative venture, were a consortium of New York and Philadelphia bankers and merchants led by the powerful Robert Morris, superintendent of finance in the recent American Revolution.

After eighteen thousand miles of sea voyage, broken by two brief stopovers, the *Empress* dropped anchor at Whampoa, the island port of Canton, on August 28. Here she remained for four months of trading, taking on a cargo of tea, silk, porcelains, and other Chinese products. On her return to New York the following May 11, the owners sold their cargo (and the ship as well) for a profit of about 25 percent. Newspapers in New York, Philadelphia, and other ports along the coast commented with approval or enthusiasm on the voyage, and the *New York News Dispatch* anticipated optimistically "a future happy period [in which we can] dispense with that burdensome and unnecessary traffick, which hitherto we have carried on with Europe."[1]

Profits from the *Empress's* voyage, though not spectacular, were satisfactory, so Morris and other investors backed more sailings to China. The *Empress* herself went out again under different ownership, and she was joined by other ships, most about her size, from Boston, Salem, Providence, New York, Philadelphia, and Baltimore. The trade had the attraction of a forbidden novelty, for until the Revolution, British navigation laws had reserved the Far East as a monopoly of the East India Company. The colonies received any Chinese goods by way of England. After the war London closed the British West Indies to profitable Yankee trade, not to be legally reopened for more than forty years. Americans, impoverished by the war, sought new commerce all over the world. During the

1. The most detailed account of the expedition is Philip Chadwick Foster Smith, *The Empress of China.* The *New York News Dispatch,* May 12, 1785, is quoted on 224–25.

late 1780s more than fifteen American ships appeared at Canton, and by 1790 the Chinese trade was well established. The Anglo-French wars that broke out in the 1790s and continued for more than two decades diverted British attention and brought rapid expansion and prosperity to Americans. The War of 1812 disrupted the China trade for a time and even caused an Anglo-American naval skirmish outside the Canton harbor, but when peace returned, trade quickly recovered, and by the late 1830s as many as forty American ships were docking at Canton in a year.[2]

From the beginning, the balance of Chinese trade was unfavorable to the United States. Tea, silk, porcelains, nankeens (a durable cotton cloth), and "notions" found a ready market at home and in Europe. In particular, tea had long symbolized the rich China trade, and the increased supply enhanced its importance to American traders. To obtain Chinese goods the Americans, like the British before them, had to send China large quantities of Spanish silver pesos—more than $70 million, it was estimated, between 1805 and 1825. From the start they sought products the Chinese would buy, such as ginseng, gathered by Indians from New England and Pennsylvania forests; sea otter and other furs from the northwest coast and the Falkland Islands; sandalwood from Hawaii; birds' nests, sea slugs, and other delicacies; and European manufactures. Their ships called at many ports to pick up freight for the Chinese trade.[3]

Shortly after 1800 they hit upon the most successful cargo of all—opium from Turkey—which was smuggled in. It soon became the real basis of American trade with China and somewhat reduced the need for specie. (This effect became more important during the 1820s, when the fall of the Spanish Empire in South America reduced the supply of silver coins.) While Americans probably never shipped into China more than one-tenth as much opium as the British East India Company before 1815, they showed great resourcefulness in organizing the complicated transactions required in smuggling and bribing government

---

2. Foster Rea Dulles, *The Old China Trade*; Kenneth Scott Latourette, "The History of Early Relations between the United States and China, 1784–1844," 10–18; Tyler Dennett, *Americans in Eastern Asia: A Critical Study of United States' Policy in the Far East in the Nineteenth Century*; Francis Ross Carpenter, *The Old China Trade: Americans in Canton, 1784–1843*, chap. 2; and Jonathan Goldstein, *Philadelphia and the China Trade, 1682–1846: Commercial, Cultural, and Attitudinal Effects*, 24–35; Conrad Edick Wright, "Merchants and Mandarins: New York and the Early China Trade," 17–25; Edward Sanderson, "Rhode Island Merchants in the China Trade," 38–44. A. Owen Aldridge, *The Dragon and the Eagle: The Presence of China in the American Enlightenment*, 100–103, 107–10, 121–23.

3. Aldridge, *Dragon and Eagle*, chap. 3, 111–19. Carpenter, *Old China Trade*, chaps. 5–10. Bennett, *Americans in Eastern Asia*, chaps. 2–4. Dulles, *Old China Trade*, 106–12, 210–11. James Kirker, *Adventures to China: Americans in the Southern Oceans, 1798*, chap. 11. Even before 1784 American ginseng was being shipped to China in large amounts by Europeans. For a breakdown of American exports to China (specie, merchandise, and bills on England) 1805–1833 see Latourette, "Early Relations," 27–28n3. The figure for specie shipments comes from U.S. Treasury records. On the significance of silver pesos to the Chinese trade system see W. E. Cheong, "Trade and Finance in China, 1784–1834: A Reappraisal," 34–56.

officials. They pacified American public opinion and their own consciences with rationalizations about Chinese depravity and xenophobia. Eventually they even got into the Indian trade too, first storing the opium on their ships and then handling it on consignment. This combination of competition and cooperation characterized Anglo-American relations in other ways too, as Americans took over much of the carrying trade between China and Europe during the Anglo-French wars, thereby earning needed specie. At the same time they began to use more bills of exchange (an early form of check) on London to replace cash transactions.[4]

During the 1820s and 1830s the American trade with China changed in other respects as well. The goods carried to Canton became more prosaic, as ginseng, sandalwood, and furs were replaced by such things as copper, candles, tobacco, beef, and New England cotton goods. Nankeens and silk declined among imports (the latter only temporarily); tea predominated by a wider margin than before. According to official figures, American imports from China reached about $5.2 million by 1821–1822, rose and fell sharply during the next two decades, and stood at about $4.9 million in 1841–1842. Even more surprising, total American trade outstripped that of the British East India Company during this period, and in 1834 the British government ended the company's monopoly and threw the trade open to all British merchants. The American advantage seems to have been due largely to greater efficiency and lower overhead, as the Americans used smaller, less expensive ships and smaller crews and achieved faster turnarounds and greater flexibility. Their insurance and freight costs were lower, their crews better behaved.[5]

In addition to distance, many obstacles beset the early China trade. Pirates infested the neighboring seas. Typhoons sometimes alternated with doldrums. The Chinese, contemptuous and a little fearful of foreigners, limited trade to one southern port, Canton, reassuringly far from the capital and the chief population centers, and placed it in the hands of the *co-hong*, a monopolistic group of merchant associations, and the often venal local officials. (Since the *co-hong* would not handle opium, a group of private traders soon appeared for that purpose.) Chinese tariffs were obscure, arbitrary, and constantly fluctuating. American unfamiliarity with the Chinese language, currency, and laws gave the Chinese further advantages. Canton was located on the delta of the Pearl River, which was

---

4. Michael Greenberg, *British Trade and the Opening of China, 1800–42,* chap. 5. Dennett, *Americans in Eastern Asia,* chap. 6. Carpenter, *Old China Trade,* chap. 10. Goldstein, *Philadelphia and China Trade,* 46–54. Charles C. Stelle, "American Trade in Opium to China, 1821–39," 68–74. Jacques M. Downs, "American Merchants and the Chinese Opium Trade, 1800–1890," 418–42. Jacques M. Downs, "Fair Game: Exploitative Role-Myths and the American Opium Trade," 142–49. Hsin-pao Chang, *Commissioner Lin and the Opium War,* 31. Opium remained China's most important import until the 1890s. Edward LeFevour, *Western Enterprise in Late Ch'ing China: A Selective Survey of Jardine, Matheson and Company's Operations, 1842–1895,* 8.

5. Dulles, *Old China Trade,* 112–18, 210–11. James R. Gibson, *Otter Skins, Boston Ships, and China Goods: The Maritime Fur Trade with the Northwest Coast, 1875–1841,* 94–95, 104–7.

usually crowded with Chinese and foreign vessels of all descriptions, especially during the autumn and winter, when silk and tea consignments were brought in from the countryside. The Chinese confined the British East India Company and other foreigners to hong-owned "factories" (offices, warehouses, and settlements) downriver from the city proper and near the main anchorage, Whampoa. Here they did business with hong merchants and other Chinese, most of them cynical, sharp bargainers but a few friendly and obliging to foreigners.[6]

The American merchants taking part in the trade were at first individuals and partners who remained at home and dealt through their own supercargoes and other agents. About 1803 they began to establish permanent branch offices in China, staffed mostly by young men who came and went for duty tours of three or four years. After the War of 1812 Boston, New York, and Philadelphia dominated the trade through tight little family-controlled merchant companies. Probably the best example was Perkins and Company at Boston, founded by Thomas H. Perkins and his brother and controlled for more than twenty years by the Perkins' nephew, John P. Cushing, who was sent out as a clerk at the age of sixteen and immediately had to take over the agency in an emergency. Through the 1820s he was a dominant figure in the commercial community of Canton. For example, in 1825 he got the local Chinese officials to reduce tonnage dues for American ships bringing rice from the East Indies and the Philippines.

By the 1830s the typical "China traders" belonged to commission houses that had evolved out of earlier partnerships. Before long most of these were centered in New York. These houses combined the capital of merchants at home with their own specialized information and local facilities and took a commission for their services, which included selling goods through Chinese merchants, buying and selling bills of exchange, and preparing market reports. Sometimes they engaged in ventures on their own account. Lacking the capital and the official backing of their larger British rivals, they were inclined to be more innovative. The most important American commission houses after 1830 were Russell and Company, successor to Perkins and Company, and also Olyphant and Company, Augustine Heard and Company, and W. S. Wetmore and Company. Of these only "the Russells" had resources and diversity to match the major British companies. Both they and Heard were very active in the opium trade, but D. W. C. Olyphant, that company's founder, was associated with the American Protestant Mission and a crusader against the drug.[7]

---

6. Greenberg, *British Trade and the Opening of China*, chap. 3 and passim. Dennett, *Americans in Eastern Asia*, chap. 3. Dulles, *Old China Trade*, chap. 2. Carpenter, *Old China Trade*, chaps. 3, 4. John King Fairbank, *Trade and Diplomacy on the China Coast: The Opening of the Treaty Ports, 1842–1854*, 48–53. Aldridge, *Dragon and Eagle*, 103–7. Wright, "Merchants and Mandarins," 37–40. Gibson, *Otter Skins, Boston Ships*, 191–203. For a good description of the intricacies of official and unofficial trade see Maurice Collins, *Foreign Mud* [i.e. opium], [etc.], 45–62. This book contains good maps of the Canton area.

7. Dennett, *Americans in Eastern Asia*, 16–18, 70–73, 91–92. Carpenter, *Old China Trade*, chap. 4. Wright, "Merchants and Mandarins," 40–41. Arthur E. Johnson and

Olyphant's attitude typified the uneasy relationship between early American merchants and missionaries in China. The American mission movement began during the 1820s in cooperation with British groups. By the mid-1830s the principal American mission leaders had arrived—Elijah C. Bridgman, the organizer, S. Wells Williams, the scholar, and Dr. Peter Parker, the first medical missionary and eventually the movement's most important political force. The Chinese government anticipated Christianity's subversive effect on Chinese traditions and did all it could to block missions, so American clerics went first to southeast Asia, especially Bangkok. Here they learned the Chinese language and culture from the many émigrés. By 1840 they had established schools and printing establishments in the Canton area and smaller centers at Singapore, Bangkok, and Batavia. Firm allies of British missionaries and enemies of the drug trade, they often treated American merchants with suspicion, but eventually the most far-sighted members of both groups came to recognize that account book and gospel were bound together in spreading western influences. At the end of the century one former missionary wrote that American businessmen could well afford to bear the entire cost of American missionary work in China for the sake of the resulting trade.[8]

It is difficult to generalize about the triangular relationship between American traders, missionaries, and the Chinese people whom they encountered. Early historians of American-Chinese relations were apt to emphasize the Americans' curiosity and admiration concerning the rich and complex civilization spread out before them, but recent writers have struck a more even balance with the disgust and impatience the Americans often felt and with the inevitable racism that lay behind these reactions. Until the 1830s the perception of China in the United States was certainly more favorable than that of merchants on the spot in Canton.[9]

Barry E. Supple, *Boston Capitalists and Western Railroads: A Study of the Nineteenth Century Investment Process*, 190–24. Robert Greenhalgh Albion, with the collaboration of Jennie Barnes Pope, *The Rise of New York Port (1815–1860)*, 198–201. On John P. Cushing see Henrietta M. Larson, "A China Trader Turns Investor—A Biographical Chapter in American Business History," 346–51. Stephen C. Lockwood, *Augustine Heard and Company, 1858–1862: American Merchants in China*, chap. 1, 21, 36–37 and passim. This book gives an excellent picture of the commission companies' operations, based on the papers of the Heard and Russell companies. For an example of how the Heards made money from the exchange rate see Frank H. H. King, *Money and Monetary Policy in China, 1845–1895*, 90.

8. Latourette, "Early Relations," chap. 4. Michael H. Hunt, *The Making of a Special Relationship: The United States and China to 1914*, 24–32. Edward H. Gulick, *Peter Parker and the Opening of China*. Chester Holcombe, "The Missionary Enterprise in China," 353–54. But not all American economic expansionists supported missions. For example, Andrew Carnegie thought them a waste and misuse of money for trying to force an alien religion on the Chinese. Andrew Carnegie to [Ella J. Newton], November 26, 1895, draft in Carnegie papers.

9. Examples of the earlier attitude are Latourette, "Early Relations," 124; and Dennett, *Americans in Eastern Asia*, 61. For a more revisionist view see Stuart Creighton Miller, *The Unwelcome Immigrant: The American Image of the Chinese, 1785–1882*, chaps. 2–4. In

Chinese attitudes toward the outsiders were similarly mixed. For about a century the Chinese government had mitigated its traditional isolationism with a real desire for foreign trade, especially if it would bring silver into the empire and remain strictly under government control. The Americans arrived at Canton just as European trade was slackening. Most Chinese had little interest in foreign businessmen beyond profit or in missionaries beyond curiosity. They welcomed the American traders for their cargoes of silver dollars, but a few genuinely liked the Yankees. One of these was the wealthy co-hong merchant Wu Ch'ung-yueh, known to foreigners as Howqua. A scrupulously honest trader whose word was his bond, he became the patron of the young John P. Cushing and, along with a small group of similar merchants, typified the best in the developing relationship.[10]

During the early decades of the Chinese trade the American government did what it could to lend support, but distance and the influence of rival economic interests at home complicated its efforts. The first American tariff law, in 1789, discriminated in favor of imports from China, especially tea, brought in American ships and directly from Canton. Later tariffs reduced the differential and allowed trade via Europe, but Americans continued to control tea imports. Congress also discriminated in favor of imports of cotton textiles until protests of domestic mill owners forced compromises in the tariff of 1816. They and other businessmen at home petitioned vigorously against the free export of specie, so much needed by the domestic economy, but China merchants were able to prevent restrictions until opium and British bills of exchange could relieve the pressure.

The government at home also gave some direct support to American traders in China. During the 1780s Congress appointed as consul Major Samuel Shaw (supercargo on the *Empress of China*'s first voyage), but the local Chinese officials refused to recognize his authority, and for many years the American consul did not have access to the Chinese government or even an interpreter for communication. Westerners in China had little protection, as was amply demonstrated by the Terranova incident of 1821, in which an Italian sailor on an American ship was accused of murder, arrested, tried secretly, and strangled. In 1819–1820, 1830, and 1832 a U.S. warship visited Canton, and during the 1830s other American naval vessels continued to establish the American presence by occasional calls. In 1839 the government created the East India Squadron to look after American interests in the vast Pacific area west of Hawaii and the Aleutians and extending across the Indian Ocean to East Africa. Business had been slow

---

an earlier article Miller examines writings of early traders and cites examples of Chinese friendliness as well as their corruption, cowardice, venality, deceit, and other objectionable qualities. Stuart Creighton Miller, "The American Trader's Image of China, 1785–1840," 375–95. See also Goldstein, *Philadelphia and China Trade*, 5–6, 69–70; Aldridge, *Dragon and Eagle*, 13–14, 119; and Hunt, *Special Relationship*, 32–40.

10. Hunt, *Special Relationship*, 41–51. Aldridge, *Dragon and Eagle*, 106; Carpenter, *Old China Trade*, chap. 4. Gibson, *Otter Skins, Boston Ships*, 86–91.

during the late 1830s, but the squadron appeared opportunely on the eve of new expansion.[11]

By that time several factors made some sort of change inevitable. The westerners' influence at Canton had increased. So had their resentment, especially among the British, at Chinese restrictions. Also the British abolition of the East India Company's monopoly eased relations with American merchants, and the panic of 1837 produced business problems in the United States. The First Anglo-Chinese War, the "Opium War" of 1839–1842, was immediately caused by a governmental effort to stamp out the expanding opium trade, which was disrupting the Chinese currency by draining off silver to India. The British blockaded Canton and withdrew their merchants from the factories, urging the Russells and other Americans to join them. The Americans, however, paid no attention, and although legal trade declined, they made great profits on opium during the hostilities. (They placated the British, however, by giving them facilities of their own for smuggling.) The Chinese were no match for the British Navy, and two peace treaties conceded nearly everything the British asked: the end of the Canton trade monopoly, four new ports opened to British trade and residence, the island of Hong Kong (offshore from Canton) ceded for a naval base, a uniform low tariff on British goods, and a most-favored-nation provision.[12]

These events finally stimulated the U.S. government to action. In 1839 American merchants in Canton had petitioned Congress for a naval force and a commercial agent to negotiate a treaty, listing desirable provisions to ensure personal security and freer trade. In the ensuing congressional discussion the cautious desire of some New England merchants not to disturb the status quo prevented diplomatic action. Much anti-Chinese opinion surfaced, led by John Quincy Adams, who blamed the war on Chinese arrogance, but Dr. Peter Parker, the medical missionary, lobbied actively among congressmen and convinced Secretary of State Daniel Webster of the need for negotiations to prevent the loss of American trade and moral influence in China.

Several events during 1842 hurried matters along. The Webster-Ashburton Treaty settled several serious outstanding Anglo-American disputes, and the first British treaty with China made clear the extent of Britain's victory. During the war Captain (later Commodore) Lawrence Kearny was sent out by Washington with two ships to protect American interests on the China coast and prevent Americans from trading in opium. Exceeding his instructions, Kearny tried to negotiate with Chinese officials for a formal commercial agreement. In this he failed, but he

---

11. Edward D. Graham, "Special Interests and the Early China Trade," 233–42. Latourette, "Early Relations," 78–79n138. Dennett, *Americans in Eastern Asia*, 62–64, 75–80, 83–89. Dulles, *Old China Trade*, 124–28, 132–38. Goldstein, *Philadelphia and China Trade*, 36, 60–61. Charles Oscar Paullin, *Diplomatic Negotiations of American Naval Officers, 1778–1883*, 167–85. E. Mowbray Tate, "American Merchant and Naval Contacts with China, 1784–1850," 179–83. Curtis T. Henson, Jr., *Commissioners and Commodores: The East India Squadron and American Diplomacy in China*, 11–17, 20.

12. Peter Ward Fay, *The Opium War, 1840–1842*, especially pt. 3.

reported vague assurances by the officials of treatment equal to that given the British. Webster and Caleb Cushing of Massachusetts, a spokesman for merchants in the China trade, induced President John Tyler to call for a diplomatic mission. Congress approved the mission in January 1843 despite the partisan opposition of Thomas Hart Benton and other Democratic territorial expansionists. After some hesitation Tyler appointed Cushing to head the mission, and Webster drew up detailed instructions with advice from Thomas H. Perkins and other leading China merchants.[13]

When Cushing arrived at Canton in February 1844, he had to undergo four frustrating months of slow bargaining with an acting provincial official before Peking sent down an experienced commissioner, Ch'iying, who had already dealt with the British. At his request, Cushing gave him a draft which became the basis of negotiations, although Ch'iying later minimized its importance in his private report. The American diplomat also smoothed his path by giving up his early demand to visit Peking (probably a bluff), which the Chinese strongly resisted, and he received much valuable aid from his translator, the missionary Dr. Peter Parker. The treaty of Wang-hsia was signed on July 3 just outside the Portuguese port of Macao.[14]

In the treaty Cushing obtained all the British privileges except a territorial cession and, in addition, extraterritoriality—the right to have American citizens accused of a crime tried under American law in an American consular court. (Naturally the British at once secured the same right through their most-favored-nation provision.) Partly in deference to missionary opinion, Cushing, unlike the British, agreed on a prohibition of the opium trade.[15] Some have credited Kearny or the British or even the Chinese with the successful negotiations. Others have

13. Dennett, *Americans in Eastern Asia,* 91–94. Latourette, "Early Relations," 110–20. Dulles, *Old China Trade,* chap. 11. Chang, *Commissioner Lin,* 206–8. Goldstein, *Philadelphia and China Trade,* 57–65. Ironically, when the war broke out, the opium trade was suffering from oversupply, and American merchants began to cut back. Hunt, *Special Relationship,* 8.

14. Dennett, *Americans in Eastern Asia,* 99–113, 134–43. Richard E. Welch, Jr., "Caleb Cushing's Chinese Mission and the Treaty of Wanghia: A Review," 128–35. Tate, "American Contacts with China," 184–87. Kenneth E. Shewmaker, "Forging the 'Great Chain': Daniel Webster and the Origins of American Foreign Policy toward East Asia and the Pacific, 1841–1852," 226–27, 230–31. Dulles, *Old China Trade,* chap. 12. J. Wade Caruthers, *American Pacific Ocean Trade; Its Impact on Foreign Policy and Continental Expansion, 1784–1860,* 99–108. On Kearny see John H. Schroeder, *Shaping a Maritime Empire: The Commercial and Diplomatic Role of the American Navy, 1829–1861,* 50–55. After a Chinese mob damaged the Augustine Heard factory at Canton, Kearny secured an assurance from the governor that China would pay the resulting claims. Some historians believe that Kearny was the real originator of the open door policy.

15. Welch, "Cushing's Chinese Mission," 335–57. Dennett, *Americans in Eastern Asia,* chap. 8. Latourette, "Early Relations," 121–44. Dulles, *Old China Trade,* chap. 13. Te-kong Tong, *United States Diplomacy in China, 1844–60,* 17–18, 21, 28–30. Eventually extraterritoriality covered some three hundred thousand foreigners. For Kearny's role in the negotiations see Henson, *Commissioners and Commodores,* chap. 4. Earl H. Pritchard, "The Origins of the Most-Favored-Nation and the Open Door Policy in China," 166–70.

argued that the treaty was unnecessary, for it did not respond to any clear-cut demand among Americans, or improper because the United States had not earned the concessions through military actions or reciprocal favors and had neither the ability nor the desire to enforce the treaty. (For example, American merchants continued to smuggle opium as before.) The treaty meant different things to the two parties. To the westerners it was a "charter of privileges," subject to later expansion, a way of bringing China into the western world. To the Chinese it was a means of putting the barbarians on an equal basis, so they could be played off against each other, a way of bringing them into the Chinese tradition.

Despite these criticisms, the Treaty of Wang-hsia was a landmark in both American and Chinese foreign policy. Superior to the British treaties in both form and content, it became at once the model for Chinese treaties with France, Norway, and Sweden. More important, the treaty opened a new era in American economic relations with China.[16]

During the first sixty years of American-Chinese trade, from 1784 to 1844, that trade never amounted to one-tenth of total American foreign trade. In its best years, 1823–1827, it reached about 6.4 percent but then dropped to about 2.1 percent annually and by the end of the century to about 1.9 percent. Imports always outweighed exports, despite the increasing American desire for the latter. In the mid-twenties exports reached about 40 percent of American-Chinese trade but fell to about 27 percent by 1840. Also the import trade, especially in its major product, tea, was highly speculative.[17]

Nevertheless, the Chinese commercial magnet exerted a remarkable influence on the economic ideology of the burgeoning United States, and the Golden East became such a widely accepted place-name that it was almost inscribed on maps. Perhaps the most important reason for this was that the trade, though speculative, could be immensely profitable. Probably most of the new fortunes amassed in the leading cities of that trade—Boston, Philadelphia, and above all New York—contained a significant Oriental element in their makeup, much of it tied up in the drug trade. Lowells, Girards, Astors, Lows, Griswolds, Copes, and many others extended their Cantonese profits and influence at home into real estate, railroads, steamship lines, and eventually politics. Perhaps the outstanding example of this capital transfer was its role in promoting early western railroads,

---

For the text of the treaty see Charles I. Bevans, comp., *Treaties and Other International Agreements of the United States of America, 1776–1949*, vol. 6, 647–68.

16. Latourette, "Early Relations," 122–30. Dennett, *Americans in Eastern Asia*, 170, 179–80. Dulles, *Old China Trade*, 201–7. Carpenter, *Old China Trade*, 104–5, 114. Miller, *Unwelcome Immigrant*, chap. 5. Fairbank, *Trade and Diplomacy*, 208–9. Schroeder, *Shaping a Maritime Empire*, 165–66. At about this time the Chinese government set up a "Barbarian Affairs Bureau" (Iwu Chu) to compile documents relating to foreign countries. Earl Swisher, *China's Management of the American Barbarians: A Study of Sino-American Relations, 1841–1861, with Documents*, 8–9.

17. Grover Clark, "Changing Markets," 127. For a glimpse of how money might be made or lost in the tea trade at this time see a letter of Joseph A. Scoville reprinted in Kenneth Wiggins Porter, *John Jacob Astor, Business Man*, vol. 2, 614–16.

first to reach the Mississippi and then to cross it, pushing toward the Pacific. Ironically, the American western movement also drew attention, investment, and manpower away from Far Eastern trade and helped to account for its persistently low percentile figures in overall trade statistics.[18]

For the purpose of this book the most significant immediate effect of the Chinese commercial magnet was felt in the Pacific basin at large. Here it drew American traders to many new places: the northwest coast of North America, the west coast of Spanish America, the Hawaiian Islands, Australia, the South Seas islands, the East Indies, Southeast Asia, and even Japan in search of products for the Chinese market. American sea captains joined the Europeans in discovering and mapping new routes and lands. In the Pacific the Chinese magnet's power had to contend with the opposing force of distance, for San Francisco lies about twenty-four hundred airline miles from both Sitka (the chief nineteenth-century settlement of Alaska) and Honolulu, nearly seven thousand miles from Manila and Canton, and more than seventy-one hundred miles from Sydney. The distances traveled from the American East Coast of course were much greater.

The product that originally attracted American ships to the northwest coast was furs, first of sea otters and later of seals, to line the clothing of wealthy northern Chinese against their cold winters. Before the Americans arrived in China, the Russians sold Siberian furs to the Chinese, first via Mongolia and then more successfully through Canton. As Siberian furs declined, Czar Peter the Great had the idea of developing a new source of supply on the North American coast and sent out an expedition that discovered the Bering Strait. During the middle decades of the eighteenth century Russians explored and traded all over the North Pacific. It was not until the end of the century, however, that Russia founded permanent settlements in Alaska—on Kodiak Island and at Novo Archangel'sk (Sitka)—and in 1799 a trading agency, the Russian-American Company. The British were also interested in the trade and sent Captain James Cook to reconnoiter that coast (1779) on his third and final exploring voyage. Some of Cook's men traded with the Indians for sea otter pelts and took them along to China, where they brought a good price.

The link between these developments and the American fur trade to China was an American sailor on Captain Cook's expedition, John Ledyard, who became excited at the profitable possibilities of the North American fur trade and tried to promote a venture. He impressed Robert Morris, Thomas Jefferson, and later John Paul Jones, but, dogged by misfortune, he was never able to carry out his plans. Instead, in 1787 a consortium of six Boston merchants sent out two small ships that rounded Cape Horn, a more dangerous route than that of the *Empress of China*, and traded for furs with the northwest Indians, who presented dangers

18. Hunt, *Special Relationships*, 11–12. Johnson and Supple, *Boston Capitalists*, chaps. 2, 3. Albion, *Rise of New York Port*, chap. 10. Goldstein, *Philadelphia and China Trade*, 40–45. Clark, "Changing Markets," 126.

of their own. One of the ships, the *Columbia,* took furs to Canton under Captain Robert Gray and became the first American ship to sail around the world. On a later voyage in the same ships Gray explored the mouth of the Columbia River, a feat that became the foundation of the later American claim to Oregon.[19]

These voyages did not earn the profits that Ledyard had foretold, but later ships did better, and Boston in particular sent out expeditions each summer to the northwest coast and Canton. During the 1780s and early 1790s the British dominated the fur trade on the northwest coast, but after that their ships virtually disappeared. The American success was due both to the energy of American seamen, some of them part owners of their ships, and to the desire of capitalists at home to escape the postrevolutionary depression. However, the Indians were becoming more hostile and the furs more scarce, so the Americans had to resort also to smuggling in California and trading supplies for furs with the Russians farther north.[20]

During the first decade of the nineteenth century the northwest fur trade and its Cantonese connections were closely bound to the career of John Jacob Astor, whose resources and business sense amply fulfilled Ledyard's dreams. After more than a decade of experience in the Canadian fur trade, Astor sent his first ship to China in 1800 but did not immediately pursue this branch of the trade. Instead he concentrated on obtaining furs for the American and European markets. In order to break up the powerful British fur monopoly in Canada, he organized the American Fur Company in 1808 and in 1811 founded a trading post and fort, Astoria, at the mouth of the Columbia River. The following year he negotiated an agreement with the Russian-American Company by which the parties would divide the fur trade on the coast and Astor would market Russian furs in China in return for supplying provisions to Sitka. Astor's plans went awry—Indians destroyed one of his fur-trading ships on the Oregon coast in 1811, and then the War of 1812 interrupted his Chinese trade. Finally his settlers at Astoria, fearing an imminent British occupation, sold out the company's holdings to the British-owned Northwest Company. By the end of the war Astor seemed to have no future on the northwest coast.[21]

19. B. P. Polevci, "The Discovery of Russian America," 13–31. James R. Gibson, *Imperial Russia in Frontier America: The Changing Geography of Supply of Russian America, 1784–1867,* 3–10. Caruthers, *American Pacific Ocean Trade,* 18–19, 30–32. Norman E. Saul, *Distant Friends: The United States and Russia, 1763–1867,* 42–48.

20. Howard I. Kushner, *Conflict on the Northwest Coast: American-Russian Rivalry in the Pacific Northwest, 1790–1867,* 4–8. Mary E. Wheeler, "Empires in Conflict and Cooperation: The 'Bostonians' and the Russian-American Company," 422–28. Dulles, *Old China Trade,* 53–55. Dennett, *Americans in Eastern Asia,* 38–40. Gibson, *Imperial Russia,* 56–58. Samuel Eliot Morison, *The Maritime History of Massachusetts, 1783–1860,* chaps. 4, 5. Caruthers, *American Pacific Ocean Trade,* 24–26. Frederick Merk, "The Genesis of the Oregon Question," 1–4. Kirker, *Adventures to China,* chap. 4.

21. Porter, *Astor,* vol. 1, chaps. 3, 6–9. Aldridge, *Dragon and Eagle,* 96–97. Nicolai Bolkhovitinov, *The Beginnings of Russian-American Relations, 1775–1815,* chap. 9. Wheeler, "Empires in Conflict and Cooperation," 428–31. Saul, *Distant Friends,* 67–68. The British

But during the war he had bought up a fleet at bargain prices, and within three months after the peace was signed, a ship of his left for Canton with nearly fourteen thousand fur skins and $39,000 in specie, to bring back a cargo of tea, silks, and other Chinese products. This began a decade of profitable fur trade with China, more complicated than the prewar trade since it also involved Europe, Hawaii, California, and the west coast of South America. Astor even became briefly involved in smuggling opium into China. Gradually, however, he concentrated on the American Fur Company's trade with Europe and the eastern United States, and between 1823 and 1825 he abandoned the China market. After another decade of fur trading mainly in the American West, Astor withdrew from the American Fur Company as well in 1834 to devote himself entirely to real estate and other fields.[22]

After the War of 1812 the United States sent the warship *Ontario* around Cape Horn to reassert the American title to the lower Columbia Valley. Boston-based fur traders returned to the northwest coast, followed by others from eastern ports, and from 1815 to 1822 ninety-six additional American trading ships arrived on the coast. By this time the Russian-American Company had established a string of fourteen food-producing settlements along the coast and islands and one ("Fort Ross") as far south as California north of San Francisco. At one time the Russians even contemplated a colony in Hawaii. On the northwest coast an odd relationship developed between Russians and Americans—the Russians depended on the Americans to supply their coastal colonies with food and trading goods, while making every effort to prevent them from trading with the Indians. This friction was intensified by rising sentiment among westerners in the American Congress for an aggressive policy toward the Oregon country.

In response to these circumstances, on September 21, 1821, Czar Alexander I issued a ukase closing the entire northwest coast as far south as the forty-first parallel (Eureka, California) to "the pursuits of commerce, whaling, and fishery, and all other industry." This of course aroused further demonstrations in Congress and the American press, but Secretary of State John Quincy Adams, a representative of New England shipping interests, a nationalist, and a former minister to Russia, managed to dampen the defiance in favor of diplomacy. During the next two years the Russians retreated from their extreme position, and in December 1823 President James Monroe incorporated a general "non-colonization" principle into his annual message as part of the Monroe Doctrine.[23]

---

traders were alarmed at Astor's activities and petitioned their government for naval support but got little except in wartime. Glynn Barratt, *Russian Shadows on the British Northwest Coast of North America, 1810–1890: A Study of Rejection of Defence Responsibilities*, 1–4. For a time, 1808–1810, the United States even considered a treaty with Russia, marking off fur-trading areas on the coast. Kushner, *Conflict*, 11–24. Gibson, *Imperial Russia*, 156–61.

22. Porter, *Astor*, vol. 1, chaps. 12–15.

23. Robert Erwin Johnson, *Thence Round Cape Horn: The Story of United States Naval Forces on Pacific Station, 1818–1823*, 4–5. Caruthers, *American Pacific Ocean Trade*, 41–64. Kushner, *Conflict*, chaps. 2, 3. Frederick Merk, *Fur Trade and Empire: George N. Simpson's*

By this time the Russian-American company was suffering from several handicaps: U.S. competition, bad management, and unreliable official support in faraway St. Petersburg. Immediately after the war it paid good dividends, but after the ukase these disappeared, in part because of the need to purchase supplies from the Americans. In 1824 and 1825 the Russian government signed boundary treaties with the United States and Britain respectively, giving up further expansion to the south and east. In 1839 the company leased most of the Alaska "panhandle" to the Hudson's Bay Company, and several years later it sold Fort Ross to the Swiss-American landowner John A. Sutter. By then the Russians' interest in the coast was fading fast. The Americans' fur trade to China also declined steadily after the 1820s as fur-bearing animals decreased, the Hudson's Bay company grew more powerful, and East Coast capitalists found other outlets for their money.[24]

Early American economic activities in Hawaii were closely bound to the northwest fur trade. The islands were discovered by Captain Cook on his last voyage in 1778, and the first American ship to visit them may have been Robert Gray's *Columbia*, which took on supplies in 1789–1790 en route to Canton. During the next two years at least five more American ships called for the same reason, and soon the central location of the islands made them "a great caravansery" for ships going in all directions. They became a wintering refuge for fur traders spending more than one season on the northwest coast; soon damaged ships were being rebuilt there. The natives received outsiders in friendly fashion under their powerful king, Kamehameha. As they became more sophisticated,

Journal [etc.], xi–xx. Wheeler, "Empires in Conflict and Cooperation," 430–35. Gibson, *Imperial Russia*, 9–13, 161–72. S. B. Okun, *The Russian-American Company*, chaps. 3, 4, 6, 7. Saul, *Distant Friends*, 96–105. The question of the defensive or offensive aims of the czar's ukase will probably never be settled to everyone's satisfaction. For an explanation of the offensive thesis see Nikolai N. Bolkhovitinov, "Russia and the Declaration of the Non-Colonization Principle: New Archival Evidence," 108–9. Anatole Mazour regards the ukase as a defensive measure intended to buy time for Russian activities in the Balkans and softened to forestall united opposition from Britain and the United States. Mazour, "The Russian-American and Anglo-Russian Conventions, 1824–1825: An Interpretation," 305–7. Henry Middleton, the American minister to Russia, reported to Adams that he had been assured that the government did not intend to enforce the ukase. Barrett, *Russian Shadows*, 15. At the time only former president Madison took an undisturbed view of the ukase. Saul, *Distant Friends*, 97n13.

24. Mazour, "Russian-American and Anglo-American Conventions," 307–10. Okun, *Russian-American Company*, chap. 10. Gibson, *Imperial Russia*, 23–29, 166–68. Kushner, *Conflict*, chap. 4. In 1824, under a provision of the new Russian-American treaty, the Russian-American Company tried in vain to forbid further American fur-trading along its coast north of 54°40'. Wheeler, "Empires in Conflict and Cooperation," 435–41. Donald C. Davidson, "Relations of the Hudson's Bay Company with the Russian-American Company on the Northwest Coast, 1829–1867," 33–51. Harold W. Bradley, *The American Frontier in Hawaii: The Pioneers, 1789–1843*, 220–23. On the American decline see Gibson, *Otter Skins, Boston Ships*, 58–61, chap. 4.

their prices rose, and the king, shrewd as a New Englander, levied port taxes and tonnage dues in imitation of other governments.[25]

As early as 1790 sailors visiting Hawaii discovered groves of sandalwood growing wild and soon realized that, as in the case of furs, the Chinese would pay a good price for the logs, for construction, furniture, and incense. Unaccountably shipments lagged for nearly twenty years, perhaps because at first Hawaiian sandalwood was regarded as inferior to that of the Marquesas and other islands. After that Americans took over the trade. As soon as Kamehameha realized its value, he decreed a royal monopoly and issued licenses, which stabilized the trade to everyone's benefit. After his death in 1819 restrictions were somewhat relaxed, and the trade reached its peak at $288,000 in 1822. But by 1830 its days were almost over.[26]

The War of 1812 brought warships and privateers of both belligerents into the Pacific to disrupt the islands' commerce, but after peace came new American participants appeared, especially Boston trading houses and John Jacob Astor's emissaries. As Spanish restrictions on California waned, Hawaii became tributary to its increasing trade. Surprisingly the U.S. government did not appoint a consul at Honolulu until 1820. During the depression of 1819 in the United States more American ships came to the islands carrying goods of all descriptions to tempt the natives, and some chiefs went deeply into debt. A civil war briefly disturbed trade in 1824, and two years later, in response to complaints to Washington by American merchants, two separate warships arrived to investigate. As a result, the Hawaiian government agreed to cover the chiefs' debts and signed a treaty of commerce and friendship (1826), including a most-favored-nation provision. Although the American government never ratified it, the Hawaiians honored the treaty anyway.[27]

By this time the whaling industry had appeared to supplement and eventually replace the fur and sandalwood trades in Hawaii's economy. Whaling figured prominently during most of New England's colonial history, but only in the Atlantic and adjacent waters. Nantucket and New Bedford whaling vessels, slow and ugly but efficient, entered the Pacific in 1791 and filled their holds off the Chilean coast. Gradually they pushed north and west across the equator but did not reach the Alaskan coast, the Bering Strait, and the Siberian coast until the 1830s and 1840s. In 1819 they began to operate out of Honolulu for supplies and soon established a regular routine of two visits a year, spring and fall. By 1830 four-fifths of shipping clearing at Hawaii (out of a total valued at about $5

25. Harold W. Bradley, "The Hawaiian Islands and the Pacific Fur Trade," 27–78, 282–86 (quotation on 282). Bradley, *American Frontier*, 1–18. Ralph S. Kuykendall, *The Hawaiian Kingdom, 1854–1874: Twenty Critical Years,* vol. 1, 81–85.

26. Bradley, *American Frontier*, 26–31, 53–71. Kuykendall, *Hawaiian Kingdom*, vol. 1, 83, 85–92. Theodore Morgan, *Hawaii, A Century of Economic Change, 1778–1876*, 65–73.

27. Bradley, *American Frontier*, 31–32, 82–89, 103–11. Kuykendall, *Hawaiian Kingdom*, vol. 1, 86–87, 89–93, 98–99. Stevens, *American Frontier*, 102. For the text of the treaty see David Hunter Miller, ed., *Treaties and Other International Acts of the United States of America, 1776–1863*, 3, 273–81.

million) was connected with the whaling industry. During the next forty years the northwest whaling grounds furnished 60 percent of American whales.[28]

Missionaries arrived in Hawaii earlier than in China (1820) and were more numerous and effective, in part because the native religion offered less formidable competition and the government was more cooperative. By 1842 there were seventy-nine American missionaries in Hawaii, operating nineteen stations all over the islands and a half-dozen schools. They were a powerful westernizing influence, although, as in China, there was considerable friction with the merchants. One of the most influential commercial outfits, Ladd and Company, however, operated under the informal patronage of the missionaries and held an extensive agricultural commission from the king.[29]

During the 1820s and 1830s several similar companies were organized in Hawaii to carry on the sandalwood trade and deal in dozens of commodities for the whalers from the United States, Europe, Latin America, China, and the Pacific Islands. In 1844 there were six commission merchants (four of them American) and eleven storekeepers (seven American). Some merchants operated their own ships. On its large government land grant, Ladd and Company established one of the first sugar plantations on the islands, pioneering in the industry, which was to replace whaling as the foundation of the whole economy. As trade expanded, barter gave way to sandalwood, then to specie, and finally to crude bills of exchange on the United States and European countries. Other capitalist trappings appeared too, such as newspaper advertisements and tariff laws.[30]

Although by the 1830s Americans dominated Hawaiian trade, British political influence was supreme under Kamehameha I and his short-lived successor, Kamehameha II, each of whom offered Britain a vague protectorate over the islands. With the accession of the boy Kamehameha III in 1825, naturalized foreigners, often American missionaries, became the principal royal advisers, supported by the Hawaiian-American treaty of 1826. The British and French, fearing American annexation, put so much pressure on the young king that in 1842 he sent two envoys to ask all three countries for recognition of Hawaiian independence. Not wanting to commit the United States beyond what was necessary to restrain Britain and France, Secretary of State Daniel Webster replied cautiously and

28. Walter S. Tower, *A History of the American Whale Fishery,* chaps. 3–5. Kushner, *Conflict,* chap. 5. Morgan, *Hawaii,* chap. 5. Kuykendall, *Hawaiian Kingdom,* vol. 1, 93–94. Bradley, *American Frontier,* 79–82, 215–19. Ernest S. Dodge, *New England and the South Seas,* chap. 2.

29. Kuykendall, *Hawaiian Kingdom,* vol. 1, chaps. 7, 11 and passim. Ralph S. Kuykendall, "American Interests and American Influence in Hawaii in 1842," 54–55, 63–65. Stevens, *American Expansion,* 8–10, 25–31. Morgan, *Hawaii,* chap. 6. Bradley, *American Frontier,* chaps. 3, 4.

30. Morgan, *Hawaii,* 98–112. Kuykendall, *Hawaiian Kingdom,* vol. 1, 93–95, 171–76. Bradley, *American Frontier,* chap. 5. A list of early merchants in Hawaii, mostly American, is in Caruthers, *American Pacific Ocean Trade,* 167–68. For a history of one of the early American companies see Josephine Sullivan, *A History of C. Brewer and Company, Limited, One Hundred Years in the Hawaiian Islands, 1826–1926.*

appointed "a consul or agent" for the islands instead of a minister plenipotentiary. In his next annual message President John Tyler announced that American dominance in commerce made it appropriate to declare that no one should annex the islands and that the United States would make "a decided remonstrance against the adoption of an opposite policy by any other power." This statement came to be called the "Tyler Doctrine," in self-conscious reference to the somewhat similar Monroe Doctrine.

The following year Tyler's pronouncement was challenged by British agents in Honolulu. The harried king, pressed by the acting British consul, offered to cede Hawaii to Britain, and the commander of a visiting British warship, Lord George Paulet, raised the Union Jack and virtually ruled the islands for five months. The apparently coincidental arrival of a U.S. warship stiffened local American resistance to the cession. Before Washington and Paris could react, the British admiral commanding the Pacific Squadron off South America hurried out to restore Hawaiian independence. A brief storm broke out in the nationalist American press, and after Anglo-French negotiations with Hawaii over European grievances, the two nations recognized Hawaiian independence, and the crisis ended without allaying anyone's suspicions.[31]

Other Pacific areas also contributed products to the Americans' trade with China. For example, in 1815 three Boston firms sent out the ship *Ophelia,* with $70,000 in specie and instructions that carried her all over the Pacific. The captain was to buy copper in Chile, then take on whale teeth in the Galápagos Islands and sandalwood in the Marquesas or Hawaii. If delayed, he was to purchase furs in Russian America or coffee at Batavia in the East Indies. After exchanging furs and sandalwood for Chinese goods, he was to bring them home with any coffee he had acquired.[32]

Adjacent to the northwest coast but presenting problems of its own was California. Beginning in 1796, the first American fur traders to visit it came around the Horn from Boston and Salem; after about 1815 a second group approached from Hawaii; and eventually a lively competition developed between the two. At first sea otter and seal furs were the principal California cargo. Since the

31. Kuykendall, *Hawaiian Kingdom,* vol. 1, 54–55, 76–80, 142–43, 164–67, chaps. 12, 13, 247–57. Stevens, *American Expansion,* 1–8, 25–29. Bradley, *American Frontier,* chap. 8. Shewmaker, "Forging the 'Great Chain,'" 231–33, 236. The Anglo-French aspects of the Paulet affair are set forth in detail by Jean I. Brookes in *International Rivalry in the Pacific Islands, 1800–1875,* chap. 7. Kuykendall, "American Interests," 48–50, 60–67. Richard W. Van Alstyne, "Great Britain, the United States, and Hawaiian Independence, 1850–1855," 15–19.

32. Kuykendall, *Hawaiian Kingdom,* vol. 1, 87–88. Dulles, *Old China Trade,* 76–79. It does not weaken the point being made that because of a series of misfortunes the *Ophelia* could not carry out any of the early transactions. She entered Canton harbor with all the specie on board, which was exchanged for a cargo of Chinese goods before she returned to Boston. For other samples of far-flung itineraries see Caruthers, *American Pacific Ocean Trade,* 80–82.

Spanish government strictly forbade the trade, the Americans became smugglers and for a time even brought in skilled Russian hunters to work the offshore islands. The independent Mexican government threw open the trade after 1821, and when furs began to decline later in the decade, other California products took their place, especially cowhides, tallow, horses, and lumber. The last of these was to remain a staple of Pacific trade for the rest of the century. Before midcentury hides and tallow were in the greatest demand—for the New England boot and shoe industry, in Hawaii, along the South American coast, and even in China. Oriental goods were brought from Hawaii to California to be traded. California also served as a supply port for whalers, and as in Hawaii, American merchants settled in Monterey, San Francisco, and San Pedro to found agencies. One of these merchants, Thomas O. Larkin, played a considerable role in bending the province toward American annexation. By the 1840s California was an American commercial outpost, and the Mexican War began a radically different chapter in its history.[33]

During the first thirty years of America's Pacific trade, ships rounding southern South America usually proceeded northward along the coast rather than heading out into the ocean, especially since they could stop for supplies at the ports of Chile or Peru. These were still under Spanish restrictions, which were gradually being relaxed by the late eighteenth century. In 1792 the first American ship, a sealer carrying some trade goods, sailed from the Cape of Good Hope to Australia, only four years after the founding there of the first convict colony. From then until 1812 about seventy American ships called at Sydney, not including whalers. The attraction of the Australian port was its demand for provisions and liquor, especially Rhode Island rum, which could be exchanged for specie before the ships went on to China. This trade, being a violation of the British East India Company's monopoly, was strictly illegal. Both British merchants and the colonials protested in vain against the restrictions, so the whole American trade was carried on through smuggling, bribery, or other evasions of the law. Eventually a few Americans even formed partnerships with their Sydney counterparts to send some Chinese goods eastward to New South Wales.[34]

The War of 1812 effectively destroyed this comfortable arrangement. The British Navy at once captured all American ships in Australian waters. In 1813 Captain David Porter, commanding the USS *Essex,* became separated from his squadron in the south Atlantic and decided to operate independently in the Pacific. Rounding the Horn, Porter resupplied his vessel at Valparaiso, then

33. Adele Ogden, "New England Traders in Spanish and Mexican California," 395–413. Robert Glass Cleland, *A History of California: The American Period,* chaps. 1–4.

34. C. Hartley Grattan, *The United States and the Southwest Pacific,* 68–80. C. Hartley Grattan, *The Southwest Pacific to 1900, A Modern History: Australia, New Zealand, the Islands, Antarctica,* 189–90. Werner Levi, *American-Australian Relations,* chap. 1. For early American sealing activities in the Indian Ocean and the South Pacific see Kirker, *Adventures to China,* chaps. 5–7.

established a base at Nukuhiva in the Marquesas Islands and virtually swept the British whaling fleet from the ocean. In 1814 he was foolhardy enough to take on the two strongest warships in the British squadron, which captured the *Essex*, but his exploits established an American naval presence in the Pacific. Australian inhabitants suffered from the stoppage of American trade, and the war created a split in their attitude toward the United States, some favoring free trade and friendship, others inwardly fearing American domination.[35]

The expansion of American influence into the South Sea islands was carried on mainly by whalers and sealers (the latter for New Zealand and more southerly islands). Although whalers operated out of sight of land for weeks or months, hunting, killing, and trying out whale oil on board ship, they needed supply ports and recreational facilities for their rowdy crews. The natives of northern New Zealand and the Galapagos, Samoan, Caroline, Society, and Fijian archipelagoes were usually quite willing to furnish these, despite the missionaries' efforts to restrain them. Tahiti in the Societies was an especially popular base, Fiji less so because of the natives' notorious cannibalism. None of these island groups approached Hawaii for the solidity or permanence of the American influence. American whalers easily outnumbered those of any other nationality, and they dominated the whole central Pacific for the first half of the century, their influence reaching a climax during the 1850s. In addition to whalers, American ships visited the smaller islands for products valued in the Cantonese market, especially shells, tortoises, sandalwood, birds' nests from the cliffs, and sea slugs from the shallow ocean floor and the coral reefs. The slugs were boiled, cured, and packed in bags for the Chinese, who made soup of them. The work was hard and sometimes dangerous, but profits might reach 700 percent.[36]

The interest of the U.S. government in the Pacific islands before the 1840s was at best sporadic, but Porter's exploits and the activities of American traders and missionaries were enough to keep Britain and France nervous, as shown by the jockeying for position in Hawaii. As early as the 1820s President John Quincy Adams and a few others favored systematic exploration of the area, and after a long campaign for support the government sent out six ships under Lieutenant Charles Wilkes on a four-year expedition (1838–1842). Wilkes covered the east half of the ocean extensively from Antarctica and Australia on the south and west

35. Kirker, *Adventures to China*, chap. 2. Arrell Morgan Gibson, with the assistance of John S. Whitehead, *Yankees in Paradise: The Pacific Basin Frontier*, 314–17. Raymond A. Rydell, *Cape Horn to the Pacific: The Rise and Decline of an Ocean Highway*, 92–95. Porter informally annexed the Marquesas, but the Senate would not confirm his action. The Australians took alarm at the groundless wartime rumor of a Franco-American plot to seize western Australia. Levi, *American-Australian Relations*, 22, 31–32. David F. Long, "David Porter: Pacific Ocean Gadfly," 177–85.

36. Levi, *American-Australian Relations*, chap. 3. Gibson, *Yankees in Paradise*, chap. 8. Rydell, *Cape Horn to the Pacific*, chap. 22, and pp. 100–101. Dodge, *New England and the South Seas*, chaps. 2, 4. Grattan, *Southwest Pacific to 1900*, 193–96, 186–87. Kirker, *Adventures to China*, chap. 9.

to Hawaii, California, and Oregon on the north and east, taking in New Zealand, Fiji, Samoa, Tahiti, Tonga, and many other islands on the way. He established firmly the continental status of Antarctica and completed a more scientific survey of the islands than Cook. But except for a few visionary statements, mainly about California and Oregon, Wilkes was less interested in the political aspects of his travels. Furthermore, he was tactless and a martinet. After his return a court martial for mistreating his men caused his remarkable expedition to be consistently undervalued by public and government alike.[37]

Except for Hawaii, the American view of the Pacific was hazy from the War of 1812 to the annexation of California. During the 1830s and 1840s the government appointed consuls for Sydney, New Zealand, Tahiti, Samoa, and Tasmania, mostly for the whalers. They and the missionaries could get a hearing among their respective interest groups at home. The islands continued to supply delicacies for the Chinese trade, but Australia did not fulfill the commercial hopes of earlier years. One reason for this was the lack of dependable staples to ship to the United States in return for the multifarious provisions and supplies that the Australians always needed. Much of their land proved ideal for sheep raising, but New England and Ohio produced their own wool and Congress restricted imports to a minimum, even before the Civil War.[38]

American trade with the East Indies began at about the same time as trade with China. As a result of the international wars accompanying the American Revolution, in 1784 the Dutch, who controlled the islands, opened them to trade with the rest of the world, and ten years later, in the Jay Treaty, Britain admitted Americans to four Indian ports. Because the Cape of Good Hope route was safer than Cape Horn, it was usually chosen for larger ships; Salem dominated this trade for a few years. Ships bound from New England for China commonly took on European cargoes, called at the Cape for supplies, and traded their way across the Indian Ocean, stopping perhaps at Indian ports or Île St. Louis (Mauritius). After passing through the Strait of Sunda between Sumatra and Java (a dangerous shortcut through the East Indian archipelago), they often called at nearby Batavia (modern Jakarta). When these ships arrived at Canton, they would have increased their supply of silver pesos or taken on coffee, pepper, sandalwood, or other items salable in China.[39]

As in the case of California and the northwest coast of North America, it was not long before many Americans were returning home with cargoes from the East Indies themselves, without going on to China. The best example was pepper, which grew wild in the interior uplands of Sumatra and became almost a Salem

37. Grattan, *U.S. and Southwest Pacific*, 93–95. Brookes, *International Rivalry*, 64–65. The most detailed account of Wilkes's exploits is William Stanton, *The Great United States Exploring Expedition of 1838–1842*, but the author attempts little criticism or analysis.
    38. Levi, *American-Australian Relations*, 33–35. Grattan, *U.S. and Southwest Pacific*, 86.
    39. Seward W. Livermore, "Early Commercial and Consular Relations with the East Indies," 31–34. Dennett, *Americans in Eastern Asia*, 24–33.

monopoly. After several reconnaissance visits during the early 1790s, the first bulk cargo was shipped to the United States in 1797, earning a reported profit of 700 percent, and soon Yankee ships were flocking to the northwest coast of the island. The trade was dangerous, for the region was ruled by warlike rival Malay sultans, and piracy was common. The island coast, near the equator, was unhealthy, and frequent storms complicated navigation. Also the British, from their strongholds in India, tried to prevent the American visits. The greatest profits from the business came from reexporting the pepper across the Atlantic to Europe. Following an initial boom, the trade slumped for a time and was completely interrupted for three years during the War of 1812.[40]

After peace returned and the British transferred their interest to Malaya, American merchants were troubled only by occasional Dutch restrictions and local Malay chiefs, and the pepper trade flourished through most of the late 1820s and 1830s. The panic of 1837 and the ensuing depression ended this prosperity and, indeed, crippled all Far Eastern trade for a time. American interest in Sumatra and pepper did not begin its final decline, however, until the late 1850s.[41]

Another East Indian commodity that enjoyed a boom during the early years was Java coffee, which largely replaced that of Haiti, the principal former supplier, after a slave uprising there in 1792. In Batavia the most important American merchants came from Providence and prospered from 1799 to 1807, taking advantage of the Anglo-French wars. Like the Salem traders in Sumatra they suffered from a combination of climate, disease, pirates, privateers, British officials, and Dutch restrictions. Jefferson's Embargo and the War of 1812 ended the early profits, but the postwar trade was brisk, and in 1819 50 out of 171 ship arrivals at Batavia were American. During the 1820s more intense Dutch competition, rising taxes, and finally a government-sponsored Dutch monopoly combined with a declining European market to end the second boom. After struggling on for another decade, the coffee trade ceased in the mid-1830s.[42]

Early American commercial activities in the Philippines were more directly associated with China than those in Sumatra or Java. Spain had carried on regular trade with Manila since 1565 by means of an annual galleon, which ran to Acapulco, Mexico. Under pressure from the English and Dutch the Spanish king opened this trade to the rest of the world in 1789, although the annual galleons continued until 1815. As elsewhere in the western Pacific, American ships promptly appeared with cargoes, the first ones about 1795 or 1796. Although a Spanish regulation restricted trade to Asiatic products, this was not rigorously enforced, and from the beginning vessels of Salem and other New England ports

40. James W. Gould, "Sumatra—America's Pepperpot, 1784–1873," 83–153. James Duncan Phillips, *Pepper and Pirates: Adventures in the Sumatra Pepper Trade of Salem,* chaps. 1–7. Morison, *Maritime History,* chap. 7.
41. Gould, "America's Pepperpot," 203–52. Phillips, *Pepper and Pirates,* 42–43, chaps. 8–15, 17.
42. Sharom Ahmat, "Some Problems of the Rhode Island Traders in Java, 1795–1836," 94–109.

brought in European and American manufactures to be sold for silver or taken on to Canton. Philippine products were also shipped back to America, such as sugar and molasses for the rum distilleries, hides for the shoe industry or for Europe, and Manila hemp (abaca), which became the main staple of trade with Salem.[43]

When American companies were finally founded in Manila during the 1820s, the two leaders reflected the ambivalent orientation of Philippine trade toward the west and toward China. Peele, Hubbell and Company grew out of the shipment of Philippine sugar, indigo, and other such products in demand at home and in Europe. In contrast, Russell and Sturgis was bound by family ties to the Perkins interests in Canton and to their successor, Russell and Company. The Philippines produced a surplus of rice, for which there was always a Chinese market, and until production declined, furs, sandalwood, sea slugs, and other Pacific products funneled through Manila into southern China. Since the English gained their own outlets onto the Asiatic continent at Singapore and later Hong Kong, they did not compete so hotly with the Americans as elsewhere in the western Pacific, and Russell and Sturgis even became the Manila agents of the London financial house of Baring Bros.[44]

Early American trade with Singapore presented an anomaly to merchants and officials. After its founding in 1819, the port rapidly became a vital commercial focus for both eastbound and westbound ships as a kind of vestibule to Canton and refuge from pirates. Unfortunately for more than a decade American ships were barred from entering Singapore. Naturally they resorted to various subterfuges, from outright smuggling to trading at Riau, a small port on a neighboring island. In 1833 the United States appointed a consul there (although he carried on much of his business in Singapore), and three years later the ban was partly lifted. American trade at Singapore suffered a slump in the early 1840s because the American tariff law of 1842 placed high duties on tea imports from other than producing countries, but after the repeal of this provision in 1846, American visits to Singapore steadily increased.[45]

During the 1820s the coasts of Siam (Thailand) and Indochina also attracted American attention. After David Porter's Pacific exploits in the War of 1812, he proposed to President James Madison that he be sent to Japan, to "introduce civilization" and develop trade, but Madison was not interested. Andrew Jackson sent Edmund Roberts, a New England merchant, to negotiate treaties with Siam and Muscat (Masqat) on the Arabian peninsula, also if possible with Cochin

---

43. William Lytle Schurz, *The Manila Galleon*, 15, 58. Thomas R. McHale and Mary C. McHale, eds., *Early American-Philippine Trade: The Journal of Nathaniel Bowditch in Manila, 1796*, 14–23. Nathaniel Bowditch, who was supercargo on one of the early Salem ships to Manila, is best known as author of *The New American Practical Navigator*.

44. Benito Legada, "American Entrepreneurs in the Nineteenth Century Philippines," 1st ser., 9, 142–50. Antonio M. Regidor y Jurado and Warren T. Mason, *Commercial Progress in the Philippine Islands* [etc.], 25–33.

45. Sharom Ahmat, "American Trade with Singapore, 1819–1865," 241–57.

China and Japan. He was to stand up to Oriental monarchical pretensions and demonstrate the virtues of American democracy. Like Matthew C. Perry later in Japan, Roberts took out gifts and displays of firearms and technology. On his first trip he signed treaties with Muscat and Siam (1835), but the Cochin Chinese would not accept his democratic procedure, and on a second voyage he died before he could visit Japan. His treaty with Siam did not bring the expected increase of trade, but his goals and methods served to prepare for the later mission of Caleb Cushing in China.[46]

Even if Roberts had survived to visit Japan, the time was not yet quite ripe for a successful American opening of that nation. What little foreign trade Japan allowed was a monopoly of the Chinese and the Dutch. An American merchant ship first visited Japanese waters in about 1791, and from then until 1807 more than a dozen Yankee traders made ingenious but vain efforts to talk their way past Japanese barriers. Then for thirty years no American ships visited Japanese waters. In 1837 Olyphant and Company of the Cantonese trade sent the *Morrison* with several Japanese castaways, along with a load of British and Dutch goods and a few missionaries to Edo (modern Tokyo) and made two landings. Local residents showed much interest, but the military fired on the Americans, and, being unarmed, the *Morrison* left. During the early 1840s the Japanese modified their hostile behavior; a few more westerners penetrated the outer defenses; and Japan received considerable publicity in the United States.[47]

However, the United States was sometimes disposed to show its strength against less powerful foes. At the end of the eighteenth century the threat of Malay pirates led President John Adams to send the frigate *Essex* to escort ships home from Batavia. In 1831, after many years of peaceful trade, Malays captured the *Friendship*, a large pepper ship at Kuala Batu on the Sumatra coast, because of an officer's carelessness, ran her aground, killed most of the crew, and made off with a large cargo of silver and trade goods. The following year President Andrew Jackson, furious at the attack and encouraged by loud press demands, sent Captain John Downes and the crack frigate *Potomac* to investigate. Downes, an admirer of the feisty David Porter, exceeded his instructions. Approaching the Sumatra coast, he disguised his ship as a merchantman, sent out a landing party that killed perhaps a hundred of the inhabitants, and burned the town. The antiadministration press denounced Downes's high-handedness, but Jackson suppressed his displeasure, and Congress quickly forgot the incident. Other punitive expeditions in 1839 and 1845 attacked the Sumatra

46. Allen B. Cole, "Captain David Porter's Proposed Expedition to the Pacific and Japan, 1815," 61–66. Dennett, *Americans in Eastern Asia*, 128–34. Henry Merritt Wriston, *Executive Agents in American Foreign Relations*, 335–39. Benjamin A. Batson, "American Diplomats in Southeast Asia in the Nineteenth Century: The Case of Siam," 47–48. Donald C. Lord, "Missionaries, Thai, and Diplomats," 414–16.

47. William L. Neumann, *America Encounters Japan, from Perry to MacArthur*, chap. 1. Paullin, *Diplomatic Negotiations*, 215–22. Shunzo Sakamaki, *Japan and the United States, 1790–1853*, chaps. 2–4.

and Indo China coast (at Danang) respectively without establishing a consistent policy.[48]

Two major events of the 1840s brought to an end the early period of American trade in the Far East and the Pacific. The first was the Treaty of Wang-hsia of 1844 with China, which greatly liberalized the terms of trade with that country and enabled both merchants and missionaries to travel more widely along its coast and eventually in its vast interior, bringing permanent changes to Chinese culture. The second major event was the American annexation of Oregon in 1846 by treaty with Britain and of California in 1848 by war and then treaty with Mexico. These acquisitions, forming with Texas and the Southwest the western third of the continental United States, gave the nation new ports on the Pacific Ocean, which encouraged greater interest in the commercial opportunities and political complexities of the Pacific and Far Eastern worlds. "Asia has suddenly become our neighbor with a placid, intervening ocean inviting our steamships upon the track of a commerce greater than that of all Europe combined," declared Secretary of the Treasury Robert J. Walker in 1848.[49] The trade benefits in China and the new territory on the Pacific coast would create a new orientation for American foreign policy hardly imagined by the founding fathers.

The Anglo-Chinese War, the U.S. treaties, and the growth of the economy at home changed the nature of American-Chinese trade in midcentury. Tea and silk became more than ever the dominant imports. A greater proportion of exports originated in the United States as outlets for the growing American agriculture and industry, especially when Americans began to embrace the "glut theory" of international economics. Britain, recovering with vigor from the temporary difficulties of the Anglo-Chinese War, continued to be a formidable rival, for its improved merchant marine and financial facilities strengthened the position of British commission houses. At the same time the perfection of the Yankee clipper ship, developed for the tea trade, temporarily neutralized some British advantages, until the American Civil War crippled all foreign trade. The Chinese loss of face in the war with Britain lowered them in American estimation, and personal relationships became less important, especially after the death of Howqua in 1843. Finally, the new conditions led to new demands from American merchants for an improved consular service and more support from the U.S. government.

The nature of American trade in the Pacific was changing too. Just before the American annexation of California and Oregon, the ebbing Russian interest in

48. David F. Long, " 'Martial Thunder': The First Official American Armed Intervention in Asia," 143–62. John M. Belohlavek, "Andrew Jackson and the Malaysian Pirates: A Question of Diplomacy and Politics," 19–29. James W. Gould, "American Imperialism in Southeast Asia before 1898," 306–8. Gould, "America's Pepper Pot," 232–47. Roberts believed that the Kuala Batu intervention made his diplomatic expedition possible. On the seizure of the *Friendship,* see Phillips, *Pepper and Pirates,* chaps. 11, 12. For a defense of Downes see Caruthers, *American Pacific Ocean Trade,* 94–97.

49. Quoted in Neumann, *America Encounters Japan,* 23.

the northwest coast of North America and the frustration of British ambitions in Hawaii created opportunities for the expansion of American influence in these two areas. The simultaneous decline of the northwest fur trade removed part of the earlier American attraction to that area, but in Hawaii sugar had already begun to replace whaling in the economy, and the islands became the principal focus of American trade in the northern and central Pacific. At the same time American interest in the southern and western Pacific islands faded in comparison, both because of greater distance and because these islands would produce no single staple as important as Hawaiian sugar. Scattered shows of force in the East Indies or Southeast Asia were less significant to American policy than the diplomatic confrontation of the early 1840s with Britain and France in Hawaii.

The first sixty years of U.S. trade in the Far East and the Pacific convinced commercial expansionists on the American East Coast of its possibilities. During those years Yankee merchants and sea captains carefully examined all likely parts of the Pacific basin except Japan, Korea, and northern China. But throughout the period American activities were experimental and improvised, and despite the changing trade conditions, they would continue so for many decades. Doubts remained in Congress, the business world, and the press about greater involvement and expenditure in this part of the world on the grounds that it was remote and strange and that peoples closer to home would be more profitable trading partners. These doubts began to disappear earliest in the Pacific areas nearest to the newly acquired California and Oregon coast. Closer economic and political ties developed first in Alaska and Hawaii.

2

Alaska
Commercial Gateway or Dead End?

AMERICAN EXPANSION into the North Pacific followed two routes—along the coast to Alaska and out across the ocean to the Hawaiian Islands. In both cases early commercial connections brought about the first political contacts, but in Alaska these contacts led very soon to outright annexation, whereas in Hawaii this took more decades to accomplish, despite almost constant mutterings about its possibility. At the end of the century Hawaii had attracted a large American population, and its value to the United States was widely recognized. But the American and, indeed, the whole white population of Alaska was still small and concentrated in a few settlements; some Americans still wondered why we had ever bothered to annex it.

Although the fur trade had faded on the northwest coast in the 1840s, whalers were flocking to that region, attracted by the rich whaling grounds off Kodiak Island and the Aleutians. By 1845 Americans had invested more than $70 million in Pacific whaling, and nearly 40 percent of the American fleet hunted in Russian American waters. The industry was speculative, but profits could rise to nearly 100 percent of invested capital. American whalers moved west from the North American coast to the Bering Sea and the Siberian coast despite every Russian effort to stop them. As late as 1870 expeditions to the Bering Sea between Alaska and Kamchatka and to the Sea of Okhotsk beyond Kamchatka kept the whaling industry alive.[1]

Meanwhile, on land the American annexation of California and Oregon provided a base for general trade with the Russian coastal settlements. In 1851 a group of San Francisco businessmen founded the American-Russian Commercial Company to import ice from Alaska, much in demand locally and to the south. During the Crimean War (1854–1856) the company took over the business of supplying food and other necessities to the Russians, cut off by the British Navy from their home base. Through most of the Civil War period the San Francisco company carried on a prosperous trade with the Alaska settlements.[2]

1. Kushner, *Conflict*, chap. 5, 120–22. Howard I. Kushner, " 'Hellships': Yankee Whaling along the Coasts of Russian-America, 1833–1852," 82.
2. Saul, *Distant Friends*, 185–93. Howard I. Kushner, " 'Seward's Folly': American Commerce in Russian America and the Alaska Purchase," 4–26. Norman E. Saul,

Another example of a California-based promotional project, this time explicitly linking Alaska with Far Eastern trade, was the Collins overland telegraph line. Perry McDonough Collins was a lawyer-promoter during the boom years of the early 1850s who became interested in cooperating with Russia to develop the trade and resources of eastern Siberia. Obtaining an appointment as American commercial agent for the Amur River region, he went to St. Petersburg in 1856 and spent more than six months traveling overland through Siberia to the Pacific. In a picturesque account of this trip and various promotional writings he described the Amur as the Asiatic counterpart of the Mississippi River, "the destined channel by which American commercial enterprise [is] . . . to penetrate the obscure depths of Northern Asia, and open a new world to trade and civilization."[3]

Collins's principal project was a telegraph line across British Columbia, Alaska, and Siberia to supersede Cyrus Field's Atlantic cable, which for nearly a decade after its first trial in 1858 seemed doomed to failure. He obtained the backing of Field's chief rival, Hiram Sibley, president of the Western Union Telegraph Company, and in 1863 reached a preliminary agreement with Russia. Collins and Sibley planned extensions to Europe, China, and Latin America—a web of telegraph wires, broken only by a short cable across the Bering Strait, that might control the communications of the whole world and would also encourage the extension of a great transpacific steamship line. The *Commercial and Financial Chronicle* anticipated that such a telegraph system would break down the European commercial monopoly and attract to San Francisco "the vast commerce which enterprise and capital will open with China." A few Americans envisioned colonies on the Amur River if Russia would grant homesteads. Western Union carried on extensive explorations along the telegraph route with aid from both American and Russian government officials and actually set up several hundred miles of line. Unfortunately, in 1867 Cyrus Field put his Atlantic cable into successful operation, and at once Western Union abandoned the Collins project.[4]

"Beverley C. Sanders and the Expansion of American Trade with Russia, 1853–1855," 156–70. E. L. Keithan, "Alaska Ice, Inc.," 121–31. During the war Britain recognized the freedom of the seas, and the United States established a "friendly neutrality." Trade between Russia and the United States continued, and missions passed between the two countries. Saul, *Distant Friends,* chap. 4.

3. Charles Vevier, "The Collins Overland Line and American Continentalism," 238–42. Corday Mackay, "The Collins Overland Telegraph," 189–90. Eldon Griffin, *Clippers and Consuls: American Consular and Commercial Relations with Eastern Asia, 1845–1860,* chap. 21. Perry McDonough Collins, *Siberian Journey down the Amur to the Pacific, 1856–1857,* 3–39.

4. Kushner, *Conflict,* 24–25. Mackay, "Collins Overland Telegraph," 190–92. Saul, *Distant Friends,* 360–70, 385–86. *Merchants' Magazine* 45 (December 1861): 598–605; 46 (February 1862): 155–57. *Commercial and Financial Chronicle* 1 (August 5, 1865): 167. William H. Dall, "The Russian-American Telegraph Project of 1866–67," 110–11. [Western Union Telegraph Company], *Statement of the Origin, Organization and Progress of the*

Two more San Francisco promotional ventures involved Alaska during the Civil War period. In 1859 Joseph Lane McDonald explored the Russian-American coastline in search of fishing grounds and founded a commercial company to obtain a fishing concession from the Russian-American Company. During the Civil War he also projected a railroad and steamship line across the United States and Alaska to Asia and as a first step issued stock in the "Puget Sound Steam Navigation Company" to carry on both fishing and trade. In 1865 another ambitious promoter, Lewis Goldstone, sought to revive the Russian-American fur trade with a lease from the Hudson's Bay Company or from St. Petersburg. Before the McDonald and Goldstone ventures collapsed, both men enlisted prestigious California capitalists and sought aid from persons in the U.S. government. In addition to these formal projects, there was also considerable smuggling and illicit fishing and whaling near the Alaska coast.[5]

Expansionists in the government had shown occasional interest in Alaska for years. Unsubstantiated rumors of annexationist proposals extended back as far as the administrations of Martin Van Buren and James K. Polk. One of California's first two senators, William McKendree Gwin (Democrat), envisioned a great Pacific empire for America, including the northwest coast, Central America to Panama, and the Pacific islands. When the Crimean War began in 1854, Gwin and Secretary of State William L. Marcy discussed the possibility of American mediation with the Russian minister, Baron Edouard de Stoeckl, as well as the sham transfer of the Russian-American Company's rights to the American-Russian Commercial Company, to prevent British seizure. This transfer proved unnecessary, for the Hudson's Bay Company and the Russian-American Company agreed to neutralize Russian America during the war, but the proposal started rumors of outright cession that continued after the war. Partly to further his own dream of steamship and telegraph lines to northern Asia, Gwin in 1859 proposed to Stoeckl the outright cession of Alaska for $5 million. Russian leaders were divided, however, and the approaching sectional crisis in America paralyzed the Buchanan administration. When the South left the Union, Gwin joined the Confederacy and dropped out of the Alaska campaign.[6]

Russian-American Telegraph Western Union Extension, Collins Overland Line via Behring Strait and Asiatic Russia to Europe, 156–57. On the abandonment of the project see U.S., Department of State, *Papers Relating to the Foreign Relations of the United States, 1866–67,* 385–88 (hereafter U.S., *Foreign Relations,* with year).

5. Kushner, *Conflict,* 124–25, 128–30. Victor J. Farrar, "Joseph Lane MacDonald and the Purchase of Alaska," 83–90.

6. Ronald J. Jensen, *The Alaska Purchase and Russian-American Relations,* chap. 1. Kushner, *Conflict,* chap. 7. Late in 1853 Russia put out feelers to the United States for covert support in a war with England and France, hoping to exploit Anglo-American coolness. Barratt, *Russian Shadows,* 55–58. On Gwin see Hallie N. McPherson, "The Interest of William McKendree Gwin in the Purchase of Alaska, 1854–1861," 28–38. Nikolai Bolkhovitinov, "The Crimean War and the Emergence of Proposals for the Sale of Russian America," 15–47.

The most influential American official in the acquisition of Alaska was William H. Seward, Republican senator from New York, secretary of state (1861–1869), and both a territorial and commercial expansionist. As senator he backed a transcontinental railroad and eventual acquisition of Hawaii. In 1852 he and Gwin obtained federal funds to survey the Bering Strait and the northern Pacific "for naval and commercial purposes." During the presidential campaign of 1860 he delivered a remarkable speech at St. Paul, Minnesota, which described Russians and Canadians establishing seaports, towns, and provinces for eventual American occupation. Although he moderated his rhetoric considerably after entering the State Department, he enthusiastically aided the Collins overland telegraph project, urging Congress to grant it a subsidy and instructing American ministers in Britain and Russia to help Collins secure construction concessions in British Columbia and Siberia.[7]

During the war period several factors operated to facilitate the eventual transfer. In the Treaty of Peking (1860) Russia obtained trading privileges with China that further decreased the value of Alaska to the czar's officials. Depredations of the Confederate raider *Shenandoah* against the whaling industry in the North Pacific emphasized to American strategists the need for more protection of American interests there. When the Russian-American Company's charter expired at the beginning of 1862, the government did not renew it, and the company operations stumbled along under an improvised arrangement. Gold discoveries in British Columbia and Canadian-American friction during the Civil War reduced British interest in the lease on the Alaska panhandle that the Hudson's Bay Company had held since 1838. Finally, Russian opposition to Anglo-French mediation in the Civil War and the opportune visit of Russian fleets to New York and San Francisco in 1863 stimulated Russo-American friendship.[8]

During 1866 the cession of Alaska took shape. The czar's brother, Grand Duke Constantine, supported by Prince Alexander Gorchakov, the foreign minister, and reinforced by arguments from Baron Stoeckl, now minister to the United States, put the case before the czar in a formal conference with the foreign ministers and others on December 16 (Old Style) and obtained his consent. The

7. Kushner, *Conflict*, chap. 7. Ernest N. Paolino, *The Foundations of the American Empire: William Henry Seward and U.S. Foreign Policy*, 35–37, chap. 3. Glyndon G. Van Deusen, *William Henry Seward*, 513–14. *The Works of William H. Seward*, edited by George E. Baker, vol. 1, 246–50; vol. 4, 159–333. U.S., 32d Cong., 1st sess., *Congressional Globe*, 1975–76; 33d Cong., 1st sess., 1566–67. William H. Seward to Zachariah Chandler, May 14, 1866. U.S., 38th Cong., 1st sess., *Senate Miscellaneous Document 123*, 6–7. John S. Galbraith, "Perry McDonough Collins at the Colonial Office," 207–14.

8. Jensen, *Alaska Purchase*, chap. 2, 39–44. *American Whale Fishery*, 77–78. Okun, *Russian-American Company*, 245–62. C. Ian Jackson, "The Stikine Territory Lease and Its Relevance to the Alaska Purchase," 292–306. Benjamin Platt Thomas, *Russian-American Relations, 1815–1867*, chap. 8. The *Shenandoah* captured 38 ships valued at $1,361,983 and took 1,053 prisoners. Benjamin Franklin Gilbert, "The Confederate Raider *Shenandoah*: The Elusive Destroyer in the Pacific and Arctic," 169–82.

principal Russian reasons for the sale combined economic and political-strategic considerations: the declining importance of Alaska in Russian commercial policy and the desire to concentrate on China, the difficulty and expense of defending remote territory, the need for money in case of war in Europe, the likelihood of filibusters and other American encroachments along the Pacific coast, and the desire to weaken Britain in Canada.[9] The mixture of motives suggests those that induced Napoleon to sell Louisiana to the United States.

On the American side, the cession was almost entirely the work of Secretary Seward, but, lacking definitive written evidence, historians disagree as to whether he was motivated primarily by land hunger, economic expansionism, a desire for a greater American role in the Far East, friendship with Russia, the desire to offset the new Dominion of Canada, or his ambition to regain popularity and crown his career with a dramatic coup. In favor of an economic interpretation, one may cite the growing American commercial status in Alaska, Seward's earlier support of naval surveys and steamship and telegraph lines in the northern Pacific area, the influence of others such as Senator Gwin, and Seward's prominent use of economic arguments in the campaign for congressional approval of the cession treaty.

Whatever his motives, Seward undoubtedly wanted to hurry negotiations after the administration's losses in the congressional elections of 1866 presaged the imminent end of his power. Accordingly, he allowed himself to be maneuvered into initiating discussions during February and March 1867, as soon as Stoeckl returned to Washington from home leave. When the Russian minister received permission to sign a treaty, it was put in final form literally overnight and signed on March 30. Although Stoeckl had earlier considered the territory worth less than $3 million, the treaty provided that the United States should pay Russia $7.2 million and receive in return Alaska with its coastal islands, the Aleutian chain, and all islands in approximately the eastern two-thirds of the Bering Sea.[10]

---

9. Jensen, *Alaska Purchase*, 48–61. Kushner, *Conflict*, chap. 9, xi–xii, 155–58. Anatole G. Mazour, "The Prelude to Russia's Departure from America," 318–19. Saul, *Distant Friends*, 388–96, 283–84, 288. Grand Duke Constantine, head of the Russian Navy, opposed the Russian-American Company and favored development of the navy and of the Amur River area. At the last moment Baron Osten-Sacken of the foreign ministry put up a vigorous argument against cession, partly on the ground of Alaska's great potential resources. Oleh W. Gerus, "The Russian Withdrawal from Alaska: The Decision to Sell," 173–75. Nikolai N. Bolkhovitinov, "How It Was Decided to Sell Alaska," 116–18. It is clear that the Russians were well aware of Alaskan gold and other mineral deposits, but this factor worked in both directions, for it led them to fear an uncontrollable American gold rush through which they might lose the area without compensation. This argument especially appealed to Stoeckl. Frank A. Golder, "Mining in Alaska before 1867," 233–38. Kushner also emphasizes this Russian feeling of compulsion. James R. Gibson also stresses the political-strategic factors. "Why the Russians Sold Alaska," 134–37.

10. Jansen, *Alaska Purchase*, chap. 4. The best case for Seward's economic orientation is put in Paolino, *Foundations of the American Empire*, 106–9 ff. Van Deusen is noncommittal (*Seward*, chap. 37). For other interpretations see Thomas A. Bailey, "Why the United States Purchased Alaska," 40; Victor J. Farrar, *The Annexation of Russian America to the United*

At once Seward submitted the treaty to the Senate, which considered it in a special executive session. The treaty suffered from initial handicaps, for both Seward and President Johnson had reached the nadir of their popularity, and the Foreign Relations Committee, presided over by Charles Sumner of Massachusetts, was controlled by Anglophile easterners, insensitive to Pacific coast interests. Surprised by the treaty, the senators knew little about Alaska except that it was cold, snow-covered, and almost unpopulated, and Sumner seemed doubtful that the United States should assume control without first consulting the few inhabitants. To help the senators decide, Seward gathered supporting statements from military leaders, the promoter Perry M. Collins, and a professor at the Smithsonian Institution. All emphasized the resources and strategic value of Alaska. Seward rushed their statements into print and lobbied personally with ten days of dinners and discussions at his home. The decisive influence on the Senate, however, seems to have been that of prominent radical Republicans Sumner, Nathaniel Banks (Massachusetts) and Representative Thaddeus Stevens (Pennsylvania), whose expansionism overcame their dislike of Seward.

After the Foreign Relations Committee had reluctantly reported the treaty, the floor debate came to a climax in a three-hour speech by Sumner on Alaskan history and resources, Far Eastern trade, the spread of democracy over the continent, and the desirability of maintaining friendship with Russia. Although it is impossible to be sure which argument moved even Sumner the most, let alone the rest of the Senate, his shotgun attack found enough targets to save the treaty, which was approved with two votes to spare on April 9.[11] Although the United States could not make payment to Russia until the House of Representatives met in December to appropriate the necessary $7.2 million, Johnson and Seward at once arranged for opening Alaskan ports to California traders. Formal transfer of sovereignty took place at Sitka on October 18; the flag flying over Alaska might well convert patriotic doubters.[12]

The American press was not much better prepared for the annexation treaty than the Senate, but it reacted at once with varied arguments that became more complex during the congressional debates. A survey of forty-eight newspapers

---

States, chap. 7; Frank A. Golder, "The Purchase of Alaska," 411–25; and Tyler Dennett, "Seward's Far Eastern Policy," 60–61. In 1870 Seward suggested that the Pacific coast with its limitless forests might be the solution to the American shipping problem. William H. Seward, "Speech on His Travels," draft, 1870. For the text of the treaty see Bevans, *Treaties,* vol. 11, 1816–19.

11. In a formal vote the treaty was approved 73–2, but a prior effort to delay consideration had been defeated by only 29–12. This latter vote may be a more accurate indication of senatorial feelings. Jensen, *Alaska Purchase,* 79–92. Farrar, *Annexation of Russian America,* chap. 4. Since no record was kept of the Senate's executive sessions, we do not know how much of Sumner's speech was actually delivered or how it was received. For the published version see Charles Sumner, *Speech of the Honorable Charles Sumner on the Cession of Russian America to the United States.*

12. Jensen, *Alaska Purchase,* 100–103. For a more detailed exposition of legal problems involved see Farrar, *Annexation of Russian America,* chap. 5.

during April and July suggests that most of the press either favored the treaty or preserved neutrality and that there were neither clear-cut party nor sectional differences, although the Middle West was somewhat less interested in the issue than the two coasts. The leaders pro and con were the *New York Times*, edited by Henry J. Raymond, a personal friend of Seward, and the *New York Tribune*, in which the redoubtable Horace Greeley, always opposed to Seward and Johnson, blasted the administration for trying to divert public attention from pressing domestic issues. He and some other editors rang the changes on the climate and barrenness of Alaska, calling it "Walrussia," "Frigidia," and "Seward's icebox." The opponents also repeated two leading antiexpansionist arguments of the 1840s and 1850s—that the United States already possessed more territory than it could govern efficiently and that the additional military and bureaucratic structure would further increase the executive's strength, already magnified by war powers.[13]

The case for the treaty was made equally by the press and by Sumner's speech, published immediately in expanded form. While Sumner had emphasized friendship with Russia, defiance to Britain, and a desire to spread democracy, the leading argument in the press seems to have been the one borne out in later history—that Alaska was a bargain at the cession price for its potential resources of fish, whales, fur, timber, and minerals and for the commercial and strategic value of its harbors. The *New York Herald*, for example, not only declared that "the fist of inevitable destiny" would give the United States all of North America but foresaw a time, soon at hand, when "the North Pacific ocean, surrounded by vast populations. . . . [would] be covered with the sails of commerce. . . . We shall find in Asia a ready and a great market for the furs, skins, ivory, fish, timber, coal, grains and metals of that region."[14]

Before that could happen, however, Alaska must be paid for, and the House of Representatives required more than six months of debate and lobbying before it would pass the necessary appropriation bill. The debate was interrupted for weeks by the impeachment of President Johnson, and it became entangled with the issue of annexing the Danish West Indies, which Seward unwisely put before Congress at the same time. He also engaged the veteran politician, Robert J. Walker, a "territory mad" expansionist, to lobby. The House recapitulated the familiar arguments already developed by the Senate and the press and gave unmerited prominence to the specious Perkins claim, an effort to divert some of the purchase money into American pockets, which opponents of the treaty

13. Richard E. Welch, Jr., "American Public Opinion and the Purchase of Russian America," 481–94. (Like many other writers on opinion, Welch really means *press* opinion.) Kushner, *Conflict*, 145–48. Virginia H. Reid, *The Purchase of Alaska: Contemporary Opinion*, 21–33. Good samples of opposition arguments cited are *New York Tribune*, April 1, 1867, 4; *Nation* 4 (April 4, 1867): 266; and *Commercial and Financial Chronicle* 4 (April 6, 1867): 422–23.

14. See citations in preceding note. *New York Herald*, April 11, May 3, and November 29, 1867. The *Herald* also favored acquiring the Danish West Indies, Hawaii, and a Japanese island.

used as a red herring. After such argument and outside pressure of all kinds, the House passed the appropriation bill on July 14, 1868, 113–43, with 44 abstaining.[15]

The victory cost the nation an incalculable amount in dignity, reputation, and internal unity. The Perkins claim eventually led to a furious Russo-American argument before it was dropped, and the Alaska debate encouraged mutual Anglo-American suspicions, already stimulated by Fenian agitation and the *Alabama* claims. Worst of all, a cloud of corruption hung over the purchase and the congressional actions, emanating from the general atmosphere of post–Civil War America and distilled as well by the unseemly haste with which the deal was closed. Probably at least $200,000 of the purchase price was distributed to legislators, lobbyists, and journalists for their help in getting the treaty approved and paid for; some opponents estimated as much as $2.2 million. Seward himself indiscreetly let out a list of the principal recipients, but even today no firm evidence exists as to the accuracy of this list or any other. Many names identified with the bribery were small fry, but included Robert J. Walker, Seward's principal lobbyist and a distinguished former senator and cabinet member, John W. Forney, a prominent newspaper publisher, and Nathaniel P. Banks, one of the principal Republican leaders in the House.[16]

That body conducted an inconclusive investigation of the case, but the accompanying attacks in the press discredited territorial expansion for many years, especially after they were reinforced by a fight over President Grant's efforts to annex the Dominican Republic. At the same time business scandals like those attached to the Pacific railroads (Crédit Mobilier) and the Pacific Mail Steamship Company fixed in the public mind a distrust of subsidies and placed obstacles in the way of better shipping, an interoceanic canal, and other items on the commercial expansionists' program.[17]

The European reaction was generally more passive, partly from ignorance about a remote corner of the world and partly from an expectation of general benefits from American occupation, as in California. Some, like Russia, hoped that Britain would be weakened. The British press was generally scornful but uneasy, and the government's suspicious opinion was conditioned by its reaction to Seward's contemporaneous effort to annex British Columbia. That province was economically tied to California and Oregon, but before the Civil War the American government had made no effort to improve these ties. During the 1860s

15. Jensen, *Alaska Purchase*, 98–99, 103–19. The Perkins claim was raised by the widow of a Yankee sea captain, Benjamin W. Perkins, who was alleged to have contracted for the delivery of munitions to Russia during the Crimean War. The shipment did not even leave New York.

16. On the later history of the Perkins claim see Allan Nevins, *Hamilton Fish*, 503–10. On the bribery question see Jensen, *Alaska Purchase*, 120–32; and Paul Holbo, *Tarnished Expansion: The Alaska Scandal, the Press, and Congress, 1867–1871*, chaps. 2, 3. Jensen feels that Stoeckl may not have been buying votes (since many recipients favored the treaty anyway) so much as purchasing other services—e.g., working to remove the Perkins claim question from the treaty discussion.

17. Holbo, *Tarnished Expansion*, chap. 4.

annexationism began to develop, especially on Vancouver Island, and Seward tried to encourage this sentiment, both by including British Columbia in proposals for settling the *Alabama* claims and by supporting the transcontinental plans of Jay Cooke's Northern Pacific Railroad. But he could raise little enthusiasm in Washington, and the formation of the Dominion of Canada in 1867 led to a promise by that government of concessions that won over the people of British Columbia.[18]

Although many Americans such as cartoonist Thomas Nast continued for years to ridicule Alaska as a frozen wasteland, more perspicacious businessmen set out at once to exploit its resources. On the same ship that carried an American official to Alaska in June 1867 to accept the transfer of the territory was a Baltimore merchant, Hayward N. Hutchinson, who reached an agreement with the general manager of the Russian-American Company for the sale of its entire property and other assets. Hutchinson and his partners then helped to organize the Alaska Commercial Company with a group of San Francisco merchants and financiers, from whom they received $1,729,000 for the Russian assets. Rightly regarding the Russian company's coastal and island fur seal fisheries as the best source of immediate profit, the Alaska Commercial Company obtained a twenty-year lease from the U.S. government for sealing rights on the Pribilof Islands in the eastern Bering Sea north of the Aleutians, undoubtedly the best fur seal grounds in the world. The contract limited the annual "take" to one hundred thousand male seals and required the company to pay the government an annual rental of $55,000 and taxes of $2.62½ per pelt.[19]

18. Henry S. Sanford to Seward, May 10, 1867, Seward papers (Sanford was minister to Belgium and reported generally on Europe). Virginia Hancock Reid, *Purchase of Alaska*, 43–46. *London Economist* 25 (April 6, 1867): 38. On American-Russian relations see Jensen, *Alaska Purchase*, 134–38. On British Columbia see Frederic W. Howay, Walter N. Sage, and Henry F. Angus, *British Columbia and the United States: The North Pacific Slope from Fur Trade to Aviation*, chap. 8; and David E. Shi, "Seward's Attempt to Annex British Columbia, 1865–1869," 319–78. Many British had long feared the American annexation of Alaska, but the "little England" government of William E. Gladstone chose this moment to withdraw all British troops from Canada except those at two major bases, Halifax and Esquimalt on the southern coast of Vancouver Island. Barratt, *Russian Shadows*, 71–72. The British minister at Washington suspected that the United States and Russia had made a deal to approve each other's advances respectively to British Columbia and Turkey. Sir Frederick Bruce to Lord Stanley, April 2, 1867, Great Britain, Foreign Office, Series 115, vol. 465 (hereafter Britain, FO, with series and volume number).

19. Frank H. Sloss, "Who Owned the Alaska Commercial Company?" 120–26. In addition to Hayward and his partners, William Kohl and Leopold Boscowitz, the early principals of the Alaska Commercial Company were Louis Sloss (president before and after Miller), Lewis Gerstle, Simon Greenewald, Albert Bostowitz, A. Wasserman, Gustave Niebaum, John F. Miller, Charles Augustus Williams, Henry P. Haven, and John Parrott. Samuel P. Johnston, ed., *Alaska Commercial Company, 1868–1940*. For the text of the lease see 9–12. The company also obtained a lease from the Russian government for seal fishing on several islands of the Komandorski group (east of Kamchatka). See also Hubert Howe Bancroft, *History of Alaska, 1730–1885*, 636–39. U.S., Department of State, *Reports from the Consuls of the United States on the Commerce, Manufactures, etc. of their Consular Districts*

As seal fur came into fashion and prices rose, the Alaska Commercial Company shipped trainloads of sealskins across the country on the transcontinental railroads, to be processed and sold in London. Within a few years after beginning operations it was also administering a chain of trading posts for other furs along the Yukon River, which runs westward through Alaska from the Canadian border to the Bering Sea. Throughout the territory the company sold or traded a wide variety of foodstuffs, textiles, and other goods, nearly all American-made. Its fleet of vessels furnished the major communications along the Alaska coast, and the company distributed the mails under a contract with the government. It maintained an efficient lobby in Washington, and one of its presidents, John F. Miller, had been collector of customs in San Francisco and U.S. senator. Before long the company's profits and power stimulated accusations of monopoly and fraud, but when a committee of the House of Representatives carried on an investigation in 1876, it pronounced the Pribilof lease perfectly legal and the company's activities above reproach—yielding a revenue of $300,000 a year to the Treasury, benefiting the poverty-stricken Indians, and in general developing the newly acquired territory.[20]

Other economic interests also contributed to that development, some in lively competition with the Alaska Commercial Company. Merchant ships traded between Alaska and California, British Columbia, Hawaii, and even South America. The North Pacific and Trading Company and many imitators developed a flourishing salmon canning industry on the offshore islands, and by the late 1880s the output of the industry was more than seven hundred thousand cases a year. Mining prospectors roamed the Yukon Valley and the neighboring mountains but could not match the successes of the fur and fishing industries. All in all, the income and revenues returned a modestly affirmative answer to the question that sometimes reappeared in a largely indifferent press: "Is Alaska a paying investment?"[21]

In the long run the annexation and assimilation of Alaska gave the United States a permanent strategic and economic base for the twentieth century. In the short run, during the late 1880s, there was some discussion of a railroad line from some point on the Northern Pacific to the Bering Strait, which would bind western

---

13 (November 1881): 50–54 (hereafter U.S. *Consular Reports,* with number, month, and year). Sealing was greatly encouraged in the early 1870s by the invention of a device for easily removing guard hairs from the sealskins. James T. Gay, "Bering Sea Controversy: Harrison, Blaine, and Cronyism," 12.

20. On the varied activities of the company see Ted C. Hinckley, *The Americanization of Alaska, 1867–1897,* 75–77, 85–88, 89–96; and Johnston, *Alaska Commercial Company,* 19–21, 31–35. On the political influence of the company, about which evidence is sketchy, see Jeannette Paddock Nichols, *Alaska: A History of Its Administration, Exploitation, and Industrial Development during its First Half Century under the Rule of the United States,* 53n48, 63–64n67. For the House investigation of 1876 see U.S., 44th Cong., 1st sess., *House Report 623.*

21. Hinckley, *Americanization of Alaska,* 69–73, 94, 121–28 and passim. Bancroft, *History of Alaska,* chaps. 30, 31. *Harper's Magazine* 44 (January 1872): 252–57.

Canada closer to the United States and even fulfill Perry M. Collins's dreams of trade with Russia.[22] This never came to pass. Instead, during the next decade Alaska provoked new diplomatic problems in which the federal government aggressively fostered American economic interests. These problems involved the fur seal fisheries of the Bering Sea and the coastal trade of the Alaska panhandle.

In the Bering Sea the Alaska Commercial Company made good use of its 1870 concession for limited sealing on the Pribilof Islands, and during the next twenty years it realized about $31 million from the sale of sealskins. When this lucrative hunting attracted Canadian rivals, the U.S. Treasury Department, doubtless at the company's urging, issued an opinion in 1881 holding that the Bering Sea was a *mare clausum*, entirely subject to American jurisdiction. Ignoring this opinion, Canadians engaged in pelagic (deep-water) sealing, destroying the company's monopoly, forcing down the price of sealskins, and eventually threatening the extinction of the island-based seal herd. In 1886 and 1887 the first Cleveland administration ordered Treasury cutters to arrest sealers on the high seas, motivated by a combination of concern for the threatened seals and for the Alaska Commercial Company and probably also by irritation with the British over a contemporaneous controversy about the Atlantic fisheries. As the *Nation* pointed out, the Americans' position in the Bering Sea was diametrically opposed to their position in the Atlantic. When London protested, Secretary of State Thomas F. Bayard, who did not support the doctrine of *mare clausum*, got the arrests stopped.[23]

The Harrison administration warned off Canadian sealers, started up arrests again, and in March 1890 transferred the expired Pribilof sealing concession to a California firm, the North American Commercial Company, two of whose founders were close friends of Secretary of State James G. Blaine.[24] His desire for a strong policy, however, was soon dampened by news that Britain had several gunboats ready on the Pacific coast to resist American revenue cutters and by the

22. U.S., 49th Cong., 1st sess., *Senate Miscellaneous Document 84*, 1–2. U.S., 49th Cong., 2d sess., *Senate Miscellaneous Document 22*. *Public Opinion* 3 (July 30, 1887): 340–41. *Bradstreet's* 19 (February 28, 1891): 136.

23. Charles Callan Tansill, *The Foreign Policy of Thomas F. Bayard, 1885–1897*, chaps. 14, 15. Tansill, *Canadian-American Relations, 1875–1911*, chaps. 1–3, 10. Hinckley, *Americanization of Alaska*, 179–84. Howay, Sage, and Angus, *British Columbia and the United States*, 320–25. For partial evidence of company connections with the Cleveland administration see Charles S. Campbell, Jr., *From Revolution to Rapproachment: The United States and Great Britain, 1783–1900*, 155–57. John W. Foster and the *Nation* blamed subordinate officials on the West Coast, controlled by the company. Even without its urging, the government would have had good reason to support the monopoly, as the Treasury received about twelve million dollars annually from the lease and duties. *Nation* 45 (October 13, 1887): 283; 52 (April 2, 1891): 277. Foster, *Diplomatic Memoirs*, 2, 22, 26–27.

24. One was Darius Ogden Mills, a California millionaire who was the father-in-law of Whitelaw Reid, a leading Blaine Republican and the party's vice presidential candidate in 1892. The other was Stephen B. Elkins, Blaine's onetime campaign manager and financial adviser and later Harrison's secretary of war. Charles S. Campbell, Jr., "The Anglo-American Crisis in the Bering Sea, 1890–1891," 396. Gay, "Harrison, Blaine, and Cronyism," 13–14.

report of a Treasury agent, an unquestioned expert on seals, that the alarming decline of the Pribilof herd was due as much to the company's slaughter on land as to the pelagic sealing of the Canadians. Bedeviled by the company and not wishing either to defy or to capitulate to Britain, President Benjamin Harrison and Blaine temporarily suppressed the embarrassing Treasury report and authorized an agreement with the British ambassador, Julian Pauncefote, signed on June 25, 1891, whereby pelagic sealing should cease, pending arbitration of the whole question, and the island kill should be restricted to seventy-five hundred a year.

The tortuous diplomacy that had produced this modus vivendi continued for the rest of the Harrison administration. The president, facing a difficult reelection campaign in 1892, may have considered risking war with Britain by taking a defiant stand. For his part, Blaine was mortally ill, about to retire, and reluctant to submit the weak American case to an arbitral board. After much backing and filling he and Pauncefote signed an arbitration treaty on February 29, 1892. The Senate approved it promptly and unanimously, and the two powers renewed the modus vivendi.[25]

Soon after Harrison left office, the arbitral tribunal began to hear the American case, which rested largely on the doctrine of *mare clausum*, American property rights in the seals, and the barbarity of the indiscriminate killings. In August 1893 the tribunal rendered an overwhelming verdict against the United States— one or both of the American representatives opposed their own government on four of the five counts! Most of the Democratic and independent press approved the verdict, and the Republicans took credit for the court's recommendations about measures to protect the seals from destruction. The Canadians grumbled because American sealers continued to operate on the Pribilof Islands. Eventually the United States paid Britain $473,151.26 for damages resulting from the seizure of Canadian sealing boats.[26]

In 1896 a gold rush to the Klondike River (a tributary of the Yukon on the Canadian side of the border), followed by another to Alaska itself, drew public attention northward and precipitated another Anglo-American-Canadian dispute with economic overtones. Americans and American companies played a major role in prospecting and mining, and the Alaska Commercial Company was one of the two leading firms, both American, that did a most profitable business shipping in supplies to the miners at inflated prices. The most practicable route to the Klondike goldfields ran across the Alaska panhandle—up the Lynn Canal, a hundred-mile fjord, and over the mountains. The transcontinental railroads

25. Tansill, *Canadian-American Relations*, chap. 11. Tyler, *Foreign Policy of Blaine*, chap. 13. Campbell, "Anglo-American Crisis," 393–414. Charles S. Campbell, Jr., "The Bering Sea Settlements of 1892," 347–67. Campbell, *From Revolution to Rapprochement*, chap. 12. The North American Commercial Company protested against the proposed modus vivendi. N. S. Jeffries to President, April 18, 1892, Harrison papers, ser. 1, reel 35. For press comments see *Literary Digest* 5 (May 9, 1891): 48–49.

26. Tansill, *Canadian-American Relations*, chap. 11. For press reactions to the settlement see *Public Opinion* 15 (August 26, 1893): 497–98.

unloaded prospectors and supplies at Seattle and Vancouver, where American and Canadian steamship lines waited to transport them to the Lynn Canal.[27]

Easy access to the goldfields depended on an unsettled interpretation of the Anglo-Russian treaty of 1824, which laid out the border between Alaska and Canada. The wording of the treaty did not make clear whether the eastern boundary of the Alaska panhandle ran across the Lynn Canal and other deep inlets or around their heads. Americans claimed the latter interpretation, intending to make the business of supply part of the American coastal trade and monopolize it for American steamers under U.S. navigation laws. Both nations naturally charged tariffs on each other's goods. In 1898 the Alaska boundary, pelagic sealing, and other outstanding Canadian-American questions were submitted to a joint commission, which discussed them at length but broke up without a settlement. After the turn of the century, when the gold rush had ended, the United States won a complete victory in the Alaska boundary question. President Theodore Roosevelt made it clear that he would not accept a compromise and in 1903 strong-armed a joint tribunal into upholding the United States on every important point at issue. During the Taft administration the United States also signed an agreement with Britain, Russia, and Japan to stop pelagic sealing in the Pacific north of 30° north latitude (about the level of Baja California).[28]

By this time American predominance in the North Pacific was permanently established. For this predominance the possession of Alaska was an absolute necessity. Clearly "Walrussia" was not a dead end, as Seward's opponents in the 1860s and 1870s jeered. But it was not a commercial gateway to the Golden East as Seward, Perry M. Collins, and many other enthusiasts expected, for few cargo vessels traveled the great circle route to the Orient. Not China trade but Alaskan resources—the fur seals and fish, minerals, and later farm and forest products—proved Seward's opponents wrong within the lifetimes of most of them. And later, in the twentieth century, it was the strategic value of Alaska, which Seward and his cohorts dimly outlined, that enabled the United States to dominate transpolar routes during World War II and the Cold War, providing first jumping-off points for attacks on the Japanese and later a defensive screen against a Soviet attack that never materialized. Seward's predictive abilities, if a little overcolored and inexact, were true enough, and his contribution to American interests formed the climax of his career.

27. Howay, Sage, and Angus, *British Columbia and the United States,* 332–36, 344–46, 354–60. Arthur Power Dudden, *America in the Pacific,* 36–37. On trade rivalries see also Norbert MacDonald, "Seattle, Vancouver, and the Klondike," 234–36.

28. On the Alaska boundary question and the joint commission of 1898–1899 see Charles S. Campbell, Jr., *Anglo-American Understanding, 1898–1903,* 65–76, chaps. 4–6, 15; and Tansill, *Canadian-American Relations,* chaps. 5–9. In the four-power sealing convention the United States agreed to divide proceeds from sealing on land. Thomas A. Bailey, "The North Pacific Sealing Convention of 1911," 2–14. After 1900 copper mining eventually replaced gold as the principal Alaskan mineral industry. Dudden, *America in the Pacific,* 38–39.

3

Hawaii
Sugar and Strategy

N 1850 THE HAWAIIAN ISLANDS were taking on most of the characteristics they were to display for the rest of the century. Sugar growing was beginning to supersede whaling as the foundation of the Hawaiian economy, but without disturbing the flourishing local trade and imports. The constant coming and going of visitors had created a polyglot society in which Americans, Europeans, and eventually Orientals would compete with the native Polynesians.

Signs of increasing American influence were apparent everywhere. American individuals or firms carried out more than three-fourths of the trade and owned the largest and best sugar plantations. Americans made up most of the missionaries, largely Protestant. The native government was advised and often controlled by foreigners, usually Americans or British. A deep-seated Anglo-American rivalry for political and military power had recently produced an American assertion of primary influence, the Tyler Doctrine (1842), and a confrontation with the British Navy, which had withdrawn on instructions from London. Suspicions remained on both sides, but neither government, far away and occupied with other matters, placed a very high priority on Hawaii.

After the late 1850s the whaling industry declined rapidly, beset by a scarcity of whales and competition from petroleum. Sugar growing and refining, which replaced it, was introduced on a systematic basis in the late 1830s by an American firm. At first crude, the industry expanded steadily in the 1850s, favored by a number of factors. For one thing, the Hawaiian government increased available land by breaking up quasi-feudal estates and allowing foreign ownership. The government also began to permit importation of contract labor. The American annexation of California and the ensuing gold rush supplied a new, profitable market for Hawaiian sugar. At the same time the old American residents on the islands and new immigrants from the United States furnished the capital, introduced the steam power and the new machinery, and developed the political contacts necessary for fast growth.[1]

1. Theodore Morgan, *Hawaii, a Century of Economic Change, 1778–1876*, chaps. 1–9. See especially 100. Kuykendall, *The Hawaiian Kingdom*, vol. 1, 135–46. Jacob Adler, *Claus*

Even before the California gold rush, in 1844, four out of six general commission houses in Honolulu were American. A good illustration is the American-Hawaiian firm C. Brewer and Company, founded by an American sailor who settled in Hawaii. After establishing a general produce trade over much of the Pacific, the company concentrated more and more on sugar exports and in 1850 acquired its first sugar lands. By the 1860s its primary business was growing and selling sugar, both on its own account and on commission, and it handled general merchandise on consignment only. A former partner, Henry A. Peirce, established one of the first large sugar plantations on the islands and became a leader among American expansionists. He served for a time as Hawaiian consul in the United States and from 1869 to 1877 as American minister to Hawaii. Another former partner, Henry A. P. Carter, was a leading Hawaiian diplomat for more than fifteen years, beginning in the mid-1870s.[2]

Except for brief setbacks, the average price of sugar rose steadily and doubled between the 1840s and the early 1860s. Despite a chronic shortage of native labor, during the decade after 1856 Hawaiian sugar exports increased from £554,895 to £17,729,161. In 1863 the U.S. minister estimated that Americans owned nearly all important Hawaiian sugar plantations and more than half of the merchant ships visiting the islands and that they controlled perhaps four-fifths of Hawaiian trade.[3]

This rapid expansion of American interest was furthered by a friendly government in the islands and erratic support from Washington. King Kamehameha III, always concerned about the danger of European intervention, relied heavily on American advisers. In 1854 the Franklin Pierce administration obtained an annexation treaty on unfavorable terms (statehood for Hawaii, annuities for the royal family), but the king died before it could be ratified. His successor, Kamehameha IV, rejected it in favor of a reciprocity treaty, which was signed the

Spreckels: The Sugar King in Hawaii, 4–10. Merze Tate, *The United States and the Hawaiian Kingdom, a Political History,* 1–10. Tate, *Hawaii: Reciprocity or Annexation?* 19–26. Stevens, *American Expansion,* 8–12, 25–28, 33. U.S., *Consular Reports* 4 (February 1881): 338–40. In the first three years after the American annexation of California, between 1848 and 1851, Hawaiian exports to American Pacific coast ports nearly doubled. For an analysis of the close relationship between California and Hawaii thereafter see Harold Whitman Bradley, "California and the Hawaiian Islands, 1846–1852," 18–27. The term "American-Hawaiian" will be used to designate American-born Hawaiians or their direct descendants.

2. Sullivan, *History of C. Brewer and Company;* Ethel M. Damon, *Sanford Ballard Dole and His Hawaii,* 34–36. Trade figures estimated by an American-Hawaiian newspaper editor. Shewmaker, "Forging the 'Great Chain,'" 229, and see 227–28 for the influence of the missionaries. Peirce urged Webster to annex Hawaii as early as 1842 and similarly supported the acquisition of Alaska in 1867. Barry Rigby, "American Expansion in Hawaii: The Contribution of Henry A. Peirce," 353–55.

3. Morgan, *Hawaii,* chap. 12. Rigby, "American Expansion in Hawaii," 356. Sullivan, *History of C. Brewer and Company,* 124. Kuykendall, *Hawaiian Kingdom,* vol. 1, 141. U.S., *Foreign Relations, 1894,* 3, 134, ff. (This volume is a convenient compilation of diplomatic correspondence concerning Hawaii.) At the same time ten times as many American whalers visited Hawaii as those of all other nationalities combined.

following year with the hearty support of American residents. Its terms were to become familiar in American-Hawaiian relations: Hawaiian sugar, molasses, and coffee to be admitted duty-free in U.S. ports, in return for similar treatment in Hawaii for a long list of American products.

American objections to the treaty were also to become familiar. The two powerful Louisiana senators, Judah P. Benjamin and John Slidell, and the wool lobby opposed setting the precedent of abolishing duties. Many thought reciprocity treaties unconstitutional because they curtailed congressional power to tax foreign trade. Some feared that Hawaii would extend the new privileges to all nations with which it had most-favored-nation agreements or bring in sugar from the Far East, to be reexported to California under a Hawaiian label. After considering the treaty over a period of eighteen months, the Senate adjourned in 1857 without acting, and the Buchanan administration abandoned the cause.[4]

The American Civil War brought a few changes in U.S.-Hawaiian relations. By shutting off the supply of Louisiana sugar, the war further encouraged American-Hawaiian trade, which helped to compensate for the continued decline in whaling. As steam power began to supplement or replace sails, Hawaii appeared in strategic discussions as a possible coaling station. In 1864 a writer in *Merchants' Magazine* referred to it as "the Cuba of the West" and "an outlying colony of California" and declared that, with a majority of the islands' foreign population and the largest capital investments, the United States had a clearer right to dominate than the British.[5]

A new Hawaiian king, Kamehameha V, and his French-born foreign minister, Charles de Varigny, were wary of American imperialism, yet fearful that a Union defeat in the war would end Hawaiian prosperity. As a precaution, the king sent his American-Hawaiian chief justice, Elisha H. Allen, to press for reciprocity and a tripartite agreement with Britain and France recognizing Hawaiian sovereignty. At the same time the American minister to Hawaii reported increasing official discrimination against Americans and urged Secretary of State Seward to negotiate for a naval base near Honolulu and send a secret agent to keep an eye on European residents. Seward favored reciprocity and eventual annexation and opposed a tripartite treaty but, being busy with wartime problems and aware of growing public hostility to an existing reciprocity treaty with Canada, he resisted all suggestions. Only at the end of the war would he go so far as to instruct

4. Tate, *United States and Hawaiian Kingdom*, 10–21. Stevens, *American Expansion*, 1–8, 12–23. On Anglo-French opposition to American annexation see Brookes, *International Rivalry*, 208–19; and Van Alstyne, "Hawaiian Independence," 19–24. Osborne E. Hooley, "Hawaiian Negotiations for Reciprocity, 1855–57," 128–47. Kuykendall, *Hawaiian Kingdom*, vol. 1, 36–46. For the text of the treaty see U.S., 56th Cong., 2d sess., *Senate Document 231*, pt. 6, 407–9. Reciprocity had already been discussed without any action in 1849 and 1852.

5. Stevens, *American Expansion*, 86–89. *Merchants' Magazine* 50 (March 1864): 170–75.

Minister Charles Francis Adams in London to inquire discreetly concerning British intentions toward Hawaii.[6]

After the Civil War an acute depression convinced Hawaiian planters, most of them American-born, that they must have reciprocity to bypass rising American tariffs. Seward sent out a new minister, Edward M. McCook, an ally alike of California sugar refiners and American-Hawaiian planters, to campaign for reciprocity so as to combat British influence and prepare for annexation. In McCook's dispatches he played down Hawaiian suspicions, praised the planters as loyal Americans, and described depression conditions and the declining native population. He declared that the poor health of the king and the uncertain succession—a chronic Hawaiian problem—made prompt action vital, before a crisis developed.[7] In November 1866 McCook took his campaign to California and then Washington. There he conferred with members of the government, to whom he supplied data for a detailed report to Congress, emphasizing trade benefits from reciprocity and avoiding mention of annexation. Meanwhile in Honolulu Foreign Minister Varigny, more sure than ever that reciprocity was the only way to maintain Hawaiian independence, sent Finance Minister Charles C. Harris, another American-Hawaiian, to negotiate.[8]

McCook and Harris met in San Francisco, far from the rumormongers of both capitals. There they consulted the local sugar refiners (one of whom had already sent an agent to Hawaii to make deals with the planters). The resulting treaty was signed on May 21, 1867. Like its predecessor of 1855 it provided for duty-free admission into the United States of Hawaiian crude and partly refined sugar (not above number 12, Dutch standard), as well as coffee, rice, furs, skins, fruits, and vegetables. In return, Hawaii would admit duty-free a great variety of American goods, including cotton and woolen cloth, agricultural implements, hardware,

6. Stevens, *American Expansion*, 95–97. Kuykendall, *Hawaiian Kingdom*, vol. 1, 65–66, 196–201. Tate, *Hawaii: Reciprocity or Annexation?* 46–49. McBride to Seward, December 10, 1863, no. 16, 56th Cong., 2d sess., *Senate Document 231*, pt. 8, 147; September 15, 16, 1864, nos. 36, 37, 52d Cong., 2d sess., *Senate Executive Document 77*, 133. Same, March 1, 1864; February 15, August 12, 1865, nos. 23, 44, 54, U.S., Department of State, Record Group 69, Despatches from United States Ministers, Hawaii, 11 (hereafter U.S., Diplomatic Despatches, with country and volume). Elisha H. Allen to [Secretary of State], Bangor, Maine, December 31, 1864. U.S., Department of State, Record Group 69, Notes from Foreign Legations, Hawaii, 2 (hereafter U.S., Notes from, with country and volume). For Seward's inquiry in Britain see Joseph G. Whelan, "William Henry Seward, Expansionist," 164–67. Kuykendall, *Hawaiian Kingdom*, vol. 1, 201–5.

7. Kuykendall, *Hawaiian Kingdom*, vol. 1, 209–10. Tate, *Hawaii: Reciprocity or Annexation?* 49–50. Edward M. McCook to Seward, September 3, 1866, no. 6, U.S., 52d Cong., 2d sess., *Senate Executive Document 76*, 133–35. None of the last six Hawaiian monarchs left a son to succeed him. Thus the succession was appointive. Twice in the 1870s a chief outside the immediate royal family was elected.

8. Kuykendall, *Hawaiian Kingdom*, vol. 1, 209–12. Tate, *Hawaii: Reciprocity or Annexation?* 50–52. McCook to the President, February 12, 1898, Day papers, box 9, U.S., 58th Cong., 2d sess., *Senate Document 231*, pt. 8, 147–52.

iron, lumber, petroleum, and many food products. According to current trade figures the relative prices of listed commodities made the treaty seem to favor the United States, but because of high American tariffs, the United States stood to lose more revenue than Hawaii. McCook wrote to Seward that the impending completion of the transcontinental railroad would make the islands a focus for American trade and shipping, both mercantile and naval. He added: "This treaty will have prepared the way for their quiet absorption."[9]

Kamehameha ratified the treaty in September, after McCook had tactfully sent away the American warship *Lackawanna,* then on a protracted visit.[10] In the United States the supporters of the treaty were many and vocal: Seward and Secretary of the Treasury Hugh McCulloch for the Johnson administration, Harris, Allen, and other envoys for Hawaii, the San Francisco and New York Chambers of Commerce, the Boston Board of Trade, its offspring, the Hawaiian Club, and dozens of individual businessmen and publicists on both coasts. The treaty had a good press, and the *New York Times* referred to it contentedly as "laying the foundations of our future national greatness." Nevertheless, for nearly three years, from July 1867 to June 1870, the Senate played cat and mouse with it before rejecting it 20–19. The small vote suggests lack of interest; not even the two Louisiana senators were present.[11]

As with the Alaska treaty, Senator Charles Sumner, chairman of the Foreign Relations Committee, was a leading advocate. The principal opponents were all Republicans—at first James W. Grimes (Iowa) and William P. Fessenden (Maine) and later two inveterate protectionists, Justin S. Merrill (Vermont) and John Sherman (Ohio). The support of the Johnson administration meant little, for it was completely discredited by 1868. After Grant's inauguration he used up much energy and political capital in a struggle to annex the Dominican Republic, and Secretary Fish was lukewarm on Hawaii.

Opponents of the 1867 treaty applied the same arguments as in 1855: the standard protectionist credo, unconstitutionality, most-favored-nation treaties with other nations, and uncompensated loss of revenue to the Treasury. Some critics objected that American planters in Hawaii, San Francisco sugar refiners, and West Coast consumers would reap the chief benefits at the Treasury's expense.

---

9. Tate, *Hawaii: Reciprocity or Annexation?* 53–54. The text was printed in the *Pacific Commercial Advertiser* (Honolulu), September 7, 1867. McCook to Seward, May 29, June 1867, no. 24, unnumbered, U.S., 56th Cong., 2d sess., *Senate Document 231,* pt. 8, 153–60. The "Dutch standard" was a crude but commonly used method for defining the purity of sugar by determining its shade, from brown to white.

10. Kuykendall, *Hawaiian Kingdom,* vol. 1, 207–8, 212–16. Tate, *Hawaii: Reciprocity or Annexation?* 55. Brookes, *International Rivalry,* 278–80.

11. Stevens, *American Expansion,* 100–104. Tate, *Hawaii: Reciprocity or Annexation?* 58–70, 72. W. Stull Holt, *Treaties Defeated by the Senate, a Study of the Conflict between President and Senate over the Conduct of Foreign Relations,* 102–5. The principal newspapers supporting the treaty were the *San Francisco Times,* the *New York Herald, Times, Evening Post,* the *Washington Post,* and *Chronicle. New York Herald,* October 4, 1867; *New York Times,* December 31, 1867.

Others were prejudiced against the Hawaiian government, monarchical and lax, or the islands' contract labor system. A few argued that the United States already enjoyed commercial supremacy in Hawaii or that American capital and citizens should be kept at home for postwar reconstruction and development. Many expansionists (including both Grimes and Fessenden) feared that a successful reciprocity treaty would actually delay annexation and urged the government instead to prepare for quick, decisive action if the Hawaiian king died and a revolution weakened native hostility to American rule.[12]

Confronted with so much opposition in the Senate, Seward did all he could to keep open American options. He had McCook offer purchase of the islands to Kamehameha as an alternative to reciprocity, but the king preferred the treaty. Also the secretary issued a general precautionary warning to American diplomats in Europe concerning possible Anglo-French interference. Meanwhile he sent out to Hawaii a special agent, Zephaniah H. Spalding, to keep him informed. However, when Spalding urged that the United States support an annexationist party and prepare for a coup, Seward had to reply that the American public was absorbed in reconstruction and other domestic problems and would never support such drastic measures.[13]

As another means of drawing Hawaii closer, the U.S. government encouraged regular connections between San Francisco and the islands. During the 1850s and early 1860s sailing vessels had furnished ample service, and projects for steamship lines were discussed but dropped. In 1866, as the American transcontinental railroad approached completion, the postmaster general awarded a ten-year mail subsidy to the Pacific Mail Steamship Company for service to China and Japan, with the provision that its ships must stop at Honolulu en route. The company complained that this requirement would add at least sixteen hundred miles to each round trip and that the Honolulu harbor was inadequate for the larger steamers proposed. Minister McCook supported the company, adding the warning

12. Kuykendall, *Hawaiian Kingdom,* vol. 1, 217–27. John Patterson, "The United States and Hawaiian Reciprocity, 1867–1870," 19–25. Tate, *Hawaii: Reciprocity or Annexation?* 56–58, 71–76. The American South, prostrated by Reconstruction and its sugar industry ruined by the war, played a small and mixed role in the debate. Stevens, *American Expansion,* 104–5.

13. Whalen, "Seward, Expansionist," 177–79, 183. Seward also had American diplomats in Europe pay close attention to a trip made to Europe at this time by Foreign Minister Varigny. Seward to McCook, September 12, 1867, unnumbered, U.S., Department of State, Record Group 69, Instructions to United States Ministers, Hawaii, roll 99 (hereafter U.S., Diplomatic Instructions, with country and volume or roll). McCook to Seward, August 5, 1867, no. 31, U.S. Diplomatic Despatches, Hawaii, 12, and September 14, 1867, unnumbered, U.S., 52d Cong., 2d sess., *Senate Executive Document 69,* 146–47. British and French reactions to the 1867 treaty are outlined in Brookes, *International Rivalry,* 281–84. At first Spalding worked among the American residents against reciprocity, but by 1870 he was urging it on the Grant administration as an anti-European measure. He stayed in Hawaii and entered the sugar trade. For his correspondence see U.S., Department of State, Record Group 69, Despatches from United States Consuls, Honolulu, 2 (hereafter U.S., Consular Despatches, with post and volume).

that a transoceanic line might drain off Hawaiian sugar to Japan, increasing British influence in Hawaii. Both urged a separate subsidy for a direct line to the islands.[14]

In 1867 the postmaster general released Pacific Mail from its Hawaiian requirement, and during the next seven years the United States paid a total of $425,000 to two successive short-lived steamship companies of mail service between San Francisco and Honolulu. The second of these, organized by the New York shipbuilder William H. Webb, was a project for steam communication between the United States and Australasia. (See chapter 4.) When it collapsed, the only regular San Francisco–Honolulu steamship connections were furnished for several years by an Australian line with subsidies from New South Wales and New Zealand for service to the United States.[15]

Although the U.S. Senate had spurned the Hawaiian treaty of 1867, the reciprocity movement continued in both countries through the early 1870s, almost without a break. The combination of high American tariffs and falling sugar prices threatened the debt-ridden sugar planters with bankruptcy, and when Kamehameha V died in 1872, there was a brief upsurge of annexationist rumors. The new king, Lunalilo, was more friendly to the United States than his predecessor, and a trio of Americans, the expansionist Henry A. Peirce, now U.S. minister, and Elisha H. Allen and Henry A. P. Carter in the Hawaiian government, circulated reciprocity arguments at large.[16]

14. Kuykendall, *Hawaiian Kingdom,* vol. 1, 17–19, 168–69. McCook to Seward, November 21, 1966, no. 15, U.S. 39th Cong., 2d sess., *House Executive Document 1,* pt. 11, 495–96. McCook to R. B. Van Valkenburgh (U.S. minister to Japan), August 3, 1867, U.S., 52d Cong., 2d sess., *Senate Executive Document 76,* 138–39. Despite some American concern about Japanese competition for Hawaiian sugar, the American minister at Tokyo helped bring about a Hawaiian-Japanese commercial treaty in 1871. Brookes, *International Rivalry,* 345.

15. Kuykendall, *Hawaiian Kingdom,* vol. 1, 169–72. Curtis, "Trade and Transportation," 133. Inter-island steamship service was mostly promoted by American residents with some financial support from the Hawaiian government. Kuykendall, *Hawaiian Kingdom,* vol. 1, 164–68.

16. Kuykendall, *Hawaiian Kingdom,* vol. 1, 229–30, 247–57. Stevens, *American Expansion in Hawaii,* 109–16. Tate, *Hawaii: Reciprocity or Annexation?* 83–88, 100–102. Carter was a thoroughgoing annexationist, for he saw in the United States the only hope for Hawaiian revival. See a letter of his dated December 19, 1872, quoted in Sullivan, *History of C. Brewer and Company,* 131–34. Ten days before Fish asked Peirce for information, the State Department had briefly discouraged Peirce's suggestion that annexation might be possible if a revolution overthrew the existing government. Davis to Henry A. Peirce, March 15, 1873; Fish to Peirce, March 25, 1873, U.S., Diplomatic Instructions, Hawaii, 2, as cited in Brookes, *International Rivalry,* 349–50, 362n13, 345–49. Peirce was also encouraging the U.S. Navy to maintain a regular "presence" in Hawaii. Rigby, "American Expansion in Hawaii," 358–59. One historian has categorically denied that a depression existed in the Hawaiian sugar industry of the 1870s, citing steady increases in sugar exports, 1865–1875, despite falling prices. Review by Theodore Morgan in *Far Eastern Quarterly* 6 (February 1947): 196–97. This denial flies in the face of the practically unanimous testimony of contemporaries and the judgment of principal writers since 1947. See, for example, Elisha H. Allen to Evarts, October 22, 1879, U.S., Notes from Hawaii, 2.

In the United States an exaggerated anxiety spread concerning British influence in Hawaii through the developing Hawaiian trade with Australia and New Zealand, especially after the expansionist premier of New Zealand, Julius Vogel, published a "Grand Scheme" for a Polynesian commercial company and a loan to Hawaii. (Neither ever materialized.) California newspapers eagerly reported the Hawaiian distress and the fancied Australasian threat.[17] In March 1873 Fish showed a sudden increase of interest and, while still doubtful about reciprocity, asked Minister Peirce for full information on Hawaiian trade, resources, and public debts. The preceding winter the War Department had sent Generals John M. Schofield and B. S. Alexander to investigate Hawaiian defensive facilities in case of war with Britain. The generals recommended acquiring purchasing rights and clearing the entrance to two deep, capacious lagoons in the mouth of the Pearl River, situated about ten miles from Honolulu and the only large natural harbor in the central Pacific.[18]

When the Hawaiian government made overtures for the renewal of reciprocity negotiations in 1873, it agreed to include control of Pearl Harbor. Native nationalists immediately opposed the cession of territory, led among others by Chief David Kalakaua and Walter M. Gibson, an American-born Mormon journalist who was to dominate the native anti-American faction on the island for more than a decade. The government had to withdraw its offer. In February 1874 the death of King Lunalilo without a direct heir brought Kalakaua to the throne by popular election. The new king accelerated the earlier campaign for a treaty, perhaps because marines from a visiting American warship helped him keep order during the unrest following his election but more likely because he saw in reciprocity the best hedge against American annexation. Less than a year after his coronation he made a ceremonial visit to the United States. Meanwhile Carter, Allen, and Peirce (home on leave) were energetically lobbying the American Congress and buttonholing Secretary Fish, alternately bored and irritated at their importunities but by now convinced that the Hawaiian situation demanded some action.[19]

17. Australia and New Zealand charged a lower duty on sugar than the United States, but after reaching a peak in 1873, their sugar imports from Hawaii declined steadily. Their populations were simply not large enough to create an attractive market, and Tate concludes that Hawaii's reputed "swing" toward the British Empire in the 1870s was more myth than reality. Tate, *Hawaii, Reciprocity or Annexation?* 102–4. For samples of California publicity reprinted on the East Coast see *New York Times,* November 8, 1872, March 15, 1873.

18. For the report of Grant's military agents see J. H. Schofield and B. S. Alexander to William W. Belknap, May 8, 1873, reprinted in *American Historical Review* 30 (April 1925): 561–65. Brookes, *International Rivalry,* 350–51. Oddly, considering the later British opposition to the transfer of Pearl Harbor, the proposal first appeared in a published letter of a British businessman in Honolulu who was concerned about the economy. Merze Tate, "British Opposition to the Cession of Pearl Harbor," 381.

19. Stevens, *American Expansion,* 116–19. Brookes, *International Rivalry,* 348–57. Tate, *Hawaii: Reciprocity or Annexation?* 86–100, 108–11. For sketches of Gibson see Tate, *United States and Hawaiian Kingdom,* 324–26; and Adler, *Claus Spreckels,* 17. On internal Hawaiian unrest and Kalakaua's succession see Brookes, *International Rivalry.* Henry A. Peirce to Fish,

In the negotiations Grant, Fish, and the cabinet were moved by both economic and political considerations. Peirce and Carter assured Fish that reciprocity would wipe out the Australasian tariff advantage and give Americans virtually complete control of the Hawaiian market. The Americans pressed for some assurance that Hawaii would not offset the American tariff concessions with export duties or extend the concessions to other countries. They also asked for political inducements such as a naval base, but while Carter agreed to forbid export duties, he parried the other requests. The treaty as signed on January 30, 1875, almost doubled the 1867 list of American products to be admitted free into Hawaii—apparently at the suggestion of Carter, who wanted to strengthen the economic tie. Coffee, cotton, and ornamental woods were omitted from the list of Hawaiian products, and sugar was defined vaguely as ordinary "Sandwich island sugar." (In practice this seems to have meant raising maximum grades of refinement from Number 12 to Number 16, Dutch standard.) The treaty was to remain in effect for seven years, and after that either government might abrogate it, giving a year's notice.[20]

Grant at once submitted the signed treaty to the Senate for approval, and since it could not take effect without appropriate changes in the American tariff, both houses then had to pass a new schedule of duties—a complicated process that lasted until the end of 1876. Admiral David D. Porter wrote to one senator that the United States must have a foothold in Hawaii to offset British influence in the North Pacific. Peirce appeared before the Senate Foreign Relations Committee, quoting Seward on the importance of the Pacific basin and predicting that the treaty would "hold those islands with hooks of steel in the interests of the United States, and . . . result finally in their annexation to the United States." To strengthen the "hooks of steel" the committee not only extended the Hawaiian free list but also, more important, added a sentence flatly forbidding Hawaii to grant preferential rates, port rights, or territory to any other country. If the United States could not have Pearl Harbor, then no one else should.[21]

When the treaty had been approved, 50–12, with these iron-bound guarantees, General Schofield wrote privately to the chairman of the House Ways and Means Committee that now the United States must carry out its part of the agreement:

February 28, 1873, no. 192, U.S., Diplomatic Despatches, Hawaii, 15. A report of Peirce's appearance before the Senate Foreign Relations Committee is in the *New York Tribune*, January 15, 1875. Henry A. P. Carter to Fish, January 11, 1875, U.S., Notes from Foreign Legations, Hawaii, 2.

20. Stevens, *American Expansion*, 120–25. Ralph S. Kuykendall, *The Hawaiian Kingdom, 1874–1893: The Kalakaua Dynasty* (vol. 2), 24–26. Carter to Fish, January 5, 1875, Fish papers, no. 17801. Fish's own views on Kalakaua's visit and the negotiation of the treaty may be followed in his diary, vols. 2, 5, 6; boxes 316, 319. Bevans, *Treaties*, vol. 8, 874–77.

21. Stevens, *American Expansion*, 125–126, 132–34. Rigby, "American Expansion in Hawaii," 364–66. David D. Porter to (Charles W.) Jones (Democrat, Florida), March 15, 1875, Letterbook, 1869–1880, 605–11, David D. Porter papers, box 21. Peirce testimony before the Senate Foreign Relations Committee, enclosed with Peirce to Fish, January 12, 1675, unnumbered, U.S., Diplomatic Despatches, Hawaii, 17.

"We cannot refuse the islands the little aid they so sorely need, and at the same time deny their right to seek it elsewhere. The time has come when we must secure forever the desired control over those islands or let it pass into other hands." The *New York Evening Post* was even more explicit—the treaty would offer the United States a strong point in the mid-Pacific and prevent British encirclement of the West Coast, giving all the benefits and no disadvantages of holding a colony.[22]

Opponents of the treaty found it difficult to answer these essentially political arguments, although a few of them likened Pearl Harbor to Samaná Bay, a base in the Dominican Republic that the Senate had recently rejected. Most of them, however, agreed that the United States must not permit British domination of the islands, and some wanted outright annexation. Therefore, they tried to focus congressional and public attention on the issue of public revenues. Chambers of commerce from southern cities lobbied hard for restoration of the sugar and rice duties, and a southern delegation in the Senate made a last stand for them. However, protectionist principles were not much emphasized. Their chief defender, Senator Justin S. Morrill, chairman of the Senate Finance Committee, played a prominent role but chose to emphasize the inordinate loss to the Treasury from the reduced customs revenue. In this he received unaccustomed support from tariff reformer David A. Wells and the *Nation,* which objected to "buying trade and paying an excessively high price for it" through contributions from the Treasury that would benefit chiefly planters and West Coast sugar refiners.

California's two senators took opposite sides in the debate on approval, for some Pacific refiners, far from welcoming the tariff reduction, feared that a competing industry in the islands might ruin them. At the same time San Francisco merchants and general California business interests supported reciprocity, expecting an increased export trade. Senator Aaron A. Sargent, who favored the treaty, predicted a flood of American emigrants, creating an American colony. The House Ways and Means Committee, remembering the Alaska treaty appropriation of the preceding decade, inquired about improper influences behind the approval bill but could discover nothing. After all the sound and fury, the congressional debate on the new duties ended in apathy, and they were easily passed. Considering the hullabaloo in the press over the renewal of the treaty a few years later, it is noteworthy that few newspapers paid much attention to the congressional debates of 1875–1876 over the original treaty and its implementation.[23]

22. H. Schofield to J. K. Luttrell, December 30, 1875. Quoted in Allen to William M. Evarts, October 22, 1879, U.S., Notes from Hawaii, 2. *New York Evening Post,* April 5, 1876. See also *New York Times,* March 12.

23. Stevens, *American Expansion,* 128–32, 134–40. Brookes, *International Rivalry,* 358–61. Edward Stanwood, *American Tariff Controversies in the Nineteenth Century,* vol. 2, 173. For a good exposition of arguments on both sides as presented in the House debate see the majority and minority reports of the Ways and Means Committee. U.S., 44th Cong., 1st sess., House Report 116. See also U.S., 44th Cong., 1st sess., *Congressional Record,* 4, 1423–26, 1490–98, 2271–83, 5486. *Cincinnati Daily Gazette,* August 3, 1873. *New*

Hawaiian planters and merchants received the reciprocity treaty with joy, somewhat tempered by native leaders' uneasiness about American influence and general dislike of new taxes that the government levied to offset the lost customs duties. European residents were furious, and the British commissioner, Major James H. Wodehouse, protested vigorously to the Hawaiian government that Britain would claim the same concessions under a most-favored-nation clause in its commercial treaty of 1851, although another article in the same treaty clearly stated that such claims must be conditioned on any reciprocal grants involved. King Kalakaua sent Carter on a conciliatory mission to Germany and Britain. He succeeded in mollifying the former government (which had no most-favored-nation treaty with Hawaii anyway), but the quarrel with Britain continued for several years until the Foreign Office abandoned it in the early 1880s. As for the Australians, they disgustedly lamented the loss of trade opportunities they were too remote and too weak to exploit.[24]

Although in considerable part politically motivated, the Hawaiian reciprocity treaty of 1875 was a milestone on the American economic advance into the Pacific basin. After decades of hesitation and divided policies concerning commerce and communications with the islands, it established a partnership between government and business in developing an economic and eventually a political satellite. By increasing trade the treaty would benefit American-Hawaiian planters and American merchants along the California coast; and by increasing American influence in Hawaii, it would furnish a substitute (or perhaps preparation) for possession of Pearl Harbor and even outright annexation of the islands.

As soon as the reciprocity treaty went into operation, it began to fulfill the principal expectations of its supporters. Within fifteen months the American minister at Honolulu reported to the State Department that the United States

---

York World, January 11, 1873. David A. Wells in Boston Evening Transcript, February 25, March 1, 1875, as cited in Tate, Hawaii: Reciprocity or Annexation? 113, 131n11. Nation 20 (March 4, 1875): 142; 82 (March 9, 1876): 152. Adler, Claus Spreckels, 14–15. There is some evidence to indicate that Hawaiian planters withheld sugar from the California market in order to coerce San Francisco refineries into withdrawing their opposition to reciprocity. Kuykendall, Hawaiian Kingdom, vol. 2, 29–30. On southern lobbying and the House committee investigation see New York Times, June 1, 1876. On apathetic press reactions see Donald Marquand Dozer, "Anti-Imperialism in the United States, 1865–1895: Opposition to Annexation of Overseas Territories," 89–90, 101–2.

24. Kuykendall, Hawaiian Kingdom, vol. 2, 40–45. Stevens, American Expansion, 147–48. For contemporary press clippings from Honolulu see enclosures with dispatches of J. Scott to William Hunter, June 5, September 9, 30, 1876. U.S., Consular Dispatches, Honolulu, 13, 14. On European efforts to obtain most-favored-nation treatment see also U.S., Reciprocity and Commercial Treaties, 110–12. Melbourne Journal of Commerce, July 13, 1875, enclosed with Peirce to Fish, October 7, 1875, no. 341, U.S. Diplomatic Despatches, Hawaii, 17. For two years before the treaty Chancellor Bismarck had told the American minister, George Bancroft, that he would be heartily glad to see the United States annex Hawaii. George Bancroft to Fish, January 25, 1873, no. 453 (secret and confidential), ibid., Germany, 3. See also U.S., Foreign Relations, 1877, 277–78.

enjoyed "every [political] benefit that it would have if the Hawaiian Kingdom were a state of the Union." The economic effects of the treaty are best measured by comparing American-Hawaiian statistics for the last two full years of operation before the treaty took effect (1875) and before it was interrupted by the McKinley tariff (1890). During that period Hawaiian annual sugar production increased more than tenfold, from 11,639 to 120,000 long tons. Hawaiian exports to the United States also rose more than tenfold (from $1,227,191 to $12,313,908), and these came to form more than 98 percent of all Hawaiian exports. The increase in American exports to Hawaii was also substantial, although less impressive—from $947,200 to $5,259,154—and the American portion of all Hawaiian imports rose from 56.3 percent to 75.5 percent.[25]

More than ever, sugar dominated the Hawaiian economy, for the increased exports brought new lands into use, and their fertility and an ideal climate reduced production costs even below those of Cuba. Between 1875 and 1890 Americans and American-Hawaiians increased their capital investment in sugar estates and refineries from about $1.5 million out of $2 million to $24,735,610 out of $33,455,990. The capital increase made possible elaborate irrigation and the heavy purchase of expensive machinery required for efficient grinding and the partial refining permitted by the treaty. Rice culture too received encouragement from the abolition of the American duty, but it lagged far behind sugar production and remained largely in Chinese hands. The advance was uneven, with bad years in 1879–1880, 1884–1885, and the early 1890s. Also, from every point of view, the native Hawaiians benefited least from the treaty. In the early 1890s, although still constituting 45 percent of the population (including half castes), they owned only 15 percent of private lands and 2 percent of invested capital.[26]

Both before and after negotiation of the treaty, its critics argued that increases in American exports were insufficient to justify the loss of customs revenue on sugar to the U.S. Treasury. Extrapolating from the slow rate of increase in the early 1870s, Merze Tate calculates that from 1875 to 1890 the United States exported at least $32,447,510 worth of goods more than it would have without the treaty. This figure included a great variety of American products: provisions, livestock, lumber,

25. U.S., *Foreign Relations*, 1882, 333. U.S., *Reciprocity and Commercial Treaties*, 122, 131, 133.

26. Lorrin A. Thurston, "The Sandwich Islands: The Advantages of Annexation," 272–73. Tate, *Reciprocity or Annexation?* 117–22, 362. Commissioner James H. Blount reported after the revolution of 1893 that $21,554,775 out of the total capital stock of $28,274,000 in sugar corporations was controlled by Americans or American-Hawaiians and that the total of American-controlled capital in all areas was $25,194,166. Stevens, *American Expansion*, 141–47, especially 147. According to Hawaiian figures, in 1894 American and American-Hawaiian corporate capital in Hawaii totaled $26,109,166 out of $36,841,000, or 70.7 percent. British and British-Hawaiian capital totaled 19.6 percent, German 5.7 percent, and Hawaiian and part-Hawaiian 1.8 percent. Weigle, "Sugar Interests," 56. Statistics on native Hawaiians are taken from the 1890 census. U.S., 53d Cong., 2d sess., *House Executive Document 47*, 80. See also *Bradstreet's* 17 (November 16, 1889): 730. For a survey of the Hawaiian economy under reciprocity see Kuykendall, *Hawaiian Kingdom*, vol. 2, chaps. 3, 4. A good case study is Sullivan, *History of C. Brewer and Company*, chap. 7.

petroleum products, iron and steel, hardware, machinery, and farm implements—but, ironically, not much machinery for sugar cultivation and grinding, which Hawaiian planters continued to import from Britain. Since the islands had a population of fewer than eighty thousand, the per capita purchases amounted to several times what the British or Canadians bought from the United States.

Moreover, the export statistics omitted many other American benefits from the treaty, such as payment for ships built to be used in inter-island and foreign trade (about sixty-five during the period of the treaty) and earnings or dividends from the many commercial, manufacturing, insurance, and other companies formed to fill gaps in the primitive island economy. The annexationist Lorrin A. Thurston did not exaggerate in his later declaration that through the reciprocity treaty the United States "secured an enormous addition to her ship-building and foreign export and carrying trade, and there has been created a prosperous, progressive American community, which is no less American because it is across an ocean and under a tropical sky."[27]

The largest amount of new capital from the mainland was brought in by Claus Spreckels, who used techniques of American "robber barons" to dominate the Hawaiian economy and government. A German-born immigrant, at first a grocer on the East Coast, he moved to California in 1856, and by the 1870s he owned the largest cane sugar refinery in the state. He imported most of his raw sugar from Hawaii, where he had favorable contracts with many of the planters. Spreckels and other California refiners opposed reciprocity, fearing that it would enable the planters to open their own local refineries. Quickly accepting the fait accompli of the treaty, however, he appeared in Honolulu just as the new duties became law to purchase the current sugar crop before prices rose and then to buy up and lease sugar plantations. He was especially interested in the unused, dry central plain of Maui. With a generous concession from the Hawaiian government, he hired an engineer to construct a thirty-mile irrigation ditch which, with tunnels, pipes, flumes, and trestles, would bring down the vital water from nearby mountains. Then, to solidify and perpetuate his landholdings, he bought out the dubious rights of a royal princess for $10,000 cash and a loan and used them to claim half of the crown lands. Eventually he got what he wanted—a clear title to his selected estates—and in the process won the firm support of King Kalakaua and Walter M. Gibson (prime minister from 1882 to 1887), who saw in him the symbol of progress and profits.

Before long, Spreckels had erected an economic empire in Hawaii and California. The most solid symbol of his power was Spreckelsville, his great plantation in central Maui, equipped with the most modern machinery, electricity (the

27. For a favorable appraisal of the efects of reciprocity, on which much of this paragraph is based, see Tate, *Hawaii: Reciprocity or Annexation?* 259–66. Tate, in turn, derives some information from Thurston, "Advantages of Annexation," 272–79 (quotation on 277). Since Thurston was writing for propagandist effect, his analysis must be used with some caution. For statistics concerning the products shipped to and from Hawaii, 1875–1896, see U.S. Bureau of the American Republics, *Commercial Directory*, 1, 892–93.

first in Hawaii), and shipping from the port of Kahalui. A prudent Englishman, William G. Irwin, managed the company that carried on purchases, sales, and general merchandising for the Spreckels empire. In some years Spreckels maintained that this company marketed more than one-half of the Hawaiian sugar crop, but probably the true figure never greatly exceeded one-third. In 1881 Spreckels founded his own steamer line, the Oceanic Steamship Company, which carried his sugar to the United States and also provided regular, fast communication between San Francisco and Honolulu. Eventually it also served Australia and New Zealand.

Retaining his refining interests in San Francisco, Spreckels incorporated the Hawaiian Commercial and Sugar Company to coordinate operations and speculate on sugar prices, and he rejected overtures from the sugar trust, recently formed in the East. Instead, it was said, through traffic agreements with the transcontinental railroads, Spreckels prevented eastern refineries from entering the Pacific coast market, which he now monopolized. He even marketed a little Hawaiian sugar and rice in the Mississippi Valley. Spreckels engaged in a trial of strength with the sugar trust between 1889 and 1892 and in the latter year had to yield a half share in his California refining company to the trust.[28]

While reciprocity strengthened American-Hawaiian economic connections, political relations remained uneasy. In Honolulu pro- and anti-American forces, usually led by H. A. P. Carter and Walter M. Gibson respectively, contended for influence with the changeable king. In 1881 and 1882 the American State Department took alarm at fancied efforts by Britain, France, and Germany to establish a protectorate or acquire Hawaiian territory. Although most Americans had hitherto paid little attention to Hawaiian contract labor, rumors began to circulate that Hawaii would import thousands of coolies from the British Empire and allow Britain to guard their welfare through special consular courts. When Kalakaua set out on a visit to Europe, Secretary Blaine, who distrusted the bibulous monarch, issued warnings to American diplomats along his route and told the American minister to Britain that if the Foreign Office wished to discuss Hawaii, he must make clear that the United States regarded it as "essentially a part of the American system of states" and would oppose "the intrusion of any non-American interest." The rumor about coolies and courts came to nothing, and Kalakaua calmed American suspicions by visiting the United States on his way home. Blaine had acted out of his chronic Anglophobia and perhaps also a desire for political capital.[29]

28. The best account of Spreckels's activities is Adler, *Claus Spreckels*, chaps. 1–12, from which these paragraphs are summarized. For brief accounts see Tate, *Hawaii: Reciprocity or Annexation?* 122–28, 169–170; and *Dictionary of American Biography*, 17, 478. On Spreckels's relations with the sugar trust, see Paul L. Vogt, *The Sugar Refining Industry in the United States, Its Development and Present Condition*, 43–45; Alfred E. Eichner, *The Emergence of Oligopoly: Sugar Refining as a Case Study*, 152–73; and Adler, *Claus Spreckels*, 21–25.

29. On Hawaiian politics and Kalakaua's round-the-world trip see Kuykendall, *Hawaiian Kingdom*, vol. 2, chaps. 7–9. Donald Rowland, "The United States and the Contract

A far more serious threat to American-Hawaiian relations than Blaine's imaginings was American opposition to the reciprocity treaty, for a campaign to abrogate it began long before the end of the seven-year probationary period. In 1878 Secretary of the Treasury John Sherman, who had opposed the treaty as a senator, reported that it was costing the Treasury more in duties than the entire gain in American exports. Thus prompted, Representative Randall L. Gibson (Democrat, Louisiana) introduced an abrogation resolution in Congress, the first gun in a long legislative campaign. At the same time the most fluent antitreaty pamphleteer began his copious publications—Henry Alvin Brown of Massachusetts, a former Treasury agent and customs supervisor who claimed to be motivated by a desire for sound tariff policy and hatred of corruption but may well have received support from business or political interests opposed to the treaty.

These interests were many and powerful, but not always fully united. Eastern sugar refiners, led by Henry O. Havemeyer, were engaged in putting together the sugar trust and saw in Spreckels a dangerous rival. Protectionists in both parties attacked reciprocity as a breaching of the tariff wall. Southern sugar and rice producers, now recovering from the Civil War, feared Hawaiian competition and favored a high tariff but also opposed the refiners' efforts to fix sugar prices in the United States. The protectionist *San Francisco Chronicle* spoke volubly for Californians who hated Spreckels, and many newspapers and business organizations all over the country criticized the treaty for fostering monopoly. On the side of the treaty were the Hawaiian government and its diplomats, Henry A. Peirce (now foreign minister), Elisha H. Allen, and Henry A. P. Carter; most American residents in the islands; Spreckels and his allies; many California business interests; navy officials; and eventually the Arthur administration. A few newspapers and periodicals that commonly advocated economic expansion, such as the *New York Tribune* and *Bradstreet's*, gave consistent support. In the Senate, which held the most immediate power over the treaty, two rivals were members of powerful committees—Justin S. Morrill, a protectionist, in the Finance Committee, and

---

Labor Question in Hawaii, 1862–1900," 250–58. For evidence of American suspicions see Evarts to Andrew D. White, October 16, 1880; Blaine to White, April 22, 1881, nos. 145, 212, U.S., *Diplomatic Instructions*, Germany, 17, 10–12, 70–72, B, no. 361, and France, 20, 265–66. Edward Thurston to Lord Granville, April 12, 1881, Paul Knaplund and Carolyn M. Clewes, eds., "Private Letters from the British Embassy in Washington to the Foreign Secretary, Lord Granville, 1880–1885," vol. 1, 128, and same, April 25, 1881, no. 132, F. O. 5/1753, 315–17. Edward F. Crapol, *America for Americans: Economic Nationalism and Anglophobia in the Late Nineteenth Century*, 154–55. David M. Pletcher, *The Awkward Years: American Foreign Relations under Garfield and Arthur*, 68–71. For the phrases quoted see U.S., *Foreign Relations, 1881*, 569–70. Blaine disclaimed any desire to annex Hawaii, but his principal press supporter, the *New York Tribune*, declared that if the Hawaiians wished to join the Union, the American government might properly override "the objections of a small class who find their profit in keeping up the present royal government." *New York Tribune*, September 19, 1881.

John T. Morgan (Democrat, Alabama), an economic expansionist, in the Foreign Relations Committee.[30]

Both in Congress and in the press, the renewed debate on the Hawaiian reciprocity treaty recapitulated old arguments, adding details and evidence, but it brought out only a few new ones. Opponents of the treaty had little to say about its political implications, except that the United States needed no quasi-colony in Hawaii or that in wartime Britain could seize it in half an hour. They complained that the treaty was being violated by the smuggling of sugar from the Far East or high-grade Hawaiian refined sugar with forged markings. Some objected that Hawaiian sugar producers oppressed wretched Chinese coolies for cheap labor, others that the rice industry was entirely in the hands of prosperous Chinese planters.

A prominent target was the great Spreckels monopoly, which was said to coerce Hawaiian planters into selling their crops cheap and maintained artificially high prices on the West Coast. The Pacific Mail Steamship Company, which reentered the Hawaiian trade about 1875, complained of unfair competition from Spreckels' Oceanic line. Citizens of Portland and other West Coast ports accused Spreckels of draining off their trade to San Francisco. The South, seeing Hawaiian sugar and rice pushing even into Louisiana and South Carolina, declared that without the treaty it could supply the nation's needs for these products. The Middle West and West called for a fair chance to develop sorghum or beet sugar industries.[31]

30. Donald M. Dozer, "The Opposition to Hawaiian Reciprocity, 1876–1888," 157–65. Stevens, *American Expansion*, 162–64. Tate, *Hawaii: Reciprocity or Annexation?* 137–39. For Sherman's report see U.S., 45th Cong., 3d sess., *House Executive Document 12*, xviii. The more comprehensive of Brown's many pamphlets were *Analyses of the Sugar Question, Comprehending Cane and Beet Sugar Production, Consumption, Classification,* [etc.] (Washington [?], 1879); *Concise Résumé of Sugar Tariff Topics in Defence of American Sugar Industries and Consumers, Commercial and Revenue Interests against Illicit Invasion, the Hawaii Treaty,* [etc.] (Washington, 1882); and *Hawaiian Sugar Bounties and Treaty Abuses Which Defraud the U.S. Revenue, Oppress American Consumers and Taxpayers* [etc.]; *Statements Made to Congress by Henry Alvin Brown . . . January, 1883* (Washington, 1883). Brown's early writings cover the whole question of the sugar import trade. Among the petitions to Congress against the treaty were many from Louisiana (sugar) and South Carolina (rice), as well as from New York City, from merchants probably associated with sugar importing and the sugar trust. U.S., 47th Cong., 1st sess., *Congressional Record,* 12, 1540, 1660, 1696, 1822, 1879. After Allen's death in January 1883, Carter became Hawaiian minister to the United States. The two men were assisted by an experienced lobbyist, George S. Boutwell, who had been a senator and Grant's secretary of the treasury.

31. Dozer, "Opposition to Hawaiian Reciprocity," 159–60. Tate, *Hawaii: Reciprocity or Annexation?* chap. 6. In addition to Brown's pamphlets, a good summary of the case against the treaty is John Ennis Searles, Jr., *A Few Facts Concerning the Hawaiian Reciprocity Treaty.* See also U.S. 47th Cong., 1st sess., *Congressional Record,* 13, Appendix, 29–37; and 2d sess., Senate Report 1013. Taussig, *Aspects of the Tariff Question,* 108–11. *Bradstreet's* 15 (August 6, 1887): 521; 16 (February 11, 1888): 92. On Spreckels see also Carter to Frederick T. Frelinghuysen, December 6, 1883; April 18, 1884, U.S., Notes from Hawaii, 21, and U.S., *Foreign Relations, 1883,* 287–88. In the midst of the controversy Spreckels's son Adolf shot and wounded the proprietor of the *Chronicle* because of its attacks on his family. *San Francisco Chronicle,* November 20, 1884.

Supporters of the treaty attacked both their opponents' facts and their logic. In 1883 the American minister to Hawaii, Rollin M. Daggett, declared that no high-grade or Chinese sugar was being smuggled into the United States, and a Treasury investigation bore him out. Allen and Carter denied that the treaty debased Hawaiian labor, and Carter skillfully juggled figures to show that the balance between American imports and exports was not as unfavorable as it seemed. San Francisco merchants declared that high freight rates would never allow much sale of Hawaiian sugar east of the Rockies and that anyway Hawaii and Louisiana together could supply only 15 percent of America's sugar needs. They blamed opposition to the treaty "not [on] public spirit but [on the] private rapacity" of eastern sugar refiners.

Because of developing national sensitivity concerning monopolies, backers of the treaty went to great lengths to explain or exonerate Spreckels. Since the world price of sugar was falling during the mid-1880s, they denied that he enjoyed a large profit margin in refining, especially after 1885, when American investors in Hawaiian plantations opened a competing refinery in California. (Consumers there complained that sugar prices remained higher than those on the East Coast.) Meanwhile Spreckels contributed to his own rehabilitation by abandoning his traffic agreements with the transcontinental railroads and lowering his own prices a little. He soon shifted his attention to competition with eastern refiners on their own ground and to the cultivation of sugar beets.

There were many other, more positive arguments for the reciprocity treaty too. Its supporters pointed out that the Treasury had an annual surplus and needed no additional duties. They cited the business that the treaty produced for American steamers, commission agents, insurance companies, and other adjuncts of the sugar industry and the $15 million that Americans had invested in Hawaii. If the treaty were abrogated, they predicted, American creditors and stockholders would be bankrupted and their property sold to the British. Then, as soon as the Canadian Pacific Railway was completed, Hawaiian trade would be diverted to Canada. This would handicap the United States in its contest for Pacific trade. As a correspondent put it to Carl Schurz: "Here is a little bit of practical Monroe Doctrine, not blustering and crowing, simple and peaceful, but eminently efficient."[32]

---

32. See the Dozer and Tate citations in notes 30 and 31. The principal pro-treaty pamphlets include: Rufus Paine Spalding, *A Bird's-Eye View of the Hawaiian Islands, with Some Reflections upon the Reciprocity Treaty with the United States;* Frederick H. Allen, *Commercial Aspects of the Hawaiian Reciprocity Treaty Prepared for the Finance Committee of the Senate;* (National Board of Trade), *A Report on the Hawaiian Treaty Presented to the National Board of Trade at Its Annual Meeting Held in Washington in January 1883;* (Anon.), *Hawaiian Reciprocity Treaty: Reasons Why It Should Not Be Abrogated. Presented on Behalf of the Merchants of San Francisco; The Hawaiian Reciprocity Treaty; The Hawaiian Treaty: A Review of Its Commercial Results; Petition to U.S. Senate and House of Representatives by Ship Builders, Ship Owners and Lumber Merchants of Pacific Coast States Relating to the Treaty of Reciprocity between the United States and the Hawaiian Islands.* Most of these are collected in Hawaiian Historical Society, "Kalakaua's Hawaii, 1874–1891; a Collection of Pamphlets

Congress intensively debated renewal of the treaty between 1881 and 1884, a period when it was also considering the "mongrel tariff" of 1883 and President Chester A. Arthur's projects for a government-sponsored Nicaragua canal and a chain of Caribbean reciprocity treaties. At Secretary of State Frederick T. Frelinghuysen's suggestion, the House Foreign Affairs Committee approved minor clarifying amendments, to prevent frauds. In the Senate Morrill's Finance Committee submitted an elaborate report in favor of abrogation, only to see the principal resulting resolution captured and buried by the Foreign Relations Committee.[33]

Meanwhile H. A. P. Carter, now Hawaiian minister at Washington, formally proposed a seven-year extension of the treaty without changes, explaining privately that the uncertainty of its future was hurting the sugar planters. The Senate Foreign Relations Committee urged Arthur to make the revised treaty more attractive by adding a longer free list of American products and a provision for an American naval base at Pearl Harbor. Since Secretary Frelinghuysen realized that the Hawaiians would oppose the latter, he advised the committee that it should be postponed for later discussion; and on December 6, 1884, he and Carter signed a simple convention extending the 1875 treaty for seven years. A month earlier Grover Cleveland had been elected president. Now a lame duck, Arthur sent the Hawaii treaty extension to the Senate with his last-minute treaties for a Nicaragua canal and reciprocity with Mexico and Cuba. All were tabled, pending Cleveland's inauguration.[34]

Unlike Arthur's other treaties, Cleveland approved of the Frelinghuysen-Carter convention for both commercial and strategic reasons and in 1886 called Hawaii

---

Dealing with the Political, Social and Economic History of Hawaii. [etc.]" For Morgan's arguments see U.S., 48th Cong., 1st sess., *Senate Report 76*. One congressman sought to carry the treaty further by introducing a resolution favoring a complete customs union with Hawaii. U.S., 47th Cong., 1st sess., *Congressional Record*, 15, 735. For statements on the Spreckels monopoly and refining rivals see Stevens, *American Expansion*, 160–61; *The Hawaiian Treaty: A Review of Its Commercial Results*, 11–15; *New York Tribune*, August 25, 1885, and *New York Times*, September 19, 1835. Spreckels built a refinery in Philadelphia during 1889. *Bradstreet's* 16 (April 7, 1888): 826; 17 (December 21, 1889): 809. For the quotation see an unidentified correspondent to Carl Schurz, April 15, 1882, Schurz papers, vol. 75.

33. Stevens, American Expansion, 165–67. Dozer, "Opposition to Hawaiian Reciprocity," 165–72. U.S. *Reciprocity and Commercial Treaties*, 113–14. Ollin Lawrence Burnette, Jr., "The Senate Foreign Relations Committee and the Diplomacy of Garfield, Arthur, and Cleveland," 93–95, 241–42. Frelinghuysen to C. G. Williams, January 10, 1883, U.S., Department of State, Record Group 69, Confidential Report Book, 15, 49–56. For the principal reports see U.S., 47th Cong., 2d sess., *House Report 1860; Senate Report 1013*. U.S., 48th Cong., 1st sess., *Senate Report 76*.

34. Stevens, *American Expansion*, 168. Burnette, "Senate Foreign Relations Committee," 242–49. Carter explained to Frelinghuysen that Spreckels was using the uncertain future of the treaty to blackmail planters into selling him sugar at low prices. Carter to Frelinghuysen, April 18 (two notes), November 17, 1884. U.S., Notes from Foreign Legations, Hawaii, 2, Frelinghuysen to Carter, May 31, 1884. U.S., Notes to Foreign Legations, Hawaii, 1, 101–3. U.S., 56th Cong., 2d sess., *Senate Document 231*, pt. 8, 242–43. For the text of the treaty see Bevans, *Treaties*, vol. 8, 898–99.

"virtually an outpost of American commerce and a stepping-stone to the growing trade of the Pacific." Nevertheless, despite Hawaiian pressure, he made no effort during 1885 to hasten Senate action. Meanwhile a new wave of attacks on reciprocity began to gather, and early in 1886 the House Ways and Means Committee held hearings on a Louisiana-sponsored proposal to negate the treaty by levying a tariff duty on Hawaiian sugar. Friends of the treaty, such as the San Francisco merchants, sprang to its defense, pointing out that seven-eighths of the capital invested in Hawaii was American, while Hawaiian sugar constituted less than 5 percent of that consumed in the United States. In April the Senate Foreign Relations Committee reported the Frelinghuysen-Carter convention with an amendment for a coaling and repair station at Pearl Harbor. At once Henry A. Brown and other opponents of reciprocity attacked the base as too remote and expensive to defend and its acquisition as a violation of existing treaties concerning Hawaii. During the year the value of Pearl Harbor and of the whole treaty became more obvious as the Hawaiian government negotiated with British bankers for a two-million-dollar loan, the Canadian government completed the Canadian Pacific Railway, and a rumor spread that Hawaii contemplated a reciprocity treaty with Canada.[35]

Because Secretary Thomas F. Bayard like Frelinghuysen feared that Hawaii would not grant a naval base at Pearl Harbor, he favored a simple renewal of the 1875 treaty, especially after Carter assured him that rumors of a Canadian treaty were false, and the Hawaiian government modified the terms of the British loan. Nevertheless in January 1887 the Senate accepted the Pearl Harbor amendment, 26–21, and then approved the whole treaty, 43–11. (Undoubtedly some foes of the treaty voted for it in the hope that the new terms would provoke Hawaii to end reciprocity altogether.) Before long Bayard came to accept the amended treaty, largely out of concern over German ambitions in the Pacific (see chapter 4) and lack of respect for the corrupt, unstable Gibson region in Honolulu. When Carter asked for a guarantee that the Pearl Harbor grant would cease if reciprocity were ever abrogated, Bayard reassured him that the Pearl Harbor provision was nonpolitical and, indeed, superfluous, since the United States already had satisfactory coaling docks at Honolulu.[36]

35. Burnette, "Senate Foreign Relations Committee," 368–72. Tate, *Hawaii: Reciprocity or Annexation?* 183–87. Tansill, *Foreign Policy of Bayard,* 372–76. *Bradstreet's* 13 (March 27, 1886): 198–99. Stevens, *American Expansion,* 171–72. James D. Richardson, comp., *A Compilation of the Messages and Papers of the Presidents, 1789–1897,* 500–501 (quotation). For Brown's arguments see his *Hawaiian Reciprocity Treaty Blunders. Immediate Abrogation a National Requirement,* 5, and *Addendum to Analyses of Hawaiian Reciprocity Treaty Blunders and the British-Hawaii Treaty of 1851–52, February 7, 1887,* 1.

36. Stevens, *American Expansion,* 172–79. Tansill, *Foreign Policy of Bayard,* 378–80. Tate, *Hawaii: Reciprocity or Annexation?* 187–97. The British loan was to have been secured by a mortgage on Hawaiian revenue. Adler, *Claus Spreckels,* chaps. 16–19. *Bradstreet's* 14 (September 25, 1886): 195; 15 (March 26, July 23, August 20, 1887): 212, 489, 553. On Bayard's support for the treaty see Thomas F. Bayard to William R. Morrison, March 16, 1986. Copy in Bayard papers, 75ff, 17622–23. To the end Cleveland's commissioner of

In the end, all doubts about Hawaiian ratification of the new treaty were settled by a bloodless revolution in June and July 1887, which overturned the Gibson cabinet, compelled Kalakaua to accept a restrictive constitution, and established a regime more friendly to the United States. Bayard assured Carter that the Pearl Harbor amendment did not affect Hawaiian sovereignty in any way, and the government in Honolulu ratified the treaty. Britain, which had protested against the Pearl Harbor amendment throughout the negotiations, now proposed a joint guarantee of Hawaiian neutrality, but Bayard replied that existing American-Hawaiian treaties made this unnecessary.[37]

Although the 1887 revolution was a movement of foreigners in general aimed at reforming the Hawaiian monarchy, many Americans in the movement harbored thoughts of establishing a republic or annexing the islands to the United States, thus anticipating the actions of the following decade. In any case, by a combination of determination, diplomacy, and economic power, the United States had established in Hawaii a position of de facto hegemony over the spirited opposition of a few British rivals, the more passive regrets of a declining Polynesian population, and the many Americans at home. The renewed reciprocity treaty and the Pearl Harbor base clearly foreshadowed coming events.

---

agriculture worked against the treaty. John T. Morgan to Bayard, January 30, 1887, and enclosed memorandum, ibid., 102ff 21046–59.

37. Tate, *Hawaii: Reciprocity or Annexation?* 17–210. On the revolution of 1897 see Kuykendall, *Hawaiian Kingdom*, vol. 2, chap. 14, and George W. Merrill to Bayard, June 6, 1886, no. 124, with enclosure, U.S., Diplomatic Despatches, Hawaii, 23. The British commissioner, James E. Wodehouse, was especially vigorous in his protest. London eventually accepted the Hawaiian assurance that British commercial needs would be filled by the port of Honolulu. Tate, "British Opposition," 386–94. The German minister to the United States was also displeased with the treaty, but Bayard told him curtly that it reflected the superior American interests in Hawaii. Stevens, *American Expansion*, 179–86. Tansill, *Foreign Policy of Bayard*, 390.

4

The Southwest Pacific
Illusion Overcomes Reality

DURING THE MEXICAN WAR, when the *Times* of London learned that the United States had occupied San Francisco and the California coast, it predicted: "From so favourable a harbour the course lies straight and obvious to Polynesia, the Philippines, New Holland [Australia], and China, and it is not extravagant to suppose that the merchants of this future emporium may open the commerce of Japan."[1] While American expansionists usually emphasized the riches of the Far East, they also believed that the vast reaches of the western and southwestern Pacific beyond Hawaii held the possibilities of profitable trade.

To reach these markets and imports, the U.S. government sponsored a transpacific steamship line as an extension of the Pacific railroad. When it fell on evil days during the depressed, scandal-ridden 1870s, Congress hastily withdrew its aid, but the steamship line managed to survive without it. At the same time that the Grant administration was negotiating a reciprocity treaty with Hawaii, one of its agents was attempting to establish a similar naval and economic strong point in the South Pacific, at the Samoan island group. These islands, he reported, have "vastly greater resources [than Hawaii] and . . . [a] tractable people who, under guidance and protection, would develop and concentrate a great trade."[2]

But the chief natural product of Samoa, copra (dried coconut meat from which oil was extracted), could not match sugar as a staple of trade. Nowhere in the southwest Pacific did efforts to develop tropical products approach the results achieved by Claus Spreckels and other American-Hawaiian planters. Also unlike Hawaii, where Europeans offered little effective resistance to the growth of American influence, the southwest Pacific became the scene of a race for colonies between England, France, and Germany, and finally during the 1880s an Anglo-German power struggle. Seeking visionary trade, the United States stumbled into this power struggle as it tried to maintain a Samoan strong point. At the same time most Americans and their government undervalued the possibilities of Australia

1. *London Times*, August 11, 1847.
2. Report of Albert B. Steinberger enclosed with his letter to Hamilton Fish dated February 13, 1874, U.S., 43d Cong., 1st sess., *Senate Executive Document 45*, 41–42. See also Stuart Anderson, " 'Pacific Destiny' and American Policy in Samoa, 1872–1899," 43–48.

and New Zealand, where, as in Canada, people of British descent, with developed tastes and purchasing power, were establishing markets for goods that American farms and factories could supply and producing raw materials that American factories could consume.

In 1894, following a decade of bickering, defiance, and compromise with the European colonial powers, the disillusioned Secretary of State Walter Q. Gresham wrote to President Cleveland: "We may well inquire what we have gained by our departure from our established policy [of noninvolvement with colonial powers] beyond the expenses, the responsibilities, and the extravagances that have so far been its only fruits." Henry Adams agreed. After a tour of the South Seas, he wrote to Senator Henry Cabot Lodge that, although entertaining, the Pacific islands were worth nothing as financial investments—"less than nothing, for they require large expenditures." He sneered at the European powers, "squabbling for possession of these wretched little lava-heaps," and concluded: "On the whole, I am satisfied that America has no future in the Pacific."[3]

Such denigration had little effect on Pacific expansionists of the 1890s. Publicists of California and the Northwest proclaimed: "We must trade with the millions in the vast empires that lie toward the setting sun. . . . Unless we do this we shall be left far behind in the race for commercial supremacy." The islands of the southwest Pacific formed one of the promising markets used to justify the construction of the Nicaragua canal during the last two decades of the century. To one observer in 1892 the awakening of China, the partition of Africa, and the division of the Pacific islands seemed clear evidence that "the theatre of stirring events" was moving to the Pacific.[4] The westward urge was as strong as ever.

In U.S.-Hawaiian relations trade, communications, and political connections could develop together, but beyond Hawaii adequate steamer service seemed a prerequisite to the spread of any other American influence. From 1865 to the 1890s the history of this service to the islands and the Far East was largely the history of one line—the Pacific Mail Steamship Company. When the Civil War ended, Pacific Mail, in alliance with the Panama Railroad, already controlled traffic between New York and San Francisco, by way of the Caribbean and Central America. Expecting to lose much of this business to the transcontinental railroad on its completion, company officials sought other areas of expansion.

At the same time Lincoln's postmaster general, Montgomery Blair, perhaps inspired by Secretary Seward, suggested that when the new railroad was in operation, trade between Europe and the Far East might be diverted through the United States if a steamship connection were provided. After a long debate, in February 1865 Congress authorized a grant of as much as $500,000 a year

3. U.S., *Foreign Relations*, 1894, Appendix 1, 513. Henry Adams to Henry Cabot Lodge, August 4, 1891, Worthington C. Ford, ed., *Letters of Henry Adams*, 1, 510–11.

4. *Tacoma Daily Ledger*, July 24, 1892, quoted in Salvatore Priscoe III, "John Barrett and Oregon Commercial Expansionism, 1889–1898," 143. Melville, "Our Future in the Pacific," 288. See also *Bradstreet's* 26 (August 20, 1898): 530.

for monthly service via Honolulu to the Far East—the "one part of the world," according to the *New York Times*, "which British enterprise has not yet covered with subsidized mail lines." Pacific Mail obtained a ten-year contract at the maximum amount and inaugurated service at the beginning of 1867.[5]

As has been seen, the government further showed its goodwill by releasing the company from its obligation to call at Honolulu, in return for expanding its service in the Far East. Also, when Pacific Mail expressed a desire for a coaling station at the two unoccupied Midway Islands west of Hawaii, the navy sent a ship to survey and take possession. In 1869 Congress appropriated $50,000 for harbor improvements at Midway, but the sum proved grossly inadequate, and the plan was abandoned. (However, the United States retained its claim to Midway.)[6]

By 1870 Pacific Mail was operating four wooden side-wheelers (the largest ever built but already outdated) on a monthly schedule from San Francisco to Yokohama and Hong Kong, with branch lines from Yokohama to Shanghai and Hakodate. Not content, company officials petitioned Congress to double its subsidy, in return for semi-monthly service to the Far East. By this time rival organizations were seeking American subsidies for service to Australia and New Zealand (to be discussed later). Also other opponents of Pacific Mail warned against monopolies, and Californians opposed the proposal, fearing increased Oriental immigration. Nevertheless, with the support of the Grant administration, in 1872 Pacific Mail received a new contract, promising an annual subsidy of $1 million.[7]

During the next two years the effects of overextension nearly destroyed Pacific Mail. On the strength of its first Far Eastern contract the company increased its capitalization from $4 million to $20 million in 1865 and 1866, thereby enriching inside speculators and causing a precipitous decline in its stock quotations. Dissension within the management brought to the presidency Alden B. Stockwell, a successful Wall Street speculator with little interest in shipping. He put through the contract of 1872 but allowed the stock manipulation to continue. Although the company's ships had hitherto enjoyed an excellent safety record, it now lost four in a single year to carelessness or ill luck. The new contract required Pacific Mail to construct iron screw steamers of at least four thousand tons in American shipyards. These proved unexpectedly difficult to finish and were delayed, so the

5. On the early history of Pacific Mail, see Pletcher, *Diplomacy of Trade and Investment*, 119–29, 189–90. Paul Maxwell Zeis, *American Shipping Policy*, 21–22. *New York Times*, February 18, 1865 (quotation); January 1, 1867. *Commercial and Financial Chronicle* 1 (October 7, 1865): 450–51.

6. Zeis, *American Shipping Policy*, 22–23. David Neal Leff, *Uncle Sam's Pacific Islets*, 12–15. Lyle B. Shelmedine, "The Early History of Midway Islands," 180–83. Rigby, "American Expansion in Hawaii," 357.

7. John Haskell Kemble, "A Hundred Years of the Pacific Mail," 131, company report of May 1870, in *Commercial and Financial Chronicle* 10 (May 28, 1870): 682–83. Zeis, *American Shipping Policy*, 23–24. John G. B. Hutchins, *The American Maritime Industries and Public Policy, 1789–1914, an Economic History*, 530. *New York Times*, December 24, 1874. For other press support of the subsidy see *New York Tribune*, January 20, 1872.

company did not receive its new subsidy. Its stock fell further, and when the panic of 1873 occurred, it was in serious trouble.[8]

But the culminating disaster was yet to come. Stung by charges of bribery, Congress in 1874 ordered an investigation of the Pacific Mail lobby, which disclosed that Stockwell had indeed paid out nearly $900,000 to obtain the new concession. The investigators were never able to prove outright bribery, since most of the money went into stock purchases to bring about an artificial rise in Pacific Mail shares for the benefit of congressmen and other insiders. Nevertheless, the Democratic press and reformers such as the *Nation* added the Pacific Mail "deal" to their growing indictment of the Grant administration. Congress withdrew the new concession and discontinued that of 1865 as soon as it expired three years later. By that time Pacific Mail had received a total of $4,583,333.32 for its Far Eastern operations.[9]

Worst of all, the scandal virtually ended government aid to American shipping for nearly two decades. For example, early in 1885 a debate broke out over a proposed clause in the annual post office appropriation, soon known as "the Pacific Mail subsidy provision," which would have authorized the postmaster general to contract with American steamship companies up to the amount of $600,000 for carrying the mails. Friends and enemies of Pacific Mail argued the merits of subsidies and the British model, the need for overseas markets, and the recent finances of the line. The Frye-Farquhar subsidy bill was finally passed in 1891, but the general manager of Pacific Mail later testified that the company received in the end practically no aid under it because of the cost of maintaining the average speed required by government contracts.[10]

Pacific Mail had originally been led to establish its line to the Far East by the impending completion of the transcontinental railroad, and it finally achieved stable operations along this route through close cooperation with the railroad and two of its leaders, Jay Gould and Collis P. Huntington. The process required a long tug-of-war between the transcontinentals and the Panama Railroad for

8. Kemble, "Hundred Years of Pacific Mail," 131, 134–35. Hutchins, *American Maritime Industries*, 530. *New York Times*, November 5, 1867; November 20, April 1, 1873; April 30, 1874; December 16, 1874; December 24, 1874. *Commercial and Financial Chronicle* 15 (October 5, 26, 1872): 451, 547; 16 (June 7, 1873): 763.

9. Zeis, *American Shipping Policy*, 24–25. For sample criticism see editorials of the *Springfield Republican* and the *Chicago Tribune* reprinted in *New York Times*, December 12, 15, 1874. *Nation* 20 (January 7, 14, 1875): 1–2, 4–5, 18. U.S., 43d Cong., 1st sess., *Senate Report 176*. For the total subsidy figures see William Eleroy Curtis, *Trade and Transportation between the United States and Spanish America*, 133. In return for this subsidy, it was pointed out, American exports to China rose only from $35,735,673 to $41,813,052 during the two decades 1856–1866 and 1867–1877. U.S., 45th Cong., 2d sess., *House Report 346*, 14–16, as cited in Zeis, *American Shipping Policy*, 35.

10. *American Exporter* 14 (February 1885): 34. U.S., 48th Cong., 2d sess., *Congressional Record 16*, 1444–46, 2508–10, 2514. Several dozen businessmen and firms, many in Pacific trade, petitioned the House for better mail service. Ibid., 1651. Testimony of H. P. Schwerin before the Merchant Marine Commission in 1904, U.S., 58th Cong., 3d sess., *Senate Report 2755*, 2, 1323, 1332.

control of the steamship line. From 1869 to 1873 Pacific Mail's relations with both parties were friendly. Then the Panama Railroad, losing more and more freight to the Union Pacific–Central Pacific, got Pacific Mail to stop issuing through bills of lading on the American roads and send its Pacific steamers with their cargoes on to Panama after only a brief stop at San Francisco. At about the same time Stockwell's mismanagement brought Russell Sage, an ally of Gould, to the presidency with plans to restore the battered company and raise the value of its stock.

Meanwhile in November 1874 the "Big Four" of the Central Pacific incorporated a rival transpacific steamer line, the Occidental and Oriental Steamship Company, to compete with Pacific Mail and force it to unload its steamers at San Francisco. Almost at once Pacific Mail, now controlled by Gould, came to terms with fixed through rates and divided the proceeds between the transcontinental railroad and the two steamer lines. Then followed about five years of rapid changes in the Pacific Mail management, as Gould came and went. When he was in control, some sort of rate agreement prevailed; when he was not, the influence of the Panama Railroad produced rate wars between Pacific Mail and the Union Pacific–Central Pacific. At the same time Pacific Mail continued to add iron screw steamers to its Far Eastern line, although it could declare no dividends and its stock fell on the market.

Finally in 1890 Gould won back control for good. The rate wars ended; the Panama Railroad ceased to dictate Pacific Mail's policy; and the American railroads guaranteed it a monthly subsidy of $110,000. In 1887 Gould's son George became president of the line, and in 1893 Collis P. Huntington, one of the "Big Four" of California railroading, succeeded him. The Occidental and Oriental Steamship Company continued running steamers to Japan and China, using the same docks and other facilities as Pacific Mail steamers and dovetailing schedules. Huntington's presidency completely united the management of the two lines.[11]

The effects of transpacific steamship lines on American economic expansion in East Asia will be examined in the next three chapters. It is necessary to turn here to communications and trade with another area: Australia, New Zealand, and the island groups of the southern and western Pacific. This area presented many problems that Americans had already faced in the Western Hemisphere. Australia and New Zealand, like Canada and Argentina, offered prosperous, Europeanized customers and temperate-climate products competing with those produced in the United States, while the Pacific islands, like tropical Latin America, could

---

11. Kemble, "Hundred Years of Pacific Mail," 135–37. Kemble, "Transpacific Railroads," 333–37. John Haskell Kemble, "The Big Four at Sea: The History of the Occidental and Oriental Steamship Company," 340–47, 350, 352. The O & O steamers were usually faster than those of Pacific Mail. The complicated maneuvers of the mid-1870s are related to Gould's railroad campaigns in Julius Grodinsky, *Jay Gould, His Business Career, 1867–1892,* 112–13, 118, 123–29, 145–48, 183–86. For the operating agreements of 1880 see U.S., 49th Cong., 1st sess., *House Executive Document 60,* 9–11.

supply much-needed sugar, coffee, and minerals but offered only buyers with low purchasing power.

In the late 1870s Americans accounted for less than $8 million of Australian–New Zealand trade totaling about $400 million, and an alert publicist bemoaned American inattention to tempting markets and resources. Since the early 1830s American whaling and merchant ships had regularly visited Australian ports. During the California gold rush fully seven thousand Australians and New Zealanders emigrated to the states, but the discovery of gold in Australia soon caused an even greater flow in the opposite direction. With encouragement from provincial governments, American-Australian trade increased during the 1850s. American merchant houses were founded, and clipper ships began to run regularly between the two countries. (Britain had already established regular steamer connections, which required transshipment by land across the Isthmus of Suez.) By cutting off American cotton shipments to England, the Civil War encouraged British cotton and wool imports from Australia, but only the latter survived the end of the war.[12]

The simultaneous completion of the American transcontinental railroad and the Suez Canal in 1869 revived general interest in communications with Australia and New Zealand. The long transit through the Red Sea and the Indian Ocean, however, encouraged the continued use of sailing ships around Africa for a time, and about a decade elapsed before the leading British steamer line, the Peninsular and Oriental Navigation Company, established frequent, dependable service to Australia. Two groups of American promoters tried to use this period of grace to create steamship lines between Australia, New Zealand, and San Francisco so as to divert Anglo-Australian trade through the United States. One of these, led by H. H. Hall, the U.S. consul at Sydney, obtained a subsidy of £1,000 a month from the governments of New South Wales and New Zealand and chartered two steamers for service from Sydney and Auckland to Honolulu, where they made connections to San Francisco through another steamship line partly subsidized by Hawaii.[13]

The leader of the second group was William R. Webb, a New York shipbuilder who had earlier been a director of Pacific Mail. His group founded the California, New Zealand, and Australia Mail Steamship Company and made a preliminary agreement with the New Zealand government. In 1871 and 1872 Webb petitioned the American Congress for a subsidy, widely supported by commercial associations and railroad conventions. The Grant administration and its minister

12. Norman Bartlett, *Australia and America through 200 Years: 1776–1976*, 99, 111, 113, 123–25, 129–32. Brian Fitzpatrick, *The British Empire in Australia: An Economic History, 1834–1939*, 124, 183, 356–59. Robert J. Creighton, "New Outlets for American Products," 572–80.

13. William Woodruff and L. McGregor, *The Suez Canal and the Australian Economy*, 7–8. John M. Maber, *North Star to Southern Cross*, 7–12, 82–83. U.S., *Foreign Relations, 1870–71*, 552–53. Kuykendall, *Hawaiian Kingdom*, vol. 1, 171. *Nation* 10 (May 19, 1870): 312.

to Hawaii, Henry A. Peirce, also urged Webb's case. When the bill came up for debate in the Senate, its supporters painted a glowing picture of future trade with the Antipodes. Senator John Sherman of Ohio, however, objected to encouraging the competition of Australian wool with that of his own state. He pointed out that Europe, the Far East, and parts of Latin America were already dependable markets for American exports and argued that the Treasury should reserve its limited funds to subsidize steamship lines in these areas. His argument was all the more effective because of intensive lobbying by Pacific Mail, which was then trying to double its subsidy. Webb's bill was defeated. Although he obtained subsidies from New Zealand and Hawaii, two Australian provinces failed to carry out their promises of aid. After two years of profitless operations between San Francisco, Honolulu, Auckland, and Sydney, Webb gave up. By that time Hall's venture had collapsed too.[14]

A third effort to establish direct steamship connections from San Francisco to Auckland and Sydney was made by the Pacific Mail Steamship Company itself. In 1875, just as the power struggle within its management was getting under way, the company contracted with the governments of New South Wales and New Zealand for monthly service in both directions between Sydney, Auckland, and San Francisco, for an annual subsidy of £90,000 (later reduced to £72,500 when an easier route was substituted). In 1879 Pacific Mail even inaugurated a through service to Britain, using the American transcontinental railroad and the Atlantic mailings of the Anchor Line. The governments of Australia and New Zealand, which were also helping subsidize two major lines to Britain via the Suez Canal, hoped that trade with the United States would increase enough to make the Pacific Mail Line profitable and that Washington would match the subsidy. But the recent Pacific Mail scandal was too much in the public mind, so the American government refused a subsidy. After the public argument over the question in 1885–1886 between Pacific Mail and Cleveland's postmaster general, New South Wales and New Zealand discontinued their subsidy, and since the San Francisco–Sydney line could not show a profit without it, Pacific Mail abandoned the service in 1886.[15] When Pacific Mail withdrew from the South Pacific, Claus Spreckels's Oceanic Steamship Company bought its ships and together with the

14. John H. Morrison, *History of American Steam Navigation*, 477–78. Kuykendall, *Hawaiian Kingdom*, vol. 1, 171–72. George Herbert Ryden, *The Foreign Policy of the United States in Relation to Samoa*, 44–49. Joseph W. Ellison, *The Opening and Penetration of Foreign Influence in Samoa to 1880*, 38. Maber, *North Star to Southern Cross*, 84–85. Sydney B. Waters, *Union Line, a Short History of the Union Steamship Company of New Zealand, Ltd.* [etc.] (Wellington, 1952[?]), 38–39. On the Senate debate see U.S., 42d Cong., 2d sess., *Congressional Globe* (1871–1872), pt. 3, 2462 ff. Webb later blamed his failure on British rivals in Australia and on Roscoe Conkling and a few southern senators in Congress. *New York Tribune*, February 7, 1881, December 6, 1887, February 4, 1889. *Dictionary of American Biography*, 19, 569–70.

15. Kemble, "Hundred Years of Pacific Mail," 132–33. Maber, *North Star to Southern Cross*, 96–97. U.S., *Consular Reports* 9 (July 1881): 45–49. U.S., *Commercial Relations*, *1882–83* 2: 778–79; *1883–84* 2: 778, *Bradstreet's* 5 (February 11, 1882): 81; (July 5, 1884): 3; 12 (August 8, 1885): 85. Curtis, "Trade and Transportation," 138–42. *Age of Steel* 57

Union Steamship Company of New Zealand maintained joint service for the rest of the century from Sydney and Auckland to Samoa, Honolulu, and San Francisco.

The American weakness and discord left the South Pacific field open to the powerful European lines using the Suez route: Peninsular and Oriental with its new, luxurious liners, Messageries Maritimes, North German Lloyd, and others. New York shippers to the Antipodes had the discouraging choice of an uncertain rail-ocean route via San Francisco, an often expensive all-sea route via Liverpool or London (both usually requiring at least one transfer), or slow sailing vessels. In 1893 *Iron Age* blamed both the U.S. government for not aiding shipping lines and American manufacturers for not putting enough pressure on the government. Instead, it remarked, cutthroat competition between New York and San Francisco steamer companies caused rate wars and disastrous gluts of American goods in Australasia. As for cable connections between San Francisco and Sydney, Americans showed little interest, although they blocked a British line from Canada by way of Hawaii.[16]

Another American handicap in trade with Australia was similar to South American trade—high tariffs. The wool lobby in Washington kept up the duties on raw wool until the mid-1890s, despite the petitions of wool manufacturers in California, who needed the fine, long-staple merino wools of New South Wales, Victoria, and New Zealand to mix with coarse American wool. The *Sydney Morning Herald* complained in the early 1880s that New South Wales paid a mail subsidy of about $300,000 a year to get its wool to San Francisco, only to find that it must pay about $300,000 more in American duties. (Some American exporters, however, also complained of New Zealand's high tariff on items not produced in the colony and the complicated interprovincial tariffs of Australia.)[17]

The obvious solution was reciprocity, but American wool producers and doctrinaire protectionists stood in the way, and no defenders of reciprocity wanted to go as far afield as the southwest Pacific. In 1878 Australian chambers

---

(August 22, 1885): 9–10. Testimony of B. Mozley (Pacific Mail Steamship Company) in U.S., 48th Cong., 2d sess., *House Executive Document 226*, 349–50. For a detailed account of New Zealand's efforts during the 1870s to obtain steamship connections with the United States see U.S., *Consular Reports* 9 (July 1881): 45–49.

16. Maber, *North Star to Southern Cross*, 13–16, 100–104, 136–40, 179, 189–90, 210–11, 216–17, 221–22, 240–42. Waters, *Union Line*, 39–40. Kuykendall, *Hawaiian Kingdom*, vol. 2, 105. *Iron Age* 51 (March 30, April 13, 1893): 756–57, 876. During the 1890s projects appeared for new lines from Canada and New York. U.S., *Consular Reports* 125 (February 1891): 238–39; 155 (August 1893): 408–11; 165 (June 1894): 335–37; 219 (December 1878): 508–11. J. F. Hogan, "A New Imperial Highway," 1–9. *Engineering and Mining Journal* 50 (September 6, 1890): 263. On cables see *Bradstreet's* 13 (April 24, 1886): 257; and U.S., 52d Cong., 2d sess., *Senate Executive Document 76*, 20.

17. On the wool trade and the needs of California manufacturers see U.S., *Consular Reports* 51 (March 1885): 576–77, 596–97; 64 (June 1886): 145–46; 86 (November 1887): 314–15. *Sydney Morning Herald*, March 17, 1882. Clipping enclosed with Charles Kahl to Davis, March 17, 1882, no. 8. (Subsidies originally stated in pounds.) U.S., Consular Despatches, Sydney, 9. G. W. Griffin to Robert R. Hitt, December 5, 1881, no. 88, ibid., Auckland, 6.

of commerce, stimulated by what some members had seen at the Philadelphia Centennial Exposition, memorialized the U.S. government for reciprocity, but when the prime minister of New South Wales visited the United States four years later, his mission was a complete failure.[18]

In the detailed, well-informed reports that several industrious American consuls submitted from Australia and New Zealand during the 1880s and 1890s, other familiar handicaps of American business were occasionally mentioned: inattention to local styles and needs, shoddy packing, and inadequate credit terms. The problem of credit was complicated by fluctuating exchange rates and long delays between order and delivery that made Australian customers prefer the faster British service. Nevertheless, insofar as statistics are available, evidence suggests that American merchants made a reasonably good showing in Australasia. American trade with New South Wales, the largest market, rose from just less than $9 million in 1883 to almost $10 million in 1890, then fell to around $6 million in 1893 as a result of the panic, which was especially severe in Australia, and rose again to almost $10 million in 1896, partly as a result of the temporary removal of the American wool duty in the Wilson-Gorman tariff of 1894.[19]

American trade with Australia and New Zealand benefited from several factors. In the first place, despite Australasian complaints, the American wool tariff was by no means airtight, and consular records show that exports of wool to the United States increased during most years of the late 1870s and 1880s, although some of it had to be shipped to London first and sold to American purchasers to comply with the law. As for exports, empire loyalties notwithstanding, Americans had almost a guaranteed market for certain products that Britain could not supply—kerosene, lumber, wheat, flour, and some canned goods, to name the most important—and these furnished a solid base for American trade. In addition, Americans shipped a great variety of other processed or manufactured goods; the list of exports to Melbourne during the 1880s runs to more than fifty categories.[20]

A few American firms, recognizing the value of Australasian customers, made serious efforts to secure them. For example, immediately after the Philadelphia

18. *American Exporter* 2 (August 1878): 14. U.S., *Commercial Relations, 1878,* vol. 1, 94. U.S., *Consular Reports* 108 (September 1889): 55–57. On the prime minister's mission see *New York Tribune,* January 30, February 10, 1882; and *London Times,* February 16, 22, 1882. In 1894 New Zealand sent a similar mission to the United States. *Bradstreet's* 31 (October 6, 1894): 632.

19. On American handicaps see *Iron Age* 31 (March 30, 1893): 756–57, U.S., *Special Consular Reports* ("Cotton Textiles in Foreign Countries"), 167–68; and U.S., *Consular Reports* 12 (October 1881): 228–29; 168 (September 1894): 32–35; 205 (October 1897): 317. The trade statistics for New South Wales are computed from statistics in pounds at a rate of five to one.

20. On the wool tariff and wool trade see U.S., *Consular Reports* 18 (April 1882): 524–26; 108 (September 1889): 9–10; 126 (March 1891): 322–23. On petroleum and lumber see ibid., 37 (January 1884): 446–47; 60 (January 1886): 18–21; and 64 (June 1886): 244–45. For long lists of American exports see ibid., 125 (February 1891): 246–49 (Melbourne statistics); 35 (November 1883): 1–6; 205 (October 1897): 317; and U.S., *Commercial Relations, 1879,* 894–95.

Exposition of 1876 the Baldwin Locomotive Company sent a sample engine free of cost. It gave such good results that a provincial government bought several. The American exhibits at the Melbourne Centennial Exposition of 1888 included impressive displays by the Elgin and Waltham Watch Companies, the Singer Sewing Machine Company, the Anheuser-Busch Brewery, and others. The Americans won perhaps their greatest victory in the area of farm machinery, and Cyrus H. McCormick thought that Australia brought greater returns on his reapers with less effort than either Britain or Europe. He and other manufacturers shipped machines there almost as soon as they went on sale in the United States and even designed one machine, the stripper-harvester, solely for the Australian market. During the 1880s and 1890s more and more American mining engineers found jobs in Australian mines, bringing with them American technology. (The most famous of these immigrants, Herbert Hoover, arrived about 1895.) By then Australian railroadmen were beginning to adopt American passenger cars and imitate American methods of transporting perishables and handling baggage.[21]

Increasingly the Americans outstripped even the British in some categories and caused alarm, especially for the British trade with New Zealand, where Americans held the advantage of distance. As in southern South America during the 1890s, British merchants called for more and better consular representation. Germany and to a lesser extent France tried to push their way into the market but could not match the Yankees.[22] Nevertheless, when one considers that in 1897 American trade with Canada was 4.5 times as large as that with Australasia ($105 million to $23.5 million), one cannot help feeling that the Americans could have done better in the Antipodes, even allowing for Canada's nearness and higher level of economic development. Beyond the turn of the century U.S. consuls were still urging manufacturers at home to pay more attention to Australasian tastes and send salesmen instead of catalogues. American cotton goods were recognized as superior, but the British sent bolts of the right width, granted better terms, and sold to more reputable retailers. With a government that opposed reciprocity and

21. *Engineering and Mining Journal* 26 (October 19, 1878): 274. On the Melbourne exposition see U.S., *Consular Reports* 106 (July 1889): 206–7; and U.S., 52d Cong., 1st sess., *Senate Executive Document 18*. On farm machinery and tools see I. W. McLean, "Anglo-American Engineering Competition, 1870–1914: Some Third-Market Evidence," *Economic History Review* 29 (August 1976): 456–63. See also U.S., *Consular Reports* 48 (December 1884): 750–52, 758–65; 50 (February 1885): 262–65; 83 (September 1887): 506–8; and Hutchinson, *McCormick*, 2, 654–60, 685n127. On hardware, mining machinery, and railroading see *Age of Steel* 57 (May 2, 1885): 12; 64 (September 15, 1888): 9–10; U.S., *Commercial Relations*, 1884–85, 540–42; U.S., *Consular Reports* 83 (September 1887): 497; 88 (January 1888): 148; *Engineering* 48 (August 16, 1889): 206–7; *Bradstreet's* 17 (September 28, 1889): 618; and Clark Spence, *Mining Engineers and the American West; the Lace-Boot Brigade, 1849–1933*, 296–99.

22. British reactions are reprinted in *Bradstreet's* 18 (June 28, 1890): 417–18. On European competition see also *U.S. Consular Reports* 68 (September 1886): 634–35; 118 (July 1890): 474–75; and 187 (April 1896): 556–57. Even at the end of this period Japanese-Australian trade was negligible.

ship subsidies and too many manufacturers who would not change their ways, the United States could not get full value from customers who shared its basic culture and temperate climate and wanted to buy American.[23]

In addition to Australia and New Zealand, the United States paid a little attention to some of the small islands lying in the South Pacific between Australia and Hawaii. After the Wilkes exploring expedition of 1838–1842 visited the principal island groups, an occasional American warship put in an appearance, and American merchant ships sailing from Honolulu to Auckland or Sydney commonly called at Samoa, Tonga, or Fiji. There was no reason to seek political control of any sort, for island colonies were outside American tradition, and before the Civil War the U.S. government felt no need for coaling stations. Consequently, Washington showed little interest in the Anglo-French rivalries that developed in this area.[24]

In the mid-1850s a new element appeared—the Hamburg firm of Johann Cesar Godeffroy und Sohn, which established a trading agency at Apia, the principal port of Samoa. The company was especially interested in coconut oil, a staple of the islands used for candies and soap. Later it shifted to copra (dried coconut meat from which the oil could be pressed), because it was easier to prepare for export. Collecting oil and copra from many surrounding islands, it shipped these products to Europe, distributing in return a variety of European goods. The Godeffroy firm soon opened sub-agencies in Tonga, Fiji, and the Marshall Islands. Especially in Samoa it began to buy up lands and establish plantation agriculture, to control the source of supply. By the late 1870s it held 4,337 acres of land and employed about 1,200 natives.

While Chancellor Otto von Bismarck supported the firm from the beginning, he warned its principal agent at Apia not to become involved in political activities, and during the 1870s he showed no disposition to enter the race with Britain and France for Pacific colonies. In 1879, when the Godeffroy company got into financial difficulties, Bismarck proposed to grant it an annual subsidy, but the Reichstag refused to make the necessary appropriation, and the firm went bankrupt. Several other German companies took its place in the South Pacific, led by the Deutsche Handelsund Plantagen-Gesellschaft der Südsee Inseln zu Hamburg (usually called the DHPG or "the long-handle company"). During the

23. U.S., 55th Cong., 2d sess., *House Document 573*, pt. 5, 1283. U.S., *Historical Statistics,* 903, 906. U.S., *Commercial Relations, 1896–97,* 1170–75, 1180–81; *1898,* 1198–99, 1212–13; U.S., *Consular Reports* 196 (January 1897): 93–97; 201 (June 1897): 295–97. U.S., Department of Commerce and Labor, [Special Agents Series, No. 11]. *Foreign Markets for the Sale of American Cotton Products,* 119–24. For a different view, blaming the American wool tariff and cheap European imports, see *New York Journal of Commerce,* July 20, 1893. However, almost to a man, consuls throughout the period favored steamship subsidies.

24. Brookes, *International Rivalry,* chaps. 8–10. William P. Morrell, *Britain in the Pacific Islands,* chaps. 1–5. Ellison, *Foreign Influence in Samoa,* 21–28. Sylvia Masterman, *The Origins of International Rivalry in Samoa, 1845–1884,* chaps. 1, 2.

mid-1880s Bismarck finally embarked on an active imperialist policy in the Pacific with the annexation of part of New Guinea and other territories.[25]

In several of these island groups Americans managed to trade without becoming embroiled in colonial rivalries. In Tahiti, for example, after some years of contact with American merchants, several chiefs, fearing British or French domination, came to the American consul in 1858 with a document formally offering annexation to the United States. British and French officials were sufficiently worried to stir up an anti-American faction among the natives, but they need not have troubled, for the Buchanan administration paid no attention whatever to the offer. In 1880 Tahiti became a French colony, but Americans continued to dominate its economy, and by 1895 the U.S. consul there reported that American goods made up about half of the local trade.[26]

In the Fiji Islands Americans had to face the colonial ambitions of Britain. The principal questions at issue involved not trade but claims for damage done to American residents and their property in native wars. American-Australian efforts to seize land in retaliation led to further argument, and U.S. warships visited the islands three times between 1855 and 1869 to investigate. In the latter year about seventy American settlers petitioned Washington for annexation, and the native king added his voice to the request. Referring to the Danish West Indies and Santo Domingo, the *New York Times* commented sarcastically: "More islands to be annexed." However, the Grant administration refused to interfere, first because Secretary Fish was anxious to settle the *Alabama* claims dispute with Britain and later because both Hawaii and Samoa seemed more desirable areas of influence. Britain's chief interest lay in calming Australian fears and maintaining a balance of power in the Pacific. It annexed the islands in 1874, largely to offset American commercial gains in the other two island groups. The United States offered no objection. Under British rule and using mostly British ships, American merchants continued to supply Fiji with many of the same products they sent to Australia and New Zealand, including California lumber, hardware, and kerosene.[27]

The United States maintained friendly relations in another manner with the Tonga Islands, lying east of Fiji and south of Samoa. This group remained under the sovereignty of a native king throughout the nineteenth century, but during

25. Mary Evelyn Townsend, *The Rise and Fall of Germany's Colonial Empire, 1884–1918*, 47–50, 72–77. Masterman, *Origins of International Rivalry*, chaps. 2, 3. Brookes, *International Rivalries*, 176, 251, 290–91, 408–11. Ellison, *Foreign Influence in Samoa*, 31–36. Stewart Firth, "German Firms in the Western Pacific Islands, 1857–1914," 11–15. On the efforts to save the Godeffroy company see also Fritz Stern, *Gold and Iron: Bismarck, Bleichröder, and the Building of the German Empire*, 390–402. Ironically, Germany's Pacific islands provided less than 1 percent of its foreign trade.

26. Brookes, *International Rivalry*, 64, 223–24. *American Mail and Export Journal* 5 (May 1880): 225. U.S., *Commercial Relations, 1894–95*, 2, 635–37. For similar French statistics see U.S., *Consular Reports* 207 (December 1897): 647; on vain efforts for steamship connections with San Francisco see 208 (January 1898): 28–29; 209 (February 1898): 214.

27. W. D. McIntyre, "Anglo-American Rivalry in the Pacific: The British Annexation of the Fiji Islands in 1874." Morrell, *Britain in the Pacific Islands*, chap. 6. *New York Times*, January 24, 1870. U.S., *Consular Reports* (April 1884): 241–44.

the 1880s the real ruler was Prime Minister Shirley W. Baker, a onetime British missionary. The Godeffroy company operated plantations here and collected copra for shipment to its headquarters at Apia. To offset British and German influence, Baker proposed a commercial treaty with the United States. There was no American consular official in Tonga, but the consuls at Apia and Auckland recommended a treaty to encourage an able native regime and stimulate the export trade from San Francisco. They said that the American population of Tonga was almost as large as that of Samoa.

Probably to reinforce American policy in Samoa, the Cleveland administration negotiated the desired treaty in 1886—a conventional commercial treaty with the provision that American warships might use any Tongan harbor as a coaling station. The United States assumed no obligations of protection or mediation, and when Baker was overthrown in a local coup during 1890, Washington resisted his entreaties to intervene. A native king continued to rule, but the islands became an informal British protectorate without American protest.[28]

On both sides of the equator between Hawaii and Samoa lay a few scattered islands, mostly uninhabited, which attracted Americans' interest just after mid-century for their deposits of guano (bird droppings used as fertilizer). In 1856 Congress authorized the president to establish American sovereignty over such islands. Representatives of two guano companies and various individuals occupied about a half dozen of these islands for a time, and the United States claimed sovereignty but did nothing to enforce this claim. Not until the 1930s did it take further interest in the islands.[29]

While the United States successfully resisted temptations to become politically involved, one way or another, in Tahiti, Fiji, Tonga, and the guano islands, its relations with Samoa followed a quite different course. Here intrigues by promoters, agitation for a coaling station, and ill-supervised consular actions, all based on the hope of future trade, gradually committed the Washington government to responsibilities it only partly understood or even recognized. By the late 1880s the Samoan question had involved the United States in the power

28. Morrell, *Britain in the Pacific Islands,* 310–29. Noel Rutherford, *Shirley Baker and the King of Tonga.* Germany and Britain also signed treaties with Tonga in 1876 and 1879. France had signed one in 1855. Thomas M. Dawson to Charles Payson, August 9, 1880; January 4, May 14, 1881, nos. 180, 213, 230, U.S., Consular Despatches, Apia, 9. Griffin to Hitt, January 3, 1881; Griffin to Frelinghuysen, July 28, 1883, nos. 89, bis 158. Ibid., Auckland, 6, 7. Alvey A. Adee, *Report No. 61,* April 12, 1881; U.S., *Reports of Diplomatic Bureau,* 5, Harold M. Sewall to William F. Wharton, July 14, December 24, 1890, nos. C, 54, U.S. Consular Despatches, Apia, 18. For the text of the treaty see Bevans, *Treaties,* vol. 11, 1043–47. On American trade with Tonga see *U.S., Commercial Relations, 1886–87,* 1088–89.

29. Leff, *Uncle Sam's Pacific Islets,* 5–8, 23–27, 30–34, 43–46, 51–54. Evarts to Edward Thornton, April 1, 1879, U.S., Notes to Britain, vol. 17, pp. 18–22. E. H. Bryan, *American Polynesia: Coral Islands of the Central Pacific,* 33–34. J. M. Ward, *British Policy in the South Pacific, 1786–1893,* 160–61.

politics of European colonialism more deeply than its relations with Hawaii, where its interests were much greater and largely unchallenged.

The Samoan group comprised fourteen islands spread out in a three-hundred-mile curve, northeast of Fiji and north of Tonga and somewhat more than two thousand miles from both Honolulu and Sydney. Upolu, one of the two largest islands, contained the principal settlement, Apia, a moderately good port. The focus of American attention, however, was the smaller island of Tutuila to the east, with its magnificent land-locked harbor of Pago Pago, comparable to Pearl Harbor but somewhat smaller. Docile and easygoing like most other Polynesians, the Samoan natives were loosely organized in a patriarchal tribal government with some democratic elements. By the late 1860s the Godeffroy firm's copra trade and plantations made its agent, Theodor Weber (also German consul) the most influential man on the islands. Expansionists in New Zealand, led by the would-be empire builder Julius Vogel, had their eyes on Samoa but were restrained by the Colonial Office in London, which was more strongly attracted to Fiji.[30]

The first important American interest in Samoa developed during the Grant administration out of promotional schemes cut from the same pattern as those that led Grant to attempt the annexation of Santo Domingo. In 1871 James B. M. Stewart and a group of speculators incorporated the Central Polynesian Land and Commercial Company in San Francisco with a capital of $100,000, and for the next two years its agents bought up as much Samoan land as they could, usually at bargain prices and especially on Tutuila, around Pago Pago. Eventually the company held title to nearly half the area of the islands.

Stewart struck a deal with the steamship promoter William H. Webb to make Samoa a port of call on his Australian line in return for land options which, however, Webb never took up. Webb expected to ship Samoan copra in competition with the Godeffroy firm and was soon planning to make Samoa the center of a trading network among the islands. For a modest outlay of stock Stewart secured the services of Senator Cornelius Cole (Republican, California) and probably other American officials, and he got Secretary Fish to appoint a company representative as commercial agent at Apia. A sea captain–trader sent out by Webb wrote an enthusiastic report on the islands, which was immediately published, and prevailed on the commander of the American Pacific squadron at Honolulu to send a warship and reconnoiter Pago Pago.[31]

30. For a detailed description of the islands, the natives, and early white visitors see R. P. Gilson, *Samoa 1830 to 1900: The Politics of a Multi-Cultural Community*, chaps. 1–4. Masterman, *Origins of International Rivalry*, 85–93. The islands lay 2,353 miles from Sydney, 2,260 miles from Honolulu, 4,161 miles from San Francisco, and 5,710 miles from Panama City. While most observers admired Pago Pago as larger and better protected than Apia, one later consul admitted that it had disadvantages too—difficult anchoring, a narrow entrance, and violent winds sweeping down from mountain gorges. Report of Consul General James H. Mulligan, September 1, 1895, U.S., *Consular Reports* 191 (August 1896): 746–58.

31. Barry Rigby, "Private Interests and the Origins of American Involvement in Samoa, 1872–1877," 75–76. Ellison, *Foreign Influence in Samoa*, 37–40. Gilson, *Samoa 1830 to*

Her captain, Commander Richard W. Meade, thought enough of the harbor to sign an agreement in 1872 with a local chieftain. This official granted its use to the United States as a naval station, in return for vague promises of advice, influence, and protection in Samoa's foreign affairs. Stewart also induced several chiefs to sign a petition for outright American annexation of all Samoa and sent it to Washington with the blessing of the expansionist American minister to Hawaii, Henry A. Peirce. Grant gave qualified approval to Meade's agreement, torn between his secretary of the navy, George M. Robeson, who was enthusiastic about Pago Pago, and Secretary of State Fish, suspicious of the commitments involved. American newspapers, taken by surprise, cited the harbor and native wishes as good reasons for annexation or a protectorate. "With enterprise and industry," declared the New York Times, "the Samoan islands may be made . . . the stepping-stones to a vast traffic in that distant region." Meade's agreement, however, was never reported by the Senate Foreign Relations Committee.[32]

Still interested, Grant decided to send out a special agent to learn more about the islands. The man he chose, Colonel Albert B. Steinberger, is still somewhat of a mystery to historians. (Even his title is dubious.) Originally recommended by Webb, he made himself congenial to the president and eventually became the close friend of Grant's notorious private secretary, General Orville E. Babcock. Opinions of Steinberger have run the gamut from unscrupulous filibuster and cryptoimperialist to sincere if impractical benefactor of the Samoan natives.[33] Fish instructed him to observe and describe Samoan harbors and resources, caution the chiefs not to sell land to foreigners, and avoid any talk about U.S. plans, as he was not a regularly accredited diplomatic agent. Whatever connection Steinberger may have had with the Central Polynesian Company, he certainly disappointed the land-hungry Stewart and his cronies by carrying out his instructions scrupulously. On his first mission he won the approval of missionaries and other European residents and submitted a detailed report advocating annexation or an American protectorate.[34]

1900, 276–85. H. Stonehewer Cooper, Coral Lands, vol. 2, 28–36. For Webb's version of his activities see New York Tribune, February 4, 1889. A great many land sales were fraudulent; by 1889 they were reported to total about 1.7 million acres—more than twice the area of the islands. Masterman, Origins of International Rivalry, 134. Fish, who was concerned at that point about German intentions in both the Caribbean and the Pacific, twice instructed the American minister at Berlin to secure denials from Bismarck of any desire to annex Samoa. Tansill, Foreign Policy of Bayard, 7–8.

32. Ryden, Foreign Policy in Samoa, chap. 3. Rigby, "Private Interests," 78–79. Ellison, Foreign Influence in Samoa, 40–44. Anderson, "'Pacific Destiny' and American Policy," 46–48. Richardson, Messages and Papers, vol. 7, 168–69. For samples of American press opinion see Boston Daily Globe, February 18, 1873; San Francisco Daily Alta California, February 21, 1873; and New York Times, September 10, 1873.

33. The most thorough combing of the sparse sources concerning Steinberger's origins is Martin Torodash, "Steinberger of Samoa," 50–52. See also Rigby, "Private Interests," 79; Gilson, Samoa 1830 to 1900, 293–96; and Ryden, Foreign Policy in Samoa, 85–86.

34. Ryden, Foreign Policy in Samoa, chap. 4. Ellison, Foreign Influence in Samoa, 46–56. Torodash, "Steinberger of Samoa," 52–53. For Fish's instructions and Steinberger's report see U.S., 44th Cong., 1st sess., House Executive Document 161, 5–11, 13–53.

Unable to interest Fish in these goals, Steinberger proceeded to Hamburg in 1874 for negotiations with the Godeffroy officials that made him virtually the company's man. Under the resulting contract he agreed to persuade the Samoan government to recognize the Godeffroy company's landholdings and copra monopoly, let it import laborers, and make it the official Samoan financial agent. In return, Steinberger was to receive a commission of "say ten percent" on all transactions between government and company. Without revealing the details of this contract, he undertook a second mission for Washington, which sent him back to Samoa on a U.S. warship for more observation and reporting. Arriving at Apia in April 1875, he presented to the impressed natives a flag and a constitution modeled on those of the United States but also providing for an all-powerful prime minister. Then he brought about the selection of a Samoan chief. Malietoa Laupepa, as king, resigned his State Department position and assumed the prime ministership himself. One of his first actions in his new office was to send off the draft of a commercial treaty to the United States.[35]

A later authority called Steinberger's brief regime Samoa's first effective government. Unfortunately, his efforts to prevent land and liquor sales antagonized Stewart's agents and most other secular residents, while his opposition to a tax that the missionaries levied on the natives alienated the powerful clergy, and discovery of his contract with Godeffroy turned non-Germans against him. The U.S. consul, who also represented the Central Polynesian Company, soon ascertained that Steinberger's instructions justified none of his acts and combined against him with British residents, the British consul, and the overbearing captain of a British warship that arrived in December 1875. The coalition prevailed on King Malietoa to dismiss Steinberger after less than seven months in office. Then the British captain arrested him and took him away in the warship's brig to Fiji, where the embarrassed governor promptly released him. With the vigorous support of the State Department Steinberger tried for a time to obtain an indemnity from Britain, but he decided that it would be futile to return to the islands.[36]

His departure left Samoa in utter confusion. The Central Polynesian Company was now bankrupt, but its successors and creditors produced a tangle of land suits and intrigues. Malietoa was overthrown, and the British and German consuls supported rival factions among the tribes. New American consular officials, some of them involved in the Central Polynesian Company's efforts, suspected both British and German intentions. On more than one occasion the American flag was raised above the house of government at Apia in the hope of restoring stability. Finally in 1876 the beleaguered Samoan legislature appointed an envoy to the

35. Ryden, *Foreign Policy in Samoa,* 112–26. Ellison, *Foreign Influence in Samoa,* 56–59. Rigby, "Private Interests," 81–85. For the text of Steinberger's agreement with Godeffroy see U.S., 44th Cong., 2d sess., *House Executive Document 44,* 129–30, 3–5. His commercial treaty contained everything necessary to promote American economic interests except the Pago Pago naval base.

36. Ryden, *Foreign Policy in Samoa,* 130–47. Gilson, *Samoa 1830 to 1900,* 297–331. Ellison, *Foreign Influence in Samoa,* 59–83, 88n91. The "later authority" was Henry C. Ide, chief justice of Samoa during the 1890s. For Evarts's defense of Steinberger see Evarts to John Walsh, May 15, 1879, no. 289, U.S., *Diplomatic Instructions,* Britain, 25, 405–10.

United States, M. K. Le Mamea, with instructions to request annexation or a protectorate. The tall, dignified Le Mamea made an immediate impression on the American press and people as the "tattooed prince," but to his chagrin President Hayes, although sympathetic, rejected his proposal. In discussions at the State Department Le Mamea then offered Pago Pago as a naval base in return for American friendship. A treaty to this effect was signed on January 17, 1878, giving the United States wide but not exclusive powers over the harbor and establishing commercial relations on a most-favored-nation basis. It also assured Samoa of American good offices in case of a dispute with a third power.[37]

Many American newspapers had sneered at Steinberger as a pretentious fraud, disguising yet another of Grant's "jobs" under bogus concern for the natives. The *New York Times* now switched sides and defended the treaty of 1878 for giving the United States a "foothold on the Southern Pacific." From Vienna the expansionist minister John A. Kasson congratulated Secretary William M. Evarts for forestalling the British in the Pacific: "That ocean does not belong to England." The Senate scrutinized the provision for good offices carefully but decided it was harmless and approved the treaty unanimously within two weeks, after attaching two minor amendments. (The House, however, defeated an appropriation for a coaling station at Pago Pago.)

The treaty, which was to entangle the United States further in Samoan affairs, rested on a fundamental misunderstanding, for the inexperienced Samoans interpreted "good offices" to mean a disguised protectorate, while contemporary American comments make clear that the Hayes administration intended nothing of the sort. The State Department assured England and Germany that the United States wanted only trade and a coaling station in Samoa, not domination. Some officials favored a joint protectorate, but Secretary Evarts, at heart a noninterventionist, agreed only to preserve order and protect foreigners. Walter Q. Gresham later suggested that the treaty was adopted largely out of "an amiable desire" to respond to the Samoans' "friendly advances."[38]

A survey of U.S. economic relations with Samoa during the following decade provides no better explanation for the treaty. Repeatedly American consuls praised the potential value of Samoan trade and the openings for American capital in

37. Ryden, *Foreign Policy in Samoa*, chaps. 6, 7. Ellison, *Foreign Influence in Samoa*, 83–93. Gilson, *Samoa 1830 to 1900*, chap. 14. Anderson, " 'Pacific Destiny' and American Policy," 49–50. Gary Alvin Pennanen, "The Foreign Policy of William Maxwell Evarts," 203–9. The text of the 1878 treaty is in Bevans, *Treaties*, 31, 437–39. For an eyewitness account of the negotiations see Frederick William Seward, *Reminiscences of a Wartime Statesman and Diplomat*, 437–41.

38. For press comments on Steinberger see *Cincinnati Daily Gazette*, December 10, 1875; *New York Tribune*, March 13, 1876; *New York Herald*, July 21, 1875; March 26, 1878; *Nation* 22 (April 27, 1878); *Boston Daily Globe*, November 11, 1877; and *New York Times*, April 14, 1876; November 29, 1877. On the treaty see *New York Times*, April 10, 1878; December 9, 1878; *New York Tribune*, April 12, 1878; and *Commercial and Financial Chronicle* 26 (April 13, 1878): 353–54. John A. Kasson to William M. Evarts, May 10, 1878, Evarts papers, 14. Gresham's statement is in U.S., *Foreign Relations, 1894*, Appendix 1, 506.

copra and cotton plantations. They predicted that after the completion of the isthmian canal, Pago Pago would dominate the principal trade route between Europe and Australasia, but after dumping a supply of coal there, the navy seldom used its new coaling station. Disputes over the Central Polynesian Company's land titles continued for a time to furnish the principal evidence of American economic activity. Early in the 1880s two San Francisco mercantile houses established flourishing agencies at Apia, and others joined them later in the decade. A few American products, such as California lumber and petroleum, dominated the Samoan market, whether sold by American, British, or German merchants. Other American goods, such as provisions, were shipped via Sydney, along with Australasian products, and Samoans obtained their textiles from Britain. In 1884 Americans furnished directly only $73,776 out of Samoa's total imports of about $200,000 and took only $25,000 of its exports, which totaled nearly $360,000. In 1867 only 6 out of 228 ships arriving at Apia were American.[39]

Many reasons for this unimpressive record were familiar enough to nineteenth-century expansionists; a few more were peculiar to the Pacific area. Although the Godeffroy company went out of business in 1879, other German companies controlled the copra trade and manipulated its prices at will. Producing large quantities on their own plantations and collecting it from other islands, they consigned it to Europe in German ships. They even introduced debased coins from Chile and Bolivia and compelled the natives to accept them in payment, at considerable profit to themselves.[40]

In addition, since both Germans and British had more ready capital than American and more experience with native tastes, they offered long-term credit and a better system of bonded goods. Not until the mid-1880s did San Francisco begin to furnish even a small market for copra. Samoa had direct steamship connections with Australia and New Zealand but not with the United States, so when it imported American goods, they had to come from San Francisco by slow sailing ship or via Auckland or Sydney, where they might wait weeks for transshipment. Pacific Mail operated steamers on the Australia–New Zealand route, which ran close to Samoa and stopped off Tutuila to discharge or take

39. D. S. Parker to Fish, January 4, 1877; Griffin to Fish, February 17, 1877; Griffin to J. A. Campbell, July 30, 1877, no. 17; Dawson to Payson, April 19, 1879, no. 57; Dawson to Evarts, September 11, 1880, no. 189; Dawson to Walker Blaine, September 15, October 17, 1881, nos. 270, 286; Theodore Canisius to Adee, May 21, 1883, no. 41; B. Greenebaum to Third Assistant Secretary of State, October 15, 1885, no. 21, all in U.S., Consular Despatches, Apia, 5, 6, 8, 10, 11. U.S., 46th Cong., 1st sess., Senate Executive Document 2, 11–29. U.S., Consular Reports 25 (November 1882): 16–18; 36 (December 1883): 227. U.S., 50th Cong., 2d sess., Senate Executive Document 31, 60–63. U.S., Commercial Relations, 1882–83, 2, 848–49; 1886–87, 1087–90. On the Central Polynesian Land and Commercial Company see Gilson, Samoa 1830 to 1900, 347–48, 373, 386, 4–6, 408.

40. Masterman, Origins of International Rivalry, 63, 79, 155–62. Ryden, Foreign Policy in Samoa, 408–11. U.S., Consular Reports 31 (July 1883): 99–101. S. S. Foster to William Hunter, February 28, 1876, no. 45; Dawson to Payson, September 27, 1880, no. 193; Sewall to George L. Rives, March 27, August 15, 1888, nos. 98, 143, U.S., Consular Despatches, Apia, 4, 7, 17.

on passengers. With a small subsidy they would have called regularly at Apia. Underlying all these problems was the widespread American feeling that South Pacific trade was not worth the effort to obtain it. According to the San Francisco *Daily Alta California* about 1876 the Hawaiian Islands "are the meat and milk of the coconut, while the Samoans and the Carolines are the husk and shell."[41]

Despite this lack of urgent concern, during the decade following the treaty of 1878 the United States became more and more deeply involved in Samoan affairs. In 1879 Germany and Britain negotiated most-favored-nation commercial treaties with Samoa, and Germany obtained an inferior naval station near Apia, which was never much used. The treaties conferred added powers on the United States because of its own most-favored-nation clause. The three nations then established a joint board composed of their consuls to govern the municipality of Apia and recognized Malietoa as ruler of the islands. To placate a rival faction, they gave its leader, Tupua Tamasese, the useless post of vice-king.[42] This unstable compromise was possible largely because Bismarck was not yet ready for a German push into the Pacific and Britain under the Liberal Gladstone regime participated in the municipal arrangement reluctantly and restrained New Zealand's desire to interfere.

The American position at this point was already obscure. State Department memoranda of 1880 and 1881 by the department factotum, Assistant Secretary Alvey A. Adee, justified American participation in this temporary protectorate as encouraging stability and "statesmanliness" among the Samoans and giving the United States a foothold in the South Pacific. Adee also suggested the extension of American influence throughout Oceania. In 1883, however, Secretary Frederick T. Frelinghuysen declared that while the United States stood in a special treaty relationship with both Hawaii and Samoa, it need not show much concern over the rest of Polynesia. Even in Samoa the United States never formally ratified the joint municipal agreement. The State Department paid little attention to developments, and a succession of consuls at Apia were appointed casually and given few precise instructions. For its part, the navy occasionally deposited coal at Pago Pago, and naval expansionists such as Commodore Robert H. Shufeldt sometimes mentioned Samoa in their writings.[43]

41. U.S., *Commercial Relations, 1875*, 1158–60; *1878–79*, 1030. U.S., *Consular Reports* 34 (October 1883): 778–80; 44 (August 1884): 624; 45 (September 1884): 100–101; 109 (October 1889): 194–96. Thomas M. Dawson to Payson, July 8, 1879, September 18, 1880, nos. 80, 191; Greenebaum to James D. Porter, July 1, 1886, no. 116; E. L. Hamilton to Porter, February 6, 1887, no. 144, U.S., Consular Despatches, Apia, 7, 8, 14. *San Francisco Daily Alta California,* no date, clipping enclosed with Greenebaum to Porter, February 9, 1886, no. 60, U.S., Consular Desatches, Apia, 14.

42. The British and German treaties were perpetual, whereas the American could be revoked by either side after ten years. Ellison, *Foreign Influence in Samoa*, 99–107. Ryden, *Foreign Policy in Samoa*, 207–76.

43. Memoranda by Adee, March 30, 1880, December 22, 1881, nos. 10, 12, 66, U.S., Reports of Diplomatic Bureau, 4, 5. This position was summarized in President Hayes's

During the mid-1880s this precarious arrangement was upset. Joint control over Apia produced a *furor consularis,* as the three consuls and their followers intrigued against each other. The Samoans were unaccustomed to a strong king, and Malietoa failed to assert himself over his rivals. Most important, in 1884 Bismarck determined on a policy of active imperialism, partly to encourage German trade and foreign investment and partly to resist Britain. In the Pacific this new policy took the form of a movement to annex New Guinea and the Bismarck archipelago and to push Samoa toward a sole German protectorate. Using New Zealand expansionism as a justification, a new German consul, Dr. O. Stübel, forced Malletoa to grant him special powers to protect German residents. Early in 1885, the Germans supported a rebellion against Malietoa and installed the vice-king Tamasese as puppet king under a German flag and protected by a German warship. John A. Kasson, recently Arthur's minister to Germany, warned Secretary Bayard just before giving up his post that Germany's encroachments in Samoa represented "calculated hostility" to American interests and lamented: "The Pacific Ocean should have been an American sea."[44]

This was the situation facing the Cleveland administration as it took office. Over the next four years Secretary of State Thomas F. Bayard's policy was firm but unprovocative. He repeatedly insisted that the United States sought no sole protectorate over Samoa but could not permit any other country to assert this control. In defense of this position he cited American treaty obligations, desire for good Samoan government, and the strategic location of the islands for trade with Australasia and the East Indies, as a result of the opening of transcontinental American railroads and the expected construction of an isthmian canal. When an American consul, Bertholde Greenebaum, declared an American protectorate and raised the U.S. flag to shield Malietoa, Bayard disavowed the act, and he discouraged King Kalakaua of Hawaii from a proposal to form an alliance or a federation with Samoa. Bismarck, surprised and puzzled by Bayard's stand, concluded that his protests were mere hypocrisy, concealing ulterior motives. American expansionists were puzzled too. One of Bayard's own agents, George

---

annual message of 1880. Richardson, *Messages and Papers,* 7, 611. The United States never ratified the agreement setting up joint control but accepted it informally. Anderson, " 'Pacific Destiny' and American Policy," 52.

44. Ryden, *Foreign Policy in Samoa,* 277–94. Masterman, *Origins of International Rivalry,* chap. 8. Paul M. Kennedy, *The Samoan Tangle: A Study in Anglo-German-American Relations, 1878–1900,* 25–50. Kennedy believes that Stübel undertook his coup on his own initiative, as Bismarck was then busily engaged elsewhere. For a pro-German account of these events see Otto zu Stolberg-Wernigerode, *Germany and the United States of America during the Era of Bismarck,* 231–40. Greenebaum to Thomas F. Bayard, September 10, 1885, no. 15, U.S., Consular Despatches, Apia, 13. The term *furor consularis* was first used by Robert Louis Stevenson in a memoir of his residence in Samoa. He applied it to the crisis period of 1888–1889, but it aptly describes conditions throughout the 1880s. Robert Louis Stevenson, *A Footnote in History: Eight Years of Trouble in Samoa,* chap. 9. Kasson to Bayard, April 13, 30, 1885, nos. 230, 235, U.S., Diplomatic Despatches, Germany, 33. Tansill, *Foreign Policy of Bayard,* 23–24.

Handy Bates, sent his master a long report in 1886 urging that Hawaii and Samoa be made exceptions to the traditional American policy of nonintervention.[45]

After much correspondence the United States, Britain, and Germany sent commissioners separately to examine the situation and held a conference on Samoa at Washington in June and July 1887. Here Bayard stubbornly proposed that the joint protectorate be made permanent and Malietoa reinstated as king, with a bicameral legislature and foreign advisers representing the three treaty powers. This solution the others rejected as naive. Bayard resisted Anglo-German efforts to recognize the dominant German position in Samoa. (Britain, concerned for its interests elsewhere, was now throwing its weight to the Germans, despite pressure from Australia and New Zealand.) Stifled by the Washington heat, the conference broke up, a failure.[46]

Soon after this the Germans issued an ultimatum to Malietoa, sent four warships to Samoa, captured him, and carried him off into exile, whereupon a more vigorous relative, Mata'afa Iosepha, assumed leadership of his faction. With support from American residents and a new U.S. consul general, Harold W. Sewall, Mata'afa started a rebellion in the bush. Within the State Department Adee warned that Samoa in the hands of a naval power could threaten the whole eastern Pacific coast from California to South America: "Samoa off-sets Pearl Harbor, and Bismarck so intends it." Bismarck, however, had his minister point out to Bayard that Germany had never taken advantage of its commercial

45. Tansill, *Foreign Policy of Bayard*, chap. 2, especially 29–31. Wehler, *Aufsteig*, 222, 229–30. Bayard's official policy is set out in three instructions to Bertholde Greenebaum (June 19, 1885), George H. Bates (July 22, 1886), and George H. Pendleton (January 17, 1888), and in a speech to the Washington Conference of 1887. U.S., 50th Cong., 1st sess., *House Executive Document 238*, 9–11, 29–33, 107–21. U.S., 50th Cong., 2d sess., *Senate Executive Document 102*, 9–21. By 1889 he was privately blaming the Samoan problem on "the greedy and quarrelsome spirit of the traders on the islands, who . . . do not care, in their hot pursuit of gain and power, whether they disturb the peace of the world." Bayard to John Sherman, February 27, 1889. Bayard to Carl Schurz, February 1, 1889. Carl Schurz, *Speeches, Correspondence and Political Papers of Carl Schurz*, 5, 7–11. At the same time Bayard was warning his minister to Germany to be on guard against German efforts to establish footholds in Central America and the West Indies. Bayard to George H. Pendleton, September 9, 1885, quoted in Tansill, *Foreign Policy of Bayard*, 29–30. Bismarck mistakenly thought Bayard was encouraging Kalakaua (Kennedy, *Samoan Tangle*, 52–53, 55, 64–65). Bayard to H. A. P. Carter, November 11, 1885, April 12, 1887, U.S., Notes to Foreign Legations, Hawaii, 1, 109–12, 110–22. For Bayard's later memory of his commercial motives see Calhoun, *Gilded Age Cato*, 164. As Bayard may not have known, Greenebaum was an agent of the Central Polynesian Company's successors. Gilson, *Samoa 1630 to 1900*, 386. For Bates's report see U.S., *Foreign Relations, 1889*, 237–38, especially the ending, 276–78.

46. Tansill, *Foreign Policy of Bayard*, chap. 3. Ryden, *Foreign Policy in Samoa*, chap. 10. Kennedy, *Samoan Tangle*, 64–66. Alfred Vagts, *Deutschland und die Vereinigten Staaten in der Weltpolitik*, vol. 1, 638–39. Memorandum of John Bassett Moore, n.d., Moore papers, box 213. Just before the conference Britain and Germany had signed a secret treaty recognizing each other's interests in Tonga and Samoa and confirming German rule in Samoa. Kennedy, *Samoan Tangle*, 62–63. On German reactions see also Wehler, *Aufstieg*, 222–23.

preponderance in Samoa as the United States had in Hawaii with its reciprocity treaty of 1875. Undeterred by either comment, Bayard continued his policy of dignified remonstrance at German aggression, although hampered by the illness of his minister at Berlin and Sewall's inexperience and impetuosity. During the hard-fought American presidential campaign of 1888 some Republicans of course used the Samoan issue to score points against Cleveland and Bayard, but it played a minor role in the campaign.[47]

After the election these two would have preferred to leave the problem to the victorious Benjamin Harrison, but Senator William P. Frye (Republican, Maine) introduced a resolution in Congress for a general investigation, and this brought forth renewed attacks on the defeated administration by the Republican press and congressional appropriations to develop a naval base at Pago Pago and defend American rights. In the midst of the hubbub Consul General Sewall returned from Samoa to add his eyewitness account to the denunciation of Germany. After his appearance before the Foreign Relations Committee the Senate voted $600,000 to defend American interests in Samoa and construct a naval base at Pago Pago.

These developments and news of further German violence in Samoa compelled Cleveland to act. First he reinforced the American naval detachment there; then on January 15 he sent relevant diplomatic and naval correspondence to Congress and turned over the problem to that body. These actions precipitated a flurry of war talk in the press. Meanwhile Bayard continued to urge restraint on the German minister, seconded by Carl Schurz, the leading German-American citizen of the day, who described for Bismarck's benefit the long-drawn-out hostilities into which the two countries might stumble. (The German admiralty was already considering this subject.) Bismarck, though annoyed at Schurz's preaching, restrained his military plans and quickly proposed another tripower conference, on which he had probably already decided. But the civil war in Samoa continued, and as Harrison took office, the presence of seven rival warships crowded into Apia Harbor—three American, three German, and one British— threatened to carry matters beyond the control of the home governments.[48]

---

47. Tansill, *Foreign Policy of Bayard*, 68–100. Adee to Bayard, November 4, 1887, Bayard papers, 120ff, 23635–36. Ryden, *Foreign Policy in Samoa*, 367–417. Kennedy, *Samoan Tangle*, 66–76. Jon David Holstine, "American Diplomacy in Samoa 1884 to 1899," 141–75. For Bismarck's remark see U.S., *Foreign Relations, 1888*, 1, 662–64.

48. Ryden, *Foreign Policy in Samoa*, 417–29. Kennedy, *Samoan Tangle*, 76–86, Holstine, "American Diplomacy in Samoa," 175–82. Tansill, *Foreign Policy of Bayard*, 100–119. Vagts, *Deutschland und die Vereinigten Staaten*, vol. 1, 648–69. Cleveland's speech to Congress on January 15, 1889, pronounced the situation in Samoa "delicate and critical." Richardson, *Messages and Papers*, 8, 804–5. Later he wrote out another message declaring that Germany's secret purpose had always been to subvert Samoan freedom. Fortunately he decided not to send it. Nevins, *Cleveland*, 445. For Frye's resolution and justification see U.S., 50th Cong., 2d sess., *Congressional Record*, 20, 106–9. For Schurz's connection with the negotiations see Schurz, *Speeches*, 5, 2–18; and Alfred Vagts, "Hopes and Fears of an American-German War, 1870–1815," 516–19. For Bismarck's reactions see Herwig, *Politics of Frustration*, 16–18. At this time Anglo-American relations were cool because of the Sackville West incident during the recent presidential campaign.

From December to February Congress and the press reviewed the Samoan question, combining political partisanship with an earnest if heavy-handed consideration of policy issues. Many harsh words were directed at Germany for trying to "brick-bat" Americans off Samoa, using well-tried British methods of colonial usurpation with "almost every conceivable insult . . . to the government of the United States." Some thought Bismarck intended to follow the same tactics in Hawaii. Others were sure that Germany, confronting French *revanche* spirit in Europe, would avoid a showdown.

Senator James N. Dolph (Republican, Oregon) eulogized Pacific trade with the promoter's familiar hyperbole, and Cleveland's commissioner George H. Bates called Samoa the key to the South Pacific as Hawaii was to the North Pacific. If the United States did not resist German pretensions in Samoa, declared the activists, it would risk its future influence among all Pacific islands and might even lose Hawaii. In particular, they said, Washington had obligations to defend the rights of American citizens on the islands, uphold the Monroe Doctrine, which covered most of the Pacific as well as the Western Hemisphere, and protect the Samoan natives "not only from disturbance by the warring factions of the islands but from the intrusion of any foreign power." Republican newspapers like the *New York Tribune* and the *Washington Post* criticized Bayard's "imbecility and pusillanimity," and called for "some old fashioned American patriotism and aggressive energy." Such critics faulted Cleveland for not upholding Greenebaum's protectorate and building a naval base at Pago Pago or at least a coaling station for merchant ships bound to the Indies. Navalists again deplored the Democrats' failure to strengthen the fighting fleet and predicted that one benefit of the Samoan crisis would be a stronger navy.[49]

Almost every one of these arguments was answered with a counterargument. Some writers decried the sudden burst of Germanophobia, blaming it on German-American dislike of Bismarck's other policies (for example, the prohibition of American pork imports). These persons pointed out that the chancellor had too many urgent concerns in Europe to start a war in Samoa. Others answered the trade expansionists by reminding them of the conspicuous American failure to lower tariffs on Australian goods and thus encourage the development of a promising market. It was ridiculous to suppose that the Monroe Doctrine extended across the ocean, for "Samoa was intended by nature to be an Australian rather than an American dependency." The United States had neither obligation nor interest in declaring war "on account of some black people thousands and

49. *Public Opinion* 3 (October 8, 1887): 351; 4 (October 15, 1887): 7; 6 (December 8, 1888, January 19, February 9, 16, 1889): 174–75, 321–22, 365–66, 388, U.S., 50th Cong., 2d sess., *Congressional Record*, 1332–33, 1337. Interview by Bates in *New York Tribune*, January 25, 1889. Ibid., October 18, 1887; November 13; January 25, 1889. *New York Times*, December 6, 1888, January 3, 1889. *Washington Post*, January 21, 1889 (quotation). *American Economist* 3 (February 1, 1889). Vagts emphasizes humanitarian, strategic, and navalist concerns in his analysis. Vagts, *Deutschland und die Vereinigten Staatan*, vol. 1, 653–69.

thousands of miles away in the Pacific." It had no mission to rescue weak nations but should save its resources for use at home; many added Hawaii or the isthmian canal as legitimate goals of foreign interest. In a mild Senate speech John Sherman conceded that a coaling station on Samoa might be useful to future trade but declared that the United States could well build it under the existing Samoan treaty, amplified by peaceful negotiations with Germany. Answering Republican sneers at Bayard's pacifism, the *New York Times* expressed concern that James G. Blaine, once settled in the State Department, might spurn such negotiations as "truckling to foreign interests."[50]

The Democrats need not have worried. Less than two weeks after Harrison took office, on March 16–17, 1889, nature intervened with a typhoon that swept across the islands and sank, beached, or crippled every warship in the cramped Apia Harbor except the one British cruiser. This catastrophe abruptly ended the crisis and gave the three powers ample time to deliberate. Before a second conference met at Berlin, British and German diplomats decided to propose a three-way cession—most of Samoa to Germany, Tonga to Britain, and Hawaii and Tutuila to the United States. Blaine rejected this proposal. As he told his agents, the defense of existing and expected American interests in the Pacific meant that "this Government cannot accept even temporary subordination." Like Bayard he would have preferred to restore some sort of native government but eventually realized that this was impossible. At the conference Britain and Germany agreed reluctantly to a treaty (signed June 15) establishing a tripartite condominium. This would involve even more joint supervision of Samoan affairs than the earlier protectorate, and the rest of the conference was given over to a discussion of details, such as the authority of a foreign-appointed supreme court, control of land titles, and taxes.[51]

With some exceptions, American reception of the Berlin treaty was just as partisan as the earlier attacks on Germany. The Senate debate was short, and after it had been made clear that the treaty did not compromise existing American rights to Pago Pago, only twelve members voted against approval. Administration newspapers praised the treaty as a triumph for Blaine, although they supposed

50. *Public Opinion* 3 (September 24, 1887): 506; 4 (October 15, 1887): 7; 6 (January 19, February 2, 1889): 300–301, 343–45. Sherman's speech is in U.S., 50th Cong., 2d sess., *Congressional Record*, 20, 1283–91, especially 1290–91. For an approving summary of the speech see *Harper's Weekly* 33 (February 9, 1889): 103. *New York Tribune*, January 18, 1889; *New York Times*, May 20, 1888, January 30, 1889; *Chicago Tribune*, January 25, 26, 1889; *Washington Post*, January 26, 1889; *San Francisco Daily Alta California*, December 13, 1888. Clipping in Bayard papers, box 228. *Nation* 45 (October 20, 1887): 302; 47 (January 31, 1889): 84–85.

51. Ryden, *Foreign Policy in Samoa*, chaps. 12, 13. Kennedy, *Samoan Tangle*, 56–97. Holstine, "American Diplomacy in Samoa," 181–87, chap. 6. U.S., Consular Despatches, Apia, 12. U.S., *Foreign Relations, 1889*, 200–201. According to German historians, Blaine told the German minister that personally he would have been willing to give up the islands but that the United States must have undisputed possession of Pago Pago. Wehler, *Aufstieg*, 233. Vagts, *Deutschland und die Vereinigten Staaten*, vol. 1, 698–700. For the text of the Berlin treaty see Bevans, *Treaties*, vol. 1, 26–28.

sourly that Bayard would claim some of the credit for it. It gave the United States, they added, all Americans needed in Samoa with a minimum of risks. Some Democrats, however, called it "the squarest back-down in the history of diplomacy," and the *Springfield Republican* pronounced it "un-American in its assumption of authority over another country, and pledging us to a system of government foreign to the spirit of our democratic institutions." The independent *New York Herald* and *Harper's Weekly* struck a balance between expansion and isolation by praising the individual provisions of the treaty while wishing that the United States could have acted alone.[52]

In little more than a decade the United States had involved itself apparently inextricably in a remote part of the Pacific without any penetrating discussion of the radically new foreign policy by Congress, press, or public. The new commitment responded to no urgent economic or strategic need. It was a product of fuzzy geography, impulsive humanitarianism, and improvisations on the spot by ambitious but inexperienced consuls. And it threatened to become a more serious international entanglement than American involvement in Hawaii, where our interests were much greater.

In the western Pacific, American economic activities were even more widely scattered than in the islands of Polynesia. However, the U.S. government made no determined stand as in Samoa until the fortunes of the Spanish-American War created an American sphere of influence in the Philippines. The important island groups of Micronesia, the Marshalls and the Carolines, illustrate this passive American attitude.

The Marshall Islands were the richest source of copra and the leading commercial center of the central Pacific. In 1885 Germany annexed the islands, and two years later two successor companies to the Godeffroy firm united to form the Jaluit Gesellschaft. It ran the islands like a company store and levied special taxes and discriminatory land lease laws on American firms, which, according to the American consular agent, did half of the islands' business, offering better goods at lower prices than the German merchants. The principal American firm, A. Crawford and Company, asked for the visit of an American warship or some other visible symbol of support. Although, as has been seen, the United States was even then defying Germany for control of Samoa, it ignored the pleas of the Crawford company. By the end of the century German merchants had a trade monopoly on the Marshalls.[53]

---

52. Summary of Senate action in *Bradstreet's* 18 (February 8, 1890): 85. *Public Opinion* 7 (June 22, 1889): 228–29; 8 (February 1, 1890): 403–4, *New York Tribune*, May 31, 1889; January 21, 23, 30, 1890; *Springfield Republican*, January 21, 1890; *New York Herald*, January 25, 1890; *Harper's Weekly* 23 (June 29, 1889): 514; 34 (February 8, 1890): 98–99. Cleveland's commissioner, Bates, continued to praise Samoa as the key to Pacific trade. *Century* 37 (August 1889): 946–49. For the generally disgruntled German press reaction see W. W. Phelps to Blaine, March 1, 1890, no. 79, U.S., Diplomatic Despatches, Germany, 50.

53. Firth, "German Firms in the Western Pacific Islands," 24–25. Townsend, *Germany's Colonial Empire*, 150–51. Francis X. Hezel, *Strangers in Their Own Land: A Century of*

American whalers, merchant ships, and missionaries were visiting the Caroline and Palau Islands regularly by 1870, and about sixty Americans lived on the islands, but the State Department did not maintain a commercial agent there. The chief American influence was Daniel Dean O'Keefe, an independent Irish-American trader on Yap Island. With his fleet of two schooners and many small boats he collected copra throughout the islands, marketed it himself in Hong Kong and Manila, and fought the Jaluit company on even terms until his death in 1901.

German firms began to penetrate the Carolines at about the same time as the Marshalls. When Bismark tried to annex these islands in the mid-1880s, Spain protested, and the Pope, intervening as arbitrator, awarded the group to Madrid. The following year the U.S. government obtained from Spain a promise to give Americans in the islands the same treatment as other foreigners. This assurance seems to have meant little at first, for missionaries continued to face obstacles to their work, and in 1890 Spain refused to certify an American consul at Ponape. Although the Spanish then relaxed their official policy, there is no evidence that any American traders except O'Keefe ever made any great profits in the islands.[54]

The German efforts to annex New Guinea and its subsequent partition between Germany and Britain in 1884 did not disturb Americans, for they had done little or no trading on the island. American commercial interests were greater in the Melanesian island groups to the east, such as the Bismarck archipelago, annexed by Germany in the mid-1880s, and New Caledonia, which had been a French colony since 1853. A. Crawford and Company was one of the San Francisco trading companies active in the Bismarcks, as in the Carolines and Marshalls. Americans established plantation agriculture there as well as trade—for example, the half-caste daughter of a onetime American consul at Apia formed a partnership with a British trader to produce copra, which they marketed through the German DHPG firm. American exports to New Caledonia, hampered by a complete lack of direct communication, consisted largely of those staples of the South Pacific, imported through Australia: California lumber, petroleum, sewing machines, agricultural

Colonial Rule in the Caroline and Marshall Islands, chap. 2. Sewall to George L. Rives, December 3, 1888, no. 164, with enclosure; Sewall to Wharton, June 5, October 21, 1890, nos. 14, 41, U.S., Consular Despatches, Apia, 17, 18.

54. George F. Seward to Secretary of State, April 7, 1869, no. 253, U.S., Consular Despatches, Shanghai, 10. Jonas M. Coe to Fish, March 31, 1870, no. 4, ibid, Apia, 3. Townsend, *Germany's Colonial Empire,* 49, 116–17. Hazel, *Strangers in Their Own Land,* chaps. 2, 3. Stolberg-Wernigerode, *Germany and the United States,* 217–25. Richard G. Brown, "The German Acquisition of the Caroline Islands, 1898–99," 137–40. Before trying to annex the Carolines, Bismarck inquired whether the United States had any claim to the islands. George H. Pendleton to Bayard, September 10, 1885, Bayard papers, 50ff, 16272–75. For American views of the Germany-Spanish quarrel see also John W. Foster's dispatches in U.S., Diplomatic Despatches, Spain, 114, 115. Pearle E. Quinn, "The Diplomatic Struggle for the Carolines, 1898," 290–92.

implements, and some provisions and canned goods. In 1893 some of these were cut off by French protective tariffs.[55]

During the mid–nineteenth century American merchants enjoyed several decades of prosperity and influence in the trade of the Philippines. When Spain relaxed its commercial policies in the 1830s, several American firms opened agencies in Manila. As seen earlier, the two leaders were Peele, Hubbell and Company, and Russell, Sturgis and Company, the latter an outgrowth of the China trade and affiliated with the powerful firm of Russell and Company.

The two American houses prospered by improving antiquated business methods in Manila, establishing a network of contracts with planters, and emphasizing the growth of Manila hemp. Encouraged by British commercial triumphs in China, however, British competitors in the Philippines began to catch up. Although Russell, Sturgis was the largest commercial house in the islands, it had to arrange credit for its customers with the aid of British banks in Hong Kong and Shanghai, which gave better terms to British merchants. The commission business, on which both houses relied, grew out of date as in China, and eventually British competitors cut into its profits so badly that in 1875 Russell, Sturgis went bankrupt. So did Peele, Hubbell twelve years later, as a result of overtrading in sugar. After that time British influence dominated Philippine trade, although Spain tried to restrict it in 1891 with a high tariff. In 1896 Spanish, British, and American trade with the Philippines was $11.7 million, $10.1 million, and $4.5 million respectively.[56]

American trade with the Philippines followed much the same pattern as trade with South America and the other islands of the southern and western Pacific. On the customs records, imports from the Philippines (mainly hemp and sugar) vastly outweighed exports to the islands—by $11,592,626 to $122,276 in 1890, the year of greatest imports from the islands. During the decade before 1897 the United States took 15 percent of the Philippines' exports and supplied only 3 percent of their imports. But these figures meant little, because the only American product shipped directly to Manila in any amount was kerosene, which had a virtual monopoly of the Philippine market. A great variety of American goods, such as flour, canned goods, furniture, carriages, coal, and others, came to the islands by way of London or Hong Kong in British or Spanish ships and over British counters, so they did not figure in American-Philippine

55. On the Germans in New Guinea see Townsend, *Germany's Colonial Empire*, 145–50; and Firth, "German Firms in the Western Pacific Islands," 20–24. For American consular comment on German efforts and on the Bismarck islands see U.S., *Consular Reports* 46 (October 1884): 192–93; 53 (June 1885): 164–65; 105 (May 1889): 134–39; 164 (May 1894): 46; and 165 (June 1894): 341. For a description of American trade with New Caledonia see U.S., *Commercial Relations, 1898*, vol. 1, 1232–33.

56. William J. Pomeroy, *American Neo-Colonialism: Its Emergence in the Philippines and Asia*, 17–18. Regidor y Jurado and Mason, *Commercial Progress*, 25–40. Lagada, "American Enterprise in the Philippines," 142–60. On British interests in 1898 see *Commercial and Financial Chronicle* 66 (May 21, 1898): 976–77. For 1896 trade figures see U.S., 56th Cong., 1st sess., *Senate Document 138*, 62.

statistics. American consuls complained that excellent American agricultural machinery was not to be found there because no one knew about it. American cotton drills were better made than British but too heavy for the climate and too expensive. A few American manufacturers sent out beautiful catalogues, while London merchants granted discounts and gave faster service. Conditions improved slightly during the 1890s, but the real changes awaited the Spanish-American War.[57]

As has been seen, Americans sent ships to the East Indies almost as early as their first ventures to China. Their trade in pepper, coffee, and other tropical products continued for a while during the last half of the nineteenth century, and, as before, the U.S. government gave occasional support to American activities. In 1850 an American official signed with the sultan of Brunei the first treaty in Southeast Asia providing for extraterritoriality only six years after Caleb Cushing had obtained that privilege from China. During the early 1850s individuals such as Commodore Matthew C. Perry and August Belmont, an expansionist American minister to the Netherlands, recommended that the United States annex outright much of the Indies and Southeast Asia. Some historians have seen in these scattered actions the germ of 1898 imperialism, but evidence is lacking of a consistent, deliberate policy, supported at home.[58]

Instead, Confederate commerce raiders during the American Civil War reduced U.S. trade in the Indies for a time and may have reinforced the government's reluctance to risk political involvement there. Seward appointed an active consul at Brunei on the island of Borneo. This man, Claude Lee Moses, with several partners formed the American Trading Company of Borneo, persuaded the sultan of Brunei to lease them a large tract, and settled perhaps sixty colonists, who cleared a few acres for rice, sugar cane, and tobacco. Perhaps hearing of this venture, the nephew of the British-born rajah of Sarawak offered to help Seward acquire the whole island. However, the Johnson administration was overrun with other problems and gave no answer or support to the colonists. Raising little food for themselves, they nearly starved and had to sell out to a British syndicate. During the Grant administration the sultan of Atjeh on Sumatra, trying to resist Dutch encroachments on his territory, appealed to Consul Augustus G. Studer at Singapore for aid, offering in exchange the strategically located island of Pulo

57. U.S., *Commercial Relations, 1880–81,* 194–95; *1885–86,* vol. 2, 1596–1603; *1886–87,* vol. 2, 1602; *1887–88,* 188–93. U.S., *Consular Reports* 26 (December 1882): 299–304; 39 (October 1889): 324. *Engineering and Mining Journal* 48 (July 6, 1889): 1, 3. For trade figures in the 1890s see *Nation* 71 (October 11, 1900): 282. U.S., *Report of the Philippine Commission to the President* (Washington, 1901), 4, 66.

58. James W. Gould, *The United States and Malaysia,* 52–53, 56–63. Seward W. Livermore, "Early Commercial and Consular Relations with the East Indies," 31–56. Ronald H. Spector, "The American Image of Southeast Asia, 1790–1865; A Preliminary Assessment," 304–5. Gould, "American Imperialism," 206–11. Gould, "America's Pepperpot," 275–349. Ahmat, "American Trade with Singapore," 3441–59.

Weh in the Malacca Strait. When Secretary Fish learned of this negotiation, he told Studer to break it off and stick to commerce.[59]

The recovery of American trade with the Indies after the Civil War was further hampered by the decline of the merchant marine, which was noticeable all over the world. In the 1850s and 1860s many American sailing ships plied Malayan waters, but when the British established steam lines, the Americans did not follow suit, and the Stars and Stripes almost disappeared from Malayan harbors. Late in the 1870s there was not a single American mercantile firm in Singapore. American products were imported via Britain or Hong Kong, and European firms in the Malayan ports handled them when it suited their interests. One casualty of this shipping change was the formerly flourishing American pepper trade in Sumatra, which ceased to use American ships after 1860 and declined rapidly in the early 1870s.[60]

American trade with the Indies and the Malay peninsula resembled trade with China in that the Indies and Malaya produced several commodities having a dependable market in the United States: spices, high-grade Sumatran coffee, tin, and crude rubber, to name the most important. American imports far outvalued American exports. Consuls at Singapore reported figures of about $7.2 million and $1.1 million respectively for 1881–1882 and $9 million and $1 million for 1897.[61] Consul Studer complained in the early 1880s of the lost opportunities for American exports, and in 1898 a successor's report was not much more encouraging. A few products found steady sales, especially among foreigners: flour, condensed milk, canned goods, tobacco, ship stores, clocks, and sewing machines. However, American textiles utterly failed to break the British monopoly.[62]

The mainstay of the American export trade in the Indies and Malaya was kerosene, which usually made up more than 80 percent of American shipments to the area and enjoyed a near monopoly until the late 1880s. In 1865 the first recorded American shipment arrived at Batavia, and by the end of the 1880s imports totaled 22.3 million gallons. The growth and the monopoly depended in part on price, in part on quality, and also on the superior American wooden packing cases of two five-gallon tins each. During much of this period a variety of small American firms competed for business, but by 1888 Standard Oil had absorbed their trade. In that year the first consignment of Russian oil arrived from

59. Gould, *United States and Malaysia,* 63–64. James W. Gould, *Americans in Sumatra,* 4–11. K. G. Tregonning, "American Activity in North Borneo, 1865–1881," 367–72. Regidor y Jurado and Mason, *Commercial Progress,* 36–37. William E. F. Krause, *American Interests in Borneo: A Brief Sketch of the Extent, Climate and Production of the Island of Borneo.* W. Brooke to Secretary of State, December 30, 1867, Seward papers.

60. George Biggers, "The Effect of the Opening of the Suez Canal on the Trade and Development of Singapore," 107–15. U.S., *Commercial Relations, 1878,* 740–43; *1879,* vol. 1, 77; *1882–83,* vol. 2, 581–87. Gould, "America's Pepperpot," 322–23, 326–30.

61. U.S., *Commercial Relations, 1882–83,* vol. 2, 583, 587; *1898,* 1157.

62. Ibid., 1874–75, 714–15; *1898,* vol. 1, 1082–83; U.S., *Consular Reports* 19 (May 1882): 29–46.

Batum, and, as in China, Standard plunged into a long-lasting trade rivalry, which forced it to improve its sales methods and shift to bulk transport and storage of petroleum products (see chapter 5). These measures proved so effective that the Russians had virtually lost the Indies market by 1898.

But the most serious threat to the American oil trade appeared in the Indies themselves, for both Sumatra and Borneo contained major deposits of high-grade crude. In 1885 a Dutchman discovered the first oil in commercial quantities, and five years later the Royal Dutch Company was founded, soon to become Standard Oil's bête noire. Ironically, American manufacturers furnished most of the early equipment for the Indies fields and American engineers the skill and labor. Royal Dutch had to operate in a tropical climate (the oil fields were almost exactly on the equator and near sea level) and during a Dutch war with the one remaining Indonesian sultanate. Nevertheless, exports began in 1892, and the oil contest in East Asia became a three-cornered affair, Americans, Russians, and Dutch.

The Dutch had neither the capital nor the manpower to develop their fields fully, so in 1895 Standard put forth feelers to buy out Royal Dutch altogether. Rebuffed, Standard made several vain efforts to acquire producing fields in Sumatra, and one campaign lasted through the Spanish-American War. It seems likely that the exclusion of Standard from the Indies oil fields was due not only to Yankeephobia and Standard's reputation but also to Dutch government support for the developing Royal Dutch monopoly, which was not matched by any action from Washington. Whatever the case, Standard did not establish production operations in the Indies until after World War I. Nevertheless, its sales held up, and in 1897 it shipped 2,009,290 cases of ten gallons, as against 495,106 shipped by the Russians and 539,589 produced in Sumatra.[63]

The last trade region to be examined in this chapter, Siam (modern Thailand), was tributary to both Singapore and Hong Kong, and, like both the Dutch East Indies and China, its foreign trade was dominated by Britain. Although Edmund Roberts negotiated a commercial treaty with Siam in 1835, the government at Bangkok imposed so many taxes and restrictions that trade did not develop, and no American ships called there from 1838 to 1855. In 1856 Townsend Harris, who two years later rendered a similar service in Japan, expanded American rights in a second treaty which not only limited Siamese tariffs and other imports but granted Americans extraterritoriality, the right to own land, consular representation, and a most-favored-nation clause. (In the same year Britain obtained a similar treaty.) During the 1880s diplomatic relations became closer, for Siam established a legation in Washington, sent a mission to the United States, which

---

63. Gould, *Americans in Sumatra*, 41–50. F. C. Gerretson, *History of the Royal Dutch*, vol. 1, chaps. 2–6; vol. 2, chap. 2. Peter Mellish Reed, "Standard Oil in Indonesia, 1898–1928," 311–13. Daniel Yergin, *The Prize: The Epic Quest for Oil, Money, and Power*, 72–76. *American Exporter* 12 (August 1883): 14. U.S., *Commercial Relations, 1884–86*, vol. 2, 1369–72. U.S., *Consular Reports* 37 (January 1884): 407–9; 78 (May 1887): 646–66; 108 (September 1889): 161–62; 144 (November 1892): 456–59; 212 (May 1898): 54–55; 220 (January 1899): 116–17.

was enthusiastically received, and negotiated a convention regulating the liquor trade. For its part, the United States raised its consulate at Bangkok to a legation, the first in eastern Asia outside China and Japan.[64]

At first the treaty of 1856 did not produce much trade, and as late as 1877 reports from the consuls were more concerned with hopes than realities. During the next two years the first shipment of American kerosene arrived at Bangkok, along with samples of sewing machines, hardware, machinery, firearms, and provisions, which all attracted customers. Since the Siamese lived largely on rice and fish, flour sales were slow, except to a few foreigners, but later Chinese bakers began to use it in cakes. Kerosene sales increased more slowly than in the Indies, and since Standard's lamps were too expensive, the Germans dominated this trade. From time to time consuls reported a familiar complaint—that great opportunities existed if only American manufacturers and merchants would show enough initiative to exploit them.[65]

After several decades of unimpressive trade with the Pacific islands and the East Indies, a publicist of the 1890s could still write that "the growing production of the United States and its swelling tide of exports, a traffic steadily augmenting, will flow from her western shores to the littoral of the Orient, to Australia, and to the Pacific islands."[66] By that time it was becoming apparent to realists that out of the many Pacific island groups only Hawaii could provide a flourishing, self-sustaining, balanced commerce to justify American trade expansionism. Hopes of creating a second Hawaii in Samoa had proved visionary by the 1890s. The Americans had not managed to win the markets of Australia and New Zealand from the British. The East Indies and parts of Southeast Asia could furnish needed raw materials, but the principal American product their people cared to buy, kerosene, was now meeting fierce competition from two rivals. If the Pacific basin beyond Hawaii held any realistic promise for Americans at the end of the century, it must be as an avenue of approach to the Orient. Eastern Asia, especially China and Japan, held the chief significance for American expansionism in the southwest Pacific.

64. Dennett, *Americans in Eastern Asia,* 130–34, 349–52. Benjamin A. Batson, "American Diplomats in Southeast Asia in the Nineteenth Century: The Case of Siam," 39–112. Donald C. Lord, "Missionaries, Thai, and Diplomats," 418–21. *New York Tribune,* July 16, 1882; May 5, 1884.

65. U.S., *Commercial Relations, 1879,* vol. 1, 80; *1880–81,* 198–99. U.S., *Consular Reports* 94 (June 1888): 557–58; 156 (September 1893): 56; 161 (February 1894): 344–46; 165 (June 1894): 310; 203 (July 1897): 475. *American Exporter* 5 (December 1879): 44.

66. Melville, "Our Future in the Pacific," 294.

5

China I
Four Hundred Million Customers

T HE MOMENTOUS EVENTS of the 1840s—the Treaty of Wang-hsia and the annexation of California and Oregon—intensified the power of the Chinese magnet for the United States. As far away as New Orleans the leading newspaper of that city, the *Bee*, declared the treaty "a circumstance of the greatest importance . . . [opening] a new and highly favorable era not only for the commerce and manufactures of the United States but particularly to the cotton planting interest of the south." Californians assumed that their state would become a commercial depot between East and West, and a rapidly growing San Francisco expected Asia to "deposit its riches in the lap of our city." These hopes were largely fulfilled, but during the 1850s New York profited even more largely from the increased China trade.[1] Other interests than commercial—missionaries, world strategists, and those in search of new sights and adventures—were also quickened by the greater attention given to the Far East.

The U.S. government reacted fitfully to pressures from American merchants and missionaries in East Asia. After the 1844 treaty it maintained a commissioner in China, first at Canton, later at Shanghai, consuls at the ports open to American trade, and finally a minister plenipotentiary at Peking. It sent Commodore Matthew C. Perry in 1853–1854 to "open" Japan to American trade, then Townsend Harris to sign a commercial treaty in 1858 and establish diplomatic relations. Thereafter for several decades it usually contented itself with a "cooperative policy" following Britain, France, and later Russia as these nations extracted privileges for their nationals, and sharing these privileges through most-favored-nation clauses in its own treaties with China and Japan. During the 1880s Washington began to take a more active interest in East Asia, especially in the area around Korea, which the American Commodore Robert W. Shufeldt "opened" to the West in self-conscious imitation of Perry. Finally, in the last years before

---

1. *New Orleans Bee*, reprinted in *Niles' National Register* 65 (January 20, 1844): 332–33; Judge Nathaniel Bennett (San Francisco, 1850) quoted in Whitelaw Reid, *Problems of Expansion, as Considered in Papers and Addresses*, 235. Albion, *Rise of New York Port*, 203. Between 1856 and 1860 annual arrivals at New York from China totaled fifty (48,500 tons), at San Francisco only thirty-three (23,400), of which many went on to New York as well.

the Spanish-American War, the State and Navy Departments began to respond to American interests in East Asia with long-range planning.

By that time more than a half century of American trade had developed only a small East Asian market, greatly inferior to those in Europe, Canada, and Latin America. Imports consistently outran exports; in 1873 and 1880 the unfavorable trade ratio was more than twenty to one. By the end of the period American trade with Japan surpassed that with China.[2] As the 1890s ended, the Americans were gaining on their chief rivals, the British, for their total trade with China amounted to only about 13 percent of British trade in 1865 but rose to nearly 64 percent in 1898.[3] American nonmissionary (i.e., business) investments in China have been estimated at about $3 million in 1830, about $7 million in 1875, and just under $20 million in 1900. (The last named figure represented only about 2.5 percent of all foreign investments in China.)[4]

This modest record naturally tempered the language of a few publicists. As early as 1880 *Bradstreet's* called Asiatic trade "a commercial superstition" and China and India "the sink-hole for British gold." Disappointed merchants and promoters came to recognize such hindrances as Chinese suspicions, xenophobia, and the "jelly-like inertia" and "soothing, whispered non commitment" of imperial officials. Some writers cautioned that while trade within China was and would remain enormous, the nation would never become a great market for American manufactures, as local producers or the newly industrialized Japanese

2. Trade figures are computed from statistics in U.S., *Historical Statistics*, vol. 2, 903–7. U.S. annual imports from and exports to China, 1821–1825, were 7.5 percent and 7.6 percent respectively of total U.S. imports and exports but fell immediately and never again reached these levels. During 1897–1901 the annual figures were 2.8 percent and 1.0 percent respectively. American imports from Japan rose from 1.0 percent of total imports, 1869–1875, to 3.7 percent in 1897–1901 and exports to Japan from 0.2 percent to 1.5 percent. Table in Peter Schran, "The Minor Significance of Commercial Relations between the United States and China, 1850–1931," 237, 245. The proportion of American business firms in China declined from 13.4 percent of all foreign business firms in 1875 to about 5 percent in 1897.

3. These figures require explanation. They are based on Chinese trade with Britain (apparently direct trade with the United Kingdom) and do not include trade with Hong Kong and British India. If trade with these areas is included, American percentages are reduced to 6.1 percent for 1865 and 12.9 percent for 1898. These are clearly too small, for a large but unspecified amount of American trade passed through Hong Kong. The figures for the two years cited are as follows (in Haekwan taels):

Year	United States	Britain	Hong Kong	British India
1865	6,347	49,377	28,043	26,402
1898	29,150	45,678	159,298	20,460

Liang-lin Hsiao, *China's Foreign Trade Statistics, 1864–1949*, 148–49, 162.
      See also Parsons, *American Engineer in China*, 158–60.
4. Remer, *Foreign Investments in China*, 245, 248–49, 260. It is worth noting, however, that Chinese trade played a much larger role in the economies of the Pacific coast states. Thomas R. Cox, "The Passage to India Revisited: Asian Trade and the Development of the Far West, 1850–1900," 97–103.

would supply most needs.[5] Nevertheless, during the 1890s optimism continued to dominate writings about the Far East. A onetime consul at Shanghai declared: "China is today the great undeveloped country of the world," and a recent legation secretary at Peking predicted that if "the electric spark of American enterprise" could be applied to the country's vast population and resources, "the trade that would spring into existence would surpass all the records of history."[6] If the trade had not yet greatly changed, neither had the expectations.

From the Treaty of Wang-hsia to the outbreak of the Civil War in the United States, American trade with China flourished in the midst of almost continuous tumult and uncertainty, benefiting from the British while competing with them. The Chinese, probably regretting the concessions made, stiffened their policies, vilified the amiable Ch'iying as a treasonous appeaser, and slid around the treaty provisions whenever they could. The British retaliated with covert threats of gunboat diplomacy. Among the Americans, only Peter Parker favored using force; most were content to "show the flag" in occasional visits by warships.[7]

Between 1845 and 1860 the total American-Chinese trade increased from about $9.5 million to about $22.5 million—imports from China nearly doubling, exports quadrupling but still behind imports. Thanks to the evolution of the speedy "China clipper," American shipping in Chinese ports rose from twenty-seven vessels (11,262 tons) in 1844 to eighty-two (78,370 tons) in 1860. Tea now completely dominated the American import trade, for both raw and manufactured silk had fallen off. This change increased the uncertainty of the trade, for tea, though popular and plentiful, was highly speculative, with fluctuating prices and grading standards. American exports were much changed from the old days, for at last the Chinese had developed a desire for American cotton goods. These, however, never reached British levels, partly because American traders were not yet closely tied to textile manufacturers. During the California gold rush gold exports to China provided a welcome balancing agent, but their effect was declining by 1860.[8]

5. *Bradstreet's* 2 (August 21, 1880): 4–5. Clarence Cary, "China and Chinese Railway Concessions," 591–605. (Quoted phrases are on 597.) For similar views from Commissioner Humphrey Marshall see his dispatch to the Secretary of State, February 7, 1853, no. 3, official, Diplomatic Despatches, China, 9.

6. Thomas R. Jernigan, "Commercial Trend of China," 63. Charles Denby, Jr., "America's Opportunity in Asia," 36. Inevitably, statisticians produced such fantasies as the estimate that if everyone in China consumed a barrel of American flour annually, they could dispose of the whole American wheat crop. Charles S. Campbell, Jr., *Special Business Interests and the Open Door Policy*, 12.

7. Henson, *Commissioners and Commodores*, 69–70. Years later Chi'ying was ordered to commit suicide. Tong, *United States Diplomacy*, 230.

8. Yuan Chung Teng, "American-China Trade, American-Chinese Relations, and the Taiping Rebellion, 1853–1858," 94–96; Earl Swisher, *The Character of American Trade with China, 1844–1860*, 166–70, 178–79. Lockwood, *Heard and Company*, 13–15, 21–22. S. G. Checkland, "An English Merchant House in China after 1842," 165–66. A small but

The opening of additional ports to the north of Canton created many opportunities for American merchants. By far the most important new port was Shanghai, near the mouth of the Yangtze River, an entrepôt through which the products of that enormous valley funneled to the sea. Almost at once cheaper tea at Shanghai drew trade away from Canton. By 1851 Shanghai, despite its difficult access, was established as the center of American business in China, with some transoceanic ships going and coming directly, instead of stopping first at Canton or Hong Kong. Americans, British, and French all developed commodious "settlements" (business and residential areas) near the waterfront and apart from the native city. Eventually these coalesced into an International Settlement administered jointly. (The French maintained a separate concession, and elsewhere the Americans were generally content to live and work in British settlements.) The most important of the other new ports was Foochow for its tea shipments. Amoy, a silk port, was also significant for its access to Taiwan, but Ningpo long remained subsidiary to Shanghai.[9]

Along with the new ports, the dissolution of the co-hong's monopoly at Canton required new efforts by the commission houses to solve language and communications problems, now more serious than ever. They soon replaced the co-hong with Chinese "compradors" (a Portuguese term), who started as interpreters and became agents, brokers, advisers, and finally semi-independent merchants. Recruiting Chinese staffs, they maintained vital connections between the commission houses and Chinese producers and wholesale merchants in ports and interior. The capital that the compradors accumulated on their own account went into trade and later steamship companies, railroads, mines, and other investments. By the 1890s they had become the nucleus of a new Chinese entrepreneurial class.[10]

---

significant trade between the American Pacific coast and China developed after 1849 in ships that had brought cargoes to California during the Gold Rush. Cox, "Passage to India Revisited," 86–87.

9. Swisher, *Character of American Trade*, 172–73. Eldon Griffin, *Clippers and Consuls: American Consular and Commercial Relations with Eastern Asia, 1845–1860*, 70–77n14, chaps. 15, 17. Hinckley, *Consular Jurisdiction*, 166–73. According to Commodore Perry, Shanghai had two dangerous shoals partly blocking the entrance to the Yangtze estuary. Matthew C. Perry to William B. Shubrick, May 15, 1853, cited in Robert Erwin Johnson, *Far China Station: The U.S. Navy in Asian Waters, 1800–1898*, 61. Americans maintained their own concession at Tientsin for several decades but never developed it into a full settlement. William Hubert Morken, "Protecting American Commerce in China: Washington's Approach to Urban Concessions, 1876–1885," 56–63. They continued to use Macao (the Portuguese colony below Canton) and especially Hong Kong as trading centers. Griffin, *Clippers and Consuls*, chap. 16. On the decline of Canton as a port see Sheila Marriner, *Rathbones of Liverpool*, 198.

10. Yen-ping Hao, "A 'New Class' in China's Treaty Ports: The Rise of the Comprador-Merchants," 446–59. For a fuller account see the same author's *The Comprador in Nineteenth Century China: Bridge between East and West*. Eventually, Americans began to have misgivings about Chinese domination of the retail trade. *New York Tribune*, March 20, 1885. Charles Denby to James G. Blaine, June 10, 1880, no. 908, U.S., Diplomatic

Some problems even the compradors could not solve for the American merchants. One was smuggling through the lax Chinese customs, which led to ruinous
price cutting. Another was currency and exchange. Nineteenth-century China had
two principal domestic units of currency, the copper "cash" and the silver "sycee,"
an oval-shaped ingot. The usual standard of measure for complex transactions
was the "tael," a unit of silver weight that varied from one mercantile center to
another. (Eventually the central government established several taels, of which
the one most used by foreigners was the "Customs" or "Haekwan" tael. During
the 1890s this was worth about an American dollar.) In everyday business the
most familiar coin was the Spanish "Carolus" peso, a dollarlike relic from the
eighteenth century, eventually replaced by its Mexican counterpart.

Fluctuations in exchange among these ill-matched units and foreign coins
caused endless problems of pricing and credit, and as late as the 1890s large cash
transactions required weighing piles of coins. The almost universal participation
in the opium trade (even American consuls were reliably suspected) arose from
exchange problems as well as from the intrinsic profits to be realized. The
shipment of opium helped finance the tea trade for both British and Americans
and prevented a ruinous drain of silver into China. Also American merchants
became bill brokers for British opium traders and acquired a dependable source
of cash to overcome their unfavorable balance of trade.[11]

Although American commercial interests on the China coast grew more complex after 1844, the U.S. government was slow to encourage them or to work
out a consistent Far Eastern policy. The State and Navy Departments issued
conflicting instructions to their officials. Traditional Anglophobia made long-term
cooperation with Britain difficult, and the State Department wavered between
supporting equal commercial access to a sovereign China (later called the "open
door") and joining the British in forcing China to grant additional concessions.
One of the government's most valuable aids to the China trade was probably
unintentional—its prevailing low tariff policy from 1846 to 1861.

Despatches, China, 85. The terms "cash," "sycee," and "tael" were apparently foreign in
origin, perhaps corruptions of Chinese words.

11. Hosea Ballou Morse, *The Trade and Administration of China,* 143–70. Checkland,
"English Merchant House in China," 176–81. Griffin, *Clippers and Consuls,* 207–17.
J. R. T. Hughes, *Fluctuations in Trade, Industry, and Finance: A Study of British Economic
Development, 1850–1860,* 248–50. Lockwood, *Heard and Company,* 14–15, 22, 26–32.
Sheila Marriner, *Rathbones of Liverpool,* chaps. 12, 14. On smuggling see 29–31. On
currency see Lien-shing Yang, *Money and Credit in China: A Short History,* 246–49. The
average value of the Haekwan tael declined from 6/3 sterling in 1867 to 4/10¼ in 1897.
Chong-su See, *Foreign Trade of China,* 284, 390. If the pound sterling–dollar ratio is
figured at 5–1, that would place the American dollar value of the tael during the 1890s
at about one dollar. This figure tallies approximately with an estimate given in the *New
York Journal of Commerce,* n.d. *Public Opinion* 17 (August 16, 1894): 473. Some observers
then and since recognized that, offsetting its helpful effects, the opium trade prevented
Chinese customers from buying cotton goods and other foreign manufactures. Le Fevour,
Western Enterprise, 8–9.

Although the United States maintained a commissioner and consuls in China, distance, economy, frequent changes in administration, and general apathy reduced the value of these officials. Some commissioners were able men, but several were impetuous expansionists, and none stayed in office long enough to make much of a mark. They welcomed the support of the East India Squadron more than either the merchants or the missionaries, but they had little real control over it, and the records are full of squabbles between commissioners or consuls and commodores. As in the rest of the world, American consuls lagged behind their British counterparts in salary, training, staff, and equipment, although extraterritoriality imposed on them judicial functions almost unknown elsewhere in the consular service. Many of them doubled as employees of the Russells. Townsend Harris pointed out the easy familiarity existing between the merchant houses, the consular officials, the naval officers, and the opium smugglers as a conflict of interest and treaty violation, but Washington did little about the situation. (For that matter, the missionaries also violated the treaty by circulating freely about the countryside.)[12]

As Chinese officials came into more contact with foreigners after 1840, their attitudes shifted. When the emperor sent an official communication abroad to another monarch he was courteous, if distant, but his subordinates were apt to treat foreigners with some contempt. The general Chinese term for foreign relations was "barbarian affairs," which the British resented more strongly than the Americans. (Both groups, however, disliked being called "foreign devils.") The Chinese officials seem to have thought foreigners inscrutable, arrogant, crafty, and greedy—all terms the Westerners frequently applied to the Chinese too. Americans especially puzzled them; eventually they accepted that these foreigners were less a threat than Europeans but learned not to count on them for more than good intentions. Pressure from the hong merchants for good relations with Westerners had some influence on officials, but they kept up their reserve and developed a policy of playing Western groups off against each other.[13]

From 1850 to 1865 China was torn apart by a series of great uprisings. The most widespread of these was the Taiping Rebellion, which, though largely confined to the interior, caused uncertainty and important long-range changes in American trade along the coast. The rebellion was both an antidynastic movement of a type familiar in Chinese history and a syncretic, quasi-Christian religious crusade,

12. Griffin, *Clippers and Consuls*, 16. Tong, *United States Diplomacy*, 32–33, 63–64. Humphrey Marshall to Secretary of State, February 7, 8, 1853, nos. 3, 4, Diplomatic Despatches, China, 9. On the commissioners' work during this period see Dennett, *Americans in Eastern Asia*, chaps. 13–14, 15, 16–18; and Tong, *United States Diplomacy*, chaps. 7–17 and passim. The only American representative with previous experience in China was the missionary Dr. Peter Parker. The most detailed account of consular problems is Griffin, *Clippers and Consuls*, pts. 2, 3. On the role of the navy see Johnson, *Far China Station*, chaps. 1–4, and Hensen, *Commissioners and Commodores*, iv–v, 11–12, 57–60, 181–85. On governement contracts see Swisher, *China's Management*, 2–5. A brief discussion of procedure is on pp. 14–16.
13. Swisher, *China's Management*, chap. 3.

whose leader claimed to be a brother of Christ. Appearing in the back country of Canton, it overran much of southern China and the Yangtze Valley. Its troops briefly besieged Shanghai but never reached Peking. By the 1860s the rebellion was on the wane, and the Chinese government stamped it out with the aid of both American and British mercenary leaders.

During the early years of the uprising the apparently pro-Christian leanings of the Taipings and their startling successes produced much support among foreign missionaries, weary of the inefficiency and corruption of the imperial government; many Westerners indeed blamed the whole rebellion on missionary activity. It was even possible that the Western powers would support the rebels and enable them to overthrow the dynasty. In the United States the Pierce administration anticipated a burst of new trade with a reinvigorated China. By 1854, however, it was becoming clear that there was little to choose from between the two regimes as to efficiency or cooperation with foreigners, so most merchants and Western diplomats decided that a victory by the imperial government was vital to Chinese stability. The East India Squadron kept a close watch along the coast, although its ships did not have the speed or shallow draft to cope with pirates, and its commander, Commodore Matthew C. Perry, was more interested in his mission to open Japan (see chap. 7). (As a consequence, Perry and the current commissioner, Humphrey Marshall, both strong-minded men, were often at odds.)[14]

The Taiping Rebellion did not permanently decrease foreign trade, but it altered the Chinese environment. On the one hand, declining purchasing power reduced imports, especially of textiles, for a few years. On the other hand, the breakdown of internal communications benefited foreign coastal shipping by forcing trade onto the sea. In the long run the rebellion further weakened the central government, increased local autonomy and probably also corruption, decreased bureaucratic efficiency, and undermined and frustrated the class of traditionalist scholar-officials. The expenses of war required new taxes and a complete overhaul of the customs procedures. Emigration to foreign countries accelerated. After the devastation of the south, the Yangtze Valley dominated the Chinese economy more than ever, and Shanghai made its position as commercial capital of the country absolute and impregnable.[15]

More important to foreigners than any of these effects, the weakness of the imperial government in the late 1850s enabled the Western powers to revise the

14. On the international aspects of the Taiping uprising see Ssu-yü Teng, *The Taiping Rebellion and the Western Powers, a Comprehensive Survey;* and Masataka Banno, *China and the West, 1858–1861: The Origins of the Tsungli Yamen,* 42–53. For merchant reactions see Teng, "American-China Trade," 98–104. Curtis Henson, Jr., "The U.S. Navy and the Taiping Rebellion," 28–40. See also his *Commissioners and Commodores,* chaps. 7, 8. The other rebellions occurred well away from the coast and apparently did not affect Westerners greatly. Mary Clabaugh Wright, *The Last Stand of Chinese Conservatism: The T'ung-Chih Restoration, 1862–1874,* chap. 6.

15. Teng, "American-China Trade," 104–9. Lockwood, *Heard and Company,* 67–69, 79–80. Griffin, *Clippers and Consuls,* 252–53, 268–73. Marriner, *Rathbones of Liverpool,* 27–28. Teng, *Taiping Rebellion,* 390–407; Wright, *Last Stand of Chinese Conservatism,* 451–53.

treaties of 1842–1844 and obtain important new concessions which they had long desired. Early in the decade two successive commissioners had tried to obtain concessions, at first independently and then in cooperation with the British, but in vain. Between 1856 and 1860 Britain and France fought two short, devastating wars against China, and in 1860 they occupied Peking. Americans and Russians, both interested observers, maintained official neutrality but struck an occasional blow. The resulting Treaties of Tientsin and Aigun (1858) and Peking (1860) considerably curtailed Chinese sovereignty. The Empire ceded to Russia the left bank of the Amur River and the Ussuri region as far as Vladivostok. It opened eleven new ports to foreign trade and residence (including four in the Yangtze Valley) and allowed foreign navigation of the river to Hankow, six hundred miles from the sea. It also specified a maximum tariff of only 5 percent ad valorem on all imports, legalized the opium trade, and provided for a maritime customs service under a foreign inspector-general and staff. At the same time China accepted the conventional Western method of carrying on diplomatic relations by permitting foreign diplomats to live permanently at Peking. In a separate action of 1861 the government created a foreign office (Tsungli Yamen) with which these diplomats might deal.[16]

As in the 1840s, Americans benefited from the forcible advances of the Europeans. Three treaties signed by the United States at Tientsin in 1858 established commercial regulations, fixed maximum tariffs, and liquidated American claims respectively. Since the first two included most-favored-nation clauses, the United States obtained many benefits granted in the treaties with other nations. The opening of the Yangtze Valley not only extended the area of American trade but created a demand for more reliable transportation than that afforded by native craft. Thus it helped slow the decline of American shipping along the coast.

The first American treaty was unusual in containing a promise that the United States would "exert their good offices" to settle amiably a question between China and some third power "if any other nation shall act unjustly or oppressively." This was inserted by the Chinese commissioners, perhaps to split the Westerners, and thereafter the Chinese regarded it as a source of reserve strength. While it was consistent with unofficial American policy, one can scarcely believe that either the American negotiator, Minister William B. Reed, or Congress regarded it as a major, binding commitment of support. Nevertheless, it was invoked and carried out in several minor cases during the 1860s and 1870s and served as a precedent for the treaty of 1882 with which the United States "opened" Korea (see chapter 8).[17]

16. Dennett, *Americans in Eastern Asia*, chaps. 17, 18. Tong, *United States Diplomacy,* chaps. 8–13. The Americans took part in an attack on Canton in 1856 and played a small role in the allied attack on the Taku forts near Peking in 1859. Johnson, *Far China Station,* chap. 6. Henson, *Commissioners and Commodores,* chaps. 11–14. On the Chinese side of these events see Wright, *Last Stand of Chinese Conservatism,* chap. 23, and Banno, *China and the West.*

17. For the text of the three American treaties see Bevans, *Treaties,* vol. 6, 659–79. For a summary of American rights and duties in China under the treaty system see U.S., *Foreign*

Although the Taiping Rebellion and the Anglo-French wars of the late 1850s increased foreign influence in China, the disturbances they set in motion also hastened the decline of the "old China trade." Also the panic of 1857 injured the business of the American commission houses, and by the end of the decade British rivals were using their surplus exchange to crowd the American houses out of Boston, New York, and other East Coast markets. In 1858 Olyphant and Company and two other American groups failed, and although Olyphant later resumed operations, the episode suggested that the old commission trade had become inadequate to the new times, and that capital was moving into investments and other adjuncts to trade. Significantly, Augustine Heard and Company brought forth plans for telegraph and railroad concessions in 1859, and the following year it and Russell and Company even negotiated with the government to take over the entire transportation of tribute rice to Peking. None of these daring ventures led to any action.[18]

Another harbinger of the new promoting spirit was a development project in Taiwan, where two energetic Americans sought to monopolize the trade in camphor and other island products. Fearing British rivalry, they got the American commissioner, Dr. Peter Parker, to propose to Washington the outright annexation of the island. The Taiwan venture failed, but before the late 1850s it would probably not have been even attempted.[19]

During the early 1860s, while the British prepared to exploit their new treaty concessions and the Chinese government renewed its efforts against the Taiping rebels, American merchants were held back by their country's Civil War. Trade in American cotton textiles had begun to decline in the 1850s as a result of the Taiping Rebellion and the depression of 1857, and this decline continued in the 1860s after southern cotton stopped moving to New England mills, so England

---

Relations, 1863–64, 426–30. On the good offices provision see Tyler Dennett, "American 'Good Offices' in Asia," 1–2, 4–17. It was invoked in cases involving Tientsin (1859), Tsushima (1861), Sakhalin (1870), the *Maria Luz* coolie ship (1872), Taiwan (1874), the Ryukyu Islands (1879), and the Franco-Chinese War (1885). Concerning tariffs, the specific duties of the 1863 tariff were supposed to approximate 5 percent ad valorem, but falling prices had raised the de facto rates. Duties were changed to an ad valorem basis to prevent further shifts. Dennett, *Americans in Eastern Asia*, 323n.

18. Griffin, *Clippers and Consuls*, 243–44. Forbes, *Personal Reminiscences*, 360–61. Lockwood, *Heard and Company*, 59–60, 77–80, chap. 9. Although the government rice contract fell through, the Heard and Russell companies undertook a more speculative rice import venture and lost heavily. On the trade of one British firm in the United States see Marriner, *Rathbones of Liverpool*, 21–22, 62, 78–80, 84, 107–8, 154, 169, 170. Note that the term "old China trade" in its British context refers to the period before the Treaty of Nanking (1842). See, for example, Greenberg, *British Trade and the Opening of China*, especially Author's Preface, chap. 1.

19. Thomas R. Cox, "Harbingers of Change: American Merchants and the Formosa Annexation Scheme," 163–84. See also Harold D. Langley, "Gideon Nye and the Formosa Annexation Scheme," 399–420; and Sophia Su-fei Yen, *Taiwan in China's Foreign Relations, 1836–1874*, chap. 3.

had a virtual monopoly by the late 1860s. For a time American merchant ships remained as popular as ever in the coastal trade, but beginning about 1863 the depredations of the Confederate raider *Shenandoah* caused most merchants to transfer their cargoes to other flags.[20]

In the United States the principal evidence of continued interest in China during the Civil War was the quickened tempo of demands for a transpacific steamship line supported by government mail subsidies. The growing population of California and the beginning of serious construction work on a transcontinental railroad caused the riches of China to figure more and more prominently in press and Congress. Memorials from the chambers of commerce of New York and San Francisco in 1860 and 1861 reminded Congress that subsidized British mail steamers had squeezed their American rivals out of the transatlantic trade and predicted that increased trade with the Pacific would create new wealth for the nation.

In 1863 Russell and Company sent a steamer on an experimental voyage to San Francisco, but without a transcontinental railroad no steamship line could operate at a profit. An American merchant advocated a steamer subsidy of $300,000 to $400,000, which, he said, would yield tenfold returns once a railroad was completed. As has been seen, Congress did indeed authorize the desired concession in February 1865, just as the Civil War was drawing to a close, and in the following year it granted the concession to the Pacific Mail Steamship Company (see chapter 4).[21]

Through the Civil War, Secretary of State Seward laid plans for postwar commercial expansion in China. His conviction as to the importance of this trade was strengthened by continual dispatches and letters from his nephew, George F. Seward, consul general at Shanghai. The secretary believed in peaceful cooperation with European powers to support Chinese independence, stability, and receptiveness to Western civilization, including trade. He would threaten force if necessary to maintain this receptiveness but use it only as a last resort.[22] Secretary Seward found an excellent agent to carry out this policy in Anson Burlingame, a rising young Republican politician whom he sent out as minister

20. W. S. G. Smith to Lewis Cass, April 26, 1860, no. 15, U.S., *Consular Despatches, Shanghai*, 5. Samuel L. Gouverneur, Jr., to Secretary of State, April 5, 1861, no. 7. ibid., *Foochow*, 2. T. Hart Hyatt, Jr., to Seward, October 1, 1861, no. 6, ibid., *Amoy*, 2. U.S., *Commercial Relations, 1860–61,* 380–81; *1861–62,* 643; *1862–63,* 572, 579; *1863–64,* 1, 710, 713; *1864–65,* 545; *1865–66,* 474. *Merchants' Magazine* 49 (September 1863): 209–18. For a concise statement of Britain's advantageous position in the mid-1860s see R. Stanley McCordock, *British Far Eastern Policy, 1894–1900,* 64–65.

21. U.S., 36th Cong., 2d sess., *Senate Miscellaneous Document 10,* passim; 67th Cong., 2d sess., *Senate Miscellaneous Document 25,* passim. U.S., *Foreign Relations, 1864–65,* 2, 422–24. See also a speech by Senator Cornelius Cole of California on February 16, 1865, just before the passage of the authorization bill. U.S., 38th Cong., 2d sess., *Congressional Globe,* pt. 2, 830–31. The experiment by Russell and Company was handicapped by the use of an old, slow, unreliable ship. *Merchants' Magazine* 50 (March 1864): 165–66.

22. Paolino, *Foundations of the American Empire,* chap. 6, especially 145–46, 152–54. Dennett, *Americans in Eastern Asia,* 407–12. Van Deusen, *Seward,* 522–23.

in 1861. Talented, magnetic, and impulsive, Burlingame had a reputation for rather superficial eloquence, broad interests, and a capacity for intensive work in short bursts. He was to develop rapidly as a diplomat during his short life.[23]

When Burlingame arrived in China, he was welcomed by the legation secretary, S. Wells Williams, an eminent missionary and Sinologist who deserves some credit for the young minister's accomplishments. Burlingame's introduction to China was further eased by a brief show of pro-American spirit accompanying the military triumphs of Frederick Townsend Ward, a popular American soldier leading the imperial troops against the Taiping rebels. After Ward's death in 1862, his successor, Henry A. Burgevine, another American, proved a failure and was dismissed, but Burlingame rode out the resulting crisis.

The American minister recognized a congenial spirit in his British colleague, Sir Frederick Bruce, who was already working to mitigate his government's time-honored aggressive policies in China. The two worked out a "cooperative policy" intended to satisfy both traders and humanitarians, and after much discussion they brought the French and Russian representatives together to approve an idealized statement of this policy. While the Western nations would jealously guard their treaty rights to trade and live in the prescribed ports, it declared, they would not threaten the territorial integrity of China or the jurisdiction of the Chinese government and would not intervene in Chinese internal affairs except to uphold the treaties. Indeed, Burlingame was so scrupulously noninterventionist that he refused to use his official position in any way to aid an American seeking a gas lighting concession for Chinese cities.

The reassurance of Burlingame and Bruce and their personal diplomacy resulted in concessions by the imperial government facilitating Western trade. China opened Nanking to the foreigners and also the coasting trade. The head of the government, Prince Kung, appointed an American geologist, Raphael Pumpelly, to survey northern China's coal deposits and also ordered a Chinese translation of Henry Wheaton's classic *Elements of International Law* for reference in future negotiations. Burlingame also prevailed on the Chinese government to warn the *Alabama* and other Confederate warships away from the Chinese coast. With less success Burlingame also pressed the State Department for a larger legation in Peking and for salaried consuls in the principal ports.[24]

23. Dennett, *Americans in Eastern Asia*, 367–68. Frederick Wells Williams, *Anson Burlingame and the First Chinese Mission to Foreign Powers*, 3–14. Martin Robert Ring, "Anson Burlingame, S. Wells Williams and China, 1861–1870: A Great Era in Chinese-American Relations," 58–67. Obituary in *New York Times*, February 24, 1870. *Dictionary of American Biography*, vol. 2, 289–90. Burlingame was first named minister to Austria-Hungary, which rejected him for having earlier supported Louis Kossuth and Hungarian independence.

24. Wright, *Last Stand of Chinese Conservatism*, chap. 3. Samuel S. Kim, "America's First Minister to China: Anson Burlingame and the Tsungli Yamen," 98–100. Samuel S. Kim, "Burlingame and the Inauguration of the Cooperative Policy," 337–54. Williams, *Burlingame*, 20–72. Ring, "Burlingame, Williams and China," 80–102. Dennett, *Americans in Eastern Asia*, 373–77. David L. Anderson, *Imperialism and Idealism: American Diplomats*

As Seward realized better than his optimistic envoy, the cooperative agreement was only a declaration of principles by individuals, and there was usually more cooperation among Westerners than between Westerners and Chinese. Nevertheless, Burlingame soon had the opportunity to proclaim some of these principles to the world at large. When he resigned his post in 1867, he suggested half seriously that he head a mission for the Chinese government that would visit the nine treaty powers and establish relations beneficial to China. At the urging of British supporters of the cooperative policy, Prince Kung and the Tsungli Yamen made the appointment. Chinese officials and students were to accompany him, as well as minor British and French diplomats, probably to allay the suspicions of their governments. Chinese official reasoning behind the mission was never clear. As a later comment by the leading Chinese member of the mission suggested, the main purpose may have been to placate the Western nations and thereby delay, not encourage, Western penetration of China. Although Burlingame's actual instructions were limited and mainly procedural and his status vague, he assumed "the first Chinese rank" and stretched his authority to the limit.[25]

Somewhat to Burlingame's nervous relief, when the mission arrived at San Francisco on April 1, 1868, it received a tumultuous welcome. The city was already resentful about Oriental immigrants, but even racists could support increased trade with China. After a month the envoys sailed via Panama for New York and more crowds. From there they visited Washington and Boston and were even entertained at Seward's home in Auburn, New York. Everywhere banquets and tours of the local sights followed each other, and the guests met President Johnson and members of Congress. Whenever they stayed at a hotel, it flew the new yellow Chinese dragon flag. Again and again in his ceremonial speeches Burlingame emphasized the Chinese intent to abandon the old seclusion and formally enter the family of nations. Once, before the House of Representatives, he was so much carried away by his oratory that he declared China eager to receive

---

in China, 1861–1898, 54. Anderson feels that Seward, being much more willing than Burlingame to follow the European lead, did not espouse a truly cooperative policy. See also Burlingame to Seward, November 11, 1862, Seward papers. For a summary of Burlingame's accomplishments see New York Times, February 18, 1868. An important diplomatic achievement was his help in bringing about the withdrawal of the Lay-Osborne flotilla, a small private English fleet of steamers purchased unnecessarily by the imperial government for use against the rebels and constituting a focus for trouble. Stanley F. Wright, Hart and the Chinese Customs, 247–48. On Burlingame's recommendations to the State Department see his dispatch to Seward, September 16, 1862, no. 25, U.S., Diplomatic Despatches, China, 20. U.S., Foreign Relations, 1861–62, 905–7. On S. Wells Williams see Ring, "Burlingame, Williams and China," 1–5; and Dictionary of American Biography, 19, 290–91.

25. Williams, Burlingame, 73–112. Ring, "Burlingame, Williams and China," 217–31, 257. Anderson, Imperialism and Idealism, 40–42. Hosea Ballou Morse, International Relations of the Chinese Empire, vol. 2, 188–90. Wright, The Last Stand of Chinese Conservatism, 277–79. Knight Biggerstaff, "The Official Chinese Attitude toward the Burlingame Mission," 682–83. Knight Biggerstaff, "A Translation of Anson Burlingame's Instructions from the Chinese Foreign Office," 277–79. Wright, Hart and Chinese Customs, 367–68.

"the holy doctrines of our Christian faith"—an entirely misleading assertion that any Chinese member of the group could have contradicted.[26]

At a climactic banquet on June 23 in Delmonico's famous New York restaurant, Burlingame set forth the Chinese desire for equality and progress in lengthy, idealistic eloquence, seasoned with a few dashes of commercialism:

> [China] finds that she must come into relations with this civilization that is pressing up around her, and feeling that, she does not wait but comes out to you and extends to you her hand. . . . She tells you that she is willing . . . to buy of you, to sell to you, to help you strike off the shackles from trade. She invites your merchants, she invites your missionaries. . . .
>
> Let her alone; let her have her independence; let her develop herself in her own time and in her own way . . . and she will initiate a movement which will be felt in every workshop of the civilized world. . . . The imagination kindles at the future which may be, and which will be, if you will be fair and just to China.

In Washington Burlingame and Seward embodied these principles in eight additional articles to the Tientsin treaty of 1858 that contained important concessions by the United States. The new articles recognized China's unmolested dominion over her territory and its residents, except as limited by earlier treaties; they conceded her control over inland trade and navigations; and they recognized the government's right to make internal improvements at its own pace, unhurried by foreign dictation. Most controversial of all, while forbidding the coolie trade, they allowed voluntary, unrestricted migration between China and the United States.[27]

On September 19 the Burlingame mission arrived in London, preceded by sour comments in the British press to the effect that it was a tool for undermining British rights in China and establishing control by Washington and Peking. After considerable delay the foreign secretary, Lord Clarendon, put his views in a letter, less official than the American treaty and couched in more general terms but containing the significant statement that Britain had no desire by applying unfriendly pressure "to induce [China] to advance more rapidly in her intercourse with foreign nations than was consistent with safety and with due and reasonable regard for the feelings of her subjects." In the face of rising British opposition to this mild statement, his lordship soon backed away and called it an experimental policy. With encouragement from the new American secretary of state, Hamilton Fish, Burlingame led his cohorts onto

26. Williams, *Burlingame*, 113–60. Ring, "Burlingame, Williams and China," 247–49. Mary Roberts Coolidge, *Chinese Immigration*, 147n3. *New York Times*, May 18, 23, 30, June 6, 10, 24, August 23, September 10, 1868; Van Deusen, *Seward*, 324 (*Auburn* [New York] *Daily Advertiser*, August 4, 1868), clipping in Seward papers.

27. Most of Burlingame's Delmonico address is reprinted in Williams, *Burlingame*, 134–39. For the text of the added articles see Bevans, *Treaties*, vol. 6, 680–84. China also obtained the right to appoint consuls in the United States, and the citizens of each country received most-favored-nation rights of travel in the other country.

the continent for visits in France (where the government was bellicose and rude), Prussia (where Bismarck was friendly), Sweden, and Holland. Then they ventured into Russia, where Burlingame contracted pneumonia. On February 23, 1870, after a brief illness, he died. Leaderless, the little delegation wandered around Europe for several months and returned to China in October 1870, after an absence of nearly three years and a journey of forty-three thousand miles.[28]

Burlingame could not have picked a better moment during the 1860s for his arrival in the United States—midway between the inauguration of Far Eastern service by the Pacific Mail Steamship Company and the completion of the Union Pacific–Central Pacific Railroad. The *New York Herald* expounded on his eloquent idealism and practical business shrewdness in waves of wishful thinking. The Pacific Ocean would become "like a mere lake"; "the vast wealth of Asiatic commerce . . . [would] flow to and across America," and New York would become "the greatest city on the globe and the financial and intellectual centre of the world," eclipsing "all the cities of ancient or modern times." More soberly others saw in the mission the ratification for past American pacifism in the Far East, a challenge to such British imperialism as had already dominated India, and a promise of more just treatment for Chinese immigrants to the United States, valuable for their labor.[29] To be sure, Californians and even a few easterners suspected that China intended the mission to prepare the way for still more immigration or predicted that cheap Chinese labor would man factories at home and shrivel the vaunted Chinese market for American products.[30] Nevertheless, a survey of American press reactions to the Burlingame mission suggests that its principal economic influence in America was to strengthen the myth of the Golden East.

Historians disagree as to the effects of Burlingame's mission and treaty on conditions in China, and some regard the treaty primarily as a unilateral statement

28. Ring, "Burlingame, Williams and China," chap. 7. Williams, *Burlingame*, 161–272. Clarendon's letter, dated December 28, 1868, is reprinted on 173–76. Morse, *International Relations*, vol. 2, 197–99. Biggerstaff, "Official Chinese Attitude," 695–701. Ratifications were exchanged on November 23, 1869. For American reprints of British press comments see *New York Times*, September 14, October 28, 1868, and *New York Herald*, September 4, 1868. A few more perceptive British deplored their government's cold reception of a group representing one-third of mankind, whereas any German princeling would have been acclaimed. *London Times*, October 16, 1868. Fish to Burlingame, September 17, 1869, in Ring, "Burlingame, Williams and China," 316. George Bancroft to Fish, March 3, 1870, no. 73, U.S., Diplomatic Despatches, Germany (Prussia), 16.

29. *New York Herald*, May 18, 1868, June 6, March 30, 1869. For more modest predictions emphasizing the new communications routes see *New York Herald*, May 27, 1868; *Merchants' Magazine* 59 (July 1868): 29–36; and *Commercial and Financial Chronicle* 6 (June 20, 1868): 775–77; 7 (July 4): 6–7. One editorial declared that the emergence of China from isolation was even more important than the transcontinental railroad for developing trade. *New York Times*, June 27, 1868; *New York Tribune*, May 19, August 25, 1868; *Chicago Tribune*, June 28, 1868.

30. *New York Times*, June 7, November 28, 1868.

of American policy on the order of the later Hay "open door" notes.[31] Certainly neither mission nor treaty improved relations between foreigners in China and the Chinese government. Both American and British merchants resented Burlingame's "wilful misrepresentations and empty declamation," imputing to them a desire to tyrannize China and enable the Chinese to hold off internal improvements indefinitely or even resume their old exclusionism. The head of Russell and Company wrote to the *Nation* that Burlingame's "system of friendly advice and help" had been an accepted policy years before his arrival and that he was merely an apologist for "a small clique of mandarins." J. Ross Browne, Burlingame's successor as minister to China, led the attack on the treaty despite instructions from Washington supporting Burlingame and had to be recalled. As for the British, they regarded Clarendon's declaration as a betrayal.[32]

The initial reaction of Chinese officials to the reception of the Burlingame mission abroad and especially to the Burlingame treaty was confused, for they had not expected their envoy to go so far. Even while the mission was under way, representatives of the Chinese and British governments were meeting to discuss revision of the 1858 treaties. During this discussion the Tsungli Yamen sent a secret circular to seventeen high Chinese officials seeking their opinion on closer diplomatic relations with foreigners, expansion of foreign missionary activities, and economic problems such as foreign-built telegraph and railroad lines, foreign trade outside the treaty ports, the use of steamships on inland waterways, and foreign participation in the salt trade and coal mining.

With few exceptions the officials replied emphatically that since the foreigners enjoyed extraterritoriality and special tax privileges, they must be restricted to

31. Mayo Smith and Morse regard the mission and treaty as largely ineffective. Williams thinks both essentially successful. Dennett sees in the mission short-term effects such as the postponement of treaty revision and a truce in foreign attacks on China. Among modern writers, Hunt thinks the mission and treaty convinced the Chinese that they needed diplomatic representation in America, the beginning of a long-range and more profound change in Chinese attitude. Anderson sees in the treaty the first equal recognition of Chinese sovereignty and responsibility. Mayo Smith, "Emigration and Immigration," as quoted in Williams, *Burlingame*, 159–60, 170–72. Morse, *International Relations*, 193–203. Dennett, *Americans in Eastern Asia*, 388–89. Hunt, *Special Relationship*, 98. Anderson, *Imperialism and Idealism*, 44–45.

32. Williams, *Burlingame*, 141–44. *Nation* 10 (January 6, 1870): 9–10. Nathan A. Pelcovits, *Old China Hands and the Foreign Office*, chap. 2. The reaction was all the more intense because of a depression in trade from 1865–1867. For examples of wholly disapproving and sympathetic British comment on the policies represented by Burlingame and Clarendon see, respectively, *Westminster Review* 93 (January 1870): 83–97; and *Broadway*, n.s., 1 (December 1868): 346–52. F. F. Low to J. C. B. Davis, March 25, 1871, Davis papers, 2023–24ff. For a sample from a disapproving American merchant see *Nation* 9 (July 29, 1869): 89–91. On Browne's opposition see Paul Hibbert Clyde, "The China Policy of J. Ross Browne, American Minister at Peking, 1868–1869," 317–19; Ring, "Burlingame, Williams, and China," chap. 6. George F. Seward to J. Ross Browne, January 22, 1869, copy in Seward papers. Burlingame to Davis, November 25, 1869, Davis papers, 5, 1038–45 ff. *New York Times*, December 14, 1869. Burlingame also warned the French against armed intervention. Bancroft to Davis, February 16, 1870, Davis papers, 5, 1190 ff.

treaty ports, where their activities could be supervised. Two or three farsighted individuals saw some value in foreign technological contributions. One of these, Tseng Kuo-fan, was willing to experiment with modernized coal mines, but he opposed steamboats and railroads because they would throw Chinese laborers out of work. When his letter leaked into the press, it seemed to bear out the worst fears of those merchants who opposed Burlingame's conciliatory policy. The ambivalent attitude of even progressive Chinese toward modern improvements has puzzled historians. One explanation, which may be the most convincing of the lot, holds that it represented a compromise between extreme reactions and was essentially defensive and temporizing.[33]

After the departure of Bruce and Burlingame and the death of Clarendon, the cooperative policy lost some of its force. Bruce's successor, Sir Rutherford Alcock, negotiated a convention in 1869 embodying the spirit of the Clarendon declaration that obtained a few concessions for each side, but British merchants were so discontented that London withheld approval. When a British consular official was murdered on a western exploring trip in 1875, however, London acted decisively. After more negotiations, Britain obtained the Chefoo convention of 1876, which opened four more coastal ports, allowed steamers to call at many points on the lower Yangtze, regularized the transit tax, and laid down clear specifications about the trial of mixed cases under extraterritoriality. Again the British merchants felt that China had not conceded enough, and their influence prevented ratification of the convention for a decade. Only gradually did the diehards become reconciled to London's policy of peacefully encouraging Chinese stability without colonial control as in India.[34]

At this time both French and Germans were content to follow the British lead, but during the late 1870s they began to push for more influence. In 1875

33. S. Wells Williams to Fish, October 1, 1859, no. 65, U.S., Diplomatic Despatches, China, 27. G. F. Seward to W. H. Seward, January 19, 1869, no. 335, U.S., Consular Despatches, Shanghai, 10. Wright, *Hart and Chinese Customs*, 373. Knight Biggerstaff, "The Secret Correspondence of 1867–1868: Views of Leading Chinese Statesmen Regarding the Further Opening of China to Western Influence," 122–36. Willams was more sympathetic with Tseng's views than was Browne. U.S., *Foreign Relations, 1867–68*, 516–18. Browne to W. H. Seward, November 25, December 5, 1868, nos. 7, 11, U.S., Diplomatic Despatches, China, 25. For modern discussions of the Chinese reaction, citing contradictory explanations, see Wright, *Last Stand of Chinese Conservatism*, chap. 8; and Sandra Sturdevant, "Imperialism, Sovereignty, and Self-Strengthening: A Reassessment of the 1870s."

34. Pelcovits, *Old China Hands*, chap. 3, 125–30. Stanley F. Wright, *China's Struggle for Tariff Autonomy, 1843–1938*, 332–88. Wright, *Hart and Chinese Customs*, 405–11. Morse, *International Relations*, chaps. 10, 14. Arthur John Sargent, *Anglo-Chinese Commerce and Diplomacy (Mainly in the Nineteenth Century)*, 193–96, 229. Young, *British Policy in China*, 4–7. Wright, *Last Stand of Chinese Conservatism*, 279–95. Historians differ as to the degree of identity between the views of British merchants and the Foreign Office. *Pacific Historical Review* 12 (February 1949): 145–46. *Nation* 10 (January 6, 1870): 9–10. In 1870 the U.S. minister helped to preserve the peace between France and China after a massacre of French missionaries at Tientsin that might have been used as revenge for concessions. Paul Hibbert Clyde, "Frederick F. Low and the Tientsin Massacre," 100–108. Frederick F. Low to Fish, June 28, 1870, Fish papers, 70. (This is not cited in the Clyde article.)

the forceful Max von Brandt became German minister to China. While always maintaining his friendship for China, he lost no opportunity to expand German influences: a steamship line, a bank, publicity on China for German industrialists, and above all blustering and blackmailing of Chinese officials. Germany would have welcomed more British support; unfortunately Von Brandt and the British minister detested each other.[35]

The British policy did not reject Burlingame's goals of cooperation and conciliation outright but tried to reconcile these goals with British interests. A symbol of the policy was Sir Robert Hart, the inspector general of the Chinese Imperial Customs Service. In 1854 the three treaty consuls and the chief customs official at Shanghai overhauled the chaotic duty-collecting system, shot through with corruption. Nine years later, after several interim arrangements, Hart, able, energetic, and fluent in Chinese, was appointed inspector general at the age of twenty-eight. He held the post for forty-six years and died just three weeks before the Chinese revolution of 1911. During his tenure he built up an elaborate centralized fiscal organization of Westerners and Chinese, collected duties honestly and rigorously (to the chagrin of many merchants), and issued reasonably reliable statistics. He also completed charting the coast, established a postal system, started schools, and advised the Chinese government on economic matters. Through all these activities he probably helped postpone its downfall. The British officials in the service always outnumbered the Americans by six or eight to one despite American complaints, in part because Hart could not find enough properly qualified Americans who could speak Chinese.[36]

On the imperial side the best example of adherence to cooperation and conciliation for reasons of self-interest was Li Hung-chang, the dominant force behind the foreign policy of the Chinese Empire. Born of an upper-class family and educated as an intellectual, he became an army officer during the Taiping Rebellion and played a major role in its final suppression. He won the patronage

---

35. On German activities and policies see John E. Schrecker, *Imperialism and Chinese Nationalism: Germany in Shantung,* 566, 80–11; and Helmuth Stoecker, "Germany and China, 1861–94." Bismarck did not always approve Von Brandt's aggressive tactics and in 1883 briefly recalled him. The chancellor wanted to retain China's friendship, but he also encouraged French and Russian expansion in the Far East to draw them away from Europe.

36. Wright, *Hart and Chinese Customs,* especially chaps. 4, 6, and pp. 853–65. Jonathan Spence, *To Change China: Western Advisers in China, 1620–1960,* 112–28. Morse, *International Relations,* vol. 2, chap. 2. Morse, *Trade and Administration,* chap. 12, especially 390–91. Hsiao, *China's Foreign Trade Statistics,* 3–7. Hart was influential in the Tsungli Yamen's decision to send out the Burlingame mission. Ring, "Burlingame, Williams and China," 217–18. On the American desire for more representation in the Imperial Customs Service see Wright, *China's Struggle,* 155–56. In 1868 there were 39 British and 6 Americans out of a total of 1,063 in the service. In 1895 the figures were 439, 52, and 4,229 respectively. Richard J. Hinton, "A Talk with Mr. Burlingame about China," 622, 623. Wright, *Hart and Chinese Customs,* 891–900. A. B. Wyckoff to John Russell Young, April 25, 1883, John Russell Young papers, 15. Minister Charles Denby had nothing but praise for Hart's administration. Denby to Blaine, April 9, 1890, no. 1092, U.S., Diplomatic Despatches, China, 87.

of important political figures, especially the Dowager Empress Ts'u-hsi, and Tseng Kuo-fan, the dominant leader at the end of the Taiping Rebellion. After filling a number of high offices, Li became at last governor-general of Chihli, the metropolitan province. He held this post from 1870 to the mid-1890s and served as de facto foreign and defense minister, for his customary residence, Tientsin, lay on the main route to Peking, and nearly every official visitor stopped to consult him. Also, as government officials and foreign diplomats alike grew weary of the Tsungli Yamen's inefficiency, they bypassed it whenever they could, and the Tsungli Yamen itself kept closely in touch with him.

Li early recognized the value of Western technology and intended eventually to use it in rolling back foreign domination, but until China could adopt it and grow strong, weakness compelled a defensive policy ("self-strengthening"). He was one of the few among the seventeen secret correspondents of the foreign office, mentioned above, who urged economic concessions to the Westerners. Alarmed at Japanese and Russian militarization, he took the lead in rearming China after the Taiping Rebellion and urged his government to follow Japan in imitating Western nations. To that end he sought to establish a system combining government supervision and merchant management (Kwan-tu-shang-pan) through which the capital of Chinese compradores and merchants might strengthen the Chinese economy—often a hard task because of Chinese conservatism. He invested his own funds in Western-style enterprises, apparently with great success, and even cooperated with such Western organizations as Jardine, Matheson and Company.

Li gave Americans the impression of favoring them above the Europeans, because, he said, the United States had no territorial ambitions in China. Beginning in 1872, he and Tseng Kuo-fan sent several groups of Chinese boys to be educated in the United States, only to discover that they would not concentrate on technology and were reluctant to return home. Li was an imposing man, more than six feet tall. American visitors often commented on his gentle, sympathetic nature, but actually he was a tough, shrewd politician, ever watchful against his many enemies among the court conservatives and skeptical about the promises of glib foreigners. Sir Robert Hart, however, thought him overrated—too optimistic and full of his own importance—and Minister Charles Denby privately criticized his arrogance and ignorance of other governments.[37]

---

37. Samuel C. Chu and Kwang-ching Liu, eds., *Li Hung-chang and China's Early Modernization*. For an overall assessment of Li see 265–78. S. M. Meng, *The Tsungli Yamen: Its Origins and Functions*, 58–60. Hunt, *Special Relationship*, 60, 115–17. Kwang-ching Liu, "Li Hung-chang in Chihli: The Emergence of a Policy, 1870–1875." For examples of Li's pro-Western writings, see Ssu-yü Teng and John K. Fairbank, *China's Response to the West, a Documentary Survey, 1837–1923*, 70–72, 74–76. On Kuan-tu shang-pan, see LeFevour, *Western Enterprise*, 40–41, 58–59, chap. 4. James Harrison Wilson, *China: Travels and Investigations in the 'Middle Kingdom,' a Study of Its Civilization and Possibilities, with a Glance at Japan*, 109–16; and John Russell Young, *Men and Memories: Personal Reminiscences*, 303–25. Less favorable is the description of Robert W. Shufeldt. Quoted in Drake, *Empire of the Seas*, 262. Fairbank et al., *I. G. in Peking*, vol. 1, 10; vol. 2, 872, 1070, 1103. Denby to Secretary of State, November 3, 1892,

* * *

For many years after the Burlingame mission and treaty the U.S. government and its representatives had to determine how much they would cooperate with European nations having rights in China and how much conciliation they would use in dealing with the Chinese government. Even before it was known that China would ratify the Burlingame treaty, Hamilton Fish declared that the Grant administration would base its policy on recognition of Chinese sovereignty, limited only by treaties, and would refuse to join the European powers in aggressive measures inconsistent with the behavior of "civilization nations." Fish later muffled this echo of Burlingame.

In 1880 the Hayes administration sent out a special commission under James B. Angell, which signed a new commercial treaty with China as part of controversial negotiations on Chinese immigration (to be discussed later). In this treaty the United States agreed to forbid the opium trade, by now insignificant, and received in return a guarantee that American ships or trade would not be assessed taxes or dues higher than those of any other nation or of China itself. (As with the Burlingame treaty, British observers suspected a secret deal.) This treaty, however, did not settle the more general question, and as late as 1883 the American minister had to ask the State Department whether the United States intended to join the other Western powers in a strong policy or break with them and "look with humanity upon China."[38]

Although cable communications with Peking via London became available about 1870, they were so expensive that the State Department held to its traditional slow, general instructions, allowing much leeway to American ministers in China. Even after communications became swifter in the 1890s, there remained many gaps between the policies of the department and those of the legation at Peking. During the decade or so after Burlingame American ministers in China were generally able, especially in reporting about the complexities of Chinese government and society. Among them Frederick F. Low and Benjamin P. Avery tended to lean toward Burlingame's more sympathetic policy, while J. Ross Browne and George F. Seward showed more mistrust of Chi-

---

no. 1600, U.S., Diplomatic Despatches, China, 92. Like some other Chinese, Li admired authoritarianism and efficiency and for a time sought an entente with Germany. Schrecker, *Imperialism and Chinese Nationalism,* 608. Li combined Western and traditional Chinese practices in managing the enterprises he controlled. Wellington K. K. Chan, "Government, Merchants, and Industry to 1911," 422–25. Some of these sources examine the subject of Li's corruption without coming to a firm conclusion.

38. Kwang-ching Liu, "America and China: The Late Nineteenth Century," 78–79. Fish's general policy statement was made in an informative dispatch to George Bancroft, the American minister to Prussia. U.S., *Foreign Relations, 1869–70,* 304–7. See also Fish's report of discussions with Grant and the cabinet. Fish diary, November 3, 1869; November 1, 1870, Fish papers, box 314, 316. For the text of the commercial treaty of 1880 see Bevans, *Treaties,* vol. 6, 688–90. For British suspicions see John A. Bingham to William M. Evarts, January 21, 1881, no. 1244, U.S., Diplomatic Despatches, Japan, 43. U.S., *Foreign Relations, 1883,* 192–93. Anderson, *Imperialism and Idealism,* 13, 168–69, chaps. 3–5.

nese officials. Those who reported on the Alcock and Chefoo conventions approved them.[39]

Perhaps more important in the long run to American economic interests than any diplomat was an unofficial American visitor, former president Ulysses S. Grant, who spent more than a month in China during 1879, near the end of a world tour he took after leaving the White House. Grant and Li Hung-chang were greatly impressed with each other, and Li naturally welcomed Grant's advice that the building of railroads and other public works would enrich and strengthen China and enable her better to resist European encroachments. At home Grant favored relaxing treaty restrictions on China. His influence on the Hayes administration is unclear, but Secretary Evarts's instructions to Commissioner Angell on extraterritoriality moderated the American position, and the 1880 commercial treaty contained a remarkably generous provision for the joint settlement of American-Chinese commercial disputes. Perhaps, as some have suggested, Grant would have redirected American Far Eastern policy had he been reelected president in 1880.[40]

The two most influential American ministers to China between Burlingame and the Spanish-American War were John Russell Young and Charles Denby, who served consecutively from 1882 to 1898. Their significance was doubtless partly due to China's increasingly complex international relations, which will be discussed in the next chapters. The two men played important roles in Chinese crises with France (1884–1885) and Japan (1894–1895). Young was a journalist who had accompanied Grant on his world tour and become his friend. He continued Grant's emphasis on Chinese independence from European influence (an emphasis he may have inspired himself), and to that end he developed a personal relationship with Li Hung-chang and urged on him modernization and economic contacts with the United States.[41] Denby, a onetime railroad lawyer and

39. Liu, "America and China," 78–87. Clyde, "China Policy of J. Ross Browne," 316–23. Clyde, "Low and the Tientsin Massacre," 100–108. Paul Hibbert Clyde, "Attitudes and Policies of George F. Seward, American Minister at Peking, 1876–1880: Some Phases of the Co-operative Policy," 387–88. William Hubert Morken, "America Looks West: The Search for a China Policy, 1876–1885," chap. 1. J. Ross Browne to Seward, November 25, 1868, no. 7; Low to Fish, May 10, 1870, no. 4, U.S., Diplomatic Despatches, China, 25, 28. G. F. Seward to Davis, February 16, 1870, no. 4, U.S., Consular Despatches, Shanghai, 11. U.S., Foreign Relations, 1870–71, 77–87. U.S., Commercial Relations, 1873–74, 205–8.

40. L. T. Remlap [Palmer], General U. S. Grant's Tour around the World, chap. 17. Young, Men and Memories, 317–23. Ulysses S. Grant to Li-Hung-chang, April 1, 1881, copy in Young papers. Morken, "America Looks West," 51–53. William M. Evarts to James B. Angell, June 7, 1880, no. 1, U.S., Diplomatic Instructions, China, 3, 113–28. Bevans, Treaties, 688–90. For press criticism of extraterritoriality see New York Herald, April 30, 1881. Secretary Seward also visited China in 1870 as part of a world tour after retirement but seems not to have produced much effect. Olive Risley Seward, ed., William H. Seward's Travels around the World, 168–70. Low to Fish, December 12, 1870, Fish papers, 74, 161–68 ff.

41. Pletcher, Awkward Years, chap. 11, especially 198–99; and Tyler Dennett, "American Choices in the Far East in 1882," 84–86. Young to Frelinghuysen, October 8, 1883, no. 267, confidential, U.S., Diplomatic Despatches, China, 66.

director, had many ties with American business, which favored his appointment, and he survived through three administrations. He believed implicitly in the great future of the Chinese market, and perhaps no one in the entire diplomatic service worked harder to further American trade and investments, although he professed to disdain the smooth-talking, "grafting" type of promoter. Handsome and charming, he was also vain and loved to be addressed as "colonel" (his Civil War rank). A more serious shortcoming, he spoke no Chinese, and although he traveled widely about China, he never acquired much feeling or respect for its people.[42]

American consuls in China were among the most miscellaneous groups of representatives ever maintained abroad by a major power. Many of them treated the Chinese with brusqueness and arrogance, but only a few left any mark. George F. Seward, consul general at Shanghai, was promoted to the Peking legation in the late 1870s. O. N. Denny, consul at Tientsin and then consul general at Shanghai, became the special friend of Viceroy Li, but when he left the service for special advisory duties in Korea, he broke with Li's pro-Chinese faction there. William N. Pethick, a very able vice consul at Tientsin with long experience in China, could not obtain promotion and resigned in about 1890 to become the confidential secretary of Li Hung-chang. This was a highly important position in which during the late 1880s and 1890s he served as intermediary between some American promoters and the Chinese government. More flamboyant than any of these was Charles W. LeGendre, consul at Amoy, who became interested in the resources of Taiwan, part of his consular district. In 1867 he led an expedition there to investigate an American shipwreck and negotiate an agreement with a native leader. After China had refused to establish a naval base on the island, LeGendre left the American consular service and led a punitive expedition for Japan against the natives. Later he ended his career as adviser in Korea, succeeding Denny.[43]

42. Views of Denby differ widely. See, for example, Healy, *U.S. Expansionism*, 178–80; Paul A. Varg, *Open Door Diplomat: The Life of W. W. Rockhill*, 12–13; and Marilyn Blatt Young, *The Rhetoric of Empire: American China Policy, 1895–1901*, 20–21. John William Cassey, "The Mission of Charles Denby and International Rivalries in the Far East: 1885–1898," vi. Charles Denby, *China and Her People: Being the Observations, Reminiscences, and Conclusions of an American Diplomat*, 1, 91. Tansill, *Foreign Policy of Bayard*, 422. Since Denby assiduously defended the rights of American missionaries, they thought well of him, and a group petitioned President Harrison to keep him at his post. *Nation* 52 (May 21, 1891): 413.

43. On Denny see Robert R. Swartout, Jr., *Mandarins, Gunboats, and Power Politics: Owen Nickerson Denny and the International Rivalries in Korea*, chap. 1 and passim. Harold J. Noble, "The United States and Sino-Korean Relations, 1885–87," 296; and Young to Thomas F. Bayard, November 4, 1886, Bayard papers, 97, 58–63 ff. On Pethick see James Harrison Wilson to Bayard, November 4, 1886, Bayard papers, and Young, *Rhetoric of Empire*, 21, 27, 52, 59, 251, 252. On LeGendre see *Dictionary of American Biography*, 6, 145–46; and Leonard H. D. Gordon, "Charles LeGendre: A Heroic Civil War Colonel Turned Adventurer in Taiwan," 65–76. For cases of consular arrogance see Robert McClellan, Jr., *The Heathen Chinee: A Study of American Attitudes toward China, 1890–1905*, 219–20.

It is remarkable that the United States got even reasonably effective service from its inadequate diplomatic and consular staffs in China, miserably neglected by a parsimonious, semi-isolationist Congress. For many years after S. Wells Williams retired, the legation at Peking had one secretary-interpreter, Chester Holcombe (like Williams a former missionary), the only officer fluent in Chinese. But for him the minister would have had to communicate with the Tsungli Yamen through the British or French legation. (Unfortunately, Li Hung-chang mistrusted him.) Conditions in even important consulates were often worse. Not a single one had a well-qualified interpreter. In 1871 a newly arrived consul at Tientsin found a wretched office with no record books or furniture, letters and dispatches "filed" in a coarse bag, most of the Chinese correspondence lost, and none of it translated. In 1865 the highest consular salaries (Shanghai and Canton) were four thousand dollars, unchanged for more than a decade. The consuls at six other posts received only a portion of fees charged, with the result that all of them were merchants or missionaries, although the Chinese made their dislike of the combined functions quite obvious. At four ports in the mid-1870s British or German officials had to represent American interests.[44]

As trade and American residents increased, the consular duties became more complicated and demanding. In the mid-1880s the consul general at Shanghai administered the whole American consular service in China, took part with other nations' consuls in the municipal government of the large foreign settlements, maintained a court to try Americans, managed a jail and a post office, handled cases of probate and divorce, and supervised American shipping. All other consuls held court from time to time in an improvised system with many abuses. Eventually appellate jurisdiction was given to California judges for cases arising in China, but reformers demanded in vain an independent court system for American residents.[45]

44. Hunt, *Special Relationship*, 169, 360n48. Morken, "America Looks West," 1, 47–50. Young to Frelinghuysen, November 28, 1884, no. 561, U.S., Diplomatic Despatches, China, 73. On the Tientsin consulate see Eli T. Sheppard to Fish, December 4, 1871; Sheppard to Charles Hale, October 16, 1872, nos. 8, 22, U.S., Consular Despatches, Tientsin, 1. On salaries and other conditions see U.S., *Foreign Relations, 1865–66*, 476–79, 482–84. F. D. Cheshire to Alvey A. Adee, November 2, 1882, no. 368, U.S., Consular Despatches, Shanghai, 33. The consul at Newchwang, in Manchuria, had no missionaries for translating, so he was obliged to have all his papers read by the British minister. Francis P. Knight to W. H. Seward, September 10, 1868, no. 5, U.S., Consular Despatches, Newchwang, 1.

45. Hinckley, *Consular Jurisdiction*, 58–63. For a summary of the duties of the consul general at Shanghai see U.S., 48th Cong., 1st sess., *House Executive Document 146*, 4. David H. Bailey to Charles Payson, January 14, 1880, no. 87, U.S., Consular Despatches, Shanghai, 29. The consul general at Shanghai reported that when the mails arrived, he had to close the doors of the consulate and set the entire staff to sorting mail for the other posts. O. N. Denny to Davis, February 13, 1882, no. 271, ibid., Shanghai, 33. For criticism of the consular court system see J. J. Henderson to Benjamin P. Avery, August 30, 1875, enclosed in Henderson to John L. Cadwalader, August 30, no. 81, U.S., Consular Despatches, Amoy, 7. U.S., 47th Cong., 1st sess., *Senate Executive Document 21*, passim; and *Senate Miscellaneous Document 89*, 13–14.

Criticism of this rickety organization was plentiful throughout the period. At the end of his world tour Grant protested so tellingly that Evarts promptly replaced seven consular officials. A member of Angell's 1880 commission, William H. Trescot, who was an experienced diplomat, drew up a long memorandum advocating a complete overhaul of the United States' Far Eastern policy, beginning with the consular system and the courts. President Garfield sent Trescot's memorandum to the Senate with Secretary Blaine's recommendations. After Garfield's assassination stimulated civil service reform, Secretary Frelinghuysen sent Congress a further bill for reform of consular courts, but some congressmen thought this smacked of colonialism. The secretary instructed Minister Young to tour the consulates and gather further information for a reform bill, but this was delayed, and Frelinghuysen's further efforts were in vain. The Pendleton Act, implementing civil service reform, did not affect the foreign service. In 1896, when twenty-four Chinese ports were open to trade, the United States maintained only eight salaried consuls in China, Britain thirty, and the total amounts spent on the two consular services were $40,000 and $200,000 respectively. The American consular service was not reformed until after 1900, and a professional American foreign service did not appear in China until 1924.[46]

Nor did the American Navy make a better showing. After its effectiveness under Perry in the early 1850s, it faded, and the East India Squadron disappeared altogether during the Civil War. Restored in 1865, it comprised five or six old gunboats in bad repair, manned by poorly disciplined crews, with perhaps one or two presentable warships. It sent only three ships up the Yangtze River to Hankow between 1873 and 1890. During this time it carried most passengers and dispatches along the coast in two old sidewheel steamers useful on rivers but not intended for ocean travel. Trescot called them death-traps, and indeed in 1883 one of them sank, killing eleven of the crew. The other was still in service during the 1890s. This sort of navy was adequate for "showing the flag" to impress weaker natives or for cooperating with European detachments so long as these were also concerned with keeping open trade lanes and not with conquering colonies.[47]

46. Morken, "America Looks West," 52–53, 132–52. *American Exporter* 5 (January 1880): 12, 16. W. H. T. [William H. Trescot], "American Interest in China, Japan, and Siam, May 1 [1881]," no. 61½. U.S., Reports of the Diplomatic Service, W. Jernigan to Edwin F. Uhl, January 16, 1896, no. 142, U.S., Consular Despatches, Shanghai, 43. John Fowler to Uhl, February 12, March 10, 1896, nos. 180, 183, ibid., Ningpo, 7. For reports on the consular service in China at the end of the century see Denby, *China and Her People*, 2, chap. 15; and Edward Bedloe to William E. Day, September 14, 1898, no. 40, U.S., Diplomatic Despatches, China, 105. At its best the Chinese foreign service was well above the American average. For a sketch of Wu T'ing-fang, Chinese minister to the United States in the late 1890s, see Michael H. Hunt, *Frontier Defense and the Open Door: Manchuria in Chinese-American Relations, 1895–1911*, 39–40.

47. A good idea of the squadron's effectiveness may be had in Johnson, *Far Eastern Squadron*, chaps. 9–15. Liu, "America and China," 51. E. Mowbray Tate, "U.S. Gunboats on the Yangtze: Historical and Political Aspects, 1842–1922," 126–27. Kenneth J. Hagan, *American Gunboat Diplomacy and the Old Navy, 1877–1889*, 9–10. *New York Herald*, February 22, 1883.

* * *

American merchants in China needed more help than these government representatives could provide, for, as in the case of both Latin America and the Pacific islands, they faced many obstacles to trade caused by distance from home and local conditions. The first was ocean transportation. When the Suez Canal was opened in 1869, almost no American sailing vessels used it because of prevalent calms on the Red Sea. Instead a British outfit, the Ocean Steamship Company, seized the initiative in developing speedy, economical steamers that quickly stole the tea trade from rivals. Soon, of course, other steam lines caught up—the older Peninsular and Oriental, the French Messageries Maritimes, several British lines new to the China trade, and finally in 1886 North German Lloyd. As competition cut into profits, in 1879 the principal steamship companies formed a "conference" to control rates and practices. In 1886 the American consul at Canton complained that monopolists made their customers boycott nonconference carriers and thereby condemned even the fastest American sailing ships to wait weeks or months in port for cargoes at miserably low rates or enter the coasting trade. Before long the conference was offering a cut rate between Hong Kong and New York via Suez to squeeze out independent steamers.[48]

This was the situation the Pacific Mail Steamship Company faced during the 1870s and 1880s. In 1870, three years after it inaugurated transpacific service, it was offering monthly sailings between San Francisco and Hong Kong, with a branch line to Yokohama and Shanghai and prompt railroad connections at San Francisco for the East Coast. The company expected to divert much of the Suez trade to the United States, but its hopes of rapid progress were dashed by its internal management problems (see chapter 4). Beginning in the late 1870s the government's restrictions on immigration of Chinese laborers cut into a lucrative eastbound traffic. Nevertheless, during the 1870s and 1880s the Pacific Mail and its competitor (later collaborator), the Occidental and Oriental Steamship Company, together provided fortnightly service to Japan and China, carrying out a variety of American products and bringing back mostly tea and silk.[49]

48. Francis E. Hyde, *Far Eastern Trade, 1860–1914*, chap. 2. U.S., *Commercial Relations, 1884–85*, 932–35. U.S., *Consular Reports* 3 (January 1881): 83–85. Charles Seymour to James D. Porter, February 5, 1886, no. 96, U.S., Consular Despatches, Canton, 10. The new route and the steamships posed problems for British merchants as well. Marriner, *Rathbones of Liverpool*, 112–13. The German government did not begin to subsidize steamers to China until 1885, but within a decade German shipping stood second to British. Schrecker, *Imperialism and Chinese Nationalism*, 8–9. J. D. Kennedy to Porter, September 10, 1886, no. 28, U.S., Consular Despatches, Shanghai, 37. U.S., *Consular Reports* 68 (September 1886): 631–32; 112 (January 1890): 44–46. Reports of special cut rates from New York continued to surface in the 1890s. *Bradstreet's* 24 (September 12, 1896): 581–82.

49. *Commercial and Financial Chronicle* 10 (May 28, 1870): 682–83; 12 (February 18, 1871): 197–98; 17 (May 9, 1874): 480–81. *New York Times*, July 8, 1877. Some American exports were staples (e.g., flour, provisions, beef, lumber, clocks, and leather), others specialties in response to Chinese demand (e.g., mercury, dried fish, silver dollars, ginseng, and seaweed).

Two scheduled ships a month, however, could hardly win the Chinese trade from the many lines using the Suez route to London, with transatlantic connections to New York. Except for the scheduled transpacific liners, steamships practically abandoned direct trips between Chinese ports and the United States, and consuls up and down the coast reported a sharp decline in American ships of any type calling at their ports. Between 1864 and 1893 British shipping annually recorded by the Chinese customs office increased from 2,862,214 tons to 19,203,978 tons, while the American figures fell from 2,609,390 tons to 78,175 tons.[50]

Consular reports were filled with dire warnings that without subsidized shipping to San Francisco and New York, American trade with China must languish indefinitely.[51] This did not happen, but British lines received most of the freight income produced by that trade, and New York, not San Francisco, became the port of entry for much Chinese tea and other Oriental goods, to the profit of eastern railroads. Adding insult to injury, congressional proponents of free ship-building materials used the poor showing of the transpacific lines to back up their arguments against ship subsidies.[52] During the late 1880s transpacific communications improved slightly as the Northern Pacific Railroad added a few steamers sailing from Tacoma. In 1886 the newly completed Canadian Pacific Railway inaugurated an ambitious steam line to the Far East by way of the northern route. A battle ensued with the American lines for freight until all parties realized that there was enough for everyone.[53]

50. U.S., *Commercial Relations, 1879–80*, 1, 794–95; *1886–87*, 2, 1226. U.S., *Consular Reports* 3 (January 1881): 82–85. E. M. Gull, *British Economic Interests in the Far East*, 58. The American decline was most rapid during the depression of the 1870s. At Shanghai between 1873 and 1878 American ships declined from 5,001 (3,483,203 tons) to 1,018 (341,942 tons), while British ships increased from 6,995 (3,645,551 tons) to 9,973 (7,439,373 tons). All figures include both oceanic and coasting trade. Table enclosed with Bailey to Payson, August 13, 1879, no. 19, U.S., Consular Despatches, Shanghai, 29. Beginning in 1875 the Japanese Mitsubishi line took over much local Japanese-Chinese trade.

51. U.S., *Foreign Relations, 1876–1877*, 112–16. U.S., *Commercial Relations, 1879–1880*, 1, 85–86. Henderson to F. W. Seward, July 13, 1878, no. 180, U.S., Consular Despatches, Amoy, 8. William L. Scruggs to Payson, April 2, 1881, no. 25, ibid., Canton, 9. Denny to Walker Blaine, October 25, 1881, no. 232, ibid., Shanghai, 22. A. G. Studer to J. C. B. Davis, March 4, 1882, no. 435, ibid., Singapore, 16. *American Protectionist* 1 (February 5, 1881): 38. In 1878 Olyphant and Company established a steamship line to transport Chinese emigrants to Peru after a Peruvian-Chinese treaty. Chinese authorities and the British at Hong Kong prevented the traffic, and the collapse of the line was partly responsible for the failure of the Olyphants later in the year. G. W. Seward to Evarts, March 9, 1878, no. 415; Holcombe to Evarts, July 5, December 26, 1878, nos. 24, 97, U.S., Diplomatic Despatches, China, 47, 48.

52. U.S., 51st Cong., 1st sess., *Congressional Record*, 21, 7175. It has been suggested that as a result of the predominance of the Atlantic-Suez route to the Far East, eastern rail interests in the United States played a crucial role in determining American Far Eastern policy in the 1890s. Stanley J. Thompson, "The Impact of the French 'Challenge' in the Isthmus of Panama on the United States' Expansion in the Caribbean, 1867–1881," 179–80.

53. William Eleroy Curtis, *The Yankees of the East, Sketches of Modern Japan*, 1, 6–7. (*New York Evening Post*), n.d., clipping in Bayard papers, 130, f. 26746a. *London Times*,

Inside China other unfavorable circumstances hampered American-Chinese trade. During the years of recovery after the Taiping Rebellion the conservative government encouraged agriculture and disparaged commerce, especially with foreign countries, lest it increase the barbarian hold on China and encourage undue wealth there.[54] Every city contained powerful guilds, often led by compradors and as tightly organized as any American trust to control trade in a given commodity, fix prices, and coordinate any necessary legal action. In many places the foreigner must buy and sell through the guild or not at all. Also the inauguration of Pacific Mail voyages enabled Chinese merchants in Hong Kong and San Francisco, some of them very wealthy, to enter into competition with American merchants, since they could now ship small consignments on a common carrier.[55]

The foreigners found it difficult to offset the Chinese guilds with their own organizations, for no Chinese laws of incorporation existed. If they wished to form a joint stock company, they must do it in Hong Kong under British law. Western-style banking facilities were also restricted to British auspices until 1889, when a German bank opened. China lacked any central banking system until 1897. As the Shanghai manager of Russell and Company explained to the *Nation*, Americans must purchase exchange through British banks or endure the delay and expense of importing hard cash from home. The days when an American commission house could carry on an exchange business of its own had gone forever.[56]

Confronted with the vagaries of Chinese currency, the chronic Chinese shortage of silver, and the resulting dependence of American merchants on British-

---

n.d., reprinted in U.S., *Consular Reports* 93 (May 1888): 375–78. *Engineering* 51 (May 22, 1891): 624. In 1894 eight steamship companies were engaged in passenger traffic to China—Via Suez: Peninsular and Oriental (55 vessels), Messageries Maritimes (59), North German Lloyd (13), Austrian Lloyd (75). Transpacific: Canadian Pacific (3), Pacific Mail-Occidental and Oriental (8), Northern Pacific (5). Four other lines carried freight and a few passengers via Suez: Glen, Shire, "Blue Funnel," and China Mutual. U.S., *Consular Reports* 184 (January 1896): 97–99.

54. Wright, *Last Stand of Chinese Conservatism,* 156.

55. U.S., *Commercial Relations, 1886–87,* 2, 1273–74. U.S., *Consular Reports* 69 (October 1886): 265–66; 83 (September 1887): 464–91. Edwin Stevens to Walker Blaine, January 9, 1881, no. 19, U.S., Consular Despatches, Ningpo, 4. *Merchants' Magazine* 58 (June 1868): 458–59.

56. U.S., *Commercial Relations, 1875–76,* 267. Albert Feuerwerker, *China's Early Industrialization: Sheng Hsuan-huai (1844–1916) and Mandarin Enterprises,* 226. Hyde, *Far Eastern Trade,* 58–60. George Cyril Allen and Audrey G. Donnithorne, *Western Enterprise in Far Eastern Economic Development,* 107–8. Schrecker, *Imperialism and Chinese Nationalism,* 10–11. Marriner, *Rathbones of Liverpool,* chaps. 3, 13, 14. Chi-ming Hou, *Foreign Investment and Economic Development in China, 1840–1937,* 52–53. H. Seldon Loring to F. W. Seward, November 14, 1877, no. 432, U.S., Consular Despatches, Hong Kong, 11. Isaac F. Shepard to Third Assistant Secretary of State, September 8, 1883, no. 126, ibid., Hankow, 5. *Nation* 16 (March 20, 1873): 195–96. For a description of business transactions in China see U.S., *Consular Reports* 43 (July 1884): 515–19. For a list of foreign bankers in China see Albert Feuerwerker, "The Foreign Presence in China," 198*n*6.

controlled exchange, the U.S. government made one ill-advised effort to help. In 1873 it created the "trade dollar," a special coin for the Far Eastern market, to supplement or even replace the popular Mexican peso. The timing of the law arouses the strong suspicion that it was largely intended to compensate for the simultaneous demonetization of the American silver dollar and provide an outlet for surplus Western silver.

Although the new coin was not intended to circulate in the United States, Congress by an oversight made it legal tender to the amount of five dollars. Also, to attract tradition-bound Chinese traders, Congress gave it a silver content 7½ percent greater than the Mexican peso. Almost $36 million worth of the new trade dollars were minted between 1874 and 1878. The experiment was a nearly total failure. For a time the trade dollars circulated in southern Chinese ports and Hong Kong (but very little in the north). Before long, however, Gresham's inexorable law asserted itself, and most of them went into the strong box or the melting pot. Also, although they ceased to be legal tender at home in 1876, many were reimported into the United States to be used informally for a decade or more. Coinage stopped altogether in 1884, and three years later Congress abolished the coin and provided for redemption at par of about $7.7 million still in circulation.[57]

Unfortunately, the United States Silver Act of 1873 approximately coincided with the beginning of a long, irregular decline in the world price of silver. Since both dollar and pound sterling were gold-based currencies and the Chinese economy was based on silver, the decline of the latter metal often encouraged the production and export of tea, silk, and other Chinese products. The fall of silver seems not to have hurt the Chinese import trade, but observers are agreed that the many unpredictable fluctuations in exchange rates increased the speculative nature of all Chinese trade. In 1889 China vainly tried to stabilize its currency by minting its own "dragon" dollar. During the following two years the Sherman Silver Purchase Act in the United States temporarily raised the value of Chinese silver, but during the 1890s the decline continued.[58]

57. P. Garnett, "History of the Trade Dollar," 91–97. Alexander E. Outerbridge, Jr., "Origin and History of the Trade Dollar," 583–96. *New York Times,* January 1, 1879. *Bradstreet's* 8 (July 7, 1883): 5. U.S., *Foreign Relations, 1875–76,* 45–46; *1877–78,* 101, 141–42. U.S., *Commercial Relations, 1876–77,* 207–8. John C. Myers to John A. Campbell, March 5, 1877, no. 61, U.S., Consular Despatches, Shanghai, 24. C. P. Lincoln to Campbell, August 12, 1877, no. 38, ibid., Canton, 8. *New York Tribune,* July 1, 1883.

58. Chong-su See, *The Foreign Trade of China,* 284–85. Sargent, *Anglo-Chinese Commerce,* 253–54, 276–77, 281–82. U.S., *Commercial Relations, 1879–80,* 1, 762–63; *1886–87,* 1, 1229–30. U.S., *Consular Reports* 74 (February 1887): 508–9. U.S., *Foreign Relations, 1889–90,* 204–6. Denby to Secretary of State, November 12, 1889, no. 1002, U.S., Diplomatic Despatches, China, 86. Denby, *China and Her People,* 2, 30–31. *Banker's Magazine* 43 (June 1889): 901–2. The international fall in the value of silver did not produce inflation within China. J. A. Leonard to Wharton, April 21, 1893, no. 262, U.S., Consular Despatches, Shanghai, 42.

As soon as American merchants sought inland markets, they encountered transportation problems similar to those of South America but even more serious. Central and southern China were well supplied with rivers, used for centuries, but some of the connecting canals had fallen into disrepair. Many roads, being full of holes or quagmires, were virtually impassable, even by crude oxcart. Perennial floods paralyzed whole provinces at a time. Overland freight charges were two to five times higher than those by water; in the most remote areas they bought the services of a porter, trotting along a path with a box or bale on his back. This primitive interior transportation made it unprofitable to send bulky or weighty products, prevented the development of a truly national market, and helped keep domestic trade in the hands of Chinese businessmen. It particularly hampered Americans, as they traded increasingly with Manchuria and northern China, poorly supplied with water routes. Naturally they reacted by proposing great railroad projects, to repeat the development of the American West.[59]

The last of the major obstacles to American-Chinese trade to be considered is Chinese internal taxation, which intensified transportation problems and caused more diplomatic argument than any other. The most objectionable tax was the likin (li-chin), a transit duty levied repeatedly on imports as they passed between the seaport and the place of final sale and also on Chinese products moving to the coast for export. Adopted temporarily in 1853 as a war measure, it soon became permanent, and even Li Hung-chang valued it as a major source of revenue. When Westerners objected that the likin violated the tariff provisions of their treaties, the Chinese government agreed that foreign-owned goods would be exempt if they paid a transit duty of 2.5 percent (half of the fixed tariff duty) and received a special pass. Unfortunately, the central government issued the transit passes; the provinces usually operated the likin stations; and sometimes both taxes were required, especially if the goods were in the hands of a native. The rates and methods of collection varied greatly from one collector to another, and the sums involved were very large. The total amount of likin collection on a long journey might exceed the original cost of the goods.[60]

59. Feuerwerker, "Economic Trends," 41–44. Paul A. Varg, *The Making of a Myth: The United States and China, 1897–1912,* 38–39. Parsons, *American Engineer in China,* 236–44. U.S., *Consular Reports* 160 (January 1894): 226–27. Shepard to Third Assistant Secretary of State, December 29, 1880, no. 82, U.S., Consular Despatches, Hankow, 5. E. J. Smithers to Adee, December 16, 1882, no. 56, ibid., Chinkiang, 4. John S. Mosby to John Davis, July 20, 1884, no. 327, ibid., Hong Kong, 15. On Chinese domination of domestic trade see Albert Feuerwerker, "Economic Trends during the Late Ch'ing Empire, 1870–1911," 50–51.

60. Wright, *Last Stand of Chinese Conservatism,* 167–70. U.S., *Foreign Relations, 1886,* 66–73, 97–99. W. W. Willoughby, *Foreign Rights and Interests in China,* 2, 748–57. Parsons, *American Engineer in China,* 155–57. During the late 1880s transit passes were most commonly used in the Yangtze Valley. U.S., *Commercial Relations, 1889–1890,* 910. In the Hankow district alone during 1883, 37,862 transit passes were issued, more than half of them to Americans. Ibid., *1882–1883,* 2094. On variations in the amounts collected see, for example, ibid., *1868–1869,* 618–20; and Denny to John Hay, February 9, 1880, private memorandum, U.S., Consular Despatches, Tientsin, 2.

Both the Alcock and Chefoo conventions were intended to deal with this problem but failed. Between 1878 and 1881 representatives of Western powers at Peking, led by Britain, fought a running battle with the Tsungli Yamen in an effort to get the government to fix a standard rate and suppress the likin stations (which it had not the power to do). The American minister played a subsidiary role in this argument, supported by Secretary Evarts. In 1882 the problem became more immediate to the Americans, as the Chinese began to impose likin duties on kerosene for the interior, but neither Frelinghuysen nor Bayard could think of any expedient that the European diplomats had not already tried. No American minister gave more attention to the much-vexed subject than Charles Denby, but in 1892 he could only report that foreign chambers of commerce and ministers were still drawing up protests for the Yamen and still receiving bland, meaningless replies.[61]

The government's conservatism was often mirrored in that of the people, who liked to continue in the old, familiar ways and were open to rumors about the insidious foreign barbarians. In many areas the small farmers at the end of the commercial chain lacked the wherewithal to buy or barter. After studying sales of cotton goods by Jardine, Matheson and Company, the largest traders in China, Edward LeFavour concludes that poverty, not principle, was the bottom cause of low sales: "Demand was often strong, though purchasing power was not, even for goods which lacked durability."[62]

On the eve of the Sino-Japanese War statistics showed the British to be still firmly in control of Chinese foreign trade. In 1893 China recorded imports totaling $143,453,650. Of these the United Kingdom supplied 21 percent, the whole British Empire 57 percent, and the United States 5.7 percent. The American record was, as usual, better for China's exports of that year, which totaled $111,595,252. Of this amount 20 percent went to the United Kingdom and 19 percent to the United States. British ships accounted for 85 percent of the tonnage of foreign ships clearing Chinese ports and 65 percent of all tonnage, including the myriad Chinese ships and boats. According to Minister Denby, out of 579 firms operating in China 373 were British and 31 American. Out of 9,945 foreign residents 3,919 were British, 1,312 American.[63]

61. For American views of foreign diplomats' efforts see John Bassett Moore, *A Digest of International Law*, vol. 5, 448–49; U.S., *Foreign Relations, 1879–80*, 167–75, 189–90, 225–26, 254–57, 264–65; *1884*, 48–50. U.S., *Consular Reports* 74 (February 1887): 510–11. Frelinghuysen to Young, September 30, 1884, no. 344; Bayard to Denby, March 8, May 3, 1886, nos. 46, 65, U.S., Diplomatic Instructions, China, vol. 3, 654–55; vol. 4, 125–32, 151–52; U.S., *Foreign Relations, 1892*, 97–99. For a British report of 1896 on various exactions see *Commercial and Financial Chronicle* 67 (August 13, 1898): 296–97. There were other hindrances to trade in China than these discussed here. For a convenient list by Minister Denby see U.S., *Consular Reports* 177 (June 1895): 338–39.

62. LeFevour, *Western Enterprise*, 40.

63. Figures for British trade and shipping are taken from British and Chinese (Imperial Maritime Customs) statistics and appear in McCordock, *British Far Eastern Policy, 1894–1900*, 71–73. American trade percentages are computed from statistics in U.S., Treasury

During the late 1880s a third commercial power, Germany, also began to increase its influence in China, as a financial syndicate located a large loan in Peking and North German Lloyd opened a steamer line to Hong Kong (1886), making faster times than its British and French rivals. German trade figures turned upward about 1889, but they did not approach the American and, of course, remained far below the British.[64] In Britain's "informal empire" China was a major province, worth much negotiation and military action. American-Chinese trade, while steadily increasing, was still peripheral to American world interests.

We must now go behind the statistics and survey the trade activities of Americans in China between the 1860s and the 1890s. During this period all the old commission houses of the pre–Civil War period ceased to function and left American business to smaller traders and a new breed of promoters. Augustine Heard and Company disappeared in 1875, Olyphant and Company in 1878, and finally Russell and Company, the most powerful of all, in 1891.

John Russell Young declared that British rivals had deliberately engineered the Russells' failure, but the reasons for the collapse of the old American houses were more complex than that. Commission houses no longer rendered a unique service to merchants and manufacturers in the United States, thanks to fast steamship lines, transcontinental railroads, and cables, which made market information quickly available and speedy action possible. New, disturbing factors reduced the certainty of profits: the increasing Chinese participation in trade, the competition of India, Ceylon, and Japan in tea and of India in cheap cottons, and the irregular fall of the gold-silver exchange rate in the 1870s and 1880s. The long-expected development of Yangtze Valley trade proved disappointing, and the Russells' briefly successful steamship venture on the river eventually failed (see chapter 6). Finally, the burgeoning American economy offered a higher yield on invested capital than Far Eastern trade. "China had no special mystique to bind them when the ledger books said go." To be sure, British companies faced many of the same problems as the Americans, but their greater resources and government support enabled them to survive and retain a dominant position in the Chinese economy. By the 1890s all that remained of the Americans' "old

---

Department, Bureau of Statistics, *Monthly Summary, 1899,* 1281. Figures of firms and residents appear in U.S., *Commercial Relations, 1891–92,* 370. Sixty percent of Chinese exports went to the British Empire, but this probably means mainly Hong Kong, from which they were reexported to Japan, Europe, and other areas that consumed Chinese tea or other products.

64. Comparable statistics for Germany are not available, as China did not break down trade figures for continental Europe until after 1898. German sea traffic to China and Japan increased from 79,000 tons in 1881–1885 to 270,700 tons in 1891–1895. Hoffman, *British and German Trade Rivalry,* 168–73, 187. According to an American consul in Germany, German exports to China increased from $5,759,600 in 1889 to $7,925,400 in 1893 and to Japan from $4,403,000 to $4,426,800. Both figures fell off somewhat the following year. U.S., *Consular Reports* 184 (January 1896): 82, also 68 (September 1886): 631–33.

China trade" was a benign memory that reinforced the continuing myth of the Golden East.[65]

The old commission houses were replaced by more specialized firms, such as export houses, investment syndicates, and Chinese firms run by onetime compradors who had learned the international trade in many cases from the commission houses and had an unparalleled knowledge of interior mercantile conditions. (With lower distribution costs, the compradors were also satisfied with lower profits.) Some of the new firms had begun years earlier as agencies for manufacturers in the United States. For example, one of the best-known organizations in the 1890s, the American Trading Company, was originally a branch office for the American Clock and Brass Work Company of Connecticut, opened in 1877. It was renamed in 1884 and broadened its interests just in time for the expansion of Japanese business, the opening of Korea, and the internationalization of Far Eastern trade. During the 1890s it played a leading commercial and investment role in Japan and Korea and competed for railroad concessions in China (see chapters 8, 9).[66]

Between the 1860s and the 1890s the American export trade grew proportionately stronger, rising from about 20 percent to more than 50 percent of the import trade. Both export and import trade followed in general the ups and downs of the American economy, turning downward in 1870 and 1873 and upward again in 1875 and 1878. Thereafter both had good years early in the 1880s and again after the short depression of 1884. The years 1888 and 1890 showed declines for both, and they rose again briefly before the panic of 1893.[67]

65. Dennett, *Americans in Eastern Asia,* 579–80. Hunt, *Special Relationship,* 144 (quotation). John K. Fairbank, "America and China: The Mid-Nineteenth Century," 27–28. For an analysis of how the changing conditions affected Jardine, Matheson and Company see LeFevour, *Western Enterprise,* chap. 3. Much of this analysis applied to Americans too. William N. Pethick to James Harrison Wilson, June 6, 1891, Wilson papers, box 16. *New York Journal of Commerce,* August 3, 1894. John Russell Young, "New Life in China," 421–23. Lockwood, *Heard and Company,* 116–19. Robert W. Lovett, "The Heard Collection and Its Story," 570–71. *New York Times,* December 24, 1877. Liu, "America and China," 26–28. Sargent, *Anglo-Chinese Commerce,* 201–4. Other harmful factors operating in the 1870s were unusual famines and floods and, in the west, political disturbances.

66. Mira Wilkins, "The Impact of American Multinational Enterprise on American-Chinese Economic Relations, 1786–1949," 262–63. Kang Chao, "The Chinese-American Cotton-Textile Trade, 1850–1930," 116–18.

67. A complete table of American exports and imports, 1865–1897, based on statistics from the Treasury Department, is in Dennett, *Americans in Eastern Asia,* 581. From it the following table of five-year averages will show general trends:

Years	Average U.S. Exports to China and Hong Kong	Average U.S. Imports from China and Hong Kong
1868–1872	$ 3,461,400	$17,195,000
1873–1877	3,583,800	17,122,200
1878–1882	6,843,600	21,516,400
1883–1887	9,384,400	19,403,200
1888–1892	9,744,900	19,002,400
1893–1897	11,127,500	21,126,900

The two leading Chinese exports to the United States were always tea and silk. Tea took an early lead and made up 60 to 90 percent of American imports from 1840 to 1860. It provided the raison d'être for the speedy clipper ships of the 1850s; and its great profits briefly fulfilled the myth of the Golden East. It also helped to centralize the import trade in New York. In 1854, as a result of the Taiping upheavals, Russell and Company sent compradors into the interior of Fukien province to buy tea directly from the growers. Heard and Company did the same in 1855, and soon the port of Foochow was dividing the tea trade with Shanghai, which had taken it over from Canton. The Taiping Rebellion, the American Civil War, and a new high American tariff on tea caused a brief depression in the trade. Tea was restored in 1872 to the American free list, where it remained to the end of the century, but the unsettlement in transportation resulting from the simultaneous opening of the American transcontinental railroad and the Suez Canal in 1869 started the trade on a long decline, broken briefly in the 1880s. Competition by Indian, Ceylonese, and especially Japanese tea then set in, and before the end of the century they were outselling Chinese tea in world markets by about 60 percent to 40 percent. By this time Pacific transportation routes had broken New York's monopoly with distribution centers in San Francisco, Chicago, and Boston.[68]

The other great Chinese export, raw silk and silk goods, formed about one-third of American imports from China, 1820–1835, but then declined sharply as tea increased. During the 1850s and 1860s Chinese raw silk shipments to France and the United States rose again for different reasons—France because a disastrous epidemic ended silkworm culture and the United States because a high tariff on silk goods during the Civil War gave a great impetus to weaving. (The American tariff on raw silk remained low because its production was too labor-intensive to be profitable, but the tariff on silk goods stayed up after the war.) During the 1860s American silk imports, almost entirely from China, began a steady rise, encouraged by the completion of the transcontinental railroad, and about 1890 silk passed tea on the customs list. As quality declined, however, other textiles, notably cottons, offered more competition in Western markets. The Japanese silk industry of the 1880s and 1890s became more mechanized than the Chinese and eventually played a larger role in trade with the United States. In addition to

68. Yen-Ping Hao, "Chinese Tea to America—A Synopsis." Robert P. Gardella, "The Boom Years of the Fukien Tea Trade, 1842–1888." Sargent, *Anglo-Chinese Commerce*, 213–18, 270–81. Allen and Donnithorne, *Western Enterprise*, 56–57. William R. Ukers, *All about Tea*, vol. 2, 258, 268, 278. Josiah C. Low to Samuel E. Huntington, February 8, November 2, 1872; Low to W. N. Condil, February 9, March 7, May 7, 1872; Low to J. B. Taylor, February 27, November 6, 1872; Low to [?]—Hurlbut, October 22, 1872, Letterbook, 74–79, 81–87, 97–107, 145–47, 158–63, 266–69, 277–90, Low-Mills family papers, box 4, U.S., *Commercial Relations 1879–1880*, vol. 1, 772–77. M. M. DeLano to Payson, June 23, 1880, no. 272, U.S., Consular Despatches, Foochow, 5. Denby to Bayard, April 5, 1886, May 17, 1887; Denby to Blaine, May 10, 1892, nos. 127, 368, 1532, U.S., Diplomatic Despatches, China, 70, 80, 92.

tea and silk, south China exported considerable sugar, but Hawaiian competition effectively shut this out of the American market.[69]

Among Western manufactures, the first to gain a foothold in midcentury China was cotton textiles. Foreign imports had to fight a long battle against local cottage looms turning out a crude but cheap cloth, and the expectations of the powerful British textile industry were largely disappointed until the 1880s. Americans thus faced two competitors; nevertheless, from about 1835 to the end of the century cotton goods often constituted half or more of American exports to China. Most of these were cheap, heavy grades of sheetings, shirtings, drills, and jeans, which could compete with the local cloth. They were especially popular in northern China to make the padded clothing needed to keep out the cold. Lacking the more sophisticated machinery and skilled labor of British mills, Americans produced fewer of the fancy light piece goods wanted in the south. The Chinese cottons trade had largely recovered from the Taiping disturbances by 1861, and American goods even outsold British in some places. By greatly increasing the price of raw cotton, the Civil War in the United States temporarily ruined the American cotton goods trade with China. The price rise somewhat handicapped European competitors as well, but cheap labor and efficient merchandising enabled them to capture the Chinese market. Also, to compensate for inferior cotton and to keep prices down, the British began to "size" their fabrics heavily with clay, which often caused them to mildew badly in transit and, of course, quickly washed out, leaving the cloth thin and sleazy.[70]

During the 1870s American manufacturers and merchants recovered much of their lost ground by building up a reputation for honest, unsized cottons, apparently aided by several years of prosperity that enabled Chinese customers to pay the higher American prices. The British fought back by imitating American labels. According to both American and British consuls, sales of American cotton goods rose rapidly during the late 1870s, perhaps as much as four times in as many years, but at the end of the decade the British were still sending about 454 million yards of piece goods of all kinds to China, as compared with only 22.6 million yards for the Americans. Also, as prosperity returned in the United States, some American mill owners lost interest in the China market. Nevertheless, during

69. Lillian M. Li, "The Silk Export Trade and Economic Modernization in China and Japan." Robert Y. Eng, *Economic Imperialism in China: Silk Production and Exports, 1861–1932*, 24–30. Min-hsiung Shih, *The Silk Industry in Ch'ing China*, 66–70. U.S., *Commercial Relations, 1879–80*, 1, 774–75.

70. Chao, "Chinese-American Cotton-Textile Trade," 103–11. Sargent, *Anglo-Chinese Commerce*, 205–7. LeFevour, *Western Enterprise*, 31–40. Melvin Thomas Copeland, *The Cotton Manufacturing Industry of the United States*, 224–25. U.S., *Commercial Relations, 1870–71*, 218; *1871–72*, 152; *1873–74*, 228–30; *1875–76*, 251–52, 268–74. American consuls exhaustively debated the merits of sizing cottons so as to bring down their price. U.S., *Consular Reports* 12 (October 1881, "Cotton Goods Trade of the World"): 299–323. The British too were much divided on the subject. *Economist* 33 (December 11, 1880): 1452. The Chinese never imported many woolen goods; indeed sales actually declined from the 1830s to the 1850s. LeFevour, *Western Enterprise*, 168n29.

the 1880s Americans tightened their hold on the market in northern China and Manchuria for coarse, heavy goods, which they controlled by a margin of nearly two to one at the end of the decade.[71]

Both British and American cotton goods were imported into China through two ports, Hong Kong (to which Canton was subsidiary) and Shanghai. At both places they were sold through Chinese brokers and compradors to native jobbers and dealers in the outports. Shanghai also had a system of public auctions. In the United States during the 1880s the milling industry of the New South competed increasingly with the older New England textile manufacturers for the export trade, especially the China market, where the southerners even sold their goods under Massachusetts labels. A sudden drop in Chinese demand during the late 1880s cut into American sales, but these recovered in 1890 and 1891. By that time American cotton goods were facing competition from Japan, India, Indo-China, and even new Chinese mills.[72]

The greatest "success story" in late-nineteenth-century American trade with China was that of kerosene, which came to equal cotton cloth in American trade figures by 1890. During the early 1870s Standard Oil sent out a few experimental shipments, which caught on, and before long an ingenious Chinese invented a cheap tin lamp for the lower-class house. (American and other merchants sold glass lamps for the more affluent.) Between 1877 and 1882 the quantity of kerosene imported at Shanghai grew fifteen times, and the increase was nearly as great at most other ports. By 1889 shipments totaled about fifteen million gallons but represented only about 2 percent of American petroleum exports.

At first Standard simply sold to exporters in the United States, but beginning in 1882 it sent a representative, William H. Libby, to carry on a systematic publicity campaign in China. Libby at once got the consul general at Shanghai to translate an advertising circular into Chinese and sent two hundred thousand copies into the interior. Kerosene was not only cheaper but also greatly superior to the dim,

71. For the period 1886–1890 the American share of sheetings and coarse drills was 68.5 percent and 60.3 percent respectively, the British share only 31.5 and 36.3, but the British controlled fine drills by 75.6 percent to 14.1 percent. British prices were usually more stable than American, probably because of a deliberate effort to please foreign buyers. Chao, "Chinese-American Cotton-Textile Trade," 111–14. Sargent, *Anglo-Chinese Commerce*, 207–8, 257–61. *Iron Age* 27 (January 20, 1881): 7. *Economist* 42 (August 6, 1884): monthly trade supplement, 4–5. U.S., *Commercial Relations, 1879–80*, 1, 763–67, 830–33. George F. Seward to Evarts, February 2, June 12, 1880, nos. 583 (with enclosure), 706, U.S., Diplomatic Despatches, China, 53, 54. E. J. Smithers to Walker Blaine, December 27, 1881, no. 35, U.S., Consular Despatches, Chinkiang, 4. Denny to Davis, February 23, 1882, no. 274, ibid., Shanghai, 33. *New York Times*, March 16, 1880; September 26, 1881; April 1, 1882; April 24, 1882.

72. Chao, "Chinese-American Cotton-Textile Trade," 114–19. U.S., *Special Consular Reports* 1 (1889): 136–41. C. F. Seward to Evarts, February 2, 1880, no. 583, U.S., Diplomatic Despatches, China, 53. Bedloe to Josiah Quincy, May 18, 1893, no. 128, U.S., Consular Despatches, Amoy, 13. Samuel L. Gracey to Walter Q. Gresham, May 29, 1893, no. 74, ibid., Foochow, 8. Hearden, "Cotton Mills of the New South," 47, 49, 53, 73–74.

smoky vegetable oils hitherto used, and the new lamps worked a kind of social revolution in Chinese life as well as releasing some of the vegetable oils for export. By 1882 one house out of six in Shanghai burned kerosene; the streets were lighted with it; and the highest-ranking Chinese official in the city (the *taotai*) used it in his office. As the trade became systematized, Standard Oil shipped kerosene to the principal ports in wooden cases, each containing two five-gallon cans. At first Americans and a few British companies carried on the retail trade, but soon in many places this passed to Chinese merchant guilds. However, Standard used its own agents instead of compradors and opened a central office at Shanghai in 1884. During the early 1890s it considered making the principal British company, Jardine, Matheson, its permanent agent, but instead it established other central offices and a marketing organization.[73]

The success of kerosene was achieved against many obstacles. A Chinese syndicate marketing the inferior native oils tried in vain to shut it out, pleading the rights of peanut growers. In some places disastrous fires owing to careless handling turned populace and officials against the "devouring evil" and brought prohibitory ordinances or crippling safety regulations until the people learned how to use it properly. Both central and local governments levied special taxes on kerosene or hampered its transportation into the interior. Young, Denby, and their consuls dealt patiently and flexibly with these hindrances, sometimes advising merchants to tolerate minor losses so as to preserve a profitable business but occasionally resisting serious impositions such as a tax that raised the price of kerosene by 40 percent and forced several ships loaded with oil to leave port without unloading. In these operations Standard's agent Libby played a key role, for no one knew more than he about the oil trade. A trusted friend of Young and Hart, he was eventually allowed to speak for the American legation in discussions with both the Chinese and Japanese governments.[74]

73. *Annals of the Academy of Political and Social Science* 13 (January–June 1899): supplement, 110. U.S., *Commercial Relations, 1879–80*, vol. 1, 767–68. U.S., *Consular Reports* 37 (January 1884): 425–29, 433–36, 441–42. *American Exporter* 5 (October 1880): 10. J. J. Frederick Bandinel to Third Assistant Secretary of State, August 17, 1882, no. 249, U.S., *Consular Despatches, Newchwang*, 2. Denby to Bayard, September 1, 1886, no. 201, U.S., *Diplomatic Despatches, China*, 77. Ralph W. Hidy and Muriel E. Hidy, *History of Standard Oil Company (New Jersey): Pioneering in Big Business, 1882–1911*, 127. Before Jardine, Matheson's negotiations with Standard it handled kerosene from America, Russia, and the East Indies under various arrangements. LeFevour, *Western Enterprise*, 144–46. Michael H. Hunt, "Americans in the China Market: Economic Opportunities and Economic Nationalism, 1890–1931," 281–82. To gain a foothold in the China market Standard priced kerosene at half the level of native bean oils, taking a loss. Chu-yuan Cheng, "The United States Petroleum Trade with China, 1876–1949," 207, 214–15, 224–25.

74. Hunt, "Americans in China Market," 282–83. Morken, "America Looks West," 94–102. U.S., *Consular Reports* 24 (October 1882): 108–409; 34 (October 1883): 676; 37 (January 1664): 426–28; 42 (June 1884): 84–85. U.S., *Commercial Relations, 1884–85*, 945. U.S., *Foreign Relations, 1888*, 266–67, 274–75. Young to Frelinghuysen, October 23, December 12, 1882, nos. 46–73, U.S., *Diplomatic Despatches, China*, 62, 63. Charles Seymour to William Wharton, February 26, 29, March 12, 25, 1892, nos. 219, 221, 222, 226, U.S., *Consular Despatches, Canton*, 12.

Eventually a longer-lasting threat appeared against which Libby and the diplomats were powerless—Russian and East Indian oil began to invade eastern Asia. Kerosene from Baku first appeared in marketable quantities about 1888, and although it was badly packed, smokier, smellier, and more dangerous to handle than American oil, its low price attracted customers. The chief marketing agent for Russian oil in East Asia was Marcus Samuel, head of the leading British merchant firm in Japan. After the Suez Canal authorities began to admit tankers in 1892, Samuel's ships carried bulk oil for greater economy, and he established a chain of storage tanks from Yokohama to Bombay. Although he soon realized that Chinese preferences would force him to sell the kerosene in tin cans, his shipments produced a sharp fall in prices throughout East Asia beginning in 1892. Standard Oil counterattacked by exporting a cheaper grade, transporting and storing its oil in bulk, introducing eight million small, cheap lamps for the common people, and setting up a network of agents and affiliates as it had in Europe and elsewhere. Undoubtedly this rivalry added tension to the international problems that pervaded the Far East during the 1890s. By 1898 Americans (mostly Standard Oil) were sending China annually about fifty million gallons of kerosene, roughly half of its total oil imports.[75]

Other American exports to China lagged behind cotton textiles and kerosene in sales. At first wheat flour, an American staple in most other parts of the world, could not compete with rice in East Asia and along with various canned goods was imported mainly for foreigners. During the depressed years of the 1870s and 1880s, when prices were low, California flour millers sent part of their supplies to China, and by the mid-1890s controlled the Chinese and Manchurian markets. These were especially welcome to the Californians, for they both reduced dependence on the highly speculative English market and disposed of lower grades in little demand elsewhere. Lumber and wood products, like flour popular in other parts of the Pacific, followed a similar pattern of sales in China, where they had to compete with inferior local and Japanese wood until, by the 1890s, the latter was almost exhausted by overcutting. The quality, plentiful supply, and easy transportation of American Pacific coast lumber might have developed a larger Far Eastern market, reported some consuls, but that many northwestern mill owners seemed more interested in San Francisco customers.

Most American machinery that sold well in Europe, Canada, and some parts of Latin America was too advanced as yet for the Chinese economy. Clocks and watches, to be sure, found a good market. Farm machinery, as all consuls

75. Hidy, *Pioneering in Big Business,* 259–61. Feuerwerker, "Foreign Presence in Chica," 196–97. D. A. Farnie, *East and West of Suez: The Suez Canal in History, 1854–1956,* 443–48. Robert Henriquez, *Bearsted: A Biography of Marcus Samuel, First Viscount Bearsted and Founder of "Shell" Transport and Trading Company.* Denby to Bayard, February 12, 1887; Denby to Gresham, December 26, 1893, nos. 544, 1772, U.S., Diplomatic Despatches, China, 80, 94. U.S., *Consular Reports* 108 (October 1889): 196–98; 115 (April 1890): 694–96; 145 (October 1892): 287–89. Bad packing and adulteration by middlemen were complaints also sometimes directed at American kerosene. Ibid., 160 (January 1894): 222–23. Remer, *Foreign Investments in China,* 251.

warned, had no chance to find customers among ultraconservative small farmers, although there was a potential market for a few improved forms of hand tools. Mining and railroad machinery was necessarily tied to investments in these fields, to be discussed later. The Chinese government occasionally bought American munitions, and the appearance of bogus Winchester cartridges on a Chinese gunboat in 1891 caused a momentary flurry.[76]

To manufacturers of these and other products American consuls in China offered the same advice as their colleagues in other parts of the world: Send out smart young agents, not just catalogues printed in English; establish connections with a firm having a branch in China; pay more attention to Chinese needs and tastes. Because coolies carried most loads, the consuls especially urged packing in sixty- to seventy-five-pound lots.

The trade figures might suggest that in most cases this advice fell largely on deaf ears. But the experiences of the Singer Manufacturing Company (sewing machines) suggest that profitable export to China required more than the consuls realized. The Singer Company, which had been remarkably successful in Europe and Latin America, established an agent in Shanghai during 1883 with so little success that the company withdrew him after four years. It then installed sample machines in industrial schools, aroused the interest in Chinese officials, including Li Hung-chang himself, and eventually even introduced a new chain-stitch machine designed for loose Chinese clothing. Although Singer's methods impressed American observers as models, after thirty years of trial and error the company was still disappointed with its results.[77] It had not located enough of the four hundred million customers.

76. Cox, "Passage to India Revisited," 88–95. *Northwestern Miller* 31 (April 24, 1891): 552. U.S., *Commercial Relations, 1879–80*, vol. 1, 768–72, 794, 801–6; *1886–87*, vol. 2, 1226–29. U.S., *Consular Reports* 3 (January 1881): 80–82; 57 (October 1885): 23–24; 144 (November 1892): 381–82; 160 (January 1894): 225–27. J. J. Henderson to Frederic W. Seward, August 16, November 30, 1878, nos. 186, 192; W. Elwell Goldsborough to John Davis, June 5, 1884, no. 174; Bedloe to William Wharton, October 23, 1891, no. 61, U.S., Consular Despatches, Amoy, 8, 10, 13. Denby to Bayard, April 25, 1988, no. 632 bis., U.S., Consular Despatches, China, 82.

77. Robert Bruce Davies, *Peacefully Working to Conquer the World: Singer Sewing Machines in Foreign Markets, 1854–1920*, chap. 7. Wilkins, "Impact of American Multinational Enterprise," 266–68.

6

China II
The Promoter's Dream, the Racist's Nightmare

ETWEEN 1865 AND 1890 American-Chinese trade grew slowly but steadily as mercantile organizations evolved from commission houses to more specialized companies. At the same time American capitalists moved into new investment fields such as steamer lines, telegraphs, and railroads. These promoters faced new problems and obstacles largely unknown to merchants of the old China trade. Traders, like missionaries, had always had to deal with popular Chinese superstitions and with the ingrown conservatism of an aristocratic government. This was particularly true if the product they introduced was completely unfamiliar, like kerosene. But promoters of investment projects, especially telegraphs and railroads, posed more intimate and intimidating threats to popular customs and religious beliefs and to the government's concern for its sovereign control over its people. Thus the promoters advanced a step beyond the traders into the heart of China.

At the same time that promoters were advancing into the interior, Chinese, mostly ordinary laborers, were moving in the opposite direction, across the Pacific and into the United States. Here they too encountered hostility born of aristocratic conservatism and popular superstition directed against the unfamiliar. American expansion and Chinese migration were two sides of the same coin—missionaries and traders helped the Chinese discover America, and mistreatment of the immigrants increased anti-Americanism in China and intensified hatred of the foreign devils. The Americans wanted the Chinese as customers and converts but not as neighbors.

During the latter half of the nineteenth century Americans showed increasing interest in a variety of noncommercial investment ventures in China. Before the 1890s this interest produced only one temporarily successful venture, a steamship line sponsored by Russell and Company. Most commission houses had operated coastal steamers during the 1850s as adjuncts to their business. The opening of the Yangtze River by the treaties of 1858 encouraged them to add river steamboats. In 1861 and 1862 Augustine Heard and Company rushed in a few and "skimmed the cream" off the river trade, but their ships carried mostly company goods. Seeing more possibilities in common carrier activities, on March 27, 1862, Russell and

Company founded a subsidiary, the Shanghai Steam Navigation Company, with a capital equivalent to $1,358,000, and set out to monopolize the carrying trade of Europeans and Chinese alike. Since officials of the parent company thought the venture risky, they refused to invest in its funds, so the stockholders were a mixture of Americans, British, and Chinese. However, Russell and Company directed operations throughout.[1]

Although in 1862 and 1863 about twenty other Shanghai firms operated at least one or two steamers on the river, the Russells' new subsidiary stifled or bought out competition, until by 1866 it carried more than half of the river trade. The following year the largest British outfit, Jardine, Matheson and Company, agreed to confine itself to coastal shipping, and the Shanghai Steam Navigation Company had a monopoly. During the next seven fat years the company charged high rates but gave good service between Shanghai and Hankow, offering sailings twice a week, a round trip of nine or ten days with intermediate stops, and clean, comfortable passenger accommodations. During those years profits were very large, and from 1868 the company declared annual dividends of 12 percent. In 1872 it operated seventeen steamers on the river and along the coast from Shanghai to Tientsin and Ningpo. Its rivals had ten steamers, only half of them on the river.[2]

The Russells' monopoly of the carrying trade then ended abruptly, as one powerful British company, Butterfield and Swire, challenged its control of the Yangtze and another, Jardine, Matheson, its coastal traffic. Local Russell officials planned a rate war with Butterfield and Swire in 1873, but the home office vetoed this plan, and early the following year the two companies signed a pooling agreement.[3]

More threatening still was the rivalry of the China Merchants Steam Navigation Company, founded in 1873 under the patronage of Li Hung-chang to lessen foreign control of trade in the heart of China and build the foundation for a strong navy. The government encouraged the new company with a contract for transporting tribute rice to Peking at a high rate, a rebate of duties on native products it carried, and, it was said, covert intimidation of native shippers. At the Russells' request the American legation entered a discreet protest but could accomplish nothing. Aware of their company's uncertain future, the shareholders of the Shanghai Steam Navigation Company sold out to the Chinese competitor for about 103 taels (perhaps $140) a share, nearly 56 percent over the market

---

1. Lockwood, *Augustine Heard and Company*, 91–97. Kwang-ching Liu, *Anglo-American Steamship Rivalry in China, 1862–1874*, chap. 1.

2. Liu, *Anglo-American Steamship Rivalry*, chaps. 2, 3. U.S., *Commercial Relations, 1873–1874*, 230–32. In 1873 British direct trade with China was 6.7 times as great as American, but thanks to the Shanghai Steam Navigation Company, the local carrying trade under the two flags was nearly equal (1,643,700 tons for American ships, 1,174,598 tons for British). Ibid., *1874–1875*, 211.

3. Liu, *Anglo-American Steamship Rivalry*, chap. 4. In 1874 the Shanghai Steam Navigation Company had fourteen ships operating in the Yangtze and along the coast, its two British rivals a total of eleven, and the China Merchants Company seven. Ibid., 114.

value. In 1876 the American company went out of business and turned over its large fleet to the China Merchants Company. During the decade after 1885 only one American river steamer docked at Shanghai.[4]

For a time foreign diplomats in China suspected that the government might have overextended itself, for the ships were not all worth the price paid for them. Chinese capitalists were slow to buy the company's stock, preferring the high returns from lending money and fearing to attract the greedy eye of the tax collector. Also China boasted few navigators or engineers. Nevertheless, the government continued its support, and the company manned its ships with Westerners. It was soon declaring dividends and had a fairly prosperous history well into the twentieth century.[5] The transfer of the fleet had a strange sequel. In 1884, during a brief war between China and France (to be discussed in chapter 8), John Russell Young helped to arrange the sale of the ships to Russell and Company, to prevent their seizure by the French. As soon as the war was over, Russell and Company resold them to the Chinese company under the terms of a secret agreement.[6]

While the Shanghai Steam Navigation Company was carrying the U.S. flag up the Yangtze River, other Americans were trying to become pioneers of telegraphy in China. Owners of Chinese junks sometimes resisted the incursions of foreign steamships, but there was a more widespread fear and hatred of telegraphs and railroads on land, which were thought to encourage evil spirits and interfere with supernatural forces in the land. In 1864 Russell and Company set up a short telegraph in Shanghai between their offices and wharves, but when a promoter

4. Benjamin P. Avery to Hamilton Fish, June 13, 1875, no. 65, U.S., Diplomatic Despatches, China, 38. U.S., *Commercial Relations, 1875–76,* 257–60; *U.S. Foreign Relations, 1876–77,* 88–91. U.S., *Consular Reports* 192 (September 1896): 68. Feuerwerker, *China's Early Industrialization,* 62, 96–99. The operating company of Butterfield and Swire was called the China Navigation Company. For its history see Sheila Marriner and Francis E. Hyde, *The Senior John Samuel Swire, 1825–98: Management in Far Eastern Shipping Trades,* chaps. 4, 5.

5. George F. Seward to William M. Evarts, May 25, August 14, 1877, nos. 257, 327, U.S., Diplomatic Despaches, China, 44, 46. David H. Bailey to Charles Payson, September 19, 1879, no. 32, U.S., Consular Despatches, Shanghai, 29. *American Exporter* 5 (April 1880): 22. The Chinese company even set up a London branch. O. H. Denny to W. Blaine, September 28, 1881, no. 224, U.S., Consular Despatches, Shanghai, 22. *Hong Kong Daily Press,* n.d., clipping enclosed with John S. Mosby to John Davis, August 2, 1884, no. 329, U.S., Consular Despatches, Hong Kong, 15. Chi-kong Lai, "Li Hung-chang and Modern Enterprise: The China Merchants' Company, 1872–1885," in Chu and Liu, *Li Hung-chang,* 218–47. Feuerwerker, *China's Early Industrialization,* 155. Wright, *Last Stand of Chinese Conservatism,* 175–77. John E. Orchard, "Contrasts in the Progress of Industrialization in China and Japan," 42. The China Merchants Company and its British rival reached a pooling agreement in 1877. Hyde, *Far Eastern Trade,* 27.

6. *New York Tribune,* November 12, 1884. John Russell Young to Frederick T. Frelinghuysen, September 4, 1884, January 7, 1885, nos. 501, 614; E. J. Smithers to Thomas F. Bayard, August 28, 1885, no. 58, U.S., Diplomatic Despatches, China, 71, 74, 76. Smithers to Alvey A. Adee, November 11, 1885, U.S., Consular Despatches, Shanghai, 36. Feuerwerker, *China's Early Industrialization,* 114, 133, 154. For the later history of the China Merchants Company see ibid., chaps. 4, 5.

erected an eight-mile line from the city to Woosung, a port at the mouth of the Yangtze, the angry natives tore it down. Burlingame tried repeatedly to secure authorization for railroads and telegraphs, but, using public opinion as an excuse, officials never gave him more than a vague oral promise. Finally, as we have seen, he concluded that the Chinese must be left to their own timing.[7]

In 1866, near the end of Burlingame's term as minister, a group of Americans interested in the Far East incorporated the East India Telegraph Company in New York, with a capital of $5 million. Among the directors were Paul S. Forbes, head of Russell and Company, and O. H. Palmer of the Western Union Telegraph Company; for a time Andrew G. Curtin, the energetic war governor of Pennsylvania, was president. The venture also had the support of Perry M. Collins and the Pacific Mail Steamship Company. The purpose was to connect the principal ports of China with each other and with assisting telegraph systems reaching eastward in Siberia and at Singapore. To evade Chinese superstitions it proposed a series of cables in the shallow South China Sea, with a short land connection to the company office in Shanghai. The company sent out an agent on reconnaissance, but although he managed to make a beginning at translating ideographic Chinese into Morse code, he failed completely to interest the Chinese government. At Secretary Seward's instructions, Burlingame made another effort with no better results. Secretary Fish too issued more general instructions for support of any American telegraphic projects. The East India Company was overly optimistic, and Minister J. Ross Browne thought its prospectus deliberately misleading about the likelihood of Chinese cooperation and patronage. Before long the company disappeared.[8]

A Danish organization, the Great Northern Telegraph Company, soon demonstrated the essential soundness of the East India Company's project. In 1871 it inaugurated cables from Shanghai to Hong Kong, connecting with a British line to Singapore, India, and Nagasaki, and with a Russian line across Siberia. After several false starts on land, a diplomatic crisis between China and Russia in 1880

7. Hinton, "A Talk with Mr. Burlingame," 620. J. Ross Browne to William H. Seward, March 1, 1869, no. 24, U.S., Diplomatic Despatches, China, 25. U.S., *Foreign Relations, 1866–67*, 483–84.

8. A prospectus giving the company's organization is enclosed with Browne to Fish, June 19, 1869, no. 43, U.S., Diplomatic Despatches, China, 26. Browne comments on its exaggerations. During the mid-1870s another New York venture, the American East India Telegraph Company, was incorporated to lay a cable from San Francisco to Hong Kong via the Aleutians and Japan. Prospectus enclosed with John A. Bingham to Fish, August 8, 1876, no. 424, U.S., Diplomatic Despatches, Japan, 32. *New York Times,* July 16, August 7, 1867. *New York Tribune,* August 24, 1868. Merle Curti and John Stalker, " 'The Flowery Flag Devils'—The American Image in China, 1840–1900," 666. Hinton, "A Talk with Mr. Burlingame," 620. W. H. Seward to Anson Burlingame, April 5, 1867, no. 196; Fish to William A. Howard, May 7, 1869, no. 2, 1869, U.S., *Foreign Relations, 1866–1867,* 455–58, 471–72. George L. Motley to Fish, Juy 30, August 11, 1869, nos. 66, 79, with enclosures, U.S., Diplomatic Despatches, Britain, 99. The Chinese suspected with reason the promoters' weak financial backing in the United States (Hunt, *Special Relationship,* 146).

demonstrated the need for quick communications, and at Li Hung-chang's urging, the imperial government commissioned the Danish company to construct a line from Peking to Tientsin and seven other cities. This and later land lines, however, were administered by a government-sponsored company.[9]

American ministers, especially Benjamin P. Avery, supported the Great Northern Company along with other foreign diplomats, since they assumed that foreign trade would benefit equally with Chinese trade from better communications. The State Department approved this support, as long as it did not lead to a monopoly by any foreign company that might discriminate against American business and later prevent the landing of an American-laid transpacific cable. In 1889, when Great Northern sought government permission for a rate-fixing cartel with the Russian and British systems, Minister Charles Denby joined other Western diplomats in a strong protest to the Chinese government, which eventually refused its approval, although an agreement of 1892 linked the Russian and Chinese systems.[10]

Railroads were to be a more important factor than telegraphs in the introduction of foreign capital for the economic development of China. As the *Commercial and Financial Chronicle* put it, a short railroad line would be the entering wedge for longer ones, which would open up inaccessible districts, elevate labor, spread knowledge, and improve the moral condition of the country. In the mid-1860s British officials suggested several short lines from Canton, Shanghai, and Tientsin and even an interior trunk line from Peking to Hankow on the Yangtze River. The Chinese officials had a standard reply to all these proposals—that the prejudices of the people, especially concerning the many graveyards along the right of way, would cause a rebellion if railroads were attempted.

Behind this rationalization officials concealed a variety of more sophisticated arguments against railroads. They would never be profitable, for the Chinese were too poor to buy tickets and would never generate enough freight, so

9. Allen and Donnithorne, *Western Enterprise*, 269. Morse, *International Relations*, vol. 2, 336–37. Feuerwerker, *China's Early Industrialization*, 63. Chu and Liu, eds., *Li Hung-chang*, 110. G. Seward to J. C. B. Davis, May 11, June 12, December 21, 1871, nos. 451, 464, 501; G. Seward to John L. Cadwalader, October 17, 1874, no. 834, U.S. Consular Despatches, Shanghai, 12, 19. U.S. *Commercial Relations, 1878–79*, 226.

10. Leslie Bennett Tribolet, *The International Aspects of Electrical Communications in the Pacific Area*, 72–76. U.S., *Commercial Relations, 1874–75*, 245–46. U.S., *Foreign Relations, 1874–75*, 223–27, 237–41, 260–61, 267–71, 274–75, 278–79, 328–31, 342–43, 412–13; *1882*, 115–17; *1883*, 142–44. James G. Blaine to Chester Holcombe, December 10, 1881, no. 142, U.S., Diplomatic Instructions, China, 3, 288–90. Holcombe to Blaine, November 29, 1881; Charles Denby to Bayard, October 6, 1887; Denby to Blaine, October 9, 24, 29, November 5, December 29, 1889; March 28, 29, April 2, June 28, October 24, 1890; Denby to Foster, January 15, 1893, nos. 21, 470, 971, 979, 986, 992, 1017, 1076, 1078, 1083, 1121, 1183, 1629, U.S., Diplomatic Despatches, China, 58, 81, 86–88, 92. British merchants strongly opposed the cartel, but the British and French governments instructed their ministers to support it. The rest of the diplomatic corps stood with Denby. See also Denby, *China and Her People*, 2, 231–33.

the railroads would go into debt and have to be rescued with subsidies. They would impoverish the country by exhausting its resources, such as coal, and by throwing millions of people out of work. Most dangerous of all, by making internal communication easy, they would facilitate foreign invasion and reduce the country to the servile state of India. Perhaps the most basic concern of officials was a conservative fear that such an earth-shaking innovation would topple the emperor and the mandarins. Li Hung-chang, who favored railroads, insisted that the Chinese must build and operate them to avoid foreign control. He cited the example of Japan to encourage China to develop her own resources.[11]

The leaders in the railroad movement were the foreign merchants at Shanghai, who wanted better communication with nearby towns, especially the port of Woosung, to which they proposed to build a railroad at their own expense. The Shanghai-Woosung project led to the first open Chinese-foreign confrontation concerning railroads. In 1872 the American vice consul at Shanghai, O. B. Bradford, discussed the subject with local British, American, and Chinese merchants, organized a company, and had a man select a provisional route. Bradford soon turned the project over to the powerful British firm of Jardine, Matheson and Company, partly because it had more available capital and partly because Consul George F. Seward, who had been out of town during the first proceedings, warned him that his participation might violate the Burlingame treaty.

Jardine, Matheson secured a permit and laid track ostensibly for an animal-drawn tramline. When a small steam locomotive was brought in, the taotai at Shanghai strongly protested. The railroad company started operations, probably hoping to bluff the local authorities into acceptance. After a man had been run down and killed (apparently through his own carelessness), the taotai ordered operations suspended, and a full-scale diplomatic argument broke out between the British legation and the Tsungli Yamen at Peking. In the end the Chinese government agreed to buy out the company. But instead of running the useful railroad itself, the government tore up the tracks and shipped rails and rolling stock to Taiwan, where they were piled up and left to rust.[12]

11. *Commercial and Financial Chronicle* 1 (September 6, 1865): 326–27. Browne to [Seward], January 28, 1867, no. 19, U.S., Diplomatic Despatches, China, 25. Blair C. Currie, "The Woosung Railroad (1872–1877)," 80. The Chinese objections to railroads are conveniently summarized in a government memorial of 1881. Chi-ming Hou, *Foreign Investment and Economic Development in China, 1840–1937*, 242, 13n29. In the secret correspondence of 1867, Li was one of only two out of seventeen in the Yamen who would consider the possibility of railroads in the future. Biggerstaff, "Secret Correspondence," 129–30. On the relationship between Li and the Tsungli Yamen in the field of telegraphs and railroads see Meng, *Tsungli Yamen*, 68–70. For the reference to Japan see Teng and Fairbank, *China's Response to the West*, 109–10. Japan was doing exactly what Li advocated. See chap. 7. For an analysis of arguments and reality concerning Chinese railroads see Ralph William Huenemann, *The Dragon and the Iron Horse: The Economics of Railroads in China, 1876–1937*, 4–44.

12. U.S., 45th Cong., 2d sess., House Miscellaneous Document 10, 4–5. Currie, "Woosung Railroad," 49–59, 71–79. Currie believes that the motives behind the Chinese actions

The first successful railroad in China was the outgrowth of a Chinese project to mine coal at K'aip'ing, about seventy miles northeast of Tientsin. This was to supply fuel for the China Merchants Steam Navigation Company. As at Woosung, the original rails were supposedly intended for mule-drawn trams to carry coal seven miles to the nearest canal, but from the beginning the tracks were laid at the standard gauge of 4'8½". One of the British engineers at the mine, Claude W. Kinder, built a crude locomotive out of scrap iron. After overcoming some local opposition, the company put this "Rocket of China" into regular service, and by 1883 the K'aip'ing Railway was running three locomotives, fifty coal trucks, and three passenger cars and a luxury car for officials on its short line. While the equipment was British-made, Li had absorbed a great deal of information about American railroading as well, by way of the Tientsin consulate and his friend Vice Consul William N. Pethick. The disastrous war with France, 1884–1885 (see chapter 8) enabled Li and Kinder to extend the short line, and in 1888 it reached Tientsin, but for a time court opposition prevented a further extension to Peking. Instead the railroad was built to the Manchurian border, and Li sent Kinder into Manchuria for further reconnaissance. By 1894 China had about 320 miles of railroad.[13]

In 1885 two Americans arrived in China who were to set in motion a drive for American railroad concessions that lasted, with interruptions, into the twentieth century. One was the new minister, Charles Denby, who could not undertake business in his own name but was prepared to support other men's projects as far as his vague instructions would allow. The Chinese government seemed to him hopelessly mired in corruption and sloth, except for a few progressive figures such as Li Hung-chang, so Denby set out to encourage these men in a campaign

---

included resentment at the company's duplicity, alarm at foreign aggressiveness, and intragovernmental jealousy of Li Hung-chang, who, in the last stages of the discussion, showed signs of wanting to run the railroad for his own benefit. According to a more recent scholar, the Chinese actions showed "that Confucian values *per se*, far from being a deterrent to modernization, could actually function as a foundation of strength and assurance upon which modernization could build"—a concern for Chinese sovereignty. Wright, *Last Stand of Chinese Conservatism*, 177–78. Sturdevant, "Imperialism, Sovereignty, and Self-Strengthening," 65–67 (quoted clause is on 67). Although Jardine, Matheson supplied most of the capital, subscribers to the Woosung company included Bradford, representatives of Russell and Company and Olyphant and Company, and other American merchants. G. Seward to Fish, September 28, 1876, no. 131, U.S., Diplomatic Despatches, China, 42. When Minister Seward was impeached (but not convicted) for misconduct, the railroad figured prominently among the charges against him. Anderson, *Imperialism and Idealism*, 102–4. For the British side of the episode see LeFevour, *Western Enterprise*, 107–10.

13. Ellsworth C. Carlson, *The Kaiping Mines, 1877–1912*, 8–11, 18–20, 24–25. Young, *Rhetoric of Empire*, 35–37. Chiang Chia-ao, *China's Struggle for Railroad Development*, 25–26. For a contemporary description of the K'aip'ing railway see Wilson, *China*, 226–30. U.S., *Consular Reports* 34 (October 1883): 825–29. A great famine in northern China during the late 1870s gave added substance to foreign arguments about the benefits of railroads. J. Stahel to John A. Campbell, January 29, 1878, no. 32, U.S., Consular Despatches, Shanghai, 26.

of unofficial persuasion. One of his first moves was to arrange for the exhibit of a model railroad in Peking.[14]

The second American railroad enthusiast was James Harrison Wilson, a one-time Civil War general with training in engineering, railroad experience, and contacts with a rising New York financier, Jacob H. Schiff, and the Grant wing of the Republican party. Wilson and Denby understood each other at once, and the promoter soon acquired the valuable friendship of Vice Consul Pethick. During the winter of 1885–1886 Wilson acted with energy, traveling about China, meeting Li Hung-chang and other notables, and laying the groundwork for a system of American railroad concessions. At the outset he planned to extend the K'aip'ing Railway to Tientsin. In a long-range outline he recommended lines from Peking to Tientsin and to Chinkiang on the Yangtze and from Hankow on the river to Canton. (This eventually became one great trunk line, Peking-Hankow-Canton.) He even thought a narrow-gauge railroad feasible on Taiwan.

Since Wilson soon realized the Chinese fear of foreign-controlled railroads and lack of capital, he suggested to Secretary Bayard that the United States might lend $50 million in silver to the Chinese government, which could then organize its own company. An intergovernmental loan was completely impracticable at this time, but Denby agreed that a Chinese-organized company was a good idea, and Wilson returned home to publicize the project and seek private capital, leaving Pethick to represent him and keep Li interested. Unfortunately, some details of the project leaked out, and the anti-railroad clique at court issued a memorial denouncing Li, Wilson, Pethick, and their Chinese friends for inflaming the people with a scheme to enrich foreigners. All plans had to be suspended for a time.[15]

At this awkward moment, what should appear on the scene but a second American project for the development of Chinese communications and resources, even more grandiose than Wilson's. The core of the new plan was to be a great bank based on both American and Chinese capital. Tax-exempt, with officials appointed by the Chinese government, it would serve as a bank of deposit, oversee the Chinese currency, and float loans for development projects. Apparently the first of these projects—perhaps chosen for its minimal effect on superstitious Chinese—was to be a company to establish telephone systems in the treaty ports.

14. U.S., *Foreign Relations, 1885*, 180–81. Denby to Bayard, January 10, February 21, March 8, 1886, nos. 69, 97, 106, U.S., Diplomatic Despatches, China, 77. Denby professed to dislike "promoters" as distinguished from more reputable "resident representatives." Anderson, *Imperialism and Idealism*, 148. Since he supported the shyster Mitkiewicz, it is difficult to appreciate his distinction.

15. Healy, *U.S. Expansionism*, 68–71, 74–76. Young, *Rhetoric of Empire*, 35. Gary Dean Best, "Ideas without Capital: James H. Wilson and East Asia, 1885–1910," 453–57. James Harrison Wilson to Bayard, October 30, 1885; Wilson to Li Hung-chang, February 10, 1886; Wilson to Liu Ming Ch'uau, June 10, 1886, James Harrison Wilson papers, boxes 5, 6, 25. Pethick to Wilson, May 16, 1886; February 11, April 1, 1887, ibid, box 18. Denby to Bayard, December 1, 1885; January 8, 10, February 21, July 13, 1886, nos. 47, 62, 69, 97, 163, U.S., Diplomatic Despatches, 77, 78. Denby stretched his instructions to the limit by drawing up a draft charter for a railroad company, basing it on the corporation law of Indiana, his home state. He and Wilson polished it and sent it to Li for his inspection.

Eventually the bank would sponsor a railroad network from Peking to Tientsin, Shanghai, Hankow, and Canton, as well as companies to open coal and iron mines and manufacture iron and steel. While the managing role of the government would safeguard Chinese sovereignty, prominent American participation would obviously open markets for American trade and fields for American investment. In the era of dollar diplomacy even the Taft administration could produce no more comprehensive blueprint; as Denby remarked, it would give its backers "the complete exploitation of China."[16]

The principal promoters of this ambitious project were an oddly matched pair—Wharton Barker, a respectable Philadelphia banker, who had recently undertaken development plans for the Russian government, and Eugene Kostka de Mitkiewicz, reputedly a Polish count but actually an international confidence man. His imposing appearance and plausible talk for a time took in Barker and many other American businessmen, State Department officials, and progressive Chinese, including Li Hung-chang himself. Barker set the plan in motion by getting preliminary subscriptions from the leading businessmen of Philadelphia. He himself stayed home, but he sent a personal agent with Mitkiewicz as a precaution. In June 1887 the "count" arrived in Shanghai with a Chinese-American entourage and a portfolio of letters of introduction, including ones from President Cleveland, Jay Gould, and the Chinese minister to the United States.

Largely ignoring Denby, Mitkiewicz set out to establish contact with Li Hung-chang, working through Li's protégé, Ma Chien-chang, and his brother. Li was more immediately interested in a bank than in railroads or mines, since this would furnish the capital China must have. Probably to give Mitkiewicz tangible proof of his interest, he obtained for him the desired telephone concession and sent him back to the United States and Europe with the Ma brothers to perfect plans for the bank and secure firm capital commitments. As soon as the European community in Shanghai and Peking learned of the new project, there was an outburst of angry protest, especially in the British-dominated English-language press. The German minister is said to have predicted angrily: "If we allow this to go on the Yankees will sweep the board." Doubtless the conservatives at the court needed no European protest to arouse them. Early in October the imperial government canceled the telephone contract and ordered Li to abandon the bank project.[17]

16. This description is a composite of several statements contained in the Wharton Barker papers, boxes 2, 5. Wharton Barker to S. P. Makiechang [Ma Chien-chang?], October 5, 1886; [Unidentified] to Chang Yen Hoon, November 28, 1886; Barker to Makiechang, January 5, 1889; Denby to Bayard, August 3, 1887, no. 426, U.S., Diplomatic Despatches, China, 81.

17. Young, *Rhetoric of Empire*, 38–47. Li envisioned the bank as a purely private venture that would not expose the government to European charges of favoritism. The negotiations in China may be followed from two contrasting viewpoints in the Barker papers and in William N. Pethick's letters in the Wilson papers. For the German minister's statement see W. A. P. Martin, *A Cycle of Cathay, or China South and North, with Personal Reminiscences,* 400. Martin had close contacts with the Tsungli Yamen and with European diplomats. Sir Robert Hart thought Mitkiewicz a Vanderbilt agent. Fairbank, *IG in Peking,* 2, 685.

The Chinese action stunned Mitkiewicz and put him on the defensive against the American press, which had already begun to question his claims and soon uncovered him as an impostor. For a time *Bradstreet's* tried to deny that anything had gone wrong, while the mugwump *Nation* raised the suspicion of a Chinese "scramble" after American silver dollars, and the *New York Sun* openly denounced Mitkiewicz as a shyster. *Engineering News* came closest to the mark when it pronounced Chinese conservatism an insuperable obstacle to Western improvements, but it unfairly criticized American diplomatic action as inadequate.[18]

Actually, Denby loyally vouched for Mitkiewicz to Chinese officials and tried to convince the Tsungli Yamen that the proposed bank would not be a monopoly such as the Chinese claimed the treaties had forbidden. After the Wilson episode he had assured Secretary Bayard that he had never said a word to secure a contract or job for anyone. Now he declared that he had acted only to protect the general reputation of the United States. Bayard was reported to favor good offices by American diplomats for any project such as Barker's, but on this occasion he mildly rebuked Denby. Although "responsible citizens whose enterprises have the practical guaranty of pecuniary ability and personal character and standing" would always receive any "practicable" support, said Bayard, "such action should originate in this department, where the opportunity for estimating the nature of the proposed enterprise and the character and responsibility of the parties proposing to embark in it can be better formed."[19]

While Li Hung-chang was angry at the "count's" imposture, he accepted Barker's good faith and for the next two years tried to persuade him to come to China in person and negotiate further, using as a lure the possibility of railroad concessions. Barker turned back to Russia instead, for apparently he wanted an iron-bound concession in advance, and this Li could not or would not obtain for him.[20] Meanwhile, the viceroy inaugurated an extension of the K'aip'ing Railway

---

It is interesting that the first German bank in China was founded less than a year later (*London Times,* January 16, 1888, clipping in Barker papers, box 4). For parallel railroad negotiations of Jardine Matheson and Company see LeFevour, *Western Enterprise,* 108–23.

18. *Bradstreet's* 15 (November 19, 1887): 759. *Nation* 45 (October 13, 1887): 283. *New York Sun,* October 6, 1887; clippings of this and other New York newspapers in Barker papers, box 3. *Engineering News* 17 (September 17, October 8, 22, 1887): 206, 251, 294.

19. Denby to Bayard, October 14, 1886; September 27, 1887, nos. 227, 461, U.S., Diplomatic Despatches, China, 81. Denby to Bayard, November 3, 1887, Bayard papers, 115, 23617–18 ff. Robert Christy to Barker, October 10, 1887, Barker papers, box 3. John Russell Young also supported the project. John Russell Young to Barker, September 26, October 11, 1887, ibid. Bayard to Denby, December 15, 1887, no. 274, U.S., Diplomatic Instructions, China, 4, 334. For a general survey of the problem see Moore, *Digest of International Law,* vol. 4, 565–70.

20. Young, *Rhetoric of Empire,* 48–52. Smithers to Porter, October 13, November 12, 1887, nos. 34, 37, U.S., Consular Despatches, Tientsin, 3. Barker to Makiechang, May 12, 1888, Letterbook, 19, 189–92, Barker papers. Barker to Li Hung-chang, August 17, 1888; Barker to Makiechang, January 5, 1889; John G. Purdon to Barker, January 18, 1889, ibid., box 4, 5. Bayard to Denby, December 15, 1887, no. 274, U.S., Diplomatic Instructions, China, 4, 334–37 (quoted section on 336). Bayard maintained that Cleveland's letter of

to Tientsin with great ceremony. Li tried to obtain its continuation to Peking, and, failing in this, he sent an agent into Manchuria in 1890 to begin reconnaissance for a northeastern extension that would counter Russian influence there. Learning of this, the Russians made a decision they had long been considering—to push the Trans-Siberian Railroad east toward Manchuria and at the same time start a second line westward from Vladivostok.[21]

Americans took no part in these projects, although the Chinese expanded line used some American rolling stock and engineering devices such as the Westinghouse air brake. As Barker and Wilson watched from the United States, William N. Pethick, now Li's confidential secretary, bemoaned the Americans' inaction.[22] But if their railroad plans had gone awry, the Europeans had done no better. The Chinese field was still open, and American promoters had made contacts that they would find useful later in the 1890s.

Early American activity in Chinese mining was more limited but no more successful than that in railroading. The geological expedition of Raphael Pumpelly that Burlingame arranged in the mid-1860s led to nothing permanent, and during the next decade Americans made some efforts to report on or work coal deposits on Sakhalin and Taiwan, but coal from Australia and Nagasaki controlled the market. Furthermore, local superstitions and government regulations hedged in foreign mining activities. In 1886 Li Hung-chang engaged John A. Church, an experienced American mining engineer, to introduce American mining methods at some old silver-lead mines in Jehol, north of the Great Wall. Apparently, Li intended to finance this project through the Barker-Mitkiewicz bank, and at first Pethick was enthusiastic about its prospects, for Church installed a modern smelter and updated the mines. But he underestimated the capital required and the local prejudices, so when his wife grew tired of the isolated settlement, he decided to go home.[23]

---

introduction in no way vouched for the count's character, but of course to the Chinese the president's signature was a magic password.

21. U.S., *Consular Reports* 81 (July 1887): 66–68; 101 (January 1889): 68. U.S., *Foreign Relations, 1889,* 79–81; *1893,* 236–37. Denby to Blaine, March 19, 1890, July 28, 1891, nos. 1070, 1362, U.S., Diplomatic Despatches, China, 78, 79. Young, *Rhetoric of Empire,* 36–38. William L. Langer, *The Diplomacy of Imperialism, 1890–1902,* vol. 1, 171–72. Robert H. Kerner, "The Russian Eastward Movement: Some Observations on Its Historical Significance," 140–42. *Railroad Gazette,* n.d., in *Public Opinion* (May 2, 1885): 470–71. China built only forty miles of track into Manchuria by 1894, as it ran out of funds. Hunt, *Frontier Defense,* 18.

22. U.S., *Foreign Relations, 1889,* 80–81. Pethick to Wilson, January 19, 1891, Wilson papers. Wilson put out a feeler for a possible loan to China in 1891, but it was rebuffed. Wilson to Pethick, March 8, 1891, Letterbook, 1889–1896, 268–71; Pethick to Wilson, March 10, June 6, 1891, Wilson papers, box 18.

23. Curti and Stainer, "Flowery Flag Devils," 668. Hinton, "A Talk with Mr. Burlingame," 618–19. U.S., *Commercial Relations, 1876–77,* 183–84. U.S., *Foreign Relations, 1875–76,* 44–45. Denny to F. W. Seward, November 28, 1878, no. 21, U.S., Consular Despatches, Tientsin, 2. Curti and Birr, *Prelude to Point Four,* 19–20. U.S., *Consular Reports* 105 (May

The open ports, especially Shanghai, offered many advantages for industrial development—cheap labor, available Chinese and foreign capital, and easy contact with outside technology and markets. During the late 1860s and 1870s Europeans and a few Americans including Russell and Company took up silk reeling and a variety of small-scale manufactures. As the legal basis of their actions they cited the French treaty of 1858, conceding the right to engage "au commerce ou à l'industrie," which other foreigners shared under their most-favored-nation clauses.

American interest in these manufacturing industries produced a diplomatic dilemma that placed commerce and industrial investment in direct opposition. During the early 1880s the Chinese government began to challenge foreign factories and made a *cause célèbre* out of the case of William S. Wetmore, head of an export-import firm, who had obtained subscriptions for a cotton-yarn mill at Shanghai. Wetmore was denied a permit to operate since a Chinese company already had a monopoly. On the one hand, the American government hesitated to press for unlimited cotton manufacturing, lest Chinese textiles, benefiting from cheap labor, crowd the American product out of Far Eastern markets. But on the other hand, Young pointed out that if the Chinese succeeded in restricting manufacturing rights, they might go on to limit trade contacts and withdraw into their old isolation. When the German minister confronted a similar situation, he called in marines who compelled the Chinese officials to stop interfering, but Young decided against coercion, partly because he felt that Americans were more interested in trade than investment. Wetmore gave up his project, and the State Department allowed the question to simmer unheeded. When Minister Denby took it up again, the department favored a do-nothing policy, but in 1893 he reluctantly joined other foreign diplomats in protesting against a Chinese ruling prohibiting the import of steam-driven machinery. The Tsungli Yamen would not yield, although by that time at least seventy-four plants were using such machinery in Shanghai alone.[24]

Part of the Chinese opposition to foreign factories was simply the conservatives' unwillingness to change, but much of it arose from a desire among more

1889): 20. Denby to Bayard, August 17, 1886, October 16, 1888, nos. 199, 731, U.S., Diplomatic Despatches, China, 78, 83. Pethick to Wilson, December 24, 1887; March 27, December 22, 1890, Wilson papers, box 18.

24. Morken, "Protecting American Commerce," 65–67. Hagan, *American Gunboat Diplomacy*, 115–18. Anderson, *Imperialism and Idealism*, 128–35. George E. Paulsen, "Machinery for the Mills of China: 1882–1896," 320–35. Gull, *British Economic Interests*, 80–81. Hou, *Foreign Investment and Economic Development*, 83. Orchard, "Contrasts in Industrialization," 20–21. Moore, *Digest of International Law*, vol. 5, 450–51. U.S., *Foreign Relations, 1883*, 129–32, 191–92. W. S. Wetmore to Denny, November 3, 1882, U.S., Consular Despatches, Shanghai, 32. Young to Frelinghuysen, August 25, 1883, no. 242, U.S., Diplomatic Despatches, China, 66. Frelinghuysen to Young, February 26, 1883, no. 86, U.S., Diplomatic Instructions, China, 3, 396–401. Denby to Secretary of State, May 27, 1889; Denby to Gresham, July 24, August 10, 1893, nos. 897, 1715, 1720, U.S., Diplomatic Despatches, China, 85, 95. Adee to Denby, August 29, 1889, no. 451, U.S., Diplomatic Instructions, China, 4, 462–63. Remer, *Foreign Investments in China*, 252–54.

progressive officials to keep Chinese industrial development under local control. Around 1880 Jardine, Matheson and Company tried to organize a cotton mill with Chinese promoters in Shanghai and some support from Li Hung-chang but failed for lack of domestic capital and too much official meddling. Two decades after the original planning a mill was finally opened under Li Hung-chang's auspices.

By 1894 Shanghai was becoming a Chinese manufacturing center, producing silk thread, paper, ironware, munitions, soap, and other minor products. As will be seen, the Sino-Japanese War of that year opened Chinese ports to Japanese-run industries, which eventually dominated manufacturing there.[25]

A final issue in Chinese-American relations during the 1870s and 1880s must be considered for its interaction with economic expansionism—the Chinese immigration question. Chinese laborers poured into California for a few years during the gold rush, reaching about twenty-five thousand in 1851, but high taxes and Australian gold discoveries greatly reduced the numbers for the rest of the decade. At first expansionists welcomed them with open arms as "the vanguard of that great Asiatic commercial army which is to pour hereafter the wealth of old dotard Custom at the feet of the youthful giant Enterprise." Whatever other Californians may have felt, their attention was somewhat diverted during the 1860s by the Civil War and the need for cheap labor to complete the transcontinental railroad. As has been seen, Anson Burlingame's mission and treaty, with its provision for free Chinese admission and residence, aroused only moderate opposition on racist grounds. Even then, however, sensational reports of Chinese atrocities against missionaries such as the Tientsin massacre of 1870 touched off new passions in the *New York Herald* and similar newspapers.

After the completion of the transcontinental railroad the tide turned. California opinion attacked the Chinese, who looked so different from other people, lived by themselves, and made no effort to assimilate. (In the Northwest, however, labor shortages preserved Chinese immigration to the end of the century.) The new railroad speeded migration from the East, and by 1870 one-fourth of the foreign-born in California were Irish. Inflammatory speeches and editorials and a grossly biased investigation by the California Senate developed an emotional and unfair case against the immigrants; their strange clothes and customs, their filth, their vices, and above all the low wages for which they would work. A new state constitution crystallized these prejudices into law.

25. Frank H. King, *A Concise Economic History of Modern China, 1840–1961,* 56–60. Allen and Donnithorne, *Western Enterprise,* 160–67. Paulsen, "Machinery for the Mills of China," 330. Sung Jae Koh, *Stages of Industrial Development in Asia: A Comparative History of the Cotton Industry in Japan, India, China, and Korea,* 721–22. LeFevour, *Western Enterprise,* 40–47. U.S., *Consular Reports* 3 (January 1881): 78–79. Denby to Blaine, May 29, 1889; August 3, 1890, nos. 901, 1138, U.S., Diplomatic Despatches, China, 85, 86. Charles Denby, Jr., to Gresham, July 17, 1894, no. 1892, ibid., 95. Denny to Payson, March 30, 1880, no. 124, U.S., Consular Despatches, Shanghai, 31. A. C. Jones to Wharton, October 1, 1890, ibid., Chingkiang, 5. *American Protectionist,* 1, 36. *Bradstreet's* 4 (November 19, 1881): 327.

The infection spread eastward, for the Reconstruction period had left racism in many corners of American life, and in a period of hot partisan rivalry California's position as a "swing" state encouraged politicians to seize on the Chinese issue as a safe if demagogic source of votes. The Western author Bret Harte popularized the epithet "heathen Chinee" and thereby fixed in place a scornful stereotype that mocked the efforts of the missionaries. The Burlingame treaty was made to seem almost treasonable, and a rumor even spread that—poetic justice!—Burlingame had died of leprosy. As anti-Chinese sentiment grew, the Peking foreign office protested to Minister George F. Seward, who warned the State Department that a national anti-Chinese law might threaten the entire foreign system in China.[26]

In 1879 Congress passed an act limiting the number of Chinese who could come to the United States in one ship—clearly an experimental approach to exclusion. President Hayes vetoed the act as a violation of the Burlingame treaty. Confronted by rising public indignation in an election year, but anxious to retain Chinese goodwill, he and Secretary Evarts then sent a special mission to China headed by James B. Angell, president of the University of Michigan, an educator who they thus thought would be acceptable to the Chinese. Thanks mainly to a Chinese-Russian diplomatic crisis in 1880 and the Chinese need for friends, the Tsungli Yamen reluctantly signed a treaty recognizing the American right to "regulate, limit, or suspend" immigration of Chinese "laborers" for a "reasonable" time. The definition of the quoted words immediately created problems. When Congress passed a bill shutting out both skilled and unskilled laborers for twenty years, President Arthur vetoed the bill as a strained interpretation of the new treaty and "a breach of national faith." Failing to pass the bill over Arthur's veto, Congress reduced the time period to ten years and provided a cumbersome system of registration by which nonlaborers might enter the United States. In 1882 Arthur signed this measure.[27]

---

26. Coolidge, *Chinese Immigration*, chaps. 1–8. McClellan, *Heathen Chinee*, chaps. 1, 2. David L. Anderson, "The Diplomacy of Discrimination: Chinese Exclusion, 1876–1882," 32–36. Hunt, *Special Relationship*, 85–90. For congressional diatribes see Coolidge, *Chinese Immigration*, 145, and U.S., 47th Cong., 1st sess., *Congressional Record*, 13, 1481–88. On sentiment in California see also Elmer Clarence Sandmeyer, *The Anti-Chinese Movement in California*, chaps. 1–4. For samples of propaganda for and against the Chinese see *United States Magazine and Democratic Review* 30 (April 1852): 321 (quotation); L. T. Townsend, *The Chinese Problem*; and M. B. Starr, *The Coming Struggle: or What the People on the Pacific Coast Think of the Coolie Invasion.* For the rumor about Burlingame see Miller, *Unwelcome Immigrant*, 164. The Burlingame treaty, while granting the Chinese free admission, explicitly denied them citizenship, but it guaranteed them most-favored-nation treatment regarding "privileges, immunities and exemptions [i.e., legal protection] in respect to travel or residence" in the United States. Bevens, *Treaties*, 680–84. On Chinese immigration into the Northwest, see Cox, "Passage to India Revisited," 96–97.

27. Coolidge, *Chinese Immigration*, chaps. 9–11. Sandmeyer, *Anti-Chinese Movement*, chap. 5. Anderson, "Diplomacy of Discrimination," 36–45. Hunt, *Special Relationship*, 100–102. After his recall, George F. Seward defended his policy in the *North American Review* 134 (June 1882): 562–77. For the principal documents concerning the treaty negotiations see Clyde, *United States Policy toward China*, 140–58. For the text of the treaty see Bevans,

During the congressional and press debates that led to the Exclusion Act both racism and trade considerations figured prominently. Many southerners joined anti-Chinese Californians in defense of racial purity, while many northerners, especially from New England, revived abolitionist arguments about freedom and racial equality. National honor and the sanctity of treaties also received much attention. A southern minority, led by Senator Joseph E. Brown (Democrat, Georgia) and the *Atlanta Constitution,* objected that the bill would hurt the sale of cotton cloth in China. The *New York Herald* declared that the paramount question with China was one of trade and that to nullify the Burlingame treaty would surrender the field to Britain. San Francisco would sacrifice her future "as a great emporium of commerce" for a "miserable petty question which has been raised by low California demagogues." The *New York Tribune* agreed. When Arthur vetoed the first exclusion act, he called Far Eastern trade "the key to national wealth and influence" and especially to the "incalculable future" of San Francisco. To protect American labor from Chinese competition and at the same time maintain this trade, he hoped that partial, compromise measures would suffice. (Throughout the debate little was said about the injuries suffered by Pacific Mail and other shipping from the loss of passage money for eastbound Chinese laborers.)[28]

Events did not conform to Arthur's hopes, for the Chinese immigration question continued to seethe through the 1880s and 1890s. Immigration figures see-sawed, reaching more than thirty-seven thousand in 1882 and falling to less than fifty from 1885 to 1888. Awkward official improvisations under the 1882 act worked further hardships on Chinese immigrants and residents, and the press continued to publicize Chinese backwardness and corruption. California xenophobes complained that a flood of new immigrants was penetrating the leaky Canadian and Mexican borders on recently completed railroads. Violence broke out in several cities and culminated in a massacre of Chinese immigrants at Rock Springs, Wyoming Territory, where a Chinese settlement was burned and about fifty killed.

Minister Denby and American consuls in the Chinese ports reported rising anti-Americanism and rioting, especially in Canton and Hong Kong, from which most of the immigrants had come. They warned that this resentment would ruin American trade and that British merchants and newspapers, hoping for this, were encouraging the Chinese to stand up for their oppressed countrymen

---

Treaties, vol. 6, 684–88. The commercial treaty already referred to (see chap. 5) was signed at the same time. British observers approved the immigration treaty but nevertheless feared an American-Chinese entente that would lead to increased American sales in China. *Economist* 38 (December 11, 1880): 1447–48.

28. Hearden, "Cotton Mills of the New South," 27–28. *New York Herald,* March 29, 1880; January 15, 1881. *New York Tribune,* May 9, 1882. Richardson, *Messages and Papers,* vol. 8, 117–18. The *New York World* declared that trade was the chief reason for Arthur's veto. *New York World,* April 5, 1882. Minister Young was especially eager for China to place an exhibition of porcelains, bronzes, and other art objects in the New Orleans Exposition of 1884 to mitigate the effects of the Exclusion Act in both countries. Young to Frelinghuysen, July 31, 1884, February 6, 1885, nos. 483, 639, U.S., Diplomatic Despatches, China, 71, 74.

in America. Denby advised Secretary Bayard to obtain an indemnity for recent outrages, press Congress for a more equitable law, and negotiate a new treaty that would prohibit emigration of Chinese laborers. This he also proposed to the Tsungli Yamen.[29]

While a senator, Bayard had expressed scorn for the Burlingame mission and treaty, and he was still inclined to resist the protests of the Chinese minister at Washington over mistreatment of immigrants. But Denby's gloomy predictions about threats to American trade and missionaries moderated the secretary's views, and with some difficulty he got Congress to appropriate $147,748.74 for indemnities (without any mention of liability). In March 1888 he and the Chinese minister even signed a clarifying treaty whereby the Chinese accepted a twenty-year exclusion of laborers in return for more clearly specified admission of nonlaborers and guarantees to Chinese residents of the United States.

These minimal concessions proved too much for a nation almost equally divided between major political parties. With a presidential election in the offing, the Senate, narrowly controlled by the Republicans, added crippling amendments, and the Chinese government rejected the treaty, amid a new round of British-encouraged riots in China. Later in the year Congress retaliated with the Scott Act, full of new and more complicated restrictions, and Chinese immigration became a burning campaign issue. Despite the urging of Bayard and Denby, Cleveland signed the act. The Harrison administration avoided the immigration issue, but in 1892, with another close presidential election approaching, Congress passed an even more restrictive law, the Geary Act, which forbade any Chinese except diplomats and their servants to enter the United States or to return if, being already residents, they left the country for any reason. Temporary admission was allowed in some cases, but the law had many unnecessarily harsh features such as a rigid system of registration and a denial of habeas corpus or bail in criminal cases. The Supreme Court promptly upheld its constitutionality.[30]

Before and after the passage of both the Scott and Geary Acts, Congress and the press thoroughly reviewed the Chinese immigration question. Racists and xenophobes mainly repeated the arguments that Californians had been polishing since the 1850s, with special attention to increasingly self-conscious labor sentiment.

29. Coolidge, *Chinese Immigration*, chap. 12. Cassey, "Mission of Denby," 50–56, 101–5. Denby to Bayard, December 8, 1885, March 10, May 17, July 16, August 4, 10, October 30, 1886, nos. 52, 107, 136, 169, 187, 195, 235, U.S., Diplomatic Despatches, China, 76–79. Seymour to George L. Rives, March 20, 1889, no. 161. Seymour to William Wharton, February 8, 1890, no. 189, U.S., Consular Despatches, Canton, 11. *New York Tribune*, August 13, 1881, January 29, 1882, December 4, 1884; *Harper's Weekly* 28 (September 30, 1884): 624. J. Thomas Scharf, "The Farce of the Chinese Exclusion Laws," 91–93.

30. Coolidge, *Chinese Immigration*, chap. 13. Cassey, "Mission of Denby," 56–81, 89–91. Bayard memorandum of conversation with Chinese minister, January 28, 1887, Bayard papers, 107, 21022–24 ff. In an involved message to Congress, Cleveland rationalized his action by citing Chinese rejection of the treaty although it had conformed to the best interests of both countries. Richardson, *Messages and Papers*, vol. 8, 630–35. After the election was over, Congress passed the McCreary amendment, which somewhat softened the Geary Act.

Opponents of exclusion appealed to humanitarianism and a sense of fair play but laid greatest stress on fear that the Chinese government and people, in their just wrath, would retaliate against the security of American missionaries and the property and profits of American business. Senate expansionists such as John T. Morgan (Democrat, Alabama), Cushman K. Davis (Republican, Minnesota), John Sherman (Republican, Ohio), William P. Frye (Republican, Maine), and others, cited raw cotton, cotton textiles, and petroleum products as endangered exports. Prompted by Collis P. Huntington, Frye predicted that the Chinese would divert both passenger and freight traffic to Canadian railroads and Vancouver, which would soon rival San Francisco, and even that exclusionists, if successful, would shut out European immigration as well, ruining American shipping lines in the Atlantic. As the *New York Herald* put it: "Neither Lord Salisbury nor Prince Bismarck . . . could have drawn a measure [the Scott Act] so well calculated to advance German and British interests in [China]."[31]

Through the din of argument at home Denby continued to describe official resentment in Peking at the congressional debates, the restrictive laws, and the mistreatment of Chinese immigrants and residents. He urged Congress to reword the laws so as to save Chinese "face" while still satisfying Californians. Several times Li Hung-chang threatened that China would retaliate against Americans if the laws continued in force. In 1892 the Tsungli Yamen refused to receive Henry W. Blair as minister on the grounds that, while a senator, he had insulted China during the immigration debates. (Thereby Denby's term of office was extended by about six years.)

But opposition seemed confined to the official classes, and the American consul at Tientsin reported that the Geary Act was not perceptibly affecting trade. When Congress amended its most objectionable provisions and the government postponed enforcement, the foreign office took no further action. In March 1894 Secretary Gresham and the Chinese minister, Yang Ju, agreed on a treaty prohibiting the immigration of Chinese laborers for ten years. During that decade Sinophobia gradually became less hysterical and more moderate, as Americans discovered some utility in the immigrants and recognized trade considerations. Also, later-arriving Japanese drew some of the fire on themselves. Nevertheless, Chinese grievances continued, so the Peking government refused to renew the treaty in 1904 and resorted to a boycott of American products that produced

---

31. Cassey, "Mission of Denby," 81–96. U.S., 50th Cong., 1st sess., *Congressional Record*, 14, 8370, 8373, 8374; 52d Cong., 1st sess., 23, 3025–32, 3479, 3481–82, 3532, 3564, 3611. *Public Opinion* 4 (April 7, 1888): 625–26; 5 (September 22, 1888): 511–12 (*Herald* quotation), 523–24; 7 (July 27, August 31, 1889): 331, 430. *Literary Digest* 5 (May 13, 1891): 48–49; 7 (May 6, 20, 27, 1893): 22–23, 80, 107–8. John Russell Young, "The Chinese Question Again," 590–602. *New York Journal of Commerce*, January 14, 1889. *Commercial and Financial Chronicle* 54 (April 30, 1892): 700. *Bradstreet's* 20 (April 9, 1892): 231. *Nation* 56 (May 25, 1893): 380–81. Expansionist senators such as Henry Cabot Lodge, who had many xenophobic constituents, had a hard time reconciling the two positions. McClellan, *Heathen Chinee*, 169, 199–200.

one of the most serious Far Eastern problems faced by the Theodore Roosevelt administration.[32]

As the 1890s began, the last vestiges of the "old China trade" disappeared, and smaller agencies and firms replaced the old commission houses. American imports from China, though increasing, had changed little in character since the 1860s. American export merchants did a flourishing trade in cotton textiles, kerosene, and a few other items, but Britain still dominated the first, and Russia was offering alarming competition in the second. American promoters had made little progress in railroading, steamships, telegraphs, mining, and industry.

Despite the rhetoric about the great potentialities of the China market often emanating from Congress and the State Department in the early 1890s, it could not be said that the U.S. government had adopted consistent or effective measures to support trade or investment. Before 1860 most American gains resulted from Anglo-French aggression and most-favored-nation clauses in the United States' treaties with China. Anson Burlingame's cooperative policy, brilliant but naive, never won the steady support of either Anglo-American merchants or diplomats. As elsewhere in the world, the American government's abandonment of shipping subsidies after the mid-1870s strengthened the near monopoly of European steamship lines over Far Eastern trade. Washington's few encouraging measures, such as the trade dollar and protests against the likin tax, were ill-conceived or ineffective.

For a time in the early 1880s conditions seemed to improve, thanks to Grant's influence, the work of the Angell commission, and the appointment of the sympathetic John Russell Young as minister to China.[33] But Congress and the State Department ignored William H. Trescot's sensible recommendations for reforms in the consular and court system. In the late 1880s, to be sure, a new business-minded minister, Charles Denby, stretched his instructions to serve as contact man for promoters of two ambitious railroad projects, but capital at home was not yet available for such extensive foreign investments.

32. For a good summary of Chinese government and popular protests see Hunt, *Special Relationship*, 96–108, 124–25. Coolidge, *Chinese Immigration*, chaps. 14, 16. McClellan, *Heathen Chinee*, chap. 4, 175–77. George E. Paulsen, "The Gresham-Yang Treaty," 281–97. George E. Paulsen, "The Abrogation of the Gresham-Yang Treaty," 457–77. The Gresham-Yang Treaty gave China a sop by temporarily approving the residence of Chinese officials, students, or merchants in the United States and by putting the registration of laborers already admitted on a reciprocal basis. Bevans, *Treaties*, vol. 6, 691–94. U.S., *Foreign Relations, 1892*, 134–35. U.S., *Commercial Relations, 1894–95*, 1, 602. Denby to Bayard, January 2, 1889; Denby to Blaine, June 4, 1891, April 7, 1892; Denby to Gresham, July 7, 1893, nos. 782, 1316, 1512, 1702, U.S., Diplomatic Despatches, China, 84, 90, 92, 93. Wharton to Denby, October 6, 1891, no. 659, U.S., Diplomatic Instructions, China, 4, 612–17. Seymour to Quincy, May 27, 1893, no. 251, U.S., Consular Despatches, Canton, 12. John Fowler to Josiah Quincy, September 16, 1893, no. 136, ibid., Ningpo, 7.

33. Morken, "America Looks West," 182–85. William H. Trescot, Memorandum, May 1, 1881. U.S., *Reports of Diplomatic Bureau*, 5.

Also, as the promoters' projects grew in scope and splendor, the fears of another group of American nationalists threatened to raise a new obstacle to American trade and investment in China. The annexation of California and the completion of the transcontinental railroad—two of the fondest dreams of midcentury economic expansionists—brought to San Francisco a pressure group of xenophobes whose hateful language could only repel Chinese customers and officials. At the same time China was becoming an international problem, as European nations and Japan probed the great empire seeking entry points for commerce, development projects, and eventually political influence. By 1890 the Far East was perhaps a little less mysterious to outward-looking Americans, but it had become a great deal more complex.

7

Japan
The Sincerest Flattery

EFORE THE 1840S the occasional encounters between American seamen and the inhabitants of the Japanese archipelago did not encourage hope of regular trade or political relations. The rise of the whaling industry and the Treaty of Wang-hsia with China, however, made increased contacts inevitable. Castaways and deserters from whalers who reached the Japanese coast were sometimes treated kindly and released, but they might be thrown into noisome prisons as suspected spies. In 1846 Commodore James Biddle was sent with two warships and a letter from the president to negotiate some sort of understanding, but he allowed himself to be insulted by his hosts, and that merely made the situation worse. The following year, however, the Japanese were greatly impressed by the American naval landing at Veracruz during the Mexican War, and in 1849 Commander James Glynn used more blunt tactics than Biddle and secured the release of several prisoners.[1]

By that time the myth of the Golden East had spread to Japan. The chief publicist for the new trade was Aaron H. Palmer, head of a New York commission house deeply involved in the China trade. He distributed through the Orient thousands of leaflets describing American manufactures, and as early as 1842 he was sending these into Japan, along with American newspapers and book catalogues, with the aid of Dutch traders. Three years later he got a congressman to introduce a House resolution calling for commercial treaties with Japan and Korea. He besieged President Polk, Congress, and the public with memorials and resolutions urging more contacts with the Far East, Siberia, central Asia, and India and a ship canal across Central America. Japan, he said, had highly cultivated agriculture, bustling trade and transportation,

---

1. Samuel Eliot Morison, *"Old Bruin": Commodore Matthew C. Perry, 1794–1858* [etc.], 30–45. Dennett, *Americans in Eastern Asia*, 249–52. Alfred Tamarin, *Japan and the United States: Early Encounters, 1791–1860*, 30–45. Sakamaki, *Japan and the U.S.*, chaps. 5–9. Paullin, *Diplomatic Negotiations*, 233–43. Peter Booth Wiley, with Korogo Ichiro, *Yankees in the Land of the Gods: Commodore Perry and the Opening of Japan*, chap. 1. For a defense of Biddle see Johnson, *Far China Station*, 40–43. The most bizarre early American landing was that of Ranaid MacDonald, who single-handedly attempted to establish friendly relations. Americans also made contact with Japanese by rescuing Japanese sailors in the open Pacific and taking them to Hawaii or Mexico. Sakamaki, *Japan and the U.S.*, chap. 11.

prosperous cities and industries, postal and coinage systems, and mines. He and other publicists stressed the islands' coal deposits, a necessity for transpacific steamer lines. Whalers reinforced Palmer's writings with complaints of Japanese mistreatment.[2]

Americans' reaction to this publicity and to knowledge of Japan's self-imposed isolation varied. Some were belligerent; for example, the *New York Express* declared: "Japan has no right to bury her treasures behind her walls. . . . She must be made to feel that she is a power on the earth, that she has means, capacities and duties, and . . . if she fails in all of these [we must] *force upon her the dawning of a better day*." But the newly founded *New York Times* deplored such a warlike attitude and denied that any nation had the right to intervene in another's domestic affairs. Because of Japan's reputed coal deposits (whose quality was somewhat exaggerated) the question of an expedition and commercial negotiations became entangled with a proposed steamer line to China on the order of the later Pacific Mail concession (see chapter 4). In May 1851 President Millard Fillmore instructed Captain John H. Aulick, just appointed commander of the East India Squadron, to negotiate a commercial treaty with Japan, arrange for the removal of shipwrecked American sailors, and provide for the purchase of coal, which Secretary Daniel Webster called grandly "a gift of Providence," deposited in Japan "for the benefit of the human family." Unfortunately for Aulick, he soon fell out with his superiors, became the victim of slanderous rumors, and was removed from command, further delaying the expedition.[3]

The British reaction to these proceedings is worth noting. After the Opium War both Japanese and Americans expected that naval power and commercial ambition would bring an immediate British intervention in Japan. However, most British merchants preferred to exploit the demonstrated trade openings in China. Also, the Admiralty doubted that its strength was adequate for an expedition to Japan, and the Foreign Office cautiously avoided expanding the diplomatic problems it was already facing in China. Instead of taking alarm at the obvious evidence of American interest, Foreign Secretary Lord Malmesbury wrote in July 1852: "Her Majesty's Government would be glad to see the trade with Japan open; but they think it better to leave it to the United States to make the experiment; and

---

2. Neumann, *America Encounters Japan*, 26–27. Dennett, *Americans in Eastern Asia*, 252–53. Schroeder, *Shaping a Maritime Empire*, 141–46. Aaron H. Palmer, *Documents and Facts Illustrating the Origin of the Mission to Japan, Authorized by the Government of the United States, May 10th, 1851* [etc.] U.S., 29th Cong., 2d sess., *House Documents 96*, especially 22–24; 30th Cong., 1st sess., *Senate Miscellaneous Document 80*, especially 102; *House Report 596*, 34–37; 31st Cong., 1st sess., *Senate Executive Document 84*.

3. *New York Express* and *New York Times* both quoted in Tamarin, *Japan and the United States*, 62–64. See also *American Whig Review*, 9, 511–15. The *Times* eventually supported the Perry expedition. On the change of American opinion during the decade preceding Perry see William L. Neumann, "Religion, Morality, and Freedom: The Ideological Background of the Perry Expedition," 747–50. On Aulick's abortive expedition see Wiley, *Yankees in the Land of the Gods*, 100–101; and Johnson, *Far China Station*, chap. 9.

if that experiment is successful, Her Majesty's Government can take advantage of its success."[4]

It is unlikely that Her Majesty's Government would have taken such a relaxed attitude toward American competition if trade with China had been involved. For both countries, China always remained the principal focus of commercial attention throughout the nineteenth century. Even after 1890, when American trade with Japan began to pass that with China, Shanghai and Canton continued to be the true gateway to the Golden East. In the world of business Japan still seemed a sideshow.

The unlucky Captain Aulick's successor in command of the Japan expedition was Commodore Matthew Calbraith Perry, younger brother of a famous naval hero in the War of 1812 and an able, experienced officer at the peak of his career. He had served on the West African coast and in the Caribbean, and during the Mexican War he had organized the successful landing at Veracruz. Ashore he had pioneered in the introduction of steamships into the navy. Perry had hoped to command the Mediterranean Squadron, but he threw himself into preparations for the Japan expedition, reading widely in the by now abundant literature on the islands.

Perry and President Fillmore agreed that the main goal of the expedition must be a commercial treaty with Japan and saw it as the first move in a great Anglo-American confrontation for control of the Pacific. His specific instructions were more limited. Fillmore gave him a formal letter to deliver to the Japanese emperor. In his projected treaty Perry was to secure protection for shipwrecked American seamen and property; permission to obtain supplies, especially coal; and access to one or more ports for trade. Since the president had no power to declare war, Perry must use persuasion and not force except in self-defense. He must be courteous, conciliatory, and patient in the face of insults, but (doubtless with Biddle in mind), he must "do nothing that will compromise . . . his own dignity or that of his country" and must "impress [the Japanese] with a just sense of the power and greatness of this country, and . . . satisfy them that its past forbearance has been the result not of timidity, but of a desire to be on friendly terms with them." In maintaining this balance between firmness and courtesy, Perry had several advantages: his well-established reputation in the service as a martinet (his nickname was "Old Bruin"), considerable experience in Third World diplomacy, and a bearing of unsmiling, portly dignity. He determined to keep a respectful distance between himself and the Japanese, whom he came to regard as incorrigibly deceitful.[5]

4. W. G. Beasley, *Great Britain and the Opening of Japan, 1834–1858*, chaps. 2, 3. The quotation from Malmesbury is on 93.
5. The best account of Perry's background and character is Morison, *"Old Bruin,"* chaps. 5–22. For Perry's instructions, drafted by the secretary of war and the acting secretary of state, see U.S., 33rd Cong., 2d sess., *Senate Executive Document 34*, 4–9.

The expedition was originally to have consisted of three war steamers and four sloops-of-war, but ships were detached or added at nearly every stage. Perry wanted to take along a scientific corps, but Congress, much divided over the whole idea, refused him the money, so he hired young deckhands with special abilities at cut rates. His interpreters, whom he picked up at Shanghai, were A. L. C. Portman, a Dutchman fluent in Japanese, and S. Wells Williams, a missionary with twenty years of experience in China. Congress managed to find funds for presents to the Japanese that would advertise American power and civilization: books of U.S. fauna and flora, liquor, firearms, machinery, and gadgets. Samuel F. B. Morse helped him assemble a primitive telegraph, and, most impressive of all, Perry took along a complete miniature (quarter size) train set—locomotive, cars, and track.

Since most of the commodore's ships were already with the East India Squadron, he made the trip out in a single steamer, by way of Cape Town, Ceylon, and Hong Kong. After collecting the rest of his squadron at Shanghai, Perry visited the Ryukyu (or Liu Ch'iu in Chinese terminology) and Bonin Islands, partly to rehearse his diplomatic technique and partly to survey them as possible American strong points. On July 6, 1853, his ships anchored in the lower part of Edo Bay, perhaps twenty-five miles south of the Japanese capital itself.

Although each side had learned much about the other, neither knew how to open proceedings. The Japanese government was two-headed, with a titular emperor at Kyoto and a de facto ruler, the shogun, at Edo; unfortunately, the latter was seriously ill at the moment. The Dutch had amply warned of Perry's approach, but a panic broke out in the capital, and Japanese officials fell into great confusion; some even wanted to fight the Americans. Perry kept himself out of sight, resisted all Japanese efforts to visit his ships, and refused to receive subordinates. He demanded that President Fillmore's letter, suggesting bases of negotiation, be taken to the "emperor" (meaning the shogun at Edo), which the horrified Japanese at first refused to do. After several days of contemplating the "black [i.e., iron-hulled] ships," however, they gave in, and with lavish ceremony Perry delivered the president's letter to two "governors" in full regalia. Eight days after his arrival he and his ships left Edo Bay, having taken soundings to within five miles of the capital and notified the Japanese that he would return the following year to begin negotiations.

Perry occupied the intervening months with return visits to Okinawa and Shanghai. There he became involved in arguments with Commissioner Humphrey Marshall and the principal American merchants, who wanted him to leave much of his squadron with them for security during the Taiping Rebellion, then just getting under way. His sense of the urgency of his Japan expedition was stimulated, however, by news of the shogun's death, the Japanese desire to delay further proceedings indefinitely, and the presence of Russian and French ships off Nagasaki. On February 15, 1854, he sailed again into Edo Bay, this time with nine ships.

Since Perry rejected all talk of delay, the new shogun appointed commissioners. Perry expected to negotiate in Edo City, but the commissioners wanted him to move his ships to Nagasaki, the Dutch port, or to unprotected anchorages near the mouth of the bay. They finally settled on Kanagawa, near Yokohama with a secure harbor. Then followed an exchange of gifts—the American railroad, telegraph, and knick-knacks in return for abundant fresh supplies—and much tipsy celebrating, as the Japanese officials developed a taste for sweetened whiskey. Japanese artists made dozens of scrolls and wood blocks of Perry, other Americans, and their ships, a vivid record of the whole visit.

The Treaty of Kanagawa, completed at the end of March, satisfied the basic requirements of Perry's instructions. It opened two ports to American ships for supply of "wood, water, provisions and coal and other articles their necessities may require, as far as the Japanese have them." The two ports were Shimoda, on the route to China and only about a hundred miles from Edo but small and inaccessible by land, and Hakodate, on the south coast of the northern island of Hokkaido, convenient to whalers. Shipwrecked sailors would be returned to Americans at either of these ports, and a consul might reside at Shimoda, but no Americans were to venture more than a few miles inland. The treaty contained a most-favored-nation clause but made no mention of extraterritoriality, religion, or naval bases.

After leaving Japan, Perry returned to Okinawa and signed the Treaty of Naha, a "wood, water, and provisions" agreement with protection for shipwrecked sailors but no mention of coal or other trade. He would have liked to go much further and in his reports recommended that the United States establish naval bases on Okinawa, the Bonin Islands, and Taiwan. He even had a subordinate take possession of some of the Bonins and bought land for himself on one of them, hoping to establish a steamer line and colonize settlers. His embarrassed superiors disavowed his actions and ignored his recommendations. In this sort of imperialism Perry may have been fifty years ahead of his time, but in most other respects he responded admirably to prevalent American needs. To be sure, his treaties gained fewer concessions than Caleb Cushing's Treaty of Wang-hsia, but except for more trade provisions and the selection of a better port than Shimoda, they were all Perry could have obtained without winning a war that the United States did not want and could not have fought.[6]

The American press gave considerable space to the Perry expedition while it was in progress, but by the time the treaty arrived, public attention had shifted to the

---

6. Good short accounts of the Perry expedition are Dennett, *Americans in Eastern Asia,* chaps. 13, 14; Neumann, *America Encounters Japan,* chap. 3; and Tamarin, *Japan and the United States,* chaps. 3, 4. More detailed accounts are Morison, *"Old Bruin,"* chaps. 21–28; and Wiley, *Yankees in the Land of the Gods,* chaps. 3–15. The last three are well illustrated with Japanese sketches. Morison emphasizes Perry's personal and naval concerns, Wiley the Japanese situation and reactions, but both cover the negotiations fully. For the text of the Treaty of Kanagawa see Bevans, *Treaties,* vol. 10, 355–60. On Perry's annexationism see Earl Swisher, "Commodore Perry's Imperialism in Relation to America's Present-Day Position in the Pacific," 30–40. On Perry's relations with Marshall in China see Henson, *Commissioners and Commodores,* chap. 8. See also William G. Beasley, *The Rise of Modern Japan,* 28–29.

Cuban question and "bleeding Kansas." Nevertheless, many journalists, including writers for the *New York Times* and *Herald,* the *Daily Alta California,* and the *North American Review* saw the Treaty of Kanagawa as a landmark. The *Alta California* called it "the entering wedge that will, ere long, open to us the interior wealth of these unknown lands." The *Herald* gloated that the great exploits of Dutch and Portuguese explorers had been reduced to nothing. Japanese curiosity about American things seemed a favorable portent for the future, but more than one writer commented on the inherent deceitfulness of Japanese officials. *Merchants' Magazine* predicted that trade would be slow to develop, as the Japanese wanted few imports and the United States would not use force like the British. A writer in Hong Kong, presumably American, thought that a coal supply would be the chief benefit of the expedition, if a transpacific steamer line were ever organized and if the British did not seize the trade first.[7]

American ships began at once to call at Japan, but the two open ports were inaccessible and small, and Japanese officials, unprepared for the inrush, interpreted the Perry treaty with narrow literalness. Critics at home unfavorably compared its trade provisions with those of the Cushing treaty. The U.S. Navy sent a scientific expedition to visit the two open ports and chart the North Pacific, but it was small, not authorized to use force, and unable to improve security conditions for whalers. By surveying the Japanese coast it stretched the treaty provisions, but its relations with the government and natives reinforced the suspicions of Perry's party. Meanwhile Britain, Russia, France, and Holland obtained somewhat broader treaties. The United States automatically shared the new concessions through its most-favored-nation provision, but the *New York Herald* and other jingoist papers began to demand action to expand American commercial rights.[8]

This action was supplied by Townsend Harris, who completed the work that Perry had started. Harris was a public-spirited New York merchant, with much trading and travel experience all over the western Pacific and the Far East, who applied for the position of consul general in Japan. On his long voyage out, he stopped in Siam on instructions to secure revision of the unsatisfactory 1833 treaty and gained a series of concessions, including extraterritoriality and a maximum

7. *New York Times,* June 13, 1854. *New York Herald,* June 12, 13, 1854; *San Francisco Daily Alta California,* n.d., quoted in Neumann, *America Encounters Japan,* 46. *North American Review* 83 (January 1856): 233–50. *Merchants' Magazine* 30 (January 1854): 19–46. *Hong Kong Register,* April 11, reprinted in *New York Herald,* June 13.

8. Payson J. Treat, *Diplomatic Relations between the United States and Japan, 1853–1895,* vol. 2, 27–36. Foster Rhea Dulles, *Yankees and Samurai: America's Role in the Emergence of Modern Japan, 1791–1900,* 132–33. Neumann, *America Encounters Japan,* 47–50. Allen B. Cole, "The Ringgold-Rodgers-Brooks Expedition to Japan and the North Pacific, 1853–1859," 152–62. Arthur Abel, "How Trade with Japan Began," 42–52. Since foreigners were prohibited from going more than about twenty-five miles from the treaty ports, they carried on trade with the interior through Japanese intermediaries, 53–54. Shin'ya Sugiyama, *Japan's Industrialization in the World's Economy, 1859–1899: Export Trade and Overseas Competition,* 52–54.

tariff of 3 percent. Harris arrived at Shimoda in August 1856, where he lived for more than a year without any attention from Washington, either a visiting warship or even a dispatch, although he was often ill and Shanghai, a center of American activity, was only seven days away.

When the Japanese refused to receive him, he used threats and persuasion to obtain a building for a consulate. In 1857 he induced the shogun's government to accept him in Edo by shrewdly contrasting the looming dangers presented by the European powers and the American rejection of Pacific imperialism. These tactics, reinforced by the Anglo-French capture of Canton, won him a convention that added Nagasaki as a trading post, granted extraterritoriality, and put American trade on almost the same footing as the Dutch.

At the end of February 1858 these and other concessions were cast in permanent treaty form. Harris had wanted a legation at Kyoto (the emperor's residence) and eight new open ports; what he got was a legation at Edo after 1862 and four new ports with consular residences. Americans might live and trade in these treaty ports as in China, but they had no freedom to travel in the interior, a prohibition that was eventually somewhat relaxed in practice. The treaty also included elaborate trade provisions, including a 5 percent maximum tariff on all major American exports. In much the same fashion as the Treaty of Wang-hsia with China, Harris's document laid the foundation for American trade thenceforth. It also contained a promise that the United States would serve as a "friendly mediator" between Japan and European nations at Japan's request—the most advanced political commitment that the United States had made anywhere in the Pacific basin and one that neither the American government nor public could have fully understood. Not surprisingly, the treaty caused a political crisis in Japan, complicated by news of the just-signed Treaties of Tientsin in China (see chapter 5) and by contemporaneous Japanese treaties with European nations on the model of Harris's treaty. The Japanese, resigned but resentful, lumped together all these agreements under the term "unequal treaties."[9]

9. Harris's diary of his residence and negotiations has been reprinted in *The Complete Journal of Townsend Harris, First American Consul General and Minister to Japan.* For the residence in Shimoda and the Edo negotiations see 199–411, 445–561. For a brief account of Harris's negotiations from the Japanese and British viewpoints see Beasley, *Rise of Modern Japan,* 30–34; and Grace Fox, *Britain and Japan, 1858–1883,* 37–41. William G. Beasley, *The Meiji Restoration,* 88–97, 105–15. Dennett, *Americans in Eastern Asia,* chap. 19. Treat, *United States and Japan, 1853–1895,* vol. 1, chaps. 2, 3. Tamarin, *Japan and the United States,* chap. 4. Beasley, *Rise of Modern Japan,* 29–34. Neumann, *America Encounters Japan,* 52–55. James E. Hoare, *Japan's Treaty Ports and Foreign Settlements: The Uninvited Guests, 1858–1898,* 4–5, 47–48, 93–95. For the provisions of Harris's treaties see Bevans, *Treaties,* vol. 9, 359–72. For the provisions of the treaties with Siam see ibid, vol. 11, 978–81. An important commercial provision of the 1858 treaty was one that straightened out the exchange rate between the dollar and the yen, which Perry had greatly overvalued. The United States soon moved its Kanagawa consulate to nearby Yokohama as it grew in size, but consuls continued to use the superscripture of Kanagawa on their dispatches for many years.

The Japanese counterpart of the Burlingame mission followed immediately. At the suggestion of Japanese officials, Harris willingly stipulated that treaty ratifications must be exchanged in Washington, and early in 1860 some seventy-seven Japanese, including retinue, set out on an American warship, preceded by the *Kanrin Maru,* a Japanese gunboat whose successful escort voyage to San Francisco greatly stimulated Japanese self-confidence. The visit anticipated that of Burlingame's Chinese by eight years and resembled it in most respects: trip via Panama to the East Coast, visit to Congress, reception by the president, and eager curiosity by crowds and press.

The Japanese, however, had more immediate, practical interests than the Chinese—formal diplomatic recognition and eventually revision of the "unequal treaties" (see below). Consequently, they eagerly observed, reported at length—not always favorably—and sketched everything new and strange. Their proud hosts showed them everything in which they expressed interest: Fort Monroe, the treasury, factories, a sugar refinery, a newspaper office, and even P. T. Barnum's Museum. The New York Chamber of Commerce lectured them on tariffs, ocean freights, and other commercial matters. Unlike the Burlingame mission, the exhausted Japanese did not visit Europe but were taken home on another American warship, via the Cape of Good Hope. The *New York Times* hoped that the Japanese mission would "set on foot a tremendous movement of progress in that prosperous and powerful realm." The immediate result of the visit was the Japanese publication of a best-seller about the American wonders, *Western Things and Affairs* (1867) by Fukuzawa Yukichi. Seven years later Japan's first learned society was beginning to publish its first journals, incorporating translations of Western books, discussions of tariffs, law reforms, and many other subjects.[10]

Harris's treaty and the Japanese mission established a basis for friendship that was severely tested during the 1860s. As in China, impulses of xenophobia and seclusion persisted among conservatives. Westerners thought Japanese laws vague and arbitrary. The sudden increase in Japan's foreign trade produced shortages in vital consumer goods and increased the local cost of living. It also brought new competition for the domestic textile industry and drained gold from the country. Even without the presence of the foreigners, the old feudal form of government associated with the shogunate was rapidly decaying, a process that produced social stresses and, in particular, set loose a class of rough professional soldiers to wander about the country and stir up trouble. Isolated foreigners were murdered along

10. Chitoshi Yanaga, "The First Japanese Embassy to the United States," 132–38. Dulles, *Yankees and Samurai,* chap. 7. *New York Times,* May 22, 1860. For Japanese accounts see Lewis Bush, *77 Samurai: Japan's First Embassy to America;* and Masao Miyoshi, *As We Saw Them: The First Japanese Embassy in the United States.* The second of these contains long contemporary accounts of the Japanese reception by President Buchanan and Townsend Harris's reception by the Mikado. For a sketch of Fukuzawa and other proponents of modernization, see Beasley, *Rise of Modern Japan,* 85–91; and William G. Beasley, *Japanese Imperialism, 1894–1945,* 17–34. Walter LaFeber, *The Clash: A History of U.S.-Japan Relations,* 37–38. Shunsuki Kamei, "The Sacred Land of Liberty: Images of America in Nineteenth-Century Japan," 56–59.

with Japanese; early in 1861 Harris's young Dutch interpreter, a great admirer of Japan, was cut down in the streets of Edo. The American legation was burned, and an American ship was fired on by forces of a feudal lord.

As Europeans suffered similar damages, Westerners became convinced that they must support their treaty rights by force, and in 1863 and 1864 they sent naval expeditions into the waters of the two principal feudatories in southern Japan. After bitter negotiations, in 1866 the Western powers imposed a punitive treaty on Japan, requiring an indemnity of $4 million. Another treaty removed a variety of obstacles to Western trade and, even more galling, limited most Japanese tariffs to 5 percent ad valorem. At about the same time the United States leased land at Yokohama for a coaling station.[11]

Up to this point Japan's relations with the West seemed to be following the same path as China's, but in 1867 and 1868 they began to diverge sharply. The shogun, long the de facto ruler in Japan but now discredited and surrounded by enemies, surrendered his powers to the young Meiji emperor, hitherto a figurehead. Aided by a group of forward-looking advisers, the emperor established a central government professing Western principles of nationality and set out to subject the hereditary clans to his authority. Two decades of political assassinations and rebellions followed, but his semimilitarist government persisted. In 1890 the first general elections were held, and a quasi-parliamentary regime came into existence under the constitution of 1889, which in Prussian style declared the emperor to be the holder of actual sovereignty.[12]

At least as important as those political reforms was Japanese importation of Western technology and attitudes, which had begun through the Dutch in the late eighteenth century. As the Japanese became aware of European imperialism, this importation accelerated in self-defense and after 1868 became almost an orgy of eclecticism. The military adopted Western-style warships, munitions, tactics, and uniforms. Perry had brought Japan a model telegraph and railroad; a real telegraph was in use by 1869, a railroad by 1872. A trial telephone line appeared in Japan only eleven years after its invention. European and American books poured from translators and printers. As the educational system was overhauled,

11. Dennett, *Americans in Eastern Asia,* chap. 21. Treat, *United States and Japan, 1853–1895,* vol. 1, chaps. 5–12; and especially 273–81. Hoare, *Japan's Treaty Ports,* 54–56. LaFeber, *Clash,* 25–29. For the American treaties see Bevans, *Treaties,* vol. 9, 375–76. On the causes of anti-foreignism see also Chitoshi Yanaga, *Japan since Perry,* 23; and George C. Allen, *A Short Economic History of Modern Japan,* 27–29. The United States played only a small role in the punitive campaigns. The maximum tariff fixed in 1866 was at about the same level as in the Chinese treaties of 1858. After the American Civil War the navy's need for a coaling station was less pressing, and it leased the land to the Pacific Mail Steamship Company. Seward W. Livermore, "The American Naval Base Policy in the Far East, 1850–1914," 114.

12. The brief German influence died after Germany joined the intervening European powers following Japan's victory over China in 1895. Masaki Miyake, "German Cultural and Political Influence on Japan, 1870–1914," 156–58. At the same time trade replaced agriculture as the most valued economic activity.

top to bottom, it incorporated the whole spectrum of natural and social sciences. Fads accompanied this learning—the "civilized" stereotype of the 1870s, slightly caricatured, was a young man at least partly dressed in Western clothes, with his hair cut and pomaded, an umbrella leaning beside him, a pocket-watch in his hand, and a plate of roast beef on the table before him. Naturally, the rapid changes sometimes drove conservatives into violent opposition, and in the late 1880s the changes brought a reaction to traditional morality and several anti-progressive measures.[13]

After the Meiji Restoration the Japanese imperial government directed, encouraged, or financed the most important economic reforms through its already well-developed bureaucracy. Confiscating large areas of feudal lands, it redistributed these and applied a systematic land tax, part of whose proceeds were used for reclamation and agricultural experiments. Disbanding the traditional guilds, it created modern corporations, directing itself industries vital to national security such as arsenals, foundries, and mines and selling or leasing others to private capitalists on easy terms. Although the shogunate of the 1850s had discouraged exports, to keep prices down, the imperial government now tried to encourage export industries, achieving greatest success with silk production. It held exhibitions at home and eventually established museums of samples abroad. Removing hidebound restrictions on internal trade and transportation, the government assumed control of railroads, telegraphs, and the postal system and subsidized the merchant marine. It created banks and standardized the currency, although a long period of depreciation produced several shifts of policy and much uncertainty.[14]

To advise about these innovations and in many cases to administer them, the government imported more than two thousand foreign specialists, mostly

---

13. A convenient brief account of political and cultural change of the Restoration Period and after is Yanaga, *Japan since Perry*, chaps. 5–9. For an analysis and explanation of the cultural imitation see G. B. Sansom, *The Western World and Japan, a Study in the Interaction of European and Asiatic Cultures*, 382–87. G. E. Hubbard, *Eastern Industrialization and Its Effect on the West with Special Reference to Great Britain and Japan*, 46–47. Thomas C. Smith, *Political Change and Industrial Development in Japan: Government Enterprise, 1868–1880*, 1–4. Recent historians do not agree as to the significance of the Meiji Restoration and deliberate government planning in this process. Hazel Jones, "The Formation of Meiji Policy toward the Employment of Foreigners," 9–30. Sugiyama, *Japan's Industrialization*, viii–xiv, 2–5. On the conservative resurgence see Byron K. Marshall, *Capitalism and Nationalism in Prewar Japan: The Ideology of the Business Elite, 1868–1914*, 61.

14. Allen, *Short Economic History of Modern Japan*, chap. 2, 50–52. E. H. Norman, *Japan's Emergence as a Modern State: Political and Economic Problems of the Meiji Period*, 127–29. M. Miyamoto, Y. Sakudo, and Y. Yasuba, "Economic Development in Preindustrial Japan, 1859–1894," 547–51. Sidney Devere Brown, "Okubo Toshimichi, His Political and Economic Policies in Early Meiji Japan," 194–97. (As home minister, Okubo directed many of these policies until his assassination in 1878.) Japan (Department of Agriculture and Commerce), *Japan in the Beginning of the Twentieth Century*, 414–17, 478–80. On the currency problem see *Bradstreet's* 27 (August 12, 1899): 510. Only in 1879 did the yen begin to replace the Mexican peso as the standard Japanese coin. U.S., *Foreign Relations, 1878–79*, 695–96.

European, whom it established in settlements as *yatoi* or hirelings.[15] Thanks in part to the discipline of Bushidō and Confucianism, businessmen largely accepted this economic statism. Although ironically that apotheosis of individualism, Samuel Smiles's *Self-Help*, was high on the list of much-read foreign books, the unrestrained pursuit of profits continued to be censured as unpatriotic.[16]

Americans provided more than one-fifth of the *yatoi*. On the one hand, the Japanese may really have felt the special regard for the United States that Americans liked to think they saw in China. On the other hand, American ministers, beginning with Charles DeLong immediately after the Meiji Restoration, made a point of urging advisers on the imperial government and Japanese missions to the United States as a means of increasing American trade. Thus, for example, in the early 1870s George Williams, an Indiana banker, helped develop banking laws and currency policy on American models, and Erastus Peshine Smith and former consul Eli T. Sheppard advised the Foreign Office on international law and urged a more assertive, less pro-British policy. Henry W. Denison and Durham H. Stevens also influenced Japanese foreign relations for years. David Murray, professor of mathematics at Rutgers College, was general adviser to the Japanese Department of Education during the 1870s; a group of American scientists established their fields at Tokyo University; and Americans held the chair of Anglo-American law there for forty years. The redoubtable Charles LeGendre helped the Japanese military in its first expansive steps after DeLong and the imperial government persuaded him to resign his commission as American consul at Amoy. Becoming for a time de facto commander of Japanese land and naval forces, he organized a punitive expedition to Taiwan in 1874. Somewhat less controversially than LeGendre, other Americans advised the imperial government on prison administration, the postal system, and the customs service.[17]

Although American missionaries in Japan were much less numerous than in China, they were more welcome, especially for their work as doctors and interpreters. Perhaps the most remarkable was Guido Verbeck, a Dutch-American

15. The total number, 1868–1900, was 2,400, including 1,034 British and 351 American. More than 200 language instructors were employed before 1868. H. B. Jones, *Live Machines: Hired Foreigners in Meiji Japan*, 1, 145. As many as 350 Japanese youths were sent abroad to study by the early 1870s, about two-thirds to the United States. Beasley, *Rise of Modern Japan*, 87–88.

16. Marshall, *Capitalism and Nationalism*, 10–11, 114–16. Yasuzo Horie, "Modern Entrepreneurship in Meiji Japan," 206–8. For a different view see Jon Halliday, *A Political History of Japanese Capitalism*, 52–53.

17. Merle Curti and Kendall Birr, *Prelude to Point Four: American Technical Missions Overseas, 1833–1938*, 40–51, 53–56. Jones, *Live Machines*, 8, 43, 46, 50, 78–79, 98–103, 112 and passim. Dulles, *Yankees and Samurai*, 153–55. Treat, *United States and Japan, 1853–1895*, vol. 2, 42–43. Robert S. Schwantes, "American Relations with Japan, 1853–1895: Survey and Prospect," 117–19. On LeGendre see also Gordon, "Charles LeGendre," 72–74; Fox, *Britain and Japan*, 576–78; Sandra Caruthers Thomson, "Filibustering to Formosa: General Charles LeGendre and the Japanese," 442–56; and Yanaga, *Japan since Perry*, 181–82. For DeLong's role see Charles DeLong to Hamilton Fish, November 22, 1872, no. 309, U.S., Diplomatic Despatches, Japan, 21.

who with several others during the 1860s founded a group of schools that eventually coalesced into Tokyo University. At Verbeck's instance the government brought to Japan other American teachers, at both university and lower levels, who introduced American books and teaching methods all over the country. American influence in this area was greatest from the first Education Act of 1872 to the late 1880s; after that time the Japanese turned to more authoritarian German methods. An educator of special interest was E. H. House, formerly an American journalist, who became professor of English language and literature. In his spare time he resumed journalism, helped found an anti-British newspaper, the *Tokyo Times,* and through articles sent home did much to arouse interest in Japan. A host of other American writers publicized Japan in books and articles and fed the American appetite for the bizarre and the exotic. At the same time American universities and colleges attracted hundreds of Japanese students during the 1870s and 1880s, some to learn Western methods, others to escape military service.[18]

A considerable amount of American advisory effort was focused on the large, sparsely settled northern island of Hokkaido, the closest approximation to a Japanese frontier. The imperial government was anxious to develop the island for its reputed mineral resources, as an outlet for surplus population, and as a strategic outpost against Russian expansion. During the 1860s the shogun sent William P. Blake and Raphael Pumpelly (before his work in China) to make a geological survey. They were followed by other American engineers, working throughout Japan, who introduced American mining machinery.

In 1870 a Japanese envoy seeking talent in America persuaded no less a man than the commissioner of agriculture, Horace Capron, to resign his post and bring a staff to Japan to organize experimental farms and advise on agricultural problems, including Hokkaido. The first model farms, located near Tokyo (renamed from Edo in 1868), flourished for a time, but Capron's agricultural colonies on Hokkaido were never successful, partly because he attempted too much and partly because of poor organization, rifts in his staff, his impatience with the Japanese, and the cold climate. He introduced many plants and animals, however, and his reports contained much sound advice on everything from farming and sheep-raising to mining. After his departure some of his followers did even more valuable work, such as Benjamin S. Lyman, who thoroughly surveyed the island's coal deposits, and William S. Clark, who developed a successful agricultural school at Sapporo, later to evolve into a major university.[19]

---

18. Curti and Birr, *Prelude to Point Four,* 40, 57–63. Jones, *Live Machines,* 77, 94–98. Dulles, *Yankees and Samurai,* 139–43. Yanaga, *Japan since Perry,* chap. 7. On E. H. House see *Dictionary of American Biography,* vol. 9, 257–58. An extensive list of American writers appears in Inazo Nitobe, *The Intercourse between the United States and Japan, an Historical Sketch,* 141–51. On Japanese students see Nitobe, 165–70. For a general appraisal of the influence of missionaries on Japanese-American relations see Schwantes, "America and Japan," 123–37.

19. Curti and Birr, *Prelude to Point Four,* 38–39, 41–53. Jones, *Live Machines,* 3, 4, 17, 74, 86, 92. Dulles, *Yankees and Samurai,* chap. 10. Spence, *Mining Engineers and the*

At the same time that cultural transfer was taking place from America westward to Japan, a reverse process was occurring more slowly as Americans were exposed to Japanese life. This process was most noticeable when Japanese sent exhibits and constructed buildings for American expositions in Philadelphia (1876), New Orleans (1885), Chicago (1893), and St. Louis (1904). Even during construction American spectators were struck by the seriousness of Japanese workers and the precise planning that went into the buildings. The colorful profusion and tasteful delicacy of the exhibits left a more lasting impression on the American visitors than any verbal description in books or magazines.[20]

Japanese progress and American contributions thereto necessarily modified the policy of the U.S. government. Secretary of State Seward was always more suspicious of Japan than of China—after the naval intervention of 1863–1864 he remarked that Japan was the only nation the United States might have to fight—and favored a policy of cooperating with European nations to keep it open to trade and Christianity, by force if necessary. Hamilton Fish made little change in this cooperative policy, and only in 1877, when William M. Evarts entered the State Department, did the United States begin at the official level to recognize Japanese progress by dissociating itself from the repressive policies of Europe.[21]

Earlier ministers carried out the cooperative policy without complaint. Seward's first minister and personal friend, Robert H. Pruyn, tempered severity with a genial disposition and managed to retain some of the personal popularity enjoyed by Townsend Harris. After Pruyn's departure in 1865, his successors came under the influence of the British minister, Sir Harry Parkes, hard-working and energetic but also choleric and overbearing, who was to dominate the diplomatic corps in Tokyo for nearly twenty years. Parkes favored a cooperative policy because it would facilitate British commercial supremacy in Japan. He took the lead in organizing the punitive expeditions of 1863–1864 and in drawing up the humiliating treaties of 1866. But Parkes also showed a keen if patronizing interest in Japan and redeemed himself in the eyes of the Meiji emperor, for almost alone among foreign representatives, he supported the imperial cause against the shogun. Thereafter he urged on the new regime the need for law, order, and civil organization. In maintaining foreign interests, Sir Harry often enjoyed the aid of the German minister to China, Max von Brandt, another domineering diplomat.[22]

American West, 282–84. John A. Harrison, "The Capron Mission and the Colonization of Hokkaido, 1868–1875," 135–42. Bogdan Mieczkowski and Seiko Mieczkowski, "Horace Capron and the Development of Hokkaido: A Reappraisal," 487–504.

20. Harris, "All the World a Melting Pot?" 24–72.

21. Dennett, *Americans in Eastern Asia,* 412–16. Paolino, *Foundations of the American Empire,* 170–94. Seward urged a joint naval demonstration as early as 1861. He was apparently aroused by Japan's unwillingness to admit missionaries. For statements by Fish supporting cooperation see Treat, *United States and Japan, 1853–1895,* vol. 1, 392. For Evarts's views soon after entering office see ibid., vol. 2, 29–30.

22. Treat, *United States and Japan, 1853–1895,* vol. 1, 128–31, 274–81, 331, 336–40. E. H. House, "The Martyrdom of an Empire," 619–20. Francis C. Jones, *Extraterritoriality*

Not until 1873 did an American minister appear in Tokyo comparable to Anson Burlingame for sympathy with the Orientals' position who held his post long enough to exert influence. John A. Bingham had been a distinguished lawyer, judge, and congressman, and his long-standing concern for human rights led him to take the side of the Japanese wherever possible against the Europeans—partly, to be sure, in order to further American interests and to thwart efforts by the British to make Japan part of their informal empire. In his efforts to bring about the revision of the 1866 treaties, which will be discussed later, he faced the systematic opposition of Parkes and Von Brandt, backed by a vociferous English-language press, and, at first, the disapproval of Secretary Fish. Bingham was sometimes criticized for not moving fast enough, but most Japanese appreciated his efforts.[23]

When former president Grant visited Japan in 1879, he was enormously impressed with Japanese progress, which seemed to him "more like a dream than a reality." Parkes wrote that the general was "turning the Japanese heads," for they neglected most other business during the visit and consulted Grant on several public questions. After James A. Garfield's inauguration, Grant tried in vain to persuade him to send Bingham to a European post and appoint John Russell Young minister, but, as we have seen, Young went to Peking instead. After Cleveland replaced Bingham in 1885, most of his successors imitated his liberal, independent policy, with one exception—John F. Swift (1889–1891), who briefly revived some suspicions of the 1860s.[24]

The United States maintained a smaller diplomatic and consular staff in Japan than in China, but its officials faced most of the same problems: a strange language, unfamiliar law and customs, too many duties, and too little pay. Bingham confided to a friend that the only way he had been able to acquire a house for his family was to get his friends in Congress to appropriate money to build a jail. Besides the legation, the United States maintained a consul general at Kanagawa (Yokohama), a consul at Nagasaki, and one at Osaka-Hiogo (Kobe). For resident and visiting Americans these officials served as judge and sometimes jailer, postmaster, and civil administrator, carrying out functions that became

---

in *Japan and the Diplomatic Relations Resulting in Its Abolition*, 93–96. On Parkes see Fox, *Britain and Japan*, 160, 540–47. In Parkes's official biography much may be read between the lines. F. V. Dickins and Stanley Lane-Poole, *The Life of Sir Harry Parkes, K. C. B., G. C. M. G., Sometime Her Majesty's Minister to China and Japan*, 2 and passim.

23. Treat, *United States and Japan, 1853–1895*, vol. 1, 526–28, 566; vol. 2, 33–34, 23–24. Bingham took every opportunity to publicize Japanese progress. For a moderate view of Bingham see Philip Ned Dare, "John A. Bingham and Treaty Revision with Japan, 1873–1895." John A. Bingham to Fish, November 2, 1875, no. 299, U.S., Diplomatic Despatches, Japan, 31.

24. Grant to Daniel Ammen, August 7, 1879, John T. Morgan papers, 1. Dickins and Lane-Poole, *Life of Parkes*, vol. 2, 278–80. *San Francisco Chronicle*, n.d., clipping enclosed with Bingham to Garfield, April 20, 1881, Garfield papers, 138, pt. 1. Treat, *United States and Japan, 1853–1895*, vol. 2, 284–85, 367.

more and more embarrassing as the Japanese established Western standards of law and public administration.[25]

At the time of the Meiji Restoration the expansionist *New York Herald* burbled: "We have interests in Japan more vital than any of the nations of Europe. Destiny has marked out the North Pacific as . . . to all intents and purposes an American lake." Thirteen years later the American consul at Nagasaki had quite another story to tell: "The United States opened the country [Japan] to the commerce of the world. Yet England and France have reaped the fruits . . . while the United States, her nearest neighbor and best friend . . . virtually does nothing."[26]

The consul was unduly pessimistic, but he was closer to the truth than the *Herald*. To be sure, the total American-Japanese trade rose from $3,295,222 in 1868 to $27,080,313 in 1892, the last undisturbed year before the depression of the 1890s and the Sino-Japanese War. One American firm, Frazar and Company, traded continuously in Japan from 1867 to 1941 and sold the Japanese their first electric light plant, streetcars, and phonographs. But during most of the late nineteenth century Japan was almost as much a British economic fief as China. Even as the *Herald* published its boast, Jardine, Matheson and the other great British commercial companies in China were establishing Japanese branches. By 1883 Britain had 98 firms of various types in Japan, the United States only 39, out of a total of 208. Consistently through the whole period Japanese censuses showed nearly half of the foreign population to be British.[27]

As in China, some problems of Japanese trade affected Europeans as much as Americans—for example, distance and the strange language and customs. The

25. James Burrell Angell, *The Reminiscences of James Burrell Angell*, 134–35. U.S., 48th Cong., 1st sess., *House Executive Document 121*, 84–86. Bingham spent his whole tour of duty trying in vain to get authorization for an adequate legation building. Treat, *United States and Japan, 1853–1895*, vol. 2, 45–46, 120, 194–95, 211–12. For an unfavorable view of American consular courts see letters by Consul Thomas B. Van Buren in *New York Tribune*, July 5, 1882; and by E. H. House in *New York Times*, January 11, 1881. A British comparison of the British and American consular establishments, much to the disadvantage of the latter, is in Hoare, *Japan's Treaty Ports*, 56–60, 74–78.

26. *New York Herald*, May 1, 1868. See also *New York Times*, January 25, 1870, for a similar but less extravagant statement. Alexander C. Jones to John Hay, January 6, 1881, no. 23, U.S. Consular Despatches, Nagasaki, 3. See also U.S., *Commercial Relations, 1884–1885*, 973–74; U.S., *Foreign Relations, 1886*, 561–64. A British survey of Anglo-Japanese trade after the midcentury helps to explain how these changes came about. Fox, *Britain and Japan*, chap. 12. Fox attributes the United States' falling behind largely to the weakening influence of the American Civil War. Ibid., 534.

27. For total trade figures see U.S., 55th Cong., 2d sess., *House Document 271*, pt. 1 (Treasury Department, Bureau of Statistics, *Monthly Summary of Trade and Finance*, November 1898), 1282. For statistics in 1883 see *Economist* 42 (November 15, 1884): Monthly Trade Supplement, 6–7. Shipping tonnages in 1883 were: British, 724,355; all others, 374,617. See also Sugiyama, *Japan's Industrialization*, 40–44. On Frazar and Company see William W. Lockwood, *The Economic Development of Japan: Growth and Structural Change, 1868–1938*, 329–30. On British firms see Hyde, *Far Eastern Trade*, 153–55; and Dickins and Lane-Poole, *Life of Parkes*, vol. 2, 29–30, 58. On populations see Hoare, *Japan's Treaty Ports*, 23.

unsteadiness of the Japanese market made long-term import orders very risky, as did the fall in the value of silver. Some recent historians believe that despite Japanese complaints against the "unequal treaties," the restrictive system they embodied actually favored Japanese merchants by preventing foreigners from expanding into the interior, while the rising Western demand for tea and silk stimulated Japanese exports.[28]

As elsewhere, one besetting American handicap was irregular, costly shipping. During the late 1860s the principal British and French steamship lines using the Suez route added Yokohama to their regular ports of call, and by the 1890s the tonnage of British ships in Japanese ports was twice that of all others put together. Pacific Mail and Occidental and Oriental could cross the ocean from San Francisco in fourteen to eighteen days, while steamers on the Suez route from London took thirty-five. For a time during the early 1870s the large size of Pacific Mail steamers enabled them to compete handily with British rivals, but after the misfortunes of 1874–1875 it sold its ships to the rising Mitsubishi line. After that New York merchants found it cheaper to ship to Yokohama via London than via San Francisco. Even in the 1890s baled cotton was carried from St. Louis to Japanese textile mills via New York and London. Usually it never left the hold of the steamer in London.[29]

Even more galling, Western European countries enjoyed favorable trade balances, in sharp contrast to the United States, which bought much but sold little. In this respect and in the principal products shipped, American trade with Japan strongly resembled that with China. After the opening of the port of Yokohama in 1859, Japanese tea exports to the United States increased at the expense of China. Sometimes at the height of the season American ships of the 1870s sailed with tea chests stacked in every unoccupied stateroom and even in the public rooms. Until 1886 most tea came to the United States via Suez; thereafter the Pacific route predominated.

Japan's raw silk production also rose during the 1870s under state sponsorship. At first much of the silk went to France, but publicity at the Philadelphia exposition of 1876 and improved direct transportation to the American East Coast on Pacific steamers and the transcontinental railroad shifted the silk trade to the United States. Eventually it surpassed the Chinese, especially as Japanese silk was of more even, dependable quality. The United States also imported smaller quantities of camphor, porcelain, and knick-knacks. By 1892 42.4 percent of Japanese exports went to American ports, 7.9 percent to British. In contrast, Britain supplied 36.9 percent of Japanese imports, the United States only 7.7 percent.[30]

28. Sugiyama, *Japan's Industrialization*, 52–76, 215–16.
29. Hyde, *Far Eastern Trade*, 158. U.S., *Commercial Relations, 1884–85*, 974; *1886–87*, 2, 1304. Fox, *Britain and Japan*, 341, 346, 347n1, 360. Curtis, *Yankees of the East*, 308–10. The American shipping situation was even worse in Japan than in China, for the latter market was larger and attracted more sailing vessels to its ports than Japan.
30. Sugiyama, *Japan's Industrialization*, 98–110, 112–18, 131–32, 146–52, 216–17. Gardella, "Fukien Tea Trade," 70. Eng, *Economic Imperialism in China*, chap. 7. Allen and

As in China, the principal American export to Japan during most of the period was kerosene, but it appeared in Japan nearly a decade earlier and became more generally used throughout the country. By 1873, the first year in which records were kept, 133,047 gallons were consumed, and in 1882 the figure had increased to 20,671,671 gallons. This phenomenal rise was due as much to the falling price of kerosene as to its usefulness. Between 1877 and 1880, when the greatest rise occurred, the price declined from an average of about $4.70 per case of ten gallons to $1.62, and thereafter it usually fluctuated around $2. Standard Oil developed a regular line of three-thousand- or four-thousand-ton sailing vessels, which took out kerosene cases to both Japanese and Chinese ports, bringing back tea, silk, and rice. As in China, the kerosene trade awakened conservative resistance and produced restrictions on storage and safety measures, which Americans thought were British-inspired.[31] In 1888 Russian kerosene appeared in Japanese ports, but it did not win much of a market during the early 1890s.[32]

The record of the American cotton goods trade in Japan was worse than in China. In 1879 the American consul general at Kanagawa reported that the Japanese imported $5,173,000 of cotton textiles from Britain, $133,000 from France, and only $73,000 from the United States. The American figures for yarn and woolen textiles were even less flattering. The ministers and consuls conceded the futility of trying to compete with low-grade British t-cloths and denims unless American producers were willing to size them heavily and give up their reputation for quality. But there seemed no good reason why American mills should not supply heavy-weight, high-grade shirtings and woolens for middle- and upper-class customers in the cold Japanese climate.[33]

Donnithorne, *Western Enterprise,* 200–203. Johannes Hirschmeier, *The Origins of Entrepreneurship in Meiji Japan,* 91–95. Ukers, *All about Tea,* vol. 2, 212. Nitobe, *U.S.-Japanese Intercourse,* 93–95. Bingham to Fish, April 8, 1875, no. 214, U.S., Diplomatic Despatches, Japan, 30. *New York Times,* September 10, 1877. *Economist* 42 (November 15, 1884): Monthly Trade Supplement, 6. Percentages for 1892 are computed from Treasury Department figures in U.S., 55th Cong., 2d sess., *House Document 575,* pt. 5, 1197.

31. Treat, *United States and Japan, 1853–1895,* vol. 2, 130, 170–72, 209, 237. U.S., *Consular Reports* 3 (January 1881): 87. Van Buren to Hay, March 9, 1880, nos. 419, 421; Van Buren to Robert R. Hitt, July 26, 1881, no. 549; G. E. Rice to Davis, December 19, 1882, no. 669; Van Buren to Davis, May 14, 1883, no. 692, U.S., Consular Despatches, Kanagawa, 10, 12, 13. Bingham to Evarts, January 18, 1881, no. 1241, U.S., Diplomatic Despatches, Japan, 43. James G. Blaine to Bingham, December 3, 1881, no. 629, U.S., Diplomatic Instructions, Japan, 3, 81–92. Curtis, *Yankees of the East,* 309. On conservative resistance see Sansom, *Western World and Japan,* 367. Not until the 1890s did Americans sell more kerosene in China than in Japan. Harold F. Williamson and Arnold R. Daum, *The American Petroleum Industry, 1859–1899: The Age of Illumination,* 675.

32. U.S., *Consular Reports* 105 (May 1889): 16–17, 61, 183–84; 153 (June 1893): 221–22. U.S., *Commercial Relations, 1889–90,* 159. Frank L. Coombs to Blaine, June 30, August 4, 1892; January 4, 1893, nos. 13, 31, 71, U.S., Diplomatic Despatches, Japan. Minister Coombs tried to hamper Russian shipments in bulk by alarming the Japanese government about the dangers of storage—a rather cynical tactic after his predecessors' protests about storage restrictions. Treat, *United States and Japan, 1853–1895,* vol. 2, 390.

33. U.S., *Commercial Relations, 1879–80,* 1, 89–90. U.S., *Consular Reports* 94 (June 1888): 486–87. Bingham to Evarts, October 8, 1877, no. 642, U.S., Diplomatic Despatches,

Outside the area of textiles, Americans developed a good trade in clocks, watches, and scales and placed mowers, reapers, and threshers on large government farms, but the Japanese market for many agricultural tools and implements declined. The efficient Singer organization sold many more sewing machines in Japan than in China. As in many other parts of the world, the British outsold Americans in steel rails and iron products of all types, and Minister Richard B. Hubbard observed that although Americans could compete in railroad rolling stock and fittings in both South America and Australasia, they sold few of these items in Japan. In the field of provisions too, American sales did not match the potentiality of the market, but American lumber producers began to dominate it in the 1890s after the Japanese had overcut their own forests.[34]

The mediocre American commercial record in Japan before the 1890s was especially ironic in that a number of progressive Japanese newspapers advocated closer trade relations with the United States, the most friendly of the Western powers. One paper remarked that the Japanese people favored contacts with the United States, while the government leaned toward Britain and, as the 1880s progressed, increasingly toward Germany as a source of industrial products. Japanese officials also favored their own nationals in disputes—for example, letting their merchant houses refuse ordered goods so as to wait for a more favorable exchange rate. Americans received little aid of this sort from their own government. The Asiatic Commercial Company got a California congressman to introduce a bill of incorporation into the House of Representatives in 1874 to give it official status in Japan, but the bill never emerged from committee. When an American importer in Yokohama complained of Japanese government discrimination, Secretary Bayard merely suggested that the American minister resort to unofficial good offices.[35]

Nevertheless, the likeliest reasons for the discouraging American sales record seem to have been much the same as in the rest of the world: lack of energy or imagination in seeking customers, failure to consult Japanese tastes, careless packing, and slow delivery. American textile manufacturers, for example, would

Japan, 35. Jones to Hay, November 15, 1880, no. 14, U.S., Consular Despatches, Nagasaki, 3. *New York Times,* September 28, November 12, 1877; *American Exporter* 2 (June 1878): 25.

34. U.S., *Commercial Relations, 1884–85,* 973–74. U.S., *Foreign Relations, 1886,* 562–64. U.S., *Consular Reports* 81 (July 1887): 58–62. Van Buren to Hay, January 19, 1881, no. 502, U.S., Consular Despatches, Kanagawa, 11. *New York Times,* January 28, 1890. *American Exporter* 5 (February 1880): 20; 29 (December 1891): 17. Davies, *Peacefully Working,* 193–94. Thomas R. Cox, *Mills and Markets: A History of the Pacific Coast Lumber Industry to 1900,* 224.

35. U.S., *Foreign Relations, 1887,* 652–53, 656. U.S., 43d Cong., 1st sess., *House Report 268.* Richard D. Hubbard to Thomas F. Bayard, January 23, 1886; May 28, June 2, 1887, nos. 105, 339, 346, U.S., Diplomatic Despatches, Japan, 34, 56, 57. Bayard to Hubbard, July 12, 1888, no. 219, U.S., Diplomatic Instructions, Japan, 3, 532–33. William Elliot Griffis, "Relations between the United States and Japan," 49–54. (A teacher and prolific writer, the *yatoi* Griffis did much to interpret Japan to Americans. Jones, *Live Machines,* 91–93.) *New York Daily Commercial Bulletin,* March 10, 1881.

not even alter their weaving machines to produce the unusually wide cloth required by the flowing Japanese garments. In 1889, when the Japanese government announced a contract for dredging machines to improve Yokohama's harbor, it could not obtain a single American bid, and the contract went to Europeans. An American importer in Yokohama put the matter in a nutshell: "The home market has hitherto been so elastic, the returns so much quicker, and their knowledge of it so much more complete, that American manufacturers have been unwilling to take the trouble or incur the risk of loss and certain expense of competing with European manufacturers for the trade of Japan." He warned that these conditions would not last forever. Other observers emphasized the importance of personal contacts even more than in most other countries and held up German sales methods as a model.[36]

While both Chinese and Japanese governments looked with suspicion on foreign investments as the harbinger of colonialism, the Chinese often extended their opposition to the public improvements themselves, especially in the interior. By contrast, the Japanese government under the Meiji regime was most anxious to build railroads, erect telegraphs, acquire a merchant marine, and develop mining and industry, but it wished either to control these activities itself or to finance them with Japanese capital. To create this capital, the government favored native business with comparatively low taxes and a repressive labor policy, and when Japanese merchants proved reluctant to invest, it often undertook the development itself. Since foreigners were encouraged to supply Japan with the necessary machinery, equipment, and technology, this economic nationalism fostered foreign trade, while it closed large fields of investment.[37]

The development of railroads offers an example. An American legation interpreter, A. L. C. Portman, obtained a concession in 1867 from the shogun's government to build a short line from Yokohama to Tokyo, but the Meiji regime transferred this to British enterprise, thanks partly to Sir Harry Parkes's influence and partly to the fact that London bankers granted a loan of £1 million. The eighteen-mile railroad, which was opened in 1872, was the first government-sponsored line in Asia under a native regime. Constructed entirely by British engineers, it cost at least $140,000 per mile, although it was only of narrow gauge and presented no great construction problems. A second railroad, from Kyoto to Osaka, opened in 1877, was also built by the British, reportedly at even greater expense.

36. Citations in notes 30 and 31 and in addition U.S., *Consular Reports* 65 (July 1886): 280–84. This contains answers to a questionnaire circulated by the consul general and includes the quoted sentence. On the instability of the Japanese market see Sugiyama, *Japan's Industrialization,* 69–71. On the dredging machines see *New York Times,* August 13, 1889. For a good description of sales methods at the turn of the century see Department of Commerce and Labor, Bureau of Manufactures [W. A. Graham Clark et al.], *Foreign Markets for the Sale of American Cotton Products,* 97–102.

37. Halliday, *History of Japanese Capitalism,* 53–57. Smith, *Political Change and Industrial Development,* chap. 4.

An American-built railroad was not opened until 1881—a twenty-three-mile line on Hokkaido, equipped with American rolling stock, which cost less than $20,000 per mile and was soon doing a flourishing freight and passenger business. Nevertheless, the Japanese government continued to hire British contractors, who, of course, used British materials and rolling stock wherever they could. During the 1880s and 1890s a government-sponsored concern, the Japanese Railway Company, carried out much of the new construction, but several dozen private companies remained in the field, all supported by Japanese capital, most using British models, and all training more and more Japanese engineers and directors. By 1896 the government controlled 870 miles of narrow-gauge track, which had to be widened in later years.[38]

The Japanese government could not establish such tight control over international cables. It allowed the Great Northern Telegraph Company of China (see chapter 6) to lay cables from Shanghai and Vladivostok to Nagasaki but retained control of land telegraph lines. Early American transpacific cable projectors got a similar reception in the 1870s. The most persistent of these was the American and East India Telegraph Company of New York, which proposed a line from San Francisco via the Aleutian Islands to several Japanese ports and thence to Shanghai and Hong Kong. None received much support from the State Department, which was mainly concerned to prevent any monopoly of landing rights. In 1880 Cyrus W. Field visited Japan with a similar project for a North Pacific line in which the Tokyo government was much interested. Nothing came of any of these ventures.[39]

---

38. Nobutaka Ike, "The Pattern of Railway Development in Japan," 217–29. Smith, *Political Change and Industrial Development*, 42–44. Hirschmeier, *Origins of Entrepreneurship*, 137–41. On British influences see Beasley, *Meiji Restoration*, 355–57; Fox, *Britain and China*, 576–78; and Wilson, *China*, 14–15, 17. Nitobe, *U.S.-Japanese Intercourse*, 137–38. *Commercial and Financial Chronicle* 10 (May 7, 1870): 586–87; 67 (August 20, 1898): 1872. DeLong to Fish, August 3, 1870, October 20, November 21, 1872, nos. 73, 295, 307; Charles A. Shepard to Fish, June 13, 1872, no. 45; Bingham to Evarts, February 9, 1881, nos. 1254, U.S., Diplomatic Despatches, Japan, no. 20, 21, 44. Van Buren to Hay, January 7, 1881, June 12, 1884, nos. 496, 810, U.S. Consular Despatches, Kanagawa, 11, 14. *New York Times*, July 24, 1872; January 19, 1873; November 5, 1877; January 24, 1881. Japanese conservatives opposed railroads, fearing increased foreign influences and profits for the Western promoters. Progressives, who hoped to develop the Japanese economy, got around the opposition by emphasizing security considerations and stability. Tokohito Tanaka, "Meiji Government and the Introduction of Railways," 771–83.

39. Tribolet, *Electrical Communications*, 224, 227. Treat, *United States and Japan, 1853–1895*, vol. 1, 382, 424, 467; vol. 2, 19, 43. Fish to DeLong, September 21, 1870, no. 34, U.S., Diplomatic Instructions, Japan, 1, 34. DeLong to Fish, August 17, 1871, no. 230, with note on docket, U.S., Diplomatic Despatches, Japan, 14. Prospectus of American and East India Telegraph Company enclosed with Bingham to Fish, August 8, 1876, no. 424; Bingham to Fish, November 21, 1876, May 7, 1877, nos. 463, 556; Bingham to Evarts, December 27, 1990, no. 1129, U.S., Diplomatic Despatches, Japan, 32–34. There is some evidence that the U.S. and Japanese governments were willing to guarantee 6 percent interest on the capital of a cable project of about 1872 in which Field was also interested. Unidentified letter fragment in J. C. B. Davis papers, 13, 2923–30 ff, 2933–34. William

It was in shipping that the Japanese government most effectively exerted its influence over American enterprises. By the late 1860s British ships had largely crowded Americans out of Japanese ports as in China, but when the Pacific Mail Steamship Company inaugurated its line to Yokohama and Hong Kong, it also established branch lines to Hakodate and via Kobe and Nagasaki to Shanghai. For a few years the latter branch line did good business in the coasting trade. In 1875, however, the Japanese government, fearing foreign domination of its ports, gave the coasting monopoly to the newly founded Mitsubishi Steamship Company, which bought four of Pacific Mail's ships, renamed them, and was soon offering prompt, efficient service to Shanghai. A decade later Mitsubishi organized other government-sponsored concerns into Nippon Yusen Kaisha (Japan Mail Steamship Company), which in the early 1890s began to send its fleet to Bombay, Australia, and Hawaii. Other smaller lines formed a network to the Chinese coast and some river ports. These ships all received state subsidies, and in 1896 a comprehensive law extended subsidies to all Japanese-owned ships over one thousand tons engaged in foreign trade.[40] A similarly exclusionist policy was followed in other sectors such as mining and banking, but these involved little American capital.

In the field of manufacturing, Americans scored a few small successes but faced the same obstacles as in transportation. The Japanese enjoyed a special advantage to a degree unique in developing countries—a flair for imitation. Japanese who visited the Philadelphia Exposition of 1876 brought back with them many agricultural implements, which the American dealers had sold them at cut rates as samples, hoping for steady customers. Instead the Japanese proceeded to reproduce their own plows, harrows, and cultivators, so that the apparently promising market never developed. For some years they continued to buy American clocks, watches, and balances, as they could not produce sufficiently accurate ones themselves, but eventually, of course, they mastered this technique too.[41]

D. Wray, *Mitsubishi and the N.Y.K., 1870–1914: Business Strategy in the Japanese Shipping Industry*, chaps. 1, 2, pp. 86, 289–90. Mitsubishi paid Pacific Mail $780,000 and Oriental and Occidental only $30,000.

40. Hirschmeier, *Origins of Entrepreneurship*, 145–46. Hyde, *Far Eastern Trade*, 158–61. Allen, *Short Economic History*, 90–92. Arthur E. Tiedemann, "Japan's Economic Foreign Policies," 120–21. J. Ross Browne to William H. Seward, October 21, 1868, no. 1, U.S., Diplomatic Despatches, China, 14. U.S., *Commercial Relations, 1874–75*, 805–6. *New York Times*, September 10, November 12, 1877. W. Tennant, "The Commercial Expansion of Japan," *Contemporary Review* 71 (January 1997): 57. Graham Clark et al., *Foreign Markets for American Cotton Products*, 94. The British were furious at being shut out of the coasting trade. *American Protectionist* 1 (June 11, 1881): 231. *Board of Trade Journal* 22 (March 1897): 300.

41. *New York Times*, September 28, November 12, 1877. The government also imitated the exposition itself at Tokyo, complete with a Machinery Hall, even though the building contained only a small Japanese-made steam engine and a little textile-making apparatus. Ibid., October 21, 1877. An example of a successful American enterprise was a pulp and paper mill at Hiogo acquired in 1877 that was soon employing about two hundred Japanese and producing thirty-six hundred pounds of paper a day. *U.S., Consular Reports*

Although Americans introduced new technology into such fields as leather making and food canning, the Japanese government exerted strong influence in industry too. A good example was cotton textiles. Japan originally imported cotton cloth from China and India. During the year of the Meiji Restoration the leading feudal lord purchased one hundred looms and spinning machinery in England. The Meiji regime established two model mills and bought machinery for ten others that it sold at a discount to private entrepreneurs. What had been essentially a cottage industry under the shogunate became centralized, especially in the Osaka district, producing mostly coarse grades with modern imported machinery. At the same time, Japanese imports of the finer American machine-made yarns increased rapidly and reached a peak in the late 1870s, about twenty-five years before this happened in China. The government floated a domestic loan in 1878 with which it purchased spinning machinery in England, established government mills, and subsidized private concerns. In 1883 the largest Japanese textile company began round-the-clock operations and five years later was paying 30 percent dividends.

During the decade after 1886 Japanese cotton spindles increased from 81,000 to 959,000. Since Japan produced little raw cotton, it had to import almost its entire supply, at first largely from India but soon a better grade from the United States, which was already shipping large quantities of cotton textiles to East Asia. The ingenious Japanese reduced their vulnerability partly by devising economical blends of cotton and other fibers and partly by creating a cartel of mills that controlled the purchase of cotton, obtained shipping and railroad rebates, and received export funds from an obliging government. Cotton mill operatives were mostly women, and both organization and machinery were British in design. However, the Japanese use of sizing struck a compromise between British and American practice. During its rapid rise the industry suffered for a time from overproduction, but by the mid-1890s it was invading the Chinese market and turning out finer cloth.[42]

The Japanese government also took a hand in developing other industries. The silk industry became, in the words of a Japanese economist, "a training school for Japanese industrialization," supplying openings for profitable investment and enforcing efficiency and economy. Many thought it owed its rapid rise to better quality control than that of Chinese filatures, but other factors were at least as

---

4 (February 1881): 230–31. This operated through the 1880s. U.S., *Commercial Relations, 1886–87*, 2, 1305–6.

42. Allen, *Short Economic History*, 71–75. Hirschmeier, *Origins of Entrepreneurship*, 90–104, 152–61. Smith, *Political Change and Industrial Development*, 11, 54–56, 60–63, chap. 6. Keizo Saki, *The Cotton Industry of Japan*, 14–19. Bruce L. Reynolds, "The East Asian 'Textile Cluster' Trade, 1868–1973: A Comparative Advantage Interpretation," 140–41. Graham Clark et al., *Foreign Markets for American Cotton Products*, 102–9. Sung Jae Koh, *Stages of Industrial Development in Asia: A Comparative History of the Cotton Industry in Japan, India, China, and Korea*, 139. *Commercial and Financial Chronicle* 66 (April 2, 1898): 643–44.

important: low prices of cocoons, low labor costs, the fast-growing American silk-weaving industry, the advantage over China in distance and transpacific steamer connections to San Francisco, and improved American rail connections. By about 1890, 56.3 percent of Japanese silk exports were going to the United States. The woolen industry, less spectacular, was even more an imitation of Western models. In 1873 the government renovated an iron smelter that had been built from Dutch drawings and laid the groundwork for an iron and steel industry. By the mid-1890s Japan was turning out electrical equipment and rolling stock for its expanding railroad system. Factories for making cement, glass, bricks, porcelain, and sugar enjoyed government support in one form or another during the nineteenth century. Although Americans dominated brewing and paper making for a time, they eventually gave way to Japanese interests. Beginning in 1880, the government sold out its industries to private companies, although in other respects it continued its nationalist policies.[43]

Nevertheless, a number of factors greatly hindered Japanese industrialization. Except for coal and copper, the islands possessed few mineral resources. Even though the government might have tolerated foreign capital in factories for a time, chronic currency depreciation (until 1886) and the examples set in railroads and the merchant marine discouraged foreign promoters and investors. Perhaps the most serious handicap was the "unequal" treaties of 1866, which forbade the government to raise its tariffs on textiles, iron and steel, and other products of the more advanced Western economies. Duties of 5 percent offered little protection to "infant industries" against Lancashire or even Massachusetts and Pennsylvania. Consequently, revision of the humiliating "unequal" treaties became the chief diplomatic goal of the Japanese government for the next three decades.

Between about 1870, when the revision movement began to gather momentum, and 1894, when new commercial treaties were finally signed, Japan and the Western powers resorted to nearly every diplomatic device that Japanese statesmen could think of: conferences, "pilot" treaties with the United States, a diplomatic mission, and innumerable bilateral discussions, drafts, and memoranda. Citing the protectionist writings of Henry C. Carey, the Japanese concentrated their efforts on the United States for the latter's demonstrated friendship and the hope of establishing a precedent for the European powers. The Americans generally recognized that there was nothing in the 1866 treaties to prevent separate action by them but that, since Anglo-Japanese trade was largest of all, no action without Britain was likely to be very effective. The principal motive stated by the Americans—sympathy with Japanese nationality—was undoubtedly genuine,

43. Smith, *Political Change and Industrial Development*, chap. 8, conclusion. Allen, *Short Economic History*, 65–67, 85–90. Beasley, *Rise of Modern Japan*, 103–14. Li, "Silk Export Trade," 78–83 (phrase quoted from Kenzo Hemmi is on p. 81). Eng, *Economic Imperialism in China*, chap. 7. Schwantes, "America and Japan," 115. For a description of a Japanese munitions factory in 1887, modeled on "Ooritch" (Woolwich), see Henry Knollys, *Sketches of Life in Japan*, 263–70.

but it was mixed with more practical considerations, such as the desire to reduce British exports to Japan.[44]

Unfortunately for Japan, a number of serious obstacles stood in the way of consent to treaty revision, even by the United States. It proved impossible to dissociate Japanese tariff autonomy from the abolition of extraterritoriality, although this antedated the 1866 treaties. Before the 1880s few Japanese objected to extraterritoriality. As their new court system developed, they tried to prove that it satisfied Western standards of reliability and fairness, but every proposal to set up mixed courts or other compromises fell between two irreconcilables—Japanese "face" and the Western powers' concern for the security of their nationals. Another noneconomic objection, appearing in the American-Japanese treaty of 1889, involved a reciprocal provision allowing immigration and land ownership in the United States. This ran afoul of the anti-Chinese fervor symbolized in the United States by the Exclusion Act of 1882 (see chapter 6).[45]

Even in the area of trade, plausible reasons prevented U.S. action. American sympathy and desire for Japanese friendship wilted when the Japanese made it clear that they proposed to levy a sizable duty on American kerosene—for revenue purposes, since Japan did not intend production. Secretary Evarts found the Japanese proposal "unfriendly and inexplicable," a strange reaction, indeed, for a high-tariff Republican. In 1887 a Japanese newspaper sensibly suggested a reciprocity treaty by which Japan would forgo a tariff on kerosene if the United States put silk textiles on the free list.[46] No one gave this idea much heed, for soon the Japanese government was releasing other tariff proposals, which the Americans pronounced downright discriminatory. These included 8 percent on cotton yarns and 5 percent on gunny bags (British and British-Indian) but 20 percent on watches (American). The average rate on American goods, said the American minister, would be twice that on British goods. Some Americans suspected the imperial government of giving fat supply contracts to British or German firms so as to influence the attitude of their governments.[47] British

44. Schwantes, "America and Japan," 122. John Bassett Moore memorandum, July 7, 1886, U.S., Reports of Diplomatic Bureau, 7, no. 14. Bingham to Frederick T. Frelinghuysen, June 6, 1884, no. 1868, U.S., Diplomatic Despatches, Japan, 50. *American Exporter* 2 (June 1878): 23. On the currency problem see Smith, *Political Change and Industrial Development,* 25–26.

45. Jones, *Extraterritoriality in Japan,* passim. Treat, *United States and Japan, 1853–1895,* vol. 1, 508–9; vol. 2, 296–98, 300–301, 337–41. Hoare, *Japan's Treaty Ports,* 64, 98, 102. The Europeans, especially the Russians, objected even to Bingham's gestures of sympathy with Japan, fearing separate American action. Marshall Jewell to Fish, July 12, 1874, no. 104; Eugene Schuyler to Fish, September 22, no. 32, U.S., Diplomatic Despatches, Japan, 26.

46. Treat, *United States and Japan, 1853–1895,* vol. 2, 105–7, 243–44, 250–51 (Evarts's quoted phrase is on 106). *Japan Gazette,* January 26, 1887, reprinted in U.S., *Consular Reports* 75 (March 1887): 630–31.

47. Bingham to Frelinghuysen, May 23, 1882, no. 1494, U.S., Diplomatic Despatches, Japan, 46. Treat, *United States and Japan, 1853–1895,* vol. 2, 333–34. Hubbard to Bayard, May 20, June 3, 1887, nos. 339, 347, U.S., Diplomatic Despatches, Japan, 56, 57. *Engineering and Mining Journal* 47 (July 13, 1889): 33.

and American publicists, led by the American Japanophile E. H. House, greatly stimulated this ill feeling by accusing each other of selfishness, hypocrisy, and lack of real concern for Japanese interests.[48]

There is no need for more than a summary of negotiations on tariff revision. In 1872 Japan sent a mission to Washington led by the foreign minister, Iwakura Tomomi, asking the United States to appoint a delegate to a conference in Europe. Secretary Fish and the Japanese discussed all points at issue as well as other trade matters and a possible loan but could not arrive at any agreement, and Fish refused to take part in a general conference.[49] Evarts, abandoning the cooperative policy, actually signed a commercial treaty in 1878, removing most restrictions, but the British minister got Japan to add a provision postponing its enforcement until European nations signed similar treaties, and this "joker" effectively nullified the whole. In 1882 Japan convened a conference in Tokyo, which Minister Bingham attended, but it proved impossible to reconcile the Japanese treaty draft with European requirements. The following year, as a mark of friendship, the United States returned to Japan the undistributed portion of an overly large indemnity it had received in 1866, but no progress was made on treaty revision.

In 1886 Japan called a second conference, which argued for months, recessed, and continued into 1887. Secretary Bayard instructed a new minister, Richard D. Hubbard, to favor revisions if they were nondiscriminatory, but the Japanese draft introduced the question of extraterritoriality, and the conference faded away in disagreement. In the last month of the first Cleveland administration, February 1889, Hubbard signed an elaborate commercial treaty with an appended schedule of tariff duties ranging from 5 to 20 percent. Unfortunately, at that point Hubbard was replaced by John W. Swift, the most anti-Japanese minister of the period, who raised every possible objection to the treaty in a series of long, ably argued dispatches and persuaded the uninformed Harrison administration to withhold it from the Senate.

The Japanese government, giving up hope for American support, turned to Britain and in 1894 obtained a promise of both tariff and judicial autonomy after a five-year transition period. The United States inconspicuously signed a similar

48. Bingham to Evarts, September 20, 1879; Bingham to Blaine, July 23, 1881; Bingham to Frelinghuysen, February 13, 1883, July 30, 1884, nos. 973, 1345, 1631, 1898, with enclosures, U.S., Diplomatic Despatches, Japan, 40, 45, 48, 51. House, "Martyrdom of an Empire," 615–17. *New York Tribune*, June 12, August 19, 1881; *New York Times*, June 27, 1882.

49. Treat, *United States and Japan, 1853–1895*, vol. 1, chap. 18. Fish suggested that Jay Cooke might be interested in the loan project, but at this time Cooke was seeking money himself for the Northern Pacific Railroad. Lewis, *America's Stake*, 334. The Iwakura embassy received red carpet treatment across the United States and further encouraged American interest in Japan. Nitobe, *U.S.-Japanese Intercourse*, 163–65. Jones, *Live Machines*, 111–12. It also opened the eyes of the Japanese to the urgent need for reforms if they hoped to change the "unequal treaties." Marlene J. Mayo, "A Catechism of Western Diplomacy: The Japanese and Hamilton Fish, 1877," 389–410. Beasley, *Meiji Restoration*, 369–70. Peter Duus, *The Abacus and the Sword: The Japanese Penetration of Korea, 1895–1910*, 14.

treaty. Japan's victory over China in 1894–1895 made any reversal unthinkable, and in 1899 the imperial government gained full control over its trade and its legal system.[50] American mercantile opinion strongly opposed the U.S. treaty, predicting that it would ruin trade, and Californians feared increased Oriental immigration.[51] Here, at least in part, American foreign policy had responded to ideological convictions and an abstract sense of justice, rather than merely economic interest.

This change suggests that by the end of the century Americans were beginning to adopt a more "modern" attitude toward the Japanese government and people as a nation on the way toward a developed status. But even though Americans' trade with Japan had actually caught up with their Chinese trade, their view of Japanese trade remained substantially what it had been in the 1850s—that it was a sideshow compared with the limitless market and fabulous image of China.

50. The most detailed account of these negotiations from an American viewpoint is Treat, *United States and Japan, 1853–1895.* Treat feels that the powers should have conceded tariff autonomy in 1872 and legal autonomy in 1887. He blames Swift primarily for the collapse of American leadership in Japan (vol. 2, 260, 367). Jones, *Live Machines,* 112. For a British sneer at the 1878 treaty see Dickins and Lane-Poole, *Life of Parkes,* vol. 2, 317. For a sample of moderate American support of the 1878 treaty see *New York Times,* July 6, 1889. In 1894 the Republican press, already furious at Cleveland and Gresham for rejecting the annexation of Hawaii, attacked the secretary for dilatoriness and even hinted that the British ambassador, Julian Pauncefote, had duped him into letting the British go first. The editors conveniently forgot Blaine's actions. *New York Tribune,* September 21, 1894. On the return of the 1866 indemnity see Treat, *United States and Japan, 1853–1895,* vol. 2, 545–59. U.S., 47th Cong., 1st sess., *Senate Report 120; House Report 138. New York Times,* January 7, 1876. *New York Tribune,* April 4, 1880. *New York Herald,* March 4, 1881. For the terms of the 1894 treaty see Bevans, *Treaties,* vol. 9, 887–96. In a manner of speaking, Japanese participation in the Columbian Exposition of 1893 at Chicago might be regarded as a celebration of Japan's new status. For a description see Harris, "All the World a Melting Pot?" 37–46.

51. *New York Journal of Commerce,* October 3, 1894. *New York Times,* October 3, December 17, 1894. But one earlier argument for revision had been that it would help American merchants compete with the British. *American Exporter* 2 (June 1878): 25. In addition to commercial objections, opponents of ratification cited the immigration issue and also rumored Japanese atrocities in the Sino-Japanese War as an indication that extraterritoriality was still necessary. *New York Times,* December 26, 1889; October 3, 1894; December 17, 1895. On immigration see *Nation* 40 (January 3, 1875): 2.

8

Korea

The Beginning of Political Involvement

W HEN THE *EMPRESS OF CHINA* sailed into Whampoa harbor in 1784, the Chinese Empire was surrounded by a ring of tributary buffer states or territories: Korea, Taiwan, Indo-China, Siam, Tibet, Sinkiang, and Mongolia. During the nineteenth century foreigners penetrated several of these buffers and threatened the empire on all sides: France from the south, Britain from the west and along the coast, Russia from the north, and Japan from the east. (Germany arrived late, at the end of the 1890s, and stayed close to the coast.) This enveloping process was already under way by the 1860s, when the United States established formal diplomatic relations with China. American merchants were accustomed to both competing and cooperating with British merchants in the coastal ports, and British activities in Burma meant little to them. American trade in Siam did not arouse much interest at home.

The possibility of political involvement in these border areas first occurred to American diplomats in East Asia and more dimly to the faraway State Department during the early 1880s. At that time Russia flexed its muscles on the Chinese northern frontier; France established a protectorate in Tongkin (northern Indo-China); and Japan showed its ambition in the offshore islands of Taiwan and the Ryukyus. Later in the decade this possibility became a reality when the United States opened the peninsula of Korea to American trade, hoping to create a second Japan. Instead, Washington found itself in the middle of a growing power struggle between Japan and China.

The Russian clouds on the northern Chinese horizon seemed remote to Westerners at first. In 1858, as has been seen, Russia took from China northeastern Manchuria, beyond the Amur River. During the 1870s Russian encroachments on Chinese Turkestan, far to the west in the territory of Ili, led to a crisis. For several months in 1879–1880 China feared war and briefly moderated its opposition to Western improvements. (At this time, for example, the imperial government first authorized construction of a telegraph line.) Somewhat to China's surprise, in 1881 Russia negotiated a peaceful settlement and evacuated Ili. Chinese officials were cocky over the victory, but they had gained only time, for the czar's government was turning its attention eastward and six years later authorized the beginning of the Trans-Siberian Railroad. This would involve Russia inextricably in East Asian affairs.[1]

Chinese self-confidence soon led to a confrontation with France on the southern border. In 1883, bitterly resenting the recently established French protectorates over Cambodia and Annam and the obvious threat to Tongkin, China sent troops across the border of Indo-China to redeem its onetime tributaries and demand French evacuation. After a series of French victories, Li Hung-chang prudently agreed to a compromise peace, only to see it rejected by nationalists in the court. France retaliated by crushing the Chinese Navy and blockading Taiwan.

The United States had taken little part in the Ili crisis, but now Li, hard-pressed by Japan in Korea (see below) asked Minister John Russell Young for good offices. Young felt compelled to intervene, fearing complete French domination over southern China and perhaps even the collapse of the imperial government. He sought to mediate but could not persuade the Chinese that their cause was lost. As an emergency measure, he helped transfer most of China's merchant marine to Russell and Company, under protection of the American flag—thereby making U.S. mediation unacceptable to France too. In the end it was Sir Robert Hart, inspector general of the Imperial Chinese Customs and perennial government adviser, who helped arrange a peace treaty in June 1885. By this treaty China lost no territory of its own but recognized French control of all Indo-China and granted special trade privileges in Yunnan province, just north of the Indo-China border.[2]

Japan's expansionism in East Asia long antedated that of France. During the sixteenth and seventeenth centuries, before the years of seclusion, Japan had instituted a tradition of foreign trade and migration, never entirely forgotten. The Meiji Restoration and the rapid modernization of Japan after 1868 coincided with European imperialization in Africa and Asia. Not surprisingly, the Japanese imitated this too, as well as the linkage between expansion and foreign trade, for they saw in trade the source of Western material strength. By the 1880s dozens or hundreds of Japanese annually were emigrating to Korea and Hawaii. A few publicists identified China as the main obstacle to Japanese progress and began to combine population pressures with trade surpluses and militarism to form an expansionist ideology that their American counterparts would have

---

1. Morse, *International Relations*, vol. 2, chap. 16. Andrew Malozemoff, *Russian Far Eastern Policy, 1881–1904*, chaps. 1, 2. In the Ili crisis the American minister to Russia, John W. Foster, at the Chinese minister's request, mentioned informally to the Russian foreign minister American hopes for peace in the Far East and interest in Chinese trade. John W. Foster to William M. Evarts, January 1, 1881, no. 77, U.S., Diplomatic Despatches, Russia, 35.

2. On the Franco-Chinese War see Morse, *International Relations*, vol. 2, chap. 17. On Young's efforts to mediate see Pletcher, *Awkward Years*, 214–18; Anderson, *Imperialism and Idealism*, 135–40; and Hagan, *American Gunboat Diplomacy*, 119–25. For Li's viewpoint see Hunt, *Special Relationship*, 133–36. During and after the war China borrowed heavily from British banks, and Jardine, Matheson tried in vain to interest the British government in mediating. LeFevour, *Western Enterprise*, 73–78.

recognized. By the 1890s a dichotomy between peaceful and forceful expansion was noticeable; it was to unsettle Japanese foreign relations for the next half century.[3]

American attitudes toward the sprouting Japanese expansionism were as hesitant and equivocal as toward the revision of the "unequal treaties." One early focus of Japanese interest was Taiwan, which had already attracted American attention (see chapter 5). Reacting to raids by Taiwanese pirates on American coastal shipping in the 1860s, Seward instructed the commander of the East India Squadron to cooperate with the British in rooting them out—a useless directive, as the American naval forces were too weak for the task. In 1867, as has been seen, Consul Charles LeGendre at Amoy led an American reconnaissance expedition to the island. Meanwhile, the Japanese government undertook a policy of probing to determine China's relationship with Taiwan and other peripheral areas. When LeGendre entered Japanese service, he led a punitive expedition in 1874 against the Taiwanese. The expedition eventually withdrew, recognizing Chinese sovereignty over the island, but not before the Japanese had ascertained the weakness of China's hold.[4]

Between that time and the 1890s American trade with Taiwan gradually increased in much the same manner as trade with the adjacent Chinese coast. The island produced excellent tea and camphor, most of which went to the United States, sugar for China and Australia, and coal for coastal steamers. Russell and Company handled some of this trade and maintained a fine modern office building in Tamsui. But the Taiwanese imported only 144,650 gallons of American kerosene in 1885—less than 1 percent of Japan. The Taiwanese bought cotton textiles mostly from Britain, and when a short railroad was built inland from Keelung, British and German interests got the contracts. There seemed no economic reasons for the Americans to care whether China or Japan controlled Taiwan.[5]

The United States had even less direct interest in the Ryukyu Islands, although Commodore Perry had negotiated for a coaling station on Okinawa. Geographically closer to China, they had been for many years de jure tributary to China but de facto subject to one of the Japanese feudal lords. LeGendre's punitive expedition of 1874 included the Ryukyus as well as Taiwan, and afterward Japan proceeded to incorporate them administratively. In 1879 Japan and China were

3. Akira Iriye, *Pacific Estrangement: Japanese and American Expansion, 1897–1911*, 17–25. Duus, *Abacus and Sword*, chap. 1.

4. Paolino, *Foundations of the American Empire*, 163–69. Sophia Su-fei Yen, *Taiwan in China's Foreign Relations, 1836–1874*, chaps. 7–9. Gordon, "Charles LeGendre," 63–76. Thomson, "Filibustering to Formosa," 442–56. Fox, *Britain and Japan*, Appendix 3, 576–78. Yanaga, *Japan since Perry*, 181–82.

5. W. Ewell Goldsborough to J. C. Bancroft Davis, June 16, 1882, no. 97, U.S., Consular Despatches, Amoy, 9. U.S., *Consular Reports* 74 (February 1887): 460–61. U.S., *Foreign Relations, 1888*, 326–38. Sales of kerosene in Japan and China for 1884 were 428,700 and 315,200 42-gallon barrels respectively. Williamson and Daum, *American Petroleum Industry*, 1, 675.

close to war over the islands. During former president Grant's visit to China, Li Hung-chang appealed to him for good offices in the quarrel as part of an informal Chinese balance-of-power policy. When Grant reached Japan, he discussed the problem with several members of the government, warned them that only the Western powers would gain from a Sino-Japanese war, and suggested that a joint commission work out a compromise solution. A Japanese commissioner departed for Peking to see what could be done.

Part of Grant's interest in the question rose from his belief that the Japanese would develop a large foreign trade if released from their treaty restrictions. When he returned home, he proposed to Secretary Evarts that the United States extend the Monroe Doctrine to the Far East and proclaim an "Evarts Doctrine" of cooperation (not alliance, he stipulated) with China and Japan against European aggression. Evarts, engaged in his own negotiations with China, wanted to keep the goodwill of both parties. He was willing to consider relaxing restrictions on China (see chapter 5) but saw no need for a public statement regarding an ominously open-ended commitment. This was just as well, for the Sino-Japanese negotiations over the Ryukyus soon broke down. Beset by the Russian crisis of 1880, one faction in the Chinese government offered to yield most of the islands, but another, more nationalistic faction refused and provoked a public outcry. After considerable delay Japan abandoned negotiations, protesting Chinese bad faith, and remained in possession. Two years later Li got John Russell Young to investigate American mediation, which Secretary Frelinghuysen refused since Japan would not agree. All Young could do was to help persuade Li to give up any idea of repossessing the Ryukyus.[6]

A more important area of Japanese expansionist probing was Korea, a peninsula strategically situated midway between Japan and northern China and uncomfortably close to Peking. The Chinese were coming to regard it as a shield against Russia and Japan, while to the Japanese, Korea was the logical complement to their modernization program. The king of Korea was traditionally independent, although he participated in tributary relations with Peking. Toward Japan he had no obligations, and he maintained a generally exclusionist policy toward

6. Yanaga, *Japan since Perry,* 182–83. Treat, *United States and Japan, 1853–1895,* vol. 1, 473–75, 568–69; vol. 2, 71–74, 141–44, 179–81. Dennett, *Americans in Eastern Asia,* 438–47. Hunt, *Special Relationship,* 118–25. Hyman Kublin, "The Attitude of China during the Liu-ch'iu Controversy, 1871–1881," 213–31. Edwin Pak-wah Leung, "Li Hung-chang and the Liu-ch'iu (Ryukyu) Controversy, 1871–1881." Morken, "America Looks West," 54–55. Pennanen, "Evarts," 225–28. Blaine also evaded a feeler for good offices, this time from Japan, after Grant's visit. John Russell Young to Evarts, March 25, 1880, Evarts papers, 27 (cited in Morken, 55). Young to Frelinghuysen, October 9, 1882, no. 33, confidential. Enclosed leter from Grant to Prince Kung, August 18, 1879, U.S., Diplomatic Despatches, China, 61. U.S. Grant to [Young], May 18, 1883, Young papers, 15. Blaine to James B. Angell, April 4, 1881, no. 82; Frelinghuysen to Young, March 16, 1883, no. 95, U.S., Diplomatic Instructions, China, 3, 214–19, 409–12.

the outside world.[7] During the 1840s and 1850s the British had tried to use the fiction of Chinese control to "open" Korea. Because of Korea's location and long coastline, American ships were occasionally cast up on its shores during the 1850s and 1860s. The crews were generally well treated, and their experiences aroused curiosity at home and some desire to open Korea to trade, as Perry had opened Japan.

During the late 1860s a series of incidents seemed to indicate that the time had come for action. In 1866, after China denied responsibility for the murder of several French missionaries in Korea, Napoleon III sent a punitive naval expedition, which the Koreans beat off. At the same time, the *General Sherman*, an American schooner under hire to a British commercial firm, grounded in a Korean river, and its crew were killed by local residents. (Years later, after much investigation, it was determined that the foreigners had provoked the fracas and largely brought their doom on themselves.)[8]

The commander of the American Asiatic Squadron sent officers to investigate the "atrocity," but Secretary Seward did not wait for their reports. Against the cautious advice of Minister Anson Burlingame in Peking, he impulsively proposed to France a joint naval expedition to avenge the injuries and open Korea. (Fortunately, the French government, involved in Mexico and Europe, declined.) In 1871 Secretary Fish sent Minister Frederick F. Low with a naval detachment to negotiate a treaty. When a Korean coastal fort fired on them, the Americans overreacted and wiped out its defenders. This bloodshed ended the mission, and its subsequent withdrawal to China was interpreted as a defeat.[9]

The episode warned some Koreans that they could no longer remain aloof from the world, and a progressive party urged the king to imitate Japan's campaign of modernization. Meanwhile, after a clash with visiting Japanese warships, in 1876 the king signed a friendship treaty with Japan that asserted Korea's independence of China, professed to restore "the amicable relations of yore" with Japan, and opened the southeastern port of Pusan to Japanese trade. During the next seven years two more ports were added. Japanese ships began to call regularly at the nearest ports, bringing in mostly British goods. At Pusan Japanese merchants

7. Korea's relationship to China and Japan is discussed in M. Frederick Nelson, *Korea and the Old Orders in Eastern Asia*, chap. 6; Yur-bok Lee, *Diplomatic Relations between the United States and Korea, 1866–1877*, 45–46; Key-hiuk Kim, *The Last Phase of the East Asian World Order: Korea, Japan, and the Chinese Empire, 1860–1882*, chap. 1; and Yur-bok Lee, *West Goes East: Paul Georg von Möllendorff and Great Power Imperialism in Late Yi Korea*, 4, 9–10.

8. Jonsuk Chay, *Diplomacy of Asymmetry: Korean-American Relations to 1910*, 17–22. Lee, *Diplomatic Relations*, 19–25. Dennett, *Americans in Eastern Asia*, 417–18. Kim, *Last Phase*, 47–55.

9. Chay, *Diplomacy of Asymmetry*, 22–33. Lee, *Diplomatic Relations*, 25–33. Dennett, *Americans in Eastern Asia*, 418–20. Anderson, *Imperialism and Idealism*, 33–34, 74–78. For the text of the French minister's report of Seward's oral protest see Tyler Dennett, "Seward's Far Eastern Policy," 34–36. Paullin, *Diplomatic Negotiations*, 287–92. Johnson, *Far China Station*, chap. 11. Kim, *Last Phase*, 55–62.

established a bank, a chamber of commerce, and a newspaper, and a government-subsidized shipping line obtained a monopoly. Soon the port was a bustling center of Japanese trade. It also attracted various Western ships, but for the time being Korea refused them admission.[10]

During the 1870s few Americans knew much about Korea, but glimmerings of interest were beginning to appear. In 1868, as a result of the *General Sherman* incident, the *New York Herald* suggested that a naval and commercial station on the peninsula might be useful and listed Korean agricultural and mineral resources. After the Low expedition of 1871 opinion was divided between admiration of Korean resources and commercial potentialities and apology for making war on "a half-civilized, feeble people, on pretexts that do not appear to have any adequate foundation."[11] In 1878 Senator Aaron A. Sargent (Republican, California) introduced a resolution appropriating $50,000 for a mission to negotiate a commercial treaty with Korea like the one with Japan. Such a treaty would help protect American merchant ships and whalers off northern China and benefit both the Pacific states and eastern manufacturers by opening a vast market. The opportunities for mining and industry and the need of instructors for the Koreans would open careers for young Americans. "It is the duty of Congress to provide means to develop our foreign commerce," Sargent concluded. "Here are twelve million people, our neighbors, who want our products. Let us invite them to be our customers."[12]

Sargent's bill died in committee, but his arguments impressed Secretary Evarts, who became convinced that Low had made a mistake in trying to open Korea by force. He and Secretary of the Navy Richard W. Thompson decided to combine a conciliatory mission with a reconnaissance tour of Africa, the Middle East, and the Indian Ocean then being planned. For this enlarged mission they chose Commodore Robert W. Shufeldt, who had already visited Korea in the 1860s,

10. The treaty also granted Japan tariff exemptions and extraterritorial rights. Li Hung-chang advised the king of Korea to negotiate with the Japanese probably because China could not afford further confrontations after Taiwan and the Ryukyus, but China refused to recognize Korean independence. Nelson, *Korea and the Old Orders,* 126–34. Lee, *West Goes East,* 19–20. Also, the vague language of a Sino-Japanese nonaggression treaty of 1871 obscured Korea's status. For the Japanese background and the negotiation of the 1876 treaty see Martina Deuchler, *Confucian Gentlemen and Barbarian Envoys: The Opening of Korea, 1875–1885,* chaps. 2, 3; Kim, *Last Phase,* chap. 6. Francis Hilary Conroy, *The Japanese Seizure of Korea, 1868–1910: A Study of Realism and Idealism in International Relations,* 31–37; Woonsung Choi, *The Fall of the Hermit Kingdom,* 9–11; and Duus, *Abacus and Sword,* 29–49, 250. On Japanese economic penetration see Deuchler, *Confucian Gentlemen,* chaps. 4, 5. William Elliot Griffis, *Corea, the Hermit Kingdom,* 424–28. For a detailed account of Korean relations with China and Japan from 1876 to 1880 see Kim, *Last Phase,* chap. 7. In 1875 Japan settled its northern boundary by acquiring the Kurile Islands from Russia in exchange for Sakhalin. Conroy, *Japanese Seizure.*

11. *New York Herald,* May 12, 1868. *Commercial and Financial Chronicle* 13 (August 26, 1871): 264. *Galaxy* 13 (March 1872): 302–13.

12. U.S., 45th Cong., 2d sess., *Congressional Record,* 7, pt. 3, 2324, 2599–601.

investigating the *General Sherman* affair, and had high hopes for its future. Shufeldt was instructed to "give special consideration" to the possibility of opening Korean ports to American trade.[13]

Arriving in 1880 after a long voyage, Shufeldt found the Koreans still unfriendly as a result of the Low expedition, so he made his way to Tokyo to consult Minister John A. Bingham and the Japanese government, which reluctantly sent a covering letter to Korea with Shufeldt's formal request for a treaty. After further waiting, he went to China at the invitation of Li Hung-chang, acting for the Tsungli Yamen. Li had been much alarmed by the Japanese annexation of the Ryukyu Islands. He wanted to repair old Chinese connections with Korea or at least establish a Western-style balance of power. For the time being, however, Li made no progress in softening up the Koreans, and Shufeldt left for the United States. On his way home he set down in memoranda and reports his conviction that treaty relations with Korea could strengthen American influence in the Pacific, already established in Alaska, Hawaii, Samoa, and Japan, to counterbalance European control of the Atlantic and become "another link which binds the East to the West."[14]

In June 1881 the commodore returned to China with a secret commission from Secretary Blaine to negotiate such a treaty. Shufeldt also apparently intended to take service with the Chinese Navy, so as to spread American influence there. But the next months provided disillusioning, for the naval appointment never materialized, and the Korean government remained unwilling to receive him. Shufeldt came to realize that Li was using him as a tool of Chinese foreign policy.[15] Only after much delay did the Koreans, fearing Russian aggression, decide to permit negotiations, and in March and April 1882 Shufeldt and Li's legal advisers hammered out a draft through many tedious revisions. (Shufeldt did not meet the Korean diplomats until the signing ceremonies.)

13. Drake, *Empire of the Seas,* 103–8. Pennanen, "Evarts," 217–20. Pennanen gives Korea more importance than Africa in the planning for Shufeldt's cruise, while Drake treats it more as an afterthought. Shufeldt had already established a reputation as a commercial expansionist, having served as consul general at Havana, 1861–1863, and as head of an expedition to survey the Tehuantepec transit route. His instructions are quoted in Paullin, *Diplomatic Negotiations,* 295.

14. Drake, *Empire of the Seas,* chap. 1. Paullin, *Diplomatic Negotiations,* 293–303. Key-Hiuk Kim, "The Aims of Li Hung-chang's Policies toward Japan and Korea, 1870–1881." Lee, *Diplomatic Relations,* 36, 38. Lee, *West Goes East,* 22–26. Deuchler, *Confucian Gentlemen,* 86–89, 111–13. Chay, *Diplomacy of Asymmetry,* 40–46. Shufeldt showed his impetuosity when the Koreans delayed their reply by preparing a naval demonstration along the coast, only to be dissuaded by Bingham and the Japanese. Frederick F. Chien, *The Opening of Korea: A Study of Chinese Diplomacy,* 72–78. Kim, *Last Phase,* 302–10.

15. Drake, *Empire of the Seas,* 261–62. Paullin, *Diplomatic Negotiations,* 303–10. Chay, *Diplomacy of Asymmetry,* 46–51. Lee, *Diplomatic Relations,* 36–39. Chien, *Opening of Korea,* 79–81. Hunt, *Special Relationship,* 126–29. Ming-te Lin, "Li Hung-chang's Suzerain Policy toward Korea, 1882–1894," in Chu and Liu, *Li Hung-chang,* 176–81. Blaine to Angell, May 9, 1881, no. 94; Blaine to Robert W. Shufeldt, November 14, U.S., Diplomatic Instructions, China, 3, 232–36, 271–77. Frelinghuysen to Shufeldt, January 6, 1882, copy in U.S., Senate, Foreign Relations Archives. On Li Hung-chang's interest in the treaty see Chester Holcombe to Blaine, December 9, 1881, no. 30, U.S., Diplomatic Despatches, 58.

The Chinese-sponsored treaty provided for the exchange of ministers and consuls and permitted Americans to trade and live in the open ports but not in the interior. It fixed maximum tariff rates of 10 to 30 percent, export duties at 5 percent, prohibited the opium trade, and granted extraterritoriality to Americans. It also forbade Americans to enter the coasting trade in Korean products, but it partly offset this restriction with the standard form of conditional most-favored-nation clause. Li had hoped to insert a statement that Korea was "a dependent state of the Chinese empire," but Shufeldt balked, and Li had to settle for an explanatory Korean letter with much less legal force. The treaty contained two controversial provisions. One was a promise that extraterritoriality would be abandoned if Koreans adopted American legal practices. Also, the first article stated that in case of unjust or oppressive treatment by other powers, both signatories would "exert their good offices . . . to bring about an amicable arrangement." This article repeated almost verbatim a provision in one of the American treaties of Tientsin with China (1858; see chapter 5).[16]

Shufeldt's treaty aroused mixed reactions among those affected by it. The governments of Korea and China were content, although Korean conservatives resented the admission of American missionaries to their ports and Li had suffered a defeat through the exclusion of his "dependent state" provision. The Japanese government and people were angry that Shufeldt had accepted Chinese sponsorship and ignored their earlier Korean treaty of 1876, even though the new treaty strengthened Korean independence. Britain, Germany, and France soon signed treaties much like the American one. Russia would have preferred keeping Korea in isolation a little longer and tried to improve its situation by securing overland trading rights with the peninsula. British merchants in China objected strenuously to Shufeldt's concessions—the exclusion from the coasting trade, the conditional most-favored-nation clause, and the promise to abolish extraterritoriality—for they suspected (probably with reason) that Li was trying to establish precedents for future negotiations between China and the Western powers.[17]

16. Deuchler, *Confucian Gentlemen*, 114–27. Kim, *Last Phase*, 310–16. Drake, *Empire of the Seas*, 282–92. Chay, *Diplomacy of Asymmetry*, 51–55. Paullin, *Diplomatic Negotiations*, 310–24. Nelson, *Korea and the Old Orders*, 140–51. Dennett, "American Good Offices," 4. C. I. Eugene Kim and Han-kyo Kim, *Korea and the Politics of Imperialism, 1876–1910*, 21–32. Chien, *Opening of Korea*, 81–89. Malozemoff, *Russian Far Eastern Policy*, 28. George Alexander Lensen, *Balance of Intrigue: International Rivalry in Korea and Manchuria, 1884–1899*, vol. 1, 17–18. For the text of the treaty see Bevans, *Treaties*, vol. 10, 470–76. Evidence indicates that the Japanese originally suggested the maximum tariff rates to Bingham. Bingham to Lucius H. Foote, June 20, 1882, enclosed with Foote to Frelinghuysen, July 25, no. 19, U.S., Diplomatic Despatches, Korea, 1.

17. Deuchler, *Confucian Gentlemen*, 122–27. Chien, *Opening of Korea*, 87–93. Drake, *Empire of the Seas*, 298–301. Holcomb to Frelinghuysen, May 29, June 12, July 13, 1882, nos. 117, 124, 146, U.S., Diplomatic Despatches, China, 60. Bingham to Frelinghuysen, July 12, 28, 1882, with enclosure, nos. 1527, 1538, ibid., Japan, 47. *London Times*, July 17, August 19, 1882.

Notwithstanding the extravagant rhetoric of Sargent and others before the negotiations, Americans were curiously apathetic or dissatisfied with the results. Minister Young was unhappy that the State Department did not consult him before approving the terms, for he felt that they were too beneficial to China and that a simple commercial treaty would have suited the circumstances better. After some grumbling about Korea's dependent status, the Senate approved the treaty but attached a resolution that no future executive agent should negotiate without Senate confirmation of his appointment.[18] As for the press, the *New York Times* conceded the commercial importance of Korea but suggested that the recognition of Korean independence and the pledge of good offices "almost amount to a political alliance." The *New York Tribune* thought the treaty useless except to the Koreans, "a kind of semi-savage bastard Chinese," as a defense against Russia, and the *Washington Post* feared that it might embroil the United States with Japan.[19]

Despite Shufeldt's hopes, the treaty of 1882 did not make him a second Perry.[20] Like the treaties of 1853 and 1858 with Japan, the new document was an expression of economic expansionism, mixed with a little humanitarianism and fascination with the exotic. It was consistent with the rising interest in Far Eastern trade expressed by the Hayes and Garfield administrations. But for several reasons it proved more of an encumbrance than an encouragement to this trade. First, the Koreans were not Japanese and could not repeat the amazing transformation that had made over a hermit nation into a flourishing market. Second, by weakening Korean-Chinese connections without clarifying the attitude of the United States toward Japan's claims, the treaty increased East Asian instability. Finally, the promise of good offices reinforced a new and dubious commitment previously extended only to China, Japan, and Samoa. It is not surprising that the Koreans wishfully regarded it as an American guarantee of their sovereignty by which the United States would replace China as Korea's protector. The treaty and the American recognition of Korea, which Secretary Frelinghuysen soon restated to Young as official policy, drew the United States closer to the East Asian cockpit.[21]

18. Young was on his way out to China to take charge of the legation when the treaty was signed. Young to Frelinghuysen, December 26, 1882, no. 85, U.S., Diplomatic Despatches, China, 63. John Russell Young, "New Life in China," 414. Ollen Lawrence Burnette, Jr., "The Senate Foreign Relations Committee and the Diplomacy of Garfield, Arthur, and Cleveland," 115–21. Henry Merritt Wriston, *Executive Agents in American Foreign Relations,* 275–78.

19. *New York Times,* July 1, 7, 1882. *New York Tribune,* July 14, 1882. *Washington Post,* July 12, 1882.

20. Indeed, Shufeldt ruined his own prospects in the Far East when, shortly before signing the treaty, he wrote an exasperated and highly indiscreet letter to former senator Sargent, denouncing the corruption and deceit of the Chinese court and even criticizing Li as a despot. Sargent, a leading opponent of Chinese immigration, published the letter. While it did not affect the treaty, the State Department promptly recalled Shufeldt, and the navy gave him a desk job. Drake, *Empire of the Seas,* 279–82, 305–11.

21. Chay, *Diplomacy of Asymmetry,* 55–57. Drake, *Empire of the Seas,* 301–4. On the Korean misunderstanding regarding the American "guarantee" see Andrew C. Nahm, *Korea: Tradition and Transformation: A History of the Korean People,* 203–4.

Events in Korea soon demonstrated the implications of the American commitment, for in July 1882 rioting broke out in Seoul, as anti-foreign mobs burned the Japanese legation and reactionaries murdered several pro-Chinese leaders in an attempted coup d'état. The Japanese sent warships, the Chinese troops, and the U.S. Navy dispatched the decrepit paddle-wheeler *Monocacy* as a tacit warning to both sides not to abridge Korean sovereignty. The king of Korea made suitable placatory gestures to his powerful neighbors and peace was restored, but for the Americans coming events had cast ominous shadows before.[22]

Since the United States had recognized Korean independence, it promptly established a legation at Seoul. For the rest of the 1880s a trio of Americans attached in one way or another to the legation served as informal advisers to the king of Korea and thereby maintained the American position at the center of the Sino-Japanese rivalry. One of these was Lucius H. Foote, a California Republican with considerable consular experience in Latin America, who was minister from 1883 to 1885. His successor in influence (although he never became minister) was George C. Foulk, a handsome, personable young navy ensign (later lieutenant) who was a skilled linguist already familiar with the Far East. Foulk served at various times as naval attaché and chargé d'affaires between 1883 and 1887 and enjoyed the confidence of King Kojong to a remarkable degree. The third American was Dr. Horace N. Allen, a medical missionary who turned to diplomacy and promotional activities. After Foote and Foulk left, Allen became adviser to the next minister, then (in 1890) legation secretary, and finally minister himself during the last years of independent Korea (1897–1905). He became skilled at coaxing concessions from King Kojong and carried on profitable intrigues without the full knowledge of the Koreans or the State Department.[23]

22. Chay, *Diplomacy of Asymmetry,* 60–63. Kim, *Last Phase,* 316–27. Pletcher, *Awkward Years,* 210–11. Morken, "America Looks West," 160–64. Lin, "Li Hung-chang's Suzerain Policy," 181–83.

23. On Foote see *Dictionary of American Biography,* vol. 6, 501–2. On Foulk see ibid., vol. 6, 559–60; and Dennett, "Early American Policy in Korea," 85–86. A very friendly account of Foulk is in Harold J. Noble, "The United States and Sino-Korean Relations, 1885–1887," 292–304. But without going into detail, Deuchler concludes that through Foote and Foulk the United States "exerted no significant influence" and "contributed little toward strengthening Korea's independence." Deuchler, *Confucian Gentlemen,* 161. On Allen a highly laudatory account is Fred Harvey Harrington, *God, Mammon, and the Japanese: Dr. Horace N. Allen and Korean-American Relations, 1884–1905.* For Allen's view of Foulk see 45–47. On Allen's influence at court see 47–54. Another briefly influential American in Korea was former consul Owen N. Denny, whom Li Hung-chang sent to advise the king along pro-Chinese lines. Denny remained almost two years, during which he broke with Li's agent, Yüan Shih-k'ai, and cooperated with Foulk in upholding Korean independence. Swartout, *Mandarins, Gunboats, and Power Politics,* chaps. 3–4. Lee, *Diplomatic Relations,* 133–35. Deuchler, *Confucian Gentlemen,* 176–77. In 1899 William F. Sands, then only twenty-five years old, became adviser to the king. For a frank, revealing account of his experiences see his memoirs, *Undiplomatic Memories,* chap. 8. This account sets forth the problem of advancing American influence in Korea. On Allen's role see also 220–24.

Foote was originally instructed, in effect, to consider Korea independent without offending China and not to interfere with Sino-Korean relations unless American treaty rights were violated. On his arrival he found a court and society of almost Byzantine complexity. The Korean upper class was divided into conservatives, who were mostly pro-Chinese, and progressives, largely pro-Japanese. King Kojong wanted to be progressive, but he was torn between his father, the former regent, an arch reactionary, and Queen Min and the Min family, at first progressive, who soon gravitated toward the Chinese faction. Intrigue was the favorite occupation at Seoul and assassination a constant danger. In 1882 and again in 1884 attempted coups covered the palace floors with blood. Both China and Japan used the first outbreak as an excuse to obtain additional privileges. On the latter occasion Dr. Allen made his first prominent appearance by sewing up the wounds of the queen's nephew, who had been nearly hacked to pieces by a pro-Japanese fanatic.

Under these circumstances King Kojong turned with almost pathetic eagerness to the sympathetic Foote for dispassionate counsel on modernizing Korea without turning it over to the Japanese or allowing Li Hung-chang to make it a Chinese province. In imitation of both China and Japan the king sent a mission to tour the United States and observe its wonders. Ensign Foulk, appointed by the U.S. Navy to conduct the mission, accompanied it back to Korea, became Foote's aide, and with Secretary Frelinghuysen's cautious approval gave Kojong much informal, tactful advice. However, bound by Foote's outmoded instructions, Foulk was no match for the aggressive Chinese. The king bombarded the State Department for teachers, technical advisers, and especially army and navy officers to drill his troops. A few teachers took up residence in Seoul, and Commodore (now Admiral) Shufeldt expressed interest in a military post, but he visited Korea only briefly. Kojong's requests became entangled in American red tape, and he got no American drillmasters until 1888. When they arrived, they proved of little value to Korean security. By then the king had become disillusioned with American delays.[24]

Others were more eager than the Americans. To regain China's lost influence in Korea, Li Hung-chang arranged for Kojong to appoint Paul von Möllendorf, a

24. This survey is based on Law, *Diplomatic Relations*, chaps. 3–6, and pp. 66–73. Chay, *Diplomacy of Asymmetry*, 66–73, 88. Harrington, *God, Mammon, and Japanese*, 25–33. Dennett, "Early American Policy in Korea, 1883–1887," 82–103; Noble, "The United States and Sino-Korean Relations," 292–304; Pollard, "American Relations with Korea, 1882–1895," 425–71; Lee, *East Goes West*, 29–32, 40–42; and George M. McCune, John R. Harrison, and Spencer J. Palmer, eds., *Korean-American Relations: Documents Pertaining to the History of the Far Eastern Diplomacy of the United States*, vol. 1, 149. For an explanation of King Kojong's trust in the United States see Yur-bok Lee, "Korean-American Diplomatic Relations, 1882–1905," 13–15. For an account of the Korean mission to the United States see also Frelinghuysen to Foote, October 16, 1883, no. 27, U.S., Diplomatic Instructions, Korea, 1, 33–38. On the abortive coups of 1882 and 1884 see Lensen, *Balance of Intrigue*, vol. 1, 19–22, 25–27; Nelson, *Korea and the Old Orders*, 152–58; and Harrington, *God, Mammon, and Japanese*, 21–25. On American military advisers see Yur-bok Lee and Wayne Patterson, eds., *One Hundred Years of Korean-American Relations, 1882–1982*, 27–31. On other American non-official advisers, see ibid., 31–34.

German diplomat with experience in the Chinese Imperial Maritime Customs, as his principal adviser. Möllendorf, a Japanophobe, bent Korea's policies in Russia's direction and soon fell out with Foote and Foulk. Another foreign contention broke out between Russia and Britain. In 1884 Russia signed a treaty with Korea for the "loan" of Port Lazareff, a warm-water harbor south of Vladivostok; the following spring Britain occupied Port Hamilton (Komundo), off the south tip of Korea, and held it for two years.[25]

Considering this four-sided rivalry and the few American interests in Korea, Secretary of State Bayard continued the policy of prudent neutrality, so when Korea requested American good offices in the Port Hamilton affair, he refused to take sides. Although both Möllendorf and Foulk favored reforms in Korea and enjoyed the king's friendship, they lost favor with China and were removed. In Möllendorf's place Li sent a tough young agent Yüan Shi-k'ai (later president of China, 1913–1916). Yüan was determined to nullify Russian and American influence. China also commissioned Owen N. Denny, formerly American consul general at Shanghai, to assist Yüan, but he mostly followed a separate policy, supporting Korean independence. During 1887–1888, despite Yüan's efforts to prevent it, a Korean legation was formally established in Washington, but in Seoul the intriguing continued.[26]

25. Chien, *Opening of Korea*, chap. 9. Lee, *Diplomatic Relations*, 93–102, 159–62. Kim and Kim, *Korea and the Politics of Imperialism*, chap. 4. Lin, "Li Hung-chang's Suzerain Policy," 183–92. Lensen, *Balance of Intrigue*, vol. 1, 17; vol. 2, 840. By 1887 the occupation of both ports had been abandoned. For a realistic contemporary British appraisal of the Korean situation—that the country offered little valuable trade but was vital to Britain for its strategic location—see *Edinburgh Review* 162 (July 1885): 284–85. Much of the American suspicion of Russia was occasioned by William Elliott Griffis in his widely read book, *Corea, the Hermit Nation*. The British reaction was determined mostly by the simultaneous Anglo-Russian crisis on the Indian border. Malozemoff, *Russian Far Eastern Policy*, 28–31. But Britain soon decided that Port Hamilton was useless as a base. The view of the Korean king as weak and vacillating, which owes much to Harrington, is challenged by Swartout. Harrington, *God, Mammon, and Japanese*, 29–30, 42–43 and passim. Swartout, *Mandarins, Gunboats, and Power Politics*, 58–60.

26. The foreign intrigues at Seoul were at their most intense between 1884 and 1888, when Foulk, Möllendorf (both of whom returned after their initial departures), Yüan Shi-k'ai, Denny, and the British, German, and Russian ministers were all pulling at King Kojong. Horace Allen accompanied Kojong's minister to the United States to advise him, but the Chinese minister maneuvered to counterbalance the new Korean legation. A Korean scholar in the United States, Yur-bok Lee, has written two separate accounts of the intrigues, *Diplomatic Relations between the United States and Korea* (1970) and *West Goes East* (1988). The first emphasizes Foulk's role, the second that of Möllendorf and Denny. McCune, Harrison, and Palmer, eds., *Korean-American Relations*, 53–65. Tansill, *Foreign Policy of Bayard*, 432, 439–40. George C. Foulk to Bayard, April 28, 1885, no. 166, U.S. Diplomatic Despatches, Korea, 2. Bayard to Foulk, August 19, 1885, no. 63, U.S., Diplomatic Instructions, Korea, 1, 111–13. Bayard to W. W. Phelps, August 19, 1885, no. 87, ibid., Britain, 17, 548–52. Bayard contributed to Foulk's difficulties not only by failing to give him adequate instructions but also by allowing a frank report by Foulk to appear in *Foreign Relations*, from which it was copied in the Korean press. Noble, "U.S. and Sino-American Relations," 300–301.

After the ratification of the 1882 treaty, President Arthur declared in his annual message that Korea "now invites the attention of those interested in the advancement of our foreign trade, as it needs the implements and products which the United States are ready to supply."[27] There seemed good reason for optimism. After the Korean mission to the United States in 1883, businessmen approached the State Department for information about commercial possibilities, and Americans (including Minister Foote himself) began to buy land in Seoul. King Kojong established a model farm along American lines and opened a consulate in New York under the management of a onetime American merchant in China. He also put out feelers for an American loan. In 1883 the Japanese government extended its telegraph system by cable from Nagasaki to Pusan, providing Korea with speedy communications to the outside world, and two years later China installed an offsetting line.[28]

Before long, however, knowledge of Korean realities dried up most of the early American interest, a process hastened by the well-publicized bloodshed of the abortive 1884 coup d'état. It is true that between 1884 and 1892 total Korean foreign trade recorded in the open ports rose from $1,737,355 (Mexican) to $7,894,975 (these figures did not include overland trade with China and much smuggling), but Americans did not enjoy much of this business. At the end of that period Britain was furnishing 55.3 percent of Korean imports, Japan 18.5 percent, and the United States only 3.5 percent.

Nor did Korean exports attract Americans as much as those of China or Japan. Rice, beans, fish (used mostly for fertilizer), cotton, hides, and other raw materials were welcome in East Asia but not worth shipping across the Pacific. The country's one good industrial product, paper, was too expensive for large sales, even in Japan. A burden on all trade was the clumsy copper currency, much inflated. Korean gold deposits in the north, among the richest in Asia, were an x factor in the economy, for production fluctuated as gold was needed to make up for the unfavorable balance of trade. Also, much of the gold produced was smuggled out and hence unrecorded. The Japanese had used their six-year head start in Korean trade to monopolize shipping and marketing. Except for a steamer of the China Merchants Steam Navigation Company from Shanghai every three weeks, only Japanese ships called at Korean ports, and most seaborne Korean trade funneled

27. Richardson, *Messages and Papers,* vol. 3, 174.

28. Foulk to Frelinghuysen, New York, November 19, 1883, Foulk papers, U.S., *Foreign Relations, 1885,* 353–54. *New York Tribune,* May 13, 1884. William Elliot Griffis, *Corea, Without and Within,* 318–20. Bingham to Frelinghuysen, September 20, 1883, no. 1744, U.S., Diplomatic Despatches, Japan, 49. On Foote's activities see Harrington, *God, Mammon, and Japanese,* 2, 128–129. Tribolet, *Electrical Communications,* 227–28. Jones to Alvey A. Adee, March 7, 1884, no. 147, U.S., Consular Despatches, Nagasaki, 4. Horace N. Allen to Blaine, June 16, 1891, no. 174, U.S., Diplomatic Despatches, Korea, 8. Deuchler, *Confucian Gentlemen,* 187–88. O. N. Denny, the American adviser to the king of Korea at this time, tried to promote a connection with the Russian telegraph system but failed to obtain the desired Japanese capital. Swartout, *Mandarins, Gunboats, and Power Politics,* 133–34.

through Nagasaki. As a result, Korean prosperity usually depended on crop and trade conditions in Japan.[29]

Nevertheless, Americans joined the handful of European merchants in Seoul, the nearby port of Chemulpo (modern Inch'on), and Pusan. James D. Morse, proprietor of a flourishing Yokohama agency for clocks and brassware, established the American Trading Company in both Japan and Korea and made his outfit one of the largest American general trading companies in the Far East. Morse also tried in vain to arrange a loan for the king of Korea and was one of the first foreigners to recognize the importance of Korean gold deposits. A onetime member of the American Trading Company in Pusan, Walter D. Townsend, moved to Chemulpo, established his own business, and imported modern rice-hulling machinery. Since Korean rice was of high quality but undervalued because of careless cleaning, he was able to compete successfully with the Japanese in exporting this staple to both Japan and China. He then used his profits to expand into other lines, became interested in mining, and obtained the Korean agency for Standard Oil. Eventually he married a Japanese woman.[30]

The principal American import handled by these companies, of course, was kerosene, whose consumption rose from 101,207 gallons in 1886 to 888,360 gallons in 1893. By the latter year the Russians were also shipping 66,559 gallons. Japanese merchants usually handled the import of cottons, and the Americans could compete with the British in heavy drills but not other fabrics. Both Foote and especially Foulk used their connections with the progressive wing of the government so that Thomas A. Edison might supply an electric light plant for the palace in 1884. This pleased the Koreans so well that they bought another plant several years later. (The equipment was transported from Chemulpo to Seoul by bull cart.) The government also bought American munitions from American companies, and no doubt Foulk could have obtained other trade for American merchants in Japan if Cleveland's State Department had approved.[31]

---

29. In 1885 and 1895 American-Korean trade was estimated at $175,000 and $200,000 respectively. Chay, *Diplomacy of Asymmetry*, 2, 78. U.S., *Foreign Relations, 1884*, 126. U.S., *Commercial Relations, 1885–86*, 2, 1283–91. U.S., *Consular Reports* 30 (April 1883): 604–7; 88 (January 1888): 162–63; 154 (July 1893): 310–14. Deuchler, *Confucian Gentlemen*, 192–97. *Bradstreet's* 32 (August 25, 1894): 542. By 1892 there were 9,132 Japanese and 1,604 Chinese living in Korea but only 79 Americans and 51 British. The Anglo-Chinese firm Jardine, Matheson also ventured into Korean mining and trade but gave up after a few years. Deuchler, *Confucian Gentlemen*, 189–90.

30. Harold J. Noble, "The Former Foreign Settlement in Korea," 768–82. Harold F. Cook, "Walter D. Townsend, Pioneer American Businessman in Korea," 74–103. Bae-tong Lee, "Competitive Mining Surveys by Foreign Powers in Korea, with Emphasis on the 1880s," 39n91, 92. In the early 1870s another American firm, a branch of the China and Japan Trading Company, was established at Chemulpo. There was one American agency in Pusan. U.S., *Consular Reports* 154 (July 1893): 313. Bingham to Frelinghuysen, September 20, 1883, no. 1744, U.S., Diplomatic Despatches, Japan, 49.

31. U.S., *Commercial Relations, 1896*, 1, 864. U.S., *Consular Reports* 105 (May 1889): 61; 154 (July 1893): 310–14. Foote to Frelinghuysen, December 18, 1883; June 9, July 31, September 4, 1884, nos. 47, 82, 101, 106, U.S., Diplomatic Despatches, Korea, 1. Allen

After 1898 a British writer was to call Korea "the happy hunting ground of the concessionists." The three Americans with the most influence on King Kojong all worked to further American investments, Foote and Foulk in Korea, while Allen also served the Korean government between 1887 and 1889 as legation secretary in the United States, publicizing opportunities for American capital. In 1884 the king told Foote that if railroad and telegraph companies could be formed in the United States, he would grant them liberal franchises. Foote himself was briefly interested in a short-line project from Seoul to Chemulpo, and Allen established contacts with James Harrison Wilson, who was principally interested in Chinese railroads. Although agents from several European countries put out feelers for mining concessions, Kojong largely followed the advice of his three American advisers on mining policy, for he seemed to regard the gold mines as a special tie between Korea and the United States. Admiral Shufeldt, representing the Union Iron Works of San Francisco, inquired about iron deposits, and a New York banking firm outlined an elaborate plan for mining and railroad concessions and a $2.25 million loan to the Korean government but could not come to terms. Other concessions were discussed or granted for a steamship line, timber cutting, and pearl fishing. But whether because of inadequate American capital or divisions within the Korean government, no important American investment materialized before the mid-1890s.[32]

By the beginning of that decade Americans had established a sizable stake in the burgeoning Japanese economy, but that of Korea proved only a pale reflection of the Japanese, both in growth and in American participation. Despite the very different economic attractions, however, American diplomacy had involved the United States intimately in the foreign policies of both countries. This involvement had come about without a corresponding increase in American armed strength along the Chinese coast and without the full understanding and approval of the American people. In the case of Korea the United States had implied in its original treaty a measure of support in international affairs only to turn away into neutrality and disinterest in Korean affairs.[33]

---

to Josiah Quincy, October 26, 1893, no. 50, U.S., Consular Despatches, Seoul, 1. Lee, *Diplomatic Relations*, 69–70, 113–14. Harrington, *God, Mammon, and Japanese*, 126, 128, 149–50. The Edison sales were made through the American Trading Company.

32. Harrington, *God, Mammon, and Japanese*, chap. 8 (quotation on 127). Lee, "Competitive Mining Surveys," 22–25, 35–41. Lee, *Diplomatic Relations*, 113–14. Foote to Frelinghuysen, July 26, September 8, 1884, nos. 97, 107; Foulk to Bayard, November 17, 1885, no. 251; Hugh A. Dinsmore to Bayard, February 7, 1888, no. 35, U.S., Diplomatic Despatches, Korea, 1, 3, 5. McCune, Harrison, and Palmer, *Korean-American Relations*, vol. 2, 187–88.

33. A good summary of the feckless American policy toward Korea from the 1880s to 1905 is Fred Harvey Harrington, "An American View of Korean-American Relations, 1882–1905," 60–67.

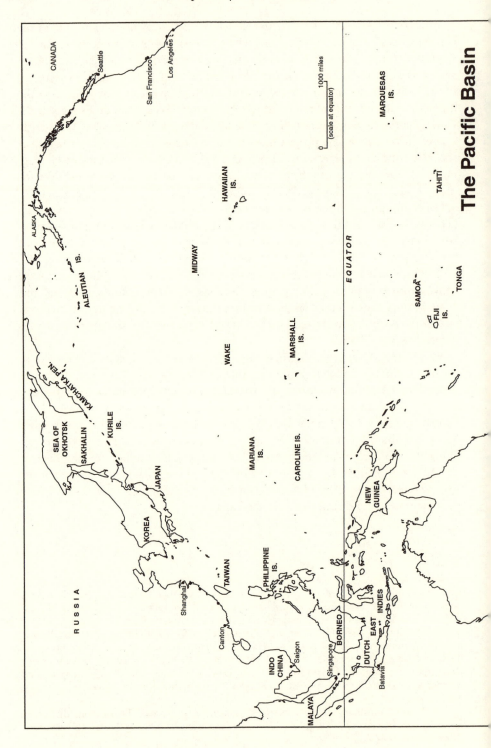

The Pacific Basin

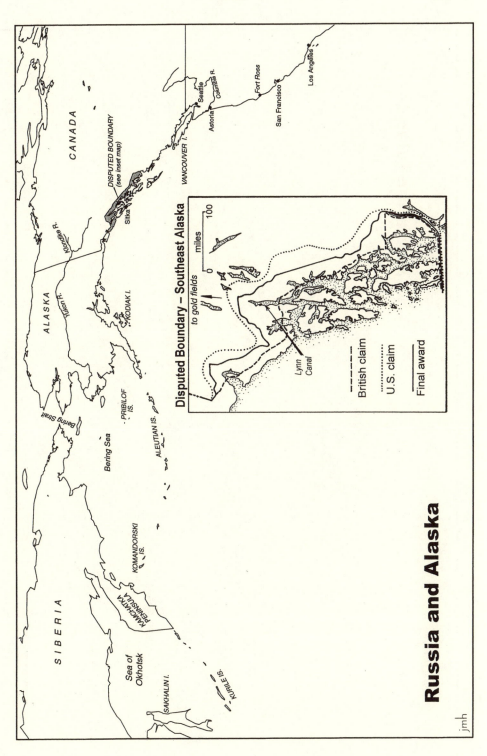

Disputed Boundary – Southeast Alaska

to gold fields

miles
0 100

Lynn Canal

British claim
U.S. claim
Final award

CANADA

DISPUTED BOUNDARY
(see inset map)

Sitka

Klondike R.

Yukon R.

ALASKA

KODIAK I.

VANCOUVER I.

Seattle

Astoria

Columbia R.

Fort Ross

San Francisco

Los Angeles

Bering Strait

PRIBILOF IS.

Bering Sea

ALEUTIAN IS.

KOMANDORSKI IS.

KAMCHATKA PENINSULA

SIBERIA

Sea of Okhotsk

SAKHALIN I.

KURILE IS.

Russia and Alaska

jmh

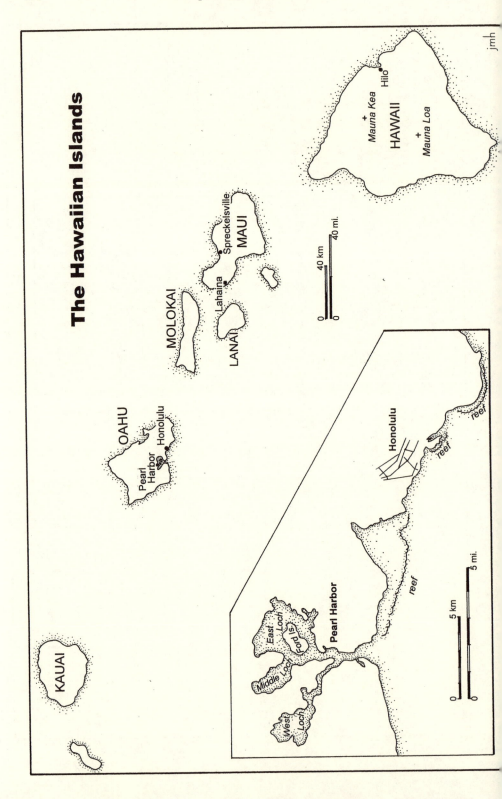

The Hawaiian Islands

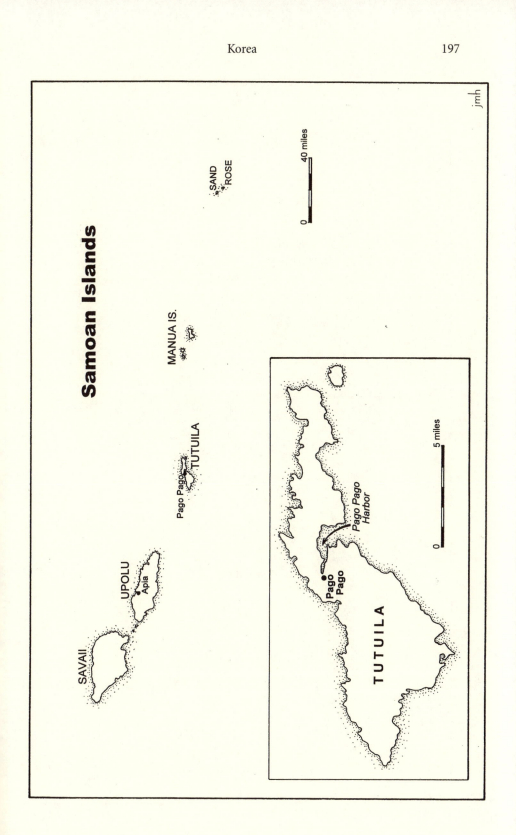

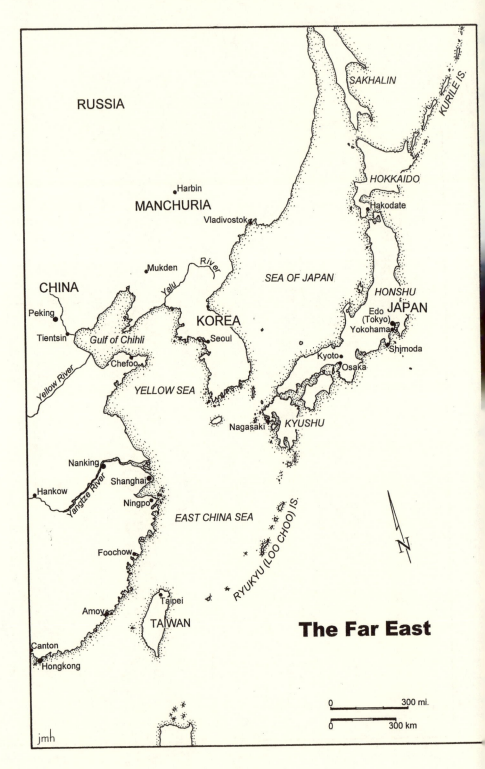

The Far East

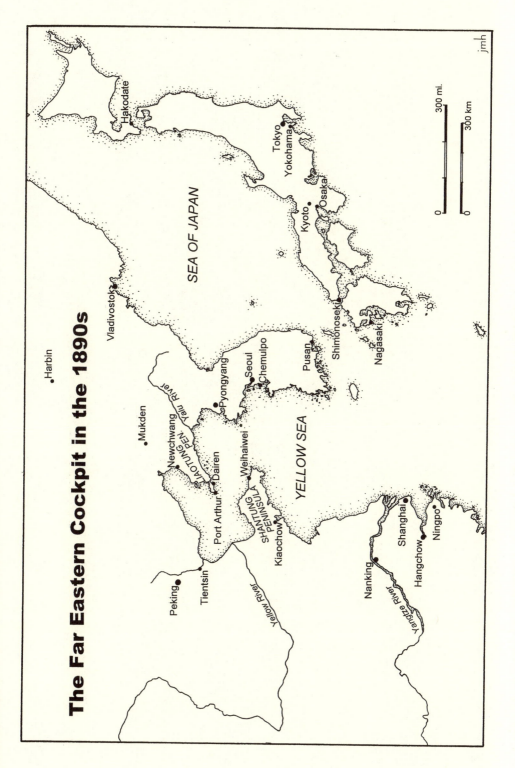

The Far Eastern Cockpit in the 1890s

Harbin

Vladivostok

Hakodate

SEA OF JAPAN

Tokyo
Yokohama
Kyoto
Osaka

Shimonoseki

Nagasaki

Pusan

Mukden

Yalu River

Newchwang
LIAOTUNG PEN.
Dairen
Port Arthur
Weihaiwei
SHANTUNG PENINSULA
Kiaochow

Pyongyang
Seoul
Chemulpo

YELLOW SEA

Peking
Tientsin

Yellow River

Nanking

Shanghai
Hangchow
Ningpo

Yangtze River

300 mi.

300 km

jmh

II

Economic Expansion *Becomes* Political Involvement, *1890-1900*

9

The East Asian Cockpit of the 1890s

NTIL THE LATTER HALF of the 1880s the American interest in the Pacific world was mostly economic and religious, focused largely on trade, attempts at investment, and missionaries. Only in Hawaii did Washington pay much attention to local politics and there only to prevent the British from gaining the upper hand with the pliable monarchy. In 1887 the United States added a lease on Pearl Harbor to its reciprocity treaty of 1875, and five months later the Hawaiians adopted a new constitution more friendly to the Americans than before. In Samoa petty consular intrigues escalated into a naval confrontation with Britain and Germany during 1889, which ended abruptly when a typhoon destroyed nearly all the warships involved. At a conference in Berlin, for want of a better arrangement, the three powers decided to experiment with a condominium.

In China the United States acted on its own and less decisively. When Secretary Bayard entered the State Department in 1885, he and his new minister to China, Charles Denby, favored the entrance of American capital into Chinese railroad and other investments, and Bayard seemed disposed to continue John Russell Young's pro-Chinese policies. But as he contemplated the developing Sino-Japanese power struggle in Korea, he enjoined strict neutrality on Denby and American diplomats at Seoul, the capital of Korea. Bayard would not unite the Peking and Seoul legations, as Denby and other Sinophiles recommended, but later he recalled one of the latter because of Chinese complaints that he was too pro-Korean. Secretary Blaine determined on a more active policy in Korea and even considered seeking a coaling station there as encouragement to both the Koreans and American investors, but he soon became disillusioned by Korean confusion and weakness and lost interest.[1]

The American press reflected the uncertainty of the government's Far Eastern policy. For example, the *New York Herald* advised even-handed support for China and Japan to prevent a war between them that might threaten American

1. Thomas F. Bayard to James Harrison Wilson, September 1, 1885, Wilson papers. Bayard to George C. Foulk, August 19, 1885, no. 63, U.S., Diplomatic Instructions, Korea, 1, 111–13. Bayard to Charles Denby, December 9, 1885, no. 19, ibid., China, 4, 86–89. John Russell Young to Wharton Barker, April 25, 1889, Barker papers, box 5. Tansill, *Foreign Policy of Bayard*, 423–25. Harrington, *God, Mammon, and Japanese*, 134–35, 246. On the problem of uniting the Peking and Seoul legations see Lee, *Diplomatic Relations*, 91–93.

commercial interests. The *Herald* would cooperate with Britain to this end, but it insisted that Europe must recognize "our essential rights on the Pacific Ocean" and declared that "the independence of China and Japan should be as much our concern as the Monroe Doctrine in America." When there was talk of European intervention in China during anti-missionary riots in 1891, however, other newspapers felt that the proper American policy was strict neutrality.[2] To judge from press comments, the American public gave far more attention during these years to the Chinese immigration question (see chapter 6) than to any other events or policies affecting East Asia.

This passivity could not long continue, for northern China, Manchuria, and Korea soon became a cockpit of European and Japanese rivalry in which military campaigns and threats brought on a race for business concessions and then political influence in what seemed to be a collapsing Chinese Empire. Swept along by these events, Americans did their best to compete for concessions and trade, while their government tried to hold to its noninterventionist policy. As the crisis with Spain over Cuban affairs loomed in 1897 and 1898, American involvement in the Far East contributed to a national sense of expanding interests. The Spanish-American War made the United States an active participant in East Asian affairs, and with the dispatch of John Hay's open door notes (1899) American Far Eastern policies were permanently changed.

The event that released these pent-up forces was the Sino-Japanese War of 1894–1895. This conflict arose from the irreconcilable Chinese and Japanese ambitions to dominate Korea and the Japanese fear that Russia intended to seize it. After the Korean crisis of 1882 Japan, alarmed at China's reaction, began to build up its armed forces. In 1894 the Tonghaks, a religious cult in Korea, shattered the frail peace of the peninsula with a rebellion, and a Korean murdered the leader of the progressive, pro-Japanese faction. The king asked China for troops with which to put down the rebellion, and Li Hung-chang sent over twenty thousand soldiers and three warships. Not surprisingly, Japan promptly occupied all the south Korean ports. In the last week of July the Japanese attacked Seoul, captured King Kojong, and forced him to declare war. A few days later both Japan and China followed suit.

Some ill-informed outsiders expected the Chinese Navy to drive back the Japanese ships, while overwhelming numbers of Chinese soldiers smothered the invaders. Nothing of the sort happened. Between July and September 1894 the crack Japanese troops won two major victories over the ill-trained, poorly led Chinese brigades and cleared nearly the whole Korean peninsula, while the two navies fought to a standstill off the mouth of the Yalu River—a battle that crippled the Chinese fleet and left Japan in control of all sea approaches to the war theater.

2. *New York Herald*, September 2, 1887, November 13, 1888. *New York Sun*, August 22, 1891, reprinted in *Public Opinion* 11 (August 29): 504–5. *Cleveland Leader*, October 4, 1891, reprinted in *Public Opinion* 12 (October 10): 5. The *Leader* was content to protect American lives and property, even if Europeans made unreasonable demands on China.

Then the victors moved west into China to attack the two peninsulas, Liaotung and Shantung, that jut into the Gulf of Chihli and control access to Manchuria and northern China respectively. In November Port Arthur (Liaotung) fell to the Japanese, in February 1895 Weihaiwei (Shantung), and with it the rest of the Chinese Navy surrendered. The Japanese paused to catch their breath and decide how best to proceed against the giant that lay before them, helpless but unwieldy. Denby wrote that the Chinese government, desperate, wanted peace at any price and the people feared that the Japanese would kill the emperor and occupy the whole country.[3]

Unlike most previous events in the Far East, the American press gave lavish coverage to the Sino-Japanese War, perhaps to divert the public from the depression and social unrest at home. Merchants were immediately concerned for the welfare of the tea and silk trades. Although racists treated both sides with condescension, a strong sentiment developed from the start that Japan, "the most civilized country in the East," was fighting for human progress against Chinese backwardness and barbarism. Social Darwinism, Japan's flattering imitation of America and Europe, and the years of diatribes against Chinese immigration all contributed to this simplistic pro-Japanese view, which was furthered by a small number of voluntary and paid propagandists, such as E. H. House. Not least among the rationalizations were suspicions that Britain and Germany were supporting China to scotch Japanese trade competition and that Russia would intervene to secure a Korean naval base. The conviction was widespread that a Japanese victory would mean "reconstruction and renovation along the whole coast of Eastern Asia . . . the development of Asiatic wealth and industry."[4]

Without waiting for Japanese victory, many American businessmen sought to profit from the war by more or less legal trade. Shipments of supplies and arms set out from the West Coast for both belligerents. Charles R. Flint and Company, one of the two largest U.S. traders with South America, was reported to have arranged the Japanese purchase of a Chilean cruiser. The Cramp Shipbuilding Company of Philadelphia, anxious for Japanese Navy contracts, was allegedly willing to sell the cruiser *Minneapolis*, which it had nearly completed for the United States. (No deal

3. For a short, satisfactory account of these events see Morse, *International Relations of the Chinese Empire*, vol. 3, 18–40. For war developments in Korea see Harrington, *God, Mammon, and Japanese,* chap. 14. Although much of the American press at the time expected an eventual Japanese victory, diplomats on the spot were overimpressed by Chinese numbers, and historical accounts were slow in appearing, allowing a myth of wrong guesses to arise. Jack Hammersmith, "The Sino-Japanese War, 1894–95: American Predictions Reassessed," 48–58.

4. Jeffery Dorwart, *The Pigtail War: American Involvement in the Sino-Japanese War of 1894–1895,* chap. 6. James Arthur Busselle, "The United States in the Far East, 1894–1905: The Years of Illusion," 11–15. Quotations are in *Literary Digest* 9 (August 18, 1894): 451; and *Commercial and Financial Chronicle* 9 (February 9, 1895): 243–44. *New York Journal of Commerce,* July 28, 1894. *Public Opinion* 17 (July 26, 1894): 393. Even the bloodthirsty Japanese attack on Port Arthur, reported in gruesome detail, had little immediate effect on pro-Japanese sentiment, for Americans remembered their own Indian wars and identified the Japanese with the white settlers.

was made.) Union Iron Works of San Francisco also angled for ship contracts, while the Carnegie and Bethlehem Iron Companies stood ready to furnish plating. Meanwhile, smaller American concerns and individuals in the Far East busily smuggled munitions and other necessities along the Chinese coast.[5]

The U.S. government was not well prepared to deal with a sudden crisis in East Asia. President Cleveland was preoccupied with domestic affairs, and Secretary of State Walter Q. Gresham was on vacation; neither in any case knew much about the area. Third Assistant Secretary William W. Rockhill was knowledgeable about the Far East and an expansionist of the Roosevelt-Lodge stripe, but like those two he despised Gresham. Minister Edwin Dun in Tokyo was well informed but not very aggressive, and Minister Denby in Peking had gone home for a kidney stone operation, leaving in charge his son, Charles Denby, Jr., the inexperienced legation secretary. Minister John M. B. Sill at Seoul was alert and sympathized with Korea, but he was at outs with his legation secretary, Horace N. Allen, a more experienced and clever missionary-diplomat. American naval strength was practically limited to one modern cruiser, the *Baltimore*. (The elder Denby returned to his post in late October 1894, and the navy eventually concentrated eight warships off the China coast to guard American interests.)[6]

As soon as hostilities began, Minister Sill got the *Baltimore* sent to Seoul. He then joined representatives of Russia, France, and Britain in asking both China and Japan to withdraw their forces from Korea. Soon after Gresham returned to Washington he abandoned this cooperative policy, thinking that it would further European but not American interests and hoping Japan would restrain its movements. When the Japanese continued to push forward, he delivered a stern protest and sent a detachment of American marines to guard the legation at Seoul. These were soon withdrawn, and after formal war broke out, the secretary announced an American policy of strict neutrality. Thereafter he resisted both British and Chinese pressure for joint intervention in one form or another, although he allowed Denby to call marines to Peking temporarily in the spring of 1895 for purely defensive purposes.[7]

With his neutrality policy Gresham combined what might be called "custodial good offices," based on the Chinese and Korean treaties of 1858 and 1882 respectively, whereby the U.S. legations undertook to uphold the interests of Japanese nationals in China and Chinese nationals in Japan. On one occasion, in November 1894, urged by the Chinese government, the secretary sounded out both belligerents on the possibility of formal American mediation, but the

5. Dorwart, *Pigtail War*, 36–37. *New York Tribune*, December 2, 21, 1894; *New York Times*, September 22, 1895. At the same time an Alabama iron manufacturer sold $370,000 of cast iron pipe to Japan for the Tokyo water works. Ibid., November 13, 1894.

6. Dorwart, *Pigtail War*, 9–14, 17–20, 59–62, 75, 132. On Dun see Treat, *United States and Japan, 1853–1895*, vol. 2, 367–68. Payson J. Treat, *Diplomatic Relations between the United States and Japan, 1895–1905*, 25–26.

7. Dorwart, *Pigtail War*, 21–27, 34, 41–42, 67–70. Dennett, *Americans in Eastern Asia*, 498–500. Treat, *United States and Japan, 1853–1895*, vol. 2, 456, 458–59, 465–66. Charles W. Calhoun, *Gilded Age Cato: The Life of Walter Gresham*, 174.

Japanese politely declined, as their victory was not yet complete and they wanted the Chinese to sue for bilateral negotiations. Gresham's policy was largely based on humanitarian concerns and the same sense of moral responsibility that had guided him and Cleveland in Hawaii (see chapter 10). It was not popular at home, especially among profiteering businessmen and Japanophiles.[8] Although Gresham urged neutrality and nonintervention on his countrymen, several of them devised plans by which the war and the probable Japanese victory might be made to advance American economic interests in the Far East. One of these was the work of the railroad promoter James Harrison Wilson and his associate, Li Hung-chang's secretary, William N. Pethick (see chapter 7). In September 1894, when Pethick was in the United States, they met to discuss the possibility of a Japanese attack on Peking, the overthrow of the Manchu dynasty, and its replacement with Li or Li's son as emperor, under the sponsorship of Japan and with the tacit approval of the United States, whose businessmen the new monarch would undoubtedly favor. The plotters made contact with Denby, who was intended to be the "Warwick" of the new dynasty, and with Japanese officials, who seemed interested but noncommittal. It is not clear whether the plotters consulted Li himself; his loyalty to the Manchus was undoubtedly too firm to be undermined. In any case, the Japanese did not send troops inland, and events soon buried the fantastic intrigue.[9]

Minister Denby meanwhile tried another tack, that of advising the Chinese government and communicating its overtures to the Japanese by way of Minister Dun in Tokyo to expedite peace negotiations. These services, as he told Gresham, would place Americans in a good position to bid for the concessions that the

8. Dorwart, *Pigtail War,* chap. 3, 73–77, 129–31. Treat, *United States and Japan, 1853–1895,* vol. 2, 492–98. George E. Paulsen, "Secretary Gresham, Senator Lodge, and American Good Offices in China, 1894," 123–42. Calhoun, *Gilded Age Cato,* 174–75. On European reactions see Langer, *The Diplomacy of Imperialism, 1890–1902,* vol. 1, 173–75. The most serious case arising from Gresham's custodial good offices involved two young Japanese students arrested in Shanghai's international settlement as spies, apparently with reason. After much argument Denby, Jr., the acting minister, turned them over to the Chinese government, which executed them, to the highly vocal horror of Cleveland's American opponents. Dorwart, *Pigtail War,* 46–55. Hunt, *Special Relationship,* 138. Treat, *United States and Japan, 1853–1895,* vol. 2, 484–90. Young, *Rhetoric of Empire,* 23–26. Calhoun, *Gilded Age Cato,* 175–77. For a sampling of American press views on mediation see *Literary Digest* 10 (November 24, 1894): 96–97; *Public Opinion* 17 (November 29, 1894): 839; and *New York Times,* November 15, 1894. For Republican attacks see Paulsen, "Gresham, Lodge, and American Good Offices," 134–35, 137–39.

9. Young, *Rhetoric of Empire,* 27–30. In the Wilson papers, where much of this intrigue is recorded, the clearest account of the plan is a letter from Wilson to Durham W. Stevens, September 23, 1894, Letterbook, 1889–1896, 385–405, Wilson papers. According to two historical accounts, Wilson expected to benefit the United States by installing a more friendly Chinese government or by preventing a foreign (mostly European) partition. Young, *Rhetoric of Empire,* 28–30. Best, "Ideas without Capital," 458–60. Busselle, "U.S. in the Far East," 55–60, 64–65. Pethick, a born plotter, soon came up with another hare-brained scheme for Britain and the United States to take over military organization of China south and north of the Yangtze River respectively. William N. Pethick to James Harrison Wilson, March 13, 1895, Wilson papers.

Chinese would have to sell after the war to raise an indemnity. The secretary approved the communication facilities as part of American good offices and allowed Denby, who was his personal friend, considerable freedom to give advice. Gresham became somewhat alarmed, however, when the Chinese engaged as special consultant John Watson Foster, Harrison's secretary of state. Foster had begun a long acquaintance with Chinese officials as minister to Russia and had helped the Chinese prepare a protest to the American government after the Rock Springs massacre of 1885. He was aware of plans for railroads, loans, and other postwar ventures as well as the Wilson-Pethick plot. Gresham repeatedly warned Denby not to violate American neutrality; over Foster, of course, he had no control.[10]

It is difficult to say how much influence Denby exerted on the Tsungli Yamen officials in his many conferences with them, both because of language problems (Denby spoke no Chinese) and because of the officials' fondness for going back and forth over the same ground. He certainly instructed them painstakingly in Western international law and diplomatic forms and tried to convince them that they must make bona fide overtures for peace. At first they offered only Korean independence and an indemnity, and they delayed action, hoping for a last-minute decision by some Western power to restrain Japan from asking too much. Denby tried to disabuse them of this hope and even asked Western diplomats to say flatly that their governments would not intervene. He felt that Western intervention would surely lead to Chinese dismemberment and that China's only chance lay in peace and making common cause with Japan against the West—former president Grant's prescription of fifteen years earlier. Denby's reports indicate that there were frequent disagreements and misunderstandings on both sides.[11]

---

10. Dorwart, *Pigtail War*, 77–78, 81–83. Denby to Gresham, December 26, 1894, no. 2072, Despatches, China, 97. For Gresham's views on the Foster appointment see his private letter to Thomas F. Bayard in England, December 24, 1894, letterbook, 48, Gresham papers. For his precautionary cables to Denby, dated February 7 and 18, 1895, see U.S., Diplomatic Instructions, China, 1. Foster described the promoters' importunities in his memoirs; historians have taken various views of the possible conflict of interest. John W. Foster, *Diplomatic Memoirs*, vol. 2, 106–9. Michael J. Devine, *John W. Foster: Politics and Diplomacy in the Imperial Era, 1873–1917*, 35–36, 77. McCormick, *China Market*, 202n7. Young, *Rhetoric of Empire*, 240–41n56.

11. Relying on Denby's dispatches, Dorwart calls him mediator in all but name. Dorwart, *Pigtail War*, 78–82. Wang Yün-sheng, a Chinese authority on the war, suggests that the Tsungli Yamen used him mainly to check documents for form. Cited in Young, *Rhetoric of Empire*, 241n60. On the basis of Chinese documentary evidence, Hunt concludes that Denby argued long with Li over tactics, advising him to yield to Japan in order to prevent European advances, but that Li, favoring a quite different plan, reduced the American legation to a message bearer. Hunt, *Special Relationship*, 139–40. Denby's own account, which naturally does not minimize his role, may be found in U.S., *Foreign Relations, 1894*, and partly in the manuscript dispatches of the Peking legation. The difficulties of his position are well illustrated in dispatches of December 1 and 20, 1894, and his policy for China is set forth in one of February 26, 1895, nos. 2042, 2066, 2146, U.S., Diplomatic Despatches, China, 97. Denby's memoirs are virtually useless. Denby, *China and Her People*, vol. 2, 130–38.

After the Japanese rejected two Chinese offers, the Tsungli Yamen called Li Hung-chang out of disgrace—although he had opposed the war, he had been blamed for the military defeats—and appointed him ambassador extraordinary with full credentials for negotiation. As soon as Li arrived in Peking to receive his instructions, he called on Denby to ask for help. Stiffened by Gresham's warnings, Denby urged Li to resign himself to territorial concessions and declared that the United States could not even give the appearance of supporting him in the negotiations.[12]

Early in March Li set out for Japan with an enormous entourage including Foster and Pethick. In his opening meeting with the Japanese, Li asked for an armistice and was told that China must first surrender three major strong points defending Peking. That night a would-be assassin shot him in the face, to the horror of the Japanese and the rest of the world. Recovering with amazing vitality, the old man exploited his injury to obtain an immediate armistice for northern China. He and Foster prepared the legal details of the negotiations and leaked them to the other powers. After the signature of the treaty, Li sent Foster to present it to the disapproving cabinet in Peking, fearing that his enemies there would destroy both it and him. He was much relieved when the treaty was ratified.[13]

Li and Foster somewhat reduced the Japanese demands, but in its final terms the Treaty of Shimonoseki, signed on April 17, 1895, was still harsh. China ceded Taiwan and the Pescadores Islands in the Taiwan Strait and leased the Liaotung peninsula, key to Manchuria. It recognized the independence of Korea, agreed to pay an indemnity of two hundred million taels ($150 million), and opened four more cities to foreign trade, including Chungking and Hangchow. Finally, China placed Japanese and Western commerce on the same basis by including a most-favored-nation clause, but since Western rights in China were by then very complicated, the treaty provided for separate negotiation of a commercial agreement.[14]

The Great Power intervention for which Li had hoped occurred eight days after the treaty was signed. Russia, Germany, and France sent the Japanese government notes "recommending" the return of the Liaotung peninsula to China, ostensibly to safeguard Peking and make genuine the independence of Korea. Actually, Russia, passive throughout the war, was now concerned for the future of Manchuria, which lay directly in the path of the partly completed Trans-Siberian Railway, and Germany hoped to keep northern China as free as possible from foreign encumbrances until its own Far Eastern policy could

12. Dorwart, *Pigtail War,* 85–86. Treat, *United States and Japan, 1853–1895,* vol. 2, 501–29. Denby to Gresham, February, 23, 26, March 5, 1895, nos. 2146, 2148, 2153, U.S., Diplomatic Despatches, China, 57. These are partly or wholly printed in Treat, *United States and Japan, 1853–1895,* vol. 2, 523–28.

13. Lensen, *Balance of Intrigue,* vol. 2, chaps. 11–12. Devine, *Foster,* chap. 7.

14. Morse, *International Relations of the Chinese Empire,* vol. 3, 43–47. Willoughby, *Foreign Rights and Interests in China,* 110–12. Beasley, *Japanese Imperialism,* 56–59.

develop. (France, interested principally in southern China, supported its new Russian ally unenthusiastically.) The Japanese government, half expecting such a demand, complied grimly and added thirty million taels ($22.5 million) to the indemnity.

The Sino-Japanese commercial treaty of 1896 required long and sometimes acerbic negotiations between the stubborn Li Hung-chang and Japanese diplomats, with several British trade experts on the sidelines, taking part to uphold their own interests. (Foster had gone home.) Chronic issues such as bonded warehouses, the notorious likin transit tax, and the most serious difference, foreign manufacturing in Chinese ports, were compromised or left vague. Japan, though victorious in battle, had to realize its partial dependence on the goodwill of the Western powers. The Japanese people, unprepared for their setback, burst out in anger, and nationalists began at once to prepare for revenge against Russia.[15] Fortunately, the United States had played a small role in the last stages of the peace settlement and, as Foster told a reporter, had "come out of it with better grace than any other [country]." By this time, however, Gresham, Denby, and other American policy makers were hoping that Japan would force China to sweep away all restrictions on foreign trade. (Denby expected to be overwhelmed by requests for concessions.) These rosy anticipations and the close participation of Denby and Foster in the peace negotiations increased American involvement in Far Eastern international politics.[16]

The Sino-Japanese War "left Pandora's Box wide open, but many Americans mistook it for the Horn of Plenty."[17] The peace treaty opened four new Chinese ports and three new rivers, allowed all foreigners to establish industrial enterprises, and gave some hope for the abolition of likin and other burdensome internal taxes. Many Americans expected that the shock of defeat would galvanize China into modernization on the order of Japan after 1868 and make it a better market than ever for cotton goods, machinery, and other American exports. Perhaps Chinese development projects might provide an outlet for capital. Americans also hoped that the peace settlement and Japan's release from the "unequal treaties" (see

15. For the execution of the Shimonoseki treaty, see Morse, *International Relations of the Chinese Empire,* vol. 3, 47–52. The background to the Russian action is shown in Malozemoff, *Russian Far Eastern Policy,* chap. 3. France received compensating privileges in southern China. For the Japanese reaction see Yanaga, *Japan since Perry,* 250–53. The Japanese minister at Washington gave the press his personal opinion that the United States should have intervened to offset the three-power alliance. *Bradstreet's* 23 (April 27, 1895): 257. On the commercial treaty see W. G. Beasley, "The Sino-Japanese Commercial Treaty of 1896," 1–15.

16. Foster's statement is in *Nation* 61 (July 18, 1895): 19. The editors agreed with him. On the hopes of Gresham, Denby, and others see Busselle, "U.S. in the Far East," 33, 70–72, 360. At the time of the war an American consultant was also advising the Japanese government. He was Henry M. Dennison, a onetime consul. For another view of postwar American reactions see Busselle, 77–79.

17. McCormick, *China Market,* 60–62.

chapter 7) would stimulate its purchase of American machinery and further open the country to American travel and other contacts with the West.[18]

Some observers were more skeptical. Many British expected only new complications. The American consul at Tientsin pointed out that the bankruptcy of Russell and Company in 1891 had left the United States without a single powerful trading firm in either Japan or China, so the marketing of American products would be left to small American outfits, European houses, or native dealers. Others feared that Japanese industry, newly freed from the restrictive tariffs of the "unequal treaties," would now flood the Chinese market. The Chinese were building their own mills; Shanghai would soon become "an Oriental Lowell." The depreciation of silver would widen the gap between the wages of Western and Oriental labor. Also, the increased Chinese imports would create an unfavorable trade balance and with the ever-mounting foreign debt, drag down the Chinese economy.[19]

The optimists had answers to many of these objections. Worthington C. Ford, the chief statistician of the State Department, saw few prospects for native-financed Chinese industry. The bogey of Japanese competition seemed more formidable, but many expected it to affect the British textile trade most of all and open markets in Japan for American machinery and raw cotton. (In any case the Japanese government decided not to establish cotton mills in China immediately.) Denby conceded that falling silver would stimulate Japanese trade in China but he pointed out that Western trade was increasing as well and that the uncertain exchange rate also worked to speed sales and reduce inventories. Expansionists called on the U.S. government to encourage development of Far Eastern markets with steamship subsidies and an isthmian canal and on American capital to show its growing strength by building its share of China's factories and railroads. *Bradstreet's* urged the establishment of cotton mills and banks in China.[20]

18. Cassey, "Mission of Denby," 181–83. U.S., Department of Agriculture, Section of Foreign Markets, Circular no. 5, "The Treaty of Shimonoseki between China and Japan of April 17, 1895, and the Possibilities of Trade with those Countries" (Washington, October 16, 1895), U.S., *Consular Reports* 180 (September 1895): 26–38. *Age of Steel* 72 (May 18, 1895): 7. *American Exporter* 35 (December 1894): 12, 14; (May 1895): 13; 36 (October 1895): 10–11. *Chicago Tribune,* May 11, 1895. Some British too were optimistic. *London Times,* October 31, 1895, quoted in U.S., *Consular Reports* 183 (December 1895): 532–36.

19. Cassey, "Mission of Denby," 180–81. Barry Lee Knight, "American Trade and Investment in China, 1890–1910," 39, 40. Report by Consul Jameson enclosed with Consul General Sir Malcolm Hannan to Lord Salisbury, April 17, 1896, Britain, Foreign Office, Annual Series, 1896, no. 1740. *Diplomatic and Consular Reports on Trade and Finance, China,* 23–28. U.S., "Treaty of Shimonoseki," 3–4. U.S., *Commercial Relations, 1896,* 1, 789–91. U.S., *Consular Reports* 166 (July 1894): 462–63. Charles Denby, Jr., to Gresham, April 26, 1894, no. 1843, U.S., Diplomatic Despatches, China, 94. *New York Times,* July 22, 1894. *San Francisco Argonaut,* n.d., reprinted in *Public Opinion* 17 (December 6, 1894): 862.

20. Worthington C. Ford, "Chinese Foreign Commerce," 14–15. Denby to Gresham, April 8, 1895, no. 2192, U.S., Diplomatic Despatches, China, 98. *Chicago Inter-Ocean,*

Confronted with this postwar expansionism, the State Department had to consider at once the role it should play in sustaining and encouraging American merchants and promoters in the Far East. Trade offered no difficulty; when Minister Denby inquired whether the United States should claim Japan's new privileges under the most-favored-nation clause in the 1858 treaty, he was told that it would expect equal and liberal trade advantages, certainly in Korea and presumably in China. He should make every effort to secure for Americans expanded commercial and residence privileges.[21] The problem of promoters seeking concessions was more difficult, and the State Department frequently answered Denby's enthusiastic reports with mere acknowledgments. In 1887, after the collapse of the Barker-Mitkiewicz railroad project (see chapter 6) Secretary Bayard had explicitly required prior department approval for "the furtherance [by the American legation] of individual plans and contracts connected with foreign governments," to prevent unworthy projects from spoiling the American reputation.[22]

During the Sino-Japanese negotiations, when Denby began to anticipate a flood of concessions, his friend Secretary Gresham gave him a gentle, private warning not to let his "generous and obliging nature" compromise him in the minds of strangers, but the first explicit instruction was a more brusque cable from Acting Secretary Edwin F. Uhl during Gresham's last illness: "You will not in any manner lend your diplomatic influence to aid the proposal for a loan [one of the first postwar American projects] and will confine your action to a formal presentation of the parties interested, if in your judgment such action appears proper."[23] Denby replied at length that this order would soon be found impracticable since a formal presentation to the Chinese court or the Tsungli Yamen would be taken to mean official American endorsement, because of the high standing enjoyed by the American legation. If the department could not choose whom to endorse and he were not allowed to choose, American businessmen would be greatly handicapped at a time of intense European competition.[24]

April 10, 1895. *New York Tribune,* August 5, 1895. *Bradstreet's* 23 (October 5, 1895): 638. For British reports see *London Times,* October 3, 1895.

21. Uhl to Denby, June 8, 1895, no. 1086, U.S., Diplomatic Instructions, China, 5, 195–96.

22. Cassey, "Mission of Denby," 174–76, 186–89. For earlier policy statements on the functions of ministers and consuls in aiding American businessmen see Francis Wharton, *A Digest of the International Law of the United States,* vol. 1, 670–71; and John Bassett Moore, *A Digest of International Law,* vol. 5, 126–27. Bayard to Denby, December 15, 1887, no. 274, U.S., Diplomatic Instructions, China, 4, 334, reprinted in Moore, *Digest of International Law,* vol. 4, 567.

23. Denby to Gresham, December 26, 1894, January 17, 1895, nos. 2072, 2104, U.S., Diplomatic Despatches, China, 97. Gresham to Denby, April 12, 1895 (telegram); Uhl to Denby, May 14, 1895 (telegram); U.S., Diplomatic Instructions, China, 5, 174, 183. Gresham to Denby, April 12, Gresham papers, box 48. It seems clear that Gresham was more concerned with preventing Denby from taking any unneutral actions in China's favor than with the problem of support for promoters.

24. Denby to Gresham, May 10, 17, 1895, personal and confidential, no. 2234, Despatches, China, 97. Denby wrote the second in answer to Uhl's telegram.

After Gresham's death Cleveland's new secretary of state, Richard Olney, tried to interpret Uhl's statement. Unfortunately, he did not resolve the dilemma. He felt that Bayard's instruction did not apply to Denby's regular duties as minister. "While American citizens, of whose character and responsibility you are satisfied, may always be introduced and vouched for as such," he added, "you should carefully abstain from using your diplomatic position to promote their financial or business enterprises." Denby should follow any different course only in an extraordinary case, having first submitted to the department all facts and reasons.[25] Olney did not suggest how Denby should drive home the unofficial character of the introduction when European diplomats made no such distinction.

For a year and a half the American minister received no further instructions on the subject. Reporting in a private letter of November 1895, he described the bold, even truculent demands of American businessmen who assumed that the legation existed to serve their every interest, and he listed the services he and his staff rendered: hearing, discussing, and revising projects involving hundreds of millions of dollars; securing interviews with foreign office functionaries; translating prospectuses and articles on the merits of American railroads; and convincing the officials that grants to American promoters would be free from the dangers of political control. A year later Denby sent a grandiose description of American promotional and financial efforts and predicted that if they were successful, "this almost limitless field of financial and industrial operations, will be occupied, dominated, and controlled by Americans."[26]

This dispatch finally drew a reply from Olney, dated December 19, 1896, when the secretary was about to leave office. In this dispatch he further loosened the restrictions on Denby:

> While agreeing with you that you should not assume directly or impliedly in the name of this Government any responsibility for, or guaranty of, any American commercial or industrial enterprise trying to establish itself in China, the Department thinks that you should use your personal and official influence and lend all proper countenance to secure to reputable representatives of such concerns the same facilities for submitting proposals, tendering bids, or obtaining contracts as are enjoyed by any other foreign commercial enterprise in the country. It is not practicable to strictly define your duties in this connection, nor is it desirable that any instructions which may have been given should be too literally followed. Your own judgment and experience, the standing of the firms who seek your assistance and of their

25. Olney to Denby, June 22, 1895 (telegram); same, June 22, unnumbered dispatch, U.S., Diplomatic Instructions, China, 5, 199–201. The quotation is from the longer dispatch. See also Gerald G. Eggert, *Richard Olney: Evolution of a Statesman*, 272–74.

26. Denby to Olney, November 25, 1895, Olney papers, 38, 6824–26 ff. Same, November 5, 1896, no. 2632 (quotation), Despatches, China. The only other dispatch on the subject in the files was a report by Charles Denby, Jr., chargé during his father's temporary absence from Peking. This briefly described the principal American promotional projects but said nothing of the legation's activities in their behalf. See also Denby, *China and Her People*, vol. 1, 91–94.

agents, must all be given due weight and your action shaped accordingly. Broadly speaking, you should employ all proper methods for the extension of American commercial interests in China, while refraining from advocating the projects of any one firm to the exclusion of others.

In the rest of the message Olney instructed Denby not to burden his staff with so much paperwork for the promoters and to send home more information about projects "if it is practicable to do so."[27]

Thus in 1895 and 1896 Gresham, Olney, and Denby edged toward dollar diplomacy. Why did they not act more openly, more explicitly, and earlier? In the first place, there was no clear distinction between trade, which ministers and consuls had always upheld, and investment promotion, for which few precedents existed. Many a railroad project, supported by speculative capital, was intended to open a great new market for machinery, rails, and supplies of all kinds. Second, the three men faced a real dilemma—neither the department nor the legation could absolutely safeguard against a second dishonest Mitkiewicz or be sure how the Tsungli Yamen might interpret a "non-diplomatic" introduction. Third, both secretaries had special reasons to trust Denby's judgment—Gresham as a personal friend and Olney as a onetime corporation lawyer with a background similar to Denby's.

Beyond the immediate problem of businessmen in China, other factors might have influenced Gresham, Olney, and Denby. Anti-missionary riots had become more numerous in China during the early 1890s, and in 1895 they had culminated in the brutal slaying of eleven missionaries at Huashan in southern China. Urged by angry protests from missionary societies, Denby repeatedly recommended cooperating with other nations in a strong policy, to which the State Department paid sympathetic attention.[28] At the same time Olney and Cleveland were giving much thought and energy to an Anglo-American crisis over a boundary question between Venezuela and British Guiana. Indeed, some of the explanations advanced by historians to account for their actions in this crisis might plausibly apply to China as well—the desire to rescue the Democratic party from Republican taunts of inaction, the dislike of encroaching British influence, and especially the hope of advancing American economic interests to counter this influence.[29]

27. Olney to Denby, December 19, 1896, no. 1376, U.S., *Foreign Relations, 1897,* 56. Eggert, *Olney,* 276–79.

28. Paul A. Varg, *Missionaries, Chinese, and Diplomats: The American Protestant Missionary Movement in China, 1890–1952,* 38–41. George E. Paulsen, "The Szechwan Riots of 1895 and American Missionary Diplomacy," 285–98. U.S., *Foreign Relations, 1895,* 1, 196–98. Denby to Uhl, June 20, 1895, no. 2269, U.S., Diplomatic Despatches, China, 98. Alvey A. Adee to Olney, August 1, 1895; Adee (as acting secretary) to Secretary of the Navy, August 10, 1895, Olney papers, 5384–88 ff, 5556–59. Press opinion was considerably divided on the subject, some newspapers calling for protection and others urging the missionaries to withdraw from the danger areas. Clippings in ibid., 33, 5794b–e ff. *Literary Digest* 11 (August 24, 1895): 483–84. *New York Tribune,* September 23, 1895. For a sample of Canadian expansionism see *Bradstreet's* 19 (October 10, 1891): 397.

29. Pletcher, *Diplomacy of Trade and Investment,* 313–21.

* * *

British economic influence in China, however, was no longer unchallenged, thanks to London's hands-off policy during the war and the tripartite intervention. The first area of open contest with Continental powers was that of lending money to the Chinese government so it could pay its war indemnity to Japan. In 1895, at the instance of the expansionist Russian minister of finance, Count Sergei Y. Witte, a Russo-French syndicate beat out Britain with a loan of $80 million. Witte also established (again with French capital) a Russo-Chinese bank, to collect taxes, coin money, and traffic in development concessions. The following year Britain and Germany countered with a joint loan of $80 million and early in 1898, after a year of wrangling with their Franco-Russian rivals, a second loan of the same amount.

In another area, railroads, the European powers pushed into the periphery of China. Witte, the creator of the Trans-Siberian Railway, was determined to build a shortcut across Manchuria to the ocean; Li Hung-chang had made plans to extend the K'aip'ing Railway to the northeast (see chapter 6). Each was determined to keep other powers out of the area. However, in 1896 Li, visiting St. Petersburg for the coronation of Czar Nicholas II, accepted the inevitable by signing the secret Li-Lobanov treaty, which granted to the Russo-Chinese Bank the right to build the desired Manchurian railroad, with suitable safeguards for Chinese sovereignty and probably a large bribe for Li. Meanwhile, Britain and France devoted their attention to southern China. In 1895 France secured permission for railroad construction across the Indo-China border toward Yunnan. Two years later Britain obtained a balancing concession to connect Burma with Yunnan. By 1898 China had pledged for loans most of her customs revenues, the usual collateral of the nineteenth-century borrower, and various internal taxes and was surrounded by encroaching railroad grants.[30]

Against this formidable competition American bankers and promoters fielded one serious loan project and three important railroad concessions in northern and central China. Only one of the four ventures was to survive beyond the Spanish-American War. The loan project involved a group of New York financiers, including by report Charles R. Flint and J. P. Morgan and Company. It was

30. Langer, *Diplomacy of Imperialism*, vol. 1, chap. 12. McCordock, *British Far Eastern Policy*, 142–76. E-tu Zen Sun, *Chinese Railways and British Interests, 1898–1911*, Introduction, chap. 1. Malozemoff, *Russian Far Eastern Policy*, 69–84. Edward H. Zabriskie, *American-Russian Relations in the Far East: A Study in Diplomacy and Power Politics, 1895–1914*, 30–39. Hunt, *Frontier Defense*, 13–16. Chia-ao, *China's Struggle*, 27–28. Huenemann, *Dragon and Iron Horse*, 50. For the role of the Tsungli Yamen in railroad construction after the war see Meng, *Tsungli Yamen*, 70. On the question of Li's bribe see Samuel C. Chu, "Li Hung-chang: An Assessment," in Chu and Ling, *Li Hung Chang*, 274–75; and Lensen, *Balance of Intrigue*, 512–13. Chapter 16 of the latter contains a detailed account of the negotiations. On the status of the K'aip'ing Railway see U.S., *Consular Reports* 184 (January 1896): 101–6. For a complete list of foreign loans to China, 1894–1913, see *Annals of the Academy of Political and Social Science* 68 (November 1915): 58–59, 64–65. By 1903 China's railroads had constructed about twenty-seven hundred miles of rail. Chia-ao, *China's Struggle*, 3.

presented by the American Trading Company, an export-import concern with extensive connections in Japan, China, and Korea, and agencies for American industrialists such as the Cramp Shipbuilding Company and the Union Iron Works. After it had failed to forestall the Franco-Russian loan of 1895, its backers offered terms in competition with the Anglo-German syndicate but could not match the more powerful Europeans and lost the contract. The American Trading Company continued to work for Chinese railroad concessions but in vain.[31]

A second comprehensive project, with somewhat more emphasis on railroads, was a revival of the Barker-Mitkiewicz proposals of the 1880s (see chapter 6), this time without the bogus count. Although Wharton Barker had passed through bankruptcy in 1890, Li Hung-chang's henchman, Ma Chien-chang, continued to correspond with him through the war period about loans and development. After the war ended, Barker raised a venture capital fund of $50,000 among his American associates and in the autumn of 1895 visited China to seek concessions. As before, Li preferred him to start a private bank to furnish capital, while Barker wanted widespread public contracts for banks, a gigantic railroad system, mines, and many other grants that would give his proposed syndicate control of the Chinese economy.

Barker's formal proposal for the railroad system will give an idea of the grandiose scope of his plans. He expected to construct about five thousand miles of trunk lines, the main one from Peking to Hankow and Canton with a branch paralleling the lower Yangtze from Hankow to Shanghai. He estimated the total cost at $125 million gold, and the net annual earnings at $8 million. If the government devoted its share of profits to systematic purchase of company bonds, it could control the railroad in twenty-five years. By that time Barker expected the system to comprise fully fifty thousand miles. Meanwhile, the sale of bonds and mortgages and income from other far-flung concessions would supply funds for construction and operations. Unfortunately, further support from American capitalists depended on persuading Li and the imperial government to grant at least one extensive railroad concession, while Li insisted that the capital must precede the concession, so Barker obtained neither. Characteristically, when he had used up his fifty-thousand-dollar fund, he went back to the United States and turned to other ventures. After his second failure in China, he had to spend a good deal of time placating those who had furnished the venture capital.[32]

31. Denby to Gresham, May 12, 14, 16, 30, 1895; Denby to Olney, March 16, 1896; Charles Denby, Jr., to Olney, May 26, nos. 2225, 2227, 2233, 2249, 2492, 2534, U.S., Diplomatic Despatches, China, 98, 100, 101. On the later, unsuccessful efforts of the American Trading Company see Sheridan P. Read to William W. Rockhill, June 1, 1896, no. 175, U.S., Consular Despatches, Tientsin, 5.

32. Young, *Rhetoric of Empire*, 62–64. Correspondence in the Barker papers gives full details of Barker's plans and activities. See also a 148-page handwritten account, apparently prepared on his return trip (Box 22). He sketched his plans several times in October 1895 to Li, Viceroy Chang Chih-tung, and the emperor, and two officials of the Imperial

A third large-scale promotional blueprint was also revived from the late 1880s—the railroad plans of James Harrison Wilson (see chapter 6). Already enjoying the support of Denby, John W. Foster, and William N. Pethick, Wilson allied himself in 1896 with James J. McCook, a noted corporation lawyer whose clients included the Pennsylvania Railroad and the Atchison, Topeka and Santa Fe. He was also a Republican party regular with ambition and a nose for intrigue who later became involved in American-Cuban relations. The two men took up an idea that a decade later fascinated Edward H. Harriman—a combined rail-sea network across the Pacific and the Eurasian land mass. The Trans-Siberian Railroad, now nearing completion, was obviously the key to such a project.

At Denby's instance McCook approached the Russian government for its cooperation, and both Wilson and McCook set out to find capital to construct an extension of the Trans-Siberian into China as far south as Peking and Shanghai. They also hoped for a Republican victory in the American elections of 1896, which might make McCook secretary of war, Wilson ambassador to Russia, and another sympathizer, Assistant Secretary of State William W. Rockhill, minister to China. The two promoters interviewed American business leaders representing Standard Oil, several railroads and manufacturers, and J. P. Morgan and Company. At the outset they obtained firm promises of support only from the Pennsylvania Railroad, the Baldwin Locomotive Company of Philadelphia, and one or two smaller firms. The Standard Oil representative objected that the proposed railroad system would funnel Russian oil into China and ruin Standard's already challenged market. Andrew Carnegie was not interested at all; Morgan preferred to await developments.[33]

The last and most successful of the four postwar American investment projects in China to be considered was incorporated in New Jersey in 1895 as the American China Development Company. Its principal creators were A. W. Bash of Seattle, leader of a group of Pacific Northwest businessmen, who did most of the leg work in China, and former senator Calvin S. Brice (Democrat, Ohio) an able railroad

---

Maritime Customs Service, Sir Robert Hart and Alfred Hippisley, approved them. The railroad project described here is taken from his formal proposal, dated October 26. Handwritten and typed copies are in Barker papers, boxes 8 and 21 respectively. After the Spanish-American War, Barker occasionally returned to his Chinese dreams, at one point trying to enlist the aid of the Russian ambassador to the United States. Young, *Rhetoric of Empire*, 250–51.

33. McCormick, *China Market*, 78–82. Healy, *U.S. Expansionism*, 77–78. Young, *Rhetoric of Empire*, 60–61. Again correspondence in the Wilson papers is the chief source of information. A good sample of Wilson's planning is his letter of October 28, 1896, to John J. McCook. Letterbook, 1896–97, 42–47. Wilson's supporters for the cabinet appointment included Jacob Schiff, Abram S. Hewitt, George Pullman, Marshall Field, and many Republican political chieftains, while Rockhill was backed by Theodore Search of the National Association of Manufacturers and Alba Johnson of the Baldwin Locomotive Company. McCormick, *China Market*, 83. However, the project may have been weakened by disunity in China, for Pethick despised Denby, whom he thought weak, narrow-minded, and typical of the inadequate American Foreign Service. Pethick to Wilson, December 15, 1895, Wilson papers, box 18.

promoter who made most of the enterprise's business contacts in the United States. During the summer of 1895 Bash talked to Denby, John W. Foster, Li, and others about railroads in northern China and with the Russian minister to China about possible connections between these Chinese lines and the Trans-Siberian Railway. Returning to the United States, he offered James Harrison Wilson a role in the project, but Wilson preferred to work with McCook and started a whispering campaign against Bash.

Meanwhile, Brice was at work in the corporation offices of New York—with much more success than Wilson. During the next two years he compiled a formidable group of backers, including former Vice President Levi P. Morton, Senator Thomas C. Platt (Republican, New York), Jacob H. Schiff of Kuhn, Loeb and Company, E. H. Harriman, and representatives of Carnegie Steel Company, American Sugar Refineries Company, the Metropolitan Life Insurance Company, and the principal New York banks. (Probably not all of these subscribed to stock at the outset, but the company's list contained enough important names by 1896 to impress the knowledgeable Denby with its prospects.) At the same time Bash and Brice obtained the services of the skilled lawyer Clarence Cary and former Senator W. D. Washburn (Republican, Minnesota).[34]

In addition to these four major projects, Americans were interested in several minor schemes, but the agents representing these had too little power to negotiate or too little capital backing.[35] The principal contest for influence in China and support at home was fought between representatives of the Wilson-McCook project and the American China Development Company. During 1896 Wilson and McCook seemed in the lead. McCook visited Russia at about the time that

34. William R. Braisted, "The United States and the American China Development Company," 148. Young, *Rhetoric of Empire,* 57–62. Campbell, *Special Business Interests,* 21–22, 26–27. Hunt, *Frontier Defense,* 26–27. B. A. Romanov, *Russia in Manchuria, 1892–1906: Essays on the History of the Foreign Policy of Tsarist Russia in the Epoch of Imperialism,* 76–77. *New York Times,* December 10, 1895. For Bash's proposal to Wilson see his letters of August 1 and October 4, 1895, Wilson papers, box 5. On Foster see Wilson to Pethick, December 7, 1896, ibid., Letterbook, 1896–97, 117–20. Washburn was a director of a prominent Minnesota flour milling company and may have been seeking a Far Eastern market for flour as a sideline. Brice also helped James R. Morse raise funds for his Korean railroad project. Harrington, *God, Mammon, and Japanese,* 177.

35. A Colonel M. R. Jeffard visited Peking during the autumn of 1895 trying to raise Chinese capital for a Peking-Hankow-Canton railroad. Read to Rockhill, June 1, 1896, no. 175, U.S., Consular Despatches, Tientsin, 5. *New York Tribune,* March 15, 1896. A syndicate was formed about a year later by an engineer, C. D. Jameson, to lend China sixteen million pounds and receive a concession for a Shanghai-Hankow line. Jameson was apparently a confidence man, for he was reported to have made unauthorized contracts with the Chinese government for the Carnegie Steel Company, the Baldwin Locomotive Company, and others. Read to Rockhill, May 11, 1897; Read to Day, October 8, 1897, nos. 221, 251, U.S., Consular Despatches, Tientsin, 6. Denby to John Sherman, October 20, 1897, no. 2814, U.S., Diplomatic Despatches, China, 103. A project of an entirely different nature was Gerow Brill's contract to establish an agricultural center. This ran into the familiar problems of language, tradition-bound peasants, and uncooperative officials. Brill eventually founded the first agricultural college in China. Curti and Birr, *Prelude to Point Four,* 28–34.

Li Hung-chang (unbeknownst to him) was negotiating the Li-Lobanov treaty concerning railroads in Manchuria. The American promoter talked to both Li and Prince M. T. Khilkov, the Russian minister of communications, and found both apparently interested in having American capital connect the Manchurian and Chinese lines. At about this time John W. Foster learned that Li planned to visit Europe on his way home from Russia and sent him a personal invitation to visit the United States too. As soon as the old man accepted, if not before, Foster informed Wilson, by now his business associate.

Although Cleveland and Olney received the news of the visit with little interest, Wilson immediately started a campaign for an official reception. Eventually he aroused Olney's enthusiasm, and Cleveland agreed to come to New York from his summer cottage in New England to meet Li. The visit, which lasted only a few days during September, was an anticlimax. Li missed the gala navy reception in New York harbor, because Wilson had met his ship and was eagerly discussing railroads and loans with him below deck. The meeting with Cleveland was brief and stiff. The viceroy's afternoon nap, which his aides dared not interrupt, kept him from a scheduled inspection of the Cramp shipyards. Having been exhausted by tours of factories, munitions plants, and naval installations in Germany, France, and Britain, Li was not much interested in what the Americans wanted to show him, although at one point he did call American railroads "the greatest he had ever seen." After touring a little on the East Coast, he left the United States at Niagara Falls and traveled across the continent on the Canadian Pacific Railroad, sailing from Vancouver to avoid Sinophobe California. (Washburn of the American China Company rode with him on the train.) No one got any firm promise of investments or trade from him, but the publicity given his visit undoubtedly stimulated American interest in China.[36]

Li was followed by another guest, Prince Khilkov, the Russian minister of communications, whom McCook and his associates wined and dined and who reciprocated with predictions of a round-the-world railroad-steamship system and American railroad equipment on Russian lines. Wilson and McCook were greatly encouraged, especially when William McKinley won the presidency, but their campaign soon began to slide downhill. An important reason was probably the narrow base of their American business support. Also, despite their strong

36. Thomas J. McCormick, "The Wilson-McCook Scheme of 1896–1897," 49–53. McCormick, *China Market*, 72–73, 80–81. Gerald C. Eggert, "Li Hung-chang's Mission to America, 1896," 240–57. Wilson to Jacob H. Schiff, September 1, 1896; Wilson to Pethick, November 25, Wilson papers, Letterbook, 1889–96, 438–41; 1896–97, 95–96. The friendly attitude of Li and Khilkov concealed basic Chinese and Russian opposition to foreign influence in northern China and Manchuria. Khilkov liked Americans, having learned railroad engineering in the United States during the 1860s. Theodore Von Laue, *Sergei Witte and the Industrialization of Russia*, 79. Li needed American capital. Also, he may have hoped that publicity during his visit would restore his reputation at home. In any case he was as evasive to the Europeans as to the Americans. He visited and was impressed by the Singer company's large sewing machine factory in Scotland. Davies, *Peacefully Working*, 195–96.

pressure on the McKinley administration, the new president would not appoint Wilson to the St. Petersburg embassy and sent Rockhill not to China but to Greece. He offered McCook the Interior Department, but the promoter preferred international affairs and became involved instead in bond issues for the Cuban revolutionary junta in New York.[37] The Wilson-McCook project was dead several months before the Spanish-American War.

For a time the American China Development Company seemed close to winning the much desired concession for a trunk railroad from Peking to Hankow. During the winter of 1896–1897 Bash and Washburn went to China and established friendly relations with Sheng Hsuan-huai, a wealthy, progressive businessman who had recently been appointed director of Chinese railroads and seemed to favor their development in northern China by the politically neutral Americans. While they negotiated, an American engineer made a preliminary survey of the proposed route, and an American expert in rolling mills took charge of an iron works near Hankow. Soon, however, a Belgian syndicate under King Leopold's patronage and allied with French interests won over the Russians and began to put pressure on the Chinese government. Minister Denby, under Olney's last, liberal instructions, waged a desperate rear-guard action, reminding the Tsungli Yamen officials (with some exaggeration) of disinterested American support for China during the war and the peace negotiations and at one point even demanding that the Tsungli Yamen instruct Sheng to close with the American China Development Company. All in vain; in May 1897 Sheng granted the Peking-Hankow concession to the Belgians.[38]

Probably the inexperienced Americans were not yet ready to compete with the Europeans in foreign investment. They may have failed because France and Russia applied stronger diplomatic pressure than could Denby, whom the McKinley administration was about to replace. But disinterest by American capitalists would seem to have been a more important factor. In October 1897 Denby reported that he had tried to arrange a one-hundred-million-dollar loan for China but could find no one in the United States willing to touch it.[39] Significantly, Bash and Wash-

---

37. McCormick, *China Market*, 80–83. Young, *Rhetoric of Empire*, 68–69. McCormick, "Wilson-McCook Scheme," 54–55. Healy, *U.S. Expansionism*, 78–79. Wilson to Denby, November 26, 1896; Wilson to Denby, Jr., November 29, December 7, 10, 1896; January 11, 1897, Wilson papers, Letterbook, 1896–97, 98–102, 104–8, 117–20, 126–30, 166–68.

38. Young, *Rhetoric of Empire*, 64–68, 251n29. McCormick, *China Market*, 74–76. Percy Horace Kent, *Railway Enterprise in China: An Account of Its Origin and Development*, 109–11. Huenemann, *Dragon and Iron Horse*, 52. U.S., *Foreign Relations, 1897*, 56–59. Denby to Olney, January 29, 1897; Denby to Sherman, March 15, April 17, May 24, 1897, nos. 2676, 2712, 2738, 2752, U.S., Diplomatic Despatches, China, 101–2. Chang Chih-tung, governor general of Hunan and Hupeh, through which the railroad would pass, considered the offer one-sided and its promoters' intentions "deceitful in the extreme." Hunt, *Frontier Defense*, 40–41.

39. Denby to Sherman, October 20, 1897, U.S. Diplomatic Despatches, China, 102. It is significant that as early as 1891 Jacob Schiff warned Wilson that the actual capital would probably have to be found in Germany. Jacob C. Schiff to Wilson, March 7, 1891. Cited in Best, "Ideas without Capital," 458.

burn had earlier rejected a Chinese offer because it did not provide enough assurance of profits for the concessionaire, and it seems doubtful that they could have bettered the very liberal Belgian terms. After the loss of the grant Clarence Cary, the company's legal adviser and a large stockholder, wrote a disillusioned magazine article, predicting that "many long years" would elapse before the completion of the Peking-Hankow line or any other extensive railroad in China. The native dislike and contempt for foreigners, he said, allowed little scope for enterprises dependent on exclusive concessions. "In business generally," Cary concluded, "China offers no greater openings than may be found at home."[40] But despite Cary's pessimism, the American China Development Company did not give up.

If Americans had suffered a setback in Chinese railroad development, they did not even attempt to compete in East Asian cables during the 1890s. At this time three operators occupied the field: the British Australasia and China Telegraph Company, connecting with the west via India; the Great Northern Telegraph Company (Danish), connecting with Russian lines to Europe; and the China Telegraph Company, controlling interior lines. Denby occasionally urged a transpacific line, which had long been an American dream. Although he managed to prevent a rate-fixing agreement between Great Northern and the Russians in 1889 (see chapter 6), the British, Danish, and Chinese companies came together in the "joint purse" agreement of July 11, 1896, the first of a series equalizing charges and, in effect, creating an ironclad monopoly over communications to China. This naturally stimulated American consideration of transpacific projects. Two companies (both chartered confusingly as the Pacific Cable Company) set out to lay a line to Hawaii (see chapter 10), and one of these, formed by the inter-American cable magnate James A. Scrymeer, also approached the Japanese government for a concession after the Spanish-American War. Neither of these schemes was carried out.[41]

American investment projects in Korea also suffered from inadequate capital backing at home, tepid State Department interest, and Japanese rivalry, strengthened by the war with China. The principal concessionaire was James R. Morse,

---

40. Young, *Rhetoric of Empire*, 65–67, 251–52*n32*. It was also objected that the language of the contract was too severe and legalistic for the simple Chinese. U.S., *Consular Reports* 206 (November 1897): 437. The earlier terms (much like those the Belgians accepted) provided government guarantees, and too little foreign control of construction and management. In the end Denby was more distressed by the secrecy of the Belgian negotiations than by the terms accepted. Denby to Sherman, May 24, October 20, 1897, no. 2752, U.S., Diplomatic Despatches, China, 102. Cary, "China and Chinese Railway Concessions," 598–604.

41. Tribolet, *Electrical Communications*, 76–80. Denby to James G. Blaine, October 24, 1890; Denby to Gresham, February 7, 1894; Denby to Olney, September 2, 1896, nos. 1183, 1806, 2590, U.S., Diplomatic Despatches, China, 88, 94, 101. The Japanese government was receptive to the Pacific cable project. Dun to Olney, February 10, 1896, no. 346, ibid., Japan, 69. *Bradstreet's* 24 (May 9, December 12, 1896): 289, 792. John Hay to Alfred E. Buck, October 24 (telegram), November 10, December 31, 1898; January 3, 14 (telegram), November 10, December 31, 1898; January 3, 14 (telegram), 1899, U.S., Diplomatic Instructions, Japan, 4, 536, 538, 543–44, 547.

president of the American Trading Company, who enjoyed the support of Minister John M. B. Sill and, even more important, of Horace N. Allen, the missionary and legation secretary, who was intriguing with the Korean government for American economic development. In 1895 Morse obtained a mining concession in the rich Un-san gold district of northwest Korea, between Pyong-yang and the Yalu River. The following year Allen secured for him a concession on generous terms for a short railroad line from Seoul to its port Chemulpo, much needed and promising to be highly profitable. The Japanese were privately dismayed, but Russia approved the grant. (Allen was on friendly terms with the Russian minister.)

These pleasing prospects soon turned sour. In 1897 Morse sold off his mining concession to a Seattle promoter, Leigh S. J. Hunt, in order to devote his time and capital to the railroad. A Denver construction company was brought in to build the line, while Morse sought more capital in the United States. Failing in this, he mortgaged the line to a Japanese syndicate of which he was a member. By the time the line was completed in 1898, he had decided to sell out to the syndicate, over Allen's earnest objections. At about the same time Japan secured another key railroad concession, from Seoul to Pusan, and, for the Russians, France got a less promising one from Seoul to the Yalu River through the Un-san district. This too soon passed to the Japanese. At the beginning of the Russo-Japanese War, in 1904, they controlled the three principal Korean lines.

Allen was somewhat consoled by the fact that Hunt and his associates continued to hold the Un-san mining concession, which Allen administered for them. In 1903 the enterprise operated several mines and mills in a district of about 750 square miles and represented a capital of about $5 million. Americans also controlled a street railway and electrical plant in Seoul, and, at Chemulpo, the largest rice mill in Korea. These few scattered businesses were the only important American investments in Korea in 1905, when the United States recognized the Japanese protectorate and closed its legation.[42]

During the mid-1890s Americans scored more notable successes in Far Eastern trade than in large-scale investments, for between 1894 and 1898 total trade

42. Harrington, *God, Mammon, and Japanese*, chaps. 9, 10. On the intricate financial relations between Allen and Morse see 165–67. On the Seoul-Chemulpo railroad see Romanov, *Russia in Manchuria*, 110–11. Sill to Uhl, August 15, 1895, no. 20, U.S. Consular Despatches, Seoul, 1. Sill to Olney, April 15, July 17, 1896; to Sherman, April 12, 1897, nos. 211, 226, 266; Allen to Sherman, December 1, 1897, February 2, May 13, 1898, nos. 12, 70, 108, U.S. Diplomatic Despatches, Korea, 12–14. Allen to Day, February 15, 1898, no. 270; Allen to Secretary of State, February 2, 1903, no. 5, 590, U.S., Consular Despatches, Seoul, 1. Although the Japanese took over most Korean enterprises after their annexation in 1911, the best Un-san mines remained in American hands until 1939. Harrington, *God, Mammon, and Japanese*, 161–67. U.S., *Commercial Relations, 1896*, 1, 865. Spencer J. Palmer, "American Gold Mining in Korea's Unsan District," 381–83. Lee, "Competitive Mining Surveys," 22–25, 35–41. Duus, *Abacus and Sword*, 142–47. *Korean Repository* 4 (August 1897): 311–15; 5 (July 1998): 272–73. The Japanese interest in Korean railroads was largely military, for army leaders expected another land war on the peninsula. Duus, *Abacus and Sword*, 138–40, 185.

with Japan increased more than 95 percent and that with China by about 30 percent.[43] These successes resulted in part from greater experience and more reliable support at home. Also, for the first time American manufacturers began to place aggressive salesmen in the Far East to drum up trade. Both the Philadelphia Commercial Museum, an active promoter of foreign trade, and the American Exporters Association sent representatives to visit Japanese chambers of commerce. An agent of the Baldwin Locomotive Company sold 120 locomotives in Japan alone, and the company was careful to dispatch a competent engineer with the delivered locomotives to help prepare them for operation. A retired army officer who represented the Bethlehem Iron Company in China tried with Denby's aid to interest the government in guns and armor plate, but in this case contrary advice from Sir Robert Hart of the Imperial Customs prevented a sale.[44]

Perhaps the best example of the new Yankee salesmanship was provided by James J. Hill, who, anticipating the completion of his Great Northern Railroad (1893), sent an agent to reconnoiter the Far Eastern market in 1892. Hill hoped to establish a transpacific steamer line, but he had to give up his plans during the depression of the mid-1890s. In 1896 he contracted with the rapidly expanding Nippon Yusen Kaisha line for service to the Great Northern terminus at Seattle. Then he arranged with Chicago steel mills for special prices on rails, persuaded Japanese textile manufacturers to experiment with American cotton, and undercut the Pacific Mail line to sell midwestern and northwestern flour in competition with that from San Francisco. At a time when depression at home and competition from Argentina and Canada for the European market were causing misery and social upheaval in the prairie states, Hill predicted that he would raise the value of the American wheat crop by one-third.[45]

43. The percentages are based on the following figures for imports and exports together: China and Hong Kong, 1894, $28,084,155; 1898, $36,603,081. Japan, 1894, $23,407,899; 1898, $45,826,691. U.S., Department of Agriculture, *Our Trade with Japan, China, and Hongkong, 1889–1899*, 16–28. The American share of Japanese imports rose from 7 percent in 1893 to 14.4 percent in 1898, while the British share fell from 32 percent to 22.6 percent. *Bradstreet's* 27 (August 19, 1899): 515.

44. *Commercial and Financial Chronicle* 63 (November 28, 1896): 952. *Board of Trade Journal* 28 (June 1896): 663. U.S., *Consular Reports* 207 (December 1897): 638–39. U.S., *Commercial Relations, 1898*, 1, 1108. Denby to Olney, February 25, 1896; Denby, Jr., to Olney, May 26, 1896, nos. 2470, 2534, U.S., Diplomatic Despatches, China, 100, 101. Hart's reason for opposing the sale was probably the depleted condition of the Chinese treasury. Japan imitated the Philadelphia Commercial Museum with a similar one in Osaka, the center of the cotton milling industry. The American consul there urged his countrymen to exhibit their products. U.S., *Consular Reports* 198 (March 1897): 372, 381.

45. Schonberger, *Transportation to the Seaboard*, 219–24. Curtis, *Yankees of the East*, 7. *New York Journal of Commerce*, July 27, 1896. *Bradstreet's* 24 (August 15, 1896): 520. U.S., Department of Agriculture, *United States Wheat for Eastern Asia*. Americans did not fear the influx of Russian wheat over the Trans-Siberian Railway, because it lay too far north of the Russian wheatfields, whose natural market was Europe via the Black Sea. U.S., *Consular Reports* 210 (March 1898): 374–76. However, Hill and the millers did have to

Between 1893 and 1898 Japanese imports and exports almost trebled and doubled respectively, and in 1895–1896 alone more than 640 million yen was invested in new enterprises (more than 340 million in railroads and 130 million in banks). In 1896 the government sent a commission to the United States to study the improvement of transportation and the increased shipment of American cotton, petroleum, and machinery. Subsidized shipyards appeared in Japan, and the merchant marine expanded. Nippon Yusen Kaisha, already a powerful force in East Asian trade (see chapter 7), increased its capital, bought new steamers, and entered the transpacific field to compete with Pacific Mail-Oriental and Occidental and the Canadian Pacific Railway's "Empress" line. By the mid-1890s the transpacific field was almost crowded, with the addition of chartered steamers operated by Northern Pacific, Oregon Railway and Navigation Company, and Central Pacific.[46]

American imports from Japan fluctuated considerably during the period, but in 1897 they stood at $24,009,756—less than $300,000 higher than five years before. In contrast, American exports to Japan increased from $3,290,111 in 1892 to $4,634,717 in 1895 and then nearly trebled during the next two years, to $13,255,478, as the Japanese prepared to impose their new tariff duties. The American share of Japanese imports doubled during these years, from about 7 percent to about 14 percent, while that of Britain fell off from about 32 percent to about 23 percent.[47] At about the same time German sales to Japan almost doubled.[48]

face Australian competition, especially as a Japanese steamship line to Australia proposed to equal American freight rates. *New York Times*, July 3, 1895. On the growth of the American-Chinese wheat-flour trade see ibid., November 28, 1897.

46. In 1896 the Japanese government described the effect of the war on the economy. For a summary of this report see *Bradstreet's* 24 (October 10, 1896): 654. Tennant, "Commercial Expansion of Japan," 54. Some of the sharp increases of Japanese imports in 1897 were doubtless caused by the expectation of higher tariffs in 1899, when the treaties of 1894 were due to take effect. *Board of Trade Journal* 22 (March 1897): 300. The Japanese commission was also instructed to investigate the purchase of land in Mexico for Japanese colonies. *Bradstreet's* 24 (July 25, 1894): 472. *Manufacturers' Record*: 30 (August 7, 1896): 21. *New York Journal of Commerce*, August 7, 1896. On the Japanese merchant marine see Meeker, "History of Shipping Subsidies," 141–45; Tennant, "Commercial Expansion of Japan," 57; *Bradstreet's* (November 28, 1896): 753; and an article in the *San Francisco Chronicle*, August 16, 1896, reprinted in *Overland Monthly* 217 (October 1896): 402–3. On the situation in the transpacific steamer field see Curtis, *Yankees of the East*, 6–7. The increase in steamers greatly complicated the shipment of Japanese tea to the United States. *New York Journal of Commerce*, June 29, 1893.

47. For American trade figures see U.S., Treasury Department, Bureau of Statistics, Monthly summary, 1899, 1282. For percentages see *Bradstreet's* 27 (August 19, 1899): 514–15. Japanese tariff raises were as high as 40 percent above earlier rates, but there was no apparent system. Increases for textiles were 10 percent and 15 percent, and a 10 percent duty was placed on kerosene. U.S., *Consular Reports* 202 (July 1897): 475–76. The American minister to Japan discussed the possibility of a reciprocity agreement, but although the foreign minister, Baron Nishi, seemed interested, Sherman could give no instructions until Japan actually carried out its new tariff. A. E. Buck to Sherman, September 20, 1897, no. 58, U.S., Diplomatic Despatches, Japan, 70. Sherman to Buck, September 14, 1897, no. 59, U.S., Diplomatic Instructions, Japan, 4, 469–70.

48. Between 1889 and 1896 German exports to Japan increased from $4,426,800 to $8,490,000. (Imports increased from $833,000 to $2,142,000.) U.S., *Consular Reports* 213

The nature of American imports from Japan changed little during the 1890s—raw silk and silk goods, tea, and a few other products. Export figures provided some surprises, for shipments of raw cotton increased from $2,341 in 1889 to $7,428,726 in 1898, when it passed kerosene and became at least temporarily the largest American export to Japan. This rise, which was most dramatic in 1896 and 1897, was due to many factors: the growth of the Japanese textile industry, Japan's removal of tariff duties, the superiority of the long-staple American fiber to those from India and China, James J. Hill's effective demonstration of that superiority, and, not least important, a temporary glut of cotton in the American South that lowered prices. For most of the 1890s British freight rates were so low that most American cotton reached the Osaka mills via London or Liverpool and the Suez route. By 1897, however, Hill's arrangement with Nippon Yusen Kaisha was beginning to shift the flow of cotton to Seattle.[49]

To the dismay of British observers, American iron and steel products began to make inroads on the Japanese market. In 1896 Carnegie Steel Company beat out British rivals for the first Japanese public tender for steel rails, followed by Illinois Steel Company. The next year significant quantities of American pig iron were sold in Japan for the first time, although the Japanese continued to prefer the British product and bought the American for its low price, to mix with British iron. The developing Japanese railroad companies, both official and private, broke their dependence on British supplies, equipment, and bridge steel, thanks largely to Hill's rail shipment and the diligence of the Baldwin Locomotive Company. The Japanese government signed contracts with the Union Iron Works and the Cramp shipyards for two new second-class cruisers.[50]

(June 1898): 227–28. One reason for the rise was that German firms managed to take over much of the small-scale export-import trade of Chinese merchants in Yokohama when the war forced the latter to leave. Ibid., 194 (March 1895): 432. Early in 1897 a German announced the publication of the first German-language newspaper in Japan. Ibid., 198 (March 1897): 399–400.

49. *Age of Steel* 77 (June 8, 1895): 7. *San Francisco Argonaut*, n.d., in *Public Opinion* 23 (September 3, 1897): 392–93. *Bradstreet's* 26 (October 15, 1898): 670. *Commercial and Financial Chronicle* 66 (April 2, 1898): 643–44. O. P. Austin, "Commercial Japan," 148–51. *American Wool and Cotton Reporter* 8 (September 27, 1894): 1210. *Board of Trade Journal* 19 (December 1895): 706–7. *Annals of the American Academy of Political and Social Sciences* 13 (January–June 1899): Supplement, 110. Curtis, *Yankees of the East*, 307–8. *New York Journal of Commerce*, December 15, 22, 1897. The well-informed Thomas R. Jernigan, onetime consul at Shanghai, believed it possible that China might eventually exploit its own excellent cotton lands and crowd Americans out of Far Eastern markets. Thomas R. Jernigan, "Commercial Trend of China," 69.

50. *Commercial and Financial Chronicle* 63 (November 28, 1896): 952. *New York Journal of Commerce*, May 19, June 1, August 14, 1896, January 2, 4, April 3, 1897. U.S., *Consular Reports* 219 (December 1898): 633–35; 220 (January 1899): 36–38. Sales of locomotives to Japan increased as follows, 1892–1897: British, 240 to 484; American, 26 to 282; German, 28 to 55. Aldcroft, *Development of British Industry*, 202. The low-tariff *New York Times* used Carnegie's success in selling steel rails in Japan to denounce the American steel duties, which forced domestic purchasers to pay seven or eight dollars per ton more than the Japanese. *New York Times*, March 27, 1896. For British reactions in diplomatic reports and trade journals see *Bradstreet's* 24 (June 13, September 5, 1896): 381, 568; 24 (July 2,

As for flour, Hill continued to increase shipments from the Northwest through the 1890s and diverted much of the West Coast wheat crop from Europe to China and Japan. Kerosene shipments also continued to rise, and in 1897 the United States supplied 70 percent of Japanese imports as against 23 percent from Russia and 7 percent from the Dutch East Indies, a new rival. Two other exports, leaf and manufactured tobacco and oil cake (for livestock feed) assumed new importance during the late 1890s. As late as 1895 British businessmen and diplomats were trying to reassure themselves that American successes resulted from a depression-inspired export campaign and nothing else, but when they continued into the better times of 1897, both the British and the Germans became more seriously alarmed.[51]

While feeling some satisfaction over these increases, the American public paid close attention during the mid-1890s to a "scare campaign" in the American and the British press against Japanese industry, which, aided by cheap labor and Japanese ingenuity, seemed to many about to crowd Westerners out of Far Eastern markets altogether and even invade the United States. Late in 1895 San Francisco newspapers feverishly described the movements of a Japanese agent who offered buttons, bicycles, matches, and various wood products at prices which, they said, would close every factory in the United States. The new transpacific sailings of the Nippon Yusen Kaisha, a proposed Japanese bounty on raw silk exports, and Japanese plans for higher tariffs all seemed ominous, especially when taken in conjunction with fears of Japanese intervention in Hawaii (see chapter 10).[52]

The State Department protested against the silk bounty as a treaty violation and eventually got it repealed, but the rumors of impending competition, while exaggerated, stirred a brief public debate with ominous overtones for the future. The National Association of Manufacturers sent Robert P. Porter, former commissioner of the census, to Japan on an inspection tour. His various reports and articles supplied arguments for both sides. On the one hand, Japan lacked

---

1898): 429–30; *Board of Trade Journal* 21 (December 1896): 727; 23 (July 1897): 22–23; *New York Times,* June 27, 1898. *New York Journal of Commerce,* August 18, 1898.

51. Department of Agriculture, *U.S. Wheat for East Asia,* 1–6. *Outlook* 55 (April 17, 1897): 1016. Canada too was lured by the Japanese market for wheat. Robert Joseph Gowan, "Canada and the Myth of the Japan Market, 1896–1911," 64–65. U.S., *Consular Reports* 207 (December 1897): 525–28. *Bradstreet's* 26 (July 2, 1898): 430. Austin, "Commercial Japan," 15–53. *Weser Zeitung,* n.d., translated and condensed in *Literary Digest* 14 (August 14, 1897): 474. Despite American successes, a consul at Yokohama sent home a British catalogue of iron and steel products written entirely in Japanese such as he had never seen from any American firm. N. W. McIver to Uhl, August 13, 1894, no. 51, U.S., Consular Despatches, Kanagawa, 20.

52. *New York Tribune,* November 25, 1895, January 11, 1897. U.S., 54th Cong., 1st sess., *Senate Document 311. Overland Monthly* 38 (June, July, October 1896): 82–91, 393, 403, 587–620. Like the Germans, the Japanese took to imitating American trademarks, marketing "Waterbury" clocks and "Eagle" pencils in India. They also offered "Belmont sperm" candles, but when a British revenue officer taxed them according to their advertised contents, the manufacturer indignantly protested that they were made in Kobe of ordinary candle wax. *New York Tribune,* February 22, 1897.

vital minerals and other raw materials, so it would be a valued customer of the United States and Europe for many years to come. On the other hand, the adaptive Japanese would exploit labor-saving machinery to the utmost. "When Japan is fully equipped with the latest machinery," Porter concluded, "It will, in my opinion, be the most potent industrial force in the markets of the world." William E. Curtis, better known for his writings on Latin America, bore him out with an article on Japan's industrial revolution. He described a small watch factory established at Osaka in 1895 by an American, who found his employees quick to learn the delicate craft.[53]

At the same time two of the most powerful economic pressure groups in the country seized upon the issue of Japanese competition and molded it to suit their purposes. Silverites, especially in the California press, declared that the cheap Japanese silver standard gave an additional advantage to Japanese employers, who already paid their labor much less than American factory-owners, and they demanded that Congress remonetize silver. Protectionists admitted the great wage differential but insisted that the only workable solution was higher tariffs on all American products that might suffer from Japanese competition. Low-tariff opponents pointed out that according to Treasury statistics, tea, raw silk, and a few specialty manufactures still made up the bulk of American imports and that the trade delegation sent by Japan in 1896 was mainly interested in American raw materials and products such as railroad supplies. The House Ways and Means Committee held hearings, gathered data, and submitted a majority report favoring protection and a minority report for remonetization. The panic blew over, and the Dingley tariff of 1897 raised duties on silks and mattings, to the dismay of the Japanese and James J. Hill. However, like a small cloud on the horizon, the Japanese trade scare of the 1890s presaged much stormy weather for twentieth-century American-Japanese relations.[54]

53. U.S., *Foreign Relations, 1898*, 442–44. On Porter see *New York Journal of Commerce*, February 19, 1897, and Robert P. Porter, "Is Japanese Competition a Myth?" 144–55 (quotation on 155). William E. Curtis, "The Industrial Revolution in Japan," 134–35. See also John Barrett, "The Plain Truth about Asiatic Labor," 620–32; and *New York Times*, February 17, 1898. A spokesman for the steel industry pointed out areas of U.S.-Japanese competition in China: fabrics, bristle brushes, matting, surgical instruments and appliances, and American-style rugs. American Iron and Steel Association, *Bulletin* 30 (April 1, 1896): 74.

54. For a good summary of the principal arguments see *Literary Digest* 13 (June 27, 1896): 261–62. On the silverite case see ibid., 12 (January 25, 1896): 363; and Henry M. Teller to Barker, August 21, 1895, typed copy in Barker papers, box 8. On the protectionist case see *New York Tribune*, January 11, 1897. See also the two House committee reports, U.S., 54th Cong., 1st sess., *House Report 2279*, pts. 1 and 2. *New York Journal of Commerce*, June 25, 1896. *New York Tribune*, January 30, 1897. Concerning the visit of the Japanese trade commission see *New York Journal of Commerce*, August 7, 1896, and *Bradstreet's* 24 (July 25, 1896): 472. The Japanese government also made efforts to attract American trade so as to ward off a higher U.S. tariff law. See Busselle, "U.S. in the Far East," 126–27. A variety of trade and other conservative journals and writers pooh-poohed the Japanese danger. *Age of Steel* 78 (September 21, 1895): 7–8. *New York Journal of Commerce*,

By the end of the decade American trade conditions in Japan had diverged more widely than ever from those in China. American imports from Japan had passed those from China and Hong Kong during the late 1880s, and in 1897 they stood at $24,009,756 and $21,837,304 respectively. Between 1892 and 1897 American exports to China and Hong Kong rose only from $10,557,546 to $17,984,472, a gain of about 70 percent as contrasted with one of about 300 percent for American-Japanese exports in the same period. The latter were also somewhat more diversified. During the 1890s American exports to China hovered around 1–1.5 percent of total exports, and they varied unpredictably from year to year.[55]

Faith in the enormous potential value of China's four hundred million customers remained, but in most other respects the differences between the two countries now favored Japan. To be sure, China furnished more extensive opportunities than Japan for developmental investment, especially in railroads, and thus more "tie-in" sales of supplies and equipment. The Japanese government, however, cooperated more willingly with foreign businessmen in purchasing their wares, regularizing taxes and laws, and providing security. French, German, and Russian merchants, some of them attracted by the Chinese railroad projects, offered more serious competition than in Japan. Above all, the ambitions of the European and Japanese governments for political control in China made that country's future extremely precarious.

During the 1890s many American goods for everyday use such as canned foods and provisions, and services such as life insurance, became widely available in Chinese ports, although one generally had to buy the goods in British or German stores, for lack of American merchants. The few small-scale American companies were often directed by British managers, and the half dozen American commercial houses in Shanghai had no branches in other ports. Away from the coast one saw almost no Americans other than missionaries. In 1891 Minister Denby and the consuls had greeted the opening of Chungking, far up the Yangtze River, with high hopes for flourishing trade and a steamship line past the notorious Yangtze rapids, but neither developed. Downriver at Hankow, in the very center of China and now the principal tea-shipping port, American representation increased very little during the two decades after 1880. In 1899 there were sixty-five missionaries in the consular district but only three or four small traders working on commission to break up river cargoes for shipment inland. Similar

---

November 26, 1895, December 18, 1896. *Bradstreet's* 25 (March 28, 1896): 197. *New York Tribune,* February 14, 1897. Hill also protested, for he had hoped to attract the silk and matting trade to Seattle and thus reduce freight rates on westbound flour. Ibid., April 9, 1897.

55. U.S., Treasury Department, Bureau of Statistics, *Monthly Summary, 1899,* 1281–82 (percentages computed from these figures). During the same period, in comparison with American exports, British exports to China and Hong Kong fell slightly from £7,581,906 in 1892 to £7,117,716 in 1897 (although the figure for 1896 was higher). *Bradstreet's* 26 (August 27, 1898): 559. In China, 1889–1898, cotton goods and refined petroleum made up about 87 percent of American sales, in Japan only about 58 percent. *Annals of the American Academy* 13 (January–June 1899): supplement, 111.

conditions existed in Manchuria, where there was only one American consulate, at the port of Newchwang (modern Yingkow). In the interior American merchants and missionaries were not to be found; American cottons, kerosene, flour, and lumber were sold by Europeans and Chinese; and customers identified the goods by trademarks without any idea of their place of origin. And although the consumption of American oil rose perhaps two and one-half times during the 1890s, sales of American-made lamps actually declined.[56]

These depressing circumstances were partly due to lack of enterprise at home and partly to lack of supporting facilities almost as serious as thirty years before. The British diplomatic and consular services were still larger and better paid—for example, the British minister received $32,000 a year, the American only $12,000. Americans had no consular representation on the island of Taiwan and in such thriving cities as Swatow, Wuchow, and Hangchow. Although transpacific shipping had improved, it was still greatly outnumbered by steamers on the longer Suez route to Europe. Also, banking facilities were still lacking, so American merchants still had to resort to the Hong Kong and Shanghai Bank or a French, German, or Russian institution. American mails were delivered only to Yokohama and Hong Kong, where they might be delayed for as long as two weeks. Any American trade increases in China during the 1890s still owed little to government aid.[57]

56. U.S., *Commercial Relations, 1897,* 1, 992–95. U.S., *Consular Reports* 6 (April 1881): 525; 194 (November 1896): 499–500; 200 (May 1897): 16; 234 (March 1900): 409. Denby to Bayard, April 27, 1887, no. 357; Denby to Blaine, March 21, 1890, no. 1071; Denby to Sherman, April 15, 1897, no. 2735, U.S., Diplomatic Despatches, China, 80, 87, 102. J. D. Kennedy to Porter, October 22, 1886, no. 41; Jernigan to Uhl, February 7, 1896, no. 145, U.S., Consular Despatches, Shanghai, 37, 43. Alexander C. Jones to Porter, March 22, 1887, no. 9, ibid., Chinkiang, 4. L. S. Wilcox to David J. Hill, August 12, 1899, no. 41, ibid., Hankow, 7. *Age of Steel* 62 (June 28, 1890): n.p. The British and French had even greater dreams for the development of the interior, first Yunnan and later Szechwan. Weekly *London Times,* March 4, 1887, reprinted in U.S., *Consular Reports* 81 (July 1887): 64–66. Warren B. Walsh, "The Yunnan Myth," 272–85. On Manchuria see Hunt, *Frontier Defense,* 20–21. Parsons, *American Engineer in China,* 175–76.

57. Knight, "American Trade and Investment in China," 42–43. Thomas R. Jernigan, "A Hindrance to Our Foreign Trade," 439–44. In 1896 British merchants subscribed three thousand pounds for a commercial mission to inquire into the decline of Anglo-Chinese trade. *Commercial and Financial Chronicle* 66 (January 29, 1898): 211. U.S., *Commercial Relations, 1896,* 1, 798–99; *1898–99,* 1, 1044. U.S., *Consular Reports* 177 (June 1897): 335; 192 (September 1896): 34–35, 66–68. In 1895 there were more than two hundred mail-passenger steamers on the Suez route between Shanghai and Britain, France, Germany, and Austria, not to mention the chiefly freight steamers. Ibid., 184 (January 1898): 97–99. In 1897 and 1898 respectively British and Japanese steamer companies established direct service between New York and East Asia. Ibid., 108–9. *New York Journal of Commerce,* February 18, 1898. John Fowler to Uhl, March 10, 1896, no. 183, U.S., Consular Despatches, Ningpo, 7. Edward Bedloe to Assistant Secretary of State, March 9, 1898, no. 10, ibid., Canton, 12. Jernigan to Uhl, February 7, 1896, no. 145, ibid., Shanghai, 43. On banking and postal facilities respectively see U.S., *Commercial Relations, 1896,* 1, 798–99, and U.S., *Consular Reports* 192 (September 1896): 1, 798–99; and 192 (September 1896): 34–35. For an interesting comparison of conditions in 1890 and 1896 see U.S.,

Although the United States shipped almost no raw cotton to China before 1898, plain gray and white cotton goods made up the largest export during the 1890s as before. Indeed, by 1897 China received about 43 percent of all American exports of cotton cloth. Between 1887 and 1897 American shipments to China increased by 59 percent in value, while those from Britain declined. In 1897 Britain and the United States furnished about 64 percent and 33 percent respectively of China's cotton goods imports, but Americans supplied as much as 80 or 90 percent of Chinese heavy cotton imports in the north. They had expected competition from Chinese and Japanese cotton mills within China after the Treaty of Shimonoseki permitted the Japanese to engage in industry. The Japanese, however, founded no mills before 1898, both to avoid Chinese taxes and to reserve the market for their home mills, and the Chinese production was small. By 1898 perhaps half a dozen western-owned yarn mills were operating in China against Japanese competition, mostly in Shanghai and including one owned by the American Trading Company.[58]

Although the most promising American trade in cotton goods was still largely concentrated in Manchuria and China north of the Yangtze River, the Americans were now beginning to contest British control of the Yangtze Valley market, selling mostly through local non-American merchants. As before, the chief advantage of American cottons was their high quality, compared to the heavily sized British article. The cotton export trade seemed particularly vital to American economic expansionists during the 1890s because the cotton industry of the American South was then expanding rapidly. During the depression years southern mill owners carried on a systematic search for customers and threatened ruinous competition with New England mills for the domestic market. The loss of flourishing textile sales in Madagascar after the French occupation of that island in 1897 and the growth of Russian influence in Manchuria made southerners especially sensitive to events in central and northern China.

The State Department attributed American textile sales in China to quality control. However, an important factor was lower prices, in part due to freight charges American cottons enjoyed on British steamers from New York via Liverpool or London and Suez—well below those levied on British shippers (see

Commercial Relations, 1897, 1, 992–95. The principal American companies with Chinese headquarters are listed in Campbell, *Special Business Interests*, 24n24.

58. Campbell, *Special Business Interests*, 19–20. Kang Chao, *The Development of Cotton Textile Production in China*, 106–16. Chao, "Chinese-American Cotton-Textile Trade," 11. Charles Denby, Jr., "Cotton Spinning at Shanghai," 50–56. U.S., *Consular Reports* 223 (April 1899): table opposite 560. U.S., *Commercial Relations, 1896*, 1, 792–93; *1898–99*, 1, 982–83. *Commercial and Financial Chronicle* 63 (November 28, 1896): 952. *New York Journal of Commerce*, June 9, 1896; May 27, 1898. Jack Blicksilver, *Cotton Manufacturing in the Southeast: An Historical Analysis*, 22. Hearden, *Independence and Empire*, 128–29. Percentages are based on value. The Americans did not compete in fancier grades. A British observer lamented that throughout the decade the British cotton goods trade with China remained practically stationary. He blamed the depreciation of silver. H. Kopsch, "Britain's Trade with China," 238–42.

chapter 5). After 1896 a direct British line from New York via Suez and multiple rail-water routes across the North Atlantic and the Pacific began to offset low British rates with faster service. However, the South and the Mississippi Valley, never satisfied, continued to agitate for the Nicaragua canal project.[59]

Whereas in cotton goods the Americans were gradually overtaking the British, in their other leading trade, kerosene, they could hear their rivals' footsteps approaching behind them. In 1891 American oil shipments were nearly four times as large as Russian, but the latter used bulk shipments and low prices to close the gap, even though their kerosene had a strong smell and a dangerously low flash point and Chinese prized the strong American tins as building material. Eventually Marcus Samuel, the principal merchandiser of Russian kerosene, was forced to market it in tins too. The Royal Dutch Company brought Sumatran oil in tankers to Hong Kong, where they packed it in old Standard Oil tins and advertised it as American until it had attracted a following for its cheapness. The three-way competition created much confusion and even crowded American kerosene temporarily out of some ports (for example, Amoy), but Standard's quality control, organization, and improved facilities for delivery in the interior helped offset its usually higher price. In 1897 American kerosene shipments to China totaled 48,212,505 gallons, Russian 36,924,825 gallons, and Dutch East Indian 14,212,278 gallons.[60]

In addition to cotton goods and kerosene, American exporters shipped smaller amounts of other goods to ports along the China coast. Efforts by James J. Hill and others to teach Chinese merchants how to make bread out of wheat flour increased sales especially in the south, where flour moved inland from Canton. At Shanghai a mill was built to grind American wheat. As with other products, most Chinese bought the cheaper grades, while the finer grades of American flour pleased discriminating customers more than that from locally grown wheat. Another promising American export was railroad supplies, thanks to the efforts of the Baldwin Locomotive Company, but as long as railroad projects remained on paper, so did plans for an iron and steel trade. Occasional consignments of such items as sugar, cigarettes, clocks, and watches, soap, and glass did not indicate that a dependable large market was likely, especially as British competitors did all they could to discredit American products. However, one of these, cigarettes, was des-

---

59. Campbell, *Special Business Interests,* 20–21. Daniel A. Tompkins, "Export Trade," 37–47. U.S., *Commercial Relations, 1894–95,* 6, 179; *1896,* 1, 280, 787. U.S., *Consular Reports* 234 (March 1900): 409. *Manufacturers' Record* 30 (July 31, 1896): 5. *Bradstreet's* 22 (August 25, 1894): 542; 26 (February 19, 1898): 113. *New York Tribune,* November 24, 1895. *New York Journal of Commerce,* August 28, 1896. After 1898, however, the Japanese gained on the Americans and British in Korea mainly because they studied the market better, responded to Korean tastes, and offered lower prices. Duus, *Abacus and Sword,* 284–85.

60. U.S., *Consular Reports* 145 (October 1892): 282–91; 188 (May 1896): 140; 189 (June 1896): 317; 218 (November 1898): 397–99; 216 (September 1898): 23–25; 223 (April 1899): 550. U.S., *Commercial Relations, 1894–95,* 1, 600–603; *1896,* 1, 787–89. *Bradstreet's* 24 (February 22, November 14, 1896): 120, 728.

tined for a great future. As early as the 1880s James Duke, founder of the "tobacco trust" at home, had seized on China as an eventual market. After opening a small-scale factory in 1891, he merged with a competitor in 1902 to form the British American Tobacco Company and created an unprecedented sales organization. By 1916 China was consuming four-fifths as many cigarettes as the United States.[61]

Although Korea remained nominally independent and Japan promptly re-opened Taiwan to foreign trade after establishing its rule there, its merchants and goods continued to dominate both areas. During and after the war the influx of Japanese customers, both military and civilian, into Korea and the departure of many Chinese stimulated a new trade in which Japanese manufactures replaced other foreign goods, especially textiles. In addition to operating the small-scale railroad and mining concessions already mentioned, Americans continued to sell kerosene and a little cloth to native Korean retailers and conducted a profitable rice business—a meager return on earlier hopes and Robert W. Shufeldt's efforts in negotiating the 1882 treaty.[62]

During the 1890s the State Department gave little encouragement to American merchants in either China or Korea. The American legation at Peking undertook no important diplomatic initiatives. Europeans, especially the Shanghai Chamber of Commerce, bitterly protested Chinese taxes on industry, but with the full approval of the State Department Denby gave little more than token support, as Americans had no great stake in industry. During 1896 the Chinese government proposed changes in the Western and Japanese treaties that would enable it to raise the low fixed tariff in return for concessions concerning internal navigation and taxation, but Denby could see no advantage in this arrangement for American trade. China deferred action the following year.[63]

61. Campbell, *Special Business Interests*, 23–24. Schonberger, *Transportation to the Seaboard*, 223–24. U.S., *Commercial Relations, 1896*, 1, 776. *Commercial and Financial Chronicle* 61 (August 3, 1895): 182. *New York Journal of Commerce*, November 24, 1897, 14. As late as 1899 Hill was convinced that the only obstacle to enormous wheat sales in China was high shipping costs, and he urged midwestern farmers to push for a bill subsidizing freight carriers. U.S., 56th Cong., 1st sess., *Senate Document 149*, 69. A sample of British discrediting tactics was a whispering campaign that American jars of beef extract contained drainings and refuse. *Bradstreet's* 22 (August 24, 1895): 542. On the cigarette industry see Sherman Cochran, "Commercial Penetration and Economic Imperialism in China: The American Cigarette Company's Entrance into the Market," chap. 6. Wilkins, "Impact of American Multinational Enterprise," 269–71.

62. Duus, *Abacus and Sword*, 261–65. *Bradstreet's* 24 (February 8, 1896): 81. U.S., *Consular Reports* 180 (September 1895): 34. U.S., *Commercial Relations, 1896*, 1, 864–65. Allen to Sherman, September 17, 1897, no. 3, U.S., Diplomatic Despatches, Kore, 13. *Korean Repository* 3 (October 1896): 411–13, 5 (August 1898): 308. Scott S. Burnette, ed., *Korean-American Relations: Documents Pertaining to the Far Eastern Diplomacy of the United States*, 3, 11, 61, 64, 82–83, 172, 213–14, 259, 281.

63. Paulsen, "Machinery for the Mills of China," 336–41. The Treaty of Shimonoseki forbade China to tax foreign industries, but when the Japanese decided to postpone building cotton mills in Chinese ports, they waived the provision. Vols. 100–110 of U.S. Diplomatic Despatches, China, contain Denby's correspondence on the questions of the industrial tax and the tariff raise. On the former question see especially U.S., *Foreign*

In Korea the Cleveland and McKinley administrations also followed a policy of avoiding questions that might embroil them with the rival powers. Minister John M. B. Sill, however, tried to bolster King Kojong's government against Japanese influence, especially after Japanese agents brutally murdered the Korean queen. Sill tried to encourage common action with the European diplomats, in particular a joint protest against Japanese efforts to create a formal monopoly over the Korean economy. Japan eventually abandoned the monopoly in favor of piecemeal control, but it was not clear that the diplomats had influenced its action. Both Olney and Sherman condemned Sill's anti-Japanese policy, and McKinley finally recalled him. Allen took his place and upheld United States' interests with more discretion.[64]

During the early and mid-1890s the United States rounded a turning point in its relations with the Far East. The Sino-Japanese War shockingly demonstrated the weakness of the Chinese empire and involved the United States in the complications of peacemaking. The war encouraged American investment projects, and these forced the State Department to formulate some sort of policy for supporting promotional interests. At the same time American Far Eastern trade increased, especially with Japan, despite the depression at home. Very soon Chinese weakness and new openings for business would whet the political appetites of the European powers and pose new policy decisions for the United States. Meanwhile, however, American policies in the Pacific were rounding turning points as well.

Relations, 1897, 88–89. On the latter question see especially Denby to Olney, August 29, 1896, no. 2587, U.S., Diplomatic Despatches, China, 101. When the Chinese government raised the likin tax on kerosene, Olney instructed Denby to make only a general protest, as trade did not seem to be suffering. Olney to Denby, January 27, 1896, no. 1235, U.S., Diplomatic Instructions, China, 5, 301–6. On the Chinese tariff proposal see also Bayard to Olney, November 30, 1896, no. 822, U.S., Diplomatic Despatches, Britain, 180.

64. Jeffery M. Dorwart, "The Independent Minister: John M. B. Sill and the Struggle against Japanese Expansion in Korea, 1894–1897," 497–500. Busselle, "U.S. in the Far East," chap. 4, 132–41. Burnette, ed., *Korean-American Relations*, 3, 9–13. The murder of Queen Min was aimed at Russian influence in Seoul after the tripartite intervention in 1895. LaFeber, *Clash*, 51. For details of the murder, Allen's reaction, and the State Department's reproof see Harrington, *God, Mammon, and Japanese*, chap. 17. Sill even provided asylum in the legation for Korean officials opposing Japan until Olney forbade this. Olney to Sill, December 31, 1895, January 11, 1896, January 5, 1897; Sherman to Sill, March 30, May 6, 15, June 16, 1897, nos. 130, 132, 166, 172, 179, 186, 189, U.S., Diplomatic Instructions, Korea, 1. For a detailed account of Sill's efforts at joint action with the Russian, German, and British ministers see Lensen, *Balance of Intrigue*, vol. 2, 553–74. Allen continued to warn the State Department about the Japanese threat to American business interests. Horace N. Allen to Secretary of State, September 13, 1898, August 23, 1900, nos. 133, 272. Burnette, *Korean-American Relations*, 61–64. However, he had no confidence in the survival of Korean independence and concluded that Japanese supervision was the best thing for the country. Duus, *Abacus and Sword*, 189, 206.

10

Contradictions in the Pacific

EVEN BEFORE THE Sino-Japanese War drew the United States into closer political involvement in the affairs of Korea and northern China, changing conditions in the Pacific were having a similar effect on American policies there. Developments in the North and South Pacific, however, were very different. In Hawaii the reformist constitution of 1887 seemed inadequate to protect the interests of American property owners. A group of activists launched a coup in 1893 to overthrow the royal government and establish a republic, with themselves in control. They expected prompt annexation under the expansionist Republican administration of Benjamin Harrison, but a new president, the moderate Democrat Grover Cleveland, thwarted their plans and left them on the doorstep of the American Union, waiting for a change of heart or president.

Although many expansionists regarded Samoa and Pago Pago as a mirror image of Hawaii and Pearl Harbor, American relations with the South Pacific islanders diverged sharply from those with Hawaiians. As has been seen, the abortive confrontation with Britain and Germany in 1889 was temporarily resolved at a conference in Berlin by creating a condominium, a little-tried method of joint government that proved unworkable from the beginning. By the late 1890s the American position in both Hawaii and Samoa was quite unsatisfactory, but for different reasons.

After the 1887 Hawaiian treaty was ratified, American opposition to reciprocity seemed to decline, and Hawaiian tension relaxed, as exports continued to increase slowly. H. A. P. Carter and other American-Hawaiians in the Honolulu government continued to press for more connections with the United States. One of their greatest desires was a cable to San Francisco. Admiral David D. Porter had proposed such a cable as early as 1870, and both Congress and the Grant administration had shown some interest. In 1879 Cyrus Field had obtained a Hawaiian concession and vainly sought capital in Britain for a line. Secretary of State Thomas F. Bayard personally favored the project but had to tell Carter, the Hawaiian minister, that the U.S. government could offer no more than moral support to a private promoter. Fearing British influence on King Kalakaua, Carter and Samuel G. Wilder, a steamship operator and former premier of Hawaii, also discussed with Bayard the possibility of a U.S. protectorate.[1]

As Carter hoped, the Harrison administration showed more interest in Hawaii. James G. Blaine, now secretary of state again, had long encouraged American influence in the islands, and in 1891 he told Harrison that Hawaii was one of the few places he favored annexing (Cuba and Puerto Rico being the others) and the only one that needed immediate attention. Naval strategists such as Captain Alfred T. Mahan, who favored developing the Pearl Harbor base, found a sympathetic ear in their new secretary, Benjamin F. Tracy.[2] Carter lost no time in proposing to Blaine a convention by which the two countries would be placed on a basis of complete free trade. In return, Hawaii would give the United States virtual control over its foreign affairs and accept American military intervention if necessary to preserve domestic peace—a protectorate on terms resembling the later Platt amendment for Cuba. The proposal aroused a storm of opposition in Hawaii, and King Kalakaua abandoned the project. Nevertheless, when a local insurrection occurred in July 1889, the Hawaiian government got the captain of an American warship in port to land seventy marines, who helped restore order.[3]

Probably the Harrison administration could not have secured Senate approval of such a drastic treaty in any case, for the McKinley tariff of 1890 struck a rude blow at American-Hawaiian relations by placing all sugar on the free list and granting a bounty to producers in the United States. Planters in Hawaii, now mostly American, lost all their previous advantage, and duties were even reimposed on rice and other Hawaiian products, in violation of the 1887 treaty. The islands plunged into a depression; within two years sugar prices dropped by 40 percent and property values by about $12 million. Planters seemed on the verge of bankruptcy. Carter began overtures again for a free-trade treaty, with added provisions for the prompt development of Pearl Harbor and an American-

1. Stevens, *American Expansion*, 187–88. Tate, *Hawaii: Reciprocity or Annexation?* 218, 223. Kuykendall, *Hawaiian Kingdom*, vol. 2, 208–10, 717n10. Tribolet, *Electrical Communication in the Pacific*, 157–58. *Blackwood's Edinburgh Magazine* 161 (February 1897): 289. U.S., *Foreign Relations*, 1887, 586. Memoranda of Alvey A. Adee, August 7, 1886, December 18, 1889, unsigned, undated note in Bayard's handwriting, U.S., *Notes from Hawaii*, 3. The *New York Herald* urged a cable, among other ties, to "the Malta of the Pacific." *New York Herald*, July 25, 1887, August 4. In 1891 Congress considered appropriating twenty-five thousand dollars for a cable survey. U.S., 51st Cong., 2d sess., *House Report 3774.*

2. Albert T. Volwiler, ed., "The Correspondence between Benjamin Harrison and James G. Blaine, 1882–1893," 174. Alfred T. Mahan, "The United States Looking Outward," 7, 8, 15, 26–27. Herrick, *American Naval Revolution*, 103. However, Tracy was more immediately interested in the Caribbean.

3. Tate, *Hawaii: Reciprocity or Annexation?* 222–32. Stevens, *American Expansion*, 196–99. Kuykendall, *Hawaiian Kingdom*, vol. 2, 434–47. Carter was motivated in the protectorate negotiations partly by Hawaiian alarm over the abortive Mills tariff debate of 1888, which had shown considerable support for placing all sugar imports on the free list. Weigle, "Sugar Interests," 49. American-Hawaiians suspected Canada of undermining treaty negotiations. Blaine apparently accepted their report. Volwiler, "Correspondence between Harrison and Blaine," 187–89. Tate, however, finds no supporting evidence. On the 1889 uprising see Tate, *U.S. and Hawaiian Kingdom*, 95–99.

Hawaiian cable but without a protectorate. The one-sidedness of his draft, Carter's death in the midst of negotiations, and the Republican defeat in the congressional elections of 1890 doomed the new project. Congress, however, removed duties on Hawaiian products in conformance with the existing treaty.[4]

Instead of alienating the Hawaiians from the United States, the McKinley tariff apparently stimulated annexationism by demonstrating the frailty of any arrangements based on Hawaiian independence. Blaine sought to encourage this sentiment by selecting as minister to Hawaii his friend John L. Stevens, a Maine newspaper editor, onetime diplomat, Anglophobe, and enthusiastic expansionist. It is not known whether the secretary gave Stevens the private instructions he sometimes provided his diplomats—indeed, Stevens felt on his arrival at Honolulu that some sort of protectorate might be preferable to annexation. But he knew his chief's sentiments, and in his dispatches he discoursed with mounting intensity on the islands' commercial and strategic importance, the instability of their government and polyglot society, Anglo-Canadian hostility to Americans, and the imminence of a crisis.[5]

Although Stevens exaggerated the threatening situation in Hawaii, there was indeed some cause for American uneasiness. After the constitutional reforms of 1887, the split between foreigners and native nationalists had widened. British capitalists, stimulated by the completion of the Canadian Pacific Railway, sought new investments; a rumor circulated that Britain would welcome a protectorate. In January 1891 King Kalakaua died suddenly while on a visit to the United States, and the regent, his sister Princess Liliuokalani, was peacefully crowned queen. More determined and stubborn than her brother, the new monarch was known to dislike the restrictive constitution of 1887, but the sugar baron Claus Spreckels and other American residents praised her abilities and anticipated no trouble. Stevens, however, suspected her intentions from the beginning and got a warship stationed indefinitely at Honolulu.[6]

4. Dozer, "Anti-Imperialism, 1885–1895," 190–97. Hilary Herbert, "Reciprocity and the Farmer," 416. Tate, *Hawaii: Reciprocity or Annexation?* 218–22, 232–35. Stevens, *American Expansion,* 201–2. Kuykendall, *Hawaiian Kingdom,* vol. 2, 57–59, 466–69, 487–500. Harold A. Wolf, "The United States Sugar Policy and Its Impact upon Cuba: A Re-appraisal," 19–20. *Bradstreet's* 9 (January 17, 1891): 36.

5. Pratt, *Expansionists of 1898,* 50–51. Kuykendall, *Hawaiian Kingdom,* vol. 2, 566–90. William Adam Russ, Jr., *The Hawaiian Revolution, 1893–1894,* 36–39. For samples of Stevens's reporting see U.S., 53rd Cong., 2d sess., *House Executive Document 48,* 49–51, 53–55, 84–86, 184–92; and John L. Stevens to Blaine, March 25, 1892, private and unnumbered, U.S., Diplomatic Despatches, Hawaii, 25. Although Stevens influenced events in Honolulu, most important negotiations were handled in Washington. Naval officers were reporting similar views but less aggressively. Stevens, *American Expansion,* 195–96, 208–10. Hawaiian annexationism was apparent at least by the early 1880s, to judge from a pamphlet arguing for it as a solution to the islands' commercial problems that would be more permanent and reliable than reciprocity. "Annexation" by "Not a member of the House of Nobles."

6. Tate, *U.S. and Hawaiian Kingdom,* 95–115. Kuykendall, *Hawaiian Kingdom,* vol. 2, chaps. 16–19. Rising British influence had been feared for years. J. H. Putnam to

When quarrels broke out among rival factions of the queen's cabinet, a group of American-Hawaiian businessmen and lawyers in Honolulu quietly formed a cabal to explore the possibilities of annexation to the United States, in the event that queen and native nationalists subverted the constitution and tried to rule by decree. Stevens worked enthusiastically with this Annexation Club and was a close friend of its leading spirit, Lorrin A. Thurston, a Hawaiian-born attorney with widespread investments in plantations and ranches. In April 1892 Thurston visited the United States, where he talked to congressmen of both parties and to Blaine. Harrison thought it prudent not to receive him in person, but according to Thurston he authorized Secretary Tracy to assure the Hawaiian that if the expected action (i.e., a revolution) occurred and "you people" came to Washington with a proposal for annexation, "you will find an exceedingly sympathetic administration here."[7]

Satisfied, Thurston left Blaine a statement of the Hawaiian situation as he saw it and returned home. During the summer of 1892 Congress discussed an appropriation for improving Pearl Harbor, and the Senate Foreign Relations Committee privately considered Thurston's annexation proposal. While press and public buzzed with anticipation, Secretary John W. Foster, who had succeeded Blaine, informed Thurston through an intermediary that his government would pay Queen Liliuokalani $250,000 to assign Hawaii to the United States—a ridiculously cheap offer that Thurston put aside with questions about its many unmentioned complications.

When the long-expected revolution finally began in January 1893, it was brought about by two interacting and partly indistinguishable groups, one wanting an independent Hawaiian republic and another seeking annexation to the United States. The immediate cause lay in two actions by Queen Liliuokalani. First she replaced a pro-American cabinet with a group of ill-qualified timeservers on whom she could rely. Then, and more important, she revealed her determination to proclaim a new constitution, increasing royal power and requiring all voters (i.e., foreigners wishing a share in the government) to become naturalized and

James D. Porter, July 28, 1887, no. 123, U.S., Consular Despatches, Honolulu, 17. Bayard memorandum, January 5, 1889, Bayard papers, 135, 27551–59 ff. During Kalakaua's visit to the United States the rumor spread that he had come to offer annexation and thus slip within the McKinley tariff barrier. *Literary Digest* 2 (December 13, 1890): 190.

7. Stevens, *American Expansion*, 203–8. Tate, *U.S. and Hawaiian Kingdom*, 115–21 (quotation on 117), 140–41, 146–48. Kuykendall, *Hawaiian Kingdom*, vol. 2, 508–14, 532–40. On Stevens's association with the Annexationist Club see Russ, *Hawaiian Revolution*, 56–57, 98–101. The authority for Harrison's assurance is Lorrin A. Thurston, in his *Memoirs of the Hawaiian Revolution* (Honolulu, 1936), 230–32. Russ accepts this evidence, Russ, *Hawaiian Revolution*, 57–58. One writer arrives at a diametrically opposed conclusion—that Harrison was reluctant to approve annexation and did so only after the arrival of the treaty. George W. Baker, Jr., "Benjamin Harrison and Hawaiian Annexation: A Reinterpretation," 295–309. On Foster's role see Michael J. Devine, "John W. Foster and the Struggle for the Annexation of Hawaii," 29–50. Devine believes that Foster took over direction of American policy toward Hawaii during Harrison's "lame duck" period.

take an oath of loyalty to her. On advice of her ministers and others she did not proclaim the constitution at once, but this was expected at any time. The queen's actions would not have produced an immediate revolution without the existence of the well-prepared Annexationist Club, confident of Harrison's favor and urged to move by the U.S. minister, John L. Stevens. Neither Stevens nor Thurston and his colleagues would have felt compelled to act at once if Cleveland had not won the American presidential election two months earlier, ending the regime of the hospitable Harrison at March 4 and raising serious doubts about U.S. actions under the Democrats.[8]

Most historians agree as to the immediate and intermediate causes of the revolution; they tend to disagree as to the most important underlying cause. Some emphasize a set of politico-social factors. One was a desire for a better government than the native monarchs could provide, a desire sometimes camouflaged by a distaste for the queen's morals. (In particular, she was said to be anti-Christian.) Related to this was prejudice against the native race by a minority of property-owning foreign whites who wanted more control over the government. A partly conflicting factor was alarm at the replacement of the declining native population by orientals, imported to supply cheap labor, and a conviction that annexation to the United States, which excluded lower-class Chinese immigrants, would ensure white supremacy in Hawaii.[9]

Historians have usually given special emphasis to economic factors without agreeing as to how they operated. Early writers accepted the argument of anti-annexationists in the United States that sugar producers had started an annexationist revolution to obtain the bounty on their product offered by the McKinley tariff to American planters—that, as the *New York Herald* put it, "Spreckels & Co." was at the bottom of any trouble in the sugar islands. The real situation was much more complex, for during the late 1880s Spreckels had balanced his Hawaiian cane sugar interests with beet sugar lands and refineries in California. He blew hot and cold on annexation, opposing it in 1891, favoring it in 1892 and early 1893, and opposing it again from May 1893 until the question had been settled.

Most important of all, the sugar trust now controlled the industry in California as the result of the arrangement of 1892 with Spreckels. Although little is known

8. On the queen's actions see Pratt, *Expansionists of 1898,* 77–80; and Tate, *U.S. and Hawaiian Kingdom,* 134–35, 155–58. On the effect of Cleveland's election see Pratt, *Expansionists of 1898,* 74.

9. The good government thesis is developed by Julius A. Pratt in "The Hawaiian Revolution: A Reinterpretation," 273–94, especially 294. It is less prominent in his book. See also Tate, *Hawaii: Reciprocity or Annexation?* 242–45. Other charges against the queen involved her support for a lottery law and her acceptance of a law licensing the sale of opium. The significance of anti-Oriental prejudice is given most prominence in William Adam Russ, Jr., "The Role of Sugar in Hawaiian Annexation," 339–50. For the history of the labor problem see Rowland, "United States and the Contract Labor Question," 249–69. The white supremacy thesis is partly refuted in Richard D. Weigle, "Sugar and the Hawaiian Revolution," 43–44, on the grounds that most of Russ's evidence came from the period after January 1893.

of the trust's attitude toward the revolution, it would seem to have had no reason to desire a change, for its sugar business on the West Coast was much more profitable than in the East, thanks to a rebate from Hawaiian planters and a system of rigged prices. At the same time in Hawaii two of the other seven leading sugar planters besides Spreckels opposed annexation consistently, and most others were lukewarm or reluctant revolutionists. The only unreserved annexationist in the group was absent during the revolution. Many sugar planters, including Spreckels, weighed the sugar bounty against fears that American laws would shut off the oriental labor supply. A more convincing economic interpretation suggests that, like Thurston, the active core of revolutionists represented property owners, professional men, and investors who saw no hope of ending the Hawaiian depression without better government and a closer connection with the American sugar market. As in the case of American annexations earlier in the century, there was undoubtedly also a crust of speculators eager for a rise in property values.[10]

The course of the revolution was considerably simpler than its causes; it lasted two days and was almost entirely bloodless. Action was precipitated by the queen's announcement that the new constitution would be introduced by legal procedure. At once a committee of safety formed by the Annexation Club carried out plans already discussed with Stevens and Captain G. C. Wiltse of the American cruiser *Boston,* then in port. Wiltse landed 154 marines to restore order—whether at Stevens's instruction or on his own initiative is not clear. One company guarded the U.S. legation; the rest took up a silently menacing position near the royal palace. (The marines also engaged in a few brawls with British sailors in port.) On the following day the committee formed a provisional government, almost entirely American-Hawaiian, with the prestigious Judge Sanford B. Dole as president, and declared the monarchy at an end. Instead of resisting, the queen withdrew her forces, probably outfaced by the marines, and let the provisional government occupy Aliiolani Hale, the traditional government buildings. Thereupon, as he had earlier agreed to do, Stevens recognized Dole's regime. During the next week the European governments followed suit, with Britain last. On January 18 Dole appointed a committee to negotiate an annexation treaty in Washington.[11]

10. For a thoroughgoing discussion of the economic question see Weigle, "Sugar and the Hawaiian Revolution," 41–58. Pratt also refuted the bounty thesis in *Expansionists of 1898,* 156–60. Russ, *Hawaiian Revolution,* 196–98. Spreckels's shifts are indicated in Adler, *Claus Spreckels,* 219, 226–27, 232–33, 241, 247–49, 253–55, 325–26n16, and Thomas J. Osborne, *"Empire Can Wait": American Opposition to Hawaiian Annexation, 1893–1898,* 17–23. Spreckels told the journalist Charles Nordhoff that the revolution was a "complete surprise" to him. *New York Herald,* May 13, 1893, quoted in Osborne, *"Empire Can Wait,"* 20. See also his statements in *North American Review* 152 (March 1891): 291, and *New York Herald,* May 4, 1893. During the queen's brief reign Spreckels's company lent her government ninety-five thousand dollars. Tate, *Hawaii: Reciprocity or Annexation?* 250. See also Adler, *Claus Spreckels,* chap. 21. For an analysis of the Hawaiian-California sugar trade in 1893 and the pricing activities of the sugar trust see *New York Journal of Commerce,* September 19, 1893.

11. Tate, *U.S. and Hawaiian Kingdom,* chap. 5. Russ, *Hawaiian Revolution,* chap. 3. Pratt, *Expansionists of 1898,* chap. 3. Hugh B. Hammett, "The Cleveland Administration

Uncertain of the future, the provisional government asked Stevens to raise the American flag and place the islands under temporary protection. He gladly complied and sent off the annexation committee with glowing accounts of their respectability and that of the revolution in general. Chartering a steamer, they raced to San Francisco, put their version of the revolution into the newspapers of January 28, and arrived in Washington on February 3 to begin negotiations with Foster. The secretary welcomed them cordially enough but disavowed Stevens's protectorate, being fully aware of congressional sensitivity. The treaty that he and the Hawaiians drew up provided for the cession of Hawaii as "an integral part of the territory of the United States" and for the extension of American laws concerning revenue and commerce to the islands within a year. However, it omitted several provisions, such as ones for statehood and a cable, that the Hawaiians desired but Foster thought too controversial. The queen and her heir were given indemnities, and the United States assumed $3.25 million of the Hawaiian debt.

For a few days in mid-February private, informal polling suggested that two-thirds of the Senate favored annexation, and on February 15, a little over two weeks before he was to leave office, Harrison submitted the treaty to the Senate. Soon, however, politicians and newspaper editors began to have second thoughts, reinforced by the arrival of Queen Liliuokalani's representative, Paul Neumann, who lobbied effectively for a full hearing of both sides. After a consultation with the incoming President Cleveland and his advisers, Democratic senators joined the doubters en masse and held up the treaty's approval.[12] Five days after inauguration, still uncertain of his course, Cleveland withdrew the Hawaiian treaty for further examination, as he had done eight years earlier with Arthur's Nicaragua canal and Spanish reciprocity treaties. He was suspicious about the background of the revolution and uncertain about the queen's rights and Hawaiian public opinion. His secretary of state, Walter Q. Gresham, went further, for he opposed the annexation of colonial territory as unconstitutional and felt that the action

---

and Anglo-American Naval Friction in Hawaii, 1893–1894," 28. On Dole's background and role see Damon, *Dole and His Hawaii;* and Helena G. Allen, *Sanford Ballard Dole, Hawaii's Only President, 1844–1926.* Fifteen out of eighteen members of the executive and advisory councils were first- or second-generation American-Hawaiians; six still claimed American citizenship. Russ, *Hawaiian Revolution,* 90.

12. Tate, *U.S. and Hawaiian Kingdom,* 194–205, 214–18. Russ, *Hawaiian Revolution,* 123–42. Pratt, *Expansionists of 1898,* 110–23. Osborne, *"Empire Can Wait,"* 5–9. Other Hawaiian desiderata omitted from the treaty were provisions for the development of Pearl Harbor and for continued admission of Chinese contract laborers into Hawaii. Devine, "Foster and the Annexation of Hawaii," 40–43. Rowland, "United States and Contract Labor," 262–64. For the text of the treaty as submitted see U.S., 52d Cong., 2d sess., *Senate Executive Document 76,* 28–40. There is some evidence of opposition to the treaty by Louisiana and western sugar interests, but the principal student of the sugar interests does not believe that they played a decisive role in the defeat of the 1893 treaty. Instead, they were more concerned about the 40 percent sugar duty in the Wilson-Gorman tariff. Weigle, "Sugar Interests," 107–8, 117–18, 122.

of the Harrison administration in subverting the Hawaiian people's rights was morally wrong.[13]

While Thurston and the other Hawaiian commissioners lobbied the administration, Congress, and the press, Cleveland appointed James A. Blount, recently retired from the chairmanship of the House Foreign Affairs Committee, as special commissioner to visit Hawaii and report on the revolution and the provisional government. The president gave Blount "paramount" authority over all American affairs in Hawaii. The Republican opposition and most of the people assumed that only a fact-finding mission was involved, but Blount believed that Cleveland wanted him to set things right if he could.

As soon as he arrived, therefore, Blount ended the protectorate, ordered the marines back to their ship, and replaced the Hawaiian flag. He spent more than four months in Hawaii, resisting all blandishments by the annexationists, listening to everyone, and saying almost nothing himself. In a series of reports Blount traced the origins of the revolution and built up a convincing case against Stevens for making it successful. Blount concluded that the natives opposed annexation by a majority of at least two to one and predicted that the provisional government, resting only on military force and the approval of a small white minority, would fall within a year or two if not aided.[14]

13. The conventional interpretation—that Cleveland was unalterably opposed to imperialism—is presented in Allan Nevins, *Grover Cleveland, a Study in Courage*, chap. 30. The evidence for a different view during his first administration comes from a series of articles by Frederic Emory, a State Department official, cited in LaFeber, *The New Empire*, 208–9. LaFeber and Hans-Ulrich Wehler, both critics of American expansionism, believe that Gresham preferred economic control over Hawaii—markets without the burden of governance—especially after the Wilson-Gorman tariff reopened the United States to Hawaiian sugar. Ibid., 203–9. Wehler, *Aufstieg*, 249–50. Calhoun rejects this interpretation and denies that Gresham was primarily influenced by economic considerations. Calhoun, *Gilded Age Cato*, Introduction, especially 4–6, also 134–36. Charles W. Calhoun, "Morality and Spite: Walter Q. Gresham and U.S. Relations with Hawaii," 295–96. (This passage is omitted from *Gilded Age Cato*.) See also Osborne, *"Empire Can Wait,"* chap. 2 and passim; and Alfred L. Castle, "Tentative Empire: Walter Q. Gresham, U.S. Foreign Policy, and Hawaii, 1893–1895," 83–96. For Gresham's own thinking on the subject see his letters: Walter Q. Gresham to Bayard, October 29, December 17, 1893; to Noble C. Butler, November 23, 1893; to John Overmeyer, July 25, 1894, Gresham papers, Letterbook, 146–53, 158–59, 171–74, 272–74, box 48. Gresham, Harrison, and Foster were all veterans of Republican politics in Indiana, and the first two had been bitter rivals.

14. Tennant S. McWilliams, "James H. Blount, Paramount Defender of Hawaii," in Tennant S. McWilliams, *The New South Faces the World: Foreign Affairs and the Southern Sense of Self, 1877–1950*, chap. 1. See also Castle, "Tentative Empire," 86–87. Tate, *U.S. and Hawaiian Kingdom*, 218–23, 228–37; Russ, *Hawaiian Revolution*, chap. 5; and Pratt, *Expansionists of 1898*, 124–25, 129–37. Blount's culminating report, dated July 17, 1893, is in U.S., *Foreign Relations, 1894. Appendix 2,* 567–605. For more details on the Blount mission see U.S., 53d Cong. 2d sess., *Senate Report 227.* Since Blount was a Georgian, his impartial treatment of racial questions involved was remarkable. During his visit Spreckels tried to discredit the provisional government by foreclosing a loan, hoping to force the government into bankruptcy. Russ, *Hawaiian Revolution*, 302–4. Adler, *Claus Spreckels,* 235–52.

This devastating judgment amply confirmed the suspicions of Cleveland and Gresham and made them determined to block annexation. At first the administration considered the possibility of reinstating the queen on her throne, and Gresham tried to hint at the use of force. An American public outcry blocked this line of action, however, and the queen rejected any thought of amnesty to the rebels. By the time she relented, Provisional President Dole, encouraged by the American outcry, rejected U.S. intervention, creating an impasse. In a special message of December 18 Cleveland laid out the whole problem and then, instead of dismissing the Hawaiian question, referred it to Congress, which conducted hearings and discussions for five months—gnawing at it, as Thurston remarked, like a dog with a bone. Finally the members left the Hawaiians to determine their own government, with the warning that the United States would regard outside interference as an unfriendly act. More pointedly, Gresham got Britain to replace an overly aggressive minister and remove its warships from Hawaiian waters by undertaking to protect British lives and property.[15] Meanwhile in Hawaii, Dole and his officials established a "permanent" de jure republic and in January 1895 handily suppressed a royalist uprising that Gresham had indirectly encouraged. By then the secretary's inability to dislodge the Dole regime and his vindictive contempt for it had offset whatever value his moral stand had in American eyes.[16]

The events just described called forth a foreign policy debate in Congress and the American press lasting several years and anticipating the even greater debates over both Hawaii and the Philippines between 1897 and 1900. No one can say how many people followed the arguments carefully—probably not more than one-fifth. Among business groups the strongest supporters of annexation were California merchants and bankers, and related interests all over the country that stood to gain from complete free trade with Hawaii. The strongest business opponents were beet sugar producers in Nebraska and California, although the

15. Tate, *U.S. and Hawaiian Kingdom*, 237–42. Russ, *Hawaiian Revolution*, chaps. 6, 8. See also his conclusions condemning both Harrison and Cleveland. Ibid., 349–51. For Gresham's actions see Calhoun, *Gilded Age Cato*, 148–57. Pratt, *Expansionists of 1898*, 137–45, 174–87. LaFeber, *New Empire*, 207–8. Osborne, "*Empire Can Wait*," chaps. 6, 8. The frustrations of Cleveland and Gresham were compounded in Honolulu by the weakness and inexperience of their minister, Albert S. Willis. While the queen always opposed recognition of the provisional government, her authorized representative had earlier told Secretary Foster that she would not object to a U.S. protectorate or annexation but preferred the former. Report of interview between Foster and Paul Neumann, February 21, 1893, Harrison papers, ser. 1, reel 38. For Cleveland's message see Richardson, *Messages and Papers*, vol. 9, 460–72.

16. A new constitution was proclaimed (without vote) that kept the government in the hands of the white minority. The uprising was made possible when the United States finally withdrew its warship from Honolulu Harbor. Apparently, it was tacitly encouraged by Gresham. There were no executions after it was suppressed, but the government took the occasion to deport its worst enemies. Pratt, *Expansionists of 1898*, 188–200. William Adam Russ, Jr., *The Hawaiian Republic, 1894–1898*, chaps. 1, 2. Calhoun, *Gilded Age Cato*, 156–61.

latter were not yet strong enough to overpower the state's mercantile bloc. In contrast, Louisiana cane sugar producers were less vocal, and the *New Orleans Times-Democrat* supported annexation on strategic grounds. The sugar trust kept silent but may have favored annexation, since it had a beneficial five-year contract with Hawaiian planters.[17]

Among politicians there seems to have been strong, bipartisan sentiment for annexation in February and early March 1893 as the only reasonable alternative to foreign domination of the islands, but when Cleveland set out to repudiate the actions of the Harrison administration, the press divided, mostly along party lines. In 1894 and 1895 Democratic opposition to Cleveland's apparent indecisiveness grew, probably because partisan editors feared a Republican victory in 1896. From the beginning such Republican newspapers as the *New York Tribune, Press, Commercial Advertiser,* and *Mail and Express,* the *Washington Post,* and the *Chicago Tribune* campaigned for annexation, as did Democratic papers such as the *New York Sun* and *World,* the *Atlanta Constitution,* and (in especially exaggerated language) the *Kansas City Times.* Independents such as the *New York Herald,* the *New York Evening Post,* and the *Boston Herald* and liberal journals such as the *Nation* and *Harper's Weekly* supported Gresham's anti-annexationist position. (Indeed, the *New York Herald* sent to Hawaii a special correspondent, Charles Nordhoff, whose investigations paralleled those of Blount and strongly influenced Gresham, Carl Schurz, and many others.) The Democratic *New York Times,* at first skeptical, soon joined the opposition. Many other Democratic papers fought annexation throughout.[18]

While it is impossible to estimate the size of various opinion groups, a survey of the principal arguments used will indicate the complex interweaving of economic and noneconomic issues. The most important annexationist argument concerned the strategic position of Hawaii, both for developing transpacific trade and for defending the U.S. coastline, and the danger that Britain or possibly Germany or Japan might somehow take over control if the United States hesitated. The

17. Pratt, *Expansionists of 1898,* chap. 5. Osborne, *"Empire Can Wait,"* 23–27, 90. Weigle, "Sugar Interests," 99–101. The principal sugar beet grower, Henry T. Oxnard, was associated with the sugar trust and worked closely with Spreckels. On the sugar trust's Hawaiian contracts see testimony of William E. Simpson, a commission merchant and promoter. U.S., 58th Cong., 2d sess., *Senate Document 231,* 1143, *New York Journal of Commerce,* September 17, 1896.

18. George F. Pearce, "Assessing Public Opinion: Editorial Content and the Annexation of Hawaii—A Case Study," 328, 330–34. Ralph Dewar Bald, Jr., "The Development of Expansionist Sentiment in the United States, 1885–1895, as Reflected in Periodical Literature," 196–99, 253–54. J. E. Wisan, *The Cuban Crisis as Reflected in the New York Press, 1895–1898,* 35–36. For summaries of the first positions taken by leading newspapers see *Washington Post,* January 30, 1893; and Russ, *Hawaiian Revolution,* 113–20. For more general surveys of newspaper attitudes see Tate, *U.S. and Hawaiian Kingdom,* 205–7; Stevens, *American Expansion,* 237–39; and Dozer, "Anti-Imperialism, 1865–95," 203–4, 217–19. San Francisco newspapers also divided, the *Morning Call* and the *Bulletin* supporting annexation and the *Chronicle* and *Newsletter* opposing it. On the Nordhoff investigation see Osborne, *"Empire Can Wait,"* 140–41n20.

New York Tribune pointed to surplus manufactures and invoked the need for new markets in South America, Australia, and the Far East. To obtain these, the United States must control isthmian transit, and that control in turn would require a defense post in Hawaii. The navalist Admiral Alfred T. Mahan devoted an entire article to the strategic advantages of Hawaii, linking annexation of the islands with construction of the Nicaragua canal and equating commercial and naval strategy. Admiral George E. Belknap and Commodore George Melville developed the naval arguments and warned against letting Britain establish a "Pacific Bermuda," reinforced from Vancouver Island, "connected by cable with Downing Street, and stored with munitions of war." The naval officers, especially Mahan, greatly influenced congressional expansionists. Many annexationists regarded Hawaii as merely the first in a chain of acquisitions: Canada, Mexico, Cuba, Santo Domingo, St. Thomas, and Samoa. (Few if any mentioned the Philippines.)[19]

In support of these basic arguments were others, at least in part rationalizations. Some echoed Manifest Destiny and European racism to proclaim Anglo-Saxons "the colonizing . . . the pioneer race," impelled by a duty to inferiors. Others inveighed against the immorality and cruelty of the queen, "the Messalina of the Pacific," doing the bidding of the sugar magnates, and praised the provisional government as "far-seeing businessmen." Others thought it un-American to help destroy a republic and force "a bedraggled and rejected dynasty . . . upon an unwilling people." A commission merchant wrote that the American assertion of paramount interests in Hawaii carried "a responsibility for maintaining law and order . . . to the end that no other power shall have cause for 'domestic interference.'" (This argument, applied to Latin America, was soon to bring forth the Roosevelt Corollary to the Monroe Doctrine.) Perhaps the most strained arguments were those that emphasized national reputation or honor—that the United States would lose face among nations if it faltered or that it was unpatriotic to haul down "Old Glory," once raised.[20]

19. *New York Tribune,* January 29, February 17, and especially February 21, 1893. An even better example linking commercial expansion, naval strategy, and Anglophobia is a speech by Representative William F. Draper (Republican, Massachusetts). U.S., 53d Cong., 2d sess., *Congressional Record,* 26, 1844–49. *Special Economist* 6 (June 1894): 361. Draper was also head of a firm manufacturing textile machinery. *Dictionary of American Biography,* vol. 3, 441–42. For a general discussion of the strategic factor see Allen Lee Hamilton, "Military Strategists and the Annexation of Hawaii, 81–91. Alfred T. Mahan, "Hawaii and Our Future Sea Power" (originally published in March 1893), reprinted in his *Interest of America in Sea Power,* 32–55. Letter of George E. Belknap, January 30, 1893, to *Boston Herald,* reprinted in U.S., 53d Cong., 1st sess., *Senate Report 227,* 169–71. For other examples of these arguments see *Literary Digest* 6 (February 11, 1893): 413; 9 (June 18, 1894): 187; and *North American Review* 160 (March 1895): 374–77. For a sample of concern about Japan see *Public Opinion* 15 (May 20, 1893): 169. A few extremists advocated annexation in preparation for a final showdown war with Britain. J. H. Sturgeon to Harrison, January 31, 1893, Harrison papers, ser. 1, reel 39. On further annexations see *San Francisco Call,* January 29, 1893, and *New York Tribune,* January 29, 1893, as cited in Pratt, *Expansionists of 1898,* 150–51.

20. *Christian Union,* February 18, 1893, as quoted in Stevens, *American Expansion,* 236. On the queen see Robert R. Hitt (Republican, Illinois) in U.S., 53d Cong., 2d sess.,

While the anti-annexationists were just as prone to rationalize or exaggerate as annexationists, at least four plausible groups of arguments against acquiring Hawaii can be found in their writings. In the first place, they said, action against the legal government and against the wishes of a popular majority on the islands would violate American traditions and international morality and probably the U.S. Constitution as well. By condoning a labor system that amounted to slavery, the Republican party would repudiate its whole Reconstruction policy toward the South. (Ironically, Spreckels was now opposing annexation precisely in order to preserve this labor system!) Liberal anti-annexationists felt that, at the very least, Hawaiians should be given a free vote on their fate in a plebiscite. After a tour through the Pacific, Asia, and Africa, Mark Twain incorporated these arguments into a blanket denunciation of European imperialism.[21]

Second, opponents of annexation called it "a huge business speculation," arranged by the sugar tycoons, despite the denials of Thurston and Dole, and offering "a heaven for our adventurers," carpet-baggers, and pork-barrel politicians. Third, they said, one annexation would lead to another until the United States had added a variety of noncontiguous territories difficult to administer and millions of degenerate tropical inhabitants impossible to dilute with Anglo-Saxons because these would not survive in the tropics. The islands, said Carl Schurz, would be not a bulwark but an "Achilles heel." Many insisted that the United States had enough territory. (For this reason some who opposed outright annexation were willing to accept a protectorate over Hawaii.)

Finally, many anti-annexationists countered their opponents' commercial and strategic arguments, declaring that in the predictable future the Atlantic, not the Pacific, would remain "the great middle sea of the world's commerce." Anyway, the United States could enjoy Hawaiian resources and harbors without assuming the responsibilities of government. The *Nation* went even further: "We do not believe that the American flag in the middle of the Pacific will make American goods either any cheaper or more desirable to the inhabitants of Australia or China and Japan, or will lower freight charges or do any of the other things that create a foreign market." As for the danger of European or Japanese attack, anti-annexationists quoted a former minister to Hawaii who thought it "extremely

---

Congressional Record, 26, Appendix, 440; Henry Cabot Lodge, "Our Blundering Foreign Policy," 8; and Pratt, *Expansionists of 1898,* 162–71. (Pratt also vindicates the queen.) *Literary Digest* 6 (February 11, 1893): 412; 8 (November 25, 1893): 78. Edward N. Brewer to "Dear Fred," November 18, 1893, Carl Schurz papers, 110, 24201–53 ff. *Public Opinion* 15 (April 22, 1893): 70. *Review of Reviews* 9 (May 1893): 515.

21. The best summary of the anti-annexationist arguments is Osborne, *"Empire Can Wait,"* chaps. 4, 5. See also *Literary Digest* 6 (February 11, 1893): 412. *North American Review* 156 (May 1893): 282–86. *Nation* 56 (February 23, March 16, 1893): 136–37, 190. *Forum* 15 (June 1893): 394–99. Gresham to Butler, November 23, 1893; to Bayard, December 17, 1893; to Overmyer, July 25, 1894, Gresham papers, Letterbook, 146–53, 158–59, 171–74, 272–74, box 48. Jacob D. Cox to Gresham, February 2, 1894, Cleveland papers, ser. 2, reel 82. Burton, *John Sherman,* 293–94. Both Harrison and Cleveland agreed that a plebiscite would be desirable. Philip S. Foner, *Mark Twain: Social Critic,* 242–46.

remote." They might have pointed out that the navy apparently agreed with them, for until 1898 it left its depot at Honolulu in charge of the American consul general there.[22]

Although many arguments for and against annexation defy exact appraisal, the danger of foreign intervention in 1893 and 1894 can be simply dismissed—there was none. American fears received some encouragement from Stevens's lurid reports of rumors, from the tactless Anglophobe statements of Admiral John G. Walker, commander at Honolulu, and from a veiled and baseless hint of the Dole regime that if the United States failed to act, it might turn to London. To be sure, Canadian nationalists, proud of their new transcontinental railroad and eager for trade with South America and Australia, complained that American control of Hawaii would cut their trade lanes and, in particular, prevent the laying of a cable across the Pacific.

The European press took a more hostile view toward annexation than the various cabinets. In Berlin the *Deutsche Rundschau* suggested that in compensation the United States should abandon its pretensions in Samoa. In Britain a few individuals and newspapers, largely Conservative, grumbled that it would be intolerable to see "another Tahiti" (a French protectorate) created in the central Pacific. However, the principal Liberal organ, *The Speaker*, encouraged approval of American actions as a step toward an Anglo-American entente. William E. Gladstone's government both publicly and privately assured Washington that it would not protest and that in its opinion the interests of British residents would be adequately protected under American rule, if this should come about. The French, German, Russian, and Japanese governments similarly indicated their acquiescence in annexation or an American protectorate.[23]

The five-year waiting period between Cleveland's rejection of annexation and the Spanish-American War brought prosperity as well as uncertainty to Hawaiian-

22. *New York Journal of Commerce*, April 6, 1895. *Baltimore Sun*, November 16, 1893. *Charleston News and Courier*, February 18, 1893, in *Literary Digest* 6 (February 25, quoted phrase): 469. Ibid. (March 11): 511. *Public Opinion* 16 (November 23, 1983): 189. *Nation* 56 (February 9, March 2, 1893): 96, 154. (The sentence quoted appears in the issue for March 2.) Carl Schurz, "Manifest Destiny," *Harper's New Monthly Magazine* 87 (October 1893): 737–45. *Harper's Weekly* 35 (February 25, March 18, April 15, 1893): 170, 246, 342. (The last two editorials were supposedly written by Schurz.) Seward W. Livermore, "American Naval Policy in the Far East, 1860–1914," 115.

23. Stevens, *American Expansion*, 240–45. Russ, *Hawaiian Revolution*, 38–43, 118–19, 158–63. Osborne, *"Empire Can Wait,"* 42–44. *Deutsche Rundschau*, March 1893, in *Literary Digest* 6 (March 25): 582–83. Merze Tate, "Great Britain and the Sovereignty of Hawaii," 539–44. Robert Lincoln to Foster, February 3, 10, 17 (telegrams), February 4, 1893, no. 907, U.S. Diplomatic Despatches, Britain, 173. The February 4 dispatch contains clippings from the principal British newspapers, including the mentioned editorial in *The Speaker*. See also Henry Vignaud to Foster, February 3, 1893, no. 129, ibid., France, 108; Andrew D. White to Foster, February 14, 1893, no. 58, ibid., Russia, 44; and Charlemagne Tower to John Sherman, June 29, 1897, no. 5, ibid., Austria, 42. Walker caused so much ill feeling in Hawaii that Cleveland recalled him. Hammett, "Cleveland Administration and Anglo-American Friction," 30. Russ, *Hawaiian Republic*, 38–41.

American relations. When Congress passed the Wilson-Gorman tariff of 1894, taking sugar off the free list and ending the bounty to American producers, it automatically restored the Hawaiian advantage under the 1887 treaty. Production continued to slump in 1895, probably because of the general depression, but during the next two years it increased sharply, as did exports to the United States, to replace Cuba's declining sugar production. By this time four American steamship lines, one Canadian, and one Japanese connected Honolulu and San Francisco with sixteen ships. In 1895 the American consul general at Honolulu observed that for the first time a significant tonnage of Hawaiian sugar was being shipped around Cape Horn to New York, mostly by Spreckels and the sugar trust.[24]

During the mid-1890s the question of a cable line between Hawaii and the North American mainland became both critical and complex. A. S. Hartwell obtained an extensive concession with a twenty-five-thousand-dollar subsidy from Hawaii in 1891 and organized a company in San Francisco but failed to get either a franchise or a subsidy from the American government. The American navy made preliminary soundings, but even after the Hawaiian revolution demonstrated the need for rapid communication with the islands, Congress was unwilling to guarantee construction costs.

Meanwhile Britain, which had long desired a Pacific cable to the Far East, approached the Hawaiian government for cession or lease of Necker islet, about 270 miles northwest of the main island group, as a landing base for a cable from Vancouver to Sydney. In the ensuing three-way negotiations the United States refused to approve alienation of Hawaiian territory (as it had a right to do under the 1875 treaty), and although Cleveland favored leasing the islet to a British company, Congress, led by Senator Henry Cabot Lodge, would not go even that far. The Senate Committee on Appropriations added a rider to the annual diplomatic and consular appropriation bill, granting $500,000 toward cable construction, but after much argument between the two houses, this was voted down. The press and public were divided between the expansionists' fear that a British cable would endanger all American influence in Hawaii and the anti-expansionists' conviction that the cable would be useful and might as well be laid by British capital as by American.[25]

24. The New York shipment was made by W. G. Irwin and Company, agents of the Western Sugar Refining Company (in which both Spreckels and the sugar trust had an interest), to the American Sugar Refining Company (official name of the sugar trust). U.S., *Consular Reports* 176 (May 1895): 169; 182 (November 1895): 386. Sugar production reached 224,218 long tons in 1896–1897. In 1897 Hawaiian exports to and imports from the United States amounted to $13,687,799 and $6,800,028 respectively. U.S., *Reciprocity and Commercial Treaties,* 122, 131, 133. *Commercial Relations,* 1895–96, 1, 1006–7.

25. Russ, *Hawaiian Republic,* 248–61. Philip E. Koerper, "Cable Imbroglio in the Pacific: Great Britain, the United States and Hawaii," 114–20. Lorrin A. Thurston, *Memorandum by L. A. Thurston Concerning a Pacific Cable, Honolulu, April 17, 1895.* Tribolet, *Electrical Communications in the Pacific,* 160–63, 168–70. "The All-British Transpacific Cable," 269–75. The question of the cable lease also became involved in Anglo-French rivalry in the Pacific, since the French were planning a cable line from New Caledonia to the United[4]

The Hawaiian government, eager for a cable but afraid of endangering annexation, awarded a concession to a group of Americans headed by a longtime resident of the islands, Colonel Zephaniah S. Spalding, who then formed the Pacific Cable Company of New Jersey with a distinguished list of stockholders including James J. Hill and Abram S. Hewitt. Almost at once a rival concern appeared, the Pacific Cable Company of New York, headed by James A. Scrymser, creator of the principal hemispheric cable system, and backed financially by J. P. Morgan and Company. Early in 1896 supporters of each company introduced a funding bill in Congress. The Senate Foreign Relations Committee reported in favor of the Spalding company, the House Committee on Interstate and Foreign Commerce in favor of the Scrymser company. In the end, the two projects killed off each other, and Hawaii did not obtain its cable until 1903.[26]

Although Cleveland considered the annexation question settled by 1894, Gresham never reconciled himself to an independent Hawaii, and Republicans in Congress, led by Senator Lodge, kept annexationism smoldering, aided by the cable issue, the abortive monarchist revolt of 1895, and rumors about filibusters and Japanese subversion. In March 1895 Lodge published an article, "Our Blundering Foreign Policy," a broadside against the Cleveland administration for worldwide "retreat and surrender," using Hawaii as a leading issue but also featuring the isthmian canal and Cuba. Lodge wrote with the campaign of 1896 in mind, of course. When this began, William McKinley, the Republican nominee, emphasized domestic issues and seems to have known or cared little about Hawaii, but the Republican platform stated that Hawaii should be "controlled" by the United States, and McKinley's victory was interpreted in both the United States and Hawaii as encouragement to the annexationists. Led by Senator Frye and former secretary Foster, they set out to educate the president-elect on the attractions of the islands.[27]

States. See press clippings enclosed with Bayard to Gresham, January 11, 1895, no. 372, U.S., Diplomatic Despatches, Britain, 179. The American minister, Harold M. Sewall, took the lead in warning against the British project. See, for example, Harold M. Sewall to John Sherman, September 23, 1897, no. 48, U.S., Diplomatic Despatches, Hawaii, 29. For Lodge's views, justifying the cable on strategic grounds, see U.S., 53d Cong., 3d sess., *Congressional Record*, 29, 3084. For refutation see ibid., 3077. For American press views about British rivalry see *Public Opinion* 18 (January 17, 1895): 52–53; *Literary Digest* 10 (January 28, 1895): 363–64; *New York Journal of Commerce*, February 14, 1895; *Outlook* 55 (January 6, 1897): 230–31; *New England Magazine* 16, n.s. (July 1897): 594–95; and *Review of Reviews* 15 (February 1897): 139. The *Nation* anticipated an eventual public expenditure of three million dollars, for which it thought there was neither public sentiment nor any possible excuse, *Nation* 60: 133, 156.

26. Others interested in the Spalding project included Grenville N. Dodge and D. O. Mills. As a young man, Spalding had been a private agent for Secretary Seward, reporting on reciprocity sentiment in Hawaii. See chap. 3, note 13. A. S. Hartwell served as advance agent of the Scrymser interests. The line was eventually laid by John W. Mackay's Commercial Cable Company. Russ, *Hawaiian Republic*, 271–79. Tribolet, *Electrical Communications in the Pacific*, 170–86. *New York Journal of Commerce*, December 9, 17, 20, 1895.

27. Pratt, *Expansionists of 1898*, 200–208, 215–16, 326. Tate, *U.S. and Hawaiian Kingdom*, 258–70. Russ, *Hawaiian Republic*, 124–28. Lodge, "Our Blundering Foreign Policy,"

Several factors favored a renewed annexationist effort in 1897. McKinley showed himself receptive to a treaty, perhaps as a means of satisfying jingoes and diverting public attention from the sensitive Cuban question. His administration included expansionists such as Theodore Roosevelt (assistant secretary of the navy) and John Hay (ambassador to Britain), who were much influenced by Mahan's strategic arguments. Plans were under way to revive the campaign for a Nicaragua canal, which had obvious relevance to the Hawaiian question. Just as important, American and Hawaiian annexationists had taken alarm at the growing power of beet sugar producers in California and Nebraska, who were strengthened by an alliance with Claus Spreckels, now extensively engaged in producing sugar beets. The annexationists realized that time might work against them. Indeed, when the Dingley tariff came up for debate in Congress during the spring, only McKinley's submission of an annexation treaty to the Senate seems to have prevented these sugar interests and other protectionists from using the bill to abrogate the reciprocity treaty and place a duty on Hawaiian sugar.[28]

The annexation treaty was drawn up secretly by Lorren A. Thurston and other Hawaiian envoys with John W. Foster. While similar to that of 1893, it was shorter and somewhat less favorable to Hawaii. Secretary of State John Sherman signed it on June 18. The sudden submission of the treaty to the Senate surprised everyone, for McKinley had earlier indicated that he would settle the tariff question before taking up Hawaii.[29]

The administration's change in timing was mainly a response to a crisis in Hawaiian-Japanese relations that came to a head in the late spring and involved the

---

8–17. McKinley had some personal interest in the islands, for his brother David had been U.S. consul at Honolulu and then Hawaiian consul at San Francisco.

28. Pratt, *Expansionists of 1898*, 215–19. Tate, *Hawaii: Reciprocity or Annexation?* 251–52. Tate, *U.S. and Hawaiian Kingdom*, 270–75. Russ, *Hawaiian Republic*, 124–28, 178–93. Herrick, *American Naval Revolution*, 199. *Review of Reviews* 15 (June 1897): 696. Historians disagree as to McKinley's attitude toward the revived treaty. LaFeber, *New Empire*, 368. Stevens, *American Expansion*, 290–91. May, *Imperial Democracy*, 122–23. Osborne, "Empire Can Wait," 154–55n36, 163–64n58. Weigle, "Sugar Interests," 125–38. On reciprocity and McKinley's intervention see reports from the Hawaiian minister, Francis N. Hatch, to his government. Russ, *Hawaiian Republic*, 15n54, 186–89; and Stevens, *American Expansion*, 285–86. For the influence of beet sugar interests see Weigle, "Sugar Interests," 128–35. *Review of Reviews* 15 (June 1897): 696. On Spreckels's ties with beet sugar see Thomas J. Osborne, "Claus Spreckels and the Oxnard Brothers: Pioneer Developers of California's Beet Sugar Industry, 1890–1900," 18–25. Spreckels was the more opposed to reciprocity because his five-year contract with Hawaiian planters was just ending. Osborne, "Empire Can Wait," 87. He urged abrogation on the ground that reciprocity favored European and Far Eastern interests in Hawaii to the detriment of California producers and labor. *San Francisco Call*, April 17, 1897, reprinted in U.S., 55th Cong., 2d sess., *Congressional Record*, 21, 6611–12. For other comments see *Public Opinion* 22 (May 6, 1897): 35–53; and *New York Journal of Commerce*, April 12, 1897.

29. For the text of the treaty see U.S., 55th Cong., 2d sess., *Senate Report 681*, 96–97. Instead of an integral part of the United States, Hawaii was merely designated as a territory, and no indemnities were provided for the queen or her heir. However, the allowable Hawaiian debt was increased to four million dollars.

United States in its first confrontation with modern Japan. The original cause of the crisis was Hawaiian alarm at the rapidly increasing Japanese population of the islands. Under a treaty of 1886 Hawaii admitted unlimited Japanese contract labor, with the result that between 1883 and 1896 Japanese residents increased from 116 to 24,407, and orientals came to form nearly half of Hawaii's total population. Given the outburst of Japanese nationalism following the Sino-Japanese War of 1894–1895, many in Hawaii and the United States feared that the imperial government sought to capture the islands by infiltration.

In February and April 1897 the Dole government, moved by a kind of panic and counting on American support, refused to admit two shiploads of immigrants on trumped-up excuses, whereupon the impetuous Japanese minister made probably unauthorized threats of coercion. Tokyo sent a warship to "show the flag" at Honolulu, and the United States increased its forces there. The State Department instructed its new minister, Harold M. Sewall, in a cipher telegram dated July 10, that if Japan resorted to force, he should land troops and declare an American protectorate over the islands. Admiral Alfred T. Mahan advised the Navy Department not to wait for provocation but to seize them at once. His chief, Secretary John T. Long, hitherto lukewarm, was converted to annexation, and a bill was introduced in Congress for the prompt development of Pearl Harbor. It was under these strained circumstances that McKinley decided on an immediate annexation treaty as a warning to Tokyo.

The suddenness of the action made the situation worse, for the Japanese minister at Washington was unprepared for the announcement. He formally protested the move on the grounds that it would endanger the peaceful status quo in the Pacific, curtail the rights of Japanese residents of Hawaii, and encourage Hawaii to put off settling outstanding Japanese claims, including those arising from the rejection of the contract laborers. Underlying this protest was Japan's chief objection—that annexation would place Hawaii under American tariff and navigation laws, thereby hurting Japanese trade and shipping. It is possible that the protest was intended largely for home consumption, and Japan explained that it had no territorial claim on the islands. Nevertheless, the possibility of an argument over a Hawaiian indemnity further increased the tension.

Secretary Sherman replied temperately that Japan had no reason to be surprised at the imminence of annexation and encouraged Hawaii and Japan to submit the new immigration claims to arbitration. The two countries found themselves unable to agree on a basis, but the American minister at Tokyo managed by the end of the year to obtain assurances from the Japanese Foreign Office that it had no objection to the American annexation of Hawaii. By that time the Japanese warship at Honolulu had been recalled, and the crisis subsided. American press comments on the imbroglio showed much suspicion regarding the intentions of "ambitious and arrogant" Japan, but Japanese writings suggest that Tokyo's intentions regarding Hawaii were limited to expansion of trade.[30]

---

30. This account is based on Thomas A. Bailey, "Japan's Protest against the Annexation of Hawaii," 46–51; Russ, *Hawaiian Republic*, chap. 4; and William Michael Morgan,

The renewed discussion of Hawaiian annexation in the American press brought out all the arguments pro and con made familiar in the earlier debate of 1893–1894, but with certain changes of emphasis occasioned by the rise of the western sugar beet industry, the Cuban revolution, European and Japanese encroachments in China (see chapter 11) and the recent Japanese protest. Expansionist journals such as the *New York Tribune*, the *Review of Reviews*, and *Overland Monthly* redoubled their efforts. While business interests were still much divided on the subject, the San Francisco Chamber of Commerce was as annexationist as ever, and *Bradstreet's* and the *New York Commercial* linked the Hawaiian question to the spread of American influence in China. Representing Hawaiian annexationists, Thurston prepared a handbook full of well-rehearsed arguments, and in January 1898 President Dole visited the United States to add his authoritative views.

The Far Eastern situation was the most important addition to the annexationists' arsenal. Mahan's exposition of Pacific Ocean strategy now embraced an Armageddon-like struggle between Western and Eastern civilizations, in which Hawaii would be a vital Western outpost. Lodge and Senator Cushman K. Davis (Republican, Minnesota), the chairman of the Foreign Relations Committee, associated the islands with the expansion of Far Eastern trade against European competition and cited their value in protecting a future Nicaragua canal as a shortcut to China. James Harrison Wilson, a promoter interested in Chinese railroads, wrote of the islands as a "naval station and a halfway house" to the "commerce of the Pacific islands and of the countries beyond." John Barrett, recently minister to Siam, predicted that annexation, added to a Pacific cable and a Nicaragua canal, would develop a flourishing cotton trade between the American South and East Asia. Some strategists warned that American control of Pearl Harbor rested only on the reciprocity treaty, which might be abrogated at any time. Such national concerns, they argued, outweighed the merely local interests of western sugar growers. As the crisis with Spain worsened, the possibility of American annexation of Cuba, with its ability to

---

"The Anti-Japanese Origins of the Hawaiian Annexation Treaty of 1897," 23–44. See also Thomas J. Osborne, "The Main Reason for Hawaiian Annexation in July, 1898," 161–64. The background of the Japanese immigration is set forth at length in Hilary Conroy, *The Japanese Frontier in Hawaii, 1866–1898*, chaps. 1–9. For extracts from Japanese press comments see *Public Opinion* 23 (July 29, 1897): 138–39; and *Literary Digest* 15 (August 7, 1897): 442. A brief modern account based on Japanese sources is Iriye, *Pacific Estrangement*, 48–54. For the navy's view see Herrick, *American Naval Revolution*, 198–201; and William Reynolds Braisted, *The United States Navy in the Pacific, 1897–1909*, 11–14. For samples of Hawaiian and American alarm at the Japanese "threat" see *Independent* 49 (April 22, 1897): 502; *Public Opinion* 22 (April 22, 1897): 488–89; 23 (July 1, 1897): 5–8; and *Literary Digest* 15 (July 17, 1897): 334–35. Some Americans felt that the Dole government had abetted the crisis in order to hasten annexation. Weigle, "Sugar Interests," 136–37. On the interaction of the Japanese and sugar questions see *Review of Reviews* 15 (June 1897): 656. Just before final annexation and on pressure from Washington, the Dole government paid Japan seventy-five thousand dollars to settle the 1897 immigration claims. The bill to develop Pearl Harbor died because of technical problems.

produce sugar more cheaply than Hawaii, gave added urgency to annexationist arguments.[31]

The anti-annexationists also reflected the earlier debate with a few new elab-
orations. The group included an even broader range of exponents than before:
Carl Schurz, Edwin L. Godkin, speaker Thomas B. Reed, the elder statesmen
Grover Cleveland and George S. Boutwell, the historian Hermann E. von Holst,
and even the English Yankeephile James Bryce. These writers decried the value of
colonies and bases, opposed any effort to amalgamate Anglo-Saxons and natives,
and thought annexation immoral, unconstitutional, and strategically foolish. In
particular, Schurz denied that Hawaii would strengthen American merchants in
faraway China, and the *New York Times* argued that a coaling station in China
would be preferable. Reed entitled a trenchant article "Empire Can Wait." The
Commercial and Financial Chronicle added the voice of business to his strictures
against colonies. Especially in California, organized labor, which had been little
interested in the Hawaiian question before 1897, now attacked the moral and economic threat of cheap contract labor and Hawaiian orientals and annexationism
as a threat to American isolation and democracy. (A few spokesmen, however, saw
in the islands, if annexed, a new job market for Americans.) Most farm editors
protested mildly.

Undoubtedly the best organized opponent of annexation at this time was the
lobby formed by Spreckels and other beet sugar refiners of California. Its members
predicted that annexation would increase the output of Hawaiian sugar and ruin
the beet industry, and they accused the McKinley administration of going back on
its party's promise to rescue them from foreign competition. Privately the refiners
offered beet growers higher prices if annexation were defeated. However, Secretary
of Agriculture James Wilson, thought to be a strong supporter of beet sugar,
shocked the lobby by declaring that Hawaii did not contain enough good land
to offer serious competition to American growers. As has been seen, throughout
the annexation struggle the position of the sugar trust remained unclear.[32]

31. Pratt, *Expansionists of 1898*, 222–24. Tate, *U.S. and Hawaiian Kingdom*, 273–79,
287–88. Russ, *Hawaiian Republic*, 202–3, 208–19, 222–24, 229–38, 240–41. LaFeber, *New
Empire*, 365–66. Wehler, *Aufstieg*, 255. Alfred T. Mahan, "A Twentieth Century Outlook"
(originally published in May 1897), reprinted in *Interest of America in Sea Power*, 217–68.
See also a speech by Senator Frye to the National Association of Manufacturers. *New York
Tribune*, January 28, 1898. John R. Proctor, "Hawaii and the Changing Face of the World,"
34–45. John T. Morgan, "The Duty of Annexing Hawaii," 1–16. John Barrett, reprinted
in U.S., 55th Cong., 2d sess., *Congressional Record*, 31, 5909. *North American Review* 156
(December 1897): 759. *Review of Reviews* 15 (June 1897): 656–57; 18 (January 1898):
12–13. *Public Opinion* 22 (June 24, 1897): 771–73. *New York Tribune*, January 10, 12, 15,
1898. During the congressional debate an American syndicate completed the purchase of
Molokai Island in Hawaii. *New York Times*, February 13, 1898.

32. Osborne, *"Empire Can Wait,"* 85–103. Tate, *U.S. and Hawaiian Kingdom*, 285–86,
288–92. Pratt, *Expansionists of 1898*, 254–57. Russ, *Hawaiian Republic*, 183–89, 375–76.
Weigle, "Sugar Interests," 141–46. E. Berkeley Tompkins, *Anti-Imperialism in the United
States: The Great Debate, 1890–1920*, 97–103. John C. Appel, "American Labor and the
Annexation of Hawaii: A Study in Logic and Economic Interests," 1–18. Dementev, *USA:*

When McKinley submitted the 1897 treaty to the Senate, that body was in special session to consider the tariff and did not take up the treaty before adjournment. During the interval before the regular session of Congress, groups of pro- and anti-annexationist congressmen visited Hawaii, and Senator Morgan even delivered a speech to a group of Hawaiians on the blessings of union with the Great Republic. When Congress again convened, the Senate debated the treaty off and on in executive session between December 1897 and March 1898, but other issues kept intruding, such as the silver question in January and the sinking of the *Maine* in February.

By the end of the latter month the annexation treaty had made such little progress that its supporters introduced a joint resolution to bypass it. This had the advantage of requiring only a majority vote but forced the issue into the House as well, where Speaker Reed was an implacable opponent. Senator Davis delivered a strong speech for annexation, and a majority of the Senate Foreign Relations Committee reported the joint resolution favorably, proposing twenty leading objections and answering them at length, but it drew a red herring across the debate by accusing Britain and Japan of intriguing against the proposal. (The Japanese minister delivered a fifteen-page protest to the State Department.) In the House annexation was occasionally debated during January and February without reaching any conclusions, but the Senate's joint resolution was not introduced there, and soon war measures occupied the attention of both houses. However, the Senate kept the treaty pending as a warning to other nations.[33]

The reasons for the failure of the second annexation effort were many: public apathy and the persistent fear of creating a "new empire" overseas, the developing crisis over Cuba, McKinley's lukewarm leadership, the lack of expected Populist support, and strong though not unanimous opposition from labor, business, and especially the beet sugar interests.[34] As will be seen in the next chapter, the needs and emotions of the war strengthened annexationist arguments, but further

Imperialists and Anti-Imperialists, 247–49. Stephen M. White, "The Proposed Annexation of Hawaii," 723–36. Schurz, "Hawaii and the Partition of China," 75. James Bryce, "The Policy of Annexation," 385–95. William B. Reed, "Empire Can Wait," 713–14. *Commercial and Financial Chronicle* 64 (May 1, June 26, 1897): 841, 1205–7; 65 (August 14, November 20, 1897): 278, 975. For other attacks on annexation see *Public Opinion* 22 (June 24, 1897): 771–73; *Nation* 64 (June 24, 1897): 468; 65 (August 5, December 16, 1897); and 66 (February 3, 1898): 80; and *Springfield* (Massachusetts) *Republican* (December 12, 1897), as reprinted in U.S., 55th Cong., 2d sess., *Congressional Record*, 31, 6270. Concerning the obscure position of the sugar trust on annexation see Osborne, *"Empire Can Wait,"* 24, 27, 90, 118, 153n18; Weigle, "Sugar Interests," 147–28; and *New York Journal of Commerce*, April 26, 1897.

33. Russ, *Hawaiian Republic*, 194–95, 206–9, 224–38, 240–47. Osborne, *"Empire Can Wait,"* 103–7. Pratt, *Expansionists of 1898*, 219–20, 225. Tate, *U.S. and Hawaiian Kingdom*, 282, 284–88. LaFeber, *New Empire*, 307–9. U.S., 55th Cong., 2d sess., *Senate Report 68*. See especially the arguments for naval and commercial expansion reprinted on 100–107 and 113–16.

34. Stevens, *American Expansion*, 290–91. Tate, *Hawaii: Reciprocity or Annexation?* 252–53.

weeks of debate were required before Congress finally approved the annexation of Hawaii by passing the joint resolution in July.

During the 1890s the experimental government in Samoa was headed in a very different direction. From the beginning the new condominium displayed most of the weaknesses of the old joint protectorate and some others too. More than a year elapsed after the Berlin treaty before the new officials were ready to function; most knew little or nothing about Samoa. The two principal Americans, Henry C. Ide (land commissioner and then chief justice, 1893–1897) and William Lea Chambers (who succeeded Ide in both positions), were effective enough, but the original chief justice, a distinguished Swedish lawyer, and the original president of the municipal council, a German nobleman, got along badly with the native government. There were many disputes over jurisdiction, especially between the municipal council and the land commission. The Samoan people were unenthusiastic about the puzzling, complicated arrangement; the worn-out, passive king, Maliatoa Laupepa, was thoroughly discredited; and the pretender Mata'afa and his supporters impatiently awaited their chance to obtain control. The three consuls sometimes cooperated with the newcomers but more often criticized and intrigued against each other. As if these troubles were not enough, a highly articulate observer reported developments in biting articles to the *Times* of London—Robert Louis Stevenson, who had come to Samoa for his health and had fallen in love with the "easy, merry, and pleasure-loving" natives.[35]

The condominium's greatest success was the work of the land commission in untangling and settling the myriad claims of the preceding two decades. The Berlin treaty had specified that bona fide purchases directly from Samoans before 1879 would be honored. After much labor the commission confirmed about 56 percent of German claims (mostly held by the DHPG company and dating back to the Godeffroy firm), only about 3 percent of British claims, and only about 7 percent of American claims (21,000 acres out of 302,746, nearly all having originated with the Central Polynesian Company.) Other problems received patchwork solutions, such as the debased currency, the municipal revenues, and the everlasting smuggling of firearms. The last-named became especially serious, for in 1893 Mata'afa revolted, supported verbally by Stevenson. After a devastating civil war the authorities persuaded the rebel to surrender, and British and German warships took him and his principal followers into exile on the Marshall Islands.[36]

35. Ryden, *Foreign Policy in Samoa*, 522–28, 533, 540–41, 549. Gibson, *Samoa, 1830 to 1900*, 415–24. Holstine, "American Diplomacy in Samoa," 231–36. Stevenson's letters to the *Times* and to others in England are reprinted in the 1969 edition of *A Footnote to History*, 253–315. An account of the condominium emphasizing international politics is Kennedy, *Samoan Tangle*, chap. 3. Annexationist sentiment was strong in Germany, and some even favored outright seizure.

36. Ryden, *Foreign Policy in Samoa*, chap. 14. Gibson, *Samoa 1830 to 1890*, chap. 16. For a more detailed and less friendly account see Vagts, *Deutschland und die Vereinigten Staaten*, vol. 1, 681–797. Holstine, "American Diplomacy in Samoa," 236–38.

While the condominium fumblingly kept order in Samoa, the United States made a few half-hearted efforts to increase its own stakes on the islands. In 1890 the Harrison administration instructed a naval lieutenant and the American consul to survey and acquire lands around Pago Pago Harbor. They made a few purchases before Mata'afa's civil war reduced the area to chaos. In 1891, encouraged by a congressional bill providing for mail subsidies, Claus Spreckels's Oceanic Steamship Company instructed its two San Francisco–Sydney steamers to make regular calls at Apia both ways. These somewhat offset the monopoly of scheduled steamer connections hitherto held by Australia and New Zealand.[37]

Nevertheless, a comprehensive report in 1895 by former consul James H. Mulligan showed no advancement of American interests. Copra prices had fallen to the lowest level in many years; the small coffee culture had been wiped out by a blight; and experiments in cotton growing had failed. The only active corporation, the DHPG, had reduced its operations, and although it released no public reports, the American consul noted that it had paid only a small dividend in 1893 and none at all in 1894. Americans owned few coconut lands except for the scanty confirmed holdings of the defunct Central Polynesian Company. Out of the 255 whites on the islands there were only 10 Americans. Two of the five leading import and retail firms were American. In 1894 the United States probably supplied nearly three-fourths of Samoan imports, although exact figures are unobtainable since most American goods came to the islands via Australia and New Zealand. All in all, Mulligan thought that the United States should maintain its influence in Samoa and develop Pago Pago, considering the likelihood of an isthmian canal in the near future.[38]

During the condominium period enthusiasm in the United States also burned low. In 1893 a merchant gathered together an exhibition of Samoan canoes and other artifacts, which, with a party of natives, he displayed at the Columbian Exposition in Chicago to publicize the islands, despite the disapproval of the State Department. After the Chicago fair he exhibited them at another exposition in San Francisco and toured other western cities. In 1897 the *North American Review* published an article by Judge Ide setting forth the expansionists' doctrine

37. On Pago Pago see Sewall to Wharton, October 17, 1890, January 19, 1891, nos. 40, 60; W. Blacklock to Josiah Quincy, April 25, 1893; Blacklock to Edwin F. Uhl, February 26, 1894, nos. 272–74, U.S., Consular Despatches, Apia, 17, 19. On the Oceanic Company's steamers see Sewall to Wharton, May 22, 1891, no. 100, and Blacklock to Wharton, September 12, 1891, no. 130, ibid., 19, and U.S., *Consular Reports* 191 (August 1898): 715–17. In 1892, hearing rumors that Britain was considering a coaling station at Samoa, Secretary Foster privately warned London away from Pago Pago, U.S., *Foreign Relations, 1892,* 243–46.

38. U.S., *Consular Reports* 191 (August 1896): 645–748. Mulligan made the report just after his resignation from his post, because of many inquiries the department had received from Americans interested in emigrating to Samoa. He strongly discouraged them. *Public Opinion* 21 (August 27, 1896): 269. Trade figures for 1890–1891 give a similar American proportion. Those for 1897 reduce it to less than three-fifths. U.S., *Consular Reports* 133 (October 1891): 233. U.S., *Commercial Relations, 1898,* 1, 1228. For a British consular report see *Bradstreet's* 22 (September 22, 1894): 596–97.

that China, Japan, Siberia, and the rest of the Pacific basin would furnish a "measureless traffic" in the eastern United States via the transcontinental railroads and the eventual isthmian canal. With the British empire paying subsidies of $4 million a year for steamship and cable communications in the Pacific and all South Pacific island groups but Samoa under European control, the United States must exploit its advantage at Pago Pago. "Samoa," he declared, "stands as a sentinel and outpost in that vast southern sea, just as Hawaii does in the northern. If it is appropriated by any foreign power, we have no foothold left south of the equator."[39]

Walter Q. Gresham, who became Cleveland's secretary of state in 1893, disagreed with this proposition as he disagreed with the Republicans' assumptions about Hawaii. Hoping to end the condominium, he took the occasion of Mata'afa's revolt to suggest a new conference to Britain and Germany. Despite Bayard's contrary arguments, Gresham managed to persuade Cleveland to reconsider the interventionist actions of his first administration that had led to the Berlin treaty. After getting administration senators to request documents and information, the secretary sent the Senate in May 1894 a devastating report on the United States' policy in Samoa since the late 1870s, as an apt illustration of its "impulse to rush into difficulties that do not concern it, except in a highly imaginary way." Cleveland urged Congress to approve unilateral withdrawal from the condominium, but Senator John T. Morgan (Democrat, Alabama), the patron of the Nicaragua canal, who feared for the Pago Pago naval base, swung the Foreign Relations Committee against the proposition. After Gresham's death, his successor, Richard Olney, took up a more aggressive policy elsewhere and ignored Samoa.[40]

Congressional and press comment on the condominium divided largely along party lines. Lodge predictably included Samoa as part of Cleveland's "blundering foreign policy," attacking both Bayard in the first administration and Gresham in the second. Republican newspapers denounced what they called Cleveland's cowardice and antipathy to foreign trade and tried to play up British and German satisfaction at American indecision. The Democratic and independent press called for noninvolvement and insisted that if the United States really needed a coaling station at Pago Pago, it could maintain one even if some other power controlled the other islands of the group, since the 1878 treaty antedated the condominium.

39. Blacklock to Assistant Secretary of State, March 28, 1893, no. 285, with memorandum by Adee disapproving the exhibition project; James H. Mulligan to Uhl, December 31, 1895, no. 93, U.S., Consular Despatches, Apia, 21. Henry C. Ide, "Our Interest in Samoa," 155–73 (quoted words on 160, 161). Statement of Charles Gibson to German minister in Vagts, *Deutschland und die Vereinigten Staaten,* vol. 1, 745.

40. Charles W. Calhoun, "Rehearsal for Anti-Imperialism: The Second Cleveland Administration's Attempt to Withdraw from Samoa, 1893–1895," 209–24. Calhoun, *Gilded Age Cato,* chap. 9. Walter Q. Gresham to the President, May 9, 1894, U.S., *Foreign Relations, 1894,* Appendix 1, 504–13 (quoted phrase on 504). Gresham to Schurz, July 11, 1893, Schurz papers, 107. Adee too recommended withdrawal. Memorandum of January 29, 1896, attached to Mulligan to Uhl, November 1, 1895, no. 79, U.S., Consular Despatches, Apia, 22. See also Vagts, *Deutschland und die Vereinigten Staaten,* 768–69.

The *Nation* denied that trade followed the flag: "Trade in our time follows cheapness and durability." It warned against "a growing disposition to shirk domestic reforms by means of a vigorous foreign policy to be carried out by a large navy."[41]

By 1897 no one was satisfied with the Samoan situation, for the condominium needed drastic revision if, indeed, it could be saved at all.[42] After the Hawaiian revolution of 1893 the German government again vainly proposed a three-way division by which it would obtain all of Samoa except Tutuila, the United States would keep Tutuila and be confirmed in its expected annexation of Hawaii, and Britain would receive Tonga, where the DHPG was closing out its interests. At the same time British cooperative sentiment was fading. Neither of the European powers approved American expansionism, but neither could afford to antagonize the Washington government.[43] When McKinley entered office, the ultimate partition of the Samoan group was dimly perceived on all sides, but its realization would depend on several external factors: American-Spanish relations in the Pacific, the fate of Hawaii, and the ebb and flow of Anglo-German rivalries, especially in Europe.

41. Lodge, "Our Blundering Foreign Policy," 10. For surveys of press comment, including some remarks on Mulligan's 1895 report, see *Literary Digest* 9 (May 26, 1894): 95; and *Public Opinion* 21 (August 27, 1896): 369–70. *Outlook* 49 (May 19, 1894): 858. *Harper's Weekly* 37 (June 23, 1894): 578. *Nation* 59 (February 22, May 17, 24, 1894): 132–33, 358–59, 380; 60 (April 11, 1895): 269 (quoted phrases, 57, 133). For a survey placing the Samoan situation in the whole context of American Pacific policy see *Review of Reviews* 9 (May 1894): 516–19.

42. For authoritative local appraisals of the condominium see Ide, "The Imbroglio in Samoa," 687–92; and H. J. Moore to Adee, January 25, 1898, U.S., State Department, Miscellaneous Letters, roll 989. Vagts, *Deutschland und die Vereinigten Staaten*, vol. 1, 780–90.

43. Kennedy, *Samoan Tangle*, 112–13. The British felt that in such a deal only Germany would gain something that it did not practically hold already.

11

The Catalyst of War

B Y THE LATE 1890S American policies in eastern Asia and the Pacific islands were poised as if on a watershed. Along the China coast the imperial government's weakness had been laid plain for all to see. Newly powerful Japan and the always menacing European nations seemed ready to close in on the helpless Chinese. Americans could not be sure how these outside threats would affect their growing trade interests and investment hopes, especially in northern China and Manchuria, the foci of international attention. In the Pacific prospects seemed brighter but still posed problems for the president, State Department, and Congress. The Hawaiian Republic was ready for American annexation if only the well-reasoned opposition of anti-imperialists could be overcome. In Samoa the condominium experiment had proved a failure, but the British and German partners seemed willing to consider a division of the islands.

Among these unresolved forces and policies, the Spanish-American War served as a kind of catalyst, speeding up a denouement and partly changing its direction. Although the war was only indirectly brought about by Pacific or Far Eastern factors, it profoundly influenced developments in that part of the world through the largely unplanned American annexation of the Philippines. Little considered by policy makers before 1898, the great archipelago, numbering more than seven thousand islands, was Spain's most important possession west of the American continents. Since it was inhabited by a mixture of alien peoples and held a strategic position off the south China coast, its occupation posed an immediate problem to the United States and plunged it further into Far Eastern politics. The war also led at once to the annexation of Hawaii and several Spanish islands of the mid-Pacific. Soon the war's influence and changing patterns in European international affairs brought about the division of the Samoan Islands as well.

Six months before the war began a crisis drew American attention to eastern Asia. Until late 1897 it had seemed possible to restrict Western and Japanese ambitions in China to the field of trade and investments. In November, however, Germany seized the long-coveted port of Kiaochow on the south coast of the Shantung peninsula, using as an excuse the murder of two German missionaries nearby. Russia, always eager for a warm-water base, might have offset this German gain with a Korean port, as Li Hung-chang, indeed, had advised in 1896. Instead it chose to send warships to Port Arthur, at the tip of the Liaotung peninsula, dominating the approaches to Peking, while its diplomats opened a long correspondence over compensations.

There followed a winter of tension in European capitals, especially between Russia and England, which feared for its trade in central China. Between February and July 1898 impotent China surrendered "spheres of influence" to all who asked. Germany received the lease of Kiaochow and economic concessions in Shantung, while Russia got the lease of southern Liaotung, including a naval base at Port Arthur, the commercial harbor of Dairen, and a rail connection to the Russian east-west line in central Manchuria. The British then insisted on a base at Weihaiwei, on the north coast of Shantung, from which they could offset Russian influence over Peking and keep a watchful eye on the Germans. Britain sought no economic concessions in Shantung but obtained a ninety-nine-year lease of Kowloon, the shoreline opposite Hong Kong, and guarantees to ensure its economic supremacy in the Yangtze Valley. France secured a base at Kwangchow in southern China and increased economic rights in Yunnan. The Japanese, more vengeful toward Russia than ever, turned toward Britain for countervailing support.[1]

The reactions of American diplomats to the German-Russian advances at Kiaochow and Port Arthur were mixed. Americans had considerable trading interests in both Shantung and Manchuria. The new American minister to Russia, Ethan A. Hitchcock, seemed to feel that the prospect of orders for American railroad supplies and coal in Manchuria would offset any dangers from increased Russian influence there. Denby at Peking had already reported the spread of Russian influence in Manchuria and suggested that American promoters try to cultivate Russian goodwill instead of always turning to Britain. The American consuls at Amoy and Chefoo, however, protested vigorously to Washington against probable German exclusionism in Shantung. They cited the case of Yung Wing, a naturalized Chinese-American who had applied for a railroad concession running through the western part of Shantung province, which the Germans rejected. Li Hung-chang was reported to favor the concession as a means of challenging the German monopoly, but the State Department refused to admit Yung Wing's citizenship or support his claim. After trying in vain to get British support, he gave up.[2]

---

1. Langer, *Diplomacy of Imperialism,* vol. 2, chap. 14. Malozemoff, *Russian Far Eastern Policy,* 93–112. McCordock, *British Far Eastern Policy,* chap. 4. Leonard K. Young, *British Policy in China, 1895–1902,* chaps. 3, 4. However, Russia partly placated Japan by recognizing its preeminent economic rights in Korea. Zabriskie, *American-Russian Relations,* 43–44.

2. Zabriskie, *American-Russian Relations,* 44. Young, *Rhetoric of Empire,* 70–71, 89–90. K. Kawai, "Anglo-German Rivalry in the Yangtze Region," 415, 418–19. Ethan A. Hitchcock to John Sherman, February 8, 1898, no. 36, U.S., Diplomatic Despatches, Russia, 51. Hitchcock was a businessman who had long worked for Olyphant and Company in China

At first Washington took a generally calm view of the whole power shift. Secretary Sherman may have been glad to see a strong stand taken against attacks on missionaries. (This was certainly the reaction of American missionaries in China.) Sherman, retreating a bit from Olney's position on supporting American investments, had recently cautioned Denby not to play up the financial resources of the American China Development Company (see chapter 9). Also, the secretary had received assurances from Germany and Russia that they would not discriminate against the trade of others, and he and McKinley were much concerned with the Cuban question by the end of 1897. A cabinet meeting of December 24 let it be known that the government would take no immediate action, and after New Year's Day Sherman even told the press that in his opinion American trade would benefit from European spheres of influence. Leading congressmen made similar statements. For a time even Denby in Peking shared the satisfaction of the missionaries, but in January he reverted to economic fears and predicted that European partition of China would destroy American business: "Divided into parcels under the control of European nations freedom of trade will not exist. . . . Our missionaries will disappear. The greatest market of the world, which we are just grasping, will be lost to us."[3]

Denby's warning matched the spirit of American business expansionists much better than Sherman's casual optimism. During the depression of the mid-1890s the Sino-Japanese War had revived the myth of the Golden East, and with prosperity returning in 1896 and 1897, China was made to seem the solution to the American problem of surplus production, especially for the rapidly growing textile industry of the New South and the older mills of New England. John Barrett, the dynamic young minister to Siam, urged the establishment at San Francisco of an Asiatic publicity center modeled on the Philadelphia Commercial Museum,

---

and also had railroad connections in the United States. Charles Denby, Jr., to Richard Olney, May 26, 1898. Charles Denby to Sherman, April 2, 1897; February 19, 21, 28, 1898, nos. 2728, 2873, 2975, 2880. Edwin H. Conger to John Hay, December 7, 1899, no. 109, ibid., China, 101, 102, 104. John Goodnow to J. B. Moore (August 31, 1898), no. 47, U.S., Consular Despatches, Shanghai, 44. John Fowler to William R. Day, December 7, 1897; March 15, April 11, August 10, 20, 1898, nos. 52, 67, 74, 92, 95, U.S., Consular Despatches, Chefoo, 3. *San Francisco Bulletin,* March 16, 1898. Clipping in U.S., State Department, Miscellaneous Letters, file microcopy 179, roll 994. Yung Wing had been educated at Yale and was well known in the United States. Hitchcock was right about Russian orders for American locomotives and railroad supplies, which materialized later in the spring. Hitchcock to Sherman, April 9, 1898, no. 28, U.S., Diplomatic Despatches, Russia, 52. *New York Journal of Commerce,* May 28, 1898.

3. McCormick, *China Market,* 97–98. Young, *Rhetoric of Empire,* 87–88, 94. Campbell, *Special Business Interests,* 30. *Washington Post,* December 25, 1897. Sherman to Denby, March 8, 1897, no. 1404, U.S., Diplomatic Instructions, China, 5, 424. Denby to Sherman, January 31, February 14, March 19, 1898, nos. 2858, 2867, 2889, U.S., Diplomatic Despatches, China, 103. (The quotation is taken from the dispatch of February 14.) The commander of the navy's little squadron on the China coast, Rear Admiral Frederick V. McNair, was passive about the European threat, but Commodore George Dewey, who succeeded him in December 1897, shared Denby's developing alarm. Braisted, *U.S. Navy in the Pacific, 1897–1909,* 19.

which was about to set up a permanent showroom for American products in Caracas. The consul at Chefoo suggested that chambers of commerce, export and manufacturers' associations, and all other business groups with interests in the Far East subscribe to a special fund to establish showrooms, an information bureau, and an American newspaper in China. Francis B. Loomis, although just appointed minister to Venezuela, wrote to Assistant Secretary William B. Day that it was time for the State Department to shift its trade emphasis from Latin America to the Far East.[4]

These rising expectations for American influence in China coincided with a number of alarming developments all over the world that seemed to threaten greater European opposition even before the coups at Kiaochow and Port Arthur. The Russian construction of the Trans-Siberian Railway, with its proposed Manchurian extension, alarmed American oil exporters even more than it pleased steel manufacturers. An impulsive German ultimatum to Haiti in the Lüders affair raised doubts about the Kaiser's intentions in the Far East as well, and new French tariffs in Madagascar, shutting out American textiles, showed the danger of protectionism if Europeans acquired spheres of influence in China. All these menacing actions were drawn together through the open defiance of American industrial competition by Count Agenor Goluchowski, the Austrian foreign minister, in 1897. While aimed at trade in Europe, the count's manifesto seemed equally applicable in China.[5]

When American businessmen read of the apparent European threats to free competition in China, some were complacent, others militant. A number of conservative publications such as the *American Banker,* the *New York Commercial,* and the *Commercial and Financial Chronicle* saw advantages in European direction of Chinese economic development. Late in December 1897, however, the *New York Journal of Commerce,* probably the nation's leading business newspaper,

4. Campbell, *Special Business Interests,* 2–5, 11–13, 15, 19–21. James J. Lorence, *Organized Business and the Myth of the China Market: The American Asiatic Association, 1898–1937,* 9–10. *North American Review* 143 (October 1896): 447. *Manufacturers' Record* 30 (July 31, 1896): 5. U.S., *Commercial Relations, 1897,* 1, 993–94. U.S., *Consular Reports* 205 (October 1897): 279–82. Francis B. Loomis to Day, November 5, 1897, William R. Day papers, box 6. Other examples of Barrett's economic expansionism in the Far East were his article "America's Interest in Eastern Asia," 257–65; and a letter to President Theodore C. Search of the NAM, reprinted in *New York Journal of Commerce,* July 7, 1897. On the Caracas showroom see Pletcher, *Diplomacy of Trade and Investment,* 254.

5. The Haitian government had imprisoned a German resident after trial. Berlin demanded an indemnity, sent a warship as a threat, and eventually obtained twenty thousand dollars and an apology. Ludwell Lee Montague, *Haiti and the United States, 1714–1938,* 255–63. For a more detailed but anti-American account see Vagts, *Deutschland und die Vereinigten Staaten,* vol. 2, 1707–27. Donald Dean Leopard, "The French Conquest and Pacification of Madagascar, 1885–1905," 222–23. Heardon, *Independence and Empire,* 130. U.S., *Commercial Relations, 1895–96,* 1, 301–3; *1898,* 1, 222–23. U.S., *Foreign Relations, 1896,* 124–25. *New York Journal of Commerce,* May 9, 1896; November 6, 1897. *Commercial and Financial Chronicle* 66 (July 16, 1898). Pratt, *Expansionists of 1898,* 259–60. *Literary Digest* 15 (December 11, 1897): 964; 17 (December 10, 1898): 686. *Public Opinion* 23 (December 2, 1897): 709–10.

called on the government to take the lead in an aggressive policy to uphold Americans' free access to Chinese markets. The *Journal* had long stood for low tariffs and governmental laissez faire in foreign trade. In 1893 it had been acquired by William Dodsworth, a trade expansionist with special concern for the southern textile market in the Far East, and since that time it had given increased space to Japan and China under the direction of its able editor, John Foord. The *Journal* especially mistrusted Russia as a nation devoted to conquest and obstructing civilization which should not be permitted to dominate the North Pacific.[6]

Stung by Secretary Sherman's complacency, Foord and Clarence Cary, the legal representative of the American China Development Company, formed a pressure group, the Committee on American Interests in China, which included at first representatives of Standard Oil and Bethlehem Iron Company and eventually many other enterprises involved in Far Eastern trade and investment. With strong support from the *New York Journal of Commerce,* the *Commercial and Financial Chronicle,* and the National Association of Manufacturers, the committee prepared a petition urging an active Far Eastern policy. After persuading sixty-eight firms (including many cotton textile exporters) to sign it, the committee circulated it among the country's chambers of commerce, which used it as a model for their own petitions to Congress, the State Department, and the press. As the New York Chamber of Commerce put it, American-Chinese trade was "destined . . . to assume large proportions unless debarred by the action of foreign governments," and it urged Congress to defend American treaty rights and protect their "important commercial interests in that Empire." In a magazine article Cary criticized Sherman's "quaint and dangerous view" and his policy of drift, and warned the government not to depend on Britain to defend American interests in China.[7]

The press debate touched off by the German and Russian coups spread across the country without much regard to party, region, or economic connections.

6. Lorence, *Organized Business,* 10–13. Campbell, *Special Business Interests,* 26. Pratt, *Expansionists of 1898,* 261–63. For the editorial announcing the *Journal's* new policy see *New York Journal of Commerce,* December 28, 1897. See also ibid., December 23, 29, 1897; January 5, 6, 24, 25, 1898. For its views on Russia see ibid., June 3, 1897. As recently as 1893 the *Journal* had written off American trade with the Far East as hopeless. Ibid., September 12, 1893. Since Russian textile exports were mostly coarse goods, American producers in the South were especially afraid of their competition in Manchuria and northern China. Hearden, *Independence and Empire,* 129–31.

7. Lorence, *Organized Business,* 15–17. Campbell, *Special Business Interests,* 30–31, 34–37. McCormick, *China Market,* 92–93. LaFeber, *New Empire,* 355–58. Clarence Cary, "China's Complications and American Trade," 35–45. New York Chamber of Commerce quoted in Campbell, *Special Business Interests,* 35. For sample petitions see U.S., State Department, Miscellaneous Letters, roll 997. About a third of the concerns represented in the committee and its successor, the American Asiatic Association, were export-import houses and commission agencies, but about 14 percent represented iron and steel manufacturers, 7 percent railroad equipment, 7 percent finance and banking, and 24 percent miscellaneous industry. Lorence, *Organized Business,* 18.

China, proclaimed the *Overland Monthly*, was a fresh world to conquer, like Cuba and Hawaii "joined to us by commercial ties more closely than Baltimore was to Boston in Washington's day." The warnings of Washington's Farewell Address, added the *New York Times*, did not apply to a situation in which future national prosperity and economic rank would depend on the growth of foreign trade. The *New York Journal of Commerce* warned that Germany and Russia intended to control and erect a tariff wall around all of China. Both to preserve an important market and to protect missionaries against the xenophobia that the Europeans would surely arouse in China, the United States must take a positive stand. Some, like the *Pittsburgh Dispatch*, called for readying the navy; others invoked the Nicaragua canal and the annexation of Hawaii. Several favored assistance to Britain, whose basic policy was similar to ours, especially after Sir Michael Hicks Beach, the chancellor of the exchequer, issued an uncompromising free trade commitment. A few, like the *Philadelphia Manufacturer*, advocated a triple alliance with Britain and Japan.[8]

As with all other expansionist questions of the century, a vigorous opposition had its say as well. Although these newspapers approved British free-trade sentiments (and, with some suspicion, a similar statement made by Germany), they regarded cooperation with Britain and Japan as that primal sin, an entangling alliance. In the past America had gained Chinese and Japanese friendship through neutrality and noninterference; why not continue these policies? "The Monroe Doctrine," declared the *New York Tribune*, "cannot be stretched to cover Asia." Since only property rights were at stake, not sovereignty, honor, or American lives, there was no need to reinforce the Far Eastern Squadron. Existing most-favored-nation treaties, said *Harper's Weekly*, would guarantee American trade. Two Baltimore newspapers, the *Sun* and the *Herald*, ridiculed expansionists' fear of German or Russian tariffs "protecting" Shantung or Manchuria, since American products continued to sell well in Europe despite similar tariffs. "We can meet this sort of competition without difficulty," declared the *Sun*, "if we will properly utilize our natural resources and advantages." Finally, the *New Orleans Picayune* raised the obvious point that two foreign policy crises at a time—Cuba and Hawaii—were enough.[9]

8. Many of the arguments and newspapers cited appear in two summaries, *Public Opinion* 24 (January 6, 1898): 5–6; and *Literary Digest* 16 (January 8, 1898): 31–33. See also *Overland Monthly* 31 (February 1898): 177–78; *Chicago Inter-Ocean,* January 5, 7, 1898; *New York Times,* December 13, 1897, February 7, 1898; *New York Tribune,* February 4, 1898; and *New Orleans Daily Picayune,* December 24, 1892. On Hicks Beach's statement see *Literary Digest* 16 (February 5, 1898): 158. On the German announcement see *Commercial and Financial Chronicle* 66 (February 12, 1898): 311–12. One statement about protection was completely frank: "While we may imitate at home the policy of commercial exclusiveness favored by Russia and Germany, we do not care to have it used against ourselves in a field where we have precisely the same rights as they." *New York Journal of Commerce,* December 29, 1897.

9. See the summaries in *Public Opinion* and *Literary Digest* cited in note 8. *New York Tribune,* December 28, 1897. *Harper's Weekly* 42 (January 8, 1898): 26–27.

Even in the midst of a developing crisis with Spain, the expansionist petitions and editorials drew responses from Congress and the McKinley administration. The chairmen of the congressional committees on foreign relations, Senator Cushman Davis (Republican, Minnesota) and Representative Nelson Dingley, Jr. (Republican, Maine) indicated their sympathy, and Senator Henry M. Telier (Republican, Colorado) contributed alarmist pronouncements. Secretary Sherman quickly backtracked from his unfortunate statement and instructed American representatives in Berlin and St. Petersburg to insist again on equal commercial rights in Shantung and southern Manchuria. Assistant Secretary Day, about to replace Sherman, privately reassured a member of the Committee on American Interests in China. McKinley withdrew the appointment of Charles P. Bryan, a politician with no diplomatic experience, as minister to China, since it had aroused much business opposition. In Bryan's place he chose the minister to Brazil, Edwin H. Conger, a former banker, lawyer, and congressman. Although Conger had little knowledge of the Far East, he convinced the Committee on American Interests in China that he would safeguard those interests adequately. Gratified by the results of their efforts, the members decided to form a permanent organization, and in June the original nucleus, now amplified, created the American Asiatic Association, officered mostly by businessmen with Foord as secretary and Cary on the executive committee.[10]

Another remarkable effect of the German-Russian coup on American Far Eastern policy was the stimulus it gave to an Anglo-American rapprochement in that area. This rapprochement had begun in the Anglo-American anxiety caused by the Venezuelan crisis of 1895 and an abortive attempt the following year for an arbitration treaty.[11] The German-Russian coup placed the British on the horns of a dilemma. They wanted to retain the exclusive control over Hong Kong that they had held since the 1840s and their dominant position in the great northern

---

10. Lorence, *Organized Business,* 16–17. Campbell, *Special Business Interests,* 37. McCormick, *China Market,* 95–96. LaFeber, *New Empire,* 359. For Teller's views see [Washington] *Evening Star,* January 3, 1898. Clipping in Day papers, box 7, *New York Journal of Commerce,* January 29, February 19, March 4, 1898. For a discussion of the significance of the free trade assurances of the European powers see Young, *Rhetoric of Empire,* 94–95, 259–60n4–6. On Conger's qualifications see Hunt, *Frontier Defense,* 29. Campbell, *Special Business Interests,* chap. 4. Lorence, *Organized Business,* 17–18, 23. The president of the association was Everett Frazar, the vice president Samuel D. Brewster, and the treasurer J. B. Patterson, all from prominent New York trading companies. Other members were James Harrison Wilson and representatives of Westinghouse Electric, southern cotton mills, and silk and locomotive interests. Hearden, *Independence and Empire,* 131. *New York Journal of Commerce,* June 17, 1898. At the same time the Philadelphia Commercial Museum announced a mission lasting up to a year to investigate Chinese markets. *Board of Trade Journal* 24 (June 1898): 665–66.

11. Joseph J. Mathews, "Informal Diplomacy in the Venezuelan Crisis of 1896." On the arbitration treaty see H. C. Allen, *Great Britain and the United States: A History of Anglo-American Relations (1783–1952),* 541–42; and Charles S. Campbell, Jr., *The Transformation of American Foreign Relations, 1865–1900,* 211–14, 219–20.

commercial hub of Shanghai. By the 1890s, however, the center of their Chinese trade and investment lay in the Yangtze Valley, the richest third of the empire, which was too large to reserve as a sphere of influence. The "open door"—equal access to Chinese trade—seemed to answer their needs, so at the beginning of 1898 Britain put out feelers for an understanding of this sort with Japan, Germany, and even Russia, but without results.

Britain then turned to the United States. Uncertain as to German and Russian intentions in northern China, Arthur Balfour and Joseph Chamberlain, the most pro-American members of the British cabinet, seconded Hicks Beach's sentiments regarding free trade in China which, as has been seen, the Americans had welcomed. In January Ambassador John Hay briefly discussed Far Eastern policy with Prime Minister Lord Salisbury. At the beginning of March Balfour and Chamberlain expressed their fear that Germany and Russia would soon adopt an exclusionist policy in Shantung and Manchuria. On March 7 the Foreign Office telegraphed to the British ambassador at Washington, Sir Julian Pauncefote, instructions to sound the United States on a joint stand to oppose "any action by foreign powers which could tend to restrict the opening of China to the commerce of all nations."[12]

The American reaction to this startling démarche was hesitant and temporizing. As McKinley and his advisers knew, there was a considerable public suspicion of close connections with Britain in an area of hot trade competition. Soon after the note of March 7, Britain decided to demand the port of Weihaiwei to balance Russia at Port Arthur and Germany at Kiaochow; this made the démarche look like hypocrisy. Probably most important, in March McKinley was approaching his final decision over war with Spain. The actual reply mentioned none of these considerations but instead feebly objected that Congress would have to determine the final policy, that no European power had yet interfered with American trade (pace Yung Wing and his Shantung railroad project), and that the United States had received assurances that the occupying powers would not seek exclusive commercial privileges. Day privately assured Pauncefote that but for the ticklish Spanish situation, the reply would have been more favorable. The question was by no means closed, for in June Hay wrote directly to McKinley at Chamberlain's request to ask if a change in attitude might be possible. (McKinley replied in the

12. Charles S. Campbell, Jr., *Anglo-American Understanding, 1898–1903,* 14–17. Campbell thinks that Balfour and Chamberlain were mainly responsible for the overture. Langer, *Diplomacy of Imperialism,* vol. 2, 490–91. Allan Nevins, *Henry White: Thirty Years of American Diplomacy,* 162–63. LaFeber, *New Empire,* 358–59. McCormick, *China Market,* 98–100. For the British background see also Young, *British Policy in China,* 65–67. For statements by Balfour and Chamberlain see *London Times,* January 11, 19, 1898. Hay to Sherman, January 11, 1898, no. 213, U.S., Diplomatic Despatches, Britain, 190. Hay to the President, January 13, 1898. Text of British overture, received March 8. Day papers, box 8. For several years Denby had hoped for a common Anglo-American policy in China to keep the door open for trade. Hunt, *Frontier Defense,* 86. For a Russian view of possible Anglo-American cooperation in Manchuria see Romanov, *Russia in Manchuria,* 152–53.

negative.) Newspapers reprinted rumors and arguments in favor of joint Anglo-American action in the Far East throughout the Spanish-American War.[13]

One more event during the spring of 1898 furthered American involvement in Far Eastern affairs. On April 14, ten days before the outbreak of the Spanish-American War, A. W. Bash of the American China Development Company signed a contract with the Chinese minister in Washington for the construction of a main-line railroad from Hankow to Canton, the logical extension of the Peking-Hankow line that the company had lost to the Belgian syndicate (see chapter 9). The terms were more liberal than the earlier contract the company had rejected; a bond issue of £4 million at 5 percent as a first mortgage on the railroad and a guarantee to the company of any profits on the bond sales, 5 percent of construction costs, and 20 percent of net profits on operations. The company might also construct extensions and branch lines, operate nearby coal mines, and even buy into the Peking-Hankow enterprise if the Belgian contract were canceled.

Fearing French interference, since the proposed line approached the French sphere of influence in southern China, Bash appealed to Day, now secretary of state, for some assurance of protection. However, Day refused to write a blank check, either alone or with British cooperation, pointing out that the United States had never adopted the practice of guaranteeing private contracts with foreign governments. The State Department did not have general instructions covering "contingencies the nature of which cannot be foreseen and which may never arise," but would take "lawful and proper" action as suited the occasion.[14]

This sort of American caution discouraged enthusiasts such as Thomas R. Jernigan, onetime consul general at Shanghai. Shortly before the American China Company's concession was announced, he learned that an Anglo-German banking group had made a sixteen-million-pound indemnity loan to the Chinese government and wrote to the *New York Journal of Commerce* bemoaning the lack of American participation in the transaction and the feeble support given American businessmen by the Peking legation, held back by orders from Washington: "The wealthiest and most capable country in the world . . . takes no substantial part in the development of China. . . . We must move or soon form the rear guard to the army of commercial progress."[15]

13. Campbell, *Anglo-American Understanding*, 19–21. McCormick, *China Market*, 99–101. On the negotiations see Young, *British Policy in China*, 67–68, 70–75. Britain also received other commitments from China. McCormick, *China Market*, 100–101. For the text of the American oral reply to Pauncefote, dated March 16, 1898, see Day papers, box 8. Hay to the President, June 30, 1898, ibid. Day to Hay, July 14, Hay papers, reel 10. *London Times*, March 29, 1898. *Hong Kong Telegraph*, May 2, 1898. Clipping enclosed with Edward Bedloe to Day, June 8, no. 25, U.S., Consular Despatches, Canton, 13. London correspondent for *New York Times*, reprinted in *Public Opinion* 18 (May 2, 1895): 470.

14. Braisted, "U.S. and American China Development Company," 148–50. Campbell, *Special Business Interests*, 28–39. Parsons, *American Engineer in China*, chap. 2. *New York Tribune*, May 14, 1899, sect. 3.

15. *New York Journal of Commerce*, April 5, 1898. This was the second Anglo-German loan; there had also been a Russo-French loan for the same purpose.

* * *

The Spanish-American War removed some of the Americans' doubts about economic expansion in the Pacific and the Far East. The war was caused by a mixture of economic, strategic, and humanitarian factors operating mainly in the Caribbean and difficult to disentangle or appraise. Many businessmen greeted the unexpected hostilities with misgivings. The great depression of the mid-1890s seemed to have ended with a pronounced business upturn during the winter and spring of 1897–1898, and they feared that a sudden shock would freeze confidence and diminish orders. After the war had begun, however, it became apparent that the recovery would continue and even accelerate. Only then did these doubters relax and give way to patriotism.[16]

The first important event of the war encouraged a shift of attention to the Far East. A week after its beginning, Commodore (later Admiral) George Dewey and the Asiatic Squadron attacked a Spanish flotilla in Manila Bay on May 1 and cut it to pieces. While the War and Navy Departments continued their plans for a campaign in Cuba, they hastily assembled an expeditionary force to occupy Manila and Luzon in conjunction with Filipino rebels, who had already been in the field for two years.

Some economic expansionists had anticipated an attack on the Philippines, but despite their later use of the victory in their propaganda, there is no evidence to suggest that they inspired Dewey's attack. Prewar trade with the Philippines was unpromising; few Americans knew anything about the islands. In 1896 Lieutenant William W. Kimball, a Naval Intelligence officer who had been instructed to draw up contingency plans for a war with Spain, recommended an attack on the Philippines along with a general blockade of Spanish colonies to cripple the enemy and acquire pawns for later negotiations. He barely mentioned trade as a secondary consideration. During the next year the Philippines attack was removed from the war plan and then replaced, as the Naval War College and the naval bureaus argued over it.

On entering the Navy Department in March 1897, Assistant Secretary Theodore Roosevelt took up the project enthusiastically, pressed it on McKinley and Secretary John D. Long, and helped secure the appointment of Commodore George Dewey to the Asiatic Squadron as an aggressive agent. The navy established a War Board to advise the president on naval policy (e.g., bases). From January to April 1898 the Navy Department sent Dewey a series of instructions, mostly signed by Long, concerning preparations for action. Only one of these, emanating from Roosevelt, is usually mentioned by historians. During this period the department

16. Pletcher, *Diplomacy of Trade and Investment,* 339–58. For prewar fears see LaFeber, *New Empire,* 390–93; Wehler, *Aufsteig,* 215–16; and Pratt, *Expansionists of 1898.* For post-declaration reassurance see *Public Opinion* 24 (April 28, 1898): 516; 25 (September 22): 380; *Bradstreet's* 26 (April 23, May 7, 21, June 19, July 2, August 20, November 19, 1898): 257, 289, 296, 321, 329, 738–39; *New York Journal of Commerce,* May 6, 9, June 2, 1898; *Commercial and Financial Chronicle* 66 (July 9, 1898): 784–86; *Wall Street Journal,* June 11, 1898.

also reinforced the commodore with the cruiser *Baltimore* and a shipload of munitions. When the war began, the Philippines were an approved part of the fighting plan, but mainly for strategic, not economic reasons, and McKinley waited three days after the declaration before ordering Dewey to Manila. The resulting assault on the Philippines was not a guaranteed American victory, for the Spanish admiral might have dispersed his ships among the islands, compelling a long chase, or the American ships might have come to grief in the narrow channel leading to Manila Bay. The battle took place on May 1; the United States learned of it next day by way of Madrid. (Dewey had no cable facilities and was not heard from until May 7.)[17]

Whatever the thinking behind the attack, its astonishing success loosed a wave of euphoria across the country that carried many sober businessmen with it. The *New York Journal of Commerce* praised the combination of circumstances that had dramatized American power in the western Pacific at the very moment when greedy European powers seemed about to monopolize Chinese trade. A week after the victory Horace N. Fisher, a prominent Boston lawyer, called the battle "a Godsend, for opening a great foreign market" and compared it to Robert Clive's victory at Plassey (1787) in imperial significance. During May and June Senator Lodge plied McKinley with economic arguments. Some business journals that had opposed the war, such as the *American Wool and Cotton Reporter* (Boston), suddenly recognized its possible commercial benefits. Through the summer the *New York Commercial* predicted that the Spanish islands would supply markets for surplus products like those Europe enjoyed in the colonies, and reporters for the *Chicago Inter-Ocean* found similar sentiments among midwestern businessmen.[18]

17. Pratt, *Expansionists of 1898*, 266. John A. S. Grenville and George Berkeley Young, *Politics, Strategy, and American Diplomacy: Studies in Foreign Policy, 1873–1917*, 267–83. David F. Trask, *The War with Spain in 1898*, 91–94. John A. S. Grenville, "American Naval Preparations for War with Spain, 1896–1898," 33–47. Ronald H. Spector, "Who Planned the Attack on Manila Bay?" 94–102. Braisted, *U.S. Navy in the Pacific, 1897–1909*, 21–25. Ronald Spector, *Admiral of the New Empire: The Life and Career of George Dewey*, 32–37. Phil Lyman Snyder, "Mission, Empire, or Force of Circumstances? A Study of the American Decision to Annex the Philippine Islands," 21–28. Theodore Roosevelt to Henry Cabot Lodge, September 21, 1897. Theodore Roosevelt, *Letters of Theodore Roosevelt*, vol. 1, 685–86. Before the war one observer suggested an attack on the islands, not to retain them but to keep Japan out. *New York Times*, March 16, 1898. According to one historian, the voyage of the *Baltimore* indicated an imperialist plot by McKinley, but this judgment lacks documentation and relies on surmise. Timothy McDonald, "McKinley and the Coming of the War with Spain," 225–39. On the timing of the final order to Dewey see a letter of John D. Long cited in Grenville and Young, *Politics, Strategy, and American Diplomacy*, 270n6. On the action at Manila Bay see Trask, *War with Spain*, chap. 5.

18. *New York Journal of Commerce*, May 25, 1898. *Commercial and Financial Chronicle* 66 (May 7, 1898): 874–75. *Outlook* 58 (April 30, 1898): 1053–54; 59 (May 14): 110–11. Horace N. Fisher to Long, May 9, 1898. Gardner Weld Allen, ed., *Papers of John D. Long, 1898–1914*, 214–15. Richard H. Werking, "Senator Henry Cabot Lodge and the Philippines: A Note on American Territorial Expansion," 234–40. On the *American Wool and Cotton Reporter* see Daniel B. Schirmer, *Republic or Empire? American Resistance to the Philippine*

It was soon apparent that the new trade opportunities would involve fundamental policy changes as well. The first to claim public attention was the annexation of territory conquered from Spain, including faraway tropical islands formerly thought undesirable. The *New York Times* and other low-tariff advocates pointed out that the high rates of the Dingley Act were scarcely compatible with commercial expansion, but some protectionist organs embraced expansionism without admitting the inconsistency. Others expected that the new possessions would drive the United States and free-trade Britain together into some kind of open door policy. The conservative *Commercial and Financial Chronicle* predicted an immediate need for an expanded diplomatic service and military forces. All in all, declared many, the war would force the United States to abandon its comfortable isolation, dig the Nicaragua canal, annex Hawaii, and give active support to business all over the world. For the next month many newspapers added a broad range of comments—the first press debate on postwar policies.[19]

Anti-expansionists also began to set forth answering arguments. They were especially strong in New England, where they could trace their intellectual descent from abolitionists and Mugwumps. Economic overtones were added by the resentment of the old commercial class toward the newer industrialists and their protectionism. The movement became public at a meeting on June 15 at Faneuil Hall, Boston, where, after several hours of speeches, the leaders founded an Anti-Imperialist Committee of Correspondence to spread propaganda. But the opposition had already appeared in other parts of the country. On June 21 former president Cleveland warned that the war might lead the country into imperialism. The *Nation* predictably foresaw a repetition of Reconstruction misgovernment if the United States tried to rule the Philippines. During May Chauncey Depew, the symbol of business, who had loudly approved McKinley's interventionist message a month earlier, saw no profits but only governmental headaches in the islands. By autumn the *Iron Age,* strongly expansionist in June, was agreeing with him. In the South and West cane and beet sugar producers opposed the acquisition of any tropical sugar lands, be they in Cuba, Puerto Rico, or the Philippines. And the silverite *Denver Republican* thought imperialism a cunning "goldbug" scheme to fasten the hated gold standard on the country for years to come.[20]

War, 60–61, 79–80. For an account of the effect of the war on American prestige in East Asia see John Barrett, "The Paramount Power in the Pacific," 166.

19. *New York Times,* May 23, 1898. *Literary Digest* 17 (July 9, 1898): 32, 37. *New York Journal of Commerce,* May 4, June 11, 1898. *Commercial and Financial Chronicle* 66 (May 14, 1898): 922–24. *Wall Street Journal,* May 3, 1898. Richard Olney, "International Isolation of the United States," 577–78. *Nation* 66 (April 28, 1898): 319; *Literary Digest* 16 (April 16, 1898): 494–95. *Public Opinion* 24 (May 19, 1898): 616–17.

20. Tompkins, *Anti-Imperialism in the United States,* 122–26. Schirmer, *Republic or Empire?* chaps. 1, 2, 65–66. *New York Tribune,* May 17, 1898. *Nation* 66 (May 19, 1898): 376–77. *Iron Age* 61 (June 23, 1898): 15. Ibid., September 29, November 24, as cited in Pratt, *Expansionists of 1898,* 272. *Literary Digest* 17 (July 9, September 24, 1898): 36, 361. For Cleveland's statement see *New York Times,* June 22, 1898.

In July the *Literary Digest* commented ironically on the contradictions and conflicts produced by the events of the war. Grover Cleveland had broken with Olney, recently his secretary of state, and the *Washington Post* caricatured the former president in an anticolonialist bed with his old foe William Jennings Bryan, whose onetime supporter, the *New York Journal,* had deserted him for imperialism. Regular Republican papers usually favored expansion, while regular Democrats opposed it, but independent journals on both sides defied the majority. In all sections differences prevailed, and such revered totems as Washington's Farewell Address and the Monroe Doctrine were sometimes exalted, sometimes discarded.[21] During the next six months a modicum of order reappeared— enough, at any rate, to permit an acceptable peace settlement—but attacks on the more deep-seated problems continued for years.

The war affected the Hawaiian annexation question more quickly in the islands than in the United States. In late March President Sanford B. Dole and his cabinet considered measures to facilitate a presumptive American occupation but, urged by foreigners and royalists, decided instead on a conventional declaration of neutrality. After Dewey's victory, the Hawaiian government nullified this declaration by providing coal depots for American warships, welcoming troops en route to the Philippines, and offering Washington any other assistance it might need, even a treaty of alliance (which McKinley put off, believing annexation imminent). The Hawaiian action risked Spanish retaliation but strengthened the case for annexation.[22]

By this time the American press and public had begun to reconsider the Hawaiian question in the light shed by the fireworks of Manila Bay. The most important new argument for annexation declared Hawaii a way station and naval base vital for communication with the Philippines. A panic among East Coast seaports during May over the remote possibility of Spanish attack gave new significance to the older argument that Hawaii might shield the Pacific coast or provide a base for enemy raids, depending on who held the islands. Other annexationists felt that Hawaii's wartime cooperation showed the good faith of its government and placed a moral obligation on the United States. An argument suggested by the British diplomat Cecil Spring-Rice to John Hay was that Germany could not object to the American annexation of Hawaii during the fighting but might insist on compensation in Samoa or elsewhere if the United States delayed until after the war. (Later research in British and German archives showed that Spring-Rice's suspicions were well founded.) Senator John T. Morgan

21. *Literary Digest* 16 (July 9, 1898): 32–38.
22. Pratt, *Expansionists of 1898,* 318–19. Thomas A. Bailey, "The United States and Hawaii during the Spanish-American War," 553–55. Harold M. Sewall to Sherman, March 30, April 12, May 10, June 9, 1898, nos. 152, confidential unnumbered, U.S., Diplomatic Despatches, Hawaii, 30, 31. European diplomats and merchants in Honolulu were all cooperative.

was especially fearful about the perils of delay and added his warnings to those of Hay and Lodge.[23]

Anti-annexationists denied that the need of a way station justified formal acquisition, for the United States already possessed Kiska in the Aleutians, on the "great circle" route to the Far East, and if this were not enough, it already had sufficient facilities at Pearl Harbor for wartime needs. Far better, they said, to wait until after the war, when Americans would presumably decide what to do with the Philippines. Hurrying the annexation under the stress of conflict would commit the United States to ill-considered decisions on such difficult issues as naval bases, repressive colonial policies, and contract labor.[24]

It is clear from the fragmentary remarks McKinley let slip from time to time that he had adopted Hawaiian annexation before or during the 1897 congressional battle and that he gave at least lip service to the arguments for wartime needs. A few ultra-annexationists such as the Hawaiian minister to the United States, Francis M. Hatch, and Senator Lodge half expected him to declare Hawaii annexed by executive authority as a wartime measure. The Hawaiian government would have welcomed this, but the canny president preferred the slower and safer method of letting Congress resume its debate and churn out a decision. He was quite willing to lobby, however, either through agents or in person, as when he called the influential Senator George F. Hoar to the White House and soothed his qualms about American imperialist intentions in China.[25]

The renewed congressional struggle over Hawaii began on May 4, when Representative Francis G. Newlands (Republican, Nevada) introduced a joint resolution for annexation in the House. For three weeks Speaker Thomas B. Reed used his commanding powers to prevent its consideration on the floor, although during that time the Foreign Affairs Committee reported it favorably. In the report the committee enclosed a statement by General J. M. Schofield that repeated some of the strategic arguments he had used twenty-three years before to justify the reciprocity treaty of 1875 (see chapter 3). A minority of the committee abjured annexation but warned off foreign nations. Rebellion against Reed's dictatorial style boiled up in the press and the House, where on May 24 many Republicans petitioned for a caucus. Probably fearing another split like that of early April on intervention in Cuba, Reed then gave in, and for four

---

23. Russ, *Hawaiian Republic,* 297–337. Bailey, "United States and Hawaii," 556–60. *Public Opinion* 24 (June 9, 1898): 707–8. *Bradstreet's* 26 (May 21, 1898): 325. *New York Tribune,* May 25, 1898. Tate, "Hawaii: Symbol of Anglo-American Rapprochment," 569–72. John T. Morgan to the President, May 23, 1898, Day papers, box 9.

24. *New York Times,* May 7, 1898, 6; July 3, 16. (*Washington Post*), May 1898. Clipping in Day papers, box 9. *New York Journal of Commerce,* June 25, 1898. *Nation* 66 (June 16, 1898): 451. Samuel Gompers to Thomas B. Reed, June 11, 1898, in U.S., 55th Cong., 1st sess., *Congressional Record, 31,* 6270. *Public Opinion* 25 (November 3, 1898): 552.

25. Margaret Leach, *In the Days of McKinley,* 213–14. Robert L. Beisner, *Twelve against Empire: The Anti-Imperialists, 1898–1900,* 145–48. Pratt, *Expansionists of 1898,* 318. Lodge and Redmond, *Lodge-Roosevelt Correspondence,* vol. 1, 302, 311. *New York Times,* June 5, 1898. George F. Hoar, *Autobiography of Seventy Years,* vol. 2, 307–9.

days, from June 11 to 15, an orderly debate unfolded. At the end the House passed the joint resolution, 209–91, with 55 not taking sides. The Louisiana and Colorado delegations voted against; the California delegation, as before, split; and the delegations of Minnesota, Wisconsin, and Utah, all increasingly interested in sugar beets, either supported the resolution or did not vote.[26]

In the Senate near the end of May Lodge and Morgan offered annexation amendments to a war revenue bill in order to start action without waiting for the House to deal with the Newlands resolution. The Vermont patriarch Senator Justin S. Morrill, who had sponsored the first Civil War protectionist tariff thirty-seven years before and opposed reciprocity and imperialism ever since, led off the debate, which soon became a filibuster by the anti-annexationists, while the supporters of Hawaii held off, confident of their majority. The Foreign Relations Committee reported the Newlands resolution favorably without further comment. Soon after the beginning of the debate Lodge began a speech on the military benefits of annexation, only to be cut off by a vote putting the Senate into executive session—a maneuver some said he had prearranged with McKinley to emphasize the vital strategic importance of Hawaii. In the last stages annexationists voted down restraining amendments and added several provisions of the 1897 treaty to the joint resolution. The Senate passed it, 42–21, with 26 not voting, and on July 7 McKinley signed it into law. Hawaii was formally annexed on August 12. The admiral in charge of the ceremonies at Honolulu tactfully maintained a low key, for the native Hawaiians were sad to see their independence extinguished.[27]

Why did Congress reverse itself on Hawaiian annexation within little more than three months? Most historians have accepted the obvious explanation that wartime needs were responsible, although some have suggested that these were exaggerated by annexationists. Recent writers emphasizing the role of economic interests in determining foreign policy have argued that commercial expansionism was either partly or largely responsible for the dramatic change. Another historian, after examining press opinion, suggests that, failing a strong public stand, the congressional vote was largely determined by party affiliation.[28]

---

26. Russ, *Hawaiian Republic,* 296–97, 339–42. Weigle, "Sugar Interests," 150–52. William A. Robinson, *Thomas B. Reed, Parliamentarian,* 366–67. For General Schofield's statement see U.S., 55th Cong., 2d sess., *House Report 1355,* 8–17.

27. Russ, *Hawaiian Republic,* 343–54. Weigle, "Sugar Interests," 155–58. Thomas J. Osborne, "Trade or War? America's Annexation of Hawaii Reconsidered," 287–92. For descriptions of the anticlimactic ceremonies in Honolulu see *Nation* 67 (August 25, September 1, 29, 1898): 139, 158, 231. Even the annexationists had mixed feelings, well expressed by a bitter-sweet editorial in the oldest annexationist newspaper. Clipping enclosed with Sewall to Day, July 18, 1898, no. 184, U.S., Diplomatic Despatches, Hawaii, 21.

28. The best examples of the traditional view are Bailey, "The United States and Hawaii"; Pratt, *Expansionists of 1898;* Russ, *Hawaiian Republic;* Tate, *United States and Hawaiian Kingdom;* and Tompkins, *Anti-Imperialism in the United States,* 118. Walter LaFeber (*The New Empire*) and Thomas J. McCormick (*China Market*) have developed the theme of commercial expansionism in the Far East. The most explicit commercial

A number of conclusions would seem reasonable. First, whether possession of Hawaii was really necessary to prosecute the war or to protect the Pacific coast from an unlikely Spanish attack, a considerable body of press and public *perceived* it as necessary, taking at face value the exaggerated opinions of military experts. In a revealing speech to the House on June 11 a young congressman, Frederick H. Gillett (Republican, Massachusetts), recalled that he had opposed annexation through the earlier debate until "the flame of actual war" broke out, which had converted him to internationalism and a big navy, and this in turn required making Hawaii "a veritable Gibraltar." It is likely that whatever they may have said on the floor, some other congressmen shifted in a similar direction before the final vote, influenced by what they heard from their constituents or read in the newspapers and, in the case of the Republicans, by pressure from McKinley.[29]

Second, while the commercial expansionist view of Hawaii as a way station toward the Golden East certainly influenced the annexationists' campaign in May and June, their arguments for Chinese trade do not seem to have changed much from earlier in the year, when the Hawaiian debate came to a halt. The fear of European domination over China aroused during the winter by German-Russian advances at Kiaochow and Port Arthur increased during the spring, but the spheres of influence granted to Russia, France, and Britain during May and June made less impression than the earlier actions, for by then the war had taken over public attention. Also at that time the most active pressure group for government aid to the China trade, the Committee on American Interests in China, was engaged in reorganizing itself into the American Asiatic Association, which did not take up the propaganda campaign until after the armistice with Spain in August.[30] The most that can be said for commercial expansionism in the final debate is that the desire for Far Eastern markets, which intensified after Dewey's victory, called attention to new possibilities, and thus indirectly encouraged Hawaiian annexation. But it would be as easy to argue that the success of the joint resolution in July did even more to facilitate the annexation of the Philippines by opening a breach in traditional anticolonialism.

---

explanation of Hawaiian annexation is contained in several works of Thomas J. Osborne: "Trade or War?" (cited in note 30); "Main Reason," 168–78; and *"Empire Can Wait,"* especially chap. 9 and Conclusion. Osborne rests his case largely on a content analysis of speeches in Congress from May to July. Concerning a partisan vote see Pearce, "Assessing Public Opinion," 340–41.

29. U.S., 55th Cong., 2d sess., *Congressional Record,* 31, 5782–83 (Gillett); 5829 (New-lands). Gillett later had a distinguished congressional career as Speaker of the House and then as senator. *Public Opinion* 24 (June 8, 1898): 707–8. *American Review of Reviews* 17 (August 1898): 124–25. For sample opinions against the military necessity argument see *Literary Digest* 16 (June 25, 1898): 752. Lewis L. Gould gives great weight to McKinley's influence in *The Spanish-American War and President McKinley,* 65.

30. For samples of press and public commercial expansionism during May see Osborne, "Trade or War?" 297–98. For samples of congressional advocacy see U.S., 55th Cong., 2d sess., *Congressional Record, 31,* 5897, 5905–6, Appendix, 534, 577–78, 582. Lorence, "Organized Business," 19. Campbell, *Special Business Interests,* 38. Indeed, Lorence mentions no connection between the Association and the annexation of Hawaii.

Perhaps the most perplexing aspect of the final Congressional debate over Hawaii was the ambivalent role of the sugar interests. Congressmen on both sides of the question accused the sugar trust of nefarious machinations on the other side, either to ruin the sugar beet growers by favoring annexation or to prevent Hawaiian producers from refining their own sugar by opposing it. Although the sugar tycoon Claus Spreckels was heavily interested in both Hawaiian cane and California beet sugar and also shared with the trust control over the principal California refinery, he consistently opposed annexation. But during the debate the Louisiana Planters Association showed a strange lack of interest in the supposed Hawaiian threat, and *Willett and Grey's Weekly Statistical Sugar Trade Journal* noted that military necessity had pushed annexation off the front page.[31]

After the passage of the resolution the *Journal* anticipated no great effect on the sugar trade, but Spreckels, ever the opportunist, headed for Washington on the morning after McKinley signed the bill to consult with him about officials for the new Hawaiian government. During the late summer and autumn confusion reigned in the Hawaiian sugar industry, as promoters including Spreckels prepared to build new refineries, anticipating the free admission of all grades of sugar into the United States. After some friction between the sugar trust and the planters, most of the latter made new contracts to sell virtually the whole Hawaiian sugar crop, and the year ended with the American Sugar Refining Company in renewed control. Since its alliance with Spreckels still held, his position in the islands did not seem greatly weakened.[32]

All in all, the success of the joint resolution was due to the war and especially to Dewey's victory—in part to the perception of military and naval needs, whether justified or exaggerated, in part to the intensification of older arguments, especially commercial, and in part to the feeling of confidence and exhilaration produced by the summer's successes. Congress, still doubtful about the Hawaiians' capacity for self-government, created a territory, although the islands had a larger population than Idaho, Nevada, or Wyoming, and appropriately Judge Dole became their first governor. An organic act of April 30, 1900, made Hawaii an incorporated territory, so its citizens as of August 1898 became American citizens automatically, and all relevant American laws, including tariffs, applied to the islands. Under the 1900 act Hawaii acquired an elected legislature, but in the monarchical tradition the executive exercised more centralized control than that

---

31. *Outlook* 59 (July 2, 1898): 503–4. For samples of references to the sugar trust in the final debates see U.S., 55th Cong., 2d sess., *Congressional Record,* 31, 5921–23, 6530, 6611–12. Weigle, "Sugar Interests," 154.

32. Weigle, "Sugar Interests," 159. Dwight Braman to McKinley, July 8, 1898, McKinley papers, ser. 1, reel 4. *Wall Street Journal,* June 16, October 14, November 4, 21, December 2, 1898; *New York Times,* August 12, September 9, October 1, 1898; *New York Tribune,* October 17, 1898. Eichner, *Emergence of Oligopoly,* 268–71. *New York Journal of Commerce,* May 24, 1898. For views of farm and labor interests see *Literary Digest* 17 (September 17, October 29, 1898): 332–33, 511–12.

of any other territory or state.[33] In the end the American disposition of Hawaii showed more system and consistency than in the cases of Cuba and Puerto Rico, mainly because it was based on years of deliberation and experience.

The disposition of the Philippines aroused more intense debate in the United States than that of Hawaii, for Congress and the public had neither experience nor clear-cut precedents on which to base decisions. After annihilating the Spanish fleet in Manila Bay, Dewey could do little more than establish shore bases, lay siege to Manila, and await reinforcements. The administration had issued general orders concerning these on May 4, three days before official news arrived of Dewey's victory. After that the army mobilized twelve thousand men in San Francisco and stepped up the embarkation schedule, but even so the occupying troops did not arrive until the end of June. Reports of a Spanish relief force caused anxiety until it was recalled en route after the Battle of Santiago.[34]

International complications also developed, for the British, the Germans, and the Japanese sent naval detachments to observe American actions and to be on hand in case the United States decided to evacuate the islands. The German flotilla was eventually almost as large as the American, and friction developed between the two commands, but there is no basis for the stubborn myth that only the British presence prevented an open break. The British government and many British business interests favored American annexation of the Philippines for the sake of regional stability and progressive development. Russia too was willing for the United States to annex the islands to keep them out of British hands and preserve the balance of power in East Asia.[35]

The position of the Japanese was more complicated than that of the other naval powers represented in Manila Bay. The Philippines lie close to Taiwan, which Japan had taken from China in the Sino-Japanese War. Not surprisingly, some Japanese nationalists hoped to add the Philippines eventually to their growing empire. Meanwhile they sought to prevent their transfer to any European nation, especially Germany, remembering bitterly the tripartite Russo-German-French intervention after the earlier war. On September 10 Count Okuma, the Japanese prime and foreign minister, informed the United States that if Spain

33. Julius W. Pratt, *America's Colonial Experiment: How the United States Gained, Governed, and In Part Gave Away a Colonial Empire*, 170, 178–83.

34. Trask, *War with Spain*, 369–88. Spector, *Admiral of the New Empire*, 68–88. Braisted, *U.S. Navy in the Pacific, 1897–1909*, 33–42. Louis J. Halle, *The United States Acquires the Philippines: Consensus vs. Reality*, 11. A. Alger, *The Spanish-American War*, 326.

35. Thomas A. Bailey, "Dewey and the Germans at Manila Bay," 59–81. Lester B. Shippee, "Germany and the Spanish-American War," 766–72. Brown, "German Acquisition," 141–42, 144–46. J. Fred Rippy, "The European Powers and the Spanish-American War," 22–52. A. E. Campbell, "Great Britain and the United States in the Far East, 1895–1903," 152–53. R. G. Neale, *Great Britain and United States Expansion: 1898–1900*, chap. 3. Geoffrey Seed, "British Views of American Policy in the Philippines Reflected in Journals of Opinion, 1898–1907," 49–60. *New York Journal of Commerce*, May 24, 1898. James K. Eyre, Jr., "Russia and the American Acquisition of the Philippines," 539–62.

could not continue to govern the Philippines, as seemed likely, Japan would favor their transfer to U.S. sovereignty. Failing that, it would favor a multilateral understanding, including Japan, to determine "a suitable government for the territory in question." For the rest of the year Okuma, other Japanese officials, and the Japanese press made it clear that this was the general Japanese position.[36]

A more immediate problem facing Dewey and soon the American government and people as well was the Philippine independence movement. This had begun in 1896 and had come under the leadership of a young nationalist, Emilio Aguinaldo, but it had nearly sputtered out by 1898, so the American consuls at Manila and Hong Kong assured the State Department that most Filipinos desired American annexation. Consul E. Spencer Pratt at Singapore, acting without authority, and later Dewey himself met Aguinaldo and obtained his support in return for oral statements of some sort regarding eventual Philippine independence. Just what they said remains unclear, but Dewey later maintained that he had made no commitments. He did not anticipate American ownership of the islands and at first thought the Filipinos more capable of self-government than the Cubans. As Aguinaldo's forces and his resistance increased, McKinley took him more seriously, and Dewey's views changed. The Americans did their best to shut out the Filipinos from the final successful attack on Manila, which capitulated on August 14 after the Spanish commander had agreed to make only token resistance. Since the peace protocol had been signed in Washington two days earlier, the Spanish later argued unsuccessfully that the city and hence the rest of the archipelago were not a legitimate prize of war.[37]

In the United States the question of annexing part or all of the Philippines remained in confusion during the fighting, while Americans informed themselves about the islands and chose sides. Between the signing of the peace protocol in August and the end of the year arguments pro and con took shape rapidly, but the issue was not formally laid before the public until the treaty was signed in

36. James K. Eyre, Jr., "Japan and the American Annexation of the Philippines," 55–71. A substantial part of the note received on September 10 is on 63–64.

37. Trask, War with Spain, 391–435, 590–91n1. Spector, Admiral of the New Empire, 47, 83–97. Schirmer, Republic or Empire? 68–72. Richard E. Welch, Jr., Response to Imperialism: The United States and the Philippine-American War, 1899–1902, 5–6, 13–14. Braisted, U.S. Navy in the Pacific, 1897–1909, 42–49, 64–69. Gould, Spanish-American War and McKinley, 65–67. After a thorough examination of the evidence, Phil Lyman Snyder concludes that Filipino leaders recognized they did not have a formal American promise of independence but maintained that their de facto working arrangement with American military forces led them to expect that the United States would follow the precedent of the Teller amendment. Snyder, "Mission, Empire, or Force of Circumstances?" 32–49, 124–26. Other Americans in the islands besides Dewey had a high opinion of Filipino leadership. Ibid., 65–66. Oscar F. Williams to Day, March 31, 1898. Rounseville Wildman to John Bassett Moore, July 18, 1898, no. 63, U.S., 58th Cong., 3d sess., Senate Document 62, pt. 1, 324, 338. For Philippine views of the Pratt and Dewey commitments see Uldarico S. Baclagon, Philippine Campaigns, 68, 78–79; and Renato Constantino, A History of the Philippines: From the Spanish Colonization to the Second World War, 207–10.

December. After that annexation was rarely out of public attention until after the election of 1900. A lineup of distinguished leaders in all fields argued for each side (and some in between, favoring caution). In general, the annexationists numbered more businessmen and church leaders, anti-annexationists more intellectuals and labor leaders, with many exceptions. Among politicians in all sections most Republicans supported annexations of some sort, while most Democrats favored delay or opposed outright.

As early as August 4 *Public Opinion* found 41.1 percent of "important" newspapers favoring "imperialism" (defined as keeping Pacific islands and Puerto Rico), 24.6 percent opposing it, and 32.3 percent wavering. Through the autumn *Literary Digest* press polls confirmed the support for some sort of annexation in all parts of the country, strongest on the West Coast and less impressive in the South and on the East Coast. In December the *New York Herald* reported 61.3 percent of newspapers in favor (out of 498 polled). The business press was divided, the *Wall Street Journal,* the *Banker and Tradesman,* the *Age of Steel,* and *Bradstreet's* urging commercial expansion through annexation, the *New York Journal of Commerce* favoring temporary annexation, and the *American Agriculturist* and the *Planter and Sugar Manufacturer* (New Orleans) opposed. Among business organizations the newly reorganized American Asiatic Association (formerly the Committee on American Interests in China) led the annexationists, followed by most chambers of commerce and the National Association of Manufacturers. The anti-imperialist movement begun in Faneuil Hall coalesced into a formal organization, the Anti-Imperialist League, by November. The head of the movement and president of the league was a successful commercial lawyer, Moorfield Storey.[38]

Most of the expansionist case for retaining part or all of the Philippines was already familiar in the cases of Cuba, Puerto Rico, and Hawaii and included ideological, humanitarian, constitutional, and other noneconomic arguments. The two principal economic justifications were the inherent value of the islands

---

38. The most useful surveys of individual leaders and of press and business opinion are Arthur M. Barnes, "American Intervention in Cuba and the Annexation of the Philippines: An Analysis of Public Discussion," especially 378–80, 386–87, 390–97, 410, 445–46; and Pratt, *Expansionists of 1898,* 266–78. These make clear the profound divisions caused by the complex issues of annexation: protectorate, naval base, Luzon, or the whole archipelago and by the mixture of economic and noneconomic arguments on both sides. Schirmer, *Republic or Empire?* 124. *Public Opinion* 25 (August 4, 1898): 135. The most detailed newspaper plebiscite was that of the *Literary Digest* 19 (September 10, 1898): 307–8. The *New York Herald,* December, is cited in Igor Petrovich Dement'ev, *USA: Imperialists and Anti-Imperialists: The Great Foreign Policy Debate at the Turn of the Century,* 148; *New York Journal of Commerce,* May 11, 1898; *New York Times,* May 15, 1898; *Wall Street Journal,* December 3, 1898; *New York Tribune,* July 30, 31, August 25, 27, 1898; *Commercial and Financial Chronicle* 66 (November 26, December 24, 1898): 1080–83, 1283–85. On the American Asiatic Association see Lorence, *Organized Business,* 17–20. On the Anti-Imperialist League see Tompkins, *Anti-Imperialism in the United States,* chaps. 9, 10; and Dementyev, *USA: Imperialism and Anti-Imperialism,* chap. 8. The German-language press was especially anti-annexationist, partly because it feared increased militarism in the United States. *Literary Digest* 17 (August 6, 1898): 156–58.

themselves and their geographic position close to the fabulous Far Eastern market. The first writings on the islands contained frothy exaggerations about "a revelation of vegetable and mineral riches" and "princely revenue poured into the lap of Spain" reminiscent of promotional literature about Latin America. Dewey himself sometimes wrote in this vein. About four months after his victory the Philadelphia Commercial Museum, a business-sponsored organization to publicize American products abroad, sent a commission to the islands to seek more precise information, and before the end of the year a special commissioner of the government produced a solid "Report on the Financial and Industrial Conditions of the Philippine Islands." By that time several leading periodicals had published enthusiastic but substantial surveys of Philippine conditions and prospects.

Almost all of them started with the Philippines' agricultural products—their flourishing hemp industry, an important source of binder twine for the United States; their sugar, held back by antiquated methods and lack of capital; their tobacco and copra, capable of great development; and their inexhaustible forests to reinforce the lumber shipments of California and Oregon throughout the Pacific and supply tropical hardwoods. One writer suggested that the Philippine sugar industry might even rescue the American consumer from the quasi-monopoly of the trust and the tariff-protected beet producers. Mineral products, such as coal, iron, lead, and alluvial gold, were also mentioned. At the same time the markets for American flour and kerosene were expected to grow, as well as the smaller consumption of American cotton cloth and yarn, hardware, canned goods, and other products.

In addition to trade opportunities, the government report hinted at openings for investment in the Philippines by pointing out that the islands had only one 192-kilometer railroad, the worst roads in the world, a primitive telegraph system, and inadequate inter-island connections. Another writer noted that the Manila street railway system already operated cars manufactured in Philadelphia. John Barrett, onetime minister to Siam and by now almost a professional expansionist, suggested that if young Britishers could develop plantations with Chinese labor, there was no reason why Americans could not follow suit. But Barrett also echoed consular advice in all tropical parts of the world by warning prospective emigrants that the Philippines were not extensions of the American West or Canada; an unacclimated laborer without capital could not expect to survive long. And some skeptical annexationists went even further by suggesting that the Philippines, once acquired, might prove more useful as trade counters to exchange with Britain for more valuable areas such as Canada or the British West Indies or even money with which to pay for the war.[39]

39. A convenient summary of principal annexationist arguments, mostly noneconomic, is Barnes, "American Intervention in Cuba," 373–77. For examples of froth see Albert J. Beveridge's maiden speech in Congress, as excerpted in Claude G. Bowers, *Beveridge and the Progressive Era*, 120; Adelbert M. Dewey, *The Life and Letters of Admiral Dewey from*

A second and even more attractive reason to retain the Philippines was their seeming importance in developing American trade with the Far East and with the world at large. The European power struggle in northern China during the preceding winter and spring had already called American attention to the area, and before the war a few expansionists had begun to urge the connection on McKinley. After Dewey's victory the newly formed American Asiatic Association launched a public education campaign of pamphlets, lectures, and press releases. The part of the world accessible from the Philippines, it appeared, held 50 percent of the world's population, with a purchasing power of a billion dollars. It was half as far from Manila to Hong Kong or Yokohama as from New York to Havana. Whereas Europe was as close as the United States to most of South America, the American Pacific coast was much closer to East Asia than Europe. According to one writer, the Far East was "practically at our back door."

Despite this geographical advantage American trade with the Far East and Australasia had always lagged far behind the British, but its recent increase (from $27 million in 1893 to nearly $63 million in 1897, according to *Bradstreet's*) gave hope of a brilliant future. This great new trade would stimulate the whole country: manufactures the East, cotton and cotton goods the South, flour the Middle West, and shipping the Pacific Coast. It would not only extend the current prosperity but permanently benefit the American economy, argued John Barrett, by liberalizing American trade policies, encouraging sound money, providing an outlet for capital, and improving the civil service. "Whatever tends to open a new foreign trade to any industry," declared *Iron Age*, "is likely to prove helpful to all."

But American advantages and prospects would go for naught, continued the annexationists, unless the United States acquired Manila for a naval base and a distributing point for American trade. Only then could investors be induced to send their capital across the Pacific. It would no longer suffice to let the British Navy protect American trade, as in the past. The more enthusiastic annexationists went even further. Given the resources of the islands and the likelihood of friction with an independent Philippine government, they said, why not demand or purchase the whole archipelago? If Americans were content with

---

Montpelier to Manila, 523; and *New York Tribune,* December 31, 1898. On the Philadelphia Commercial Museum see ibid., September 20, 1898. For Edward H. Harden's report see U.S., 55th Cong., 3d sess., *Senate Document 169,* 3–34. Department of Agriculture, *Trade of the Philippine Islands,* 9–15. U.S., 55th Cong., 3d sess., *Senate Document 169.* John Barrett, "The Problem of the Philippines," 266. Barrett, "The Value of the Philippines," 694–98; Pratt, *Expansionists of 1898,* 267n94. *Scribner's Magazine* 24 (July 1898): 18–19. Frank A. Vanderlip, "Facts about the Philippines with a Discussion of Pending Problems," 559–61. *Literary Digest* 17 (October 22, 1898): 505. *New York Times,* June 20, 1898. *New York Tribune,* September 9, 1898. *Annals of the American Academy* 13 (May 1899, supplement): 156–57. Russell Hastings to McKinley, August 22, 1898, McKinley papers, ser. 1, reel 4. Roosevelt to James Harrison Wilson, July 12, 1899, in Roosevelt, *Letters of Theodore Roosevelt,* vol. 2, 1032. *New York Times,* December 11, 1898. Some British observers were disposed to cede the British West Indies to the United States already since competition for the world sugar market with American-held territories would be ruinous. *Blackwood's Edinburgh Magazine* 164 (November 1898): 714–16.

Manila or Luzon, they might find themselves with British or German neighbors in the other islands or partners in an unwieldy protectorate like Samoa. From the beginning of the annexationist campaign, its most extreme publicists added the Philippines to a list incorporating the fondest dreams of expansionists for the past two decades: Hawaii, the Nicaragua canal, a Pacific cable, Cuba, and a chain of naval bases across the Pacific and the Caribbean. The Baltimore *Manufacturers' Record* proclaimed with some exaggeration: "Behind the successes of the arms of the United States is a solid phalanx of business interests determined to seize every advantage that may be gained under the prestige of victory in sharp competition with other nations of the world."[40]

The commercial arguments for retaining part or all of the Philippines soon involved protectionists in the dilemma of the "open door." The United States had long supported the principle of equal access to Chinese trade; so had Britain from time to time. After Dewey's victory many expansionists cited the open door to justify annexing part or all of the Philippines. At once the *New York Journal of Commerce* pointed out that the United States must then set a proper example with its trade policies in the Philippines. "We cannot stand for an 'open door' in China and close the door in the Philippines," it declared, and referring to French tariffs in Indochina asked: "Is Manila to become another Hong Kong or another Saigon?" The *Journal* even hoped that the United States could "establish a reign of peaceful competitive commerce the world over." More realistically, the *New York Times* pointed out that an open door policy would ensure the support of Britain against other powers' designs on the Philippines.

Other newspapers, especially tariff reformers, and the American Asiatic Association took up the argument during the summer. In his instructions to the American peace commission McKinley even included a general statement favoring the open door principle throughout the Orient and its application to the Philippines. A shrewd British observer guessed that McKinley was responding to western sugar-beet interests who wanted an excuse to raise a tariff against Philippine sugar. But the American consul at Hong Kong warned that an open door would allow Britain and Germany to absorb three-fourths of the islands' trade. During the autumn Nelson Dingley, the principal author of the 1897 tariff, visited the islands and on his return explained that the open door did not mean free trade but simply equal treatment for the United States and other trading nations. He reminded his hearers of British imperial preference and added that

40. Lorence, *Organized Business,* 18–19. Campbell, *Special Business Interests,* 44. Pratt, *Expansionists of 1898,* 266–71. Schirmer, *Republic or Empire?* 67. *New York Journal of Commerce,* May 13, 1898. *Wall Street Journal,* May 5, December 14, 1898. *Literary Digest* 17 (September 24, 1898): 361–63. (Baltimore *Manufacturers' Record* quoted on 362.) *North American Review* 166 (June 1898): 759–60; 167 (September 1898): 264–65. *Century Magazine* 56 (August 1898): 555–63. *Arena* 22 (November 1899): 570–75. *Harper's Weekly* 44 (July 28, September 22, 1900): 702–3, 885. *Iron Age* 61 (June 23, 1898): 15. *Bradstreet's* 26 (June 4, 25, December 17, 1898): 356–57, 404, 803–4. *Financial Review,* May 1898, reprinted in *National Geographic Magazine* 9 (June 1898): 304. *Manufacturers' Record,* October 20, 1899, reprinted in Gardner, *Different Frontier,* 60–65.

if the Philippines became an American territory, the open door would have to be reconciled with the U.S. Constitution. Thus encouraged, protectionist newspapers denounced a Philippine open door as preposterous, and at the signing of the peace treaty a brief but furious controversy broke out in the press.[41]

Anti-annexationists rested their positive case primarily on humanitarian, ideological, and constitutional arguments, dramatically or emotionally presented—the rights of the Filipinos to self-rule and the damage to American traditions and the Constitution of suppressing such rights. Their economic arguments were usually negative, rejecting the tempting advantages offered by the annexationists as hollow or counterbalanced by disadvantages. One such argument was used against acquiring any tropical territory—that its sugar producers and migrant labor would compete disastrously with Americans. Although labor generally supported the war for patriotic reasons at its beginning, it split on annexation, as some unions accepted the businessmen's expansionism, while others opposed militarism and high taxes for the sake of new foreign markets and cheap Oriental workers. Samuel Gompers feared also that an enlarged army, flushed with victory over the Filipinos, would turn to strike-breaking. Some anti-annexationists questioned the value of the Philippine market in comparison with Latin America. The *Nation* refuted the rosy predictions of Senator Morgan and other southern expansionists that Manila would funnel cotton textiles into the China market. Shanghai and Hong Kong, it said, were better distribution points for northern and southern China respectively.[42]

41. *New York Journal of Commerce,* May 26, June 11, October 25, 1898 (quoted phrases from May 26 and June 11 issues). *American Wool and Cotton Reporter,* June 30, 1898, cited in Schirmer, *Republic or Empire?* 79–80. *New York Times,* July 28, 29, 31, September 10, 1898; *New York Tribune,* May 14, 1898; *Nation* 67 (November 24, 1898): 379. A few newspapers suggested a joint Anglo-American regime in the Philippines. *The Manufacturer,* n.d., reprinted in *New York Times,* August 28, 1898. On the American Association see Lorence, *Organized Business,* 20–21; and a letter of John Foord in the *New York Times,* June 25, 1898. For McKinley's instructions see Whitelaw Reid, *Making Peace with Spain: The Diary of Whitelaw Reid, September–December 1898,* 236–37. Wildman to Hay, January 6, 1899, quoted in Tyler Dennett, *John Hay: From Poetry to Politics,* 287. The "shrewd British observer" was the publicist A. Maurice Low in *National Review* 32 (January 1899): 685. For Dingley's statement see *New York Tribune,* November 26, 1898. For the press debate see ibid., November 28; and *Literary Digest* 17 (December 10, 1898): 680–82. For a British free trade reaction see Lord Farrar in *New York Tribune,* July 24, 1898. Aside from this group, Europeans seem to have viewed American annexation of the Philippines principally for its effect on American involvement in Far Eastern political relations. A. E. Campbell, "Great Britain and the United States in the Far East, 1895–1903," 164–67.

42. A convenient summary of anti-annexationist arguments is Barnes, "American Intervention in Cuba," 367–73. Pratt, *Expansionists of 1898,* 272–73. McGee, "Gompers and Imperialism," 191–98. Gompers's views are also summarized in Healy, *U.S. Expansionism,* 220–21. Dement'ev, *USA: Imperialists and Anti-Imperialists,* 258–68. Louisiana Planter and Sugar Manufacturer (New Orleans), reprinted in *Literary Digest* 17 (September 24, 1898): 361. Edward Atkinson, "Eastern Commerce: What Is It Worth?" 295–304. *Nation* 71 (July 26, 1900): 66. Carl Schurz, *The Policy of Anti-Imperialism,* 21–22. George G. Vest, "Objections to Annexing the Philippines," 112–19. Richard Olney, "Growth of Our Foreign Policy," 295–96. *Public Opinion* 29 (August 9, 1900): 167–68.

Others went further and challenged the propaganda of the American Asiatic Association and other enthusiasts concerning the value of the China trade. The strength of this skepticism is suggested by the efforts of Secretary Day from 1898 to 1900 to get a congressional appropriation of $20,000 for a commission to investigate trade opportunities in China. Although several dozen business leaders and every important expansionist pressure group supported the bill, it was vainly introduced twice and finally disappeared during the Boxer Rebellion.[43]

Some anti-annexationists complained that the Philippines were so far away that protecting them at all would be risky and expensive, requiring larger armed forces. Instead, many suggested that control of Manila would be adequate for a naval base and transshipment center without the need to govern and defend the rest of the archipelago. Since the Philippines could probably never become states or even territories under the Constitution, they would have to be ruled as colonies, but experience with Canada and Latin America had demonstrated that profitable trade did not depend on colonial rule. Why not follow that experience and enjoy the fruit without the husk? In the war just ended Spain's far-flung colonies had been nothing but a handicap, and recent American trade increases suggested that even Britain's empire might not continue to be a great advantage. Edward Atkinson, a textile mill owner and a rabid anti-annexationist, argued that advanced nations made the best customers, and nineteenth-century trade statistics certainly bore him out. The statistician Worthington C. Ford demonstrated that the possibilities of greatly enlarging exports to the West Indies were much better than to East Asia. A few economic arguments bordered on the social and moral—for example, that imperialism abroad would encourage monopoly at home and benefit business, not labor or that American lower-class poverty made any talk of exporting a surplus to foreigners "both an economic absurdity and an arraignment of our American civilization at the bar of humanity and justice."[44] All in all, it would be fair to say that the economic arguments

43. Campbell, *Special Business Interests*, 38, 63–66. McClellan, *Heathen Chinee*, 191–92. U.S., 55th Cong., 2d sess., *House Document 536. Literary Digest* 17 (July 16, 1898): 66–67. *New York Times*, June 15, July 4, 1898.

44. Richard E. Welch, Jr., "Motives and Policy Objectives of Anti-Imperialists, 1898," 119–29. Healy, *U.S. Expansionism*, 232–33, 242–43. Pratt, *Expansionists of 1898*, 272–73. Beisner, *Twelve against Empire*, 87. Göran Rystad, *Ambiguous Imperialism: American Foreign Policy and Domestic Politics at the Turn of the Century*, 26. Carl Schurz, "The Issue of Imperialism," in Frederic Bancroft, ed., *Speeches, Correspondence and Political Papers of Carl Schurz*, vol. 6, 6–9, 26–29. Edward Atkinson, "Treatise Submitted at the Meeting of the American Association for the Advancement of Science . . . August 25, 1899," 31–32. W. P. Treat et al., "In Re Imperialism," 483–91. Vest, "Objections to Annexing," 119. *Arena* 22 (April 1900): 338–41. Andrew Carnegie, "Distant Possessions—The Parting of the Ways," 240–43. *New York Times*, October 21, 22, 24, 1898. *Harper's Weekly* 42 (October 22, 1898): 1046. On the presumed benefits of annexation to the American South see *Nation* 71 (July 26, 1900): 66. Quotation from an address by Charles A. Towne, at that time a Silver Republican from Minnesota. U.S., 55th Cong., 3d sess., *Senate Document 161*, 11. John Sherman to James P. Munroe, November 18, 1898. Draft "for publication," Sherman papers, box 5964. (Senator) John C. Spooner to Day, n.d., Day papers, box 10.

against annexation were as numerous and as widely circulated as those in favor of it.

The press and public debate over the Philippines virtually drowned out comment on the American acquisition of other Spanish islands in the Pacific. Within ten days of Dewey's victory the Naval War Board got Secretary Long to order the seizure of Guam in the Mariana group (then called the Ladrones), and a warship en route to reinforce Dewey accomplished this without resistance. Indeed, its commander might have seized Saipan and the rest of the group had he not interpreted his orders narrowly. At about the same time another reinforcing warship took possession of uninhabited Wake Island, between Guam and Midway. (The United States had held Midway since 1867.)

The Caroline Islands to the south attracted a little more attention because of missionary troubles there in the 1880s, although the Germans had dominated trade (see chapter 4). A few individuals urged the incorporation of the Carolines, either as a connecting link between Hawaii and the Philippines or as a substitute for the latter. In October an economics professor at the University of Michigan made a case for the Carolines much like expansionist arguments about Hawaii—that they were "fertile, well wooded and well watered, with a healthful oceanic climate and magnificent harbors," suitable for cable and coaling stations, commercial ports, or naval bases. If the United States did not take them, another strong power would. German traders and strategists were more interested than Americans, and it became clear that the fate of the Carolines would depend on that of the Philippines in the peace negotiations.[45]

President McKinley's attitude toward Philippine annexation has puzzled historians as much as his decision to intervene in Cuba. At opposite extremes are those who believe he intended to annex the islands even before the outbreak of the war and those who regard the "decision" as the result of undirected drift.[46] The majority hold that, in his characteristically cryptic fashion, McKinley gradually evolved from desire for a naval base at or near Manila through several stages:

45. William R. Braisted, "The Philippine Naval Base Problem, 1898–1909," 21. Leslie W. Walker, "Guam's Seizure by the United States in 1898," 1–12. Quinn, "Struggle for the Carolines," 290–94. Pratt, *Expansionists of 1898*, 274, 302–4. William E. Dodge to Moore, May 23, 1898, Moore papers, box 186. Edward Van Dyck Robinson, "The Caroline Islands and the Terms of Peace," 1046–48 (quotation). Laff, *Uncle Sam's Pacific Inlets*, 11–15, 21–22. Commander E. D. Taussig formally claimed Wake for the United States on January 17, 1899. Braisted, *U.S. Navy in the Pacific, 1897–1909*, 56–57.

46. For examples of the two extremes mentioned see on the one side McCormick, *China Market*, 107–17; and Wehler, *Aufstieg*, 365; and on the other Louis J. Halle, *Dream and Reality: Aspects of American Foreign Policy*, 189–90; and Halle, *U.S. Acquires the Philippines*, passim. Good discussions of the problem are Trask, *War with Spain*, 615–16n18. Brian P. Damiani, "Advocates of Empire: William McKinley, the Senate, and American Expansion, 1898–1899," 1–5; Snyder, "Mission, Empire or Force of Circumstances?" 247–49 (see especially 237–42). An encyclopedic discussion of historiography is Ephraim K. Smith, "William McKinley's Enduring Legacy: The Historiographical Debate on the Taking of the Philippine Islands," 205–49.

retention of the city, of Luzon island, and eventually of the whole archipelago. The evidence for this evolution is found in the timing and wording of orders to send an occupying force (May 4), Secretary Long's instructions to Dewey (May 26), the cabinet's discussions of peace terms (July 28–30), the State Department's receipt of the Japanese note suggesting courses of action (September 10), McKinley's instructions to the peace commissioners (September 16), and his revised instructions for outright annexation (October 26 and 28), along with various elusive statements made in conversation with intimates or visitors and later reported by them.[47]

The evidence regarding McKinley's motives is similarly incomplete and partly conjectural. As has been seen, the original decision for Dewey to attack Manila was apparently made for reasons of naval strategy, and the early orders to send reinforcements and seize the city seem to have been primarily motivated by military considerations. After Dewey's victory he and the Naval War Board presented to McKinley the case for a permanent base at Subic Bay, near Manila, and from then through the summer public and private writings also impressed on him the value of a commercial center in the islands to encourage the developing China trade. At the same time the German, British, and Japanese interest in the islands and reports by geological and commercial commissions established the difficulty of retaining Manila without Luzon and Luzon without the other islands. Last but not least among the motivating factors was the rapidly developing public expansionism. The principal evidences of this were the congressional passage of the much-vexed Hawaiian annexation bill in early July and popular enthusiasm for the carefully worded references to expansion in McKinley's campaign speeches during a midwestern tour in October. Around all these arguments shone a

---

47. Trask, *War with Spain,* 382–85, 404, 428, 431, 439–43, 452–56. Welch, *Response to Imperialism,* 3–10. Morgan, *McKinley and His America,* 396–413 et passim. Gould, *Spanish-American War and McKinley,* 62–64, 67, 84–90, 99–110. Paolo E. Coletta, "McKinley, the Peace Negotiations, and the Acquisition of the Philippines," 341–45. Robert C. Hildebrand, *Power and the People: Executive Management of Public Opinion in Foreign Affairs, 1897–1921,* 34–36, 37–41. Granville and Young, *Politics, Strategy, and American Diplomacy,* 285–88. Grunder and Livezey, *Philippines and United States,* 30–33. The instructions of October 26 were not delivered; those of October 28 were essentially the same. Snyder, "Mission, Empire, or Force of Circumstances?" 105–6. For views of possibly influential advisers see Grenville and Young, *Politics, Strategy, and American Diplomacy,* 291–94; Werking, "Lodge and the Philippines," 234–40; Widenor, *Lodge and Search for Foreign Policy,* 115; undated memorandum by Lodge in Day papers, box 9; Schirmer, *Republic or Empire?* 72–73; Kenton J. Clymer, "Checking the Sources: John Hay and Spanish Possessions in the Pacific," *The Historian,* 88–89. John Davis Long, *America of Yesterday, as Reflected in the Journal of John Davis Long,* 213–15; and Alger, *Spanish American War,* 326. In mid-August, well before the instructions to the commissioners to keep Luzon, McKinley asked for and obtained from Dewey information about the resources of the different islands. Correspondence reported in U.S., 56th Cong., 1st sess., *Congressional Record,* 33, 895. The new minister to China added his arguments for keeping the islands or at least Manila. E. H. Conger to Day, August 26, 1898, no. 31, U.S., Diplomatic Despatches, China, 104. For an example of hearsay evidence regarding McKinley's opinions see Pritchett, "Recollections of McKinley," 400–401.

beneficent though patronizing humanitarianism toward the Filipinos but no appreciation of Aguinaldo's nationalism or willingness to arrange with him a compromise form of government. As with the original intervention in Cuba, the evidence suggests that economic considerations were important but probably not decisive in McKinley's determination to annex the Philippines.[48]

In mid-September, while the president was still making up his mind, he appointed a peace commission, tilted toward annexation: Secretary Day, who resigned from the State Department, as chairman; two Republican expansionist senators, Cushman K. Davis (Minnesota, chairman of the Foreign Relations Committee) and William P. Frye (Maine); a Democratic anti-expansionist senator, George Gray (Delaware); and the Republican journalist-politician-diplomat Whitelaw Reid. At the outset Frye and Reid favored annexing all the Philippines, Davis Luzon, and Day and Gray opposed acquiring any Pacific territory, but they all accepted McKinley's instructions to obtain Puerto Rico, Luzon, and an island in the Marianas (presumably Guam).

For weeks the negotiations centered on responsibility for the enormous Cuban colonial debt. Meanwhile, after the election campaign McKinley issued revised instructions to demand the whole Philippine archipelago and urge haste. The commission complied, Day and Gray regretfully, and after some resistance by the Spaniards, a treaty was signed on December 10. It provided $20 million in compensation for Spain and equal commercial treatment in the Philippines for ten years. Meanwhile, Germany had secretly obtained from Spain conditional options on two bases in the Carolines, Kusaie and Yap. The Americans made a bid for Kusaie and might have acquired all the Marianas and Carolines, but McKinley would not grant further trade concessions in exchange. Germany finally purchased both groups, excepting Guam, to the later sorrow of a whole generation of Americans.[49]

48. See sources cited in preceding note. A good summary of McKinley's motives is Coletta, "McKinley and the Philippines," 345–47. See also Snyder, "Mission, Empire, or Force of Circumstances?" 71 ff. The neat outline McKinley himself presented to a group of missionaries, according to his biographer, Charles S. Olcott (*The Life of William McKinley,* vol. 2, 109–11) has been widely, often cynically, quoted but may have been at least a partial fabrication. Gould, *Spanish-American War and McKinley,* 108–10. For a list of possible business and other economic influences on the president see McCormick, *China Market,* 117–20. Concerning a futile conversation between McKinley and the Filipino representative Felipe Agoncillo see Trask, *War with Spain,* 443; and Morgan, *McKinley and His America,* 405–6. On naval arguments see Braisted, "Philippine Naval Base Problem," 22–23. On economic factors in the Cuban intervention see Pletcher, *Diplomacy of Trade and Investment,* 340–54.

49. Trask, *War with Spain,* 435–68. Hildebrand, *Power and the People,* 36–37, 41–42. For Reid's perceptive account in his diary see Reid, *Making Peace with Spain,* especially 26–31. For McKinley's original instructions and the opinions of the commissioners at the end of October see ibid., 233–42. The text of the treaty is in Bevans, *Treaties,* vol. 2, 615–21. Spain also ceded Puerto Rico. On the Spanish-American-German diplomacy concerning the Carolines and Marianas see Quinn, "Diplomatic Struggle," 294–302, and Brown, "German Acquisition," 143–44, 146–52. McCormick states that at one point Spain

A month before the treaty was signed the United States held midterm elections, confirming the Republican control of both houses and adding six new Republicans in the Senate, which would have to approve the treaty by a two-thirds majority. During November and December the NAM, the National Businessmen's League, and boards of trade in New York, Minnesota, Minneapolis (flour milling), and Lowell, Massachusetts (textiles), petitioned Congress in favor of the treaty. In December McKinley made a week-long speaking tour of the South, the least annexationist section of the country, where crowds applauded his discreet mixture of patriotism and expansionism. On this occasion in particular it was difficult to determine who was leading whom. Elsewhere, the Northeast mildly approved new territories, and the West, especially the Pacific coast, was enthusiastic, but public opinion at large was far from settled.[50]

The Senate was more evenly divided than the press, both parties being split on annexations. Both sides hoped for fast action, the administration to avoid embarrassment or continued negotiations with Spain, its opponents because they would be weaker in the new Senate, if McKinley had to call a special session. During the debate, carried on in executive session, anti-annexationists seized the initiative with a series of speeches repeating all the arguments developed since the preceding summer. Both sides cited economic factors, playing up or decrying Philippine and Chinese trade. At the outset opponents of the treaty showed their internal disunity with several conflicting resolutions and amendments, either opposing all annexations for constitutional reasons or accepting temporary control in one form or another but promising independence to the Philippines. William Jennings Bryan may have changed a few Democratic votes by favoring the treaty, probably in the interest of peace, although many accused him of partisan motives. Henry Cabot Lodge and other administration stalwarts as well as the president himself exerted more influence on doubtful Republicans. And from the outside pressure groups made their presence felt, such as two dozen elder statesmen, business, and labor leaders who sent an anti-annexationist petition to

---

offered the United States both groups in exchange for "open door status for Spain in Cuba and Puerto Rico." McCormick, *China Trade,* 123. The account in Reid's published diary is less clear-cut. Reid, *Making Peace with Spain,* 186–96. In accordance with the Teller amendment to the congressional war resolution the instructions made no reference to the annexation of Cuba.

50. Gould, *Spanish-American War and McKinley,* 105–6, 110–12. Barnes, "American Intervention in Cuba," 403–4. Hildebrand, *Power and the People,* 42–43. The Republicans lost seventeen seats in the House, a normal midterm phenomenon. A sampling of press opinion on the election showed considerable disagreement as to the public attitude toward annexations. *Literary Digest* 17 (November 19, 1898): 596–97. *New York Tribune,* October 21, December 8, 1898. See also evidence of anti-annexationist sentiment in the *Merchants' and Manufacturers' Board of Trade.* Ibid., December 10. Among business journals the cautious *Commercial and Financial Chronicle* was still wary of "colonialism," while *Bankers' Magazine* and the *Wall Street Journal* were optimistic about the future. *Commercial and Financial Chronicle* 66 (November 26, December 10, 1898): 1080–83, 1185–87. *Bankers' Magazine* 57 (December 1898): 886–88. *Wall Street Journal,* November 22, 1898.

the Senate. Finally, just before the Senate's vote, open fighting broke out with the Filipino rebels.

At the end of January the outcome was still uncertain. Press and public were impatient at the delay as unworthy of the war's glorious victories, but the stock market, then in the midst of a boom, hardly wavered. Finally on February 6 the treaty was approved, 57–27, with only one vote to spare. Anti-annexationists were not satisfied, so debate continued over two more resolutions. One abjured the annexation of Cuba, approximating the language of the Teller amendment in April. It was defeated by the tie-breaking vote of the vice president. The other, pronouncing in vague language against permanent annexation "as an integral part of the United States," was passed, 26–22, but nearly half of the senators abstained. Since the House never took it up, it had no effect.

Clearly the Senate was still as divided as before; one analyst counted twenty-nine senators opposed to expansion, thirty-four imperialists, sixteen moderates, and eleven uncertain. Historians have never been able to agree on what or who produced the winning margin for the treaty—the issues, McKinley, his cohorts, Bryan, or hostilities in the Philippines.[51] Whatever the case, the "splendid little war," in John Hay's callous phrase, ended on a note of uncertainty.

51. Pratt, *Expansionists of 1898*, 345–58. Trask, *War with Spain*, 168–70. Morgan, *American's Road to Empire*, 101–9. Tompkins, *Anti-Imperialism in the United States*, chap. 12. Stuart Creighton Miller, *"Benevolent Assimilation": The American Conquest of the Philippines, 1899–1903*, 26–30. Schirmer, *Republic or Empire?* chap. 9., especially 124. Gould, *Spanish-American War and McKinley*, 111–18. Paolo E. Coletta, "Bryan, McKinley, and the Treaty of Paris," 138–46. Snyder, "Mission, Empire, or Force of Circumstances?" 199–207. Damiani, "Advocates of Empire." Hildebrand, *Power and the People*, 43–44. For economic arguments in the debate see U.S., 55th Cong., 3d sess., *Congressional Record*, 32, 438, 449–51, 641–42, 925, 1831–32. William J. Pomeroy, *American Neo-Colonialism: Its Emergence in the Philippines and Asia*, 57–62. Richard E. Welch, Jr., believes that if Hoar and Bryan had collaborated early in the debate to present a bipartisan plan for a Philippine protectorate and a guarantee of eventual independence, they might have headed off the annexationists. Richard E. Welch, Jr., "Senator George Frisbie Hoar and the Defeat of Anti-Imperialism, 1898–1900," 362–80, especially 379. On the work of Lodge see Richard E. Welch, Jr., "Opponents and Colleagues: George Frisbie Hoar and Henry Cabot Lodge, 1898–1904," 191. On the pressure group, which included Grover Cleveland, Andrew Carnegie, and Samuel Gompers, see *New York Tribune*, February 6, 1899. For press comment on the debate and treaty see *Public Opinion* 26 (February 2, 1899): 133–35; *New York Tribune*, February 2, 4, 1899. *Commercial and Financial Chronicle* 68 (February 11, 1899): 251–52. On the stock market see *Wall Street Journal*, January 31, February 8, 1899. For an analysis of Senate opinions see Grunder and Livezey, *Philippines and United States*, 46–47. On historiographical differences regarding the outcome see, for examples, Trask, *War with Spain*, 622n58. A similar disagreement concerns Bryan's reasons for supporting a treaty he disliked. Some believe that he wanted to remove imperialism from politics and wage the election of 1900 mainly on the silver issue, others that he wanted to make imperialism the principal issue for 1900 and regarded the silver question as dead.

12

Unfinished Business and New Directions

LL WARS LEAVE unfinished business behind them—boundaries, indemnities, veterans' benefits, and many other matters, tangible and intangible. Some of them also present new directions and opportunities, usually to the victors. The Spanish-American War left unsettled the problems of occupying and ruling the Philippines and of finding some substitute for the unworkable condominium over Samoa. In northern China the European and Japanese spheres of influence, comprising naval bases and areas of economic dominance, threatened American trade and investments. This threat seemed to require new American policies that would uphold the idea of an open door to economic opportunities in Asia, and these policies in turn seemed to require increased involvement in Far Eastern politics.

During the two years after the peace treaty the United States fought a civil war in the Philippines, settled the Samoan question, announced an open door policy for China, and intervened to help put down a rebellion in that country. Then it was time for another presidential election, which apparently ratified what had been done.

When the Senate approved the peace treaty with Spain, war was breaking out in the Philippines. Its underlying causes were distance, unfamiliarity with the islands, and the indeterminate American intentions after the Battle of Manila Bay. The immediate cause was the failure of the American government and its military leaders to come to an explicit understanding with Emilio Aguinaldo, leader of the Filipino rebel movement and presumed ally. While McKinley's representatives carried on negotiations with the Spanish in Paris, Aguinaldo organized a constitutional government over most of the islands. At the same time American army leaders set up a temporary occupation in Manila, which they cleaned up and policed.

There was still opportunity for cooperation with the rebels, who were disunited and had alienated some of the populace. The principal force holding them together during this time was fear of the Americans, for Spanish propaganda had given them a lurid picture of American cruelty toward Indians and blacks, and their fear was increased by occasional skirmishes with the American troops and the haughtiness of the American commander, General Elwell S. Otis. President

McKinley, hampered by slow communications and poor advice, was largely out of touch with the islands. He was determined not to concede Philippine independence, and his otherwise benevolent intentions toward the Filipinos were overencouraged by Otis's exaggerated reports of annexationist sentiment among the upper classes. During January 1899 General Otis made several efforts to negotiate with the rebels surrounding Manila, but he stipulated recognition of U.S. sovereignty. Aguinaldo insisted on complete independence, so no compromise was possible. On February 4 hostilities broke out spontaneously, but the Americans were too few to overcome the besieging forces and were limited to raids until they could receive reinforcements.[1]

Two weeks later McKinley spoke at length about America's benevolent intentions toward the Filipinos, but he also made clear that he would hold no plebiscite for an indefinite time. He had already appointed an investigating commission led by President Jacob Gould Schurman of Cornell University, who had opposed annexation publicly but was an economic expansionist, and including others with some knowledge of the islands. The Schurman Commission arrived in Manila during March and immediately appealed to prosperous, educated, upper-class Filipinos (ilustrados) by detailing plans for reform and participation in an American-controlled regime. However, commission members quarreled with each other and with the army leaders. Their final report to the president contained useful information about the islands, but it did not recommend much more than suppression of the revolt and continued American rule by civilians.[2] During the summer McKinley appointed a brilliant, conservative New York corporation lawyer, Elihu Root, as secretary of war, intending him not only to overhaul the maladministered War Department but also to supervise the new colonies. After intensive study of British colonial administration Root concluded that if the United States were to continue holding the Philippines, it must reconcile its basic principles of government, especially those relating to individual freedom, with "the customs and business and social life of the islanders."[3]

Needless to say, the army had trouble conforming its disciplinary codes and traditions to these high-minded intentions, although its leaders recognized that

1. Grunder and Livezey, *Philippines and United States*, 51–55. John Morgan Gates, *Schoolbooks and Krags: The United States Army in the Philippines, 1898–1902*, chaps. 1, 2. Welch, *Response to Imperialism*, 14–23. Bonifacio S. Salamanca, *The Filipino Reaction to American Rule, 1901–1913*, 22–29. For a more anti-American account see Pomeroy, *American Neo-Colonialism*, 69–70.

2. Peter W. Stanley, *A Nation in the Making: The Philippines and the United States, 1899–1921*, 54–60. Pomeroy, *American Neo-Colonialism*, 70–83. LaFeber, *American Search*, 165–67. Miller, "Benevolent Assimilation," 131–33. Welch, *Response to Imperialism*, 28–30. The commission also included General Otis, Admiral Dewey, Charles Denby, former minister to China, and Dean C. Worcester, a Michigan zoologist who had lived in the Philippines. For the commission's report see U.S., 56th Cong., 1st sess., *Senate Document 112*.

3. Philip C. Jessup, *Elihu Root*, vol. 2, chaps. 16–17 (quoted phrase on p. 346). Glenn Anthony May, *Social Engineering in the Philippines: The Aims, Execution, and Impact of American Colonial Policy, 1900–1913*, 5–8.

the prospect of reforms would further weaken the already divided rebels. Receiving reinforcement, the Americans extended their control to several of the smaller islands and during the dry season of fall and winter 1899–1900 occupied most of northern Luzon. By the end of 1899 Washington believed that the rebellion was almost quelled. McKinley appointed a second commission to implement a permanent government for the Philippines. Its director was William Howard Taft, a distinguished Ohio lawyer with little knowledge of or interest in public administration. He was to control the colonial system for more than a decade as commissioner, civil governor, secretary of war, and president of the United States. In March 1900 Root drew up instructions for the Taft Commission, carefully dividing functions between military and civilians, laying out municipal governments, and emphasizing education, especially in English. In May Otis transferred command of army forces to General Arthur MacArthur, who optimistically issued a proclamation of amnesty.[4]

But during the 1899 campaign Aguinaldo had realized the futility of open battles with the Americans and shifted to an organized guerrilla campaign. Although at first the Americans underestimated its effectiveness, they soon responded in kind. Most of the officers and men had gained their experience in Indian wars at home, and many regarded the Filipinos as "niggers"—little better than animals. Atrocities occurred on both sides. Some Americans soon resorted to torture, and the American commanders tried to censor reports of the fighting. Aguinaldo's propagandists made a great play of American hypocrisy, while anti-annexationists at home, still smarting from the recent battles over the peace treaty, took up the cry eagerly and organized the Anti-Imperialist League, fighting off charges of treason. When the Taft Commission arrived in June, they found a rapidly worsening situation, which the impatient Taft blamed on General MacArthur. The optimism of six months before was replaced by an oxymoron, "beneficent pacification" as the chief aim of America's Philippine policy. Finally, on July 4, 1902, President Roosevelt declared the Philippine War formally ended.[5]

Since Philippine resources and trade had made up one of the most potent arguments for annexation, one might have expected a vigorous commercial policy

4. Gates, *Schoolbooks and Krags*, chaps. 3, 4. Welch, *Response to Imperialism*, 24–32. May, *Social Engineering*, 8–19. Stanley, *Nation in the Making*, 61–65. The Taft Commission included Luke W. Wright (later governor general), Worcester, Henry Clay Ide (who had served in the Samoan condominium government), and Bernard Moses, a historian of colonial Latin America.

5. Gates, *Schoolbooks and Krags*, chap. 5. James A. LeRoy, *The Americans in the Philippines: A History of the Conquest and First Years of Occupation with an Introductory Account of the Spanish Rule*, vol. 2, chaps. 23, 24. Pomeroy, *American Neo-Colonialism*, 84–93. For intimate accounts of the guerrilla warfare see Russell Roth, *Muddy Glory: America's "Indian War" in the Philippines*; Glenn A. May, *Battle for Batangas: A Philippine Province at War*; and Welch, *Response to Imperialism*, vol. 2, chap. 9. On the Anti-Imperialist League see Tompkins, *Anti-Imperialism in the United States*, chap. 10; and Welch, *Response to Imperialism*, chap. 3.

to be one of the first American measures after defeating Spain. On the capture of Manila in August 1898 McKinley announced that the port would be open to all American and neutral trade in noncontraband. For convenience's sake the military commander retained the existing complicated Spanish tariff duties (removing the preference for Spanish goods), but these duties soon had to be revised, especially since they bore too heavily on Filipinos in the city. Exporters in the United States soon pressed the government for lower rates, but the peace treaty required that duties on American and Spanish imports into the islands be kept equal for ten years, and other nations having most-favored-nation treaties with the United States would surely invoke them as well.

Clearly a general tariff revision was needed. Although Congress passed the Foraker Act on April 12, 1900, establishing a system for Puerto Rico, the Filipino rebellion prevented General Otis and the Schurman Commission from doing more than tinkering with the Spanish tariff. To make matters worse, after the Americans began to occupy other Philippine ports, Otis and Admiral Dewey could not agree on whether they were to be opened to foreign trade. Not until September 1901 did the Taft Commission establish uniform rates for the islands, and on March 8, 1902, Congress enacted these into law. In 1909 the Payne-Aldrich Act established free trade between the United States and the Philippines with a few exceptions, and four years later these were removed.[6]

The success of the free trade system was more apparent than real. By 1930 the Philippines were receiving 63 percent of their imports from the United States and sending 77 percent of their exports there. Filipino production of sugar, copra, coconut oil, tobacco, and Manila hemp (abacá) expanded rapidly. During 1925–1930 the Philippines bought an average of $75 million worth of American goods. But this flourishing trade made the islands dependent on their big customer, so the ever-present independence movement, which was mainly political and psychological in origin, worked against their major economic interests. At the same time the powerful sugar, tobacco, and dairy industries in the United States supported Philippine independence under a liberal cloak. The resulting division of motivation complicated an already difficult relationship for the next half century. At the same time the growing Japanese menace emphasized the remoteness and vulnerability of the islands. As early as 1907 Theodore Roosevelt himself was privately admitting that they had turned out to be an Achilles heel.[7]

* * *

6. Pedro S. Abelarde, *American Tariff Policy towards the Philippines, 1898–1946*, 4–36. LeRoy, *Americans in the Philippines*, vol. 2, 73–76.
7. Pratt, *America's Colonial Experiment*, 291–97. Grunder and Livezey, *Philippines and United States*, 211–18. American investments in agriculture, mining, and manufacturing were slow in appearing before 1913. Railroads, which appeared earlier, earned disappointingly low profits. An agricultural bank of the same period failed in its purpose to help the small farmer. Stanley, *Nation in the Making*, 226–31. Grunder and Livezey, *Philippines and United States*, 89–93. American investments in the Philippines reached about two hundred million dollars by 1935. Ibid., 200n5. On the vulnerability of the Philippines see Roosevelt to William Howard Taft, August 21, 1907, cited in Griswold, *Far Eastern Policy*, 35n2.

The Spanish-American War helped dispose of the Samoan condominium by dissipating the fog that surrounded a partition settlement. The first direct effect of the war was a decision by the U.S. Naval War Board in August 1898 to develop the American-held harbor of Pago Pago into a coaling base. This produced an outburst of jealous Yankeephobia in the German press and responsive grumbling in American newspapers. The ramshackle condominium was further strained in the same month by the death of Malietoa Laupepa, the weak figurehead king who had generally favored the British and Americans. The German government allowed his rival, Mata'afa Iosefa, to return from exile and gather a following. In the ensuing civil war the commander of the American naval forces, Admiral Albert Kautz, rejected Mata'afa's German-sponsored government and in March 1899 bombarded a coastal village under his control, while both British and American forces engaged in fracases with the Samoans that were widely reported at home.

As early as January 1899 Kaiser Wilhelm's government made conciliatory approaches to Britain for a partition settlement such as Britain and Germany had put forward ten years before. McKinley approved their proposal for a joint investigating commission in the islands to gain time and calm tempers. (Also, Admiral Kautz was recalled.) The commission abolished the Samoan monarchy and divided the government among the various tribes under the supervision of the three consuls. By summer several factors favored partition: British involvement in European and African problems, further conviction on all sides of the condominium's unworkability after the civil war, and a subsiding of German-American hostility in the presses of both countries.[8]

From the earliest suggestion of partition in the 1880s, the Germans hoped to retain the two largest islands in the west end of the group, Savaii and Upolu, which contained the capital city, Apia, most of the native population, and the principal German-owned property. Since the United States held rights to and territory around Pago Pago harbor on Tutuila Island to the east, that was to be the American share, while Britain would leave Samoa and be confirmed in possession of the Tonga group. Neither British nor Americans felt that their share was large enough, but an Admiralty memorandum on the value of Tonga brought the British Foreign Office around, and the United States was offered a bonus of several small islands east of Tutuila that no one else wanted. A tripartite treaty was signed on December 2, 1899, and quickly approved by the American Senate.[9]

---

8. This account of events leading up to the partition of Samoa is largely based on Kennedy, *Samoan Tangle*, chaps. 4, 5; Ryden, *Foreign Policy in Samoa*, chaps. 13–15; and Holstine, "American Diplomacy in Samoa," chaps. 7–8. See also Vagts, *Deutschland und die Vereinigten Staaten*, vol. 1, 797–938. McKinley's reaction was partly occasioned by the recent collapse of Anglo-American negotiations over the Alaska boundary (see chap. 2). Campbell, *Anglo-American Understanding*, 151–56.

9. For the terms of the treaties see Bevans, *Treaties*, vol. 1, 373–77. The European and African aspects of Anglo-German negotiations are well covered in Kennedy, *Samoan Tangle*, chap. 5. Fiji was Britain's most important possession in the southwest Pacific,

American press opinion on the settlement echoed some arguments from the debate on Philippine annexation, but the dominant sentiments were relief—"good riddance" to the condominium—and self-congratulation at obtaining the one island America wanted. Some remarked that the question had taught the country the value of a navy and a coaling station; others thought we had no business meddling so far away from home. As for the Samoans, the *New York Tribune* rationalized: "The civilization of the world requires that the islands of the sea should be made safe stopping-places for peaceful commerce, and civilization has rights that even barbarism is bound to respect." Undoubtedly the most important long-range effects of the Samoan affair were to encourage a developing Anglo-American rapprochement and to widen, even if slightly, a crack in German-American friendship. One newspaper regarded the latter as part of the high price paid for Tutuila.[10]

On the continent of Asia the Spanish-American War activated the American government into taking a stand toward the Euro-Japanese threat to China that had developed during the late 1890s (see chapters 9, 10). The debate over disposing of the Philippines became closely associated with Chinese trade. A proposal for an open door policy in the Philippines faced insuperable opposition from traditional protectionists, but the open door in China was not necessarily inconsistent with protectionism at home. One writer laid out an elaborate program for Anglo-American cooperation in maintaining "the integrity of Chinese trade." The *New York Journal of Commerce* incorporated the policy into the mainstream of American expansionism: "The genius of our people, their detestation of oppression, their respect for international justice, their consciousness of a great commercial destiny, all bind the United States to sympathy with the cause of the 'open-door.' "[11]

---

and its population was closely related ethnically to that of Tonga. The additional islands received by the United States included the small Manua group and the uninhabited Sand and Rose atolls. They were not formally ceded until 1904 and were virtually ignored thereafter. Ryden, *Foreign Policy in Samoa*, 576–77. Under a treaty of 1886 with the king of Tonga the United States had a right to a naval station there, but this was allowed to fade away without formal action. Kennedy, *Samoan Tangle*, 282–84.

10. Kennedy, *Samoan Tangle*, 254–58. *Public Opinion* 26 (February 2, April 6, 1899): 135–36, 421; 27 (August 10, November 16): 167–68, 616–17; 28 (January 25, 1900): 101. *Literary Digest* 18 (April 8, 1899): 389–90; 19 (November 18): 606–7. *New York Tribune*, January 21, February 10, 11, March 24, 31, April 13, November 11, 1899 (quotation in issue of April 13). *New York Commercial Advertiser*, January 19, 1899; *Bradstreet's* 26 (November 18, 1899): 726–27. A few publicists persisted in the idea that Samoa had great potential commercial importance as a way station between Panama, Australasia, and the Orient. O. P. Austin, "The Commercial Importance of Samoa," 218–20. For German press reactions see *Literary Digest* 17 (August 27, October 29, 1898): 264, 532. The effect of Samoa on relations between the United States, Britain, and Germany is analyzed at some length in Kennedy, *Samoan Tangle*, 285–306.

11. Pratt, *Expansionists of 1898*, 266–71. *Bradstreet's* 26 (December 17, 1898): 803–4. *American Wool and Cotton Reporter*, June 30, 1898, cited in Schirmer, *Republic or Empire?*

As a press campaign took form, other factors began to work for an open door policy. Evidence appeared of increased government interest: a proposal by Secretary Day for a commission to investigate Chinese trade, the appointment of the Anglophile expansionist John Hay in September 1898 as secretary of state; and the protectionist McKinley's statement of support in his instructions to the peace commissioners at the same time: "Asking only the open door [in the Orient] for ourselves, we are ready to accord the open door to others." Events in China showed the need for some sort of action, as rioting in the Peking area led Hay to send two gunboats to the adjacent coast and similar unrest in Manchuria caused fear of Russian repression. Cotton goods manufacturers and exporters in New England and the South petitioned the government for "a vigorous policy" in an area that accounted for half of their sales in China. Early in 1899 Hay was instructed to "act energetically" on behalf of one company.[12]

For a time during late 1898 and early 1899 some Americans were tempted to follow the Europeans' example and ask China for a sphere of influence. McKinley's new minister to China, Edwin H. Conger, impelled by the Russian threat to American trade in Manchuria, naively suggested one in Chihli, around Tientsin, at the very heart of the empire, but this seemed so unlikely that Hay did not give it a second thought. More plausible was a report by Consul A. Burlingame Johnson of Amoy, the principal link between China and the Philippines, recommending a naval base there, but Tokyo already regarded the port with special concern for its closeness to Taiwan, and Hay rejected the report. All Johnson could do was block the Japanese effort to obtain a grant of the whole port area of Amoy. During the summer and autumn of 1898 the American China Development Company agitated for special privileges at Canton, the terminus of its railroad concession from Hankow, to give the line an outlet to the sea. Failing to interest the State Department, the company, which needed more capital anyway, signed an agreement on February 1, 1899, with the British and Chinese corporation, sharing control over the Hankow-Canton and Canton-Kowloon lines.[13]

79–80. Mark B. Dunnell, "Our Policy in China," 396–409. *New York Times,* July 28, 1898. *The Manufacturer,* n.d., reprinted in ibid., August 28. *New York Journal of Commerce,* June 21, 22, 23 (quotation), October 23, 1898. *New York Tribune,* August 14, 1898.

12. The phrase quoted from McKinley's instructions is in Reid, *Making Peace with Spain,* 237. Campbell, *Special Business Interests,* 46–47. William A. Williams, "Brooks Adams and American Expansion," 223–24. *New York Times,* October 26, November 3, 1899.

13. Young, *Rhetoric of Empire,* 98–106. Consul John Fowler at Chefoo also suggested that port as a naval base. Braisted, "American China Development Company," 150. For an unfavorable appraisal of Conger see Hunt, *Frontier Defense,* 29–30. Conger to Day, November 3, 1898, no. 82, U.S., Diplomatic Despatches, China, 105. A. Burlingame Johnson to David J. Hill, January 12, March 14, 1899, nos. 38, 45, U.S., Consular Despatches, Amoy, 14. On the British side, the alliance with the weaker American China Development Company was partly intended to safeguard their interests in the Yangtze Valley. Young, *British Policy in China,* 91–93. *New York Tribune,* July 14, 1899. At one point

Although a few government officials and businessmen sought spheres of influence and naval bases, most Americans interested in China looked to some sort of open door policy as the solution to their problems. The advocates were remarkable for their diversity. In 1898–1899 the guiding force was undoubtedly the American Asiatic Association, led by the journalist John Foord and Clarence Cary, a lawyer for the American China Development Company who also represented American manufacturers and exporters. In December 1898 they were joined by a group of Shanghai merchants, the American Association of China, and at home there were other allies such as the National Association of Manufacturers and the New England Cotton Manufacturers Association.

Other advocates were less openly allied with business. One group of expansionist publicists were former diplomats such as John Barrett and Charles Denby, father and son, who wrote with authority of things they had seen. They shared the pages of upper-class periodicals with intellectuals like Brooks Adams, academics such as C. K. Adams (University of Wisconsin) and E. R. Johnson (University of Pennsylvania), Assistant Secretary of State John Bassett Moore, and the arch anti-imperialist Carl Schurz. Finally, a touch of cosmopolitanism was added by two British publicists, Archibald R. Colquhoun and Lord Charles Beresford, who wrote popular books and articles on the breakup of China. Beresford was especially influential, a hearty, confident after-dinner speaker who toured the Chinese ports and then the United States, spreading his message of alarm, opportunity, and Anglo-American solidarity.[14]

As with so much other rhetoric on commercial expansion, the case for an open door policy began with a recitation of unmatched Chinese resources—"a reservoir of untouched wealth," as John Foord put it, " . . . side by side with an industrious and docile population ready, under proper direction, to utilize it." The State Department statistician Worthington C. Ford countered with the prediction that as China industrialized, it would consume fewer American manufactures, but John Foord replied that instead Europeanization would develop new wants among the Chinese. Expansionists argued that the United States deserved a generous share of the new opportunities for trade and development, partly because the Spanish-American War made it, in John Barrett's words, "the paramount power

---

a rumor spread that the Continental powers had invited the United States to claim a share of Chinese territory but that the United States had declined. *London Times,* November 6, 1899. There is no further evidence of the démarche.

14. Young, *Rhetoric of Empire,* 109–10, 118–21. Campbell, *Special Business Interests,* 50–51. Lorence, *Organized Business,* 19–23. McCormick, *China Market,* 137–41. Prisco, *John Barrett,* 39–45. Archibald R. Colquhoun, *China in Transformation.* Charles Beresford, *The Break-Up of China, with an Account of Its Present Commerce . . . and Future Prospects.* Beresford's activities had the approval of Ambassador John Hay. Dennett, *John Hay,* 286–88. *New York Tribune,* December 10, 1898; March 25, 1899. *New York Times,* May 14, 1899. The American Asiatic Association managed to inset a "China Day" into the schedule of the International Commercial Congress at Philadelphia. Ibid., October 19, 1899. The broad appeal of the issue is apparent from the fact that both low-tariff and high-tariff newspapers such as the *New York Times* and *Tribune* respectively supported the open door.

of the Pacific" and partly because in the past it had always treated the Chinese government with consideration—the mailed fist in a velvet glove.

Given American incentives and merits, the next problem was how best to guarantee the American share against the perceived Euro-Japanese threat. A few believed hopefully with the *New York Evening Post* that Russia would not dare risk British enmity or destroy its traditional friendship with the United States by closing the door to Manchuria, but more agreed with Professor Frederick Wells Williams of Yale and Charles A. Conant that the czar aimed at a monopoly over all China if possible. Since Americans were almost unanimously opposed to hostilities in Asia, Barrett proposed to the New York Chamber of Commerce three choices in descending priority. The first was a strong stand for the integrity of China, "because we have much to lose and nothing to gain by its breaking up." The other two were assertion of American rights under the Treaties of Tientsin (1858)—i.e., the open door—and acquisition of a port in northern China for a naval base. The open door, he felt, would be impossible to maintain in a partitioned China, because of the difficulty in apportioning transportation and communication rights and police powers in the vast interior. But China could not hope to maintain its integrity unaided, as the loss of Port Arthur, Kiaochow, and Weihaiwei had shown all too clearly.

With these harsh truths in mind, trade expansionists proceeded to consider the possibilities of a cooperative policy, undeterred by the fate of a similar effort in Samoa, which in the spring of 1899 was in the last stages of collapse. Britain seemed the logical partner, with Japan included for additional weight. Indeed, scolded the *New York Times,* the Anglo-Americans might have prevented the partition of China a year earlier by uniting to forbid it. (The *Times* conveniently overlooked the developing crisis with Spain.) But it was not too late for a united stand against discriminatory trade laws in the spheres of influence. The optimistic Beresford also wanted to overhaul the imperial government and even anticipated a general Anglo-American commercial alliance, apparently unaware of American tradition. He was disappointed to report in England that he had seen no desire on the part of American businessmen to make any practical effort to safeguard Chinese trade. The likelihood of formal cooperation between the two powers decreased when Britain and Russia exchanged notes in April 1899, agreeing not to seek railway concessions in Manchuria and the Yangtze Valley respectively. To be sure, the open door was generally supposed to apply only to trade, but to many Americans the language of the agreement sounded ominously like a cry of "Every man for himself!"[15]

15. The sources from which these paragraphs have been compiled include those cited in note 13 and the following: Speech of John Barrett and comments thereon. *New York Tribune,* June 2, 1899. John Barrett, "The Paramount Power of the Pacific," 165–79. *Journal of the American Asiatic Association* 1 (June 10, 1899): 50–53. *Annals of the American Academy of Political and Social Science* 13 (May 1899, supplement): 124–53, 158–60, 191–93 (articles by Worthington C. Ford, Robert T. Hill, John Foord, E. R. Johnson, and F. W. Williams). *Literary Digest* 17 (September 3, 1898): 272–74.

While public sentiment for an open door was growing, the same was happening within the American government. As late as the spring of 1899 Secretary John Hay favored a passive reaction, probably reflecting McKinley's preference and his own fear of Senate opposition. Having little knowledge of the Far East, in April Hay brought his friend William W. Rockhill to Washington as adviser. Rockhill had lived in China, Korea, and Mongolia from 1884 to 1892 but was out of touch with recent developments. He disliked Beresford's bluff Anglo-Saxonism and his prejudice against the Chinese government. Rockhill believed sincerely in the open door principle and, although little concerned for merchants or missionaries, he wished to forestall the breakup of China. He supplied Hay with facts and arguments mostly received from an old friend, Alfred E. Hippisley, in a detailed correspondence that lasted all summer. Hippisley, whom some regard as the true author of Hay's open door notes, was a British veteran of the Chinese Imperial Customs and like Sir Robert Hart preached the integrity of China and free trade. Thus Hippisley and through him Rockhill and Hay represented the old British mercantile tradition in China, antedating partition.[16]

During July and August 1899 several developments brought the McKinley administration to the point of action. One was a set of public pronouncements by Jacob Gould Schurman, head of the first Philippine commission, who had just returned from the islands with an increased concern for the future of China, both its independence and the free access of all foreigners to its trade. Schurman added little new information to the debate, but his official position and friendship with McKinley gave weight to his generalizations. Another development seemed to suggest that the Russian threat might have been overemphasized. The July issue of *North American Review* carried a plea for Russo-American understanding,

---

A more alarmist prediction than Frederick Wells Williams about Russian intentions is Charles A. Conant, "The United States as a World Power," 618–22. "Southern Trade in China," *The Manufacturers' Record,* October 20, 1899, reprinted in Gardner, ed., *A Different Frontier,* 60–65. *New York Times,* January 26, March 13, 17, 1899. *New York Tribune,* December 10, 1898; February 25, May 2, 1899. *New York Journal of Commerce,* October 31, 1898. Beresford, *Break-Up of China,* 443–44. *Atlantic Monthly* 85 (August 1899): 278–79. Dennett, *John Hay,* 286–87. On the Anglo-Russian negotiation see McCordock, *British Far Eastern Policy,* 277–91; Langer, *Diplomacy of Imperialism,* vol. 2, 682–84; and Philip Joseph, *Foreign Diplomacy in China, 1894–1900: A Study in Political and Economic Relations with China,* chap. 17. *New York Tribune,* May 2, 1899. Andrew D. White, onetime minister to Russia and ambassador to Germany, thought that the agreement was favorable to American interests since it would hasten the enormous transpacific commerce in which we hoped to share. Ibid., May 3.

16. Griswold, *Far Eastern Policy,* 61–68. Young, *Rhetoric of Empire,* 115–18, 123–25. Hay to Paul Dana, March 16, 1899. William R. Thayer, *The Life and Letters of John Hay,* vol. 2, 241. Hay to Rockhill, August 7, 1899, cited in McCormick, *China Market,* 137, 216n14. The influence of the American Asiatic Association may also have helped move Hay. Lorence, *Organized Business,* 22–23. As historians have apportioned credit for the open door notes between Hay, Rockhill, and Hippisley, some have disagreed as to whether Rockhill influenced Hippisley or vice versa. For contrasting views see Dennett, *John Hay,* 289–92; Paul A. Varg, "William Woodville Rockhill and the Open Door Notes," 378–80; and Harvey Pressmen, "Hay, Rockhill, and China's Integrity: A Reappraisal," 61–79.

prefaced by a statement from a prominent Russian newspaper editor, who was also a nobleman and reputed friend of the czar. About a month later the czar issued a ukase dated August 15, creating a free port at Dairen on the Liaotung peninsula, an important gateway to Manchuria. Hay at once asked Rockhill for a memorandum on the new situation, which became the basis for a series of open door notes dispatched to Britain, France, Germany, Russia, and Japan. (Italy was added at the last moment.)[17]

These notes, drafted by Hay and Rockhill and sent out with McKinley's approval, withheld American recognition of any spheres of influence, since these might pose conflicts with existing treaty rights of other nations. To prevent this, the United States asked each power to make a declaration and urge other powers to follow suit, affirming the following points. First, there should be no interference with "any treaty port or vested interest within any 'sphere of influence' or leased territory." Second, the old Chinese treaty tariff should be applied to all merchandise landed at ports (except free ports) within the sphere of influence. Third, a country holding a sphere of influence should levy no higher harbor dues or railroad charges on vessels or goods of foreign countries within this sphere of influence than on "vessels of its own nationality . . . [or] merchandise belonging to its own nationals." The note also referred favorably to the czar's recent ukase on Dairen and an earlier German statement that Kiaochow was a "free port." Hay did not mention investments; presumably these were still subject to restrictions. However, the note to Britain did refer briefly to the desirability of maintaining Chinese integrity "in which the whole western world is alike concerned" and to that end the urgency of "administrative reforms."[18]

Although Hay had limited his notes to a minimal definition of the open door, the reaction of most powers was a mixture of hesitation and outright opposition, and he had to tread a careful path through their replies. He had hoped for simultaneous negotiations, but he wisely decided to issue the notes over a period of several weeks, from September to November. Japan and Italy agreed without contest. Britain, which had indirectly helped to inspire the notes, now balked at including its Hong Kong protectorate, and Hay had to work out an exception for leased "military station(s)" that would not apply to other holdings. Germany and France accepted nearly everything, provided all other powers also agreed, but they objected to guaranteeing equal railroad rates, and Hay devised compromise wording. Russia proved the principal stumbling block, although Hay and Rockhill

17. Griswold, *Far Eastern Policy*, 68–76. Young, *Rhetoric of Empire*, 125–31, 133–34. McCormick, *China Market*, 140–44. Vladimir Holstrom, *"Ex Oriente Lux! A Plea for Russo-American Understanding,"* with introduction by Prince E. Ouktomsky, 6–32. *New York Tribune*, August 17, 1899. For the text of Rockhill's memorandum see Griswold, *Far Eastern Policy*, 475–91.

18. For the correspondence (notes and replies) see Bevans, *Treaties*, vol. 1, 278–95. U.S., *Foreign Relations, 1900*, 299. The dates of the dispatch of the notes were as follows: Germany, Russia, and England, September 6; Japan, November 13; Italy, November 17; and France, November 21. Ibid., *1899*, 128–43.

had expected Russian cooperation because of the czar's ukase on Dairen. Foreign Minister Count Muraviev found the note vague and confusing. Count Sergei Witte, minister of finance and leader of Russian expansionists, decided that it was intended to shut Russia out of Manchurian trade and at first refused any consent. Hay transferred negotiations to St. Petersburg and after weeks of discussions, by a mixture of bluff and persistence, managed to pry from Russia grudging consent to the tariff provisions. In order to hold his other signatories fast, he announced at the beginning of 1900 that the powers would give written agreements and then dispatched a circular note, dated March 20, proclaiming all replies "favorable . . . final and definitive."[19]

The dominant reaction of the American press to Hay's notes was triumphant approval. By assuring the future of American trade in the Far East, the United States had won, said the *New York Times,* "a diplomatic success . . . by purely diplomatic methods at nobody's expense," and without aggressive intent but in the name of the whole world. The notes would almost enforce themselves; they were a sign that the United States could operate successfully in international affairs without alliances. According to the *Philadelphia Press,* they were possibly more important than the war itself. Against this chorus of hosannas the most scathing reply was that of the *Springfield Republican,* which thought Hay intellectually shallow for having accepted mere assurances that meant nothing and changed nothing: "Underneath this showy concern for the interests of American trade and capital in the Far East there is a steady movement toward militarism." Other skeptics agreed that a formal written agreement would have been preferable and pointed out that now the United States would have to open the door in the Philippines and admit Chinese more freely into California. The *Boston Journal* remarked realistically that American power in the Philippines, not the appeal of its principles, had made the "triumph" possible.[20]

Few state papers in America's development have been subjected to a wider range of historical interpretations than Hay's open door notes of 1899. Most writers have agreed that the events of 1898, especially the annexation of the

19. Griswold, *Far Eastern Policy,* 76–78. McCormick, *China Market,* 146–53. Young, *Rhetoric of Empire,* 131–35. Hunt, *Frontier Defense,* 30–32. Zabriskie, *American-Russian Rivalry,* 54–60. Romanov, *Russia in Manchuria,* 74–76. McCordock, *British Far Eastern Policy,* 301–7. Dennis, *Adventures in American Diplomacy,* 187–95. Beasley, *Japanese Imperialism,* 70–71. For a sampling of foreign press reactions see *Literary Digest* 20 (May 5, 1900): 556. On the Russian attitude see Busselle, "U.S. in the Far East," 209–11. According to Hay, Muraviev initially promised that Russia would do what France did but later angrily repudiated the commitment. Hay to Henry White, April 2, 1900, quoted in Thayer, *The Life and Letters of John Hay,* vol. 2, 243.

20. Dennis, *Adventures in American Diplomacy,* 194–95 (quotation from *New York Times*), *Public Opinion* 27 (November 23, 1899): 643–44; 28 (January 11, April 5, 1900): 37–38, 419–21. *Literary Digest* 20 (January 13, 1900): 35–36 (quotation from *Springfield Republican*). *New York Times,* January 6, 1900. *Bradstreet's* 28 (March 31, 1900): 194. Other similar expressions during the same weeks anticipated an increase of prosperous Far Eastern trade.

Philippines, helped stir the United States to some sort of action. Until about 1920 historians, lacking access to most pertinent sources, praised Hay's diplomatic coup as a lasting advance in American foreign policy. During the 1920s writers continued to praise Hay's tactics, but some doubted the permanence of his solution since the intentions of the United States could never be relied on. Tyler Dennett, whose comprehensive history of American Far Eastern policy (1922) was a classic for several generations of scholars, convinced most of them that the notes largely restated and expanded traditional American policy in China. But Dennett also described the notes as "a purely temporary expedient to meet a specific situation."[21]

The frustrations of the Manchurian Incident of 1931 and the later world developments of the 1930s soon produced interpretations more critical of Hay. In his textbook (1936) Samuel Flagg Bemis called American Far Eastern policy at the turn of the century a "great aberration" committing the United States inevitably to force in defense of largely European and Japanese interests in China. A. Whitney Griswold (1938) declared that Hay, far from promoting useful cooperation, merely oriented American policy toward more intervention in the Far East, starting several cycles of advances and retreats that kept everyone off balance. The classic statement of this unfavorable interpretation was a couple of lectures by George F. Kennan in 1950 that caught the public eye and established a stubborn conviction that American Far Eastern policy in the twentieth century consistently outran the nation's military capabilities and interests.[22]

Although the American business stake in China remained small during the mid–twentieth century, historians of the 1950s began to find in Hay concern for this stake that made his policies seem less muddle-headed and more purposeful than Bemis, Griswold, and Kennan had thought. Charles A. Campbell focused attention on the influence of the American Asiatic Association. Thomas McCormick saw in Hay's notes a realistic effort to prevent partition of the Chinese Empire and enable the United States and Britain to shut out other competitors for the Chinese market. Somewhat more sinister, William A. Williams called the notes "a classic strategy of noncolonial imperial expansion" and later "an imperial strategy of great power and consequence," combining anti-imperialism with "the endless expansion of the American frontier in the name of self-determination, progress, and peace."[23]

---

21. John A. Garraty, "American Historians and the Open Door Notes." Ernest R. May, "Factors Influencing Historians' Attitudes: Tyler Dennett," 4–9, 32–37. Dennett, *Americans in Eastern Asia*, 645–49. Dennett later guessed but offered no proof that the notes were part of a tacit bargain whereby Britain withdrew from the Caribbean. Dennett, *John Hay*, 206. See also Paul H. Clyde, "The Open-Door Policy of John Hay," 212–23.

22. Garraty, "American Historians," 9–11. Robert H. Ferrell, "The Griswold Theory of Our Far Eastern Policy." Waldo H. Heinrich, "The Griswold Theory of Our Far Eastern Policy: A Commentary," in Borg, *Historians and American Far Eastern Policy*, 22–31, 39–41. Samuel Flagg Bemis, *A Diplomatic History of the United States*. Griswold, *Far Eastern Policy*, chap. 2, 7, 87. George P. Kennan, *American Diplomacy, 1900–1950*, chaps. 2, 3.

23. Campbell, *American Business Interests*. McCormick, *China Market*, 129, 134–37, 153–54. William A. Williams, *The Tragedy of American Diplomacy*, 43. William A. Williams, *Empire as a Way of Life*, 128.

Most recent interpretations have tried to compromise among the earlier ones. Raymond Esthus split the difference between realism and the lack of it by describing Hay's notes as based on recognition of America's limitations. He blamed later interventions on expansion of the notes, first by Hay himself and Roosevelt, by Root, and especially by Taft and Knox. Marilyn Blatt Young and Michael Hunt played down the notes as deliberately ambiguous. Young saw them as "limited objectives upon which vast claims might later be based," while to Hunt they were "a token nod to the future of the Chinese market and a tribute to the influence and persistence of American pressure groups. But not much more." Others saw the notes as a substitute for an Anglo-American alliance that Hay knew to be impossible or as a device to avoid a congressional debate in an election year.[24] As ambitious American policies in East Asia unfold, Hay's modest efforts will doubtless undergo further metamorphoses.

Less than three months after Hay pronounced the powers' replies to his notes "final and definitive," the United States was called on to make good its implied commitment. During the spring and summer of 1900 a Chinese nationalist, antiforeign uprising boiled up—the Boxer rebellion. This was organized by secret societies (one of which was mistranslated as "Fists of Righteous Harmony") with some approval from the dowager empress, who controlled the government. The Western powers drew up a useless joint protest, and after the German minister had been murdered by a Chinese soldier, diplomats, missionaries, and other Western residents of northern China sought safety in the legation compounds of Peking. Thus began a fifty-five-day siege, from June to August, during which the foreigners ate their polo ponies and took turns, men and women alike, shooting at Boxers who ventured too close to their walls.

From the beginning the United States participated freely in naval and military efforts to raise the siege and return China to order, the more willingly since Washington by now had seventy-five thousand soldiers and accompanying naval units in the Philippines, fighting Filipino rebels. The United States furnished twenty-one hundred troops out of about twenty thousand for a joint relief expedition to Peking, and by the end of August there were more than six thousand American soldiers in China. Hay seized the opportunity to send a circular note to the European leaders and Japan, dated July 3, expressing the long-term American goals of suppressing the Boxer rebellion: safety and peace for China, the preservation of Chinese territorial and administrative integrity, the protection of existing foreign trade rights, and the principle of equal and important trade. Although this was often called Hay's "second open door note,"

24. Raymond A. Esthus, "The Changing Concept of the Open Door, 1899–1910," 435–37, 452–54. Raymond A. Esthus, "The Open Door and the Integrity of China, 1899–1922: Hazy Principles for Changing Policy," 48–74. Marilyn Blatt Young, "American Expansion, 1870–1890: The Far East," 181–92. Hunt, *Frontier Defense*, 33–34. Hunt, *Special Relationship*, 153. Kenton J. Clymer, *John Hay, The Gentleman as Diplomat*, 148–49. Howard I. Kushner and Anne Hummel Sherill, *John Hay: The Union of Poetry and Politics*, 110–11.

it was both more and less extensive than his notes of 1899—more, because he now explicitly advocated preserving Chinese territorial integrity, less, because the note was only an expression of American views without any request for a reply.

In keeping with Hay's July 3 circular, the United States threw its influence on the side of moderation during the Boxer intervention, and after the rebellion collapsed it did what it could to get all the troops out as soon as possible and minimize the indemnity and other punishments imposed on the Chinese. The principal dangers were the Japanese desire to occupy Amoy and the Russian intention to convert Manchuria into a virtual protectorate. Hoping to gain leverage from lenience, the czar's government suddenly proposed a general withdrawal immediately after hostilities ended. This threw American policy makers into confusion—some, like Elihu Root, most army officers, and a substantial bloc in Congress, wanted prompt withdrawal, while others, including Hay, Assistant Secretary Alvey A. Adee, and many missionaries, hoped for continued Western military cooperation. At one point Washington departed so far from the open door idea as to investigate a possible naval base at Samsah Bay on the Fukien coast, only to find that Japan objected. By the end of 1902 most foreign troops had left China.[25]

During the Boxer intervention a prescient article appeared by Josiah Quincy, writer, historian, and member of a distinguished Massachusetts family. Quincy predicted that the open door commitments and the sending of troops would lead inevitably to political action in China. This would upset the balance existing there among the European nations and Japan and require closer relations between the United States and those nations. We "must act with the fullest attainable knowledge, with the amplest consideration," he warned. Quincy was wrong in some particulars, but his words foreshadowed new policies and attitudes for the century about to begin.[26]

The open door policy met its first test, thanks in part to the presence of American troops near the China coast and to the determination of American leaders. In the midst of the crisis the United States, as it had four years before, proved its essential stability by conducting a hotly contested presidential election without wavering in its response to the crisis. Yet, despite the outcome of the election, a decisive administration victory, the intensity of the opposition suggested that the American people were not yet wholly converted to the new emphasis on foreign policy.

While the campaign and election of 1900 are interpreted as having revolved around "imperialism," the word was not clearly defined at the time. It usually

25. For more detailed accounts of these events see Griswold, *Far Eastern Policy*, 78–86. Young, *Rhetoric of Empire*, chaps. 7–9; McCormick, *China Market*, chap. 6; Zabriskie, *American Russian Rivalry*, chap. 4; and Hunt, *Frontier Defense*, chap. 4. Richard D. Challener, *Admirals, Generals, and American Foreign Policy, 1898–1914*, 3–8, 37, 182–83, 185, 187–90. For the text of Hay's circular note of July 3 see U.S., *Foreign Relations, 1903*. Appendix 1, 12.
26. Josiah Quincy, "The United States in China," 183–95.

referred to the status of the Philippines—colony, protectorate, or independent nation—and Hawaii and Puerto Rico were only occasionally mentioned. The applicability of "imperialism" to the continent of North America was doubtful. Theodore Roosevelt virtually called Thomas Jefferson the first imperialist but he also denounced William Jennings Bryan, the anti-imperialist Democratic candidate, as a hypocrite for wringing his hands over the Filipinos and ignoring American blacks.[27] The issue of racism, still largely unspoken in American politics, hung over the imperial issue in both parties. Neither party called for more conquests in the future, although the Republicans thought a few more naval bases might be necessary, and both parties supported the construction of the Nicaragua canal. The role of trade and investments in furthering imperialism was more often implied than specified, and both supporters and critics tended to repeat or intensify the arguments already developed in 1898 during the debate over the peace treaty. In general leaders of large-scale industries such as cotton textiles or boots and shoes were more optimistic about the Philippines and the China market than small or regional producers, who thought more about the expense of pacification. Habitual expansionists such as Frederic Emory or John Barrett thought that commercial expansion into underdeveloped areas offered the most promising outlets for American industry and capital. Skeptics such as Worthington C. Ford saw no hope of trade with the Philippines that would repay the costs of the war and felt that they might as well be thrown open to free trade. Other pessimists saw little chance of increased sales to the conservative Chinese that alone would make a Chinese rail system profitable or predicted that if they were ever stirred out of their torpor, the Chinese would become disastrous competitors in the world markets.[28]

Although the presidential candidates of the two parties were already determined, their conventions set the tone for the whole campaign. The Republican nominating speeches contained no surprises—prideful complacency at the country's prosperity and good intentions for the newly acquired territories. George A. Knight of California eulogized his state's expansive past and the acquisition of Pacific islands, predicted the dismemberment of China, and called the Philippines "a great depot in the Pacific for the distribution of the output of our inventive genius and industrial hand." But McKinley in his acceptance speech denied that the Philippines had been acquired for trade or commerce—"not for exploitation, but for humanity and civilization." Bryan sought to fly free silver, his battle-flag of 1896, on the same standard as anti-imperialism; he added antitrust legislation but rejected civil service reform. His arguments against imperialism were moral

27. Walter LaFeber, "Election of 1900," 1897–98. Roosevelt, *Letters of Theodore Roosevelt*, vol. 2, 1365.

28. Welch, *Response to Imperialism*, 76–78. Frederic Emory, "Our Commercial Expansion," 538–44. John Barrett, "What America Has at Stake in China," 744. Worthington C. Ford, "Trade Policy with the Colonies," 300–303. Frank Doster, "Will the Philippines Pay?" 465–70. John P. Young, "Will Chinese Development Benefit the Western World?" 348–62.

and humanitarian, not economic, and neither side mentioned the tariff despite many complaints about the Dingley Act.[29]

During the campaign both parties had to deal with contradictions and problems. The Republican nomination of Roosevelt for vice president was a clear symbol of expansion, and he supplied activity and dynamism, making a reported 673 speeches in twenty-four states and covering more than twenty-one thousand miles, while McKinley conducted his usual front-porch campaign. The president worried over Russian intervention in China and ordered the withdrawal of American troops from Peking, arousing a storm of criticism at home. Perhaps because of this the Republican campaign began to emphasize prosperity over imperialism as a lure for voters.

Democratic problems were far more serious. Bryan's free silver flag was anathema to many conservative anti-imperialists, in part because it would have required a stronger president than they could tolerate. (Unlike Bryan, they also preferred civil service to antitrust reform.) There was an economic case to be made for anti-imperialism—that prosperous trade did not require colonial rule. But in the one speech he devoted to anti-imperialism, Bryan characteristically contented himself with a social aphorism, "the expense [of imperialism] is borne by the people, while the profits are enjoyed by a few"—army contractors, ship owners, franchise holders, and officials. Most of the speech was devoted to political and religious morality. Many anti-imperialists, despairing, contemplated a third party, and for a time Andrew Carnegie considered subsidizing it, but he withdrew, and the movement collapsed.[30]

In the end McKinley was reelected by an electoral vote of 292–155 and a popular vote of 7.2 million to 6.4 million. It was a clear-cut Republican victory but not a landslide; a shift of fewer than thirty thousand votes, properly distributed, would have made Bryan president. Present-day historians are largely agreed that McKinley's election was a victory for prosperity rather than imperialism, a cautious unwillingness to experiment with change. Of course there were other factors: Bryan's inferior organization, his insistence on "the Jonah of 16 to 1" and trust-busting instead of civil service, the Democratic fight over the vice presidential nomination, Bryan's feeble war record, and the

---

29. Republican National Convention, *Official Proceedings of the Twelfth Republican National Convention, Held in the City of Philadelphia, June 19, 20, and 21, 1900* [etc.]. The phrases quoted from George A. Knight and William McKinley are on 126 and 187 respectively. Rystad, *Ambiguous Imperialism*, chap. 6. Schirmer, *Republic or Empire?* chap. 14. LaFeber, "Election of 1900," 1881, 1889–90. McKinley's acceptance letter promised expanded foreign trade, ship subsidies, and support for an isthmian canal. Ibid., 221–23. On the tariff see Albert Shaw, "The American Presidential Election," 620–21.

30. Rystad, *Ambiguous Imperialism*, 271. LaFeber, "Election of 1900," 1881–82, 1889, 1894, 1898–1900, 1906. Tompkins, *Anti-Imperialism in the United States*, 217–18. Welch, *Response to Imperialism*, chap. 4. For Bryan's only full statement on imperialism, at Indianapolis, see William Jennings Bryan, *Speeches of William Jennings Bryan Revised and Arranged by Himself*, vol. 2, 17–49 (quoted phrase on 42). On Carnegie see also Beisner, *Twelve against Empire*, 181–82.

greater electoral weight of the East Coast, which was relatively uninterested in Pacific matters.[31]

The most immediate effect of the Republican victory was felt not in the United States but in the Philippines. The rebels were fully aware of the two parties' positions on the war, and anti-imperialist writings, combined with their own hopes and rhetoric, convinced them that Bryan had a good chance of winning. Aguinaldo staged an offensive, and terrorism increased against collaborators, who naturally fell away. The Republican victory was a crippling blow; guerrilla surrenders increased sharply; and Aguinaldo's capture the following March, though not a result of the election victory, virtually ended the active rebellion.[32]

Gōren Rystad, a perceptive Swedish historian acting perhaps as a "man from Mars," has perceived broader implications in the election of 1900 than most Americans. Nearly half of the electorate either opposed or saw serious flaws in imperialism. Indeed, Republicans and Democrats proved to be not so far apart in foreign policy as they had seemed. On the one hand, the humanitarian case for Philippine annexation was damaged by the Filipino revolution with its atrocities and by Britain's contemporaneous Boer War. On the other hand, expansionist businessmen came to realize that colonies were not necessary for foreign trade or investments. In a sense both anti-imperialists and imperialists lost ground in the electoral conflict, for both were chasing will-o-the-wisps. The anti-imperialists looked backward to an illusory past, for Americans had always been an expansive people, whether crossing the Alleghenies or the Pacific. At the same time the imperialists looked forward to an illusory future. Their humanitarian, democratic ideals for the Philippines would not be realized, and their economic interests in the islands and in China would not develop as they hoped.[33]

31. Rystad, *Ambiguous Imperialism,* chap. 9. LaFeber, "Election of 1900," 1907–16. Paolo E. Coletta, *William Jennings Bryan,* vol. 2, 278–85. Welch, *Response to Imperialism,* 72–74. Schirmer, *Republic or Empire?* chap. 15. The patchwork of contemporary press opinion is well shown in *Public Opinion* 29 (November 15, 1900): 123–17; and *Literary Digest* 21 (November 17, 1900): 575–76. On the role of the blacks see William B. Gatewood, Jr., *Black Americans and the White Man's Burden, 1898–1903,* 232–60.

32. John M. Gates, "Philippine Guerrillas, American Anti-Imperialists, and the Election of 1900," 51–64.

33. Rystad, *Ambiguous Imperialism,* 309–11. See also LaFeber, "Election of 1900," 1916–17.

13

Conclusion

The Diplomacy of Involvement

URING THE TWO YEARS between the end of the war and the election of 1900 expansionists surpassed themselves with predictions for the glorious future of American economic relations with the Pacific islands and the Far East. Whitelaw Reid, who had already done all he could for the peace treaty, declared that American possession of the Philippines would "fence in the China Sea" and, with American control over the west coast of North America, would enable the United States "to convert the Pacific Ocean almost into an American lake." John Barrett embroidered this theme in several widely read articles, and John Foord, editor of the *New York Journal of Commerce*, and a variety of other publicists predicted that Westerners had merely "scratched the surface" of Chinese trade. Every section of the country would benefit, they said, and regional writers played up advantages to the New South (via James J. Hill's rail-steamer system) and California, "the Golden Coast."[1]

A few skeptics had their say even this early. James Harrison Wilson and John J. McCook, both expansionists of the preceding decade, were wary of Japan and thought Russia a better trade partner for the future. The anti-expansionist Henry Adams also favored a more pro-Russian policy, fearing that the czar's government was "sailing into another French revolution," which might "smash the whole civilized world." Senator Albert J. Beveridge, also an expansionist, predicted Russian rivalry in Manchuria, and a consul at Newchwang painted a dismal picture of America's interests there, with few of its citizens living in the bustling new town of Harbin and little petroleum or cotton goods sold there. Wharton

---

1. McClellan, *Heathen Chinee*, chap. 6. Reid, *Problems of Expansion*, 42. Barrett, "Paramount Power," 165–79. John Barrett, "America in the Pacific and Far East," 918–29. Barrett, "What America Has at Stake in China," 744. John Barrett, "The Crisis in China: Its Meaning for Engineering Interests," 804–8. John Barrett, "America in the Pacific," 487–90. John T. Foord, "China in Regeneration: An Epoch and an Opportunity," 655–60. Melville, "Our Future in the Pacific," 292–96. "The Commerce of the Pacific," *Age of Steel*, reprinted in *Public Opinion* 25 (July 7, 1898): 28. *Bradstreet's* 26 (August 20, 1898): 530. Benjamin Taylor, "The Coming Struggle in the Pacific," 666–67. [Chauncey M. Depew], *Orations, Addresses, and Speeches of Chauncey M. Depew*, vol. 1, 218–19. Gilbert Reid, "American Opportunities in China," 237–42. Robert T. Hill, "Commercial Relations of the United States with the Far East," 136–43. Austin, "Commercial Development of Japan," 329–37.

Barker now felt that the Chinese could not be made into large-scale customers of Western goods and farsightedly urged Americans to unite with Chinese capitalists in creating infrastructure (he did not use the word) for a future Chinese industrial society.[2] In 1903, however, the U.S. government raised some hope for increased trade by negotiating a commercial treaty in which China agreed to substitute a 12½ percent surtax on imports for the much-hated likin transit tax and opened the two principal cities of Manchuria to American trade.[3]

As the Russo-Japanese War (1904–1905) approached, fears of American political involvement increased, and the Japanese victory did not reassure commercial expansionists or those who had hoped for an alliance with Britain and Japan to preserve a Far Eastern balance. The Japanese public bitterly resented American mediation to end the war, and writings on Japanese competition and the term "yellow peril" began to appear in the United States as early as 1905. James J. Hill, completely disillusioned about the prospects for Far Eastern trade, aired his disappointment in the press. Other writers seized upon consular accounts of missed opportunities. The chaos attending the Chinese revolution of 1911 completed the discomfiture of the trade expansionists.[4]

Statistics bore out the publicists' shifting opinions. The commercial treaty of 1903 with China should have improved facilities for trade, but the Chinese almost immediately started a boycott of American products, finally spurred by their resentment at mistreatment of immigrants in the United States. American exports to China rose only slightly between 1900 and 1910, from $15,259,167 to $16,320,612, which was less than 1 percent of all American exports in each year. Although Chinese foreign trade doubled between 1900 and 1913, the American share of this trade declined and remained in third place behind that of Britain and Japan. By 1913 Russia too had nearly caught up. (In contrast, American exports to Japan exceeded $40 million by that time.)[5] The Americans' worst commercial failure in China was cotton goods, formerly the largest export, which rose to 35

2. LaFeber, *Clash*, 78–79. Ford, ed., *Letters of Henry Adams* (1938), 409–10 (quotation). Adams's solution was to stop the search for Asian markets and raise a tariff against Asian goods. Wharton Barker, "The Industrial Interests of the United States in the Far East," 7–12. See also *Forum* 28 (November 1899): 348–62, for a similar but more alarmist warning and (January 1900): 592–99, for a reply by a commercial expansionist. Albert J. Beveridge, *The Russian Advance*. Hunt, *Frontier Defense*, 34–38. Henry B. Miller, "Russian Development of Manchuria," 113–27.

3. For the text of the treaty see Bevans, *Treaties*, vol. 6, 675–708. For press comments see *Public Opinion* 36 (January 21, 1904): 70; *Outlook* 75 (October 17, December 26, 1903): 394–95, 976–77.

4. *Living Age* 240 (Febrary 6, 1904): 372–74. John Hays Hammond, "The Menace of Japan's Success," 6273–75. Edmund G. Bogart, "Japan Winning the Pacific," 10937–44. Day Allen Willey, "America in the Orient: A Word Concerning Our Neglected Opportunities," 410–14. Thomas T. Millard, "America in China," 67–89. James J. Hill, "The Future of Our Oriental Trade," 6465–67. James J. Hill, "A Lost Opportunity in the Pacific," 12482–503. For a good account of American reaction to the "yellow peril" see Iriye, *Pacific Estrangement*, chap. 6.

5. Knight, "American Trade and Investment in China," 125–33. In 1910 total U.S. trade with China was $46,310,982, with Japan $88,358,071. Ibid., 143–45. Frederick McCormick,

percent of the Chinese market in 1905 but fell to 5.7 percent in two years and never fully recovered.[6] In contrast, Standard Oil improved its position until a general industry-wide price war broke out in about 1910.[7]

During this period American direct and portfolio investments in East Asia (i.e., excluding missions) increased from $19.9 million in 1900 to about $49.3 million in 1914.[8] What attracted attention, however, was a series of spectacular failures in China associated with prominent business and government leaders. The first of these involved the American China Development Company, a survivor from the 1890s (see chapters 9, 11). In 1898 it received a nontransferable concession for a railroad between Hankow and Canton. As the company encountered problems, it violated its concession by transferring stock to Belgian interests and finally gave up. After tortuous financial diplomacy involving J. P. Morgan and finally President Roosevelt, the Chinese government had to pay $5.75 million to indemnify bondholders and cover property claims. For this it received the outstanding bonds and about thirty miles of track.[9]

The second conspicuous American failure was a projected "round-the-world" rail and steamer line of E. H. Harriman, an American railroad tycoon who was one of the original shareholders of the American China Development Company. As a connecting link through Manchuria he wanted to build a railroad under a Japanese concession in the aftermath of the Russo-Japanese War. When the Japanese insisted on their own railroad, Harriman planned a parallel line, but the recession of 1907 and Harriman's death two years later intervened, and the project collapsed.[10]

A third unhappy venture was the Hukuang project to float loans for the Chinese government and build the Hankow-Canton railroad abandoned in the

"American Defeat in the Pacific," 67–73. Chao, "Chinese-American Cotton-Textile Trade," 121. Remer, *Foreign Investments in China,* 261.

6. Hunt, "Americans in China Market," 286–88. Hunt, *Frontier Defense,* 108–11, 185. May and Fairbank, *America's China Trade,* 119–25. Dana G. Munro, "American Commercial Interests in Manchuria," 157–65. Baltimore *Manufacturers' Record,* cited in Lorence, "Organized Business," 9. U.S. Department of Commerce and Labor, Bureau of Manufactures, Special Agents Series, no. 11, *Foreign Markets for the Sale of American Cotton Products,* 14–109. U.S., *Consular Reports* 347 (August 1909): 47; 349 (October 1909): 151–53.

7. Hidy, *Pioneering in Big Business,* 497–503, 547–53. Williamson and Daum, *American Petroleum Industry,* 252–53, 258–60.

8. Remer, *Foreign Investment in China,* 260, 264, 274. Mira Wilkins, *The Emergence of Multinational Enterprise: American Business Abroad from the Colonial Era to 1914,* 107. William W. Lockwood, *The Economic Development of Japan: Growth and Structural Change, 1868–1938,* 322–23.

9. Braisted, "U.S. and American China Development Company," 147–65. Howard K. Beale, *Theodore Roosevelt and the Rise of America to World Power,* 200–211. Chia-ao, *China's Struggle,* 34–35. Hunt, *Frontier Defense,* 41–44, 92–93. Huenemann, *Dragon and Iron Horse,* 53. E-Tu Zen Sun, *Chinese Railways and British Interests, 1989–1911,* 74–76.

10. Charles Vevier, *The United States and China, 1906–1913: A Study of Force and Diplomacy,* chap. 2, 48–50, 120–28. Walter V. Scholes and Marie V. Scholes, *The Foreign Policies of the Taft Administration,* 117–23, 131. Hunt, *Frontier Defense,* 153–58, 206.

American China debacle. British capital originally resuscitated the plan, and after much jockeying an Anglo-French-German consortium was formed. Although American capitalists had originally shown no interest in Hukuang, the newly organized Taft administration took it up. After some persuasion the Europeans agreed to admit an American group of bankers led by Morgan and Jacob Schiff of Kuhn, Loeb, and Company. The Hukuang loan project immediately ran into complications; no formal contract was signed until 1910; and early in the Woodrow Wilson administration the American Group withdrew in reaction to the new president's disapproval. President Taft and Secretary of State Philander C. Knox also tried to increase American economic influence in China with a plan to neutralize Manchurian railroads under group control and a loan to stabilize Chinese currency. These failed too, partly because no other nation interested in Chinese development would support the United States and partly because the Chinese revolution of 1911 tore the country apart.[11]

The myth of the Golden East survived the Spanish-American War as glittering as ever. Events of the first decade in the new century, however, showed that it remained an inadequate guide for American business and government in China. An atmosphere of trial and error continued to surround Roosevelt's mediation in the Russo-Japanese War, the Hukuang consortium, and the rest of Taft's "dollar diplomacy," as presidents and businessmen tried to mature the inchoate policies inherited from the nineteenth century.[12] A final appraisal of the early policies will help to explain why these men fell short of their goals.

The basic problems of relations and policies in the North Pacific had been solved by the end of the nineteenth century with the organization of territorial government in Alaska and Hawaii. Both annexations illustrate the interaction between economic expansion and American foreign relations, since both areas were desired for their raw materials and for controlling the North Pacific routes to the Far East. Both created diplomatic problems, Alaska with its offshore seals and boundary controversy, Hawaii with its booming sugar trade and its labor problems. But the annexation of Alaska was largely the work of one man, William H. Seward, not the culmination of a public movement, economic or otherwise, and the sealing and boundary questions also involved only limited economic interests.

In contrast, the strengthening American tie with Hawaii was intertwined for four decades with reciprocity, one of the most frequently proposed expedients of

11. Vevier, *United States and China,* chaps. 3–4, 214–19. Scholes, *Foreign Policies of the Taft Administration,* chaps. 8–14. Hunt, *Frontier Defense,* 188–90, chaps. 12–14. Vincent P. Carosso, with the assistance of Rose C. Carosso, *The Morgans: Private International Bankers, 1854–1913,* 550–78. Remer, *Foreign Investments in China,* 266–72. The name "Hukuang" was a composite of the three Chinese provinces in which the railroads were to operate: Hunan, Hupeh, and Kwangtung.

12. For a penetrating analysis of American policies toward China, in part from the Chinese viewpoint and with special reference to Manchuria, see Hunt, *Frontier Defense,* 245–57.

economic expansionism, and American-Hawaiian relations involved a variety of American business interests, including sugar production and refining, landowning, shipping, and general merchandising. Reciprocity and annexation called forth repeated debates on economic expansion in which the executive, Congress, and the press participated heatedly. To be sure, economic arguments mingled confusingly with strategic, political, constitutional, and humanitarian considerations. Also, it was never fully clear that economic expansion required outright annexation of the islands. Nevertheless, the history of American-Hawaiian relations furnishes one of the best available examples of the interaction between diplomacy, trade, and investment during the last third of the nineteenth century.

In the southern and western Pacific, diplomacy led instead to involvements that were clearly against American interests, whether economic, political, or social. The United States' entanglement in Samoa stood the rationale of economic expansion on its head. Here the nation risked a brush with Germany for islands that produced only an unimportant product, copra, shipped mainly to Europe, and had a small, underdeveloped population of unlikely customers. One of the islands, to be sure, contained a magnificent harbor suitable for a naval base. Unfortunately, this harbor lay far from the principal trade lanes leading anywhere but to Australia and New Zealand. The government in Washington was so little interested in that region that it would not support reciprocity, shipping subsidies, or any other means to encourage a promising trade.

The explanations of the irrational American involvement in Samoa do no credit to the intelligence or prudence of policy makers: their failure to restrain consular impulses, overreliance on the Hawaiian model, imitation of European colonialism, and sentimental sympathy for native friendliness. By the mid-1880s a South Pacific crisis had crept up on the first Cleveland administration. Later, after a confrontation and an unsuccessful three-power experiment in cooperative colonialism, the participants rescued the situation with partition—and the United States never made use of its share thereafter.

Involvement in the Philippines came about even more quickly than that in Samoa, as the product of a crisis in American-Spanish relations that developed in the 1890s over the Cuban question. The attack on the Philippines was part of the military strategy planned against Spain. After the surprisingly easy victory, President McKinley considered and rejected the available alternatives to annexation more quickly than in Samoa, largely because of the pressures of war and because the Samoan experience ruled out a cooperative solution. The Philippines' resources and their location near the China coast seemed to make annexation more attractive, but distance and tradition were deterrents as powerful as in Samoa and more compelling than in Hawaii. The active opposition at home and the suppression of the Filipino rebellion on the islands tainted the annexationist decision, and the geopolitical hazards of their exposed position soon made them seem an Achilles heel. However, economic interests, partisan stubbornness, and a concern to save face delayed a reversal of the misguided policy until after World War II.

* * *

In all the cases of Pacific expansion—Alaska, Hawaii, Samoa, and the Philippines—the Far Eastern magnet exerted a powerful attraction, first to American trade and later to investment as well. The resulting American involvement in East Asia remained a major concern long after successes and failures in the Pacific had become history. Eventually, East Asia became a permanent subdivision of American foreign relations on a par with European and hemispheric affairs.

Political involvement in the Far East developed in large part from earlier activities of merchants and missionaries and to a lesser degree from the projects of later nineteenth-century promoters of railroads and other communications. Early American expansionists motivated Caleb Cushing's diplomacy, by which the United States shared in the advantages won by Britain in the Opium War, and the combination of force and persuasion, by which Commodore Matthew C. Perry and Townsend Harris opened Japan to American diplomacy and trade. After the Chinese Empire established regular foreign relations on the Western model, Anson Burlingame placed these relations on a basis of friendship and mutual attraction, not always realistic.

American diplomats of varying abilities continued a gradual rapprochement with both China and Japan until the 1880s, when a newly developed Japanese expansionism began to reach out to territories formerly tributary to China. Without much realization of this change, the United States, seeking trade opportunities, opened diplomatic and commercial relations with the Korean kingdom. American diplomats in Seoul took an active part in the intrigues of this small capital until in 1894–1895 the Sino-Japanese War spread the Oriental power struggle over Manchuria and northern China, site of the most important American trade and investment ambitions in East Asia.

At this point the European powers, alarmed, stirred to action, and the United States, much to its surprise, found itself at the center of a diplomatic storm like those in the Old World that it had usually avoided until now. In 1899–1900 concern over the Euro-Japanese threat to American economic interests and the decision to annex the Philippines resulted in more positive and advanced statements of American Far Eastern policy than we had ever made before and a cooperative military expedition to help the Europeans and Japan put down a violent rebellion in China. The United States was in East Asia to stay.

Anyone seeking to explain this progressive American involvement must first examine the factors that shaped mercantile and governmental policies in the Far East between 1784 and 1900. The most obvious and fundamental factor was geographical distance. From 1784 past the mid–nineteenth century, communication with the Far East had to follow a long sea route from New York or Boston around South America or Africa. During most of that time it depended on ordinary trading vessels proceeding to the China coast directly or after zigzagging around Europe or the Pacific islands in search of cargo. In the 1850s sailing vessels reached their peak of speed and efficiency in the China clippers, serving the tea trade. After 1869 faster routes to the Far East became available through the Suez Canal by steamer and across the North American continent and the central Pacific by train and steamer.

Distance and slow communications threw an unusual amount of responsibility on business or political agents from the days when supercargoes on the *Empress of China* and her successors handled trade matters for their superiors at home, or merchants became U.S. consuls in their spare time. Some cases were extreme. In one of these the sixteen-year-old John P. Cushing took over a commercial agency in Canton because, on his arrival, he found that the incumbent had died. In another case Townsend Harris, the first American consul in Japan, spent eighteen months in seclusion without hearing from the State Department. Concerned for their profits, business houses on the American East Coast sent out a series of young men to learn the Chinese trade from more experienced supervisors in China who functioned practically on their own without many modern advantages. For example, they never solved the problem of replacing cash with more convenient credit transactions except by reliance on British banks, the allies of their trade rivals.

In the case of the State Department, distance encouraged ignorance and inattention to Far Eastern affairs, with a few exceptions such as William H. Seward in the 1860s. Good luck sometimes placed able diplomats in the Far East who could take initiatives on their own with a degree of continuity, such as John A. Bingham in Tokyo or John Russell Young or Charles Denby in Peking. As for the navy, it sent ships occasionally into the Pacific at first, then established an informal patrol for the East Indies in the 1830s, and finally created the Asiatic Squadron in 1866. Although responsible for both East Africa and Asia, the squadron devoted increasing attention to China and Japan.[13] Some naval commanders, such as Matthew C. Perry, assumed the functions of ministers and consuls or operated even more independently.

Distance was even more significant in the case of the American public. Through churches and missionaries, people at home developed a humanitarian but patronizing attitude toward the "benighted heathen" without much real appreciation of the complex Chinese culture. Tea and silk, the principal imports, did not greatly affect the material life of most persons, so more immediate economic concerns at home drew their attention away from Pacific and Far Eastern commercial matters. Not surprisingly, the majority paid little attention to the increasing American political involvement in the Sino-Japanese power struggle over Korea until the press brought it to their attention in the 1890s.

A second factor, somewhat related to geographical distance, might be called cultural distance. Orientals and Westerners were strange to each other. On the one hand, the Chinese and Japanese cultures were ancient, self-centered, once strong but weakened by isolation and tradition. On the other hand, the Western cultures had recently developed and were expansive and impetuous. Both peoples were proud of their accomplishments. In China the Westerners made a two-

13. Johnson, *Far China Station.*

pronged advance, the mercantile, already familiar to the Chinese and thought to be manageable, and the missionary, despised as a symbol of inferior culture and feared as subversive to ancient morals.[14] (In Japan, however, trade considerations predominated.) Both governments reacted similarly at first, begrudging limited contacts through restricted trading posts. The Chinese resisted further Western influence and yielded concessions only to military force, while the Japanese opened their doors and set out to imitate everything they needed from Western culture.

In both countries the British and Americans took the lead in spreading Western trade and religion, the British in China and the Americans briefly in Japan. From the beginning both sought peaceful economic and social relations, but the British, more experienced in the Third World, appreciated that force must be anticipated as a last resort. Americans' convictions were divided. They were willing to benefit from gains the British made by fighting and even added the precaution of extraterritoriality to British-won concessions in the 1840s. At the same time they assumed that the Chinese preferred to deal with them because of their peaceableness. When some Chinese called the United States "the flowery flag republic" in reference to the Stars and Stripes, Americans took it as a significant sign of friendship rather than a graceful but superficial compliment.

Occasionally the cultural gap was bridged, as, for example, by the farsighted Chinese merchant, Howqua, who eased relations with the first generations of American merchants. Soon their successors resorted to a Chinese go-between, the comprador, who adjusted currency problems and governmental contacts and in the process formed the nucleus of a new Chinese capitalism. But cultural distance never disappeared in either business or politics. During the 1860s the first important American diplomat in China, Anson Burlingame, fancied that he could institute a cooperative policy between Americans, British, and Chinese and so impressed his hosts that the Peking government entrusted him with a mission to present their case to the United States and Europe. A similar misunderstanding handicapped the relations between Li Hung-chang and early American railroad promoters in the 1880s, especially Wharton Barker and James Harrison Wilson. In both cases each side wanted what the other could not give, restrained by the differences between the two systems.[15]

The Americans aggravated misunderstandings like these with their mounting anti-Chinese prejudices, both in China and at home. After the 1840s their increased contact with the Chinese created a stereotype of the "heathen Chinee"— backward, unreliable, deceitful, and immoral, perhaps not even human. Until around 1870 Chinese immigration into the United States was tolerated, even encouraged as a source of cheap labor, but thereafter prejudices produced exclusion laws which by the 1890s the Chinese were beginning to resent. Anti-Japanese prejudices also existed, but the greater respectability of the government, the

14. Tong, *United States Diplomacy,* 78–81.
15. A good case study of American-Japanese misunderstanding is the frustrating five-month negotiations of the Iwakura mission with Secretary of State Hamilton Fish in 1872. Mayo, "Catachism of Western Diplomacy," 389–410.

flattering Japanese imitation of Western culture, and the limited flow of Japanese immigrants reduced their effect.

A third important factor shaping American policies was the rise of Japan to political, economic, and military power. As soon as the Japanese had abolished the shogunate and completed the Meiji restoration, they set out to reform their political, military, economic, and educational systems along Western lines, importing products, methods, and instructors from America and Europe as guides. They read widely in Western liberal writings, but although books on individualism sold well, the government instituted rigorous controls over business, lest foreign investments lead to foreign control over industry, mines, railroads, and steamship lines as in China or India. Trade with Americans and other foreigners was encouraged when the Japanese could not supply the products for themselves.

The relationship of the United States to this Japanese renaissance was ironic. Not only had an American naval officer opened the Japanese gate to the outside world with his ships, guns, and model railroads, but also when Japan began to put in motion an expansionist policy toward neighboring territories, it could turn to American manifest destiny for supporting arguments, while its burgeoning foreign trade followed British and American models. Even the shrewdest Yankees could not have expected such an outcome from the models, samples, and teachings that they had willingly furnished to these diligent pupils. The Japanese capped the climax of their rise to regional power by expanding their influence onto the Korean peninsula and humiliating China in the Sino-Japanese War. This rearranged the balance of power in northern China and Manchuria and drew the United States into Far Eastern affairs.

So far the factors complicating American–Far Eastern relations arose from the environment or the inherent nature of Orientals and Westerners, but a few were produced by actions of the Americans themselves. One of these was overexpectation. The "myth of the Golden East" accompanied the growth of American foreign trade from colonial times. Part of the myth was the belief in fabulous Chinese wealth, passed down in Europe from the days of Marco Polo; part of it was simply the enormous Chinese population, expected to be eager customers for Western wares. (The fact that much of this population lived far inland seldom received much consideration.) It would not be too much to say that the vision of the Golden East was a major motivating force in nineteenth-century American history, as it was largely responsible for exploration and trade in the Pacific Ocean, for American interest in an isthmian canal, and in part for the whole western movement.

Combined with overexpectation was a phenomenon that might be called underpreparation. The first generations of China traders were remarkably successful, combing Europe and the Pacific for goods to take the place of their scarce silver: furs, sandalwood, and most successfully opium. Their commission houses in Canton and other open ports were well adapted to conditions along the Chinese coast and rivaled those of the more powerful British.

After changes in the 1870s and 1880s forced the breakup of the old houses, however, Americans were inclined to rely on European or Chinese sales outlets instead of establishing their own, as new inland cities were opened to foreign trade. Manufacturers of cotton goods were content to produce coarse, heavy fabrics for northern China and Manchuria and neglected finer goods such as the British had for sale. Frequently, American mill owners would not consult Chinese or Japanese tastes as to color or width of goods, or even issue advertisements that their customers could understand. (As an exception, however, Standard Oil seldom missed an opening in its contest with Russian and East Indian oil.) When American promoters appeared with high-flown plans for railroads and telegraphs, their capital backing was too weak for them to compete on even terms with Europeans in the search for Chinese concessions.

Behind this underpreparation, most American business showed a lack of intense interest in the Far East as a market or investment field. The *New York Journal of Commerce* put it well: "The American merchant has been so busy attending to the trade demands of his own country from which he has been deriving such unparalleled profit that he has given little thought to the commerce beyond the seas." This was noticeable even in areas much closer and more familiar than China or Japan, such as Canada, Mexico, or the Caribbean.[16] If American industrialists and exporters were reluctant to seek out these more accessible markets, why should they respond to the fulsome publicity of Pacific expansionists and change their business methods or risk their capital across a broad ocean and among a strange people? Indeed, the most imaginative and forceful expansionists were politicians, journalists, or missionaries, not solid businessmen or periodicals such as the *Commercial and Financial Chronicle,* which published an occasional news article about the Far East but seldom any editorials, although most issues were filled with facts and opinions about Canada and Mexico.[17]

A few cases suggest that careful attention to and diligent pursuit of the attractive Chinese market were not in themselves guarantees of immediate business success. After several decades of disappointing sales in northern China, the vice president of Singer Manufacturing Company cautiously put aside the enthusiastic predictions he received at the turn of the century and continued to carry on public relations by the company's traditional practice of escorting prominent visitors around Singer's sewing machine factories in America and Europe. Not until 1904 did the company abandon the outmoded commission house method of sales in favor of a company-controlled subsidiary. It had learned the need for patience and perseverance in the Chinese market.[18]

16. *New York Journal of Commerce* quoted in Knight, "American Trade and Investment in China," 118–19. On trade and investment in Canada, Mexico, and the Caribbean, see Pletcher, *Diplomacy of Trade and Investment,* passim.

17. McClellan, *Heathen Chinee,* 192–93, 201–2.

18. Davies, *Peacefully Working,* 194–205. The analysis is hampered by incomplete statistics of sales.

Like many businessmen operating in the Far East, government officials were influenced by the complementary factors of overexpectation and underpreparation and improvised goals and policies without much desire for more complete evidence or regard for available resources. Although expansionists in the government talked grandly of the Golden East, they appointed commissioners and consuls as patronage required and sent them out with small pay and almost without instructions. Usually the U.S. Navy was poorly represented by a few inferior vessels appearing from time to time in Chinese ports. Perry's expedition to Japan was its only large-scale operation and its only real success. Throughout the nineteenth century the American legation in Peking and the consulates had to rely for translations on former missionaries, sometimes even on British diplomats, and few Americans were qualified to serve with the omnipresent British in the Chinese Maritime Customs because they could not speak fluent Chinese. As a result, British advisers predominated in Peking and Tokyo, such as the imperious Sir Harry Parkes, who overshadowed several early American ministers in Japan.

The opening of Korea in the early 1880s was haphazardly planned in Washington without adequate consultation with the American legation in Peking. The State Department only partly understood the responsibilities it assumed by becoming involved in the contest between China and Japan for control of the Korean peninsula, and it was completely taken by surprise in 1894 when the contest erupted into war. After the Japanese victory, Washington could not give American merchants or investors accurate information about new power relationships in northern China and, indeed, had not even determined the extent to which it would support applications of promoters for concessions. When Germany and Russia demanded spheres of influence in 1897, the secretary of state reacted passively and then had to reverse himself in response to an outcry from alarmed merchants and promoters.

The Spanish-American War brought together most of the factors that had shaped nineteenth-century American relations with the Far East. Probably the war should have been confined to the Caribbean, where it broke out. But the accident of Spain's residual hold on the Philippines, the myth of the Golden East, and the alarm felt in mercantile circles over the German-Russian threat to northern China combined to extend American influence from the Asiatic mainland to the Philippine islands.

Having attacked the Philippines as a strategic gambit and won a surprisingly overwhelming and much publicized victory, McKinley could not easily withdraw. The public and the press expanded the subject in a furious debate. Within weeks the modest idea of a naval base in Manila escalated into a full-fledged island colony nearly seven thousand miles from the California coast and on the very brim of the Far Eastern caldron. With economic stakes in northern China and Manchuria and an army operating at least temporarily in the Philippines, the United States' commitments were now well ahead of its policies. In reaction to this new situation it dispatched the open door notes and joined in putting down the Boxer rebellion in China.

The hope of the McKinley administration in undertaking these unfamiliar policies may have been to regain the apparent stability of the early 1890s, when China had seemed in control of its own affairs and Japan had seemed content with islands and trade. But in 1901 chance brought the activist Theodore Roosevelt to the White House to erect a much more ambitious Far Eastern policy on the frail nineteenth-century foundations. At the same time Japan's resentment against Russia channeled its expansion into a war, in which it won another smashing victory, confirming its dominance in Manchuria and northern China.

Thus in the early 1900s the United States found itself deeply involved in East Asia through a variety of factors: spreading economic interests, alarm at foreign competition, intermittent public attention, and elements of chance. After the open door notes and the Boxer rebellion extrication would have required a long-term effort, forbearing leadership, and public determination that did not exist.

By 1906 and 1907 an American-Japanese rivalry was beginning to take shape, encouraged in the United States by a press campaign against the "yellow peril." This surrounded any reasoned debate with emotion in the as yet little understood Far East question. World War I temporarily removed the Europeans from East Asian affairs and largely diverted American attention, allowing Japan to enhance its position. Even in the 1920s an American-Japanese showdown was probably not inevitable, but neither country had the foresight or restraint to avoid it. Certainly the casual American business contacts of the nineteenth century, the loose, improvised official policies, and the American public attitude toward the Far East—both unrealistic and uncertain—had proved a poor preparation for the problems of the new century.

Bibliography

I. Manuscript Sources

1. UNITED STATES OFFICIAL PAPERS, NATIONAL ARCHIVES

Department of State, Foreign Affairs Section (Record Group 59, microfilm)
Instructions to United States Ministers
Despatches from United States Ministers
Consular Instructions
Consular Despatches
Notes to Foreign Legations
Notes from Foreign Legations
Reports of Bureau Officers
Miscellaneous Letters

2. GREAT BRITAIN OFFICIAL PAPERS, PUBLIC RECORDS OFFICE, LONDON

Foreign Office (microfilm, Library of Congress)
Series 5 (United States)

3. PRIVATE PAPERS

Barker, Wharton, Papers, Library of Congress
Bayard, Thomas F., Papers, Library of Congress
Carnegie, Andrew, Papers, Library of Congress
Cleveland, Grover, Papers, Library of Congress
Davis, J. C. Bancroft, Papers, Library of Congress
Day, William R., Papers, Library of Congress
Evarts, William M., Papers, Library of Congress
Fish, Hamilton, Papers, Library of Congress
Gresham, Walter Q., Papers, Library of Congress
Harrison, Benjamin, Papers, Library of Congress
Hay, John, Papers, Library of Congress
McKinley, William, Papers, Library of Congress
Moore, John Bassett, Papers, Library of Congress
Olney, Richard, Papers, Library of Congress
Porter, David D., Papers, Library of Congress
Schurz, Carl, Papers, Library of Congress

Seward, William H., Papers, University of Rochester, New York
Sherman, John, Papers, Library of Congress
Wilson, James Harrison, Papers, Library of Congress
Young, James Russell, Papers, Library of Congress

4. DISSERTATIONS

Bald, Ralph Dewar, Jr. "The Development of Expansionist Sentiment in the United States, 1885–1895, as Reflected in Periodical Literature." Ph.D. diss., University of Pittsburgh, 1953.

Barnes, Arthur M. "American Intervention in Cuba and the Annexation of the Philippines: An Analysis of Public Discussion." Ph.D. diss., Cornell University, 1948.

Belcher, Jack B. "Economic Initiatives of the United States Congress on American Foreign Policy: A Quantitative Analysis, 1886–1896." Ph.D. diss., Georgetown University, 1976.

Brinker, William John. "Robert W. Shufeldt and the Changing Navy." Ph.D. diss., Indiana University, 1973.

Burnette, Ollin Lawrence, Jr. "The Senate Foreign Relations Committee and the Diplomacy of Garfield, Arthur, and Cleveland." Ph.D. diss., University of Virginia, 1952.

Busselle, James Arthur. "The United States in the Far East, 1894–1905: The Years of Illusion." Ph.D. diss., University of Virginia, 1975.

Calhoun, Charles W. "'The Ragged Edge of Anxiety': A Political Biography of Walter Q. Gresham." Ph.D. diss., Columbia University, 1977.

Cassey, John William. "The Mission of Charles Denby and International Rivalries in the Far East, 1885–1898." Ph.D. diss., University of Southern California, 1959.

Damiani, Brian P. "Advocates of Empire: William McKinley, the Senate, and American Expansion, 1898–1899." Ph.D. diss., University of Delaware, 1987.

Dare, Philip Ned. "John A. Bingham and Treaty Revision with Japan, 1873–1895." Ph.D. diss., University of Kentucky, 1975.

Dozer, Donald Marquand. "Anti-Imperialism in the United States, 1865–1895: Opposition to Annexation of Overseas Territories." Ph.D. diss., Harvard University, 1936.

Hearden, Patrick Joseph. "Cotton Mills of the New South and American Foreign Relations, 1865–1901." Master's thesis, University of Wisconsin, 1966.

Holstine, Jon David. "American Diplomacy in Samoa 1884 to 1899." Ph.D. diss., Indiana University, 1971.

Kim, Samuel S. "Anson Burlingame, a Study in Personal Diplomacy." Ph.D. diss., Columbia University, 1966.

Knight, Barry Lee. "American Trade and Investment in China, 1890–1910." Ph.D. diss., Michigan State University, 1968.

Leopard, Donald Dean. "The French Conquest and Pacification of Madagascar, 1885–1905." Ph.D. diss., Ohio State University, 1966.

Matthews, John Herbert. "John Sherman and American Foreign Relations, 1883–1898." Ph.D. diss., Emory University, 1976.

Morken, William Hubert. "America Looks West: The Search for a China Policy, 1876–1885." Ph.D. diss., Claremont Graduate School, 1974.

O'Horo, Thomas Kevin. "American Foreign Investments and Foreign Policy: The Railroad Experience, 1865–1898." Ph.D. diss., Rutgers University, 1977.

Pennanen, Gary Alvin. "The Foreign Policy of William Maxwell Evarts." Ph.D. diss., University of Wisconsin, 1969.

Ring, Martin Robert. "Anson Burlingame, S. Wells Williams and China, 1861–1870: A Great Era in Chinese-American Relations." Ph.D. diss., Tulane University, 1972.

Snyder, Phil Lyman. "Mission, Empire, or Force of Circumstances? A Study of the American Decision to Annex the Philippine Islands." Ph.D. diss., Stanford University, 1972.

Specter, Allan B. "Harrison and Blaine: Foreign Policy, 1889–1893." Ph.D. diss., Rutgers University, 1967.

Stutz, Frederick H. "William Henry Seward, Expansionist." Master's thesis, Cornell University, 1937.

Thompson, Stanley J. "The Impact of the French 'Challenge' in the Isthmus of Panama on the United States' Expansion in the Caribbean, 1867–1881." Ph.D. diss., American University, 1974.

Weigle, Richard D. "The Sugar Interests and American Diplomacy in Hawaii and Cuba, 1893–1903." Ph.D. diss., Yale University, 1939.

Whelan, Joseph G. "William Henry Seward, Expansionist." Ph.D. diss., University of Rochester, 1959.

Wolf, Harold A. "The United States Sugar Policy and Its Effect upon Cuba: A Re-appraisal." Ph.D. diss., Indiana University, 1958.

II. Published Sources—Primary

1. OFFICIAL PAPERS

United States

SD Senate Document
SED Senate Executive Document
SMD Senate Miscellaneous Document
SR Senate Report
HD House Document
HED House Executive Document
HMD House Miscellaneous Document
HR House Report
28th Cong., 2d sess., *HD 138.*

29th Cong., 2d sess., *HD 96.*

30th Cong., 1st sess., *SMD 80.*
  2d sess., *HR 596.*

31st Cong., 1st sess., *SED 84.*

36th Cong., 2d sess., *SMD 10.*

38th Cong., 1st sess., *SMD 123.*

39th Cong., 2d sess., *HED 1.*

43d Cong., 1st sess., *SED 45; SR 116.*

44th Cong., 1st sess., *HR 116, 623; HED 161.*
  2d sess., *HED 44.*

45th Cong., 2d sess., *HED 226; HMD 10.*
  3d sess., *HED 12.*

46th Cong., 1st sess., *SED 2.*

47th Cong., 1st sess., *SR 120; HR 138.*

48th Cong., 1st sess., *HED 121.*

49th Cong., 1st sess., *SMD 84; HED 60.*
  2d sess., *SMD 22.*

50th Cong., 1st sess., *HED 238.*
  2d sess., *SED 102, 311.*

51st Cong., 2d sess., *HR 377.*

52d Cong., 1st sess., *SED 18.*
  2d sess., *SED 69, 76, 77.*

53d Cong., 1st sess., *SR 227.*
  2d sess., *HED 47, 48.*

54th Cong., 1st sess., *HR 2279.*

55th Cong., 2d sess., *SR 68, 681; HD 271, 536, 573, 575; HR 1355.*
  3d sess., *SD 61, 169.*

56th Cong., 1st sess., *SD 112, 149.*
  2d sess., *SD 138, 231, 373.*

58th Cong., 2d sess., *SD 231.*
  3d sess., *SD 62; SR 2755.*

67th Cong., 2d sess., *SMD 7, 10.*

Bevans, Charles I. *Treaties and Other International Agreements of the United States of America, 1776–1949.* 12 vols. Washington, D.C.: Government Printing Office, 1968–1972.

Congressional Record.

Department of Agriculture, Section of Foreign Markets, Circular No. 17. Frank H. Hitchcock, *United States Wheat for Eastern Asia.* Washington, D.C.: Government Printing Office, 1897.

———. Bulletin No. 14. Frank H. Hitchcock, *Trade of the Philippine Islands.* Washington, D.C.: Government Printing Office, 1898.

———. Bulletin No. 18. Frank H. Hitchcock, *Our Trade with Japan, China, and Hongkong, 1889–1899.* Washington, D.C.: Government Printing Office, 1900.

Department of Commerce, Bureau of the Census. *Historical Statistics of the United States. Colonial Times to 1970.* 2 vols. Washington, D.C.: Government Printing Office, 1975.

Department of Commerce and Labor. Special Agents Series, No. 11. *Foreign Markets for the Sale of American Cotton Products.* Washington, D.C.: Government Printing Office, 1907.

Department of State. *Commercial Relations of the United States with Foreign Countries.* Washington, D.C.: Government Printing Office, 1856–1914.

―――. *Papers Relating to the Foreign Relations of the United States.* Washington, D.C.: Government Printing Office, 1862–.

―――. *Reports from the Consuls of the United States on the Commerce, Manufactures, etc. of their Consular Districts.* Washington, D.C.: Government Printing Office, 1880–.

Miller, David Hunter. *Treaties and Other International Acts of the United States of America.* Washington, D.C.: Government Printing Office, 1931–1943.

Moore, John Bassett. *A Digest of International Law.* 8 vols. Washington, D.C.: Government Printing Office, 1906.

Richardson, James D., comp. *A Compilation of the Messages and Papers of the Presidents, 1789–1897.* 10 vols. Washington, D.C.: Government Printing Office, 1896–1899.

Tariff Commission. *Reciprocity and Commercial Treaties.* Washington, D.C.: Government Printing Office, 1919.

Treasury Department, Bureau of Statistics. *Monthly Summary of Commerce and Finance of the United States, 1899.* Washington, D.C.: Government Printing Office, 1900.

―――. October 1901. Washington, D.C.: Government Printing Office, 1901.

―――. *Statistical Abstract of the United States, 1899.* Washington, D.C.: Government Printing Office, 1900.

Wharton, Francis. *A Digest of the International Law of the United States.* 3 vols. Washington, D.C.: Government Printing Office, 1886.

Other

Burnette, Scott S., ed. *Korean-American Relations: Documents Pertaining to the Far Eastern Diplomacy of the United States.* Vol. 3, *The Period of Diminishing Influence, 1896–1905.* Honolulu: University of Hawaii Press, 1989.

Hsaiao, Liang-lin. *China's Foreign Trade Statistics, 1864–1940.* Cambridge, Mass.: East Asian Research Center, Harvard University Press, 1974.

Japan, Department of Agriculture and Commerce. *Japan in the Beginning of the Twentieth Century.* London, 1904.

McCune, George M., John R. Harrison, and Spencer J. Palmer, eds. *Korean-American Relations: Documents Pertaining to the History of the Far Eastern Diplomacy of the United States.* 2 vols. Berkeley: University of California Press, 1951.

2. MEMOIRS, PRIVATE CORRESPONDENCE, PAMPHLETS, ETC.

Adams, Brooks. *American Economic Supremacy.* New York: Macmillan, 1900.

———. "The Spanish War and the Equilibrium of the World." *Forum* 25 (August 1898): 641–51.

Alger, Russell A. *The Spanish-American War.* New York and London: Harper, 1901.

Allen, Frederick H. *Commercial Aspects of the Hawaiian Reciprocity Treaty.* Washington, D.C.: Government Printing Office, 1885.

Angell, James Burrell. *The Reminiscences of James Burrell Angell.* New York and London, 1912.

Anon. "The All-British Transpacific Cable." *Blackwood's Edinburgh Magazine* 161 (February 1897): 269–75.

Anon. *Annexation, by Not a Member of the House of Nobles.* [Honolulu, 1882?].

Anon. *Hawaiian Reciprocity Treaty. Reasons Why It Should Not Be Abrogated. Presented on Behalf of the Merchants of San Francisco.* Washington, D.C., 1868.

Apostol, José P. "The American-Philippine Tariff." *Philippine Social Science Review* 3 (August 1900): 42–47.

Atkinson, Edward. *Address . . . on the Export of Cotton Goods at the Meeting of the New England Cotton Manufacturers Association, April 26, 1876.* N.p., 1876.

———. "Eastern Commerce: What Is It Worth?" *North American Review* 170 (February 1900): 195–304.

———. "Treatise Submitted at the Meeting of the American Association for the Advancement of Science . . . August 25, 1899." *Anti-Imperialist* 1 (June 3, 1899).

Austin, O. P. "The Commercial Development of Japan." *National Geographic Magazine* (September 1899): 329–37.

———. "The Commercial Importance of Samoa." *National Geographic Magazine* 10 (May 1899): 218–20.

Baldwin, F. Spencer. "Some Gains from Expansion." *Arena* 20 (November 1899): 572–75.

Bancroft, Frederic, ed. *Speeches, Correspondence, and Political Papers of Carl Schurz.* 6 vols. New York: G. P. Putnam's Sons, 1913.

Bancroft, Hubert Howe. *The New Pacific.* New York, 1900.

Barker, Wharton. *The Great Issues.* "Reprints of some Editorials from *The American,* 1897–1900." Privately printed, 1908.

———. "The Industrial Interests of the United States in the Far East." *Engineering Magazine* (October 1898): 7–19.

Barrett, John. "America in China, Our Position and Opportunity." *North American Review* 75 (November 1902): 655–63.

———. "America in the Pacific." *Forum* 30 (December 1900): 478–91.

———. "America in the Pacific and Far East." *Harper's Monthly* 99 (November 1899): 917–26.

———. "America's Interest in Eastern Asia." *North American Review* 162 (March 1896): 257–65.

———. "The Crisis in China: Its Meaning for Engineering Interests." *Engineering Magazine* 19 (September 1900): 804–8.

———. "The Paramount Power in the Pacific." *North American Review* 160 (August 1899): 165–79.

———. "The Plain Truth about Asiatic Labor." *North American Review* 143 (November 1896): 620–32.

———. "The Problem of the Philippines." *North American Review* 167 (September 1898): 359–67.

———. "The Value of the Philippines." *Munsey's Magazine* 21 (August 1899): 689–709.

———. "What America Has at Stake in China." *Harper's Weekly* 44 (August 11, 1900): 744.

Beresford, Charles. *The Break-Up of China, with an Account of Its Present Commerce . . . and Future Prospects.* New York and London: Harper, 1899.

———. "China and the Great Powers." *North American Review* 168 (May 1899): 530–32.

Beveridge, Albert J. *The Russian Advance.* New York: Harper and Bros., 1904.

Biggerstaff, Knight. "A Translation of Anson Burlingame's Instructions from the Chinese Foreign Office." *Far Eastern Quarterly* 1 (May 1942): 277–79.

———. "The Secret Correspondence of 1867–1868: Views of Leading Chinese Statesmen Regarding the Further Opening of China to Western Influence." *Journal of Modern History* 22 (June 1950): 122–36.

Bogart, Edmund G. "Japan Winning the Pacific." *World's Work* 16 (November 1908): 10937–44.

Brown, Henry Alvin. *Addendum to Analyses of Hawaiian Reciprocity Treaty Blunders and the British-Hawaii Treaty of 1851–52, February 7, 1887.* Washington, D.C., 1887.

———. *Analyses of the Sugar Question, Comprehending Cane and Beet Sugar Production, Consumption, Classification,* [etc.]. Washington, D.C., 1879.

———. *Concise Résumé of Sugar Tariff Topics in Defence of American Sugar Industries and Consumers, Commercial and Revenue Interests against Illicit Invasion, the Hawaii Treaty,* [etc.]. Washington, D.C., 1882.

———. *Hawaiian Reciprocity Treaty Blunders. Immediate Abrogation a National Requirement.* Washington, D.C., 1886.

———. *Hawaiian Sugar Bounties and Treaty Abuses Which Defraud the U.S. Revenue, Oppress American Consumers and Tax Payers* [etc.]. Washington, D.C.: Judd and Detweiler, 1883.

Bryan, William Jennings. *Speeches of William Jennings Bryan Revised and Arranged by Himself.* 2 vols. New York, 1911.

Bryce, James. "The Policy of Annexation." *Forum* 33 (August 1897): 385–95.

Butler, S. P. "A Modern Railroad System for China." *Harper's Weekly* 41 (November 27, 1897): 1687.

Carnegie, Andrew. "Americanism *versus* Imperialism." *North American Review* 168 (January 1897): 362–72.

————. "Distant Possessions—The Parting of the Ways." *North American Review* 147 (August 1898): 240–43.

Cary, Clarence. "China and Chinese Railway Concessions." *Forum* 24 (January 1898): 598–604.

Christlieb, Theodore. *Protestant Foreign Missions, Their Present State: A Universal Survey Translated by D. K. Reed.* Boston: Congregational Publishing House, 1880.

Cleveland, Grover. *Presidential Problems.* New York: Century, 1904.

Collins, Perry Macdonough. *Siberian Journey down the Amur to the Pacific, 1856–1857.* Edited with an introduction by Charles Vevier. Madison: University of Wisconsin Press, 1969.

Colquhoun, Archibald R. *China in Transformation.* New York: Harper's, 1898.

Conant, Charles A. "The United States as a World Power." *Forum* 29 (July 1900): 628–32.

————. *The United States in the Orient: The Nature of the Economic Problem.* Boston and New York: Houghton Mifflin and Company, 1901.

Cooper, H. Stonehewer. *Coral Lands.* 2 vols. London, 1880.

Creighton, Robert J. "New Outlets for American Products." *International Review* 11 (December 1881): 572–79.

Curtis, William Eleroy. "The Industrial Revolution in Japan." *Bureau of Labor Bulletin* 2 (January 1896).

————. *Trade and Transportation between the United States and Spanish America.* Washington, D.C.: Government Printing Office, 1889.

————. *The Yankees of the East, Sketches of Modern Japan.* 2 vols. New York: Stone and Kimball, 1896.

Denby, Charles. *China and Her People: Being the Observations, Reminiscences, and Conclusions of an American Diplomat.* 2 vols. Boston, 1906.

————. "The Influence of Mission Work on Commerce." *Independent* 53 (December 12, 1901): 2960–62.

————. "Shall We Keep the Philippines?" *Forum* 26 (November 1898): 279–81.

————. "Why the Treaty Should Be Ratified." *Forum* 22 (February 1899): 641–49.

Denby, Charles, Jr. "America's Opportunity in Asia." *North American Review* 156 (January 1898): 32–39.

————. "Cotton Spinning at Shanghai." *Forum* 28 (September 1899): 50–56.

Depew, Chauncey M. *Orations, Addresses, and Speeches of Chauncey M. Depew.* Edited by John Denison Champlin. 8 vols. New York: Privately printed, 1910.

Dewey, Adelbert M. *The Life and Letters of Admiral Dewey from Montpelier to Manila.* Akron, Ohio: Werner Co., 1899.

Dicey, Edward. "The New American Imperialism." *Nineteenth Century* 44 (September 1898): 487–501.

Dingley, Nelson, Jr. "How to Restore American Shipping." *North American Review* 148 (June 1889): 687–96.

Doster, Frank. "Will the Philippines Pay?" *Arena* 25 (May 1901): 465–70.

Dunnell, Mark B. "Our Policy in China." *North American Review* 167 (October 1898): 396–409.

———. "The Settlement with China." *Forum* 22 (February 1902): 643–61.

Emory, Frederic. "Our Commercial Expansion." *Munsey's Magazine* 11 (January 1900): 530–44.

Fairbank, John K., et al., eds. *The I.G. in Peking, the Letters of Robert Hart, Chinese Maritime Customs, 1868–1907.* Introduction by L. K. Little. 2 vols. Cambridge, Mass.: Harvard University Press, 1975.

Feng, Wu Ting. "The United States and China." *Ainslee's Magazine* (June 1900), summarized in *Public Opinion* 28 (June 14, 1900): 741–42.

Flint, Charles R. *Memories of an Active Life: Men and Ships, and Sealing Wax.* London: G. P. Putnam, 1923.

Foord, John T. "China in Regeneration: An Epoch and an Opportunity." *Engineering Magazine* 19 (August 1900): 655–60.

Forbes, Robert B. *Personal Reminiscences.* 2d ed., rev. Boston: Little, Brown Co., 1882.

Ford, Worthington C. "Chinese Foreign Commerce." *Harper's Weekly* 34 (January 5, 1895): 14–15.

———. "Commercial Superiority of the United States." *North American Review* 166 (June 1898): 75–84.

———. *Letters of Henry Adams.* 2 vols. Boston and New York: Houghton Mifflin, 1900.

———. "Trade Policy with the Colonies." *Harper's Magazine* 96 (July 1899): 293–303.

Foster, John W. *Diplomatic Memoirs.* 2 vols. Boston and New York: Houghton Mifflin, 1909.

Gale, Esson M. "President James Burrill Angell's Diary as United States Treaty Commissioner and Minister to China, 1880–1881." *Michigan Alumnus, Quarterly Review* 49 (1942–1943): 195–208.

Gardner, Lloyd C., ed. *A Different Frontier: Selected Readings in the Foundations of American Economic Expansionism.* Chicago, 1966.

Giddings, Franklin Henry. *Democracy and Empire, with Studies of Their Psychological, Economic, and Moral Foundations.* New York: Macmillan, 1900.

———. "Imperialism?" *Political Science Quarterly* 13 (December 1898): 585–605.

Griffis, William Elliot. *Corea, the Hermit Nation.* 2d ed. New York: Charles Scribner's Sons, 1885.

———. *Corea, Without and Within.* Philadelphia, 1885.

———. "Relations between the United States and Japan." *Magazine of American History* 17 (June 1892): 49–54.

Hammond, John Hays. "The Menace of Japan's Success." *World's Work* 10 (June 1905): 6273–75.

Harris, Townsend. *The Complete Journal of Townsend Harris, First American Consul General and Minister to Japan.* Edited by M. E. Congenza. New York, 1930.

Harrison, Benjamin. *Speeches of Benjamin Harrison . . . : A Complete Collection of His Public Addresses from February, 1888, to February, 1892. . . .* Compiled by Charles Hedges. New York: U.S. Book Company, 1892.

Hart, Robert. "China and Her Foreign Trade." *North American Review* 172 (January 1901): 59–71.

The Hawaiian Reciprocity Treaty. Washington, D.C.: Judd and Detweiler, 1882.

Hawaiian Reciprocity Treaty: Reasons Why It Should Not Be Abrogated. Presented on behalf of the merchants of San Francisco. Washington, D.C.: Freeman and Money, 1886.

The Hawaiian Reciprocity Treaty. A Review of Its Commercial Results. N.p., n.d.

Herbert, Hilary. "Reciprocity and the Farmer." *North American Review* 154 (April 1892): 414–23.

Hill, James J. "The Future of Our Oriental Trade." *World's Work* 10 (August 1905): 6465–67.

———. "A Lost Opportunity in the Pacific." *World's Work* 19 (January 1910): 12482–503.

Hill, Robert T. "Commercial Relations of the United States with the Far East." *Annals of the American Academy of Political and Social Science* 13 (May 1899): 136–43.

Hinton, Richard J. "A Talk with Mr. Burlingame about China." *Galaxy* 6 (November 1868): 613–23.

Hoar, George F. *Autobiography of Seventy Years.* 2 vols. New York: Charles Scribner's Sons, 1903.

Hogan, J. F. "A New Imperial Highway." *Westminster Review* 141 (January 1894): 1–9.

Holcombe, Chester. "The Missionary Enterprise in China." *Atlantic Monthly* 98 (September 1906): 348–54.

Holstrom, Vladimir. *"Ex Oriente Lux!* A Plea for Russian-American Understanding," with introduction by Prince E. Ouktomsky. *North American Review* 169 (July 1899): 6–32.

Horstmann, Henry. *Consular Reminiscences.* Philadelphia: J. B. Lippincott and Co., 1886.

House, E. H. "The Martyrdom of an Empire." *Atlantic Monthly* 47 (May 1881): 610–23.

Ide, Henry C. "The Imbroglio in Samoa." *North American Review* 168 (June 1899): 687–93.

———. "Our Interest in Samoa." *North American Review* 65 (August 1897): 155–73.

Jernigan, Thomas R. "Commercial Trend of China." *North American Review* 156 (July 1897): 63–69.

———. "A Hindrance to Our Foreign Trade." *North American Review* 163 (October 1896): 438–47.

Johnson, Donald B., and Kirk Porter. *National Party Programs, 1840–1972.* Urbana: University of Illinois Press, 1973.

Kidd, Benjamin. "The United States and the Control of the Tropics." *Atlantic Monthly* 62 (June 1902): 400–408.

Knaplund, Paul, and Carolyn M. Clewes, eds. "Private Letters from the British Embassy in Washington to the Foreign Secretary, Lord Granville, 1880–1885." *American Historical Association, Annual Report for the Year 1941.* 3 vols. Washington, D.C.: Government Printing Office, 1942.

Knollys, Henry. *Sketches of Life in Japan.* London: Chapman and Hall, Ltd., 1887.

Kohlsaat, Herman H. *From McKinley to Harding, Personal Recollections of Our Presidents.* London, 1923.

Kopsch, H. "Britain's Trade with China." *Empire Review* 2 (September 1901): 238–42.

Krause, William E. F. *American Interests in Borneo, a Brief Sketch of the Extent, Climate and Productions of the Island of Borneo.* 2d ed. San Francisco: H. H. Bancroft and Company, 1867.

LeRoy, James A. *The Americans in the Philippines: A History of the Conquest and First Years of Occupation with an Introductory Account of the Spanish Rule.* 2 vols. Boston and New York: Houghton Mifflin, 1914.

Lodge, Henry Cabot. "Our Blundering Foreign Policy." *Forum* 19 (March 1895): 8–17.

———, and Charles H. Redmond, eds. *Selections from the Correspondence of Theodore Roosevelt and Henry Cabot Lodge, 1884–1918.* 2 vols. New York, 1925.

Long, John Davis. *America of Yesterday, as Reflected in the Journals of John Davis Long.* Edited by Lawrence Shang Mayo. Boston: Atlantic Monthly Press, c1923.

———. *Papers of John D. Long, 1897–1904.* Selected and edited by Gardner Weld Allen. Boston: Massachusetts Historical Society, 1937.

McCormick, Frederick. "American Defeat in the Pacific." *Outlook* 96 (January 14, 1911): 67–73.

McHale, Thomas R., and Mary C. McHale, eds. *Early American-Philippine Trade: The Journal of Nathaniel Bowditch in Manila, 1796.* New York: Southeast Asia Studies, 1962.

McKinley, William. *Speeches and Addresses of William McKinley from His Election to Congress to the Present Time.* New York: Appleton and Co., 1894.

———. *Speeches and Addresses of William McKinley, from March 1, 1897 to May 30, 1900.* New York: Doubleday and McClure Co., 1900.

Mahan, Alfred T. "Hawaii and Our Future Sea Power." *Forum* 15 (March 1893): 1–11.

———. *The Interest of America in Sea Power: Present and Future.* New York: Little, Brown and Co., 1898.

———. "The Isthmus and Sea Power." *Atlantic Monthly* 72 (October 1893): 459–72.

———. "The United States Looking Outward." *Atlantic Monthly* 66 (December 1890): 816–24.

Martin, W. A. P. *A Cycle of Cathay, or China, South and North, with Personal Reminiscences.* New York: Fleming H. Revell Co., 1896.

Melville, George W. "Our Future in the Pacific—What We Have There to Hold and Win." *North American Review* 166 (March 1898): 281–96.

Millard, Thomas T. "America in China." *Forum* 44 (July 1910): 67–89.

Miller, Henry B. "Russian Development of Manchuria." *National Geographic Magazine* 15 (March 1904): 113–27.

Morgan, John T. "The Duty of Annexing Hawaii." *Forum* 25 (March 1898): 1–16.

Mulhall, Michael D. "Thirty Years of American Trade." *North American Review* 165 (November 1897): 572–78.

Munro, Dana G. "American Commercial Interests in Manchuria." *Annals of the American Academy of Political and Social Sciences* 35 (January 1912): 157–65.

National Board of Trade. *A Report on the Hawaiian Treaty Presented to the National Board of Trade at Its Annual Meeting Held in Washington in January 1883.* Boston: Tolman and White, 1883.

Nordhoff, Charles. *Northern California, Oregon, and the Sandwich Islands.* New York: Harper and Brothers, 1874.

Olney, Richard. "Growth of Our Foreign Policy." *Atlantic Monthly* 75 (March 1900): 289–301.

———. "International Isolation of the United States." *Atlantic Monthly* 81 (May 1898): 577–88.

Outerbridge, Alexander E., Jr. "Origin and History of the Trade Dollar." *Bankers' Magazine* 58 (March 1899): 383–86.

Palmer, Aaron H. *Documents and Facts Illustrating the Origin of the Mission to Japan* [etc.]. Washington, D.C.: H. Polkinhorn, 1857. Reprt., Wilmington, Del.: Scholarly Resources, 1973.

Perkins, George C. "The Competition of Japan." *Overland Monthly* 28 (October 1896): 393–403.

Petition to U.S. Senate and House of Representatives by Ship Builders, Ship Owners and Lumber Merchants of Pacific Coast States Relating to the Treaty of Reciprocity between the United States and the Hawaiian Islands. San Francisco, 1886.

Porter, Robert P. "Is Japanese Competition a Myth?" *North American Review* 143 (August 1896): 44–55.

Proctor, John R. "Hawaii and the Changing Face of the World." *Forum* 24 (September 1897).

———. "Isolation or Imperialism?" *Forum* 26 (September 1898): 14–26.

"Proposed Railroad in China." *Scientific American* 29 (January 11, 1890): Supplement, 11687.

Quincy, Josiah. "The United States in China." *Contemporary Review* 78 (August 1900): 183–95.

Reed, Thomas B. "Empire Can Wait." *Illustrated American* 22 (December 4, 1897): 713–14.

Regidor y Jurado, Antonio M., and J. Warren T. Mason. *Commercial Progress in the Philippine Islands [etc.].* Manila: Chamber of Commerce of the Philippine Islands, April 1925.

Reid, Gilbert. "American Opportunities in China." *Forum* 27 (April 1899): 237–42.

Reid, Whitelaw. *Making Peace with Spain: The Diary of Whitelaw Reid, September–December 1898.* Edited by H. Wayne Morgan. Austin: University of Texas Press, 1965.

———. *Problems of Expansion, as Considered in Papers and Addresses.* New York: Century Co., 1900.

Remlap [Palmer], L. T. *General U. S. Grant's Tour around the World.* Chicago: J. Fairbanks and Co., 1880.

Republican National Convention, Held in the City of Philadelphia, June 19, 20, and 21, 1900 [etc.]. Philadelphia, 1900.

Robinson, Edward Van Dyck. "The Caroline Islands and the Terms of Peace." *Independent* 50 (October 13, 1898): 1046–48.

Rockhile, William W. "The United States and the Future of China." *Forum* 29 (May 1900): 324–31.

Roosevelt, Theodore. *The Letters of Theodore Roosevelt.* Selected and edited by Elting E. Morison et al. 8 vols. Cambridge, Mass.: Harvard University Press, 1951–1954.

Scharf, J. Thomas. "The Farce of the Chinese Exclusion Laws." *North American Review* 146 (January 1898): 91–93.

Schofield, J. R., and B. S. Alexander. "Report on Pearl Harbor, 1873." *American Historical Review* 30 (April 1925): 564–65.

Schurman, Jacob Gould. *Philippine Affairs: A Retrospect and Outlook, an Address.* New York: Scribner's Sons, 1907.

Schurz, Carl. "Hawaii and the Partition of China." *Harper's Weekly* 42 (January 22, 1898): 75.

———. "Manifest Destiny." *Harper's* 37 (October 1893): 737–45.

———. *The Policy of Anti-Imperialism.* Chicago, 1899.

———. *Speeches, Correspondence and Political Papers of Carl Schurz.* Edited by Frederic Bancroft. 10 vols. New York: G. P. Putnam's Sons, 1910.

Searles, John Ennis, Jr. *A Few Facts Concerning the Hawaiian Reciprocity Treaty.* Washington, D.C., 1886.

Seki, Keiza. *The Cotton Industry of Japan.* Tokyo: Society for the Promotion of Science, 1956, 1966.

Seward, Frederick William. *Reminiscences of a Wartime Statesman and Diplomat, 1830–1915.* New York and London: G. P. Putnam's Sons, 1916.

Seward, George F. *Chinese Immigration, in Its Social and Economical Aspects.* New York: Charles Scribner's Sons, 1881, 1970. Reprt. ed., New York: Arno Press and *New York Times,* 1970.

Seward, Olive Risley, ed. *William H. Seward's Travels around the World.* New York: D. Appleton and Company, 1873.

Seward, William Henry. "Speech on His Travels." Draft, 1870. *William H. Seward Papers.* Rhees Library, University of Rochester.

———. *The Works of William H. Seward.* Edited by George E. Baker. 5 vols. New York: Redfield, 1853–1884.

Shaw, Albert. "The American Presidential Election." *Contemporary Review* 78 (November 1900).

Shufeldt, Robert W. *The Relation of the Navy to the Commerce of the United States. March 23, 1878.* Washington, D.C.: Government Printing Office, 1878.

Spalding, Rufus Paine. *A Bird's-Eye View of the Hawaiian Islands, with Some Reflections upon the Reciprocity Treaty with the United States.* Cleveland, 1882.

Starr, M. B. *The Coming Struggle: or What the People on the Pacific Coast Think of the Coolie Invasion.* San Francisco: R and E Research Associates, 1873.

Stevenson, Robert Louis. *A Footnote in History: Eight Years of Trouble in Samoa.* Geneva: Edito-Service, S. A., 1969.

Sumner, Charles. *Speech of the Honorable Charles Sumner on the Cession of Russian America to the United States.* Washington, D.C.: *Washington Globe,* 1867.

Taylor, Benjamin. "The Coming Struggle in the Pacific." *Nineteenth Century* 44 (October 1898): 656–72.

Taylor, H. C. "The Control of the Pacific." *Forum* 30 (1887): 407–16.

Teng, Ssu-yü, and John K. Fairbank. *China's Response to the West, a Documentary Survey, 1837–1923.* Cambridge, Mass.: Harvard University Press, 1954.

Thurston, Lorrin Andrew. *Memorandum . . . Concerning a Pacific Cable.* Honolulu: Printed by the *Hawaiian Star,* 1895.

———. "The Sandwich Islands: The Advantages of Annexation." *North American Review* 156 (May 1898): 272–73.

Tompkins, Daniel. "Export Trade." In *American Commerce, Its Expansion* [etc.] (Charlotte, N.C., 1900), 37–47.

Townsen, L. T. *The Chinese Problem.* San Francisco: R and E Research Associates, 1870.

Treat, W. P., et al. "In Re Imperialism." *Sewanee Review* 6 (October 1898): 483–91.

Trescot, William H. "The Administration of Our Foreign Affairs." *International Review* 8 (March 1880): 308–322.

———. "American Interests in China, Japan, and Siam." Report No. 61½, May 1, 1881. Reports of the Diplomatic Bureau, vol. 5. *SD59.*

Vanderlip, Frank A. "Facts about the Philippines with a Discussion of Pending Problems." *Century Magazine* 56 (August 1898): 559–61.

Vest, George G. "Objections to Annexing the Philippines." *North American Review* 168 (January 1899): 112–20.

Volwiler, Albert T., ed. "The Correspondence between Benjamin Harrison and James G. Blaine, 1882–1893." *Proceedings of the American Philosophical Society* 80 (1938).

Western Union. *Statement of the Origin, Organization and Progress of the Russian-American Telegraph Western Union Extension, Collins Overland Line via*

Behring Strait and Asiatic Russia to Europe. Rochester, N.Y.: Evening Express Book and Job Printing Office, 1866.

White, Stephen M. "The Proposed Annexation of Hawaii." *Forum* 24 (December 1897): 723–36.

Willey, Day Allen. "America in the Orient: A Word Concerning Our Neglected Opportunities." *Putnam's Monthly* 4 (July 1908): 410–14.

Wilson, James Harrison. "America's Interests in China." *North American Review* 166 (February 1898): 129–41.

———. *China: Travels and Investigations in the "Middle Kingdom," a Study of Its Civilization and Possibilities, with a Glance at Japan.* New York: 1887; reprt. ed., Wilmington, Del.: Scholarly Resources, 1975.

Young, John P. "The Question of Japanese Competition." *Overland Monthly* 28 (July 1896): 82–93.

———. "Will Chinese Development Benefit the Western World?" *Forum* 28 (November 1891): 348–62.

Young, John Russell. "The Chinese Question Again." *North American Review* 154 (May 1892): 590–602.

———. *Men and Memories: Personal Reminiscences.* Edited by May D. Russell Young. 2 vols. New York: F. T. Neely [c. 1901].

———. "New Life in China." *North American Review* 153 (October 1893): 121–22.

3. DAILY NEWSPAPERS

United States

Baltimore Sun
Boston Daily Globe
Chicago Inter-Ocean
Chicago Tribune
Cincinnati Daily Gazette
New Orleans Daily Picayune
New York Daily Commercial Gazette
New York Evening Post
New York Herald
New York Journal of Commerce
New York Sun
New York Times
New York Tribune
New York World
San Francisco Alta California
San Francisco Call
San Francisco Chronicle
Springfield Republican
Wall Street Journal

Washington Post

Foreign

The Economist (Br.)
The Times (Br.)

4. OTHER PERIODICALS

General Interest

American Economist
American Review
Annals of the American Academy of Political and Social Science
Arena
Atlantic Monthly
Blackwood's Edinburgh Magazine (Br.)
Broadway (Br.)
Century Illustrated Magazine
Contemporary Review
Empire Review (Br.)
Forum
Harper's New Monthly Magazine
Harper's Weekly
Illustrated America
International Review
Korean Repository (Korea)
Literary Digest
Magazine of American History
Michigan Alumnus, Monthly Review
Munsey's Magazine
Nation
National Geographic Magazine
New England Magazine
Niles' National Register
Nineteenth Century (Br.)
North American Review
Outlook
Overland Monthly
Public Opinion
Putnam's Monthly
Review of Reviews
Westminster Review (Br.)
World's Work

Specialized Interest

Age of Steel
American Exporter
American Mail and Export Journal
American Protectionist
American Wool and Cotton Reporter
Banker's Magazine
Board of Trade Journal
Bradstreet's
Commercial and Financial Chronicle
Engineering: An Illustrated Weekly Journal (Br.)
Engineering and Mining Journal
Engineering Magazine: An Industrial Review
Engineering News and American Railway Journal
Iron Age
Manufacturers' Record
Merchants' Magazine and Commercial Review (Hunt's Merchants' Magazine)
Northwestern Miller
Scientific American
Additional newspapers and periodicals not listed were used through clippings in public or private papers and reprints in other publications.

III. Published Sources—Secondary

1. BOOKS

Abelarde, Pedro H. *American Tariff Policy towards the Philippines, 1898–1946.* New York: King's Crown Press, 1947.

Adler, Cyrus. *Jacob H. Schiff, His Life and Letters.* 2 vols. Garden City, N.Y.: Doubleday, Doran, 1928.

Adler, Jacob. *Claus Spreckels: The Sugar King in Hawaii.* Honolulu: University of Hawaii Press, 1966; reprt., Honolulu: Mutual Publishing Paperback Series, 1966.

Albion, Robert Greenhalgh, with the collaboration of Jennie Barnes Pope. *The Rise of New York Port (1815–1860).* New York: Charles Scribner's Sons, 1930.

Aldridge, A. Owen. *The Dragon and the Eagle: The Presence of China in the American Enlightenment.* Detroit: Wayne State University Press, 1993.

Akagi, Hidemichi. *Japan's Foreign Relations, 1546–1936: A Short History.* Tokyo: The Hokuseido Press, 1936.

Allen, George C. *A Short Economic History of Modern Japan.* Rev. ed. London: George Allen and Unwin, 1972.

Allen, George Cyril, and Audrey C. Donnithorne. *Western Enterprise in Far Eastern Development.* London: George Allen and Unwin, 1954, 1962.

Allen, H. C. *Great Britain and the United States: A History of Anglo-American Relations (1783–1952)*. New York: St. Martin's Press, 1955.

Allen, Helena G. *Sanford Ballard Dole, Hawaii's Only President, 1844–1926*. Glendale, Calif.: A. H. Clark Co., 1988.

Anderson, David L. *Imperialism and Idealism: American Diplomats in China, 1861–1898*. Bloomington: Indiana University Press, 1985.

Baclagon, Uldarico S. *Philippine Campaigns*. Manila: Graphic House, 1952.

Bancroft, Hubert Howe. *History of Alaska, 1730–1885*. San Francisco: History Company, 1880; reprt., New York: Antiquarian Press, 1960.

Banno, Masataka. *China and the West, 1858–1861: The Origins of the Tsungli Yamen*. Cambridge, Mass.: Harvard University Press, 1964.

Barratt, Glynn. *Russian Shadows on the British Northwest Coast of North America, 1810–1890: A Study of Rejection of Defence Responsibilities*. Vancouver: University of British Columbia Press, 1983.

Barrows, Chester L. *William M. Evarts: Lawyer, Diplomat, Statesman*. Chapel Hill: University of North Carolina, 1941.

Bartlett, Norman. *Australia and America through 200 Years: 1776–1976*. Sydney: S.U. Smith at the Fine Arts Press, 1976.

Beale, Howard K. *Theodore Roosevelt and the Rise of America to World Power*. Baltimore: Johns Hopkins University Press, 1956.

Beasley, William G. *Great Britain and the Opening of Japan*. London: Luzac and Company, 1951.

———. *Japanese Imperialism, 1894–1945*. Oxford: Oxford University Press, 1978.

———. *The Meiji Restoration*. Stanford, Calif.: Stanford University Press, 1972.

———. *The Rise of Modern Japan*. New York: St. Martin's Press, 1990.

Becker, William H. *The Dynamics of Business-Government Relations: Industry and Exports, 1893–1921*. Chicago: University of Chicago Press, 1982.

Beisner, Robert L. *Twelve against Empire: The Anti-Imperialists, 1898–1900*. New York: McGraw-Hill, 1968.

Bemis, Samuel Flagg. *A Diplomatic History of the United States*. New York: Henry Holt and Company, 1936.

Blicksilver, Jack. *Cotton Manufacturing in the Southeast: An Historical Analysis*. Atlanta: Bureau of Business and Economic Research, 1959.

Bolkhovitinov, Nikolai. *The Beginnings of Russian-American Relations, 1775–1815*. Translated by Elena Levin. Cambridge, Mass.: Harvard University Press, 1975.

Bowers, Claude G. *Beveridge and the Progressive Era*. New York: Literary Guild, 1932.

Bradley, Harold W. *The American Frontier in Hawaii: The Pioneers, 1787–1843*. Palo Alto, Calif., 1940.

Braisted, William Reynolds. *The United States Navy in the Pacific, 1897–1909*. Austin: University of Texas Press, 1958.

Brookes, Jean I. *International Rivalry in the Pacific Islands, 1800–1875*. Berkeley:

University of California Press, 1941; reprt., New York: Russell and Russell, 1972.

Brown, John K. *The Baldwin Locomotive Works, 1831–1915: A Study in American Industrial Practice*. Baltimore: Johns Hopkins University Press, 1995.

Bryan, Jr., E. H. *American Polynesia: Coral Islands of the Central Pacific*. Honolulu: Tongg Publishing Company, 1941.

Bush, Lewis. *77 Samurai: Japan's First Embassy to America*. Tokyo: Kodasha International, 1968.

Cairncross, A. K. *Home and Foreign Investment, 1870–1913*. Studies in Capital Assimilation. Cambridge, England: Cambridge University Press, 1953.

Calhoun, Charles W. *Gilded Age Cato: The Life of Walter Gresham*. Lexington: University Press of Kentucky, 1988.

The Cambridge History of China. Edited by John K. Fairbank. 12 vols. New York: Cambridge University Press, 1978–1998.

Campbell, Charles S., Jr. *Anglo-American Understanding, 1898–1903*. Baltimore: Johns Hopkins University Press, 1957.

———. *From Revolution to Rapprochement: The United States and Great Britain, 1783–1900*. New York: John Wiley and Sons, 1974.

———. *Special Business Interests and the Open Door Policy*. New Haven: Yale University Press, 1951.

———. *The Transformation of American Foreign Relations, 1865–1900*. New York: Harper's, 1976.

Carlson, Ellsworth C. *The Kaiping Mines, 1877–1912*. Cambridge, Mass.: Harvard University Press, 1957.

Carosso, Vincent P., with the assistance of Rose C. Carosso. *The Morgans: Private International Bankers, 1854–1913*. Cambridge, Mass.: Harvard University Press, 1967.

Carpenter, Francis Ross. *The Old China Trade: Americans in Canton, 1784–1843*. New York: Coward, McCann and Geoghegan, 1976.

Caruthers, J. Wade. *American Pacific Ocean Trade; Its Impact on Foreign Policy and Continental Expansion, 1784–1860*. New York: Exposition Press, 1973.

Challener, Richard D. *Admirals, Generals, and American Foreign Policy, 1898–1914*. Princeton, N.J.: Princeton University Press, 1973.

Chandler, Charles Lyon. *Inter-American Acquaintances*. Sewanee: University Press of Sewanee, Tennessee, 1917.

Chang, Chia-ao. *China's Struggle for Railroad Development*. New York: John Day Company, 1943.

Chang, Hsin-pao. *Commissioner Lin and the Opium War*. Cambridge, Mass.: Harvard University Press, 1964.

Chang, Richard T. *From Prejudice to Tolerance: A Study of the Japanese Image of the West, 1826–1864*. Tokyo: Sophia University, 1970.

Chao, Kang. *The Development of Cotton Textile Production in China*. Cambridge, Mass.: Harvard University Press, 1977.

Chay, Jongsuk. *Diplomacy of Asymmetry: Korean-American Relations to 1910.* Honolulu: University of Hawaii Press, 1990.

Chien, Frederick F. *The Opening of Korea: A Study of Chinese Diplomacy.* Hamden, Conn.: Shoe String Press, 1967.

Choi, Woonsung. *The Fall of the Hermit Kingdom.* Dobbs Ferry, N.Y.: Oceana Publications, 1967.

Chu, Samuel C., and Kwang-ching Liu, eds. *Li Hung-chang and China's Early Modernization.* Armonk, N.Y.: M. E. Sharpe, 1994.

Cleland, Robert Glass. *History of California: The American Period.* New York: Macmillan Co., 1922.

Clymer, Kenton J. *John Hay, the Gentleman as Diplomat.* Ann Arbor: University of Michigan Press, 1975.

Cole, Arthur Harrison. *The American Wool Manufacture.* Cambridge, Mass.: Harvard University Press, 1926.

Coletta, Paolo E. *William Jennings Bryan.* 3 vols. Lincoln: University of Nebraska Press, 1964–1969.

Collins, Maurice. *Foreign Mud* [etc.]. New York: Alfred A. Knopf, 1941.

Collins, Perry McDonough. *Siberian Journey down the Amur to the Pacific, 1856–1857.* Edited with an introduction by Charles Vevier. Madison: University of Wisconsin Press, 1962.

Conroy, Francis Hilary. *The Japanese Frontier in Hawaii, 1868–1898.* Berkeley: University of California Press, 1951.

————. *The Japanese Seizure of Korea, 1869–1910: A Study of Realism and Idealism in International Relations.* Philadelphia: University of Pennsylvania Press, 1960.

Constantino, Renato. *A History of the Philippines: From the Spanish Colonization to the Second World War.* New York: Monthly Review Press, 1975.

Coolidge, Mary Roberts. *Chinese Immigration.* New York: Henry Holt and Co., 1909.

Cooling, Benjamin Franklin. *Benjamin Franklin Tracy: Father of the American Fighting Navy.* Hamden, Conn.: Anchor Books, 1973.

————. *Grey Steel and Blue Water Navy: The Formative Years of America's Military-Industrial Complex, 1881–1917.* Hamden, Conn.: Anchor Books, 1979.

Copeland, Melvin Thomas. *The Cotton Manufacturing Industry of the United States.* Cambridge, Mass.: Harvard University Press, 1912.

Cox, Thomas R. *Mills and Markets: A History of the Pacific Coast Lumber Industry to 1900.* Seattle: University of Washington Press, 1974.

Crapol, Edward F. *America for Americans, Economic Nationalism and Anglophobia in the Late Nineteenth Century.* Westport, Conn.: Greenwood Press, 1973.

Curti, Merle, and Kendall Birr. *Prelude to Point Four: American Technical Missions Overseas, 1833–1938.* Madison: University of Wisconsin Press, 1954.

Damon, Ethel M. *Sanford Ballard Dole and His Hawaii.* Palo Alto, Calif., 1957.

Davies, Robert Bruce. *Peacefully Working to Conquer the World: Singer Sewing Machines in Foreign Markets, 1854–1920.* New York: Arno Press, 1976.

DeConde, Alexander, ed. *Encyclopedia of American Foreign Policy*. 3 vols. New York: Scribner's, 1978.

Deerr, Noël. *The History of Sugar*. 2 vols. London: Chapman and Hall, 1949–1950.

Dement'ev, Igor Petrovich. *USA: Imperialists and Anti-Imperialists: The Great Foreign Policy Debate at the Turn of the Century*. Translated by David Skvirsky. Moscow: Progress Publishers, 1979.

Dennett, Tyler. *The Americans in Eastern Asia: A Critical Study of United States' Policy in the Far East in the Nineteenth Century*. New York: Macmillan, 1922; reprt., New York: Barnes and Noble, 1963.

———. *John Hay: From Poetry to Politics*. New York: Dodd, Mead and Company, 1933.

Dennis, Alfred L. P. *Adventures in American Diplomacy, 1896–1906*. New York: E. P. Dutton and Company, 1928.

Deuchler, Martina. *Confucian Gentlemen and Barbarian Envoys: The Opening of Korea, 1875–1885*. Seattle: University of Washington Press, 1979.

Devine, Michael J. *John Watson Foster: Politics and Diplomacy in the Imperial Era, 1873–1917*. Athens: Ohio University Press, 1981.

Dickins, F. V., and Stanley Lane-Poole. *The Life of Sir Harry Parkes, K. C. B., G. C. M. G., Sometime Her Majesty's Minister to China and Japan*. 2 vols. London: Macmillan and Co., 1894.

Dobson, John A. *Reticent Expansionism: The Foreign Policy of William McKinley*. Pittsburgh: Duquesne University Press, 1988.

Dodge, Ernest S. *New England and the South Seas*. Cambridge, Mass.: Harvard University Press, 1935.

Dorwart, Jeffery. *The Pigtail War: American Involvement in the Sino-Japanese War of 1894–1895*. Amherst: University of Massachusetts Press, 1975.

Drake, Frederick C. *The Empire of the Seas: A Biography of Rear Admiral Robert Wilson Shufeldt, USN*. Honolulu: University of Hawaii Press, 1984.

Dudden, Arthur Power. *The American Pacific: From the Old China Trade to the Present*. New York: Oxford University Press, 1992.

Dulles, Foster Rhea. *The Old China Trade*. Boston and New York: Houghton Mifflin, 1930; reprt., New York: AHS Press, 1980.

———. *Yankees and Samurai: America's Role in the Emergence of Modern Japan, 1791–1900*. New York: Harper and Row, 1965.

Duus, Peter. *The Abacus and the Sword: The Japanese Penetration of Korea, 1895–1910*. Berkeley: University of California Press, 1995.

Eastman, Lloyd E. *Throne and Mandarins: China's Search for a Policy during the Sino-French Controversy, 1880–1885*. Cambridge, Mass.: Harvard University Press, 1967.

Eggert, Gerald G. *Richard Olney: Evolution of a Statesman*. University Park: Pennsylvania State University Press, 1974.

Eichner, Alfred S. *The Emergence of Oligopoly: Sugar Refining as a Case Study*. Baltimore: Johns Hopkins University Press, 1969.

Ellison, Joseph W. *The Opening and Penetration of Foreign Influence in Samoa to 1880.* Corvallis: Oregon State College Monographs in History, 1938.

Eng, Robert Y. *Economic Imperialism in China: Silk Production and Exports, 1861–1932.* Berkeley: University of California Press, 1986.

Fairbank, John. *Trade and Diplomacy on the China Coast: The Opening of the Treaty Ports, 1842–1854.* Cambridge, Mass.: Harvard University Press, 1953; reprt., Stanford, Calif.: Stanford University Press, 1969.

Farnie, D. A. *East and West of Suez: The Suez Canal in History, 1854–1956.* Oxford: Clarendon Press, 1969.

Farrar, Victor J. *The Annexation of Russian America.* Washington, D.C.: W. F. Roberts Co., 1937; reprt., 1966.

Fay, Peter Ward. *The Opium War, 1840–1842.* Chapel Hill: University of North Carolina Press, 1995.

Feuerwerker, Albert. *China's Early Industrialization: Sheng Hsuan-huai (1844–1916) and Mandarin Enterprise.* Cambridge, Mass.: Harvard University Press, 1958.

Fitzpatrick, Brian. *The British Empire in Australia: An Economic History, 1834–1939.* 2d ed. Melbourne: Melbourne University Press, 1949.

Foner, Philip S. *Mark Twain: Social Critic.* 2d ed. New York: International Publishers, 1960.

Fox, Grace. *Britain and Japan, 1858–1883.* Oxford: Clarendon Press, 1969.

Fry, Joseph A. *John Tyler Morgan and the Search for Southern Autonomy.* Knoxville: University of Tennessee Press, 1992.

Gates, John Morgan. *Schoolbooks and Krags: The United States Army in the Philippines, 1898–1902.* Westport, Conn.: Greenwood Press, 1973.

Gatewood, William B., Jr. *Black Americans and the White Man's Burden, 1898–1903.* Urbana: University of Illinois Press, 1975.

Gerretson, F. C. *History of the Royal Dutch.* 4 vols. Leiden: E. J. Brill, 1953–1957.

Gibson, Arrell Morgan, with the assistance of John S. Whitehead. *Yankees in Paradise: The Pacific Basin Frontier.* Albuquerque: University of New Mexico Press, 1993.

Gibson, James R. *Imperial Russia in Frontier America: The Changing Geography of Supply in Russian America, 1784–1867.* New York: Oxford University Press, 1976.

———. *Otter Skins, Boston Ships, and China Goods: The Maritime Fur Trade with the Northwest Coast, 1785–1841.* Seattle: University of Washington Press, 1992.

Gilson, R. P. *Samoa 1830 to 1900: The Politics of a Multi-Cultural Community.* Melbourne, 1970.

Goldstein, Jonathan. *Philadelphia and the China Trade, 1682–1846: Commercial, Cultural, and Attitudinal Effects.* University Park: Pennsylvania State University Press, 1978.

Gould, James W. *Americans in Sumatra.* The Hague: Martinus Nijhoff, 1961.

———. *The United States and Malaysia.* Cambridge, Mass.: Harvard University Press, 1969.

Gould, Lewis L. *The Spanish-American War and President McKinley.* Lawrence: University of Kansas Press, 1982.

Grattan, C. Hartley. *The Southwest Pacific to 1900, A Modern History: Australia, New Zealand, the Islands, Antarctica.* Ann Arbor: University of Michigan Press, 1963.

———. *The United States and the Southwest Pacific.* Cambridge, Mass.: Harvard University Press, 1961.

Greenberg, Michael. *British Trade and the Opening of China, 1800–42.* Cambridge, England: Cambridge University Press, 1951.

Grenville, John A. S., and George Berkeley Young. *Politics, Strategy, and American Diplomacy: Studies in Foreign Policy, 1873–1917.* New Haven: Yale University Press, 1966.

Griffin, Eldon. *Clippers and Consuls: American Consular and Commercial Relations with Eastern Asia, 1845–1860.* Ann Arbor, Mich.: Edwards Brothers, 1938.

Griswold, A. Whitney. *The Far Eastern Policy of the United States.* New York: Harcourt Brace, 1938; reprt., New Haven, Conn.: Yale University Press, 1962.

Grodinsky, Julius. *Jay Gould, His Business Career, 1867–1892.* Philadelphia: University of Pennsylvania Press, 1957.

———. *Transcontinental Railroad Strategy, 1869–1893: A Study of Businessmen.* Philadelphia: University of Pennsylvania Press, 1962.

Gulick, Edward H. *Peter Parker and the Opening of China.* Cambridge, Mass.: Harvard University Press, 1973.

Gull, E. M., *British Economic Interests in the Far East.* Oxford: Oxford University Press, 1943.

Hagan, Kenneth J. *American Gunboat Diplomacy and the Old Navy, 1877–1889.* Westport, Conn.: Greenwood Press, 1973.

———. *This People's Navy: The Making of American Sea Power.* New York: Free Press, 1991.

Halle, Louis J. *Dream and Reality: Aspects of American Foreign Policy.* New York: Harper, 1959.

———. *The United States Acquires the Philippines: Consensus vs. Reality.* Lanham, Md.: University Press of America, 1985.

Halliday, Jon. *A Political History of Japanese Capitalism.* New York: Pantheon Books, 1975.

Han, Sang-joo, ed. *After One Hundred Years: Continuity and Change in Korean-American Relations.* Seoul: Korea University, Asiatic Research Center, 1982.

Hao, Yen-ping. *The Comprador in Nineteenth Century China: Bridge between East and West.* Cambridge, Mass.: Harvard University Press, 1970.

Harrington, Fred Harvey. *God, Mammon, and the Japanese: Dr. Horace N. Allen and Korean-American Relations, 1884–1905.* Madison: University of Wisconsin Press, 1944.

Healy, David. *U.S. Expansionism: The Imperialist Urge in the 1890s*. Madison: University of Wisconsin Press, 1970.

Henriquez, Robert. *Bearsted: A Biography of Marcus Samuel, First Viscount Bearsted and Founder of "Shell" Transport and Trading Company*. New York: Viking Press, 1960.

Henson, Curtis T., Jr. *Commissioners and Commodores: The East India Squadron and American Diplomacy in China*. University: University of Alabama Press, 1982.

Herrick, Walter R., Jr. *The American Naval Revolution*. Baton Rouge: Louisiana State University Press, 1966.

Hezel, Francis X. *Strangers in Their Own Land: A Century of Colonial Rule in the Caroline and Marshall Islands*. Honolulu: University of Hawaii Press, 1955.

Hidy, Ralph W., and Muriel E. Hidy. *History of Standard Oil Company (New Jersey): Pioneering in Big Business, 1882–1911*. New York: Harper and Row, 1955.

Hildebrand, Robert C. *Power and the People: Executive Management of Public Opinion in Foreign Affairs, 1897–1921*. Chapel Hill: University of North Carolina Press, 1981.

Hinckley, Ted C. *The Americanization of Alaska, 1867–1897*. Palo Alto, Calif.: Pacific Books, 1972.

Hinkley, Frank E. *American Consular Jurisdiction in the Orient*. Washington, D.C.: W. H. Lowdermilk, 1906.

Hirschmeier, Johannes. *The Origins of Entrepreneurship in Meiji Japan*. Cambridge, Mass.: Harvard University Press, 1964.

Hoare, James E. *Japan's Treaty Ports and Foreign Settlements: The Uninvited Guests, 1858–1899*. Richmond, Surrey: Curzon Press, 1994.

Hoffman, Ross J. S. *Great Britain and the German Trade Rivalry, 1875–1914*. Philadelphia: University of Pennsylvania Press, 1933; reprt., New York: Russell and Russell, 1964.

Holbo, Paul. *Tarnished Expansion: The Alaska Scandal, the Press, and Congress, 1867–1871*. Knoxville: University of Tennessee Press, 1983.

Holt, W. Stull. *Treaties Defeated by the Senate, a Study of the Conflict between President and Senate over the Conduct of Foreign Relations*. Baltimore: Johns Hopkins University Press, 1933.

Hou, Chi-ming. *Foreign Investment and Economic Development in China, 1840–1937*. Cambridge, Mass.: Harvard University Press, 1965.

Howay, Frederic W., Walter N. Sage, and Henry F. Angus. *British Columbia and the United States: The North Pacific Slope from Fur Trade to Aviation*. Toronto and New Haven: Ryerson Press for the Carnegie Endowment for International Peace, 1942.

Hoxie, Alexander. *Manchuria: Its People, Resources and Recent History*. New York: Charles Scribner's Sons, 1904.

Hsu, Immanuel, C. Y. *China's Entrance into the Family of Nations: The Diplomatic Phase, 1858–1880*. Cambridge, Mass.: Harvard University Press, 1968.

Hubbard, G. E. *Eastern Industrialization and Its Effect on the West with Special Reference to Great Britain and Japan.* Oxford: Oxford University Press, 1935.

Huenemann, Ralph William. *The Dragon and the Iron Horse: The Economics of Railroads in China, 1876–1937.* Cambridge, Mass.: Harvard University Press, 1984.

Hughes, J. R. T. *Fluctuations in Trade, Industry, and Finance: A Study of British Economic Development, 1850–1860.* Oxford: Clarendon Press, 1960.

Hunt, Michael H. *Frontier Defense and the Open Door: Manchuria in Chinese-American Relations, 1895–1911.* New Haven, Conn.: Yale University Press, 1973.

——. *The Making of a Special Relationship: The United States and China to 1914.* New York: Columbia University Press, 1983.

Hutchins, John G. B. *The American Maritime Industries and Public Policy, 1789–1914, an Economic History.* Cambridge, Mass.: Harvard University Press, 1941.

Hutchinson, William T. *Cyrus Hall McCormick.* 2 vols. New York: Century Co., 1935.

Hyde, Francis E. *Far Eastern Trade, 1860–1914.* London: Adam and Charles Black, 1973.

Iriye, Akira. *Pacific Estrangement: Japanese and American Expansion, 1897–1911.* Cambridge, Mass.: Harvard University Press, 1972.

Jensen, Ronald J. *The Alaska Purchase and Russian-American Relations.* Seattle: University of Washington Press, 1975.

Jessup, Philip C. *Elihu Root.* 2 vols. New York: Dodd, Mead and Company, 1938.

Johnson, Allen, and Dumas Malone, eds. *Dictionary of American Biography.* 22 vols. New York: Scribner's, 1928–1935.

Johnson, Arthur E., and Barry E. Supple. *Boston Capital and Western Railroads: A Study of Nineteenth Century Railroad Investment Process.* Cambridge, Mass.: Harvard University Press, 1967.

Johnson, Robert Erwin. *Far China Station: The U.S. Navy in Asian Waters, 1800–1898.* Annapolis, Md.: Naval Institute Press, 1979.

——. *Thence Round Cape Horn: The Story of United States Naval Forces on Pacific Station, 1818–1823.* Annapolis, Md.: Naval Institute Press, 1979.

Johnston, Samuel P., ed. *Alaska Commercial Company, 1868–1940.* Privately printed, 1940.

Jones, Francis C. *Extraterritoriality in Japan and the Diplomatic Relations Resulting in Its Abolition.* New Haven, Conn.: Yale University Press, 1941.

Jones, H. B. *Live Machines: Hired Foreigners in Meiji Japan.* Vancouver: University of British Columbia Press, 1980.

Joseph, Philip. *Foreign Diplomacy in China, 1894–1900: A Study in Political and Economic Relations with China.* London: G. Allen and Unwin, 1928; reprt., New York, 1971.

Kennan, George F. *American Diplomacy, 1900–1950.* Chicago: University of Chicago Press, 1951.

Kennedy, Paul M. *The Samoan Tangle: A Study in Anglo-German-American Relations, 1878–1900*. New York: Barnes and Noble, 1994.

Kent, Percy Horace. *Railway Enterprise in China: An Account of Its Origin and Development*. London: Arnold, 1908.

Kim, C. I. Eugene, and Han-kyo Kim. *Korea and the Politics of Imperialism, 1876–1910*. Berkeley: University of California Press, 1967.

Kim, Key-hyuk. *The Last Phase of the East Asian World Order: Korea, Japan, and the Chinese Empire, 1860–1882*. Berkeley: University of California Press, 1980.

King, Frank H. H. *A Concise Economic History of Modern China, 1840–1961*. New York: Frederick A. Praeger, 1969.

———. *Money and Monetary Policy in China, 1845–1895*. Cambridge, Mass.: Harvard University Press, 1965.

Kirker, James. *Adventures to China: Americans in the Southern Oceans, 1792–1812*. New York: Oxford University Press, 1970.

Koh, Sung Jae. *Stages of Industrial Development in Asia: A Comparative History of the Cotton Industry in Japan, India, China, and Korea*. Philadelphia: University of Pennsylvania Press, 1966.

Krause, William E. F. *American Interests in Borneo: A Brief Sketch of the Extent, Climate and Production of the Island of Borneo*. 2d ed. San Francisco, 1967.

Kushner, Howard I. *Conflict on the Northwest Coast: American-Russian Rivalry in the Pacific Northwest, 1790–1867*. Westport, Conn.: Greenwood Press, 1975.

———, and Anne Hummel Sherill. *John Hay: The Union of Poetry and Politics*. Boston: Twayne Publishers, 1977.

Kuykendall, Ralph S. *The Hawaiian Kingdom, 1854–1874: Twenty Critical Years*. Honolulu: University of Hawaii Press, 1954.

———. *The Hawaiian Kingdom, 1874–1893: The Kalakaua Dynasty*. Honolulu: University of Hawaii Press, 1967.

LaFeber, Walter. *The American Search for Opportunity, 1865–1913. The Cambridge History of American Foreign Relations*, vol. 2. New York: Cambridge University Press, 1991.

———. *The Clash: A History of U.S.-Japan Relations*. New York: W. W. Norton and Co., 1997.

———. *The New Empire, an Interpretation of American Expansionism, 1860–1898*. Ithaca, N.Y.: Cornell University Press, 1963.

Langer, William L. *The Diplomacy of Imperialism, 1890–1902*. 2 vols. New York and London: Alfred A. Knopf, 1935.

Laughlin, J. Laurence, and H. Parker Willis. *Reciprocity*. New York: Baker and Taylor Company, 1903.

Leach, Margaret. *In the Days of McKinley*. New York: Harper and Brothers, 1959.

Lee, Yur-bok. *Diplomatic Relations between the United States and Korea, 1866–1887*. New York: Humanities Press, 1970.

———. *Establishment of a Korean Legation in the United States, 1887–1890. A Study of Conflict between Confucian World Order and Modern International Relations*. Urbana: Center for Asian Studies, University of Illinois, 1983.

————. *West Goes East: Paul Georg von Möllendorff and Great Power Imperialism in Late Yi Korea.* Honolulu: University of Korea Press, 1988.

————, and Wayne Patterson, eds. *One Hundred Years of Korean-American Relations.* University: University of Alabama Press, 1986.

LeFevour, Edward. *Western Enterprise in Late Ch'ing China: A Selective Survey of Jardine, Matheson and Company's Operations, 1842–1895.* Cambridge, Mass.: Harvard University Press, 1968.

Leff, David Neal. *Uncle Sam's Pacific Islets.* Stanford, Calif.: Stanford University Press, 1940.

Lensen, George Alexander. *Balance of Intrigue: International Rivalry in Korea and Manchuria.* 2 vols. Tallahassee: University Presses of Florida, 1982.

Levi, Werner. *American-Australian Relations.* Minneapolis: University of Minnesota Press, 1947.

Lewis, Cleona, assisted by Karl T. Schlotterbeck. *America's Stake in International Investments.* Washington, D.C.: Brookings Institution, 1938.

Liu, Kwang-chang. *Anglo-American Steamship Rivalry in China, 1862–1874.* Cambridge, Mass.: Harvard University Press, 1963.

Lockwood, Stephen C. *Augustine Heard and Company, 1858–1862: American Merchants in China.* Cambridge, Mass.: Harvard University Press, 1971.

Lockwood, William W. *The Economic Development of Japan: Growth and Structural Change, 1868–1938.* Princeton, N.J.: Princeton University Press, 1954.

Long, David. "Pacific Ocean Gadfly." In James C. Bradford, *Command under Sail: Makers of the American Naval Tradition, 1775–1850* (Annapolis, Md.: Naval Institute Press, 1985), 177–85.

Lorence, James J. *Organized Business and the Myth of the China Market: The American Asiatic Association, 1898–1937.* Philadelphia: American Philosophical Society, 1981.

Maber, John M. *North Star to Southern Cross.* Prescot, Lancashire: T. Stephenson and Sons, Ltd., 1967.

Malozemoff, Andrew. *Russian Far Eastern Policy, 1881–1904.* Berkeley: University of California Press, 1958.

Marriner, Sheila. *Rathbones of Liverpool.* Liverpool: Liverpool University Press, 1961.

————, and Francis E. Hyde. *The Senior John Samuel Swire, 1825–98: Management in Far Eastern Shipping Trades.* Liverpool: Liverpool University Press, 1967.

Marshall, Byron K. *Capitalism and Nationalism in Prewar Japan: The Ideology of the Business Elite, 1868–1914.* Stanford, Calif.: Stanford University, 1967.

Masterman, Sylvia. *The Origins of International Rivalry in Samoa, 1845–1884.* Stanford, Calif.: Stanford University Press, 1934.

Mattox, Henry E. *The Twilight of Amateur Diplomacy: The American Foreign Service and Its Senior Officers in the 1890s.* Kent, Ohio: Kent University Press, 1989.

May, Ernest R., and John K. Fairbank, eds. *America's China Trade in Historical Perspective.* Cambridge, Mass.: Harvard University Press, 1966.

————, and James C. Thomson, eds. *American–East Asian Relations: A Survey.* Cambridge, Mass.: Harvard University Press, 1972.

————. *Imperial Democracy: The Emergence of America as a Great Power.* New York: Harcourt, Brace and World, 1961.

May, Glenn Anthony. *Battle for Batangas: A Philipppine Province at War.* New Haven, Conn.: Yale University Press, 1991.

————. *Social Engineering in the Philippines: The Aims, Execution, and Impact of American Colonial Policy, 1900–1913.* Westport, Conn.: Greenwood Press, 1980.

McClellan, Robert, Jr. *The Heathen Chinee: A Study of American Attitudes toward China, 1890–1905.* Columbus: Ohio State University Press, 1970.

McCordock, R. Stanley. *British Far Eastern Policy, 1894–1900.* New York: Columbia University Press, 1931.

McCormick, Thomas J. *China Market: America's Quest for Informal Empire, 1893–1901.* Chicago: Quadrangle Books, 1967.

McKee, Delbert. *Chinese Exclusion versus the Open Door Policy, 1900–1906: Clashes over China Policy in the Roosevelt Era.* Detroit: Wayne State University Press, 1977.

McWilliams, Tennant S. *The New South Faces the World: Foreign Affairs and the Southern Sense of Self, 1877–1950.* Baton Rouge: Louisiana State University Press, 1988.

Meng, S. M. *The Tsungli Yamen: Its Origins and Functions.* Cambridge, Mass.: Harvard University Press, 1962.

Merk, Frederick, ed. *Fur Trade and Empire: George N. Simpson's Journal* [etc.]. Cambridge, Mass.: Harvard University, 1931; rev. ed., 1968.

Miyoshi, Masao. *As We Saw Them: The First Japanese Embassy to the United States, 1860.* Berkeley: University of California Press, 1979.

Miller, Stuart Creighton. *"Benevolent Assimilation": The American Conquest of the Philippines, 1899–1903.* New Haven, Conn.: Yale University Press, 1982.

————. *The Unwelcome Immigrant: The American Image of the Chinese, 1785–1882.* Berkeley: University of California Press, 1969.

Montague, Ludwell Lee. *Haiti and the United States, 1714–1938.* Durham, N.C.: Duke University Press, 1940.

Morgan, H. Wayne. *America's Road to Empire: The War with Spain and Overseas Expansion.* New York: John Wiley, 1965.

————. *William McKinley and His America.* Syracuse, N.Y.: Syracuse University Press, 1963.

Morgan, Theodore. *Hawaii, a Century of Economic Change, 1778–1876.* Cambridge, Mass.: Harvard University Press, 1948.

Morison, Samuel Eliot. *The Maritime History of Massachusetts, 1783–1860.* Boston: Houghton Mifflin, 1921; reprt., 1961.

————. *"Old Bruin": Commodore Matthew C. Perry, 1794–1858* [etc.]. Boston: Little, Brown and Co., 1957.

Morrell, William P. *Britain in the Pacific Islands.* Oxford: Clarendon Press, 1960.

Morrison, John H. *History of American Steam Navigation*. New York: W. A. Sametz and Co., 1903; reprt., New York: Stephen Daye Press, 1958.

Morse, Hosea Ballou. *International Relations of the Chinese Empire*. 3 vols. London and New York: Longmans, Green and Co., 1910–1918.

———. *The Trade and Administration of China*. Rev. ed. London: Longmans, Green and Co., 1913.

Myers, Ramon H., and Mark R. Peattie, eds. *The Japanese Colonial Empire, 1895–1945*. Princeton, N.J.: Princeton University Press, 1984.

Nahm, Andrew C. *Korea: Tradition and Transformation: A History of the Korean People*. Elizabeth, N.J.: Holly, 1988.

The National Encyclopedia of American Biography. New York: J. T. White, 1898.

Neale, R. G. *Great Britain and United States Expansion, 1898–1900*. East Lansing: Michigan State University, 1966.

Nelson, M. Frederick. *Korea and the Old Orders in Eastern Asia*. Baton Route: Louisiana State University Press, 1948.

Neumann, William L. *America Encounters Japan, from Perry to MacArthur*. Baltimore: Johns Hopkins University Press, 1963.

Nevins, Allan. *Grover Cleveland, a Study in Courage*. New York: Dodd, Mead and Co., 1933.

———. *Hamilton Fish: The Inner History of the Grant Administration*. New York: Dodd, Mead and Co., 1937.

———. *Henry White: Thirty Years of American Diplomacy*. New York: Harper, 1930.

Nichols, Jeanette Paddock. *Alaska: A History of Its Administration, Exploration, and Industrial Development during Its First Half Century*. Cleveland: Arthur H. Clark Co., 1924.

Nitobe, Inazo (Ota). *The Intercourse between the United States and Japan, an Historical Sketch*. Baltimore: Johns Hopkins University Press, 1891.

Norman, E. H. *Japan's Emergence as a Modern State: Political and Economic Problems of the Meiji Period*. New York: Institute of Pacific Relations, 1940.

Offner, John L. *An Unwanted War: The Diplomacy of the United States and Spain over Cuba, 1895–1898*. Chapel Hill: University of North Carolina Press, 1992.

Okun, S. B. *The Russian-American Company*. Translated by Carl Ginsburg. Cambridge, Mass.: Harvard University Press, 1951.

Olcott, Charles S. *The Life of William McKinley*. 2 vols. Boston, New York: Houghton Mifflin Company, 1916.

Osborne, Thomas S. *"Empire Can Wait": American Opposition to Hawaiian Annexation, 1893–1898*. Kent, Ohio: Kent State University Press, 1981.

Paolino, Ernest N. *The Foundations of the American Empire: William Henry Seward and U.S. Foreign Policy*. Ithaca, N.Y.: Cornell University Press, 1973.

Paullin, Charles Oscar. *Diplomatic Negotiations of American Naval Officers, 1778–1883*. Baltimore: Johns Hopkins University Press, 1912; reprt., Gloucester, Mass.: Peter Smith, 1967.

Pelcovits, Nathan A. *Old China Hands and the Foreign Office.* New York: King's Crown Press, 1948.

Phillips, James Duncan. *Pepper and Pirates: Adventures in the Sumatra Pepper Trade of Salem.* Boston: Houghton Mifflin, 1949.

Plesur, Milton. *America's Outward Thrust: Approaches to Foreign Policies, 1865–1890.* DeKalb: Northern Illinois University Press, 1971.

Pletcher, David M. *The Awkward Years: American Foreign Relations under Garfield and Arthur.* Columbia: University of Missouri Press, 1962.

———. *The Diplomacy of Annexation: Texas, Oregon, and the Mexican War.* Columbia: University of Missouri Press, 1973.

———. *The Diplomacy of Trade and Investment: American Economic Expansion in the Hemisphere, 1865–1900.* Columbia: University of Missouri Press, 1998.

Pomeroy, William J. *American Neo-Colonialism: Its Emergence in the Philippines and Asia.* New York: International Publishers, 1970.

Porter, Kenneth Wiggins. *John Jacob Astor, Business Man.* 2 vols. Cambridge, Mass.: Harvard University Press, 1931.

Pratt, Julius W. *America's Colonial Experiment: How the United States Gained, Governed, and In Part Gave Away a Colonial Empire.* New York: Prentice-Hall, 1950.

———. *Expansionists of 1898: The Acquisition of Hawaii and the Spanish Islands.* Baltimore: Johns Hopkins University Press, 1936; reprt., Chicago, 1964.

Prisco, Salvatore, III. *John Barrett, Progressive Era Diplomat: A Study of a Commercial Expansionist, 1887–1920.* University: University of Alabama Press, 1973.

Pyle, Joseph Gilpin. *The Life of James J. Hill.* 2 vols. Garden City, N.Y.: Doubleday, Page and Company, 1917.

Regidor y Jurado, Antonio M., and Warren T. Mason. *Commercial Progress in the Philippine Islands* [etc.]. London, 1905; reprt., Manila, 1925.

Reid, Virginia H. *The Purchase of Alaska: Contemporary Opinion.* Long Beach, Calif.: Press-Telegram, 1940.

Remer, Charles F. *Foreign Investments in China.* New York: Macmillan, 1933.

Robinson, William A. *Thomas B. Reed, Parliamentarian.* New York: Dodd, Mead and Company, 1930.

Romanov, B. A. *Russia in Manchuria, 1892–1906: Essays on the History of the Foreign Policy of Tsarist Russia in the Epoch of Imperialism.* Translated by Susan Wilbur Jones. Ann Arbor, Mich.: J. W. Edwards, for the American Council of Learned Societies, 1952.

Roth, Russell. *Muddy Glory: America's "Indian War" in the Philippines, 1898–1935.* West Hanover, Mass.: Christopher Publishing House, 1981.

Russ, William Adam, Jr. *The Hawaiian Republic, 1894–1898.* Selinsgrove, Pa.: Susquehanna University Press, 1961.

———. *The Hawaiian Revolution, 1893–1894.* Selinsgrove, Pa.: Susquehanna University Press, 1959.

Rutherford, Noel. *Shirley Baker and the King of Tonga*. New York: Oxford University Press, 1971.

Rydell, Raymond A. *Cape Horn to the Pacific: The Rise and Decline of an Ocean Highway*. Berkeley: University of California Press, 1952.

Rydell, Robert W. *All the World's a Fair: Visions of Empire at American International Expositions, 1876–1916*. Chicago: University of Chicago Press, 1984.

Ryden, George Herbert. *The Foreign Policy of the United States in Relation to Samoa*. New Haven: Yale University Press, 1933.

Rystad, Göran. *Ambiguous Imperialism: American Foreign Policy and Domestic Politics at the Turn of the Century*. Stockholm: Esselte Studium, 1975.

Sakamaki, Shunzo. *Japan and the United States, 1790–1853*. Wilmington, Del.: Scholarly Resources, 1978.

Salamanca, Bonifacio S. *The Filipino Reaction to American Rule, 1901–1913*. Hamden, Conn.: Shoe String Press, 1968.

Sandmeyer, Elmer Clarence. *The Anti-Chinese Movement in California*. Urbana: University of Illinois Press, 1939.

Sands, William Franklin. *Undiplomatic Memories*. New York: McGraw-Hill, 1930.

Sansom, George. *The Western World and Japan, a Study in the Interaction of European and Asiatic Cultures*. London: Cresset Press, 1950.

Sargent, Arthur John. *Anglo-Chinese Commerce and Diplomacy (Mainly in the Nineteenth Century)*. Oxford: Clarendon Press, 1907.

Saul, Norman E. *Distant Friends: The United States and Russia, 1763–1867*. Lawrence: University Press of Kansas, 1991.

Schirmer, Daniel B. *Republic or Empire? American Resistance to the Philippine War*. Cambridge, Mass.: Harvard University Press, 1972.

Scholes, Walter V., and Marie V. Scholes. *The Foreign Policies of the Taft Administration*. Columbia: University of Missouri Press, 1970.

Schonberger, Howard B. *Transportation to the Seaboard: The Communication Revolution and American Foreign Policy, 1860–1911*. Westport, Conn.: Greenwood Press, 1971.

Schrecker, John E. *Imperialism and Chinese Nationalism: Germany in Shantung*. Cambridge, Mass.: Harvard University Press, 1971.

Schreiner, George Abel. *Cables and Wireless and Their Role in the Foreign Relations of the United States*. Boston: Stratford Company, 1924.

Schroeder, John H. *Shaping a Maritime Empire: The Commercial and Diplomatic Role of the American Navy, 1829–1861*. Westport, Conn.: Greenwood Press, 1985.

Schurz, William Lytle. *The Manila Galleon*. New York: E. F. Dalton and Company, 1939.

See, Chong-su. *The Foreign Trade of China*. New York: Columbia University, Longmans, Green and Company, 1919.

Shenton, James P. *Robert J. Walker: A Politician from Jackson to Lincoln*. New York: Columbia University Press, 1961.

Shih, Min-hsiung. *The Silk Industry in Ch'ing China.* Translated by E-tu Zen Sun. Ann Arbor: University of Michigan Press, Center of Chinese Studies, 1976.

Sievers, Harry. *Benjamin Harrison, Hoosier President: The White House and After.* Indianapolis, 1968; reprt., New York: New York University Publishers, 1968.

Siracusa, Joseph M. *New Left Diplomatic Histories and Historiana: The American Revisionists.* Port Washington, N.Y.: Kennikat Press, 1973.

Skaggs, Jimmy M. *The Great Guano Rush: Entrepreneurs and American Overseas Expansion.* New York: St. Martins Griffin, 1995.

Smith, Philip Chadwick Foster. *The Empress of China.* Philadelphia: Philadelphia Maritime Museum, 1984.

Smith, Thomas C. *Political Change and Industrial Development in Japan: Government Enterprise, 1868–1880.* Stanford, Calif.: Stanford University Press, 1955.

Spector, Ronald. *Admiral of the New Empire: The Life and Career of George Dewey.* Baton Rouge: Louisiana University Press, 1974.

Spence, Clark. *Mining Engineers and the American West: The Lace-Boot Brigade, 1849–1933.* New Haven: Yale University Press, 1970.

Spence, Jonathan. *To Change China: Western Advisers in China, 1620–1960.* Boston: Little, Brown, [1958].

Stanley, Peter W. *A Nation in the Making: The Philippines and the United States, 1899–1921.* Cambridge, Mass.: Harvard University Press, 1974.

Stanton, William. *The Great United States Exploring Expedition of 1838–1842.* Berkeley: University of California Press, 1975.

Stanwood, Edward. *American Tariff Controversies in the Nineteenth Century.* 2 vols. Boston and New York: Mifflin and Company, 1903.

Steigerwalt, Albert K. *The National Association of Manufacturers: A Study in Business Leadership, 1873–1914.* Grand Rapids, Mich.: Dean Hicks Company, 1964.

Stern, Fritz. *Gold and Iron: Bismarck, Bleichröder, and the Building of the German Empire.* New York: Knopf, 1977.

Stevens, Sylvester K. *American Expansion in Hawaii, 1842–1898.* Harrisburg, Pa.: Archives Publishing Company of Pennsylvania, 1945.

Stolberg-Wernigerode, Otto zu. *Germany and the United States of America during the Era of Bismarck.* Translated by Otto E. Lessing. Reading, Pa.: Janssen Foundation, 1937.

Sugiyama, Shin'yo. *Japan's Industrialization in the World's Economy, 1859–1879: Export Trade and Overseas Competition.* Atlantic Highlands, N.J.: Athlone Press, 1988.

Sullivan, Josephine. *A History of C. Brewer and Company, Limited, One Hundred Years in the Hawaiian Islands, 1826–1926.* Boston: Walton Printing Company, 1926.

Sun, E-tu Zen (I-tu Jen). *Chinese Railways and British Interests, 1898–1911.* New York: King's Crown Press, 1954.

Sung, Betty Lee. *Mountain of Gold: The Story of the Chinese in America*. New York: Macmillan, 1967.

Swartout, Robert S., Jr. *Mandarins, Gunboats, and Power Politics: Owen Nickerson Denny and the International Rivalries in Korea*. Honolulu: Asian Studies Program, University of Hawaii, 1980.

Swisher, Earl. *The Character of American Trade with China, 1844–1860*. Boulder: University of Colorado Press, 1941.

———. *China's Management of the American Barbarians: A Study of Sino-American Relations, 1841–1861, with Documents*. New Haven, Conn.: Far Eastern Publications, 1951.

Tamarin, Alfred. *Japan and the United States: Early Encounters, 1791–1860*. London: Macmillan, 1970.

Tansill, Charles Callan. *Canadian-American Relations, 1875–1911*. New York: Carnegie Endowment for International Peace, 1943; reprt., Gloucester, Mass.: Peter Smith, 1964.

———. *The Foreign Policy of Thomas F. Bayard, 1885–1897*. New York: Fordham University Press, 1940.

Tate, Merze. *Hawaii: Reciprocity or Annexation?* East Lansing: Michigan State University Press, 1968.

———. *The United States and the Hawaiian Kingdom, a Political History*. New Haven, Conn.: Yale University Press, 1965.

Taussig, Frank W. *Some Aspects of the Tariff Question*. Cambridge, Mass.: Harvard University Press, 1915; reprt., New York: Greenwood Press, 1959.

———. *The Tariff History of the United States*. 7th ed. New York, London: G. P. Putnam's Sons, 1923.

Temin, Peter. *The Jacksonian Economy*. New York: Norton, 1969.

Teng, Ssu-yü. *The Taiping Rebellion and the Western Powers, a Comprehensive Survey*. Oxford: Clarendon Press, 1971.

Terrill, Tom E. *The Tariff, Politics, and American Foreign Policy, 1874–1901*. Westport, Conn.: Greenwood Press, 1979.

Thayer, William Roscoe. *The Life and Letters of John Hay*. 2 vols. London: Constable and Company; Boston: Houghton Mifflin, 1915.

Thomas, Benjamin Platt. *Russian-American Relations, 1815–1867*. Baltimore: Johns Hopkins University Press, 1930.

Thomas, Lately [Robert V. P. Steele]. *Between Two Empires: The Life Story of California's First Senator, William McKendree Gwin*. Boston: Houghton Mifflin, 1969.

Thurston, Lorrin A. *Memoirs of the Hawaiian Revolution*. Honolulu, 1938.

Tikhmenev, P. A. *A History of the Russian-American Company*. Translated by Richard A. Pierce and Alton S. Donnelly. Seattle: University of Washington Press, 1978.

Tompkins, E. Berkeley. *Anti-Imperialism in the United States: The Great Debate, 1890–1920*. Philadelphia: University of Pennsylvania Press, 1970.

Tong, Te-kong. *United States Diplomacy in China, 1844–60*. Seattle: University of Washington Press, 1964.

Tower, Walter S. *A History of the American Whale Fishery*. Philadelphia: Published for the University, 1907.

Townsend, Mary Evelyn. *The Rise and Fall of Germany's Colonial Empire, 1884–1918*. New York: Macmillan, 1930.

Trask, David F. *The War with Spain in 1898*. New York: Macmillan, 1981.

Treat, Payson J. *Diplomatic Relations between the United States and Japan, 1853–1895*. 2 vols. Stanford, Calif.: Stanford University Press, 1932.

———. *Diplomatic Relations between the United States and Japan, 1895–1905*. Stanford, Calif.: Stanford University Press, 1938.

Tribolet, Leslie Bennett. *The International Aspects of Electrical Communications in the Pacific Area*. Baltimore: Johns Hopkins University Press, 1939.

Tyler, Alice Felt. *The Foreign Policy of James G. Blaine*. Minneapolis: University of Minnesota Press, 1927.

Ukers, William H. *All about Tea*. 2 vols. New York: Tea and Coffee Trade Journal, 1935.

Vagts, Alfred. *Deutschland und die Vereinigten Staaten in der Weltpolitik*. 2 vols. New York, 1935.

Van Deusen, Glyndon G. *William Henry Seward*. New York: Oxford University Press, 1967.

Varg, Paul A. *The Making of a Myth: The United States and China, 1879–1912*. East Lansing: Michigan State University Press, 1968.

———. *Missionaries, Chinese and Diplomats: The American Protestant Missionary Movement in China, 1890–1952*. Princeton, N.J.: Princeton University Press, 1958.

———. *Open Door Diplomat: The Life of W. W. Rockhill*. Urbana: University of Illinois Press, 1952.

Vevier, Charles. *The United States and China, 1906–1913: A Study of Finance and Diplomacy*. New Brunswick, N.J.: Rutgers University Press, 1955.

Vogt, Paul L. *The Sugar Refining Industry in the United States, Its Development and Present Condition*. Philadelphia: Published for the University, 1908.

Von Laue, Theodore. *Sergei Witte and the Industrialization of Russia*. New York: Columbia University Press, 1963; reprt., New York: Atheneum, 1974.

Wall, Joseph Frazier. *Andrew Carnegie*. New York: Oxford University Press, 1970.

Ward, J. M. *British Policy in the South Pacific, 1786–1893*. Sydney: Australasian Publishing House, 1948.

Wardle, Arthur C. *Steam Conquers the Pacific: A Record of Maritime Achievement, 1840–1940*. London: Hodder and Sloughton, 1940.

Waters, Sydney B. *Union Line, a Short History of the Union Steamship Company of New Zealand* [etc.]. Wellington, New Zealand, 1952.

Wehler, Hans-Ulrich. *Der Aufstieg des amerikanischen Imperialismus: Studien zur Entwicklung des Imperium Americanum, 1865–1900*. Göttingen: Vanderhoek and Ruprecht, 1974.

Welch, Richard E., Jr. *Response to Imperialism: The United States and the Philippine-American War, 1899–1902.* Chapel Hill: University of North Carolina Press, 1978.

Werking, Richard Hume. *The Master Architects: Building the United States Foreign Service, 1890–1913.* Lexington, Ky., 1977.

Widenor, William C. *Henry Cabot Lodge and the Search for an American Foreign Policy.* Berkeley: University of California Press, 1990.

Wiley, Peter Booth, with Korogo Ichiro. *Yankees in the Land of the Gods: Commodore Perry and the Opening of Japan.* New York: Viking, 1990.

Wilkins, Mira. *The Emergence of Multinational Enterprise: American Business Abroad from the Colonial Era to 1914.* Cambridge, Mass.: Harvard University Press, 1970.

Williams, Frederick Wells. *Anson Burlingame and the First Chinese Mission to Foreign Powers.* New York: Scribner's, 1917.

Williams, William Appleman. *Empire as a Way of Life.* New York: Oxford University Press, 1980.

———. *The Tragedy of American Diplomacy.* Rev. ed. New York: Dell Publishing Company, 1962.

Williamson, Harold F., and Arnold R. Daum. *The American Petroleum Industry, 1859–1899: The Age of Illumination.* Evanston, Ill.: Northwestern University Press, 1959.

Willoughby, W. W. *Foreign Rights and Interests in China.* 2 vols. Baltimore: Johns Hopkins University Press, 1927.

Wisan, J. E. *The Cuban Crisis as Reflected in the New York Press, 1895–1898.* New York: Octagon Books, 1934.

Woodruff, William, and L. McGregor. *The Suez Canal and the Australian Economy.* Melbourne: Melbourne University Press [Carlton], 1957.

Wray, William D. *Mitsubishi and the N.Y.K., 1870–1914: Business Strategy in the Japanese Shipping Industry.* Cambridge, Mass.: Harvard University Press, 1984.

Wright, Mary Clabaugh. *The Last Stand of Chinese Conservatism: The T'ung-Chih Restoration, 1862–1874.* Stanford, Calif.: Stanford University Press, 1959; reprt. ed., New York, 1966.

Wright, Stanley F. *China's Struggle for Tariff Autonomy, 1843–1938.* Shanghai: Kelly and Walsh, 1938.

———. *Hart and the Chinese Customs.* Belfast: Wm. Mullen and Sons, 1950.

Wriston, Henry Merritt. *Executive Agents in American Foreign Relations.* Baltimore: Johns Hopkins Press, 1929.

Yanaga, Chitoshi. *Japan since Perry.* New York: McGraw Hill, 1949; reprt. ed., Hamden, Conn.: Shoe String Press, 1960.

Yang, Lien-shing. *Money and Credit in China: A Short History.* Cambridge, Mass.: Harvard University Press, 1953.

Yen, Sophia Su-fei. *Taiwan in China's Foreign Relations, 1836–1874.* Hamden, Conn.: Shoe String Press, 1965.

Yergin, Daniel. *The Prize: The Epic Quest for Oil, Money, and Power.* New York: Simon and Schuster, 1991.

Young, John Russell. *Man and Memories: Some Reminiscences.* Edited by May D. Russell Young. 2 vols. New York, 1901.

Young, Leonard, K. *British Policy in China, 1895–1902.* Oxford: Clarendon Press, 1970.

Young, Marilyn Blatt. *The Rhetoric of Empire: American China Policy, 1895–1901.* Cambridge, Mass.: Harvard University Press, 1958.

Younger, Edward. *John A. Kasson: Politics and Diplomacy from Lincoln to McKinley.* Iowa City, Iowa, 1955.

Zabriskie, Edward H. *American-Russian Relations in the Far East: A Study in Diplomacy and Power Politics, 1895–1914.* Philadelphia, 1941; reprt., Westport, Conn.: Greenwood Press, 1976.

Zeis, Paul Maxwell. *American Shipping Policy.* Princeton, N.J.: Princeton University Press, 1938.

2. ARTICLES

Abel, Arthur. "How Trade with Japan Began." *Pacific Historian* 11 (winter 1967): 42–52.

Adler, Jacob. "The Oceanic Steamship Company; a Link in Claus Spreckels' Hawaiian Sugar Empire." *Pacific Historical Review* 29 (August 1968): 257–70.

Ahmat, Sharom. "American Trade with Singapore, 1819–1865." *Journal of the Malaysian Branch, Royal Asiatic Society* 19 (December 1965): 241–57.

———. "Some Problems of the Rhode Island Traders in Java, 1799–1836." *Journal of Southeast Asian History* 7 (March 1965): 94–106.

Alexander, R. S. "Report on Pearl Harbor, 1873." *American Historical Review* 30 (April 1925): 561–65.

Anderson, David L. "Anson Burlingame, American Architect of the Cooperative Policy in China, 1861–1871." *Diplomatic History* (summer 1971): 239–55.

———. "The Diplomacy of Discrimination: Chinese Exclusion, 1876–1882." *California History* 7 (spring 1978): 32–45.

Anderson, Stuart. " 'Pacific Destiny' and American Policy in Samoa, 1872–1899." *Hawaiian Journal of History* 12 (1978): 45–60.

Appel, John C. "American Labor and the Annexation of Hawaii: A Study in Logic and Economic Interests." *Pacific Historical Review* 23 (February 1954): 1–18.

Bailey, Thomas A. "Dewey and the Germans at Manila Bay." *American Historical Review* 45 (October 1939): 59–81. (Also in Alexander De Conde and Armin Rappaport, eds., *Essays Diplomatic and Undiplomatic of Thomas A. Bailey,* 103–39.)

———. "Japan's Protest against the Annexation of Hawaii." *Journal of Modern History* 3 (1931): 46–61.

————. "The North Pacific Sealing Convention of 1911." *Pacific Historical Review* 4 (March 1935): 2–14.

————. "The United States and Hawaii during the Spanish-American War." *American Historical Review* 36 (April 1931): 552–60.

————. "Why the United States Purchased Alaska." *Pacific Historical Review* 3 (1934): 39–49.

Baker, George W., Jr. "Benjamin Harrison and Hawaiian Annexation: A Reinterpretation." *Pacific Historical Review* 33 (August 1964): 295–309.

Baron, Harold. "Anti-Imperialism and the Democrats." *Science and Society* 12 (summer 1951): 422–39.

Batson, Benjamin A. "American Diplomats in Southeast Asia in the Nineteenth Century: The Case of Siam." *Journal of the Siam Society* 64 (July 1978): 39–112.

Bauer, K. Jack. "The Korean Expedition of 1871." *United States Naval Institute Proceedings* 74 (February 1948): 196–203.

Beasley, W. G. "The Sino-Japanese Commercial Treaty of 1896." In T. C. Fraser and Peter Lowe, eds., *Conflict and Amity in East Asia: Essays in Honor of Ian Nish*. Houndmills, Basingstoke: Macmillan Academic and Professional, 1992, 1–15.

Becker, William H. "American Manufacturers and Foreign Markets, 1870–1900: Business Historians and the 'New Economic Determinists.'" *Business Historical Review* 47 (winter 1993): 466–81.

————. "Foreign Markets for Iron and Steel, 1893–1913: A New Perspective on the Williams School of Diplomatic History." *Pacific Historical Review* 44 (May 1975): 233–48.

Belohlavek, John M. "Andrew Jackson and the Malaysian Pirates: A Question of Diplomacy and Politics." *Tennessee Historical Quarterly* 36 (spring 1977): 19–29.

Best, Gary Dean. "Ideas without Capital: James H. Wilson and East Asia, 1885–1910." *Pacific Historical Review* 49 (August 1980): 453–70.

————. "James J. Hill's Lost Opportunity on the Pacific." *Pacific Northwest Quarterly* 64 (January 1973): 8–11.

Biggers, George. "The Effect of the Opening of the Suez Canal on the Trade and Development of Singapore." *Journal of the Malaysian Branch, Royal Asiatic Society* 28 (March 1955): 107–15.

Biggerstaff, Knight. "The Official Chinese Attitude toward the Burlingame Mission." *American Historical Review* 41 (July 1936): 682–702.

Bolkhovitinov, Nikolai. "The Crimean War and the Emergence of Proposals for the Sale of Russian America, 1855–1861." *Pacific Historical Review* 59 (February 1990): 15–49.

————. "How It Was Decided to Sell Alaska." *International Affairs* 8 (August 1988): 116–26.

————. "Russia and the Non-Colonization Principle: New Archival Evidence." *Oregon Historical Quarterly* 72 (June 1971): 101–26.

Bradley, Harold W. "California and the Hawaiian Islands, 1846–1852." *Pacific Historical Review* (February 1947): 18–29.

———. "The Hawaiian Islands and the Pacific Fur Trade." *Pacific Northwest Quarterly* 30 (July 1939): 27–29.

Braisted, William R. "The Philippine Naval Base Problem, 1898–1909." *Mississippi Valley Historical Review* 41 (June 1954): 21–40.

———. "The United States and the American China Development Company." *Far Eastern Quarterly* 11 (February 1952): 147–55.

Brauer, Kinley J. "1821–1860: Economics and the Diplomacy of American Expansionism." In William H. Becker and Samuel F. Wells, Jr., *Economics and World Power: An Assessment of American Diplomacy* (New York: Columbia University Press, 1984), 15–118.

Brown, Richard G. "The German Acquisition of the Caroline Islands, 1898–99." In John A. Moses and Paul M. Kennedy, eds., *Germany in the Pacific and the Far East, 1870–1914* (St. Lucia, Queensland: University of Queensland Press, 1977).

Brown, Sidney Devere. "Okubo Toshimichi, His Political and Economic Policies in Early Meiji Japan." *Journal of Asian Studies* 21 (February 1962): 183–97.

Calhoun, Charles W. "Morality and Spite: Walter Q. Gresham and U.S. Relations with Hawaii." *Pacific Historical Review* 52 (August 1983): 292–311.

———. "Rehearsal for Anti-Imperialism: The Second Cleveland Administration's Attempt to Withdraw from Samoa, 1893–1895." *Historian* 48 (February 1986): 209–24.

Campbell, A. E. "Great Britain and the United States in the Far East, 1895–1903." *Historical Journal* 1, no. 2 (1958): 154–75.

Campbell, Charles S., Jr. "The Anglo-American Crisis in the Bering Sea, 1890–1891." *Mississippi Valley Historical Review* 48 (December 1961): 393–414.

———. "The Bering Sea Settlements of 1892." *Pacific Historical Review* 22 (November 1963): 347–68.

Cardella, Robert P. "The Boom Years of the Fukien Tea Trade, 1842–1888." In Ernest R. May and John King Fairbank, *America's China Trade in Historical Perspective* (Cambridge, Mass.: Harvard University Press, 1986).

Castle, Alfred L. "Tentative Empire: Walter Q. Gresham, U.S. Foreign Policy, and Hawaii, 1893–1895." *Hawaiian Journal of History* 29 (1995): 83–96.

Chan, Wellington K. K. "Government, Merchants, and Industry to 1911." In Doris Twitchett and John K. Fairbank, gen. eds., *The Cambridge History of China* (Cambridge, England: Cambridge University Press, 1972–), vol. 2, pt. 1.

Chang, Richard T. "General Grant's 1879 Visit to Japan." *Monumenta Nipponeca* 24 (1969): 373–92.

Chao, Kang. "The Chinese-American Cotton-Textile Trade, 1850–1930." In Ernest R. May and John King Fairbank, *America's China Trade in Historical Perspective* (Cambridge, Mass.: Harvard University Press, 1986).

Cheng, Chu-yuan. "The United States Petroleum Trade with China, 1876–1949."

In Ernest R. May and John King Fairbank, *America's China Trade in Historical Perspective* (Cambridge, Mass.: Harvard University Press, 1986).

Cheong, W. E. "Trade and Finance in China, 1784–1834: A Reappraisal." *Business History* (Liverpool) 7 (January 1965): 34–56.

Checkland, S. G. "An English Merchant House in China after 1842." *Business History Review* 27 (September 1953): 158–89.

Chu, Samuel C. "Li Hung-chang: An Assessment." In Samuel C. Chu and Kwan-Ching Liu, *Li Hung-chang and China's Early Modernization* (London: M. E. Sharpe, 1994).

Clark, Grover. "Changing Markets." In Joseph Barnes, ed., *Empire in the East*. New York: Doubleday Press, 1934.

Clyde, Paul Hibbert. "Attitudes and Policies of George F. Seward, American Minister at Peking, 1876–1880: Some Phases of the Cooperative Policy." *Pacific Historical Review* 2 (1933): 387–404.

———. "The China Policy of J. Ross Browne, American Minister at Peking, 1868–1869." *Pacific Historical Review* 1, no. 3 (1932): 312–23.

———. "Frederick F. Low and the Tientsin Massacre." *Pacific Historical Review* 2 (March 1933): 100–108.

———. "The Open-Door Policy of John Hay." *Historical Outlook* 22 (May 1931): 210–14.

Clymer, Kenton J. "Checking the Sources: John Hay and Spanish Possessions in the Pacific." *Historian* 48 (November 1985): 82–87.

Cochran, Sherman. "Commercial Penetration and Economic Imperialism in China: The American Cigarette Company's Entrance into the Market." In Ernest R. May and John King Fairbank, *America's China Trade in Historical Perspective* (Cambridge, Mass.: Harvard University Press, 1986).

Cole, Allen B. "The Ringgold-Rodgers-Brooke Expedition to Japan and the North Pacific, 1853–1859." *Pacific Historical Review* 16 (May 1947): 152–62.

———, ed. "Captain David Porter's Proposed Expedition to the Pacific and Japan, 1815." *Pacific Historical Review* 9 (March 1940): 61–65.

Coletta, Paolo E. "Bryan, McKinley, and the Treaty of Paris." *Pacific Historical Review* (May 1957): 131–46.

———. "McKinley, the Peace Negotiations, and the Acquisition of the Philippines." *Pacific Historical Review* 30 (November 1961): 341–50.

Cook, Harold F. "Walter D. Townsend, Pioneer American Businessman in Korea." *Royal Asiatic Society, Korean Branch, Transactions* 43 (August 1973): 74–103.

Cox, Thomas R. "The Passage to India Revisited: Asian Trade and the Development of the Far West, 1850–1900." In John A. Carroll, ed., *Reflections of Western Historians* (Tucson: University of Arizona Press, 1969).

———. "Harbingers of Change: American Merchants and the Formosa Annexation Scheme." *Pacific Historical Review* 42 (May 1993): 163–84.

Currie, Blair C. "The Woosung Railroad (1872–1877)." *Papers on China*. Cambridge, Mass.: Center for East Asian Studies, Harvard University: 1966, 49–85.

Curti, Merle. "America at the World Fairs, 1841–1893." *American Historical Review* 55 (July 1950): 833–56.

————, and John Stalker. " 'The Flowery Flag Devils'—The American Image in China, 1840–1900." *Proceedings of the American Philosophical Society* 96 (1932): 66–90.

Dall, William H. "The Russian-American Telegraph Project of 1866–67." *National Geographic* 7 (March 1976): 110–11.

Davidson, Donald C. "Relations of the Hudson's Bay Company with the Russian-American Company on the Northwest Coast, 1829–1867." *British Columbia Historical Quarterly* 5 (January 1941): 33–51.

Degada, Benito. "American Enterprise in the Nineteenth Century Philippines." *Explorations in Entrepreneurial History,* 1st ser., 9 (1957): 142–60.

Dennett, Tyler. "American Choices in the Far East in 1882." *American Historical Review* 30 (October 1924): 84–108.

————. "American 'Good Offices' in Asia." *American Journal of International Law* 16 (January 1922): 1–24.

————. "Early American Policy in Korea, 1883–1887." *Political Science Quarterly* 38 (March 1923): 82–103.

————. "The Open Door." In Joseph Barnes, ed., *Empire in the East* (Garden City, N.Y., 1934), 269–97.

————. "The Open Door Policy as Intervention." *Annals of the American Academy of Political and Social Science* 168 (July 1933): 78–83.

————. "Seward's Far Eastern Policy." *American Historical Review* 27 (October 1922): 45–62.

Devine, Michael J. "John W. Foster and the Struggle for the Annexation of Hawaii." *Pacific Historical Review* 46 (February 1971): 29–50.

Dorwart, Jeffery M. "The Independent Minister: John M. B. Sill and the Struggle against Japanese Expansion in Korea, 1894–1897." *Pacific Historical Review* 44 (November 1975): 485–502.

Downs, Jacques N. "American Merchants and the Chinese Opium Trade, 1800–1890." *Business History Review* 42 (winter 1968): 418–42.

————. "Fair Game: Exploitative Role-Myths and the American Opium Trade." *Pacific Historical Review* 41 (May 1972): 133–49.

Dozer, Donald M. "Anti-Expansionism during the Johnson Administration." *Pacific Historical Review* 12 (September 1943): 253–75.

————. "The Opposition to Hawaiian Reciprocity, 1876–1888." *Pacific Historical Review* 14 (June 1945): 157–83.

Eggert, Gerald G. "Li Hung-chang's Mission to America, 1896." *Midwest Quarterly* 18 (April 1977): 240–57.

Esthus, Raymond A. "The Changing Concept of the Open Door, 1899–1910." *Mississippi Valley Historical Review* 46 (December 1959): 435–54.

————. "The Open Door and the Integrity of China, 1899–1922: Hazy Principles for Changing Policy." In Thomas H. Etzold, ed., *Aspects of Sino-American Relations since 1784* (New York, 1978), 48–74.

Eyre, James K., Jr. "Japan and the American Annexation of the Philippines." *Pacific Historical Review* 11 (March 1942): 55–71.

———. "Russia and the American Acquisition of the Philippines." *Mississippi Valley Historical Review* 28 (March 1942): 539–62.

Fairbank, John K. "America and China: The Mid-Nineteenth Century." In Ernest R. May and James G. Thomson, Jr., eds., *American-East Asian Relations: A Survey* (Cambridge, Mass.: Harvard University Press, 1973), 19–33.

Farrar, Victor J. "Joseph Lane MacDonald and the Purchase of Alaska." *Washington Historical Quarterly* 12 (April 1921): 83–90.

Ferrell, Robert H. "The Griswold Theory of Our Far Eastern Policy." In Dorothy Borg, comp., *Historians and American Far Eastern Policy* (New York: Columbia University East Asia Institute, 1966), 14–21.

Feuerwerker, Albert. "Economic Trends during the Late Ch'ing Empire, 1870–1911." In Doris Twitchett and John K. Fairbank, gen. eds., *The Cambridge History of China* (Cambridge, England: Cambridge University Press: 1972–), vol. 11, pt. 2, 1–69.

———. "The Foreign Presence in China." In Doris Twitchett and John K. Fairbank, gen. eds., *The Cambridge History of China* (Cambridge, England: Cambridge University Press: 1972–), vol. 11, pt. 2.

Firth, Stewart. "German Firms in the Western Pacific Islands, 1857–1914." *Journal of Pacific History* 8 (1973): 10–28.

Galbraith, John S. "Perry McDonough Collins at the Colonial Office." *British Columbia Historical Review* 17 (July–October 1953): 207–14.

Gardella, Robert P. "The Boom Years of the Fukien Tea Trade, 1841–1868." In Ernest R. May and John King Fairbank, *America's China Trade in Historical Perspective* (Cambridge, Mass.: Harvard University Press, 1986).

Garnett, P. "History of the Trade Dollar." *American Economic Review* 7 (March 1917): 91–97.

Garraty, John A. "American Historians and the Open Door Notes." In Borg, *Historians and American Far Eastern Policy,* 4–13.

Gates, John M. "Philippine Guerrillas, American Anti-Imperialists, and the Election of 1900." *Pacific Historical Review* 46 (February 1977): 51–64.

Gay, James T. "Bering Sea Controversy: Harrison, Blaine, and Cromyism." *Alaska Journal* 3 (winter 1973): 12–19.

Gerus, Oleh W. "The Russian Withdrawal from Alaska: The Decision to Sell." *Revista de Historia de America* 75–76 (December 1973): 154–75.

Gibson, James R. "Why the Russians Sold Alaska." *Wilson Quarterly* 3 (summer 1979): 179–88.

Gilbert, Benjamin Franklin. "Lincoln's Far Eastern Navy." *Journal of the West* 8 (July 1969): 355–68.

———. "The Confederate Raider *Shenandoah:* The Elusive Destroyer in the Pacific and Arctic." *Journal of the West* 4 (April 1965): 169–82.

Golder, Frank A. "Mining in Alaska before 1867." *Washington Historical Quarterly* 7 (July 1916): 233–38.

———. "The Purchase of Alaska." *American Historical Review* 25 (April 1920): 411–25.

Gordon, Leonard H. D. "Charles LeGendre: A Heroic Civil War Colonel Turned Adventurer in Taiwan." *Smithsonian Journal of History* 3 (winter 1968–1969): 63–76.

Gough, Barry M. "James Cook and the Origins of the Maritime Fur Trade." *American Neptune* 38 (July 1978): 217–24.

Gould, James W. "American Imperialism in Southeast Asia before 1898." *Journal of Southeast Asian Studies* 3 (September 1972): 306–14.

———. "The Filibuster of Walter Murray Gibson." *68th Annual Report of the Hawaiian Historical Society for the Year 1959* (1960): 7–32.

———. "Sumatra—America's Pepperpot, 1784–1873." *Essex Institute Historical Collections* 90 (April–July–October 1956): 83–153, 203–52, 275, 349.

Gowan, Robert Joseph. "Canada and the Myth of the Japan Market, 1896–1911." *Pacific Historical Review* 39 (February 1970): 63–83.

Graham, Edward D. "Special Interests and the Early China Trade." *Michigan Academician* 6 (fall 1973): 233–42.

Grenville, John A. S. "American Naval Preparations for War with Spain, 1896–1898." *Journal of American Studies* 2 (April 1968): 33–47.

Hamilton, Allen Lee. "Military Strategists and the Annexation of Hawaii." *Journal of the West* 15 (April 1976): 81–91.

Hammersmith, Jack. "The Sino-Japanese War, 1894–95: American Predictions Reassessed." *Asian Forum* 4 (January–March 1972): 48–55.

Hammett, Hugh B. "The Cleveland Administration and Anglo-American Naval Friction in Hawaii, 1893–1894." *Military Affairs* 40 (February 1976): 27–32.

Hao, Yen-ping. "Chinese Tea to America—A Synopsis." In Ernest R. May and John King Fairbank, *America's China Trade in Historical Perspective* (Cambridge, Mass.: Harvard University Press, 1986), 11–31.

———. "A 'New Class' in China's Treaty Ports: The Rise of the Comprador-Merchants." *Business History Review* 44 (winter 1980): 446–59.

Harrington, Fred Harvey. "An American View of Korean-American Relations, 1883–1905." In Yur-bok Lee and Wayne Patterson, eds., *One Hundred Years of Korean-American Relations, 1882–1982* (University: University of Alabama Press, 1986), 46–67.

Harris, Neil. "All the World a Melting Pot? Japan at American Fairs, 1876–1904." In Akira Iriye, ed., *Mutual Images: Essays in Japanese-American Relations* (Cambridge, Mass.: Harvard University Press, 1975).

Harrison, John A. "The Capron Mission and the Colonization of Hokkaido, 1868–1875." *Agricultural History* 25 (July 1951): 135–42.

Heinrich, Waldo H. "The Griswold Theory of Our Far Eastern Policy: A Commentary." In Dorothy Borg, comp., *Historians and American Far Eastern Policy* (New York: Columbia University East Asia Institute, 1966).

Henson, Curtis T., Jr. "The U.S. Navy and the Taiping Rebellion." *American Neptune* 36 (January 1978): 28–40.

Hezel, Francis X. "A Yankee Trader in Yap: Crayton Philo Holcomb." *Journal of Pacific History* 10 (1975): 3–19.

Hooley, Osborne E. "Hawaiian Negotiations for Reciprocity, 1855–57." *Pacific Historical Review* 7 (June 1938): 128–47.

Horie, Tasuzo. "Modern Entrepreneurship in Meiji Japan." In William W. Lockwood, ed., *The State and Economic Enterprise in Japan: Essays in the Political Economy of Growth* (Princeton, N.J.: Princeton University Press, 1965), 183–208.

Hunt, Michael H. "Americans in the China Market: Economic Opportunities and Economic Nationalism, 1890–1931." *Business History Review* 51 (autumn 1977): 277–307.

———. "The Forgotten Occupation: Peking, 1900–1901." *Pacific Historical Review* 48 (November 1979): 501–29.

Ike, Nobutaka. "The Pattern of Railroad Development in Japan." *Far Eastern Quarterly* 14 (February 1955): 217–29.

"An Iowan at Singapore." *Annals of Iowa* (April 1954): 302–4.

Jackson, C. Ian. "The Stikine Territory Lease and Its Relevance to the Alaska Purchase." *Pacific Historical Review* 36 (August 1967): 289–306.

Jones, Hazel. "The Formation of Meiji Policy toward the Employment of Foreigners." *Monumenta Nipponica* 23, no. 1 (1968): 9–30.

Kawai, K. "Anglo-German Rivalry in the Yangtze Region." *Pacific Historical Review* 8 (December 1939): 413–19.

Keithan, E. L. "Alaska Ice, Inc." *Pacific Northwest Quarterly* 36 (April 1945): 121–31.

Kemble, John Haskell. "The Big Four at Sea: The History of the Occidental and Oriental Steamship Company." *Huntington Library Quarterly* 3 (April 1949): 339–57.

———. "The Genesis of the Pacific Mail Steamship Company." *California Historical Society Quarterly* 13 (September, December 1934): 240–54.

———. "A Hundred Years of the Pacific Mail." *American Neptune* 12 (April 1950): 123–43.

———. "The Transpacific Railroad, 1869–1915." *Pacific Historical Review* 23 (August 1949): 331–43.

Kerner, Robert K. "The Russian Eastward Movement: Some Observations on Its Historical Significance." *Pacific Historical Review* 17 (May 1948): 135–48.

Kim, Key-Hiuk. "The Aims of Li Hung-chang's Policies toward Japan and Korea, 1870–1881." In Samuel C. Chu and Kwang-Ching Liu, eds., *Li Hung-chang and China's Early Modernization* (London: M. E. Sharpe, 1994), 145–61.

Kim, Samuel S. "America's First Minister to China: Anson Burlingame and the Tsungli Yamen." *Maryland Historian* 3 (spring 1972): 89–104.

———. "Burlingame and the Inauguration of the Cooperative Policy." *Modern Asian Studies* 5 (October 1971): 337–54.

Knight, Melvin P. "Britain, Germany and the Pacific, 1880–87." In John A. Moses and Paul M. Kennedy, eds., *Germany in the Pacific and the Far East, 1870–1914* (St. Lucia, Queensland: University of Queensland Press, 1977), 61–88.

Koerper, Philip E. "Cable Imbroglio in the Pacific: Great Britain, the United States and Hawaii." *Hawaiian Journal of History* 9 (1975): 114–20.

Kublin, Hyman. "The Attitude of China during the Liu-ch'iu Controversy, 1871–1881." *Pacific Historical Review* 17 (May 1949): 213–31.

Kuo, Ping Chiu. "Caleb Cushing and the Treaty of Wanghsia, 1844." *Journal of Modern History* 5 (March 1933): 34–54.

Kushner, Howard I. " 'Hellships': Yankee Whaling along the Coasts of Russian-America, 1835–1852." *New England Quarterly* 45 (March 1972): 81–95.

———. "The Russian-American Diplomatic Contest for the Pacific Basin and the Monroe Doctrine." *Journal of the West* 15 (April 1976): 65–70.

———. " 'Seward's Folly': American Commerce in Russian America and the Alaska Purchase." *California Historical Society Quarterly* 54 (spring 1975): 4–26.

Kuykendall, Ralph S. "American Interests and American Influence in Hawaii in 1842." *Thirty-ninth Annual Report of the Hawaiian Historical Society for the Year 1930.* Honolulu, 1931.

———. "Negotiation of the Hawaiian Annexation Treaty of 1893." *Fifty-First Annual Report of the Hawaiian Historical Society for the Year 1942* (September 1943): 5–64.

LaFeber, Walter. "Election of 1900." In Arthur M. Schlessinger, Jr., ed., *History of American Presidential Elections, 1789–1968* (New York, 1971), vol. 3, 1877–1917.

Lai, Chikong. "Li Hung-chang and Modern Enterprise: The China Merchants' Company." In Samuel C. Chu and Kwang-ching Liu, eds., *Li Hung-chang and China's Early Modernization* (Armonk, N.Y.: Mast-Sharpe, 1994).

Langley, Harold D. "Gideon Nye and the Formosa Annexation Scheme." *Pacific Historical Review* 34 (November 1961): 397–420.

Larson, Henrietta M. "A China Trader Turns Investor—A Biographical Chapter in American Business History." *Harvard Business Review* 12 (April 1934): 345–58.

Latourette, Kenneth Scott. "The History of Early Relations between the United States and China, 1784–1844." *Transactions of the Connecticut Academy of Arts and Sciences* 22 (1917): 1–209.

Lee, Bae-tong. "Competitive Mining Surveys by Foreign Powers in Korea, with Emphasis on the 1880s." *Journal of Social Sciences and Humanities* (Seoul), 36 (June 1972): 13–41.

Lee, Yur-bok. "Korean-American Diplomatic Relations, 1882–1905." In Yur-bok Lee and Wayne Patterson, eds., *One Hundred Years of Korean-American Relations, 1882* (University: University of Alabama Press, 1986), 12–45.

Legada, Benito. "American Entrepreneurs in the Nineteenth Century Philippines." *Explorations in Entrepreneurial History,* 1st ser., 9 (1957): 147–60.

Leung, Edwin Pak-wah. "Li Hung-chang and the Liu-ch'iu (Ryukyu) Controversy, 1871–1881." In Samuel C. Chu and Kwang-Ching Liu, eds., *Li Hung-chang and China's Early Modernization* (London: M. E. Sharpe, 1994).

Lewis, Charles L. "Our Navy in the Pacific and the Far East of Long Ago." *United States Naval Institute Proceedings* 69 (June 1943): 857–64.

Li, Lillian M. "The Silk Export Trade and Economic Modernization in China and Japan." In Ernest R. May and John King Fairbank, *America's China Trade in Historical Perspective* (Cambridge, Mass.: Harvard University Press, 1986), 77–99.

Lin, Ming-te. "Li Hung-chang's Suzerein Policy toward Korea, 1882–1894." In Chu and Liu, *Li Hung-chang and China's Early Modernization,* 176–94.

Liu, Kwang-ching. "America and China: The Late Nineteenth Century." In Ernest R. May and James C. Thompson, *American–East Asian Relations: A Survey* (Cambridge, Mass.: Harvard University Press, 1972), 34–96.

———. "Li Hung-chang in Chihli: The Emergence of a Policy, 1870–1875." In Albert Feuerwerker, Rhoads Murphey, and Mary C. Wright, eds., *Approaches to Modern Chinese History* (Berkeley: University of California Press, 1967), 68–104.

Livermore, Seward W. "The American Naval Base Policy in the Far East, 1850–1914." *Pacific Historical Review* 13 (June 1944): 113–35.

———. "American Strategy Diplomacy in the South Pacific, 1890–1914." *Pacific Historical Review* 12 (March 1943): 33–51.

———. Early Commercial and Consular Relations with the East Indies." *Pacific Historical Review* 15 (March 1946): 31–58.

Long, David F. " 'Martial Thunder': The First Official American Armed Intervention in Asia." *Pacific Historical Review* 42 (1973): 143–62.

Lord, Donald C. "Missionaries, Thai, and Diplomats." *Pacific Historical Review* 35 (November 1966): 413–31.

Lovett, Robert W. "The Heard Collection and Its Story." *Business History Review* 35 (winter 1961): 570–71.

MacDonald, Norbert. "Seattle, Vancouver, and the Klondike." *Canadian Historical Review* 49 (September 1968): 234–46.

Mackay, Corday. "The Collins Overland Telegraph." *British Columbia Historical Quarterly* 10 (July 1946): 187–215.

Mathews, Joseph J. "Informal Diplomacy in the Venezuelan Crisis of 1896." *Mississippi Valley Historical Review* 50 (September 1963): 195–212.

May, Ernest R. "Factors Influencing Historians' Attitudes: Tyler Dennett." In Dorothy Borg, comp., *Historians and American Far Eastern Policy* (New York: Columbia University East Asia Institute, 1966).

Mayo, Marlene J. "A Catechism of Western Diplomacy: The Japanese and Hamilton Fish, 1877." *Journal of Asian Studies* 26 (May 1967): 389–410.

Mazour, Anatole G. "The Prelude to Russia's Departure from America." *Pacific Historical Review* 10 (September 1841): 311–19.

———. "The Russian-American and Anglo-Russian Conventions, 1824–1825: An Interpretation." *Pacific Historical Review* 14 (September): 303–10.

McCormick, Thomas J. "Insular Imperialism and the Open Door: The China Market and the Spanish-American War." *Pacific Historical Review* 32 (May 1963): 155–69.

———. "The Wilson-McCook Scheme of 1896–1897." *Pacific Historical Review* 31 (February 1967): 47–58.

McDonald, Timothy. "McKinley and the Coming of the War with Spain." *Midwest Quarterly* 7 (spring 1966): 225–39.

McIntyre, W. D. "Anglo-American Rivalry in the Pacific: The British Annexation of the Fiji Islands in 1874." *Pacific Historical Review* 29 (November 1960): 361–80.

McKee, D. L. "Samuel Gompers, the A.F. of L., and Imperialism, 1895–1900." *Historian* 21 (February 1959): 187–99.

McLean, I. W. "Anglo-American Engineering Competition, 1870–1914: Some Third-Market Evidence." *Economic History Review* 29 (August 1976): 4456–63.

McPherson, Hallie. "The Interest of William McKendree Gwin in the Purchase of Alaska, 1854–1861." *Pacific Historical Review* 3 (March 1984): 28–38.

Merk, Frederick. "The Genesis of the Oregon Question." *The Oregon Question: Essays in Anglo-American Diplomacy and Politics.* Cambridge, Mass.: Harvard University Press, 1967.

Mieczkowski, Bogdan, and Seiko Mieczkowski. "Horace Capron and the Development of Hokkaido: A Reappraisal." *Journal of the Illinois State Historical Society* 27 (November 1954): 487–504.

Miller, Stuart Creighton. "The American Trader's Image of China, 1785–1840." *Pacific Historical Review* 36 (November 1967): 375–95.

Miyake, Masaki. "German Cultural and Political Influence on Japan, 1870–1914." In John A. Moses and Paul M. Kennedy, eds., *Germany in the Pacific and the Far East, 1870–1914* (St. Lucia, Queensland: University of Queensland Press, 1977).

Miyamoto, M., Y. Sakudo, and Y. Yasuba. "Economic Development in Preindustrial Japan, 1859–1894." *Journal of Economic History* 25 (December 1965): 541–64.

Morgan, William Michael. "The Anti-Japanese Origins of the Hawaiian Annexation Treaty of 1897." *Diplomatic History* 6 (winter 1982): 23–44.

Morken, William Hubert. "Protecting American Commerce in China: Washington's Approach to Urban Concessions, 1876–1885." *Historian* 40 (November 1977): 53–69.

Nelson, James Wharton. "Congressional Opinion in Missouri on the Spanish-American War." *Missouri Historical Review* 51 (April 1957): 245–56.

Neumann, William L. "Determinism, Destiny, and Myth in the American Image of China." In George L. Anderson, ed., *Issues and Conflicts: Studies in Twen-*

tieth Century American Diplomacy (Lawrence: University Press of Kansas, 1959).

————. "Religion, Morality, and Freedom: The Ideological Background of the Perry Expedition." *Pacific Historical Review* 23 (August 1954): 247–57.

Noble, Harold J. "The Former Foreign Settlement in Korea." *American Journal of International Law* 23 (October 1929): 766–82.

————. "The Korean Mission to the United States in 1883." *Transactions of the Korean Branch of the Royal Asiatic Society* 18 (1929): 1–27.

————. "The United States and Sino-Korean Relations, 1885–1887." *Pacific Historical Review* 2 (September 1933): 292–304.

Ogden, Adele. "New England Traders in Spanish and Mexican California." In Adele Ogden and Engel Sluiter, eds., *Greater America: Essays in Honor of Herbert Eugene Bolton* (Berkeley: University of California Press, 1943), 395–413.

Orchard, John E. "Contrasts in the Progress of Industrialization in China and Japan." *Political Science Quarterly* 52 (March 1937): 18–20.

Osborne, Thomas J. "Claus Spreckels and the Oxnard Brothers: Pioneer Developers of California's Beet Sugar Industry, 1890–1900." *Southern California Quarterly* 54 (summer 1972): 117–25.

————. "The Main Reason for Hawaiian Annexation in July, 1898." *Oregon Historical Quarterly* 71 (June 1970): 161–78.

————. "Trade or War? America's Annexation of Hawaii Reconsidered." *Pacific Historical Review* 50 (August 1981): 289–309.

Palmer, Spencer J. "American Gold Mining in Korea's Unsan District." *Pacific Historical Review* 31 (November 1963): 379–91.

Parry, Albert. "Cassius Clay's Glimpse into the Future." *Russian Review* 2 (spring 1953): 52–67.

Patterson, John. "The United States and Hawaiian Reciprocity, 1867–1870." *Pacific Historical Review* 7 (March 1939): 19–26.

Paulsen, George E. "The Abrogation of the Gresham-Yang Treaty." *Pacific Historical Review* 40 (November 1971): 4457–77.

————. "The Gresham-Yang Treaty." *Pacific Historical Review* 27 (August 1968): 281–97.

————. "Machinery for the Mills of China, 1882–1896." *Monumenta Serica* 27 (1968): 320–42.

————. "Secretary Gresham, Senator Lodge, and American Good Offices in China, 1894." *Pacific Historical Review* 36 (May 1967): 123–42.

————. "The Szechwan Riots of 1895 and American Missionary Diplomacy." *Journal of Asian Studies* 23 (February 1969): 285–98.

Pearce, George F. "Assessing Public Opinion: Editorial Content and the Annexation of Hawaii—A Case Study." *Pacific Historical Review* 43 (August 1974): 324–41.

Polevci, B. F. "The Discovery of Russian America." In S. Frederick Starr, ed.,

Russia's American Colony (Durham, N.C.: Duke University Press, 1987), 13–31.

Pratt, Julius W. "The Hawaiian Revolution: A Reinterpretation." *Pacific Historical Review* 1 (September 1932): 273–94.

Pressman, Harvey. "Hay, Rockhill, and China's Integrity: A Reappraisal." *Papers on China* 13 (1959): 61–79.

Pritchard, Earl H. "The Origins of the Most-Favored-Nation and the Open Door Policies." *Far Eastern Quarterly* 1 (February 1942): 161–72.

Quinn, Pearle E. "The Diplomatic Struggle for the Carolines, 1898." *Pacific Historical Review* 2 (September 1945): 290–302.

Rea, Kenneth W. "China's View of American Diplomacy, 1844–1860." *Chinese Culture* 16 (June 1975): 79–88.

Reed, Peter Melish. "Standard Oil in Indonesia, 1898–1928." *Business History Review* 32 (autumn 1958): 311–27.

Reynolds, Bruce L. "The East Asian 'Textile Cluster' Trade, 1878–1973: A Comparative Advantage Interpretation." In Ernest R. May and John King Fairbank, *America's China Trade in Historical Perspective* (Cambridge, Mass.: Harvard University Press, 1986).

Rigby, Barry. "American Expansion in Hawaii: The Contribution of Henry A. Peirce." *Diplomatic History* 4 (fall 1980): 353–69.

———. "The Origins of American Expansion in Hawaii and Samoa, 1865–1900." *International History Review* 10 (May 1988): 211–27.

———. "Private Interests and the Origins of American Involvement in Samoa, 1872–1877." *Journal of Pacific History* 8 (1973): 75–87.

Rippy, J. Fred. "The European Powers and the Spanish-American War." *Historical Studies* 19 (1927): 22–52.

Rowland, Donald. "The United States and the Contract Labor Question in Hawaii, 1862–1900." *Pacific Historical Review* 2 (1933): 249–69.

Russ, William A., Jr. "The Role of Sugar in Hawaiian Annexation." *Pacific Historical Review* 12 (December 1943): 339–51.

Sanderson, Edward. "Rhode Island Merchants in the China Trade." In Linda Lotridge Levin, ed., *Federal Rhode Island: The Age of the China Trade, 1790–1820.* Providence, R.I., 1978.

Saul, Norman E. "Beverley C. Sanders and the Expansion of American Trade with Russia, 1853–1855." *Maryland Historical Magazine* 67 (summer 1972): 153–70.

Schran, Peter. "The Minor Significance of Commercial Relations between the United States and China, 1850–1931." In Ernest R. May and John King Fairbank, *America's China Trade in Historical Perspective* (Cambridge, Mass.: Harvard University Press, 1986), 237–58.

Schwantes, Robert S. "American Relations with Japan, 1853–1895: Survey and Prospect." In Ernest R. May and James C. Thompson, *American–East Asian Relations: A Survey* (Cambridge, Mass.: Harvard University Press, 1972).

Seed, Geoffrey. "British Views of American Policy in the Philippines Reflected in Journals of Opinion, 1895–1907." *Journal of American Studies* 2 (April 1968): 49–60.

⌄Sharrow, Walter G. "William Henry Seward and the Basis for the American Empire." *Pacific Historical Review* 36 (April 1967): 325–42.

Shelmedine, Lyle S. "The Early History of Midway Islands." *American Neptune* 8 (July 1948): 179–95.

Shewmaker, Kenneth E. "Forging the 'Great Chain': Daniel Webster and the Origins of American Foreign Policy toward East Asia and the Pacific, 1841–1852." American Philosophical Society, *Proceedings* 129 (September 1985): 225–59.

Shi, David E. "Seward's Attempt to Annex British Columbia, 1865–1869." *Pacific Historical Review* 47 (May 1978): 217–38.

Shippee, Lester B. "Germany and the Spanish-American War." *American Historical Review* 30 (July 1925): 754–77.

Shunsuki, Kamei. "The Sacred Land of Liberty: Images of America in Nineteenth Century Japan." In Akiro Iriye, ed., *Mutual Images: Essays in American Japanese Relations* (Cambridge, Mass.: Harvard University Press, 1995).

Sloss, Frank H. "Who Owned the Alaska Commercial Company?" *Pacific Northwest Quarterly* 66 (July 1977): 120–30.

Smith, Ephraim K. "William McKinley's Enduring Legacy: The Historiographical Debate on the Taking of the Philippine Islands." In James C. Bradford, ed., *Crucible of Empire: The Spanish American War and Its Aftermath* (Annapolis, Md.: Naval Institute Press, 1993).

Spector, Ronald H. "The American Image of Southeast Asia, 1790–1865: A Preliminary Assessment." *Journal of Southeast Asian Studies* 3 (September 1972): 299–305.

———. "Who Planned the Attack on Manila Bay?" *Mid-America* 53 (April 1971): 94–102.

Stanley, Peter. "The Making of an American Sinologist: William W. Rockhill and the Open Door." *Perspectives in American History* 11 (1977–1978): 419–60.

Stelle, Charles C. "American Trade in Opium to China, 1821–39." *Pacific Historical Review* 10 (March 1941): 57–74.

Stoecker, Helmuth. "Germany and China, 1861–94." In John A. Moses and Paul M. Kennedy, eds., *Germany in the Pacific and the Far East, 1870–1914* (St. Lucia, Queensland: University of Queensland Press, 1977), 26–37.

Sturdevant, Sandra. "Imperialism, Sovereignty, and Self-Strengthening: A Reassessment of the 1870s." In Paul A. Cohen and John E. Schrecker, eds., *Reform in Nineteenth Century China* (Cambridge, Mass.: Harvard University Press, 1976), 63–70.

Swisher, Earl. "Commodore Perry's Imperialism in Relation to America's Present-Day Position in the Pacific." *Pacific Historical Review* 16 (February 1977): 30–40.

Tanaka, Tokohito. "Meiji Government and the Introduction of Railways." *Con-*

temporary Japan: A Review of Far Eastern Affairs 28 (1966–1967): 567–88, 750–88.

Tate, E. Mowbray. "American Merchant and Naval Contacts with China, 1784–1850." *American Neptune* 31 (July 1971): 177–91.

———. "U.S. Gunboats on the Yangtze: Historical and Political Aspects, 1842–1922." *Studies on Asia* 7 (1966): 121–32.

Tate, Merze. "British Opposition to the Cession of Pearl Harbor." *Pacific Historical Review* 29 (November 1960): 387–94.

———. "Canada's Interest in the Trade and Sovereignty of Hawaii." *Canadian Historical Review* 44 (March 1963): 20–42.

———. "Great Britain and the Sovereignty of Hawaii." *Pacific Historical Review* 31 (November 1962): 327–48.

———. "Twisting the Lion's Tail over Hawaii." *Pacific Historical Review* 36 (February 1967): 27–46.

Teng, Yuan Chung. "American-China Trade, American-Chinese Relations, and the Taiping Rebellion, 1853–1858." *Journal of Asian History* 3 (1969): 93–117.

Thomson, Sandra Caruthers. "Filibustering to Formosa: General Charles Le-Gendre and the Japanese." *Pacific Historical Review* 40 (November 1971): 442–56.

Tiedemann, Arthur E. "Japan's Economic Foreign Policies, 1868–1893." In James W. Morley, ed., *Japan's Foreign Policies, 1868–1941, a Research Guide* (New York: Columbia University, 1974).

Tompkins, E. Berkeley. "Seylla and Charybdis: The Anti-Imperialist Dilemma in the Election of 1900." *Pacific Historical Review* 36 (May 1967): 143–61.

Torodash, Martin. "Steinberger of Samoa." *Pacific Northwest Quarterly* 67 (April 1977): 49–59.

Tregonning, K. G. "American Activity in North Borneo, 1865–1881." *Pacific Historical Review* 23 (November 1954): 357–72.

Vagts, Alfred. "Hopes and Fears of an American-German War, 1870–1915." *Political Science Quarterly* 54 (December 1939): 514–35.

Van Alstyne, Richard W. "Great Britain, the United States, and Hawaiian Independence, 1850–1855." *Pacific Historical Review* 4 (1935): 15–24.

Varg, Paul A. "William Woodville Rockhill and the Open Door Notes." *Journal of Modern History* 24 (December 1952): 375–80.

Vernon, Manfred C. "The Dutch and the Opening of Japan to the United States." *Pacific Historical Review* 18 (February 1959): 39–48.

Vevier, Charles. "American Continentalism: An Idea of Expansion, 1845–1910." *American Historical Review* 65 (January 1960): 323–35.

———. "The Collins Overland Line and American Continentalism." *Pacific Historical Review* 28 (August 1959): 237–53.

Volwiler, Albert T. "Harrison, Blaine, and American Foreign Policy, 1889–1893." *Proceedings of the American Philosophical Society* 79 (1938): 637–48.

Walker, Leslie W. "Guam's Seizure by the United States in 1898." *Pacific Historical Review* 14 (March 1945): 1–12.

Walsh, Warren B. "The Yunnan Myth." *Far Eastern Quarterly* 2 (May 1943): 272–85.

Weigle, Richard D. "Sugar and the Hawaiian Revolution." *Pacific Historical Review* 16 (February 1947): 41–58.

Welch, Richard E., Jr. "American Public Opinion and the Purchase of Russian America." *American Slavic and East European Review* 17 (December 1958): 481–94.

———. "Caleb Cushing's Chinese Mission and the Treaty of Wanghia, a Review." *Oregon Historical Quarterly* 58 (December 1957): 328–57.

———. "Motives and Policy Objectives of Anti-Imperialists, 1898." *Mid-America* 51 (April 1969): 119–29.

———. "Opponents and Colleagues: George Frisbie Hoar and Henry Cabot Lodge, 1898–1904." *New England Quarterly* 39 (June 1966): 182–209.

———. "Senator George Frisbie Hoar and the Defeat of Anti-Imperialism, 1898–1900." *Historian* 26 (May 1964): 362–80.

Werking, Richard H. "Senator Henry Cabot Lodge and the Philippines: A Note on American Territorial Expansion." *Pacific Historical Review* 42 (May 1973): 234–40.

Wheeler, Mary E. "Empires in Conflict and Cooperation: The 'Bostonians' and the Russian-American Company." *Pacific Historical Review* 40 (November 1971): 419–41.

Whittaker, William G. "Samuel Gompers, Anti-Imperialist." *Pacific Historical Review* 28 (November 1969): 429–56.

Wilkins, Mira. "The Impact of American Multinational Enterprise in American-Chinese Relations, 1786–1949." In Ernest R. May and John King Fairbank, *America's China Trade in Historical Perspective* (Cambridge, Mass.: Harvard University Press, 1986), 259–83.

Williams, William A. "Brooks Adams and American Expansion." *New England Quarterly* 25 (June 1952): 217–32.

Worthy, Edmund. "Yung Wing in America." *Pacific Historical Review* 34 (August 1965): 265–87.

Wright, Conrad Edick. "Merchants and Mandarins: New York and the Early China Trade." In David Sanctuary Howard, *New York and the China Trade* (New York: New York Historical Society), 19–23.

Yanaga, Chitoshi. "The First Japanese Embassy to the United States." *Pacific Historical Review* 4 (June 1940): 113–38.

Index

DATE DUE

il: 3479215			
d: 2/7/02			
MAR 1 8 REC'D			
GAYLORD			PRINTED IN U.S.A.